Researching National Security and Intelligence Policy

Researching National Security and Intelligence Policy

Bert Chapman

CQ Press

*A Division of Congressional Quarterly Inc.
Washington, D.C.*

CQ Press
1255 22nd St., N.W., Suite 400
Washington, D.C. 20037

Phone, 202-729-1900
Toll-free, 1-866-4CQ-PRESS (1-866-427-7737)

www.cqpress.com

Copyright © 2004 by CQ Press, a division of Congressional Quarterly Inc.

All rights reserved. No part of this publication may be reproduced or transmitted in any form or by any means, electronic or mechanical, including photocopy, recording, or any information storage and retrieval system, without permission in writing from the publisher.

∞ The paper used in this publication exceeds the requirements of the American National Standard for Information Sciences—Permanence of Paper for Printed Library Materials, ANSI Z39.48-1992.

Cover design: Richard Pottern
Composition: Sheridan Books

Printed and bound in the United States of America

08 07 06 05 04   5 4 3 2 1

Library of Congress Cataloging-in-Publication Data
Chapman, Bert.
  Researching national security and intelligence policy / Bert Chapman.
    p. cm.
  Includes bibliographical references and index.
  ISBN 1-56802-855-5 (alk. paper)
 1. National security—United States—Study and teaching. 2. Intelligence service—United States—Study and teaching. 3. Military intelligence—United States—Study and teaching. 4. National security—Study and teaching. 5. Intelligence service—Study and teaching. 6. Military intelligence—Study and teaching. I. Title.

UA23.C5135 2004
025.06′355033573—dc22

2004010645

For Becky, my best friend and love of my life

Summary Contents

Contents ix

Boxed Features xx

Preface xxi

1 National Security Educational Institutions 1

2 Executive Branch Agencies—Department of Defense 25

3 Other Executive Branch Agencies 72

4 Military Agencies 136

5 Independent Agencies 188

6 Intelligence Agencies 207

7 Congress and Congressional Support Agencies 229

8 Commissions and Advisory Organizations 253

9 Legal and Regulatory Resources 277

10 Research Institutions and Think Tanks in Washington, D.C. 296

11 Research Institutions and Think Tanks outside Washington, D.C. 311

12 Foreign and International Government Organizations 327

13 Foreign Research Institutions 359

14 Selected Indexes, Journals, Series, and Scholars 380

Acronyms 405

Index 413

Citations of Authors 448

Contents

Summary Contents   vii

Boxed Features   xx

Preface   xxi

Chapter 1 National Security Educational Institutions   1

Armed Services Academies   2
   U.S. Air Force Academy   2
   U.S. Coast Guard Academy   2
   U.S. Military Academy   2
   U.S. Naval Academy   3
Military Graduate Schools   3
   Air University   3
   U.S. Army War College   4
   Army Command and General Staff College   5
   Marine Corps University   7
Naval War College   8
Naval Postgraduate School   10
Joint Education   11
   National Defense University   13
   Industrial College of the Armed Forces   13
   Joint Forces Staff College   14
   National War College   15
Skelton Panel   16
Conclusion   18
Notes   18

Chapter 2 Executive Branch Agencies—Department of Defense   25

Office of the Secretary of Defense   25
   Assistant Secretary of Defense for Networks and Information Integration   26
   Assistant Secretary of Defense for Legislative Affairs   26
   Assistant Secretary of Defense for Public Affairs   27
   Assistant to the Secretary of Defense for Intelligence Oversight   27
   Director of Administration and Management   27
   Director of Defense Research and Engineering   28
   Director for Operational Test and Evaluation   28
   Director of Program Analysis and Evaluation   28
   Office of the Executive Secretary   29
   Office of Inspector General   29
   Undersecretaries of Defense   29
   Assistant Secretary of Defense for International Security Affairs   31
Other Defense Agencies   33
   Defense Advanced Research Projects Agency   33
   Defense Commissary Agency   34
   Defense Contract Audit Agency   34
   Defense Contract Management Agency   34
   Defense Finance and Accounting Service   35

Defense Information Systems Agency   35
Defense Logistics Agency   36
Defense Policy Board   37
Defense Science Board   37
Defense Security Service   38
Defense Technical Information Center   39
Defense Threat Reduction Agency   40
Joint Chiefs of Staff   40
Missile Defense Agency   42
Additional Defense and Affiliated DOD Institutions   43
   Anthrax Vaccine Immunization Program   43
   Asia-Pacific Center for Security Studies   44
   Computer Emergency Response Team   44
   Defend America   45
   Defense Advisory Committee on Women in the Services   45
   Defense Environmental Network and Information Exchange   45
   Defense Information Technology Testbed   46
   DefenseLink Freedom of Information Act   46
   Defense Modeling and Simulation Office   47
   Department of Defense Forms Program   47
   Depleted Uranium Library   47
   Deputy Undersecretary of Defense for Industrial Affairs   48
   Directorate for Information Operations and Reports, Statistical Information Analysis Division   48
   DOD Communications and Directives Directorate   49
   George C. Marshall Center for European Security Studies   49
   Gulf War Illnesses, Gulflink   50
   Joint Total Asset Visibility   51
   Joint Vision 2020   51
   National Defense University   52
   Office of Counterproliferation and Biological Defense   61
   Office of Economic Adjustment   61
   Office of Net Assessment   62
   Public Key Infrastructure Program Management Office   62
   Space Policy Directorate   63
   TriCare   63
   Western Hemisphere Institute for Security Cooperation   64
Notes   64

Chapter 3 Other Executive Branch Agencies   72

Department of Commerce   72
   Bureau of Industry and Security   72
   Critical Infrastructure Assurance Office   73
   National Institute of Standards and Technology   74
   National Technical Information Service   75
   Office of Inspector General   75
Department of Energy   76
   Argonne National Laboratory   76
   Brookhaven National Laboratory   77
   Chemical and Biological Defense Program   77
   Closing the Circle—DOE Office of Environmental Management   77
   Directives, Regulations, Policies, and Standards   78
   DOE Representative to the Defense Nuclear Facilities Safety Board   78
   Energy Information Administration   79
   Environment, Safety, and Health Researchers Workstation   79
   Idaho National Engineering and Environmental Laboratory   79
   Initiatives for Proliferation Prevention   80
   International Nuclear Safety Program   80
   Kansas City Plant   81
   Knolls Atomic Power Laboratory   81
   Lawrence Berkeley National Laboratory   81
   Lawrence Livermore National Laboratory   82
   Los Alamos National Laboratory   82
   National Nuclear Security Administration   83
   National Spent Nuclear Fuel Program   83
   National Transportation Program   84
   Nevada Operations Office   84
   New Brunswick Laboratory   85
   Nuclear, Energy, Science, and Technology Office   85

Nuclear Explosion Monitoring, Research, and Engineering Program   86
Oak Ridge National Laboratory   86
Office of Civilian Radioactive Waste Management   88
Office of Environmental Management   88
Office of Independent Oversight and Performance Assurance   89
Office of Inspector General   89
Office of Policy and International Affairs   90
Office of Scientific and Technical Information   90
Office of Site Closure   91
OpenNet   91
Pacific Northwest Laboratory   92
Pantex Plant   92
Sandia National Laboratories   93
Savannah River Site   93
Strategic Petroleum Reserve   94
Yucca Mountain Project   95
Environmental Protection Agency   96
Department of Health and Human Services   96
　Centers for Disease Control Emergency Preparedness and Response   96
　Food and Drug Administration Counterterrorism   97
　National Disaster Medical System   97
　National Institute of Allergy and Infectious Diseases   98
　National Library of Medicine Biodefense and Bioterrorism   98
　Office of Inspector General   98
Department of Homeland Security   99
　Animal and Plant Health Inspection Service   99
　Citizenship and Immigration Services   100
　U.S. Coast Guard   101
　U.S. Customs and Border Protection   101
　Federal Law Enforcement Training Center   102
　Office of Domestic Preparedness   102
　Plum Island Animal Disease Center   103
　U.S. Secret Service   103
　Transportation Security Administration   104
Department of Justice   104

Computer Crime and Intellectual Property Section   105
Counterespionage Section   105
Drug Enforcement Administration   105
Executive Office for Immigration Review   106
Federal Bureau of Investigation   106
National Drug Intelligence Center   108
Office of Inspector General   108
Office of Intelligence Policy and Review   108
Office of International Affairs   109
Department of State   109
　Bureau of Arms Control   110
　Bureau of Diplomatic Security   110
　Bureau of International Narcotics and Law Enforcement Affairs   111
　Bureau of Nonproliferation   111
　Bureau of Political-Military Affairs   112
　Bureau of Verification and Compliance   112
　Coordinator for Counterterrorism   113
　Directorate of Defense Trade Controls   113
　Historian's Office   114
　Office of Inspector General   114
　Office of War Crimes   115
Department of Transportation   115
　Federal Aviation Administration   115
　Maritime Administration   116
　Office of Assistant Secretary for Aviation and International Affairs   116
　Office of Inspector General   117
Department of the Treasury   117
　Office of Enforcement   117
　Office of Foreign Assets Control   118
　Office of Inspector General   118
Executive Office of the President   119
　Presidential Speeches, Proclamations, and Executive Orders   119
　National Security Council   121
　Office of Management and Budget   121
　Office of National Drug Control Policy   122
　Office of Science and Technology Policy   123
　President's Critical Infrastructure Protection Board   123
　White House Military Office   123
Notes   124

Chapter 4 Military Agencies 136

Unified Combatant Commands 136
  Central Command 137
  European Command 137
  Joint Forces Command 138
  Northern Command 138
  Pacific Command 139
  Southern Command 139
  Special Operations Command 139
  Strategic Command 140
  Transportation Command 140
  Unified Command Plan 141
U.S. Air Force 141
  AF News: The Air Force News Agency 141
  Air Force Link 142
  Air Combat Command 142
  Air Command and Staff College 142
  Air National Guard 143
  Air University 143
  Air Force Academy 144
  Air Force Academy Institute for National Security Studies 144
  Air Force Audit Agency 145
  Air Force Command and Control and Intelligence, Surveillance, and Reconnaissance Center 145
  Air Force Communications Agency 145
  Air Force Doctrine Center 146
  Air Force Flight Test Center 146
  Air Force Historical Research Agency 146
  Air Force History Support Office 147
  Air Force Information Warfare Center 147
  Air Force Institute of Technology 148
  Air Force Office of Scientific Research 148
  Air Force Research Laboratory 148
  Air Force Safety Center 149
  Air Force Senior Leadership 149
  Air Force Space Command 149
  Deputy Undersecretary of the Air Force—International Affairs 150
  Space and Missile Systems Center 150
U.S. Army 150
  Aberdeen Proving Ground 151
  American, British, Canadian, and Australian Armies Program 151
  Armor School 151
  Army Chemical School 152
  Army Leadership 152
  Army Mountain Warfare School 152
  Army National Guard 152
  Army Newspapers 153
  Army Research Institute for the Behavioral and Social Sciences 153
  Army Research Laboratory 154
  Army Science Board 154
  Army War College 154
  Assistant Secretary of the Army (Acquisition, Logistics, and Technology) 155
  Center for Army Lessons Learned 156
  Center for Military History 156
  Central Identification Laboratory 157
  Command and General Staff College 157
  Corps of Engineers 157
  Field Artillery School 158
  General Dennis J. Reimer Training and Doctrine Digital Library 158
  Human Resources Command 158
  Infantry School 159
  Medical Research Institute of Chemical Defense 159
  U.S. Military Academy 159
  National Simulation Center 160
  Office of Army International Affairs 160
  Official Department of the Army Publications and Forms 160
  Ordnance Corps 160
  Soldier and Biological Chemical Command 161
  Space and Missile Defense Command 162
  Training and Doctrine Command 162
U.S. Marine Corps 162
  Headquarters 163
  Plans, Policies, and Operations Department 163
  Chemical Biological Incident Response Force 163
  History and Museums Division 163
  Installations and Logistics Departments 164
  Logistics Command 164
  Manpower and Reserve Affairs 164
  Marine Air Ground Task Force Staff and Training Program 164
  Marine Aviation 165
  Marine Corps Combat Development Plan 165
  Marine Corps Doctrine Division 165
  Marine Corps Institute 166
  Marine Corps Systems Command 166
  Marine Corps University 166

Marine Corps Warfighting Laboratory 167
Programs and Resources Department 167
Safety Division 167
Training and Education Command 168
U.S. Navy 168
   Chief of Naval Operations 168
   FOIA Online 169
   Military Sealift Command 169
   U.S. Naval Academy 169
   Naval Aerospace Medical Research Laboratory 170
   Naval Air Systems Command 170
   Naval Cost Analysis Division 170
   Naval Facilities Engineering Command 171
   Naval Historical Center 171
   Naval Medicine Online 171
   U.S. Naval Observatory 172
   Naval Postgraduate School 172
   Naval Research Laboratory 173
   Naval Sea Systems Command 173
   Naval Surface Warfare Center 173
   Naval Treaty Implementation Program 174
   Naval Undersea Warfare Center 174
   Naval Vessel Register 174
   Naval War College 175
   Navy International Programs Office 175
   Navy Personnel Research, Studies, and Technology 176
   Navy Warfare Development Command 176
   Network Centric Innovation Center 176
   Office of Naval Research 177
   Space and Naval Warfare Systems Command 177
   Surface Warfare Directorate 177
Notes 178

Chapter 5 Independent Agencies 188

Chemical Safety and Hazard Investigation Board 188
Defense Nuclear Facilities Safety Board 189
Federal Emergency Management Agency 189
Federal Maritime Commission 190
General Services Administration 190
U.S. Institute of Peace 191
U.S. International Trade Commission 191
National Academy of Sciences 192
National Archives and Records Administration 192
   Information Security Oversight Office 193
   Presidential Libraries 194
Nuclear Regulatory Commission 201
Nuclear Waste Technical Review Board 202
Selective Service System 203
Notes 203

Chapter 6 Intelligence Agencies 207

Central Intelligence Agency 207
Directorate of Intelligence 208
   Directorate of Science and Technology 208
   Center for the Study of Intelligence 209
   Electronic Freedom of Information Act 210
   National Intelligence Council 211
   Foreign Broadcast Information Center 211
Defense Intelligence Agency 212
Military Intelligence Agencies 214
   Air Force Intelligence—Air Intelligence Agency 214
   Army Intelligence 215
   Marine Corps Intelligence Center 216
   Naval Intelligence 217
National Geospatial Intelligence Agency 219
National Security Agency 219
National Counterintelligence Executive 220
National Reconnaissance Office 221
Department of Energy Intelligence Agencies 221

Department of State Bureau of Intelligence and Research   222
Department of Transportation Office of Intelligence and Security   223
National Cyber Security Division   223
President's Foreign Intelligence Advisory Board   224
Notes   225

Chapter 7 Congress and Congressional Support Agencies   229

Congressional Bills and Resolutions   229
Congressional Committee Hearings   230
Congressional Committee Reports   231
Legislative Calendars   233
Committee Activity Reports   233
Floor Debate   233
Congressional National Security Committees   234
  House Appropriations Committee   234
  House Armed Services Committee   234
  House Budget Committee   235
  House Energy and Commerce Committee   236
  House Government Reform Committee   236
  House Permanent Select Intelligence Committee   237
  House International Relations Committee   237
  House Judiciary Committee   238
  House Select Committee on Homeland Security   239
  Senate Appropriations Committee   239
  Senate Armed Services Committee   239
  Senate Budget Committee   240
  Senate Energy and Natural Resources Committee   240
  Senate Foreign Relations Committee   241
  Senate Governmental Affairs Committee   242
  Senate Select Committee on Intelligence   242
  Senate Judiciary Committee   243
  Senate Caucus on International Narcotics Control   243
Commission on Security and Cooperation in Europe   244
Congressional Support Agencies   244
  Congressional Budget Office   244
  General Accounting Office   245
  Library of Congress—Congressional Research Service   246
  Office of Technology Assessment   247
Notes   247

Chapter 8 Commissions and Advisory Organizations   253

Ronald Reagan Administration   253
  Commission on Integrated Long-Term Strategy   254
  Commission on Merchant Marine and Defense   254
  Military Manpower Task Force   254
  National Advisory Committee on Oceans and the Atmosphere   255
  National Bipartisan Commission on Central America (Kissinger Commission)   255
  President's Blue Ribbon Commission on Defense Management (Packard Commission)   255
  President's Commission on Strategic Forces (Scowcroft Commission)   256
  President's Private Sector Survey on Cost Control (Grace Commission)   256
  President's Special Review Board (Tower Commission)   256
George H. W. Bush Administration   257
  Defense Conversion Commission   257
  House Armed Services Committee Panel on Military Education   257
  President's Commission on Aviation Security and Terrorism   258
  President's Commission on Catastrophic Nuclear Accidents   258
  President's Council of Advisors on Science and Technology   259
  Presidential Commission on the Assignment of Women in the Armed Forces   259
Bill Clinton Administration   260
  Advisory Committee on Human Radiation Experiments   260

Advisory Panel to Assess Domestic Response Capabilities for Terrorism Involving Weapons of Mass Destruction (Gilmore Commission) 261
U.S. Commission on National Security/21st Century (Hart-Rudman Commission) 261
Commission on Protecting and Reducing Government Secrecy 262
Commission on Roles and Capabilities of the U.S. Intelligence Community (Brown-Rudman Commission) 262
Commission on Roles and Missions of the Armed Forces 263
Commission to Assess the Organization of the Federal Government to Combat the Proliferation of Weapons of Mass Destruction (Deutch-Specter Commission) 263
Commission to Assess U.S. National Security Space Management and Organization 264
Defense Base Closure and Realignment Commission 265
IC21: The Intelligence Community in the 21st Century 265
Interagency Commission on Crime and Security in U.S. Seaports 266
National Commission for the Review of the National Reconnaissance Office 266
National Commission on Terrorism (Bremer Commission) 267
National Partnership for Reinventing Government/National Performance Review 267
President's Advisory Committee on Gulf War Veterans Illnesses 268
President's Commission on Critical Infrastructure Protection 268
White House Commission on Aviation Safety and Security (Gore Commission) 269
George W. Bush Administration 269
Commission on the Future of the U.S. Aerospace Industry 269
National Commission on Terrorist Attacks Upon the United States 270
U.S.-China Economic and Security Review Commission 270
Notes 271

Chapter 9 Legal and Regulatory Resources 277

U.S. Laws 277
U.S. Statutes at Large 278
United States Code 278
Federal Court System 279
U.S. Supreme Court 279
Foreign Intelligence Surveillance Court 280
Freedom of Information Act and Electronic Freedom of Information Act 281
Military Law 282
Uniform Code of Military Justice 282
U.S. Court of Appeals for the Armed Forces 283
Judge Advocates General 283
Other Military Legal Affairs Resources 286
U.S. Government Documents Regulatory Issues 290
Federal Register 290
Code of Federal Regulations 291
Lists of Sections Affected 292
Notes 292

Chapter 10 Research Institutions and Think Tanks in Washington, D.C. 296

American Enterprise Institute for Policy Research 296
ANSER Institute for Homeland Security 297
Arms Control Association 297
Atlantic Council of the United States 297
British-American Security Information Council 298
Brookings Institution 298
Carnegie Endowment for International Peace 299
Cato Institute 299

Center for Defense Information   299
Center for Security Policy   300
Center for Strategic and Budgetary
    Assessments   300
Center for Strategic and International
    Studies   300
Chemical and Biological Arms Control
    Institute   301
Federation of American Scientists   301
Global Security   302
Henry L. Stimson Center   302
Heritage Foundation   303
Institute for Defense Analyses   303
Institute for Policy Studies   304
Jewish Institute for National Security
    Affairs   304
National Institute for Public Policy   304
National Security Archive   305
Nuclear Control Institute   305
Potomac Institute for Policy Studies   306
Russian American Nuclear Security Advisory
    Council   306
Terrorism Research Center   307
Wisconsin Project on Nuclear Arms
    Control   307
Woodrow Wilson International Center for
    Scholars   308
Notes   308

Chapter 11 Research Institutions and Think Tanks outside Washington, D.C.   311

Belfer Center for Science and International
    Affairs   311
Center for Civilian Biodefense
    Strategies   312
Center for Global Peace and Conflict
    Studies   312
Center for Infectious Disease Research and
    Policy   313
Center for International Security and
    Cooperation   313
Center for International Trade and
    Security   313
Center for Nonproliferation Studies   314
Columbia International Affairs Online   314
Declassified Documents Reference
    System   315
East-West Center   315
Foreign Policy Research Institute   316
Hoover Institution on War, Revolution, and
    Peace   316
Hudson Institute   317
Institute for Foreign Policy Analysis   317
John M. Olin Institute for Strategic
    Studies   318
Johns Hopkins Center for Strategic and
    Advanced International Studies   318
MIT Security Studies Program   318
National Bureau of Asian Research   319
Nautilus Institute   319
Pacific Institute Studies in Development,
    Environment, and Security   320
Program in Arms Control, Disarmament,
    and International Security   320
Program on Science and Global
    Security   320
Project on Defense Alternatives   321
RAND Corporation   321
Ridgway Center for International Security
    Studies   323
Stratfor   323
Triangle Institute for Security Studies   324
Notes   324

Chapter 12 Foreign and International Government Organizations   327

Australia   328
    Department of Defence   328
    Australian Intelligence Agencies   330
    Australian National Audit Office   332
    Australian Parliament   332
Canada   333
    Department of National Defence   334
    Canadian Intelligence Agencies   335
    Canadian Parliament   336
    Office of Auditor General   337
United Kingdom   338
    Prime Minister's Office   338
    Cabinet Office—Intelligence Security
        Committee   338

Home Office 339
Ministry of Defence 339
British Intelligence Agencies 340
National Archives—Public Records Office 341
National Audit Office 342
Parliament 342
Other Foreign Governments 344
  India 344
  Israel 344
  New Zealand 344
  Singapore 345
  South Africa 345
International Government Organizations 345
  European Parliament—Committee on Foreign Affairs, Human Rights, Common Security, and Defence Policy 346
  European Union Common Foreign and Security Policy 346
  North Atlantic Treaty Organization 347
  Organization for Security and Co-operation in Europe 347
  United Nations 348
Notes 351

Chapter 13 Foreign Research Institutions 359

Australia 359
  Australian Defence Studies Centre 359
  Australian Strategic Policy Institute 360
  Strategic and Defence Studies Centre 360
Bulgaria—Institute for Security and International Studies 360
Canada 361
  Canadian Institute of Strategic Studies 361
  Centre for Security and Defence Studies—Carleton University 361
  Conference of Defence Associations 362
  Council for Canadian Security in the 21st Century 362
  Research Group in International Security 363
  University of Calgary—Centre for Military and Strategic Studies 363
  University of Manitoba—Centre for Defence and Security Studies 363
  York Centre for International and Security Studies 364
Denmark—Danish Institute of International Affairs 364
Finland—Finnish Institute of International Affairs 365
Germany—German Institute for International Politics and Security 365
India 365
  Institute for Defence Studies and Analysis 366
  Institute for Peace and Conflict Studies 366
Israel 366
  Begin-Sadat Center for Strategic Studies 366
  Institute for Advanced Strategic and Political Studies 367
  Jaffee Center for Strategic Studies 367
Japan—Institute for International Policy Studies 368
New Zealand—Centre for Strategic Studies 368
Pakistan—Institute of Strategic Studies–Islamabad 368
Singapore—Institute of Defense and Strategic Studies 369
South Africa 369
  Centre for Conflict Resolution 369
  Institute for Security Studies 369
Sri Lanka—Regional Centre for Strategic Studies 370
Sweden—Stockholm International Peace Research Institute 371
Switzerland 371
  Center for Security Studies 371
  Geneva Centre for Security Policy 372
  International Relations and Security Network 372
Taiwan—Taiwan Security Research 373
United Arab Emirates—Emirates Center for Strategic Studies and Research 373
United Kingdom 373
  Acronym Institute for Disarmament Diplomacy 374
  Civil-Military Relations in Central and Eastern Europe Internet Resource Center 374

Conflict, Security, and Development Group 374
Conflict Studies Research Centre 375
International Institute for Strategic Studies 375
Jane's Information Group 376
Lancaster University—Centre for Defence and International Security Studies 376
Royal United Services Institute 376
Notes 377

Chapter 14 Selected Indexes, Journals, Series, and Scholars 380

Periodical Indexes 380
  "Air University Library Index to Military Periodicals" 380
  America: History and Life 381
  "Catalog of Government Publications" 381
  Congressional Information Service Index 381
  "Ebsco Host's Military and Government Collection" 381
  Historical Abstracts 381
  LexisNexis Government Periodicals Index 382
  Public Affairs Information Service International 382
  "Staff College Automated Periodicals Index" 383
  Worldwide Political Science Abstracts 383
Scholarly Journals 383
  Armed Forces and Society 384
  Astropolitics: The International Journal of Space Power and Policy 384
  Civil Wars 384
  Cold War History 384
  Comparative Strategy 384
  Contemporary Security Policy 385
  CQ Weekly Report 385
  Defence Studies 385
  European Security 385
  Intelligence and National Security 385
  International Journal of Intelligence and Counterintelligence 386
  International Peacekeeping 386
  International Security 386
  Journal of Battlefield Technology 386
  Journal of Cold War Studies 387
  Journal of Conflict and Security Law 387
  Journal of Contingencies and Crisis Management 387
  Journal of Military Ethics: Normative Aspects of the Use of Military Force 387
  Journal of Military History 388
  Journal of Slavic Military Studies 388
  Journal of Strategic Studies 388
  Low Intensity Conflict and Law Enforcement 388
  National Interest 388
  National Journal 389
  Proceedings: U.S. Naval Institute 389
  Security Studies 389
  Small Wars and Insurgencies 389
  Studies in Conflict and Terrorism 390
  Survival 390
  Terrorism and Political Violence 390
  Global Crime 390
Monographic Series 391
  Annals of Communism—Yale University Press 391
  BCSIA Studies in International Security—Massachusetts Institute of Technology Press 392
  Cambridge Studies in International Relations 392
  Contributions in Military Studies 392
  Cornell Studies in Security Affairs 392
  Eastern European Studies—Texas A&M University Press 393
  Foreign Policy, Security, and Strategic Studies—McGill-Queen's University Press 393
  Modern War Studies—University Press of Kansas 394
  The New Cold War History—University of North Carolina 394
  Nuclear Age Series—Stanford University Press 394
  Princeton Studies in International History and Politics 395
  Smithsonian History of Aviation and Spaceflight Series 395
  Studies in Canadian Military History—University of British Columbia Press and Canadian War Museum 395
  Studies in International Security and Arms Control—Stanford University Press 396

Studies in War, Society, and the Military—
 University of Nebraska Press   396
Texas A&M University Military History
 Series   397
Scholars   397
 Eliot Cohen   397
 Anthony Cordesman   398

James Corum   399
Colin Gray   399
John Mearsheimer   400
Michael O'Hanlon   401
Barry Posen   401
Larry Wortzel   402
Notes   402

Acronymns   405
Index   413
Citations of Authors   448

Boxed Features

Goldwater-Nichols Act   12
Department of Defense   26
Freedom of Information Act   30
1947 National Security Act   41
Department of Homeland Security   100
USA PATRIOT Act   107
National Security Council Documents   120
Military Acronyms   137
Intelligence Community   208
Central Intelligence Agency   209
Intelligence Acronyms   210
National Intelligence Estimates   212
President's Daily Brief   213
Congressional Oversight of National Security Policy   231
Posse Comitatus Act   278
Courts-Martial   283
Law of War   285
Military Commission Trials   289
Superintendent of Documents Classification System   382
Library of Congress Subject Headings   391
Dewey Decimal Classification System   393
Library of Congress Classification System   396

Preface

The September 11, 2001, attacks compelled Americans and the rest of the international community to think about national security issues. However, a limited reference literature exists to assist in conducting substantive research on national security policy. This is not an easily navigated area. For example, such policy consists of how and why nations go to war, how they assess their military forces as well as those of their opponents, what determines the capabilities and limitations of individual weapons systems, and how the psychological behavior of policymakers affects the entire process.

Researching National Security and Intelligence Policy covers these subjects but also goes one step further. The book takes a much more expansive view of the multiple factors that compose national security policy than do other texts. This includes an introduction to resources on such topics as the public health responses to incidents that involve weapons of mass destruction and the contractual and accounting details involved in purchasing a military weapons system. In addition, this reference examines the process of introducing and guiding national security legislation through a legislative body, the implementation of regulations to carry out legislative intent for a particular statute, and court cases. Export controls on items considered sensitive for national security are explored as are health care for military service members and their families, the role of environmental subjects—such as nuclear waste—in formulating national security policy, and cutting-edge scientific and technological research.

This volume covers works from governmental and scholarly publications that represent a variety of methodological, partisan, and ideological viewpoints. Its scope is global and includes publicly accessible English-language governmental publications and research institution publications from a number of countries, including Australia, India, Singapore, South Africa, and the United Kingdom. Publications from international governmental organizations, including the European Union and the United Nations, also are represented. The United States is the world's preeminent military power in the early twenty-first century. This does not mean, however, that Americans and others interested in the study of national security policy can afford to be unfamiliar with non-American viewpoints on national security issues in addition to the vast variety of opinions on these subjects held by Americans and U.S. institutions.

The national security policy materials available in U.S. federal depository libraries are a particularly valuable resource. Numbering more than twelve hundred nationwide, these libraries are part of the Federal Depository Library Program (FDLP) operated by the U.S. Government Printing Office (GPO). The FDLP provides free access to government information resources. A directory of these libraries is available at www.gpoaccess.gov/libraries.html.

Two other valuable reference services are available on the GPO's website. The Catalog of U.S. Government Publications site (www.gpoaccess.gov/cgp) offers bibliographic information about U.S. government publications distributed by the GPO to federal depository libraries from January 1994 to the present. In addition, it provides links to the full text of an increasing number of publications and includes listings of depository libraries that may have a copy of them. The New Electronic Titles site (www.access.gpo.gov/su_docs/locators/net) provides full-text electronic access to U.S. government publications dating from July 2000 to the present that the GPO has included in the FDLP.

In democratic countries, national security policy research also involves the perennial conflict between the right of citizens to be informed and the need to formulate and execute sensitive military and intelligence operations. A balanced compromise is not always possible when secrecy is required to protect the lives and operational methods used to carry out such covert activities. Readers should recognize that much national security policy information is classified. This is done to protect operational sources and methods used to formulate and implement governmental national security policy. Although practices and statutory declassification procedures vary in democratic countries, most national security information produced by such countries will eventually be declassified and publicly accessible in some format. Such declassification, however, may not occur until decades after the occurrence of the events or policy decisions being examined.

Researching National Security and Intelligence Policy emphasizes the availability of free, high-quality national security policy information on the Internet. However, print, microform, and archival resources also are reviewed, in part because of the Internet's limited coverage of historical material. This book uses and critically examines such works. It eschews the trumpets-and-drums approach taken by some right-wing publications as well as the myopic, naïve, and dangerous hostility to national security issues and institutions taken by individuals and organizations on the far left side of the political spectrum. It is not a soapbox for propagating my views or those of anyone else. Rather, its intent is to show how individuals—students, scholars, or anyone else interested in national security issues—can conduct intellectually substantive research on these issues. It does not advocate a particular methodological or theoretical paradigm for conducting such research.

The book begins with a historical overview of national security policy education within the United States, focusing on the service academies, military war colleges, and joint service institutions. Later chapters describe the publicly available national security policy resources produced by U.S. executive branch agencies, including the Department of Defense and the armed services; resources produced by independent government agencies; materials originating in Congress and congressional support agencies; and governmental legal and regulatory resources.

Other chapters discuss national security resources produced by international government organizations and U.S. and foreign research institutions. In these the emphasis is on national security research, key scholarly journals, and the works of selected security studies scholars.

I have made all reasonable efforts to verify the accuracy of uniform resource locators (URLs) for government agencies and nongovernmental resources cited in this book. However, changing governmental, academic institution, and private sector organization identities and website administrative practices means that some URLs may have changed. Often, users will be redirected to the new site. If not, use search engines, such as the U.S. government's www.firstgov.gov, for federal agency resources and commercial search engines, such as www.searchmil.com, www.google.com, or your favorite search engine, to locate the new URLs.

Acknowledgments

Numerous individuals influenced whatever writing abilities and intellectual erudition that may appear in this book. My parents, Albert and Mildred Chapman, who are retired teachers, have shaped me in innumerable ways and impressed upon my brother, Brent, and me the importance of a quality education and effective communication. Many other teachers enhanced my ability to think critically and transmit those thoughts into written words, including Steve Hoffmann, Larry Wilcox, and Alan Winquist, among others.

Chris Anzalone, Colleen McGuiness, January Layman-Wood, and Lorna Notsch of CQ Press have guided me through the intricacies of book publishing with consummate professionalism.

My career as a professional librarian has been ably directed by effective supervisors such as Juanita Weisel, Mark Tucker, and Judy Nixon. I also have been blessed to work at Purdue University's Humanities, Social Sciences, and Education Library—its collegial atmosphere encourages intellectual and scholarly advancement. Throughout my career as a government documents librarian, I have been fortunate to have a solid support staff, among them Bernice Lesmeister, Trina Boykin Nolen, Lori Bryant, Linda Fidelle, Amy Fox, Jan Glascock, and Janyne McWilliam.

Other librarians provided professional support, including many working as government documents librarians at U.S. federal depository libraries. Although not a government documents librarian, an associate who has been particularly encouraging and supportive of my professional growth is Pam Rebarcak, who is both a colleague and a cherished friend.

Most importantly, I want to thank my wife, Becky, who keeps me focused on the important things in life and whose love gives me the greatest confidence and security found in this world.

Bert Chapman
Lafayette, Indiana

CHAPTER 1

National Security Educational Institutions

Countries other than the United States—such as Germany, Russia, and the United Kingdom—have developed educational institutions to instruct military personnel and officers in the skills and values that they regard as essential in producing effective commanders, strategists, and warfighters to fulfill vital national security objectives. However, an examination of the historical evolution of U.S. national security policy educational institutions is instructive, owing to the domestic and international influence they have on contemporary professional military education. The American institutions are highly regarded internationally because the United States is generally seen as providing a model political-military relationship with effective civilian authority. Additional factors prompting high appraisals of U.S. national security educational institutions include their ability to provide political and military authorities in emerging democracies with exposure to the U.S. democratic political culture with its augmented interaction between military and civilian policymakers and the desire of foreign military personnel to gain greater insight into U.S. military performance in combat and humanitarian operations, to learn about innovative practices in military management and operations, and to experience the freedom to explore innovative ways of solving operational and strategic problems that might not be possible in their indigenous political-military institutional culture.[1]

A quote from a 1998 article appearing in the Joint Chiefs of Staff journal *Joint Force Quarterly* provides valuable intellectual and historical context to the factors that have brought on the growth of modern professional military education (PME) in the United States.

> A number of influences led to increased interest in the subject in the United States at the end of the 19th century. The impressive, effortless Prussian victories of 1866 and 1870 supported the arguments of reformers such as William Tecumseh Sherman and Emory Upton that it was essential to military effectiveness. But the benign security environment of the day removed all urgency from the issue of educational reform. At

the turn of the century, however, two new factors sped it up. The first was the increasing identification of professions such as law, medicine, and engineering with educational preparation. Officers realized that to be considered professional they would have to institute a substantial program of education. Second, the Spanish-American War revealed major deficiencies in military organization and introduced imperial commitments that demanded study. Americans, least of all their military, could no longer hide behind notions of isolationism.[2]

Armed Services Academies

The armed services academies—U.S. Air Force Academy, U.S. Coast Guard Academy, U.S. Military Academy, and U.S. Naval Academy—influence professional U.S. military education.

U.S. Air Force Academy

Located in Colorado Springs, Colorado, the U.S. Air Force Academy (USAFA) was established in 1954 and is responsible for providing undergraduate education to approximately four thousand cadets. The academy's mission is to develop aerospace officers with the resources and skills required to lead the air force.[3] Nineteen academic departments offer thirty academic majors—twenty disciplinary, four divisional, and six interdisciplinary in scope. The majors include aeronautical and astronautical engineering, history, legal studies, meteorology, military strategic studies, physics, and political science.[4]

U.S. Coast Guard Academy

The U.S. Coast Guard Academy (CGA) is located in New London, Connecticut, and its mission is preparing men and women with the technical skills and character to be commissioned Coast Guard officers.[5] CGA's origins date back to 1876, when a School of Instruction for the Revenue Marine was established near New Bedford, Massachusetts. The academy's modern institutional incarnation began with the 1915 merger of the Life Saving Service and the Revenue Cutter Service. The CGA moved to its present location in 1932, and nearly five thousand applicants seek appointments each year. Admission is based on an annual national competition instead of the congressional appointments required for the other military academies.[6]

CGA awards bachelor of science degrees in eight majors: civil engineering, electrical engineering, mechanical engineering, naval architecture and marine engineering, operations research and computer analysis, marine and environmental science, government, and management. The academy also commissions about 175 ensigns during its annual May graduation ceremonies.[7]

U.S. Military Academy

The U.S. Military Academy (USMA), in West Point, New York, was established in 1802. Its mission is providing undergraduate education and training for cadets who are commissioned as second lieutenants in the army upon graduation. USMA's cadet corps personnel number four thousand, and they can choose academic instruction from twenty-two majors and twenty-five fields of study ranging across the liberal arts, sciences, and engineering.[8]

USMA remains an important player in American national security education, and its motto "Duty, Honor, and Country" is deeply ingrained in U.S. military culture.

U.S. Naval Academy

The U.S. Naval Academy (USNA) is located in Annapolis, Maryland. Established in 1845, USNA's mission is serving as the navy's undergraduate educational institution and promoting the overall education of its student body who are called midshipmen. USNA initially consisted of fifty midshipmen; its current enrollment is nearly four thousand, including women, who were first admitted to the service academies in 1976. The academy awards bachelor's degrees in twenty-five subjects, including naval architecture, ocean engineering, oceanography, mathematics, history, and political science.[9]

Military Graduate Schools

A number of U.S. military institutions provide graduate-level educational and training for U.S. military officers, foreign military officers, and select U.S. government civilians and award graduate degrees such as the master of strategic studies. Such officers and civilians are likely to be individuals destined to hold significant operational command positions within the U.S. military, national militaries if they are from outside the United States, or prominent civilian policy-making positions with national security aspects.[10]

Each of the U.S. armed services has educational institutions that cover education and training in the educational and operational issues that officers need to be successful leaders in their respective services. Some of these institutions are war colleges for the entire service, while others cover specific aspects of leadership within a particular military service such as the U.S. Army Command and General Staff College (CGSC). Meanwhile, joint military education stresses the need to work with two or more military departments or services to conduct activities and operations.[11]

Air University

Air University (AU) is located at Maxwell Air Force Base near Montgomery, Alabama. Established in its contemporary form in 1946, AU's mission is conducting professional military, graduate, and continuing education for officers, enlisted personnel, and civilians to prepare them for leadership, command, staff, and management responsibilities.[12]

Component entities within AU include the Air Command and Staff College (ACSC); Air War College (AWC); College of Aerospace Doctrine, Research, and Education (CADRE); Ira C. Eaker College for Professional Development; and School of Advanced Air and Space Studies (SAASS).

ACSC serves as the air force's intermediate PME school. It is responsible for preparing field grade officers, international officers, and U.S. civilians to assume positions of increased responsibility in the military and other governmental areas. It is geared toward teaching the skills required for aerospace operations supporting joint campaigns as well as leadership and command. ACSC's academic environment promotes free expression of ideas and independent, analytical, and creative thinking. Its curriculum evolves from a lecture-based to a seminar-centered active learning and problem-solving environment over a ten-month cycle.[13]

AWC serves as the air force's senior professional military school. It prepares 265 resident and more than 3,500 nonresident students from U.S. military services, federal agencies, and forty-five countries to provide leadership in a strategic environment emphasizing joint operations and the use of aerospace power to support national security. It also serves as a resource to promote learning and dialogue on national and international aerospace issues.[14]

CADRE mission objectives include advancing the theory and application of aerospace power through professional education, research, and training and the publication of the journal *Air and Space Power Journal*.[15]

The Ira C. Eaker College for Professional Development provides professional continuing education and technical training to air force and Department of Defense (DOD) personnel as well as international officers. It offers eighty-three resident and distance education courses for chaplains, manpower managers, comptrollers, historians, human resource managers, and judge advocate generals.[16]

The SAASS mandate is educating strategists in aerospace warfare's art and science. SAASS faculty teach a graduate-level curriculum covering the theories, history, applications, design, and effective expression of aerospace strategies, operational concepts, and related policies in the context of conflict, deterrence, and war. This curriculum encompasses forty-eight weeks in classes meeting two hours four times a week in a graduate colloquium format. Student preparation for these sessions averages six to eight hours and is augmented by a weekly reading demand of twelve hundred to fifteen hundred pages. Students are also required to prepare a thesis structured on original source documents.[17]

U.S. Army War College

The U.S. Army War College (USAWC) is located in Carlisle Barracks, Pennsylvania. Its mandate includes preparing selected military, civilian, and international leaders for strategic leadership responsibilities; educating current and future leaders on landpower's development and use in joint, multinational, and interagency environments; conducting and publishing research on national security and military strategy; and supporting the army's strategic communication efforts.[18]

USAWC was established in Washington, D.C., in 1903 and moved to its present location in 1951. It includes divisions such as the Strategic Studies Institute (SSI) established in 1954, the Military History Institute (MHI) established in 1967, and the Center for Strategic Leadership (CSL) established in 1994. CSL carries out USAWC's educational mission for a student body whose graduating class numbered 321 in

1997. USAWC students must be active-duty colonels or lieutenant colonels with at least sixteen and no more than twenty-three years of service when classes begin.[19]

CSL is responsible for serving as an educational center and high-technology laboratory. Its activities include focusing on decision-making processes at interagency, strategic, and operational levels to support USAWC, combatant commanders, and senior army leadership. Specific CSL objectives include expanding and refining the study of landpower's strategic use and its application in joint and combined operations while helping senior army leaders resolve strategic problems by using cutting-edge technology.[20]

MHI is responsible for organizing and preserving historical army materials and providing access to these materials for the defense community, academic researchers, and the public to expand understanding of the army's role in U.S. history and the future.[21]

SSI serves as the army's research institute for analyzing national security policy and military strategy. Its personnel include civilian research professors, military officers, and a professional support staff. The Art of War Department examines global, regional, and functional issues with particular emphasis on army transformation. The Regional Strategy and Planning Department analyzes regional strategic issues. The Academic Engagement Program develops and sustains collaborative partnerships with the global strategic community.[22]

Other USAWC academic components include the Department of Command, Leadership, and Management (DCLM), the Department of Military Strategy, Planning, and Operations (DMSPO), and the Department of National Security and Strategy (DNSS). DCLM seeks to prepare students to operate in a strategic environment by developing understanding of strategic leadership responsibilities derived from group learning, creative and critical thinking, strategic leadership competence, joint and army systems and processes, and critical self-appraisal.[23]

DMPSO is responsible for educating officers to translate national military strategy into short-term and intermediate-term plans and programs. It seeks to do this by developing and conducting instruction on theater strategic planning; campaign planning through a multiplicity of military operations; joint, multinational, and interagency plans and operations; military operations other than war; and joint and Army doctrine.[24]

DNSS aims to develop and conduct instruction in national military strategy and national security. Its curricular content utilizes economics, history, international relations, politics, national and international security studies, and regional studies to prepare students for senior national security establishment positions.[25]

Army Command and General Staff College

The U.S. Army Command and General Staff College (CGSC) is located at Fort Leavenworth, Kansas. Formally established as the School of Application for Cavalry and Infantry, CGSC acquired its current name in 1947 and received congressional authorization to award the master of military science degree to its graduates in 1974. It has a projected student body of nearly thirty-three thousand army and other service officers, Army Department civilians, and almost one hundred international officers from seventy countries.[26]

CGSC's mission revolves around educating leaders in professional military values and practices, being the primary agent for the Leadership Development Program, developing army doctrinal guidance, and supporting and advancing the growth of military art and science. It carries out these mandates through a master of military art and science degree program; developing, coordinating, and executing army leader development action plans; regularly reviewing doctrine to maintain its currency and validity; stimulating and developing doctrinal concepts and ideas; ensuring the internal and external integration of military art and science advancements; and researching, writing, and publishing works supporting the advancement of military art and science.[27]

A variety of institutions enable CGSC to fulfill its educational and research objectives: the Center for Army Lessons Learned (CALL), Combat Studies Institute (CSI), Combined Arms and Services Staff School (CAS3), Combined Arms Research Library (CARL), School for Command Preparation (SCP), and School of Advanced Military Studies (SAMS).

CALL is responsible for collecting and analyzing data from current and historical sources dealing with army operations and training and for producing lessons about these events for military commanders, staff, and CGSC students.[28]

CSI presents military history instruction by examining the evolution of military theory, the art of war, and nature of battle with discussion groups of approximately eighteen officer students. CSI also serves as the historical studies advocacy agency for the Training and Doctrine Command (TRADOC) and possesses a Military History Instructional Support Team and a research and publications section.[29]

CAS3 is responsible for educating and training junior army leaders to function as staff officers. Its institutional objectives include improving the ability of these officers to analyze and solve military problems, increasing their communication skills, enhancing their ability to interact and coordinate as a staff member, and improving their understanding of army organizations, operations, and procedures during six-week course sessions.[30]

CARL collects and maintains various information resources to support the instructional and research needs of CGSC students, faculty, and the overall military community. It provides descriptions of its holdings and links to a variety of digitized resources including selected historical class lectures through its website (www.cgsc.army.mil/carl/resources/).[31]

SCP coordinates and conducts battalion- and brigade-level pre-command training for active and reserve command selectees. This is accomplished through four one-week courses: Pre-Command Course, Command Team Seminar, Tactical Commanders Development Course, and Battle Commanders Development Course. These courses emphasize experiential learning and stress visualizing, describing, and directing military unit actions during combat operations using tools such as the "Think Like a Commander" CD-ROM and other forms of simulation-enhanced tactical training.[32]

The institutional intent of SAMS is providing graduate officer education in military art and science to produce leaders with the flexibility required to solve complex problems of peace and war. These objectives are carried out by the Advanced Military Studies Program (AMSP) and the Advanced Operational Arts Studies Fellowship (AOASF). AMSP curriculum focuses on planning, preparing, and executing operations in joint, multinational, and interagency situations; features the integrated study of military history, theory, and execution-based practical exercises; and helps students develop cognitive problem-solving skills to surmount difficult operational challenges at war's tactical and operational levels.[33]

AOASF serves as a SAMS capstone program and is a two-year course preparing senior officers for colonel-level command and operational planning assignments in combatant and service component commands. Program year one sees fellows adhering to a curriculum incorporating graduate military art and science studies, visits to combatant and service component commands, guest speakers, and practical exercises in campaign and major operations planning. Program year two fellows serve as CGSC faculty members with emphasis on being AMSP seminar leaders.[34]

Marine Corps University

Marine Corps University (MCU) is located in Quantico, Virginia. The newest of the armed services higher educational institutions, MCU was founded in 1989, although U.S. Marine Corps (USMC) higher educational programs date back to the 1891 establishment of the School of Application in Washington, D.C.[35] MCU's mission involves developing, executing, and evaluating professional military education for marines by focusing on leadership and core competencies through resident and distance education programs to enable students to meet current and future operational challenges.[36]

MCU pedagogical objectives are carried out by several component entities including Marine Corps War College (MCWAR), Command and Staff College (CSC), School of Advanced Warfighting (SAW), Expeditionary Warfare School (EWS), Enlisted Professional Military Education (EPME), and School of Marine Air Ground Task Force (MAGTF) Logistics.

MCWAR provides a one-year program educating senior officers and civilians for decision making during war and military operations other than war in joint, interagency, and multinational environments. Sixteen students were enrolled in this program during 2003. Its graduates are trained to assume senior leadership positions of increasing complexity through their study of national and theater military strategies and plans and to provide military support to such strategies in the context of national security policies, decision making, objectives, and resources.[37]

CSC, with 184 students in 2003, seeks to provide intermediate and advanced-intermediate professional military education to USMC field grade officers and officers from other services and foreign countries and to prepare them for command staff duties with MAGTFs and for assignment with joint, multinational, and high-level service organizations.[38]

SAW is a second-year supplement to CSC and had twenty-four students in 2003. It focuses on the link between the operational art of what warfighters must do to win campaigns and how they prepare themselves to achieve this goal. The objectives are accomplished through a dynamic curriculum and active learning methodologies and through the production of officers who can think independently.[39]

EWS provides career-level professional military education to selected U.S. Marine, other service, and international officers and emphasizes command and control, warfighting skills, and combined arms operations and MAGTFs in expeditionary operations to prepare graduates to serve as commanders and staff officers within operational forces. Two hundred forty-one students were enrolled in this program in 2003.[40]

EPME strives to develop, execute, and evaluate professional military education and training focusing on leadership and USMC core competencies through resident and distance education programs to prepare students to meet present and future operational challenges. This program had 903 Sergeants Course graduates, 718 Career Course graduates, and 353 Advanced Course graduates in 2003.[41]

The School of MAGTF Logistics enrolled 291 students in 2003. Its mission is providing logistics education programs to company and field-grade logisticians and establishing a liaison with Marine Corps Combat Development Command (MCCDC) to develop logistics doctrine and educate and prepare USMC logisticians for enhanced logistics responsibilities.[42]

An additional component of MCU is the Marine Corps Research Center (MCRC). Established in 1993, MCRC is made up of an archive, a conference center, and a library. MCRC's mission is supporting the study of expeditionary and amphibious warfare in the corps by providing comprehensive storage, retrieval, analysis, and distribution of warfighting information. It seeks to provide its constituents with timely access to books, journals, historically significant archival documents, current scholarly research, and the USMC professional military education process and to stimulate the development and implementation of concepts, doctrine, tactical techniques, and procedures that further corps education and training.[43]

Naval War College

The Naval War College (NWC), in Newport, Rhode Island, was established in 1884. NWC's mission includes enhancing the professional capabilities of its students to make sound decisions in combat, staff, and management positions in naval, joint, and combined environments; providing solid understanding of military strategy and operational art; instilling joint attitudes and perspectives; and serving as a research and gaming center to develop advanced strategic, warfighting, and campaign concepts for future deployment of maritime, joint, and combined forces.[44]

Important NWC academic components are the College of Distance Education (CDE), College of Naval Command and Staff (CNCS), College of Naval Warfare (CNW), Naval Command College (NCC), and Naval Staff College (NSC).

CDE is an extension of NWC's CNCS and provides educational services to nonresident military officers and selected government employees through evening seminars and web-based correspondence programs.[45]

CNCS is a multidisciplinary program for U.S. Navy and Coast Guard lieutenant commanders, other armed services majors, and civilians with equivalent seniority from various federal agencies in annual classes of 240–260 students. Individuals selected to attend CNCS by their respective services have bachelor's degrees, nearly half have master's degrees, and they will have earned outstanding performance appraisals during their twelve to fifteen years of service. CNCS students pursue studies in NWC's three core areas: Joint Maritime Operations, National Security Decision Making, and Strategy and Policy. The ultimate CNCS program objective is preparing students for increased responsibilities as commanders or lieutenant colonels and junior captains or colonels.[46]

CNW is also a multidisciplinary program designed for U.S. Navy and Coast Guard captains or commanders, other armed service colonels or lieutenant colonels, and civilians of equivalent seniority from various federal agencies in annual classes of 200–225 students. Those attending have bachelor's degrees, more than half have master's degrees, and 3 percent hold doctorates. Furthermore, they have earned outstanding performance appraisals during their fifteen to twenty years of service. They study NWC's core areas in the following order: National Security Decision Making, Policy and Strategy, and Joint Military Operations. The key CNW program objective is preparing these students for higher executive responsibilities as senior captains or colonels and flag or general officers.[47]

NCC is the NWC component providing education for international naval officers from countries allied with the United States. Its institutional goals include enabling selected international naval officers to develop national security decision-making skills, build strategy and policy analytical structures, gain expertise in joint warfighting doctrine, increase their understanding of U.S. societal institutions, promote friendship and cooperation, prepare for higher command responsibilities in their militaries, and promote international naval cooperation for the peaceful use of the seas, for lessening crises, and for fighting and winning wars.[48]

NSC seeks to train international naval officers in developing the professional and managerial skills required to assume command and staff responsibilities within their own navies. This is accomplished through a five-and-a-half-month academic curriculum, offered twice a year beginning in January and July. Areas emphasized by this curriculum include naval planning and decision making and augmenting officers' knowledge of seapower's role in international affairs. A key component of NSC instruction is visiting economic, educational, governmental, and nongovernmental institutions to interact with civilian and military leaders to discuss issues and promote a more balanced understanding of U.S. society.[49]

An important NWC research component is the Center for Naval Warfare Studies (CNWS). This entity complements NWC curriculum by serving as a forum for researching professional issues that inform and stimulate classroom faculty and students as well as naval and policy-making civilians. Carrying out this professional research are the Strategic Research Department, Warfare Analysis and Research Department, War Gaming Department, International Law Department, Advanced Research Program, Naval War College Press, Office of Naval Intelligence Detachment, and Strategic Studies Group.[50]

Naval Postgraduate School

The Naval Postgraduate School (NPS) is located in Monterey, California. Its contemporary institutional organization dates from a 1945 law making it a fully accredited graduate institution. NPS has nearly fifteen hundred students representing thirty countries. These students are U.S. military service officers, U.S. government employees, and foreign government employees. They are pursuing master's and doctoral degrees in subjects as varied as aeronautical engineering, applied physics, information technology management, meteorology, national security affairs, and physical oceanography in ways appropriate to U.S. Navy and Defense Department requirements.[51] Besides curricular degree programs, NPS has numerous research centers performing innovative research on national security–relevant issues. Examples are the Cebrowski Institute for Information Innovation and Superiority (CINFINIS), Center for Civil-Military Relations (CCMR), Center for Contemporary Conflict (CCC), Center for Information Systems Security Studies and Research (NPS CISR), Center for Joint Services Electronic Warfare (CJSEW), Center on Terrorism and Irregular Warfare (CTIW), and Spacecraft Research and Design Center (SRDC).

CINFINIS seeks to engage in pathbreaking research and education in information technologies, operations, and strategies emphasizing their national security development and applications. This research is carried out by CINFINIS and by component organizations such as the Center for Information Security (INFOSEC) Studies and Center for the Study of Mobile Devices and Communications. Specific focus areas of CINFINIS research include technical developments facilitating trustworthy collection, location, and analyses of electromagnetic emissions for National Technical Intelligence capability infrastructure; constructing and using computing resources to control and share information depending on its importance and sensitivity; showing how infrastructure threats are developed and pursued over time by highly organized adversaries; developing experimental methods for communicating with information adversaries and their infrastructure; and synthesizing, disseminating, processing, and displaying information in a trustworthy infrastructure.[52]

CCMR seeks to strengthen civil-military relations in democratic countries through various U.S.-funded education and training programs. It conducts programs assisting recipient countries in areas such as defense decision making, strategic planning and restructuring, peace support operations, and fighting terrorism. CCMR programs also cover geographic regions such as Africa, Asia-Pacific, Europe, Latin America, and the Middle East and produces various instructional resources and research publications documenting its work.[53]

CCC conducts research on current and emerging security issues and transmits its findings to U.S. and allied policymakers and military forces. Research areas generally focus on key emerging security issue areas such as asymmetric conflict including terrorism and information operations, the proliferation of weapons of mass destruction and nonproliferation initiatives, regional instability including peacekeeping and humanitarian missions, and strategic nuclear policy highlighting deterrence doctrine, command and control, arms control, and missile defense.[54]

NPS CISR strives to assist warfighters' information assurance needs and seeks to accomplish this by bringing together vital educational and research elements of a DOD university. It conducts research and academic outreach, holds classes and workshops, offers information assurance courses, and sponsors lectures by noted authorities to accomplish these objectives. More than four hundred students use its laboratories annually, and the center supports more graduate student thesis information assurance research than any other U.S. program in this area.[55]

CJSEW is a focal point for industrial and DOD electronic warfare research. It assists the Joint Services Electronic Warfare Program and the NPS information warfare curriculum while also hosting simulation and modeling tools and hardware research supporting national electronic warfare strategy. Examples of CJSEW research areas include atmospheric modeling, communications and radar jamming, high-speed signal processing, information warfare strategies, laser and radar cross-section engineering, missiles and missile simulation surveillance systems, and shipboard self-protection systems.[56] CTIW produces contemporary, innovative, and interdisciplinary analysis on terrorism and irregular warfare. Center researchers examine domestic and international terrorism and other types of irregular warfare waged by established governments and substate groups including special operations. As part of this study, CTIW researchers emphasize the impact of such conflicts on communication and information systems while also examining emerging threats to national infrastructures. Application of this research produces formal methods for evaluating and simulating the decision processes and actions effecting the interactions of governments and substate groups.[57]

SRDC engages in research in space system design, spacecraft testing, attitude and structural control, adaptive smart structures, and space robotics. SRDC laboratories are used for students and researchers to conduct experiments on assorted high-technology and aerospace applications and collaborate on joint ventures with organizations such as the Navy Satellite Operations Center and Naval Research Laboratory.[58]

Joint Education

The individual armed service war colleges have developed their own institutional traditions and can point to accomplishments and setbacks during their respective institutional historical evolution. This same spirit of service individualism also characterized an often insular and parochial attitude by the armed services in national security policy making and education. Individual services seek to advance their interests within DOD, with Congress, and by the conduct and control of military operations at the expense of other armed service branches. Concern over this rivalry in Congress, exacerbated by serious operational command problems and disputes during Operation Urgent Fury in Grenada in 1983 and earlier U.S. military operations, led Congress to pass the Goldwater-Nichols reform act in 1986.[59]

Named for its sponsors, Sen. Barry Goldwater (R-Ariz., 1953–1965, 1969–1987)

> ## Goldwater-Nichols Act
>
> The 1986 Goldwater-Nichols Act, sponsored by Arizona senator Barry Goldwater and Alabama representative Bill Nichols, is one of the most significant laws in U.S. national security policy-making history. Passed over concern about the lack of interservice cooperation during U.S. military operations, Goldwater-Nichols sought reforms to enhance the ability of U.S. military forces to operate in a joint or multiservice operation.
>
> Examples of these reforms are reorganizing the Department of Defense (DOD) and strengthening civilian authority; improving military advice provided to the president, secretary of defense, and National Security Council; placing clear responsibility on unified and specified combatant commands for accomplishing assigned missions; ensuring that command leaders have the authority to execute their assigned missions; increasing military attention on strategy formulation and contingency planning; using defense resources more efficiently; improving joint officer management policies; increasing the importance of joint assignments in professional military education; and enhancing the overall effectiveness of military operations and improving DOD administrative management.
>
> The overall success of Goldwater-Nichols would be demonstrated, for example, in Operation Desert Storm, Operation Enduring Freedom, and Operation Iraqi Freedom.

and Rep. William F. Nichols (D-Ala., 1967–1988), this legislation had several objectives including strengthening the authority of the Joint Chiefs of Staff (JCS) and unified combatant commands such as Central Command (CENTCOM). Where PME was concerned, control of senior military education moved from individual services toward joint military organizations such as the JCS. The following assessment describes how Goldwater-Nichols affected national security education, as provided by the war colleges, and responsibility for joint military education as required by the legislation.

> The question represented more than a school-curriculum issue for each of the four services, for it affected the promotion potential and career paths for its officers. The Goldwater-Nichols legislation had dramatically changed the rules. Joint duty became a prerequisite for high command and rapid advancement for an officer, where in the past an assignment outside the service command channels could sidetrack an officer's career. And, with joint professional military education a requirement for key joint-duty positions, getting this joint certification became an important goal for individual officers and for the parent service. No longer could concern over what was taught at the service war colleges be left to the colleges to decide; no longer could a service, as the navy had, give little notice to which and how many of its officers had attended a war college. The change in joint education's importance signaled in one more way the shift in power to the joint system.[60]

Goldwater-Nichols strengthened the importance of existing joint military educational institutions such as National Defense University (NDU) and its component units the Industrial College of the Armed Forces (ICAF), Joint Forces Staff College (JFSC), and National War College (NWC).

National Defense University

National Defense University is located at Fort McNair, in Washington, D.C., and was created in 1976 from ICAF and NWC. Its educational institutional mission is to

- Prepare selected commissioned officers and civilian officials from the Department of Defense, Department of State, and other agencies of the government for command, management, and staff responsibilities in a multinational, intergovernmental, and joint national security setting;
- Prepare, through the Joint Forces Staff College curriculum, mid-career officers for joint and staff duty;
- Promote, through the Information Resources Management College, excellence in information resources management education for executive users of information systems at senior and intermediate levels;
- Provide, through the Information Resources Management College, research and gaming resource symposia for the benefit of the Secretary of Defense; the Joint Staff, National Defense University and other Federal departments and agencies involved in national security;
- Conduct short and long-range studies of national security policy, military strategy, and management of resources for national security, and civil-military affairs; and
- Promote understanding and teamwork among the Armed Forces and between those agencies of Government and industry that contribute to national security.[61]

The U.S. Department of Education reviewed ICAF and NWC programs and in 1992 recommended that NDU seek the authority to award graduate degrees. A 1993 law granted NDU's president the authority to award a master of science degree in national resource strategy to ICAF graduates and a master of science in national security strategy to NWC graduates. These degrees were first conferred at NDU's June 15, 1994, graduation ceremonies, and NDU gained accreditation from the Commission on Higher Education of the Middle States Association in 1997.[62]

Industrial College of the Armed Forces

ICAF was established in 1924 as the Army Industrial College, acquired its present name in 1946, and became part of NDU in 1976. Its mission is preparing selected military officers and civilians for senior leadership and staff positions by engaging in postgraduate executive-level research on national security strategy and resource component aspects of national power and how acquisition and joint logistics are integrated into national security strategy.[63]

ICAF accomplishes its curricular and research objectives through six academic departments covering acquisition, economics, grand strategy and mobilization, leadership and information systems, military strategy and logistics, and political science and elements of natural power along with an affiliated Center for Strategic Leadership Development (CSLD).

The Acquisition Department program has two components covering a core acquisition program for all students and a congressionally mandated course for defense acquisition professionals. Departmental curriculum seeks to promote an augmented understanding of the defense acquisition process and how defense acquisition policies and practices affect the U.S. industrial base, economic outlook, and national security strategy.[64]

Economics Department instruction and research cover macroeconomic approaches for analyzing and creating economic policy in the context of a globally interdependent economy; resource allocation in the U.S. economy's business, defense, and public sectors; and product and factor markets that may be influenced or regulated by governmental policies to shape national economic strategy.[65]

CSLD seeks to support ICAF's teaching, research, and outreach programs relating to strategic leadership development by leveraging educational and information technology to promote joint and interagency perspectives on strategic issues supporting ICAF's learning experience.[66]

Joint Forces Staff College

Joint Forces Staff College (JFSC) is an NDU component located in Norfolk, Virginia. It was established in 1946, and its institutional mandate is educating staff officers and other leaders in joint operational–level planning and warfighting to produce a professional commitment to joint, multinational, and interagency teamwork, attitudes, and perspectives.[67]

During 2001, 752 U.S. military officers completed their educational program at JFSC. The institution has been accredited by the Middle States Association of Colleges and Schools since February 1997, and that accreditation was reconfirmed in October 2001.[68]

Students participate in various programs and courses with representative samples including the Joint and Combined Warfighting School (JCWS), which has intermediate and senior levels; the Joint Command, Control, and Information Warfare School (JCIWS); Joint Planning Orientation Course (JPOC); and Homeland Security Planners Course (HLSPC).

JCWS seeks to instruct and acculturate joint and multinational warfighters to plan and lead at war's operational level according to JCS directives. It accomplishes this through a twelve-week interactive executive seminar, which uses case studies and other interactive pedagogical methods such as video teleconferencing to discuss and review joint aspects of military operations including operations other than war.[69]

JCIWS seeks to prepare students for joint service within the command, control, communications, computers, and intelligence (C4I) and information warfare communities. Coursework in this area consumes four weeks and covers C4I concepts in a joint environment, how DOD's organization supports the C4I process, and managerial and operational procedures of existing C4I systems.[70]

JPOC seeks to have students become familiar with the commands, agencies, procedures, and techniques used in planning time-sensitive military activities. Students learn about the joint planning process in peacetime and during international crises. They become familiar with the process for developing a contingency plan for the JCS chairman and the process used by DOD's Joint Planning and Execution Committee (JPEC) to develop timely recommendations for the president or secretary of defense involving the possible use of U.S. military forces.[71]

HLSPC is a forty-hour certificate-granting course on homeland security with an interagency emphasis that enrolls military and civilian students. It provides a military perspective on homeland security and seeks to prepare military and federal civilian officials to participate in homeland security planning and response programs.[72]

National War College

The National War College (NWC) was established in 1946 as a replacement for the combined Army-Navy Staff College, which existed from 1943 to 1946. NWC has produced more than seventy-five hundred graduates who have assumed positions in the U.S. military or government and foreign militaries and governments.[73] Its mission is preparing future armed forces leaders, State Department officials, other civilian government agency leaders, and selected foreign fellows for high-level policy, command, and staff responsibilities through a senior-level curriculum emphasizing joint and interagency perspectives and research in national security policy and strategy.[74]

NWC's curriculum consists of a core program, elective courses, and regional studies. All students are required to complete the core curriculum consisting of zero to twelve class contact hours weekly. Courses contained in this curriculum include Fundamentals of Strategic Logic, Military Thought and the Essence of War, The National Security Strategy Process, The Global Security Arena, Doing National Military Strategy, Field Studies and National Security, and a Crisis Decision Exercise year-end practicum emphasizing active learning. The last course involves students working in small groups to resolve a future national security crisis scenario. It requires students to analyze the crisis, evaluate existing domestic and international situations, determine U.S. interests and objectives, evaluate threats, and formulate strategies and mobilize resources in an effort to address the crisis as it evolves.[75]

The core curriculum and other NWC electives and research and writing programs seek to emphasize that national security strategy and policy are created and implemented within changing policy processes and competing interests, that the presence of finite governmental resources requires policymakers to prioritize between competing domestic and international interests, and that national security objectives and strategies must be formulated and implemented within ethical parameters that can constrain policy-making freedom of action. Additional NWC course themes include stressing that national security strategy must identify national interests and challenges to those interests, that policy instruments for meeting challenges to those interests must be organized within a cohesive strategy to meet desired national objectives, and that military strategy and operations require that armed forces develop a joint culture fostering teamwork, joint warfighting, and multinational endeavors to plan and successfully execute military operations.[76]

Skelton Panel

Numerous appraisals have been made of U.S. national security education. Such instruction has been held in high international regard. However, other less laudatory assessments exist of U.S. national security institutional infrastructure. While generally favorable of Naval War College curriculum and standards, a leading military historian in the late 1980s was critical of the absence of exams or graded papers at the Air and Army War Colleges, confusion over proper curriculum and institutional mission at these colleges, and conflicting visions for these institutions between their civilian service departmental secretary and the war colleges leadership.[77]

The 1986 Goldwater-Nichols act sought to strengthen the importance of joint educational efforts in U.S. PME. Military officers aspiring to high command positions were required to complete joint education coursework to attain promotion and other forms of professional advancement. The House Armed Services Committee in 1987 created a Panel on Military Education to examine the military's efforts to implement Goldwater-Nichol's statutory requirement for greater joint education and to assess the ability of the existing military education system to produce military thinkers, planners, and strategists.[78] Chaired by Rep. Ike Skelton (D-Mo., 1977), this forum, known as the Skelton Panel, from late 1987 through 1988 conducted a series of hearings on the U.S. PME system and released its findings in an April 21, 1989, report. The Skelton Panel determined that DOD's basic military educational system was sound and compared favorably with European military schools but that significant improvements could be made to the U.S. PME system.[79]

The Skelton Panel proposed nine improvements.

1. Establishing a PME framework for DOD schools that specifies and relates primary pedagogical objectives for each PME level;
2. Improving faculty quality at these institutions by amending the law to hire civilian faculty and ensure that only high-quality military instructors receive faculty appointments at these institutions;
3. Establishing a two-phase joint specialist officer education program with the first phase taught in service colleges and the second phase taught at the Joint Forces Staff College;
4. Converting the National War College to a National Center for Strategic Studies;
5. Making national military strategy the primary focus of senior service colleges and increasing the number of military faculty and students from other armed services at these individual institutions;
6. Implementing a substantive capstone course at the National Center for Strategic Studies that integrates studying national military strategy and national security strategy;

7. Reviewing naval military education to determine whether navy officers should attend both intermediate and senior colleges and whether Naval War College schools should have more distinct curriculum;
8. Establishing a position of director of military education on the JCS chairman's staff to support JCS responsibilities for joint PME and for formulating military education coordination policies; and
9. Requiring intermediate and senior PME school students to complete frequent essay examinations and write papers and reports that are thoroughly reviewed, critiqued, and read by faculty.[80]

The Skelton Panel also concluded that the key goal of PME is employing combat forces and warfighting, with leadership and management assuming secondary roles. Panel members said that as military officers become responsible for larger units the schools they attend will focus on larger operations. Consequently, the commission urged that the first tier of PME focus on branch or warfare specialties, that intermediate schools such as the service war colleges expand officers' knowledge to cover branches besides their own service and incorporate joint perspectives into their training, and that senior schools such as National War College focus on national military strategy.[81]

The Skelton Panel in 1991 held follow-up hearings on implementation of its PME recommendations to review General Accounting Office (GAO) reports seeking to quantify DOD's progress. GAO found that PME schools had taken some positive action on 90 percent of Skelton Panel recommendations, that navy PME schools were the only ones meeting panel recommendations of incorporating faculty from other services at their schools, and that army school officials believed that letter grades fostered competition instead of cooperation. The agency cited other examples of progress and noncompliance with panel recommendations.[82]

The status and performance of the U.S. national security educational system remains the subject of ongoing debate and scrutiny. A Center for Strategic and International Studies (CSIS) panel, chaired by former defense secretary Dick Cheney (1989–1993), issued its report *Professional Military Education: An Asset for Peace and Progress* in 1997. The report examined PME during a time of military downsizing and in light of increased societal demographic diversity and permissiveness. It stressed emphasizing preventative defense in PME curriculum to prepare soldiers for nontraditional missions such as peacekeeping. Other report recommendations included establishing mandatory ethics and leadership development courses at PME institutions; establishing technological core competencies at each PME level; providing officers strong technological backgrounds by emphasizing applied science, math, and engineering and by encouraging foreign languages, international affairs, world history, and conflict resolution in PME; maintaining strong funding for PME; adapting to changing societal demographics in student enrollment patterns; maintaining separate academies for individual services; and increasing activities and cooperation among services and developing synergy between service academies and training programs, such as Reserve Officers Training Corps.[83]

Also in 1997, Representative Skelton presented a generally positive appraisal of the progress made in implementing panel PME recommendations. He favorably noted the role of joint planning and operations by U.S. forces in Operation Desert Storm in 1991 against Iraq but expressed concern at the slow progress being made by military service schools to achieve greater interservice faculty and student integration.[84]

A June 1998 DOD inspector general report evaluating a joint PME program made several recommendations. It advocated that air force, Marine Corps, and navy personnel managers increase the practice of sending officers to JFSC en route to joint assignments, that the navy give more officers joint assignments after attending JFSC, that the JCS designate a single contact point to coordinate last-minute Phase II course substitutions, and that the possibility of shortening this course be examined without compromising joint educational quality and still retaining the benefits of multiservice acculturation.[85]

Conclusion

The U.S. PME system has evolved from tentative beginnings to a massive and complex system incorporating the service academies, war colleges for each armed service, and the multifaceted institutions of National Defense University to educate and prepare present and future U.S. military and civilian leaders for national security decision-making and policy-making responsibilities.

An individual examining the publicly available instructional and research resources produced by these institutions through printed materials and websites cannot help but be impressed by their numerical quantity and intellectual quality. These materials cover the wide variety of topics faced by historical, current, and future U.S. national security policymakers and present a variety of traditional and provocative opinions on national security policy issues. Attendance at these war colleges and joint service institutions by numerous foreign military officers also testifies to the international influence and respect the U.S. national security education system has earned.

Literature about contemporary U.S. PME offers appraisals of its strengths, weaknesses, and future prospects.[86] PME literature and assessments of U.S. PME quality will continue to be produced and will influence the value of national security policy information forthcoming from the U.S. military. This literature also will affect the analyses of national security issues produced by the U.S. and foreign government agencies, international government organizations, and U.S. and foreign research institutes and offered in scholarly monographs and journals.

Notes

1. John A. Cope, *International Military Education and Training: An Assessment,* McNair Paper 44 (Washington, D.C.: National Defense University, Institute for National Strategic Studies, 1995), 2, 14–15 (www.ndu.edu/inss/McNair/mcnair44.pdf), accessed November 21, 2003.

2. Leonard Holder Jr. and Williamson Murray, "Prospects for Military Education," *Joint Force Quarterly,* 18 (Spring 1998): 82. Additional introductory background can be found in Russell F.

Weigley, *The American Way of War* (New York: Macmillan, 1973), 77–91. Another perspective on professional military education is provided by Scott Efflandt and Brian Reed, "Developing the Warrior Scholar," *Military Review*, 81 (4) (July/August 2001): 82–89.

3. The Air Force Academy's organic statute is PL 83-325, "To Provide for the Establishment of a United States Air Force Academy, and for Other Purposes," 68 *U.S. Statutes at Large*, 47–49. The academy's mission statement can be found at www.uwafa.af.mil/misvis/, accessed November 25, 2003. Historical coverage of developments in the academy's first quarter century is available in John P. Lovell, *Neither Athens Nor Sparta? The American Service Academies in Transition* (Bloomington: Indiana University Press, 1979), 59–90.

4. See U.S. Air Force Academy, "Academic Major" (n.d.) 1 (www.academyadmissions.com/academics/ majors/), accessed November 26, 2003; U.S. Air Force Academy, "Fact Sheet: Academics" (2003), 1 (www.usafa.af.mil/pa/factsheets/academic.htm), accessed November 26, 2003; and U.S. Air Force Academy, "Fact Sheet: A Quick Look at the U.S. Air Force Academy" (2002), 1 (www.usafa.af.mil/pa/factsheets/quickloo.htm), accessed November 26, 2003.

5. U.S. Coast Guard Academy, "About the Academy" (n.d.), 1 (www.cga.edu/about/about.htm), accessed November 26, 2003.

6. U.S. Coast Guard Academy, "Academy History" (n.d.), 1 (www.cga.edu/about/academyhistory/academyhistory.htm), accessed November 26, 2003. Additional historical information is provided in Lovell, *Neither Athens Nor Sparta?*, 34–37, 125–157.

7. See U.S. Coast Guard Academy, "Academics" (n.d.), 1 (www.cga.edu/academics/academics.htm), accessed November 26, 2003; and U.S. Coast Guard Academy, "About the Academy."

8. For general historical background, see Theodore J. Crackel, *West Point: A Bicentennial History* (Lawrence: University Press of Kansas, 2002); and Lovell, *Neither Athens Nor Sparta?*, 16–26, 91–124. For academic information and U.S. Military Academy (USMA) mission statements, see U.S. Military Academy, "About the Academy" (n.d.), 1–2 (www.usma.edu/about.asp), accessed November 26, 2003; U.S. Military Academy, "USMA Mission" (n.d.), 1 (www.usma.edu/ mission.asp), accessed November 26, 2003; and U.S. Military Academy, "Academic Development" (n.d.), 1 (www.usma.edu/admissions/prosp_acad.asp), accessed November 26, 2003. For an example of USMA strategic educational planning and forecasting, see U.S. Military Academy, Academic Affairs Division, Office of the Dean, *Educating Future Army Officers for a Changing World: Operational Concept for the Academic Program of the United States Military Academy* (West Point, N.Y.: U.S. Military Academy, 2002) (www.dean.usma.edu/aad/EFAOCW.pdf), accessed November 26, 2003.

9. For historical background, see Jack Sweetman, *The U.S. Naval Academy: An Illustrated History* (Annapolis, Md.: Naval Institute Press, 1995). For enrollment and curricular details, see U.S. Naval Academy, "About USNA" (n.d.), 1 (www.nadn.navy.mil/about.htm), accessed December 1, 2003; U.S. Naval Academy, "A Brief History of the United States Naval Academy" (n.d.), 1–2 (www.usna.edu/VirtualTour/150years/), accessed December 1, 2003; and U.S. Naval Academy, "Office of the Academic Dean and Provost Class of 2004 Majors Programs" (2001), 1–2 (www.usna.edu/acdean/majors/2004/04majors.html), accessed December 1, 2003.

10. For an overview, see Thomas A. Keaney, "The War Colleges and Joint Education in the United States," in *Military Education: Past, Present, and Future*, ed. George C. Kennedy and Keith Neilson (Westport, Conn.: Praeger, 2002), 149–165.

11. U.S. Joint Chiefs of Staff, *Joint Doctrine Encyclopedia* (Washington, D.C.: U.S. Joint Chiefs of Staff, 1997), 357 (www.dtic.mil/doctrime/jrm/encyi_l.pdf), accessed December 1, 2003.

12. See Air University, "Fact Sheet: Air University" (2003), 1–5 (www.au.af.mil/au/facts.html), accessed December 1, 2003. For more detailed historical overviews and analysis, see Jerome A. Ennels, *A Short History of Air University, 1946–2001* (Maxwell Air Force Base, Ala.: Air University Office of History, 2001); Richard L. Davis and Frank P. Donnini, eds., *Professional Military*

Education for Air Force Officers: Comments and Criticisms (Maxwell Air Force Base, Ala.: Air University Press, 1991) (http://aupress.au.afmil/Books/Davs_Donnini/Davis_Donnini.pdf), accessed November 25, 2003; Mark R. Grandstaff, "Muir Fairchild and the Origins of Air University, 1945–46," *Airpower Journal,* 11 (4) (Winter 1997): 29–39; and Wesley Phillips Newton and Jerome A. Ennels, "Air University Recovers from Vietnam and Regains Respect," *Airpower Journal,* 11 (4) (Winter 1997): 60–68.

13. Air University, Air Command and Staff College, "About ACSC" (2003), 1 (www.acsc.max well.af.mil/About/about.htm), accessed December 1, 2003.

14. Air University, Air War College, "AWC Commandant's Welcome" (n.d.), 1 (www.maxwell.af.mil/au/awc/wel comes/welcome.htm), accessed December 1, 2003.

15. Air University, "Fact Sheet" (2003), 4 (www.au.af.mil/au/facts.php), accessed December 1, 2003.

16. Air University, Ira C. Eaker College for Professional Development, "What We Do" (2003), 1 (www.maxwell.af.mil/au/cpd/nav.htm), accessed December 1, 2003.

17. See Air University, School of Advanced Air and Space Power Studies, "Mission" (n.d.), 1 (www.maxwell.af.mil/au/sass/mission.htm), accessed December 1, 2003; and Air University, School of Advanced Air and Space Power Studies, "Curriculum" (n.d.), 1–2 (www.maxwell.af.mil/au/sass/curriculum1.htm), accessed December 1, 2003.

18. U.S. Army War College, "U.S. Army War College Mission Statement" (n.d.), 2 (www.carlisle.army.mil/stratplan.asp), accessed December 3, 2003.

19. See U.S. Army War College, "History" (n.d.), 11–12 (www.carlisle.army.mil/history.htm), accessed December 3, 2003; Harry P. Ball, *Of Responsible Command: A History of the United States Army War College* (Carlisle Barracks, Pa.: Alumni Association of the United States Army War College, 1994); and Judith Hicks Stiehm, *U.S. Army War College: Military Education in a Democracy* (Philadelphia: Temple University Press, 2002), 49. For U.S. Army War College admission requirements, see U.S. Army War College, *Distance Education Catalogue for the Class of 2003* (Carlisle Barracks, Pa.: U.S. Army War College, Department of Distance Education, 2003), 21 (http://dde.carlisle.army.mil/catalogues/2003cat.pdf), accessed December 3, 2003.

20. U.S. Army War College, Center for Strategic Leadership, "CSL Mission" (n.d.), 1 (www.carlisle.army.mil/usacsl/Mission.asp), accessed December 3, 2003.

21. U.S. Army War College, U.S. Army Military History Institute, "About MHI," (n.d.), 1 (www.carlisle.army.mil/usamhi/ 1aboutmhi.html), accessed December 3, 2003.

22. U.S. Army War College, Strategic Studies Institute, "About SSI" (n.d.), 1 (www.carlisle.army.mil/ssi/ about.html), accessed December 12, 2003.

23. U.S. Army War College, "Department of Command, Leadership, and Management" (n.d.), 1 (www.carlisle.army.mil/usawc/dclm/Welcome.html), accessed December 3, 2003.

24. U.S. Army War College, "Department of Strategy, Planning, and Operations" (n.d.), 1 (www.carlisle.army.mil/usawc/dmpso/), accessed December 3, 2003.

25. U.S. Army War College, "Department of National Security and Strategy" (n.d.), 1 (www.carlisle.army.mil/usawc/dnss/), accessed December 3, 2003.

26. U.S. Army, Command and General Staff College, "CGSC History and Chronology" (2003), 2, 6–7 (www.cgsc.army.mil/history.asp), accessed December 3, 2003. For more detailed historical background, see Boyd L. Dastrup, *The U.S. Army Command and General Staff College: A Centennial History* (Manhattan, Kan.: Sunflower University Press, 1982); and Timothy K. Nenninger, *The Leavenworth Schools and the Old Army: Education, Professionalism, and the Officer Corps of the United States Army, 1881–1918* (Westport, Conn.: Greenwood Press, 1978).

27. U.S. Army Command and General Staff College, "About the Command and General Staff College" (2003), 1–2 (www.cgsc.army.mil/about.asp), accessed December 3, 2003.

28. U.S. Army Command and General Staff College, Center for Army Lessons Learned, "Welcome" (2003), 1 (http://call.army.mil/mission.htm), accessed December 3, 2003.

29. U.S. Army Command and General Staff College, Combat Studies Institute, "Homepage" (2003), 1 (www.cgsc.army.mil/CSI/), accessed December 3, 2003.

30. U.S. Army Command and General Staff College, Combined Arms and Services Staff College, "About the Combined Arms and Services Staff School" (2003), 1 (www.cgsc.army.mil/cas3/about.asp), accessed December 3, 2003.

31. U.S. Army Command and General Staff College, Combined Arms Research Library, "Resources at CARL" (2003), 1 (www.cgsc.army.mil/carl/resources/), accessed December 3, 2003.

32. U.S. Army Command and General Staff College, School for Command Preparation, "Our Mission" (2003), 1–2; (www.cgsc.army.mil/scp/), accessed December 4, 2003.

33. See U.S. Army Command and General Staff College, School of Advanced Military Studies, "Homepage" (2003), 1 (www.cgsc.army.mil/sams/), accessed December 4, 2003; and U.S. Army Command and General Staff College, School of Advanced Military Studies, "Advanced Military Studies Program" (2003), 1 (www.cgsc.army.mil/sams/amsp/), accessed December 4, 2003.

34. U.S. Army Command and General Staff College, School of Advanced Military Studies, "Advanced Operational Arts Studies Fellowship" (2003), 1 (www.cgsc.army.mil/sams/aoasf/), accessed December 4, 2003.

35. U.S. Marine Corps, Marine Corps University, "History" (n.d.), 1 (www.mcu.usmc.mil/mcu/History/about.htm), accessed December 4, 2003.

36. U.S. Marine Corps, Marine Corps University, "Our Mission" (n.d.), 1 (www.mcu.usmc.mil/), accessed December 4, 2003.

37. See U.S. Marine Corps, Marine Corps University, *Marine Corps University Factbook 2004* (Quantico, Va.: Marine Corps University, 2003), 13 (www.mcu.usmc.mil/mcu/Staff-Sections/VPAA/ MCUFactbook2003.pdf), accessed December 4, 2003. For background on the Marine Corps War College's mission and curriculum, see U.S. Marine Corps, Marine Corps University, *Marine Corps University Catalog Academic Year 2002–2003* (Quantico, Va.: Marine Corps University, 2002), 16–30 (www.mcu.usmc.mil/Catalog/MCWAR.pdf), accessed December 4, 2003.

38. See U.S. Marine Corps, Marine Corps University, *Marine Corps University Factbook 2004*, 15; and U.S. Marine Corps, Marine Corps University, *Marine Corps University Catalog Academic Year 2002–2003*, 31–51.

39. U.S. Marine Corps, Marine Corps University, *Marine Corps University Factbook 2004*, 18.

40. U.S. Marine Corps, Marine Corps University, *Marine Corps University Factbook 2004*, 20.

41. U.S. Marine Corps, Marine Corps University, *Marine Corps University Factbook 2004*, 23.

42. U.S. Marine Corps, Marine Corps University, *Marine Corps University Factbook 2004*, 24.

43. Marine Corps University, Marine Corps Research Center, *Marine Corps Research Center Strategic Plan 1999–2004* (Quantico, Va.: Marine Corps Research Center, 1998), 2 (www.mcu.usmc.mil/MCRCweb/abouta.htm), accessed December 4, 2003.

44. U.S. Naval War College, "NWC Mission" (n.d.), 1 (www.nwc.navy.mil/aboutnwc/mission.htm), accessed December 4, 2003. Historical background on the Naval War College is provided in Ronald H. Spector, *Professors of War: The Naval War College and the Development of the Naval Profession* (Newport, R.I.: Naval War College Press, 1977); and John B. Hattendorf and others, *Sailors and Scholars: The Centennial History of the U.S. Naval War College* (Newport, R.I.: Naval War College Press, 1984).

45. See Naval War College, College of Distance Education, "Welcome to CDE" (n.d.), 1. (http://cde.nwc.navy.mil/welcome.htm), accessed December 4, 2003; and Naval War College, College of Distance Education, "CDE's Mission" (n.d.), 1 (http://cde.nwc.navy.mil/mission.htm), accessed December 4, 2003.

46. Naval War College, "College of Naval Command Staff" (n.d.), 1, (www.nwc.navy.mil/academics/colleges/cncs.htm), accessed December 4, 2003.

47. Naval War College, "College of Naval Warfare" (n.d.), 1 (www.nwc.navy.mil/academics/colleges/cnw.htm), accessed December 4, 2003.

48. Naval War College, Naval Command College, "Mission" (n.d.), 1 (www.nwc.navy.mil/ncc/NCC%20mission_files/slide0002.htm), accessed December 4, 2003.

59. Naval War College, Naval Staff College, "About NSC: Facts about Naval Staff College" (n.d.), 1 (www.nwc.navy.mil/nsc/About%20NSC/facts.htm), accessed December 4, 2003.

50. Naval War College, "Center for Naval Warfare Studies" (2003), 1–2 (www.nwc.navy.mil/cnws/), accessed December 4, 2003.

51. Naval Postgraduate School, "NPS at a Glance" (Monterey, Calif.: Naval Postgraduate School Public Affairs Office, 2001), 1–2 (www.nps.navy.mil/PAO/ at_a_glance.htm), accessed December 5, 2003.

52. See Naval Postgraduate School, Cebrowski Institute for Information Innovation and Superiority, "Homepage" (2003), 1 (http://i2si.nps.navy.mil/), accessed December 5, 2003; and Naval Postgraduate School, Cebrowski Institute for Information Innovation and Superiority, "Projects" (2003), 1 (http://i2si.nps.navy.mil/projects.html), accessed December 5, 2003.

53. Naval Postgraduate School, Center for Civil-Military Relations, "CCMR 2003 Program and Course Catalog" (2003), 1 (www.ccmr.org/public/library_file_proxy.cfm/lid/2049/), accessed December 5, 2003.

54. Naval Postgraduate School, Center for Contemporary Conflict, "About the CCC" (2003), 1 (www.ccc.nps.navy.mil/about.asp), accessed December 5, 2003.

55. Naval Postgraduate School, Center for Information Systems Security and Research, "Mission Statement" (2003), 1 (http://cisr.nps.navy.mil/mission.html), accessed December 6, 2003.

56. Naval Postgraduate School, Center for Joint Services Electronic Warfare, "Center for Joint Services Electronic Warfare" (n.d.), 1 (www.nps.navy.mil/cjsew/), accessed December 6, 2003.

57. Naval Postgraduate School, Center on Terrorism and Irregular Warfare, "Welcome to the Naval Postgraduate School Center on Terrorism and Irregular Warfare" (n.d.), 1 (www.nps.navy.mil/ctiw/), accessed December 6, 2003.

58. Naval Postgraduate School, Spacecraft Research and Design Center, "Introduction" (n.d.), 1 (www.aa.nps.navy.mil/~agrawal/srdc/introduction.html), accessed December 6, 2003.

59. For an authoritative history on the challenges involved in getting this seminal statute enacted, see James R. Locher III, *Victory on the Potomac: The Goldwater-Nichols Act Unifies the Pentagon* (College Station: Texas A&M University Press, 2002).

60. See Thomas A. Keaney, "The War Colleges and Joint Education in the United States," in *Military Education: Past, Present, and Future,* ed. George C. Kennedy and Keith Neilson (Westport, Conn.: Praeger, 2002), 158; and James R. Locher III, "Taking Stock of Goldwater-Nichols," *Joint Forces Quarterly,* 13 (Autumn 1996): 10–17.

61. National Defense University, "Mission and Vision of NDU" (n.d.) (www.ndu.edu/info/mission.cfm), accessed April 14, 2004.

62. For the National Defense University's graduate degree–granting authority, see PL 103-160, "National Defense Authorization Act for Fiscal Year 1994," 107 *U.S. Statutes at Large,* 1730–1731. For degree awarding and accreditation information, see National Defense University, "History of the National Defense University" (n.d.), 1 (www.ndu.edu/info/history.cfm), accessed December 6, 2003.

63. See National Defense University, *Class of 2004 Student Handbook: ICAF History* (Washington, D.C.: Industrial College of the Armed Forces, 2003), 1 (www.ndu.edu/icaf/handbook/history.htm}, accessed December 6, 2003; and National Defense University, "ICAF Mission" (n.d.), 1 (www.ndu.edu/icaf/mission/), accessed December 6, 2003.

64. National Defense University, Industrial College of the Armed Forces, "Academic Departments: Department of Acquisition" (2003), 1 (www.ndu.edu/icaf/departments/acquisition/), accessed December 6, 2003.

65. National Defense University, Industrial College of the Armed Forces, "Department of Economics" (n.d.), 1 (www.ndu.edu/icaf/departments/econ/), accessed December 6, 2003.

66. National Defense University, Center for Strategic Leadership Development" (n.d.), 1 (www.ndu.edu/icaf/center/), accessed December 6, 2003.

67. See National Defense University, Joint Forces Staff College, "History" (n.d.), 1 (www.jfsc.ndu.edu/about/history.asp), accessed December 8, 2003; and National Defense University, Joint Forces Staff College, "Overview" (n.d.), 1 (www.jfsc.ndu.edu/about/overview.asp), accessed December 8, 2003.

68. See National Defense University, Joint Forces Staff College, "College Demographics" (2001), 18 (www.jfsc.ndu.edu/current_students/documents_policies/documents/stakeholdersreport/2001/page18.htm), accessed December 8, 2003; and National Defense University, Joint Forces Staff College, "Accreditation" (n.d.), 1 (www.jfsc.ndu.edu/about/accreditation.asp), accessed December 8, 2003.

69. National Defense University, Joint Forces Staff College, "Overview of JCWS-S" (n.d.), 1–2 (www.jfsc.ndu.edu/schools_programs/jcwss/overview.asp), accessed December 8, 2003.

70. National Defense University, Joint Forces Staff College, "Joint C4I Staff and Operations Course" (n.d.), 1 (www.jfsc.ndu.edu/schools_programs/jciws/c4i/general_info.asp), accessed December 8, 2003.

71. National Defense University, Joint Forces Staff College, "Overview of JPOC" (n.d.), 1 (www.jfsc.ndu.edu/schools_programs/jpoc/overview.asp), accessed December 8, 2003. For an explanation of the Joint Planning and Execution Committee and military planning, see Richard W. Goodale Jr., "Planning for War: A System," *Joint Force Quarterly,* 5 (Summer 1994): 106–110.

72. National Defense University, Joint Forces Staff College, "Homeland Security Planners Course: Overview" (n.d.), 1 (www.jfsc.ndu.edu/schools_programs/homeland_security/overview.asp), accessed December 8, 2003.

73. National War College, "History of the National War College" (n.d.), 1 (www.ndu.edu/nwc/history/), accessed December 9, 2003.

74. National War College, "Mission" (n.d.), 1 (www.ndu.edu/nwc/mission/), accessed December 9, 2003.

75. National War College, "NWC Student Handbook AY 2003" (2003), 1–5 (www.ndu.edu/nwc/handbook/studenthandbook/Part3.html), accessed December 9, 2003.

76. National War College, "NWC Student Handbook AY 2003," 2.

77. Williamson Murray, "Grading the War Colleges," *National Interest,* 6 (Winter 1986–1987): 12–19.

78. U.S. Congress, House Committee on Armed Services, Panel on Military Education, *Professional Military Education,* 101st Cong., 2d sess., 1990, 1. Transcripts of this panel's hearings covering 1987–1988 contain extensive testimony, reports, and supplemental materials on the military's educational system totaling 1,464 pages.

79. U.S. Congress, House Committee on Armed Services, Panel on Military Education, *Report of the Panel on Military Education of the One Hundredth Congress,* 101st Cong., 1st sess., 1989, 2.

80. U.S. Congress, House Committee on Armed Services, Panel on Military Education, *Report of the Panel on Military Education of the One Hundredth Congress,* 2–7.

81. U.S. Congress, House Committee on Armed Services, Panel on Military Education, *Report of the Panel on Military Education of the One Hundredth Congress,* 7–8.

82. U.S. Congress, House Committee on Armed Services, Military Education Panel, *Professional Military Education*, 6, 15, 19. For progress on implementing overall Skelton Commission recommendations and commission recommendations on joint profession military education, see pp. 31–101 and 103–171. For an example of an evaluative report, see U.S. General Accounting Office, *Army Status of Recommendations on Officers' Professional Military Education* (Washington, D.C.: General Accounting Office, 1991).

83. Center for Strategic and International Studies (CSIS), "CSIS Panel, Former Defense Secretary Call for Strengthening Professional Military Education to Respond to Technological Challenges, New Missions" (1997), 1–2 (www.csis.org/press/pr97_1.html), accessed December 9, 2003.

84. Ike Skelton, "JPME: Are We There Yet?" *Military Review,* 77 (1) (January/February 1997): 96–101.

85. U.S. Department of Defense, Office of Inspector General, *Evaluation Report: Joint Professional Military Education Phase II* (Washington, D.C.: Department of Defense, 1998), ii (www.dodig.osd.mil/audit/reports/fy98/98-156.pdf), accessed December 9, 2003.

86. For examples of these appraisals, see Holder and Murray, "Prospects for Military Education," 81–90; Robert A Vitas, "Civilian Graduate Education and the Professional Officer," *Military Review,* 79 (3) (May/June 1999): 47, 54–55; Steven H. Kenney, "Professional Military Education and the Emerging Revolution in Military Affairs," *Airpower Journal,* 10 (3) (Fall 1996): 53; and William F. Burns, "The Education of a Modern Major General," *Naval War College Review,* 57 (1) (Winter 2004): 20–33.

CHAPTER 2

Executive Branch Agencies— Department of Defense

The principal formulators of U.S. national security policy are executive branch agencies, which are also major producers of national security policy information. Heading the executive branch is the president of the United States, who also is designated by the Constitution as commander in chief of U.S. armed forces.[1] The Department of Defense (DOD) and its multiple component parts are the largest single governmental producer of national security policy information.[2] Comprehensive access to all Defense Department and armed services branches is provided through www.defenselink.mil/.[3]

Office of the Secretary of Defense

The Office of the Secretary of Defense (OSD) website (www.defenselink.mil/osd/) provides biographical information about the secretary of defense and the deputy secretary of defense. It also includes the text of speeches and press interviews given by the defense secretary and his deputy as well as the text of general DOD reference publications such as *Defense Almanac,* which provides a detailed overview of OSD organizational components and their missions.

The OSD website also features links to information about the assistant secretary of defense for networks and information integration; assistant secretary of defense for legislative affairs; assistant secretary of defense for public affairs; assistant to the secretary of defense for intelligence oversight; director of administration and management; director of defense research and engineering; director of operational test and evaluation; director of program analysis and evaluation; executive secretary of the Department of Defense; general counsel of the Department of Defense; inspector general; undersecretary of defense (comptroller); undersecretary of defense for acquisition, technology, and logistics; undersecretary of defense for personnel and

> **Department of Defense**
>
> The Department of Defense (DOD) was created as the National Military Establishment by the 1947 National Security Act before assuming its present name in 1949. DOD is responsible for providing the military forces needed to deter war and protect U.S national security. DOD jurisdiction covers the individual U.S. armed forces, joint combatant commands, and DOD civilian employees and departments.
>
> Some entities within DOD such as the Office of the Secretary of Defense (OSD) control policy-making offices such as those headed by the undersecretary of defense for acquisition, technology, and logistics; the undersecretary of defense for personnel and readiness; and the undersecretary of defense for policy.
>
> DOD agencies include the Defense Intelligence Agency, Defense Security Cooperation Agency, Defense Threat Reduction Agency, and National Security Agency.
>
> Each branch of the U.S. armed services has its own institutional bureaucracy headed by a secretary, who is a presidentially appointed and Senate-confirmed civilian. For instance, the Department of the Army is headed by a secretary of the army whose administrative responsibilities are facilitated by an inspector general and assistant secretaries covering fields such as civil works, installations, and the environment. The secretary of the army is also in charge of uniformed command entities such as the Army Corps of Engineers and U.S. Army Europe and 7th Army.

readiness; and undersecretary of defense for policy. However, links are not available to information about the director of force transformation or the director of net assessment.

Assistant Secretary of Defense for Networks and Information Integration

The assistant secretary of defense for networks and information integration is responsible for ensuring that information superiority is achieved and maintained for DOD missions and that U.S. adversaries are unable to obtain a comparable level of intelligence about U.S. military operations.[4] *Disposition of Unclassified DoD Computer Hard Drives* (2001) is an example of a publication accessible through the office's website (www.defenselink.mil/nii/).

Assistant Secretary of Defense for Legislative Affairs

Responsibilities of the assistant secretary of defense for legislative affairs include giving support to the secretary of defense in his interactions with the White House, cabinet members, Congress, and the State Department.[5]

Information resources on this office's website (www.defenselink.mil/la/) include a listing of National Guard and reserve units from individual states and territories called to active-duty service for Operation Enduring Freedom (Afghanistan) as of

December 5, 2001, biographical information on the assistant secretary, seating charts and listings of members for relevant congressional oversight committees, and the current week's roster of office legislative affairs personnel scheduled to testify before congressional committees and subcommittees.

Assistant Secretary of Defense for Public Affairs

The assistant secretary of defense for public affairs serves as the primary adviser and assistant to the secretary and the deputy secretary of defense and is responsible for providing information about DOD activities to the public in multiple formats.[6] The office sponsors www.defenselink.mil, and its components include the Directorate for Press Operations, which supplies news releases and photos to the media and general public; the Directorate for Public Inquiry and Analysis, which answers questions from the public such as how to apply for a security clearance or locating the address of someone in the military; and the American Forces Information Service (AFIS), which provides information to an internal military audience in the form of print, television, radio, and Internet dissemination—some of which is publicly accessible through the office website (www.defenselink.mil/pubs/almanac/asdpa.html).

Examples of information resources available through the website are transcripts from interviews with major DOD officials or military officers including some audio and video webcasts dating back to 1994, briefing slides (often in PowerPoint) given by these officials at public press briefings, daily information on defense contracts valued at $5 million or higher awarded by individual armed services, and the option of subscribing to receive free e-mail updates of various DOD announcements.

Assistant to the Secretary of Defense for Intelligence Oversight

The assistant to the secretary of defense for intelligence oversight (ATSDIO) is responsible for ensuring that all DOD-related intelligence activities adhere to federal law, executive orders, and departmental directives, regulations, and policies.[7] Publicly accessible resources on ATSDIO's website (www.dod.mil/atsdio/) include DOD directives on departmental intelligence policy, such as *DOD Directive 5240.1-R: Procedures Governing the Activities of DOD Intelligence Components that Affect United States Persons* (1982), *DOD Directive 5240.1: DOD Intelligence Activities* (1988), and *DOD Directive 5148.11: Assistant to the Secretary of Defense for Intelligence Oversight* (1994).

Director of Administration and Management

DOD's director of administration and management, under the supervision of the deputy secretary of defense, is the primary assistant and adviser to the secretary and deputy secretary on DOD organizational and administrative management issues. These issues encompass developing and maintaining organizational charters and overseeing programs such as DOD's Management Headquarters and Historical Office programs, being the focal point for DOD quality management issues, and analyzing and controlling OSD manpower requirements.[8]

Resources accessible through the director of administration and management website (www.defenselink.mil/odam/) include an office organizational chart, the organizational charters for various DOD advisory committees such as the Defense Advisory Committee on Women in the Services (DACOWITS) and the Joint Advisory Committee on Nuclear Weapons Surety, DOD directives such as *DOD Directive 3150.6: United States Nuclear Command and Control System Support Staff* (2001), and Historical Office publications including *Public Statements of William J. Perry, Secretary of Defense* (1994), *The Department of Defense 1947–1997: Organization and Leaders* (1997), and *Missions and Functions Guidebook* (2002).

Director of Defense Research and Engineering

The director of defense research and engineering (DR&E) is responsible for seeing that current and future U.S. warfighters have superior and affordable technology to support their missions and win wars they need to fight.[9] Publicly accessible materials on DR&E's website (www.defenselink.mil/ddre/) include an organizational chart, the director's biography, information on DR&E's International Technology Programs Office describing DOD defense science relationships with other countries and international organizations such as the North Atlantic Treaty Organization (NATO), information on collaborative relationships between DR&E and U.S. organizations, and publications such as *Defense Science and Technology Budget and Investment Focus* (2002) and *Technology: A Foundation for Transformation* (2002).

Director for Operational Test and Evaluation

The director for operational test and evaluation (DOT&E) is responsible for issuing DOD operational test and evaluation policy and procedures, reviewing and analyzing the results of these tests and evaluations conducted for significant DOD acquisition programs for the secretary of defense, and ensuring the adequacy of DOD operational test and evaluation programs for effectiveness and suitability for combat use.[10]

Some of the contents of the DOT&E website (www.dote.osd.mil/) have been removed for national security reasons. Nevertheless, significant resources remain, including reports such as *Defense Acquisition Trend Metrics in the Department of Defense* (2000) and *Fiscal Year 2002 Annual Report Extracts* (2002), an organizational chart, links to various military test and evaluation websites including the Ronald Reagan Ballistic Missile Test Site at Kwajolein Atoll and the U.S. Army's Aberdeen Test Center in Aberdeen, Maryland, links to articles on live fire programs such as "Joint Live Fire Program Tests Full-Up Stinger Missile against F-14 Tomcat" (1999), presentations by DOT&E personnel, and a listing of testing and evaluation programs reviewed in 2002 such as the air force's *Hard-Deeply Buried Target Defeat Capability* and the army's *Battlefield Command Information System*.

Director of Program Analysis and Evaluation

The Office of the Director, Program Analysis and Evaluation (PA&E) provides analytic advice to the secretary of defense on possible alternative weapons systems and force structures, defense systems cost-effectiveness, and advice in areas such as military medical care, information technology, and defense economics.[11]

Although some resources of PA&E's website (www.pae.osd.mil/) are accessible to military users only, a number of publicly accessible materials can be found, including lists of various PA&E project areas such as operations other than war, weapons performance analysis, and command and control satellite analysis, along with reports such as *Performance Contracting in DoD* (1998) and *Projected Defense Purchases: Detail by Industry and State: Calendar Years 2000 through 2005* (2000).

Office of the Executive Secretary

The executive secretary provides direct administrative support to the secretary and deputy secretary of defense.[12] The website www.defenselink.mil/execsec/ contains information about the office's operations and the secretary of defense's *Annual Report to the President and Congress* from 1996 to 2001.

Office of Inspector General

DOD's Office of Inspector General (DODIG) evaluates DOD programs for the secretary of defense and Congress. DODIG personnel prepare numerous reports documenting the performance of DOD programs.[13] Materials documenting DODIG activities can be accessed through statements of DODIG personnel before congressional oversight committee hearings; the text of DODIG semiannual reports to Congress chronicling agency activities from the October 1, 1996–March 31, 1997, report to the present; links to other military inspectors general and law enforcement sites; and documents contained in DODIG's Freedom of Information Act (FOIA) electronic reading room such as *Instruction 4630.2: Internet Use Policy* (1999).

The most substantive resource on DODIG's website (www.dodig.osd.mil/) is the evaluation and audit reports on DOD programs, which date back to federal fiscal year 1990, beginning on October 1, 1989. These reports provide detailed analysis of various DOD programs and insight into DOD's administrative and policy-making processes. Examples of these reports are *Tracking Security Clearance Requests* (2000), *Report on Quality Control Review of PriceWaterHouseCoopers LLP and Defense Contract Audit Agency for Office of Management and Budget Circular No. A-133 Audit Report of Massachusetts Institute of Technology Fiscal Year Ended June 30, 1999* (2001), *FY 2001 DOD Information Security Status for Government Information Security Reform* (2001), *Meteorological and Oceanographic Support in the European Theater* (2001), *Logistics: Delivery and Receipt of DoD Cargo Inbound to the Republic of Korea* (2002), and *Acquisition: V-22 Osprey Hydraulic System* (2002).

Undersecretaries of Defense

Four undersecretaries of defense also produce useful national security–related information.

The undersecretary of defense (comptroller) serves as the secretary of defense's chief adviser for departmental budget, financial management, and accounting

> ### Freedom of Information Act
>
> The Freedom of Information Act (FOIA) was enacted in 1966 to require federal executive branch agencies to make government records publicly accessible. The 1996 Electronic Freedom of Information Act (EFOIA) extended this level of public access to government information to cover electronic format records.
>
> These acts established procedures for requesting records from government agencies, which also include military departments, independent regulatory agencies, and government-controlled operations. These statutes do not apply to the president, vice president, members of Congress, the federal judiciary, state or local governments, private companies, or individuals receiving federal contracts or grants.
>
> Some information categories are exempt from FOIA and EFOIA including current information classified for foreign policy or national security reasons, investigative information, personnel records, and materials containing trade secrets or confidential business information.
>
> The Justice Department's Office of Information and Privacy website (www.usdoj.gov/oip/oip.html) serves as a gateway to federal FOIA and EFOIA policy documentation. It also provides access to other agency EFOIA websites that can contain reports on national security policy matters.

matters.[14] Further information about this office can be found at www.dtic.mil/comptroller/, including an organizational chart with biographical information on key personnel, the text of DOD financial management regulations, detailed defense spending breakdowns by program, audited financial statements for individual DOD programs such as those covering military retirement funds and Department of the Navy general funds, and individual reports such as *Department of Defense Charge Card Task Force Final Report* (2002).

Responsibilities of the undersecretary of defense for acquisition, technology, and logistics include serving as the secretary of defense's principal adviser on military acquisition matters, research and development, production, military construction, and procurement.[15] The website www.acq.osd.mil/ features numerous information resources useful to those wanting to learn how defense acquisition and procurement affect national security policy formulation. Site resources include congressional testimony and speeches by the undersecretary. Numerous defense acquisition publications may also be found, such as *Unmanned Aerial Vehicles Roadmap 2000–2025* (2001), *Guide to Incentive Strategies for Defense Acquisitions* (2001), *Intellectual Property: Navigating through Commercial Waters: Issues and Solutions When Negotiating Intellectual Property with Commercial Companies (Version 1.1)* (2001), and the reference manual *Defense Acquisition Deskbook* (2002).

DOD's undersecretary for personnel and readiness is responsible for civilian and military personnel policy, career development, training, education, retirement pay, mobilization planning, and numerous other subjects.[16] This office's website (www.dod.mil/prhome/) is a rich resource for military personnel demographic information. Besides including speeches by the undersecretary, site contents include reports such as *Career Progression of Minority and Women Officers* (1999), *Population Representation in the Military Services, Fiscal Year 2000* (2001), *Military Personnel Human Resources Strategic Plan* (2001), *Department of Defense Personnel and Readiness 2001–2006 Strategic Plan,* and *Report of the Ninth Quadrennial Review of Military Compensation* (2002).

The undersecretary of defense for policy serves as the secretary of defense's principal staff assistant for overall international security policy and political-military affairs covering issues as divergent as NATO matters, foreign military sales, arms control, and regional security affairs.[17] Accessible at www.defenselink.mil/policy/, this office's website features biographical information about and speeches by the undersecretary and an organizational chart featuring links to departmental components such as the assistant secretary of defense for international security affairs, the Defense Prisoner of War/Missing Personnel Office (DPMO), the Defense Security Cooperation Agency (DSCA), and the assistant secretary for special operations and low-intensity conflict.

Assistant Secretary of Defense for International Security Affairs

The assistant secretary of defense for international security affairs (ISA) is responsible for advising the undersecretary of defense for policy on international political-military affairs for all areas of the globe except NATO, Europe, and the former Soviet Union.[18] ISA's website (www.defenselink.mil/policy/isa/) provides information about the office, a biographical portrait of the assistant secretary, and links to ISA regional offices for African Affairs, Asian and Pacific Affairs, Near East and South Asian Affairs, and Western Hemisphere and links to the websites for the ISA-controlled offices of the Defense Prisoner of War/Missing Personnel Office, Defense Security Cooperation Agency, and International Negotiations and Regional Affairs (INRA).

ISA—African Affairs

This office is responsible for developing and implementing U.S. national security interests and programs in sub-Saharan Africa.[19] Publicly accessible resources available through its website (www.defenselink.mil/policy/isa/africa/afrindex.html) include the text of an April 2, 2002, Pentagon news briefing on office responsibilities, the text and a Real Audio clip of a July 25, 2002, Voice of America report on a U.S. military training program for sub-Saharan Africa, and the reports *DOD Strategy for Sub-Saharan Africa* (2001), *Critical Factors in Demobilization, Demilitarization, and Reintegration: An Analysis of Ethiopia, Liberia, Mozambique, and Zimbabwe* (2002), and *Policy Options for United States Support to Demobilization, Demilitarization, and Reintegration in Sub-Saharan Africa* (2002).

ISA—Asian and Pacific Affairs

This office covers international security affairs and policy for the Asia-Pacific region. Its website (www.defenselink.mil/policy/isa/asiapacific/apindex.html) contains the phone numbers for various country desk officers and links to other U.S. government Asian policy resources. However, no reports or text on national security–related subjects were available as of mid-April 2004.

ISA—Near East and South Asian Affairs

This office is responsible for coordinating U.S. international security polices for the Middle East and South Asia. Its website (www.defenselink.mil/policy/isa/nesa/nesa_index.html) features an organizational mission statement, links to government and nongovernment resources on these regions, and the report *United States Strategy for the Middle East* (1995), plus the arms control and nuclear nonproliferation sections of the Clinton administration's *A National Security Strategy for a New Century* (1999) produced by the National Security Council (NSC).

ISA—Western Hemisphere Affairs

Charged with coordinating U.S. security policies toward the Western Hemisphere, this office maintains a website (www.defenselink.mil/policy/isa/western/western_hemisphere_affairs.html) currently limited to an October 2001 PowerPoint presentation on the office's organizational role in U.S. national security policy making and a listing of country desk officers. The site otherwise is still under construction.

Defense Prisoner of War/Missing Personnel Office

This office is responsible for investigating and recovering U.S. military personnel missing in action from countries around the world.[20] Numerous resources on American prisoners of war (POWs) and missing in action (MIA) are provided through the website www.dtic.mil/dpmo/.

Resources on this site include information on POWs and MIAs from the Korean and Vietnam Wars plus the cold war. Databases for these conflicts include incident descriptions and dates, listings of personnel involved, and breakdowns of these personnel by state. Additional resources on this site include material on the uses of DNA (deoxyribonucleic acid) in identifying POWs and MIAs, 2002 and 2003 DPMO meetings providing updates on POW/MIA family members on DPMO recovery efforts, a sample agenda for these meetings, and reports such as *The Gulag Study* (2002) and earlier editions of this same work investigating instances in which U.S. military personnel may have been placed in Soviet labor camps.

Defense Security Cooperation Agency

The agency was established in 1971, and its mandate includes directing and administering approved U.S. security assistance plans and programs such as military assistance, international military education and training, and foreign military sales.[21] Its website (www.dsca.osd.mil/) provides access to numerous information resources including an organizational chart with links explaining the functions of individual DSCA components; a 2002 PowerPoint presentation entitled "Introduction to Security Assistance," which describes the roles played by DOD and the State Department in U.S. security assistance programs; information on defense trade security initiatives; and announcements about various defense trade shows. Publicly accessible DSCA reports include *Customer Guide to U.S. Security Assistance Programs* (2001), *Guidelines for Foreign Military Financing of Direct Commercial Contracts* (2001), and *Defense Acquisition Deskbook* (2002).

Office of International Negotiations and Regional Affairs

This office is part of ISA and is responsible for securing basing and access rights to U.S. forces deployed abroad and for ensuring legal protection for these forces.[22] INRA's website (www.defenselink.mil/policy/isa/inra/) contains additional information about its institutional purpose and the text of a December 31, 2000, announcement by President Bill Clinton about the United States signing the International Criminal Court Treaty; a January 10, 2001, letter from Secretary of Defense William S. Cohen to Senate Foreign Relations Committee chairman Jesse Helms (R-N.C., 1973–2003) concerning the International Criminal Court; and a listing of countries with which the U.S. military has international force–basing agreements.

Other Defense Agencies

Several other DOD agencies help formulate national security policy and produce useful information resources. These agencies play roles as diverse as delivering military supplies, auditing defense programs, feeding military base personnel, and evaluating the scientific potential of weapons systems.

Defense Advanced Research Projects Agency

The Defense Advanced Research Projects Agency (DARPA) is controlled by the undersecretary of defense for acquisition, technology, and logistics. It engages in advanced and applied research and development programs for DOD and conducts prototype projects that may be incorporated into future DOD or military programs.[23] Established in 1958, DARPA had 240 employees and an annual budget of nearly $2 billion as of 2001.[24]

Its highly specialized work is carried out by technical and support offices such as the Advanced Technology Office, Information Exploitation Office, and Microsystems Technology Office. Research and development specializations carried out by these offices include special operations, information assurance, biological warfare defense, advanced mathematics, national security warning and decision making, next-generation computational and information systems, sensors and sensor exploitation, surface target interdiction, precision kill capabilities, defenses against low-cost and low-technology air vehicles and missiles, and defenses against global position satellite (GPS) jamming.[25]

A variety of resources are present on DARPA's website (www.darpa.mil/) including a technical staff directory, news releases, recent budget request messages to Congress, information about the operational activities of individual DARPA components, and the text of some reports including *DARPA On-Site Contractor Security Guidance* (n.d.) and *DARPA Technology Transition* (1997), which provides a historical overview of DARPA programs and their accomplishments.

Defense Commissary Agency

The Defense Commissary Agency (DCA) runs nearly 280 commissaries globally that provide groceries to U.S. military personnel, retirees, and their families at discounted prices.[26] The website www.commissaries.com provides information about DCA operations and various information resources. Some of these resources include fact sheets on foot and mouth disease and e coli bacteria, press releases, and information on reporting fraud, abuse, or waste at commissaries to the DCA inspector general. Website contents also include the text of *Vision Magazine* and publications such as *Civilian Employee Handbook* (1998), *Director's Policy: Information Technology* (2001), *Comparing Commissaries, Exchanges, and Ships' Stores* (2002), and *History of U.S. Military Commissaries* (2002).

Defense Contract Audit Agency

Established in 1965, the Defense Contract Audit Agency (DCAA) performs contract audit responsibilities for DOD along with accounting and financial advisory services to all DOD entities engaging in procurement and contract administration.[27]

DCAA's website (www.dcaa.mil/) contains information on agency activities and its accounting and auditing practices and procedures. Accessible materials include an organizational guide and history, the current DCAA strategic plan, audit guidance documents such as *Audit Guidance on the Cost of Money Rate for July 1, 2002, through December 31, 2002* (2002), and audit preparation materials such as *Audit Program on Contractor Billing System and Related Internal Controls* (2001). Other features of the website are publications such as *DCAA Report on Activities* (2001), *DCAA Catalog of Training Courses* (2002), and *Contract Audit Manual* (2002). Such resources can help illustrate the importance of sound accounting and auditing procedures in formulating and implementing national security policy.

Defense Contract Management Agency

The Defense Contract Management Agency (DCMA) is an independent DOD combat support agency serving as the department's contract manager and charged with ensuring that federal acquisition programs, supplies, and services get delivered on time, within cost, and meet DOD performance requirements.[28]

Publicly accessible resources on its website (www.dcma.mil/) include news releases; the *DCMA Communicator* newsmagazine and *DCMA Communicator Express* headquarters employees newsletter; information on DCMA's Plant Clearance

Automated Reutilization Screening System (PCARSS) with which DCMA intends to create a paperless contracting environment for reporting, screening, and disposing of excess government property on contractor facilities; and additional resources on the defense contracting process.

Defense Finance and Accounting Service

The Defense Finance and Accounting Service (DFAS) was established by the secretary of defense in 1990 and is responsible for standardizing DOD's financial and accounting information, functions, and services.[29] Numerous materials on defense accounting and financial practice are accessible on the DFAS website (www.dfas.mil/). Available are information on relevant financial accounting legislation before Congress such as the text of H.R. 5094, a bill introduced in July 2002 to establish a federal Accounting Standards Advisory Board; DFAS press releases; information about DFAS e-commerce activities; and information about efforts to provide its physically disabled employees with access to information technology equipment as provided to employees without physical disabilities.

DFAS publications accessible on its website include a variety of reports and agency manuals, such as *Contractor Payment Information Handbook* (2000), *DOD Finance and Accounting Data Model Version 3.0* (2001), *Annual Audited Financial Statements Fiscal Year 2001* (2002), and *Annual Report FY 2001*. Such DFAS publications can provide enhanced understanding of the important role quality financial accounting must play in formulating and executing national security policy.

Defense Information Systems Agency

The Defense Information Systems Agency (DISA) originally was called the Defense Communications Agency when established by the secretary of defense in 1960 and was given its current name in 1991.[30] The importance of DISA's institutional mandate has increased given the continually growing influence of information operations and security in national security policy.

> The DISA is responsible for planning, developing, and supporting command, control, communications (C3), and information systems that serve the needs of the National Command Authorities (NCA) under all conditions of peace and war. It provides guidance and support on technical and operational C3 and information systems issues affecting the Office of the Secretary of Defense (OSD), the Military Departments, the Chairman of the Joint Chiefs of Staff and the Joint Staff, the Unified and Specified Commands, and the Defense Agencies (hereafter referred to collectively as "the DOD Components"). It ensures the interoperability of the Worldwide Military Command and Control System (WWMCCS), the Defense Communications System (DCS), theater and tactical command and control systems, North Atlantic Treaty Organization and/or allied C3 systems, and those national and/or international commercial systems that affect the DISA mission. It supports national security emergency preparedness telecommunications functions of the National Communications System (NCS), as prescribed by Executive Order 12472.[31]

These multifaceted responsibilities are executed by an organizational structure that includes the White House Communications Agency; DISA directors for interoperability, network services, operations, strategic plans, programming, and policy; and DISA field and line organizations located in the Washington, D.C., area and around the world such as the Defense Information Technology Contracting Organization, the Joint Interoperability Test Command, DISA Europe Field Command, and DISA Strategic Command Field Office.[32]

A number of resources are publicly accessible through DISA's website (www.disa.mil/). These include descriptions of DISA's organizational structure and websites of DISA component entities and descriptions of DISA core mission areas such as information assurance, Common Operating Environment, the Defense Information System Network, Defense Message System, Global Combat Support System, Global Command and Control System, and DISA's e-commerce activities.

Publications from DISA include information circulars such as *Physical Security Measures for DCS Facilities* (1983), *Radio Frequency Spectrum Management and Use* (1997), and *Satellite Communications (SATCOM) Equipment Reporting System* (1998). Additional DISA website contents include listings of agency job announcements and contracts along with information on DISA internship and student worker programs.

Defense Logistics Agency

The Defense Logistics Agency (DLA) was formally established in 1977 when its name was changed from the Defense Supply Agency. Its organizational history began during World War II, when massive U.S. military increases required large-scale munition and supplies purchasing.[33] DLA's current administrative authorization dates from 1988.

> The DLA shall function as an integral element of the military logistics system of the Department of Defense to provide effective and efficient worldwide logistics support to the Military Departments and the Unified and Specified Commands under conditions of peace and war, as well as to other DoD components, Federal Agencies, foreign governments, or international organizations as assigned.[34]

Resources accessible through DLA's website (www.dla.mil/) include information about DLA's headquarters and regional offices such as the Defense Supply Center in Columbus, Ohio, opportunities for businesses to buy from and sell products to the military, an archive of news releases from December 1997 to the present, congressional testimony by DLA leaders, and the ability to download software such as DLA's "Environmental Reports Logistics System."

Specific publications that are publicly accessible include policy reports for Congress such as *Strategic and Critical Materials Report to Congress: Operations under the Strategic and Critical Materials Stock Piling Act during the Period October 2000 through September 2001* (2002) and agency promotional materials such as *Defense Logistics Agency Strategic Plan 2002–2007* (2002). Other accessible publications include environmental policy reports such as *DOD Environmental Quality Program Review: Data Request for First Half of FY 1999 (Oct. 98–Mar. 99)* and agency directives and manuals such as *Weapons Support System Program (WSSP) Users Handbook* (n.d.), *Military Engineering Data Asset Locator System* (1987), *Instructional Guide for Basic Military Preservation and Packing* (1990), *DLA Weapons Support System Program* (1999), and *Trade Security Control Procedures Applicable to Department of Defense Surplus Property and Foreign Excess Personal Property* (2001).

Such publications illustrate the vitally important role played by logistical operations in executing national security policy by agencies such as DLA and demonstrate the complex variety of issues required for military forces and agencies to achieve the goals set by their national political and military leaderships.

Defense Policy Board

The Defense Policy Board, consisting of former governmental policymakers such as former vice president Dan Quayle (1989–1993), former secretaries of defense James R. Schlesinger (1973–1975) and Harold Brown (1977–1981), and former House Speakers Thomas S. Foley (D-Wash., 1989–1995) and Newt Gingrich (R-Ga., 1995–1999), serves as an informal advisory board on national security issues to DOD. During the summer of 2002, it was revealed that the board hosted a briefing by a RAND Corporation official who described Saudi Arabia as a hostile state and recommended that the U.S. take hostile action against that country unless it stopped supporting terrorism.[35] The Defense Policy Board (DPB) has no website, and it holds its meetings in secret. Mention of its meetings may be found through a search of DOD's defenselink.mil website. Having a publicly accessible website might enable DPB to have a mechanism for providing a straightforward presentation of its activities and for minimizing the impact of controversies such as that resulting from the briefing on Saudi Arabia.

Defense Science Board

The Defense Science Board (DSB) was created in 1956 with a civilian and military membership. Its responsibilities included reporting to the assistant secretary of defense for research and development on how scientific knowledge could assist in providing information and knowledge on cutting-edge weapons systems. DSB's basic mission has remained unchanged, and its membership currently consists of thirty-two authorized members and seven ex officio members (the chairs of the individual armed service branches and Missile Defense Agency (MDA) and Defense Intelligence Agency advisory committees). These individuals are appointed to terms of one to four years and are chosen based on their prominence in science and technology and the application of these to military operations, research, engineering, manufacturing, and acquisition processes.[36]

Numerous noteworthy information resources can be found on DSB's website (www.acq.osd.mil/dsb/). These include DSB's organizational history and institutional charter, links to armed services scientific research center websites, and a quarterly newsletter from February 1998 to the present chronicling ongoing DSB activities. The most riveting feature of the website is the research reports DSB has produced on diverse defense science topics, such as *Submarine of the Future* (1998), *Tritium Production Technology Options* (1999), *DoD Supercomputing Needs* (2000), *The Creation and Dissemination of All Forms of Information in Support of Psychological Operations (PSYOP) in Time of Military Conflict* (2000), *Protecting the Homeland: Defensive Information Operations, 2000 Summer Study Vol. II* (2001), *Improved Fuel Efficiency of Weapons Platforms* (2001), and *High Energy Laser Weapons Systems Applications* (2001).

Defense Security Service

The Defense Security Service (DSS) was established by the secretary of defense in 1972 and currently operates under DOD Directive 5105.42 dated June 14, 1985. The institutional mandate of DSS is administering DOD's personnel security program, which aims to ensure that individuals working for DOD with access to sensitive information are loyal to the United States and possess trustworthy moral character.[37] Besides conducting background personnel investigations through its Personnel Security Investigations Program, DSS responsibilities encompass the National Industrial Security Program, which is responsible for ensuring that defense contractors' facilities and personnel have requisite security clearances to perform their work, and the Security, Education, Training, and Awareness Program, which runs the Defense Security Service Academy and the DOD Polygraph Institute as part of its efforts to promote departmental awareness of security education, training, professional development support, and counterintelligence issues.[38]

These multifaceted missions are performed by nearly twenty-five hundred DSS employees in the United States and Puerto Rico. Nearly half of this workforce consists of special agents conducting nearly 400,000 personnel security investigations annually, and 220 DSS employees are industrial security representatives who direct, advise, and assist more than 11,000 contractor facilities involved in classified contracts or research and development initiatives.[39]

Additional information about DSS and its activities may be found on its website (www.dss.mil/). Resources are generally grouped into categories covering DSS's core missions involving personnel and industrial security. Procedures for applying for jobs with DSS are also listed on this website as are various news releases.

The best feature on the DSS website is the "Security Library" containing reports and articles on defense personnel and industrial security topics. Examples of these resources are *Arrangements for the International Hand Carriage of Classified Documents, Equipment, and/or Components* (1991), *Terminator VIII: How to Destroy Your Classified Materials* (1992), *International Industrial Security Requirements Guidance Annex* (n.d.), *Industrial Security Letters* (1995–present), *Secure Telephone Unit, Third Generation (STU-III) Type I Handbook for Industry* (1997), *DOD Guide to Marking Classified Documents* (1997), *Suspicious Indicators and Security Countermeasures for Foreign Collection Activities Directed against the U.S. Defense Industry* (1997), *Scholarly Approaches to Collecting Scientific and Technical Information from Cleared Defense Companies* (1998), and the annual reports *Technology Collection Trends in the U.S. Defense Industry* (1997–present).

Defense Technical Information Center

The Defense Technical Information Center (DTIC) started just after World War II out of the need to translate captured German and Japanese military scientific and technical information.[40] It was formally established as the Central Documents Office on October 13, 1948, by the secretaries of the Navy and Air Force, and it became DTIC in October 1979.[41] DTIC's responsibilities include serving as a specialized provider of domestic and international scientific technical reports with particular emphasis on information resources having military applications for DOD and managing thirteen Information Analysis Centers with experienced information and scientific subject specialists who assist users in locating unclassified information and eligible users in locating classified materials.[42]

DTIC's website (www.dtic.mil/) contains a number of useful information resources accessible to the general public. Visitors to this site will find information on registering for DTIC products, links to other military scientific and technical information (STI) sites, and links to DTIC's "Defense Virtual Library," which features the text of technical reports, still images, and moving images on defense STI matters. Also on the site are DTIC organizational information documents such as *DTIC 2001: Report to Our Customers* and the journal *DTIC Review,* which abstracts various defense STI research.

Additional components of DTIC's website include general reference resources such as the regularly published and updated *DOD Index of Specifications and Standards,* which provides technical specifications for various military products, and the "Militarily Critical Technologies List," which describes cutting-edge research in disciplines such as directed and kinetic energy technology, information systems technology, lasers and optics, and sensory technology.

The preeminent information resource provided by DTIC is the Scientific and Technical Information Network (STINET), which provides access to the full text of many reports on defense STI from defense contractors and military agency components. Examples of these reports whose subject coverage encompasses the spectrum of defense STI research are *System/Design Trade Study Report for the Navigation of the Airborne, Ground Vehicular, and Man-Portable Platforms in Support of the Buried Ordnance Detection, Identification, and Remediation Technology* (1995), *Information Fusion Battlespace Dominance* (1998), *A Moderate Course for USAF (United States Air Force) UAV (Unmanned Aerial Vehicle) Development* (1998), *E Pluribus Unum: Enhancing Intelligence Support in the Network Centric Environment* (1999), *Secure Continuous Biometric-Enhanced Authentication* (2000), and *Soldier Performance Course of Action Visualization Aids* (2000). An additional laudable feature of STINET is the "Research and Development Network" research summary of ongoing defense STI research from federal fiscal year 1996 (October 1, 1996–September 30, 1997) to the present.

Defense Threat Reduction Agency

The Defense Threat Reduction Agency (DTRA) was created on October 1, 1998, from the previously existing Defense Special Weapons Agency.[43] DTRA's institutional responsibilities include protecting the United States and its allies by reducing the threat from weapons of mass destruction such as chemical, biological, radiological, nuclear, and high explosives.[44] These activities are carried out by DTRA personnel and resources concentrating on the areas of cooperative threat reduction, technology development, on-site inspection, technology security, combat security, and threat control and reduction on a global scale.[45]

Further information about DTRA operations and activities can be found on its website (www.dtra.mil/). These resources include a Quicktime video describing DTRA activities, information on DTRA involvement in enforcing various arms control and security agreements such as the Intermediate Nuclear Forces (INF) Treaty between the United States and the former Soviet Union, the Conventional Forces in Europe (CFE) Treaty, the Nuclear Nonproliferation Treaty (NPT), and the Strategic Arms Reduction Talks (START) Treaty with the Russian Federation. A "Cooperative Threat Reduction Scorecard" section of DTRA's website lists nuclear weapons destroyed in Kazakhstan, Russia, and the Ukraine as a result of DTRA enforcement activities, projections of future nuclear weapons destruction in the former Soviet Union, and detailed program descriptions of DTRA disarmament activities. Additional DTRA website content includes fact sheets on the United Nations Special Commission on Iraq, the Bomb Line Unit (BLU-118/B) Thermobaric Warhead, and a *Threat Reduction Reduction Bibliography* listing and, in some cases, providing links to journal articles, websites, and various U.S. government and international government organization reports on reducing the proliferation of weapons of mass destruction.

DTRA's website includes a variety of historical and contemporary reports documenting its activities. Examples of these include *On-Site Inspections under the INF Treaty: A History of the On-Site Inspection Agency and INF Treaty Implementation, 1988–1991* (1993), *On-Site Inspections under the CFE Treaty: A History of the On-Site Inspection Agency and CFE Treaty Implementation, 1990–1996* (1996), *Defense Special Weapons Agency 1947–1997: The First 50 Years of National Service* (1996), *Nuclear Weapons Accident Response Procedures* (1999), *Customer Report for Mock Urban Setting Test* (2002), and *Corrective Measures Study/Feasibility Study for the Disposition of Metal/Concrete Debris and Radioactive Coral (above 13.5 pCi/g) Located in the Radiological Control Area on Johnston Island, Johnston Atoll* (2002).

Joint Chiefs of Staff

The Joint Chiefs of Staff (JCS) was established in 1949 amendments to the 1947 National Security Act. Its membership consists of a chairman from one of the armed services appointed by the president and confirmed by the Senate for one two-year term with eligibility for an additional biennial term, the U.S. Army's chief of staff, the chief of naval operations representing the U.S. Navy, and the U.S. Air Force's chief of staff. The JCS reports to the president and the secretary of defense and serves as principal adviser to them and the National Security Council on national security issues. JCS responsibilities specified in its enabling statute include

1. Preparation of strategic plans and provision for the strategic direction of the military forces;
2. Preparation of joint logistic plans and assignment to the military services of logistics responsibilities in accordance with such plans;
3. Establishment of unified commands in strategic areas;
4. Review of major material and personnel requirements of the military forces in accordance with strategic and logistic plans;
5. Formulation of policies for joint training of the military forces;
6. Formulation of policies for coordinating the military education of members of the military forces; and
7. Provision of United States representation on the Military Staff Committee of the United Nations in accordance with the provisions of the Charter of the United Nations.[46]

This organizational structure generally remained in place until the passage of the Goldwater-Nichols Department of Defense Reorganization Act of 1986.[47] Enacted in

1947 National Security Act

The 1947 National Security Act is responsible for most of the early twenty-first century U.S. national security establishment. It transferred the existing War and Navy Departments into the Department of Defense under the secretary of defense's leadership. Subsequently, each military department—U.S. Army, U.S. Navy, and U.S. Air Force—would have its own service secretary. A 1949 amendment gave the secretary of defense enhanced power over individual armed services and their secretaries.

The legislation also created the Central Intelligence Agency (CIA) out of the Office of Strategic Services and other existing intelligence organizations. The CIA was entrusted with serving as the U.S. government's primary civilian intelligence-gathering organization.

The 1947 law also provided for the National Security Council (NSC). The NSC, consisting of the president, vice president, secretaries of state and defense, and director of central intelligence, was charged with providing the president with advice on immediate and emerging national security issues compiled from U.S. government agencies.

The NSC would develop its own professional staff under the direction of the president's assistant for national security affairs. The NSC's role and influence have varied in different presidential administrations and was affected by passage of the 2002 Homeland Security Act.

response to growing concern by Congress and governmental commissions over deficiencies in the JCS operating structure, the Goldwater-Nichols act increased the authority of the JCS chairman by making him, instead of the corporate JCS, the primary military adviser to the president, secretary of defense, and NSC; established the position of vice chairman of the JCS; endowed military theater commanders in chief with expanded powers; increased the prestige and rewards of serving in joint military commands; and defined the military chain of command as extending from the president to the secretary of defense to the military commanders in chief with the president having the discretion of allowing his communications to the secretary of defense and these commanders to go through the JCS chairman.[48]

Public documentation of JCS activities is provided through a variety of printed publications and through the JCS website (www.dtic.mil/jcs/). Examples of the resources accessible through this Internet portal include descriptions of JCS directorates covering issues such as force structure, intelligence, manpower, operations, strategic plans, and the various unified combatant commands. The JCS website features biographical information on and speeches by the JCS chairman, general overviews on protecting U.S. military forces from anthrax and terrorism, the text of the Goldwater-Nichols reform law, links to DOD news and press releases, and information on joint warfare doctrine.

Publications accessible through the JCS website include the journal *Joint Forces Quarterly* from 1993 to the present, *The Development of the Base Force, 1989–1992* (1993), *Operation Just Cause—Panama* (1995), *The History of the Unified Command Plan, 1946–1993* (1995), *The Chairmanship of the Joint Chiefs of Staff* (1995), and *National Military Strategy: Shape, Respond, Prepare Now—A Military Strategy for a New Era* (1997). These and other publications illustrate the history of the JCS and how its areas of emphasis will likely continue to focus on achieving greater cooperation between the individual armed service branches as they strive to execute U.S. national security policy.

Missile Defense Agency

The Missile Defense Agency was created in January 2002 as a new incarnation of the Ballistic Missile Defense Organization, which was created during the Clinton administration to replace the Strategic Defense Initiative Organization set up during the Reagan administration.[49] MDA became the primary agency for directing U.S. missile defense programs. Secretary of Defense Donald H. Rumsfeld stressed what he saw as DOD's primary missile defense priorities.

   a. First, to defend the U.S., deployed forces, allies, and friends.
   b. Second, to employ a Ballistic Missile Defense System (BMDS) that layers defenses to intercept missiles in all phases of their flight (i.e., boost, midcourse, and terminal) against all ranges of threats.
   c. Third, to enable the Services to field elements of the overall BMDS as soon as practicable. To that end, we have started to deploy the Patriot Advanced Capability-3 system [in 2002], after successful testing, as the first line of defense against short-range missiles.

d. Fourth, to develop and test new technologies, use prototype and test assets to provide early capability, if necessary, and improve the effectiveness of deployed capability by inserting new technologies as they become available or when the threat warrants an accelerated capability.[50]

Numerous resources describing how MDA carries out these mandates are available on the agency's website (www.acq.osd.mil/bmdo/). These materials include RealPlayer and Quicktime videos of missile defense system tests; news releases; agency budget information; an organizational chart featuring links describing MDA departments such as Test and Evaluation and Systems and Engineering; a link to the Joint National Integration Center (www.jntf.osd.mil/), which provides testing, modeling, simulation, and analysis of ballistic missile testing; and fact sheets on various MDA programs including *Airborne Laser Test Program* (2002), *Ballistic Missile Approach* (2002), *Patriot Advanced Capability-3* (2002), and *Theater High Altitude Area Defense (THAAD)* (2002).

MDA's website also contains reports and reference sources covering various aspects of missile defense. Representative samples include *Ballistic Missile Defense Glossary Version 3.0* (1997), *National Missile Defense Review Committee Report* (1999), *Summary of Report to Congress on Utility of Sea-Based Assets to National Missile Defense* (1999), *Ballistic Missile Defense: A Brief History* (2000), *Harnessing the Power of Technology: The Road to Ballistic Missile Defense from 1983–2007* (2000), *Ballistic and Cruise Missile Threat* (2000), *BMDO Fiber-Optic Technologies for Telecommunications Part II: Optical Switches and Circuitry* (2001), and *Missile Defense Technologies to Counter Terrorism* (2002).

Additional Defense and Affiliated DOD Institutions

Many additional agencies affiliated to varying degrees with DOD provide national security policy resources. These agencies include academic institutions such as the National Defense University (NDU) and its various components, specific programs such as the Anthrax Vaccination Immunization Program (AVIP), advisory bodies such as the Defense Advisory Committee on Women in the Services, military doctrinal resources such as the Joint Electronic Library (JEL), and policy-oriented entities such as the Space Policy Directorate.

Anthrax Vaccine Immunization Program

The appearance of anthrax in congressional and other governmental offices in the Washington, D.C., area during the fall of 2001 provided a vivid demonstration of how dangerous this chemical is and the national security implications its widespread dissemination could cause. The Anthrax Vaccine Immunization Program (AVIP) has been around for many years and received a June 28, 2002, reauthorization in the wake of concern over the vaccine's safety expressed in Congress and elsewhere.[51]

AVIP's website (www.anthrax.osd.mil/) contains a variety of resources describing the programs administering this vaccine to U.S. military personnel. Materials on this site include information on released lots of anthrax vaccines from their manufacturing plants, various medical forms, links to article citations and the full text of some articles on anthrax from journals such as the Centers for Disease Control's *Emerging Infectious Diseases* and the *Journal of the American Medical Association*.

Publications accessible on AVIP's website include *Policy for Reporting Adverse Events Associated with the Anthrax Vaccine* (1999), a link to the army field manual *Treatment of Biological Warfare Agent Casualties* (2000), *Medical Management of Biological Casualties,* 4th ed. (2000), *Policy on Clinical Issues Related to Anthrax Vaccination* (2002), *Policy on Administrative Issues Related to the Anthrax Vaccine Immunization Program* (2002), and *Vaccine Program to Protect against Anthrax* (2002).

Asia-Pacific Center for Security Studies

The Asia-Pacific Center for Security Studies (APCSS) was authorized by fiscal year 1995 defense spending legislation, and APCSS officially opened on September 4, 1995. Its purpose is building and strengthening existing bilateral relationships between the U.S. military's Pacific Command and armed forces of Asian-Pacific nations by focusing on multilateral approaches to deal with regional security issues.[52]

The website www.apcss.org/ contains information resources about APCSS programs as well as numerous publications. Available resources include information about the College of Security Studies, where senior military and civilian officials from Asian-Pacific nations take classes on regional security issues and gain expanded insights into the national security policy perspectives of these individuals and nations; an alumni newsletter; listings of center graduates and e-mail links to many of these individuals; reports from selected center-sponsored conferences; and information about upcoming conferences held under center auspices.

The publications accessible on the APCSS website reflect the diverse and complex nature of Asian-Pacific security issues. A representative sampling of these materials is *Islam in Asia* (1999), *Report from the Seminar on China's Internal Challenges and Their Implications for Regional Stability* (2000), *Nuclear Weapons Challenges in Asia* (2000), *Asia-Pacific Space and Missile Security Issues* (2000), *Domestic Determinants and Security Policy-Making in East Asia* (2000), *Security Policy in Indonesia: By Guess, or by Golly?* (2001), *Rethinking Education, National Security, and Social Stability in China* (2001), *East Asia/Pacific Military Cooperation since 9/11* (2002), *Chemical and Biological Weapons in East Asia: Prospects for Cooperation* (2002), and *Tentacles of Terror: Al-Qaeda's Southeast Asian Network* (2002), which also includes an accompanying PowerPoint presentation.

Computer Emergency Response Team

The Computer Emergency Response Team coordinates military and DOD responses to computer and information security emergencies. Its website homepage (www.cert.mil/) is publicly accessible, but site content is restricted to authorized U.S. government users.[53]

Defend America

The Defend America website (www.defendamerica.mil/) provides one-stop access to coverage of U.S. military efforts in the war against terrorism. Site contents include links to relevant government agency websites such as the White House and Federal Emergency Management Agency, military websites such as www.defenselink.mil/ and individual armed service branch websites, and links to volunteer organizations such as the Red Cross and Salvation Army. Additional Defend America resources include news coverage (including audio and video webcasts), military operation photos, and background fact sheets on Afghanistan, Osama Bin Laden, and al Qaeda. The website also has information on Pentagon reconstruction, special operations, and unmanned aerial vehicles; Iraq situation updates; instructions on how to send a message of support to U.S. military forces; individual weapons system fact sheets; and memorial biographies and photographs of those killed in the September 11, 2001, attack on the Pentagon.

Defense Advisory Committee on Women in the Services

The Defense Advisory Committee on Women in the Services (DACOWITS) advises and makes recommendations to the secretary of defense on issues and policies concerning the recruitment, retention, treatment, employment, integration, and well-being of professional women in the armed forces and related advice on family issues regarding military recruitment and retention.[54]

A variety of information resources can be located on the DACOWITS website (www.dtic.mil/dacowits/), such as quarterly executive committee reports from September 2000 to September 2001, links to military and nonmilitary sites on the roles women play in the military, and press releases. Additional content includes an organizational chart, the names of DOD personnel who are ex officio DACOWITS members, individual military service liaisons to DACOWITS, semiannual conference issue books from 1998 to 2001, and policy recommendations submitted to the secretary of defense from the 1970s to the present.

Defense Environmental Network and Information Exchange

The Defense Environmental Information Network and Information Exchange (DENIX) is part of the Office of the Deputy Under Secretary of Defense for Installations and Environment. This office provides oversight and policy guidance for managing worldwide DOD installations and for DOD's global environmental, occupational safety, and health programs including cleanup at active and closing military bases, compliance with environmental laws, conservation of natural and cultural resources, pollution prevention, fire protection, explosive safety, and pest management.[55]

The DENIX website (https://www.denix.osd.mil/) provides a variety of resources on DOD's environmental programs and activities as well as links to environmental publications produced by individual armed services branches. Materials include an organizational chart, biographical information on the deputy undersecretary of defense for installations and the environment, and links to U.S. and foreign environmental laws and regulations.

The DENIX site is a particularly rich resource for defense environmental policy publications. Posted are *History of Environmental Security in the Department of Defense* (n.d.), *DOD Commanders' Guide to Biodiversity* (n.d.), *Defense Environmental Quality Program Annual Reports to Congress* (fiscal years 1994–2000), *Defense Environmental Restoration Program Annual Reports to Congress* (fiscal years 1994–2001), *DOD Directive 4715.3: Environmental Conservation Program* (1996), *DOD Report on Base Alignment and Closure* (1998), *Environment, Safety, and Occupational Health in the Department of Defense* (2000), *DOD Occupational Health Guidance for Handling Suspicious Letters and Packages* (2001), *Interim Recommendations for Cleanup of Commercial and Residential Buildings Following Bacillus Anthracis Spore Release* (2001), and *Report of the DOD Munitions Plan* (2002). These and other publications illustrate the increasingly important role played by environmental issues in national security policy formulation, implementation, and assessment.

Defense Information Technology Testbed

The Defense Information Technology Testbed (DITT) received its organizational charter from the assistant secretary of defense for command, control, communications, and intelligence (ASD-C3I) on March 23, 1997. DITT's mission includes establishing a multimedia system for electronic records management with easy access and retrieval gateways to select and transfer appropriate commercial technologies to DOD.[56]

This emphasis on information resources management is reflected in the contents of DITT's website (http://call-ditt.leavenworth.army.mil/) located on the U.S. Army's Fort Leavenworth, Kansas, server. Site contents include overviews of DITT projects in areas as varied as information lifestyle, metadata, and pilot systems. Information is also provided on other military information resource management activities along with access to DITT-produced publications such as *Multimedia Analysis and Archives System* (n.d.), *The Once and Future Portal: Integration, Knowledge Access, and Exploitation with Enterprise Document and Record Management* (2000), *Functional and System Use Cases for Records Management Application Environment* (2000), and *Archiving Public Web Sites Final DOD Guidance* (2001).

DefenseLink Freedom of Information Act

The DefenseLink Freedom of Information Act website (www.defenselink.mil/pubs/foi/) provides information about DOD activities relevant to its administration of the Freedom of Information Act. Resources on this site include a DOD Freedom of Information briefing, DOD FOIA guidelines and regulations, the text of the *Department of Defense (DOD) Freedom of Information Act Handbook* (n.d.), annual DOD FOIA program reports from 1996 to 2001, and a link to the electronic reading room of the Office of the Secretary of Defense and Joint Chiefs of Staff featuring additional FOIA materials.

Defense Modeling and Simulation Office

The Defense Modeling and Simulation Office (DMSO) serves as DOD's official representative for modeling and simulation (M&S) activities, coordinates M&S activities with other federal agencies and armed services, promotes initiatives and demonstrations to fill crucial technological M&S deficiencies in military requirements, and serves as a contact on M&S technical issues with NATO countries.[57]

DMSO's website (https://www.dmso.mil/public/) contains a variety of publicly accessible materials including news releases, information about its activities in warfighting areas such as asymmetric warfare, joint programs, and military transformation and information about DMSO areas of technological emphasis including dynamic environments, human performance, and knowledge integration.

Examples of DMSO publications are *DOD Directive 5000.59: DOD Modeling and Simulation (M&S) Management* (1994), *DOD Modeling and Simulation Glossary* (1998), and *The Transformation Process: Modeling and Simulation Is a Key Enabler* (2001).

Department of Defense Forms Program

Forms are essential to fulfilling the work requirements of any organization whether it be a small business, educational institution, or DOD. The DOD Forms Program website (http://web1.whs.osd.mil/icdhome/FORMTAB.HTM) provides information about and access to many forms produced by DOD, the secretary of defense, individual armed service branches, and the National Guard as well as to other federal agency forms. DOD forms are arranged in numerical order and constitute the largest portion of the website. They include *DD 2329: Record of Trial by Summary Court Martial* (1984), *DD 2346: Official Combat Area Individual Name Listing of Casualties* (1998), *DD 1879: DOD Request for Personnel Security Investigation* (1999), *DD 1384: Transportation Control and Movement Document* (2000), and *DD 1419: DOD Industrial Plant Equipment Requisition* (2000).

Depleted Uranium Library

The Depleted Uranium Library website (http://deploymentlink.osd.mil/du_library/) is part of DOD's Deployment Health Support Directorate and provides access to medical and environmental information, data, and training materials on depleted uranium. Depleted uranium consists of leftover isotopes of highly radioactive uranium formerly serving as nuclear fuel or used as nuclear weapons. It provides protection for military weapons such as Abrams tanks.[58]

The site contains a variety of materials from DOD, other U.S. government agencies, and selected foreign government resources on depleted uranium's military use and possible health effects. Accessible resources include a depleted uranium general awareness training video in Quicktime and RealPlayer formats; the text of news releases, speeches, and press briefings by DOD and armed services personnel; and summaries of ongoing depleted uranium research findings such as *Carcinogenic Potential of Depleted Uranium and Tungsten Alloys.*

Among the numerous reports featured on the website are *Health and Environmental Consequences of Depleted Uranium Use in the U.S. Army* (1995), *Management of Equipment Contaminated with Depleted Uranium or Radioactive Commodities* (1999), *Analysis of Transuranics and Other Contaminants in Depleted Uranium Armor* (2000), and *Depleted Uranium Environmental and Medical Surveillance in the Balkans* (2001).

Deputy Undersecretary of Defense for Industrial Affairs

The deputy undersecretary of defense for industrial affairs is responsible for seeing that a sufficient defense industrial base exists and oversees defense production to meet current, future, and emergency requirements. He or she also advises the undersecretary of defense for acquisition, technology, and logistics on defense industry acquisition, consolidations, and mergers.[59]

Materials on the office's website (www.acq.osd.mil/ip/) include an organizational chart showing the two overall divisions covering industrial consolidation and globalization and industrial base capabilities and readiness along with their component parts covering global industrial integration initiatives, mergers and acquisition review, and defense industry financial analysis and metrics. Publicly accessible resources include *DOD Directive 5000.60: Defense Industrial Capabilities Assessment* (1996), *DOD Directive 5000.60-H: Assessing Defense Industrial Capabilities* (1996), *DOD Directive 5000.62: Impact of Mergers on Acquisition of Major DOD Suppliers on DOD Programs* (1996), and *Annual Industrial Capabilities Report to Congress* (2002–present).

Directorate for Information Operations and Reports, Statistical Information Analysis Division

The Statistical Information Analysis Division (SIAD) of DOD collects, processes, and publishes DOD military and civilian workforce information and supports various workforce reporting systems within DOD's Directorate for Information Operations and Reports.[60]

Numerous data-based reports are available on the SIAD website (http://web1.whs.osd.mil/). Specific publications include *Distribution of Personnel by State by Selected Locations* (fiscal years 1994–present), *DOD Active Duty Military Personnel Levels Fiscal Years 1950–2000* (n.d.), and *Worldwide Manpower Distribution by Geographic Area* (2001). Topics covered in these and other SIAD publications include statistical military strength breakdowns by military and civilian personnel by rank, grade, and geographic area; breakdowns of military casualties from the Korean War to the present; and a glossary of DOD labor force terms such as *casualty, enlistment,* and *operating location.* This site once featured a roster listing general flag officers worldwide, but this information was likely removed for security reasons after the September 11, 2001, terrorist attacks.

DOD Communications and Directives Directorate

The Communications and Directives Directorate is responsible for providing a single uniform system of DOD issuances and directives to carry out departmental policies and procedures.[61] A multitude of DOD policy documents such as military commission orders, instructions, and departmental directives are accessible through the directorate's website (www.dtic.mil/whs/directives/) and browsable in numeric order.

Examples of site contents include the text of *Military Commission Order No. 1: Procedures for Trials by Military Commissions of Certain Non–United States Citizens in the War against Terrorism* (2002) and an accompanying fact sheet. Numerous DOD instructional documents can be viewed, such as *DOD Instruction 1110.1: Defense Manpower Requirements Report* (1979), *DOD Instruction 1308.3: DOD Physical Fitness and Body Fat Programs Procedures* (1995), and *DOD Instruction 3000.4: Capabilities-Based Munitions Requirements Process* (2001).

DOD directives are the most important policy documents accessible on this site because they contain information required by law, the president, and the secretary of defense in initiating, governing, or regulating actions and conduct by DOD entities within their areas of responsibility.[62] A representative sampling on the website includes *DOD Directive 1100.18: Wartime Manpower Mobilization Planning* (1986), *DOD Directive 3115.8: Collection of Information on Non–U.S. Persons outside the United States at Request of U.S. Law Enforcement Agencies* (2000), *DOD Directive 3150.2: DOD Nuclear Weapons System Safety Program* (1996), *DOD Directive 5100.1: Functions of the Department of Defense and Its Major Components* (2002), *DOD Directive 5105.68: Pentagon Force Protection Agency* (2002), and *DOD Directive 5205.10: Department of Defense Treaty Inspection Readiness Program* (2001).

George C. Marshall Center for European Security Studies

The George C. Marshall Center for European Security Studies was established by DOD Directive 5200.34 in November 1992.[63] Named for former secretary of state (1947–1949) and defense (1950–1951) George C. Marshall, the center's mission is to increase understanding and appropriate defense cooperation within a context of political and economic democracy, human rights, and freedom by

1. Serving as a venue for defense contacts.
2. Providing defense education to U.S. civilian and military personnel and to such personnel from European countries including newly independent states once part of the former Soviet Union.
3. Conducting research on security issues affecting the United States, Europe, and former Soviet states.
4. Conducting conferences, seminars, and information exchange activities with

U.S. civilian and military personnel along with European and former Soviet civilian and military personnel.
5. Conducting foreign area officer and language training according to military department requirements.
6. Supporting North Atlantic Treaty Organization activities involving European nations and former Soviet states.[64]

The Marshall Center is located in Garmish Partenkirchen, Germany, and carries out its mission through various educational programs including the College of International Security Studies and the Foreign Area Officer Program. The program trains military officers with regional expertise, foreign language skills, and knowledge of foreign political-military relationships to integrate their experience into policy-making and analytical positions.[65]

The center's website is accessible at www.marshallcenter.org/ in English, German, and Russian and has a number of materials about center programs and listings of writings done by center faculty. A weakness of the website is the presence of a number of broken links. Examples of works accessible through the website are four Marshall Center papers on European security topics: *Europe's New Defense Ambitions: Implications for NATO, the U.S., and Russia* (2000), *The Transformation of Russian Military Doctrine: Lessons Learned from Kosovo and Chechnya* (2000), *Cooperative Security: New Horizons for the International Order* (2001), and *Western Unity and the Transatlantic Security Challenge* (2002).

Another feature is links to security studies papers by Marshall Center alumni including *Strange War in Southern Kyrgyzstan* (n.d.) and *Defence Budgeting (Planning, Programming, and Budgeting) System in Lithuania* (n.d.). A link to the Partnership for Peace Consortium website (www.pfpconsortium.org/) contains works of defense education and research institutes from forty-two American and European countries.

Gulf War Illnesses, Gulflink

Executive Order 12961, issued on May 26, 1995, established a Presidential Advisory Committee on Gulf War Veterans Illnesses.[66] This committee issued a report on illnesses suffered by Persian Gulf War veterans as a result of suspected chemical exposures they experienced during Operation Desert Storm. The position of special assistant for Gulf War illnesses subsequently was created within DOD to oversee and disseminate research and possible treatments for these ailments.[67] Gulflink was set up under the auspices of the special assistant.

The website www.gulflink.osd.mil/ serves as a content-rich resource for materials and data on Gulf War illnesses and their historical, scientific, and political implications on national security planning and policy making. An important feature on Gulflink's homepage is a link to Medsearch, the Gulf War Medical Research Library. Medsearch is a collaborative effort among DOD, the Department of Heath and Human Service, and the Department of Veterans Affairs. It provides access to project summaries of ongoing research into Gulf War illnesses and links to some full text reports and scientific journal articles.

Gulflink site contents also feature press briefings and transcripts dating back to 1994 and congressional committee testimony on Gulf War illnesses by governmental and military officials. The most important feature of this site is the reports containing case studies and other analyses of the effects chemical exposures may have had on U.S. personnel participating in the Persian Gulf War. Examples of these reports include *Inhibited Red Fuming Nitric Acid* (1999), *Vaccine Use during the Gulf War* (2000), *Environmental Exposure Report: Oil Well Fires* (2000), *Possible Post-War Use of Chemical Warfare Agents against Civilians by Iraq* (2000), *Environmental Exposure Report: Pesticides* (2001), *Case Narrative: 11th Marines Final Report* (2001), *Case Narrative: Al Jubayl, Saudia Arabia Final Report* (2001), *Possible Mustard Release at Ukhaydir Ammunition Storage Depot* (2001), *Case Narrative: Chemical Warfare Agent Release at Muhammad-iyat Ammunition Storage Site Final Report* (2002), and *Technical Report: Modeling and Risk Characterization of U.S. Demolition Operations at the Khamisiyah Pit* (2002).

Additional site contents include declassified intelligence and operational documents on the Persian Gulf War.

Joint Total Asset Visibility

Joint Asset Total Visibility (JTAV), part of the Office of Under Secretary of Defense for Acquisition, Technology, and Logistics, has its origins in a November 1995 Defense Total Asset Visibility Implementation Plan. JTAV's mission is providing "timely and accurate information on the location, movement, status, and identity of units, personnel, equipment, and supplies" while working to improve DOD logistical performance practices.[68]

Further details about JTAV programs can be gleaned from its website (www.defenselink.mil/acq/jtav/). The site has background historical information, press briefings, and reports such as *Defense Total Asset Visibility Plan* (1995), *Joint Total Asset Visibility System Architecture* (1997), *Joint Total Asset Visibility Strategic Plan* (1999), *Joint Total Asset Visibility Program Baseline and Economic Analysis* (2001), *Ground Control Satellite System (GCSS) Family of Systems Update Brief* (2001), and *JTAV Information Brief* (2001).

Joint Vision 2020

Joint Vision 2020 reflects the Joint Chiefs of Staff's conception of joint warfare involving all U.S. armed services branches. It builds upon the scope of its predecessor planning program, Joint Vision 2010, to guide the ongoing technological and operational transformation of the U.S. military.[69] Joint Vision 2020's strategic planning document makes the following declaration underlying its institutional modus operandi.

> If our Armed Forces are to be faster, more lethal, and more precise in 2020 than they are today, we must continue to invest in and develop new military capabilities. . . . As first explained in *JV 2010,* and dependent upon realizing the potential of the

information revolution, today's capabilities for maneuver, strike, logistics, and protection will become dominant maneuver, precision engagement, focused logistics, and full dimensional protection. The joint force, because of its flexibility and responsiveness, will remain the key to operational success in the future. The integration of core competencies provided by the individual Services is essential to the joint team, and the employment of the capabilities of the Total Force (active, reserve, guard, and civilian members) increases the options for the commander and complicates the choices of our opponents. To build the most effective force for 2020, we must be fully joint: intellectually, operationally, organizationally, doctrinally, and technically.[70]

Further information about Joint Vision 2020 and its conceptual thinking on the nature of future warfare can be found at www.dtic.mil/jv2020/. Resources include PowerPoint slides for a briefing explaining doctrinal attributes of Joint Vision 2020 such as full spectrum dominance, links to individual armed service branch visions of joint military operations, a link to the Joint Electronic Library and its joint warfare doctrinal documents, and a link to various joint vision historical documents such as *Joint Vision 2010* and *Concept for Future Joint Operations* (1997).

National Defense University

National Defense University (NDU) and its component parts train selected military and civilian personnel for responsibilities in national security policy-making positions.[71] NDU's research missions seek to disseminate and expand understanding of U.S international security issues.[72] The NDU website (www.ndu.edu/) provides access to additional information about NDU programs and access to national security policy research produced by, for example, the Africa Center for Strategic Studies (ACSS), Center for Counterproliferation Research (CCR), and Institute for National Strategic Studies (INSS).

Africa Center for Strategic Studies

The Africa Center for Strategic Studies seeks to enhance African democratic governance by providing senior African civilian and military leaders rigorous academic programs in civil-military relations, national security strategy, and defense economics. Additional ACSS goals include stressing the vital importance of civilian control and military professionalism in the democratic process, examining how civilian-military relationships function in developing and implementing national security strategy, and maintaining ongoing and long-term interaction with participants in ACSS programs.[73]

The ACSS website (www.africacenter.org/) provides additional information about center activities including data on meetings and programs, biographical information and academic credentials of ACSS leaders, and links to U.S. government agency and academic research sites pertaining to Africa. A forthcoming feature of the website will be presentations, research papers, and speeches by ACSS faculty.

Center for Counterproliferation Research

The Center for Counterproliferation Research (CCR) conducts research and educational programs on assessing U.S. efforts to address and counteract the proliferation of weapons of mass destruction: nuclear, chemical, and biological. CCR research and programs seek to increase the awareness of military leaders and defense civilians as to how the threat of proliferation affects defense policy, programs, and military operations.[74]

CCR's website (www.ndu.edu/centercounter/) provides information about the center's mission and links to publications produced by CCR personnel. Examples include *Radiological Dispersal Devices: Assessing the Transnational Threat* (1998), *Deterrence and Defense in a Nuclear, Biological, and Chemical Environment* (1999), *Bioterrorism and Biocrimes: The Illicit Use of Biological Agents since 1900* (2001), *The Counterproliferation Imperative: Meeting Tomorrow's Challenges* (2001), *Adversary Use of NBC Weapons: A Neglected Challenge* (2001), and *Chemical, Biological, Radiological, and Nuclear Terrorism: The Threat According to the Current Unclassified Literature* (2002).

Center for Hemispheric Defense Studies

North and South American defense ministers, meeting in 1995 in Williamsburg, Virginia, expressed concern over the limited number of civilians in their countries who could deal substantively with military and defense issues. Former U.S. secretary of defense William J. Perry (1994–1997) proposed creating a center to address these concerns during the defense ministers' 1996 conference in Bariloche, Argentina. The Center for Hemispheric Defense Studies (CHDS) thus was established. Its mission is developing academic programs to educate civilians in security planning and management, increasing their familiarity with professional military issues, and studying the overall defense policy-making process.[75]

CHDS provides information about its mission and research through its website (www3.ndu.edu/chds/) in English, Portuguese, and Spanish. Materials available are an academic calendar, the annual report for federal fiscal year 2000, the names of current academic fellows and their country of origin, press releases, biographical and professional information on center faculty, and links to Latin American research center websites.

Research-related resources include issues of the center's e-journal *Security and Defense Studies* with sample articles including "The Military and Media in Canada since 1992" (2001), "Security, Sovereignty, and Public Order in the Caribbean" (2002), and "Mission Reconfiguration, Environmental Change, and the Reconfiguration of the Jamaican Security Forces" (2002). Another noteworthy feature on the website is the text of papers from the 2001 Research and Education in Defense and Security Studies Seminar (REDES) held in Washington, D.C., and the 2002 REDES seminar held in Brasilia, Brazil. Examples of English language papers presented during the 2002 seminar include "Intelligence Professionalism in the Americas," "Post-September 11 Anti-Terrorist Efforts by the Organization of American States,"

"Brazil's Amazon Surveillance System (SIVAM): Promoting Cooperation against International Crime and Terrorism," "Roles, Missions, and Activities of Chile in the Antarctic Continent," "New Democracy, Old Arrangement: The Civil-Military Relations under Fox," and "The USA-Brazil Implementing Arrangement on the International Space Station: Interpretation and Application."

Center for the Study of Chinese Military Affairs

The Center for the Study of Chinese Military Affairs is part of NDU's Institute for National Strategic Studies and was created by Congress in 1999 as part of the fiscal year 2000 defense spending act.[76] The center's mission is serving as a national resource for multidisciplinary research and information exchange on China's national goals and strategic posture and on China's ability to develop and deploy its military in support of national strategic goals. In performing this mission, the center informs DOD officials, other federal policymakers, and Congress of the results of its findings and maintains an active outreach program to promote expanded knowledge of Chinese military affairs by American and international analysts.[77]

The center provides information about its work and publications through its website (www.ndu.edu/inss/China_Center/CSCMA_frames.htm). Materials accessible through this website include translations of Chinese media stories about the foreign travels of the People's Liberation Army (PLA), a list of recommended readings on China's military, and assorted research reports on China's military and military activities. Examples of these reports are *The South China Sea: Future Source of Prosperity or Conflict in Southeast Asia* (1996), *The Chinese People's Liberation Army: "Short Arms and Slow Legs"* (1999), *China's Military Capabilities* (2000), *Assessing Chinese Military Development: What Are the Important Questions? A Criteria of Relevance* (2000), and *Questions about the Air Battle Dimension of the PLA's Developing Information Strike Combine* (2000).

Center for Technology and National Security Policy

The Center for Technology and National Security Policy (CTNSP) was established at NDU in 2001 to analyze and assess scientific and technological developments as applied to national security policy.[78] CTNSP's website (www.ndu.edu/ctnsp/) contains a number of useful national security policy resources. These include information about center faculty, descriptions of CTNSP research activity in homeland security, information technology studies, DOD laboratory performance, computational science modeling, biotechnology, and military transformation studies. News events are also covered including conferences such as "Homeland Security: The Civil-Military Dimension," which was held in September 2002 and was jointly sponsored by NDU and the University of Maryland.

CTNSP has also produced a number of publicly accessible reports that are part of its Defense Horizon reports series. Samples of these resources are *Resurrecting Transformation for the Post–Industrial Era* (2001), *Maritime Access: Do Defenders Hold All the Cards?* (2001), *Small Security: Nanotechnology and Future Defense* (2002), *Redis-*

covering the *Infantry in a Time of Transformation* (2002), *The Airborne Laser from Theory to Reality* (2002), *Biological Weapons: Toward a Threat Reduction Strategy* (2002), and *The Virtual Border: Countering Seaborne Container Terrorism* (2002).

Industrial College of the Armed Forces

Established in 1924 as the Army Industrial College, the Industrial College of the Armed Forces (ICAF) acquired its current name in 1946 and became part of NDU in 1976.[79] ICAF's institutional mandate is to prepare selected military officers and civilians for senior leadership and staff positions by engaging in postgraduate and affiliated research on national security strategy and industrial resources with particular emphasis on how acquisition and joint logistics are integrated into national security strategy.[80]

ICAF's website (www.ndu.edu/icaf/) contains additional information about the college's programs and research. The website provides links to ICAF's academic departments including acquisition, economics, grand strategy and mobilization, leadership and information strategy, military strategy and logistics, and political science and elements of national power. These departmental links provide descriptions about the courses offered at ICAF, such as NATO Europe, Mediterranean Littoral, Economics and Information Technology, Economics and National Security, Macroeconomics for National Security Strategy, Economic Diplomacy and Economic Warfare, Acquisition Policy I, and Domestic Emergency Response Operations.

Particularly noteworthy publications on ICAF's website are detailed analyses of various defense industries done by ICAF students for the years 2000–2003. Defense industry studies for 2000 include *Electronics, Information Systems, Land Combat,* and *Strategic;* 2001 industry studies, *Agribusiness, Aircraft, Shipbuilding, Space,* and *Transportation.* The *ICAF Handbook Class of 2003* (2002) rounds out the publications output available on ICAF's website and helps national security policy students understand the important role of industrial logistics, mobilization, and production in implementing national security policy objectives.

Information Resources Management College

NDU's Information Resources Management College (IRMC) was established on November 10, 1988, by a joint memorandum from the DOD comptroller and the NDU president as a response to a congressional mandate to establish a graduate-level institution to educate military leaders on information resources management responsibilities. IRMC's mission is preparing leaders to use computers and information technology and to manage and allocate these resources for strategic advantage. The areas of curricular and research emphasis are business process reengineering, information resource management policy, information technology, information security, acquisition reform, and managing acquisition processes.[81] IRMC's website (www.ndu.edu/irmc/) provides additional information about the college's mission and programs. A current course catalog is accessible along with descriptions of course offerings such as Assuring the Information Infrastructure; Critical

Information Systems Technologies; Developing Enterprise Security Strategies, Guidelines, and Policies; Homeland Security; and Managing Information Security in a Networked Environment.

Institute for National Strategic Studies

The Institute for National Strategic Studies (INSS) was established in 1984. Its primary missions are as follows.

- Policy research and analysis and other support to the Joint Chiefs of Staff, Office of the Secretary of Defense, unified commands, and other U.S. Government agencies in developing and advancing national security strategy and defense policy;
- Support of NDU educational missions, other professional military education institutions, and interagency training programs by providing regional/functional expertise and of state-of-the-art strategic gaming and simulation exercises; and
- Outreach activities, including an extensive program of publications and conferences, to inform the national security and defense policy debate in the U.S. and abroad.[82]

INSS is divided into several parts, including the Center for Counterproliferation Research and Center for the Study of Chinese Military Affairs. Also under the INSS umbrella is a Research Directorate, which analyzes strategic trends throughout the world and conducts defense strategy studies evaluating these trends; a Conference Directorate, which hosts several events each year on global and regional security issues; and a Publications Directorate, which produces books and papers on national security policy. The National Strategic Gaming Center (NSGC) also is a component of INSS.[83] Access to INSS-produced resources is available through www.ndu.edu/inss/insshp.html. Product examples are presentations or excerpts from symposia sponsored by the directorate such as the 1998 European Symposium "NATO 2010: A Strategic Vision," the 2001 Pacific Symposium "Enhancing Regional Cooperation through New Multilateral Initiatives," the 1999 Topical Symposium "After Kosovo: Implications for U.S. Strategy and Coalition Warfare," the 2001 Topical Symposium "National Security in the Global Era," the 2001 Joint Operations Symposium "After September 11: Implications for Strategy, Transformation, and Homeland Security," and the 2002 Joint Operations Symposium "Homeland Security: The Civil-Military Dimensions."

The Publications Directorate offers NDU-produced books and other information resources through the National Defense University Press. The directorate's website (www.ndu.edu/inss/press/nduphp.html) provides information on ordering NDU Press products and the full text of many of its materials. These publications include individual book-length studies, books that are part of monographic series such as the McNair Papers, and succinct analyses of national security policy issues such as the Strategic Forum series.

Examples of these publications, reflecting the diverse and prolific output of the NDU Press, include the annual *Strategic Assessment* (1995–1999), *The Bear Went over the Mountain: Soviet Combat Tactics in Afghanistan* (1996), *Defensive Information Warfare* (1996), *Shock and Awe: Achieving Rapid Dominance* (1996), *Modern U.S. Civil-Military Relations: Wielding the Terrible Swift Sword* (1997), *Chairman of the Joint Chiefs of Staff Strategy Essay Competition* (1998–present), *U.S.-Russian Partnership: Meeting the New Millennium* (1999), *China Debates the Future Security Environment* (2000), *Strategic Challenges for the Bush Administration* (2001), *Asian Perspectives on the Challenges of China* (2001), *Agricultural Bio-Terrorism: A Federal Strategy to Meet the Threat* (2002), *Anticipating Strategic Surprise on the Korean Peninsula* (2002), *Beyond Containment: Defending U.S. Interests in the Persian Gulf* (2002), and *Colombia's War: Toward a New Strategy* (2002).

Joint Electronic Library

The Joint Electronic Library (JEL) website (www.dtic.mil/doctrine/) contains information about the military doctrines of individual armed services branches as well as theoretical and operational aspects involving the joint collaboration of all military forces. Produced through the auspices of the Defense Technical Information Center (DTIC), JEL has information intended to promote joint doctrine awareness and management among U.S. armed forces to enhance joint, interagency, and multinational interoperability while enhancing military warfighting capabilities.[84]

Consequently, a variety of resources dealing with military doctrine, education, and training are accessible through the JEL website. Materials include publications such as the research journal *Joint Forces Quarterly* and general military monographs such as *American Civil–Military Relations: New Issues, Enduring Problems* (1995).

A particular JEL emphasis is on publications stressing how two or more armed service branches seek to integrate missions and objectives in military operations. Representations of these are *Joint Publication 3-01.5: Doctrine for Joint Theater Missile Defense* (1996), *Joint Military Operations Historical Collection* (1997), *Joint Publication 3-07.2: Joint Tactics, Techniques, and Procedures for Antiterrorism* (1998), *Joint Publication 2.0: Doctrine for Intelligence Support to Joint Operations* (2000), *Handbook for Joint Urban Operations* (2000), and *Joint Publication 3-02: Joint Doctrine for Amphibious Operations* (2001).

JEL also provides access to selected doctrinal publications produced by the individual armed services. Those produced by the U.S. Air Force include *Air Force Doctrine Document (AFDD) 2-1.7: Aerospace Control in the Combat Zone* (1998) and *AFDD Organization and Employment of Aerospace Power* (2000). U.S. Army publications include *Field Manual (FM) 100-7: Decisive Force: The Army in Theatre Operations* (1995) and *FM 100-8: The Army in Multinational Operations* (1997). Marine Corps entries include *Marine Corps Doctrinal Publication MCDD) 1: Warfighting* (1997) and *MCDD 3: Expeditionary Operations* (1998). U.S. Navy doctrinal contributions on the JEL website include *Navy Doctrine Publication (NDP) 6: Naval Command and Control* (1995) and *NDP 4: Naval Logistics* (2001).

Joint Forces Staff College

Located in Norfolk, Virginia, the Joint Forces Staff College (JFSC) was established in 1946.[85] It describes its mission as educating staff officers and other leaders in joint operational–level planning and warfighting to produce a professional commitment to joint, multinational, and interagency teamwork, attitudes, and perspectives.[86]

JFSC's website (www.jfsc.ndu.edu/) contains further information about its mission, curriculum, and programs. Website contents include information about the Joint and Combined Staff Officer School; the Joint and Combined Warfighting School; the Joint Command, Control, and Information Warfare School; a professional reading list of joint operations literature from JFSC's commandant; and the text of the Henry Hofheimer Lecture Series on national security policy making by individuals such as retired Marine Corps general Anthony Zinni and Rep. Ike Skelton (D-Mo., 1977–), who serves on the House Armed Services Committee.

Additional features of JFSC's website are information on and presentations from college-sponsored conferences such as "Multinational Operations Symposium" (2000), course descriptions, and specific publications including *Joint Staff Officer's Guide* (2000) and *Joint Forces Staff College 2001 Stakeholders Report: Educating Joint Warriors for the 21st Century* (2001).

National Defense University Library

The National Defense University (NDU) Library possesses more than 500,000 print and microform volumes and 50,000 classified documents as part of collections emphasizing national security, strategy, international relations, management, national resource mobilization, and other topics supporting NDU's military educational mission.[87]

The website for NDU's library (www.ndu.edu/library/library.html) contains resources that can be useful to national security policy students and scholars. One of these resources is subject bibliographies prepared by NDU Library personnel on subjects such as asymmetric warfare, information assurance, logistics and mobilization in the future, military forces in the Asia-Pacific region, and small wars. The bibliographies list books and articles, and they provide links to web-based resources on these subjects.

A highlight of the NDU Library website is the access it provides to digitized collections of historical national security policy-making materials. Examples include materials from the President's Blue Ribbon Commission on Defense Management (Packard Commission) during the 1980s; resources on the Goldwater-Nichols Department of Defense Reorganization Act of 1986, including the text of most congressional committee hearings and reports on this statute from 1981 to 1986; National War College (NWC) student papers from 1995 to 1999; and nearly twenty-one hundred lectures delivered at the Industrial College of the Armed Forces between 1924 and 1965.

National Security Education Program

The National Security Education Program (NSEP) was established in December 1991 by the National Security Education Act.[88] This statute established a National Security Education Program, National Security Education Fund, and National Security Education Trust Fund to administer and implement NSEP objectives. These objectives include giving Americans an understanding of less commonly taught foreign languages so the United States can remain an integral part of international global security issues, building a critical base of future national leaders who have fostered international relationships and worked and studied in other countries, developing a cadre of highly skilled professionals with superior knowledge of foreign cultures to assist in national security policy decision making, and enhancing the institutional capacity of U.S. educational institutions and increasing the number of faculty at these institutions who are capable of educating U.S. citizens in the achievement of these goals.[89]

NSEP is administered by the secretary of defense in cooperation with the National Security Education Board. This body consists of thirteen members, seven of whom are from presidential cabinet-level agencies such as the Department of Energy and six appointed by the president subject to Senate confirmation. This board provides awards to U.S. university students interested in national security aspects of international affairs who will also incur an obligation to work for a federal agency involved in national security policy making.[90]

Further information about NSEP programs can be found on its website (www.ndu.edu/nsep/). Examples of accessible resources include listings of institutional grant recipients from 1994 to 2001, a 2000 NSEP newsletter, information on undergraduate scholarships and graduate fellowships, and reports such as *National Security Education Program* (2001) and *National Briefing on Language and National Security* (2002).

National Strategic Gaming Center

The National Strategic Gaming Center (NSGC)—part of NDU's INSS—designs, develops, and delivers games, simulations, and exercises that provide experiential learning for NDU enrollees and supports research and outreach by DOD and other federal agencies.[91]

NGSC's website (www.ndu.edu/inss/nsgc_internet_site/) provides access to a limited number of resources. These include information on the computer systems and software it uses in war-gaming and simulation exercises; descriptions of its classes and programs, such as the June 25, 2002, "Silent Prairie" exercise attended by fifteen members of Congress, Secretary of Defense Donald H. Rumsfeld, and Secretary of Agriculture Ann M. Veneman; information on its programs with other federal national security policy agencies; visitors information; and links to other military modeling and simulation websites.

National War College

The National War College (NWC) was established in 1946 as an augmented replacement for the combined Army-Navy Staff College, which existed from 1943 to 1946, and has produced more than seventy-five hundred graduates who went on to assume positions in the U.S. military or government and foreign militaries and governments.[92] NWC's mission is preparing future armed forces leaders, State Department officials, and leaders for other civilian governmental agencies for high-level policy, command, and staff responsibilities through senior-level curriculum and research in national security policy and strategy from an eligible student body of U.S. and foreign candidates.[93]

NWC's website (www.ndu.edu/nwc/) provides a variety of information resources explaining the college's institutional mission. The site has descriptions of course offerings such as Fundamentals of Strategic Logic, Nature of War, Doing National Military Strategy, and Institutions of National Security Strategy; an image gallery of clip art featuring U.S. and foreign military logos; military equipment photographs; institutional insignia; and biographical information on NWC faculty and their areas of expertise.

Accessible general NWC publications include *Officer Professional Military Education Policy* (2000) and *Student Academic Handbook—Academic Year 2003* (2002). The highlight of NWC's website is the presence of student research papers that reflect the topical diversity of NWC curriculum. Representative samples are "The Encryption Export Policy Controversy: Searching for Balance in the Information Age" (2000), "Mahan's Elements of Sea Power Applied to the Development of Space Power" (2000), "Saddam Hussein and the Iran-Iraq War" (2001), "Geostrategic Security Analysis of Israel" (2001), "Political Foot-Soldier: Colin Powell's Interagency Campaign for the Base Force" (2002), "From Successful Invasion to Failed War: An Analysis of Soviet Military Strategy in Afghanistan, 1979–1989" (2002), "Water Conflict in the Jordan River Basin: What Should Strategists Ask?" (2002), and "Threat Analysis: North Korean Nuclear Program" (2002).

Near East-South Asia Center for Strategic Studies

NDU's Near East South Asia Center for Strategic Studies (NESA-CSS) was formed in 2000. Countries participating in its programs range from the Atlas Mountains to the Himalayas, including nations as diverse as Algeria, Bangladesh, India, Israel, and Morocco.[94] The mission of NESA-CSS is to enhance Near East and South Asian stability by fostering an academic environment conducive to addressing important regional security issues, promoting mutual understanding, forging partnerships, improving security-related decision making, and strengthening cooperation between civilian and military security professions from the United States and NESA-CSS participating countries.[95]

The NESA-CSS website (www.ndu.edu/nesa/) contains information about center activities. Resources accessible include listings of center faculty and staff, news releases, and a schedule of upcoming events. A limited number of publications are available, including journal articles written by NESA-CSS faculty such as "Swords and Shields: Ballistic Missiles and Defenses in the Middle East and South Asia" (2002) and "War and the Iraq Dilemma: Facing Harsh Realities" (2002). One research report is available: *Water and Security Policy: The Case of Turkey* (2002).

School for National Security Executive Education

NDU's School for National Security Executive Education (SNSEE) provides education for civilians involved in national defense in hopes of fostering awareness of the emerging national security environment, promoting communication between government agencies, and developing an educated and flexible workforce capable of responding to multiple national security threat environments.[96]

Additional information on SNSEE can be found on its website (www.ndu.edu/snsee/). The website contains no research reports by SNSEE faculty, but it does have information about SNSEE faculty and descriptions of courses they teach, including Geopolitics and Defense Policy, National Security Decisionmaking, and Leadership Competencies and National Security.

Office of Counterproliferation and Biological Defense

The Office of Counterproliferation and Biological Defense is headed by the deputy assistant secretary of defense, counterproliferation and chemical and biological defense programs. Its mission is to serve as a single point within DOD for overseeing, coordinating, and integrating chemical and biological defense, counterproliferation support, chemical demilitarization, and Assembled Chemical Weapons Assessment (ACWA) programs.[97]

The website www.acq.osd.mil/cp/ has numerous publicly accessible information resources from the Office of Counterproliferation and Biological Defense, including *Biological and Genetic Engineering: Implications for the Development of New Warfare Agents* (1996), *Report on Activities and Programs for Countering Proliferation and Nuclear, Biological, and Chemical (NBC) Terrorism: Executive Summary* (1994–2002), *DOD Chemical and Biological Defense Program Annual Report to Congress* (1997–2003), *Joint Service Chemical and Biological Defense Program Overview* (2000–2002), *Chemical and Biological Defense Primer* (2001), and *Integrated Chemical and Biological Defense Research, Development, and Acquisition Plan: Chemical and Biological Point Detection and Decontamination* (2002).

Office of Economic Adjustment

President George H. W. Bush on January 15, 1992, signed an executive order creating an interagency Economic Adjustment Agency to assist communities, regions, and states negatively affected by major DOD program changes.[98] The Economic Adjustment Agency evolved into the Office of Economic Adjustment (OEA), which is located within the Office of the Secretary of Defense. OEA manages and directs the Defense Economic Adjustment Program in light of major DOD program changes such as base expansions, closures, or realignments; major defense contract changes resulting in significant worker layoffs; and other personnel reductions or increases. OEA works with affected communities and regions in problem assessment, identifying and evaluating possible solutions, determining requirements for solving these problems, and assisting in developing strategies and action plans to enable the communities and regions to help themselves.[99]

Numerous materials describing OEA's activities are accessible on its website (http://oea.osd.mil/). Site contents include descriptions of OEA's four program areas: base realignment and closure, joint land use, defense industry adjustment, and international programs. The base realignment and closure section lists military bases and installations closed by state and armed service branches, the joint land use section focuses on developing cooperative land use planning between the military and adjacent local communities to accommodate military needs and municipal growth, the defense industry adjustment section covers direct economic assistance to affected communities, and the international programs section briefs foreign officials whose nations may be contemplating similar military spending reductions.

Publicly accessible OEA publications include *Defense Base Closure and Realignment Commission Report to the President* (1995), *Coping with the Human Aspects of Base Closure and Defense Industry Downsizing: Community Guidance Manual* (1996), *Policy on Land Use Controls Associated with Environmental Restoration Activities* (2001), and *Base Reuse Success Stories* (2002).

Office of Net Assessment

The Office of Net Assessment (ONA) is responsible for developing and coordinating net assessments concerning the current standing and future prospects of U.S. military capabilities while providing objective analysis and advice on military policy, doctrine, strategy, goals, and objectives.[100] ONA does not have a website, and much of its work is classified. Its origins may date to 1954, when a Net Evaluation Capabilities Subcommittee was established in the Office of the Secretary of Defense.[101] However, a 1997 DOD official history says ONA was established during the 1969–1973 tenure of Secretary of Defense Melvin Laird.[102]

ONA and its director received significant media attention during the early days of the George W. Bush administration for the office's role in fostering the revolution in military affairs in then emerging Bush national security policy planning.[103] Despite its secretive nature, ONA is an important institutional player in U.S. national security policy circles. Paying attention to articles written about ONA in the *New York Times* and *Washington Post* is a good way to track the office's influence.

Public Key Infrastructure Program Management Office

The Public Key Infrastructure Program Management Office is part of the Office of the Assistant Secretary of Defense for Command, Control, Communications, and Intelligence and was created through an April 9, 1999, memorandum by the ASD-C3I.[104] Public Key Infrastructure (PKI) is the mechanism used to support vital DOD applications with public key certificates. Such applications provide authentication and confidentiality to communications and network transactions along with verifying the data integrity and nonrepudiation of such transactions.[105]

Detailed information on PKI programs can be found on the website www.c3i.osd.mil/org/sio/ia/pki/. Site contents include an organizational chart, biographies of key personnel, announcements, and links to other governmental PKI sites, although only those produced by the National Institute of Standards and Technology are publicly accessible. PKI publications include *Smart Card Adoption and Implementation* (1999), *Public Key Enabling of Applications, Web Servers, and Networks for the Department of Defense* (2001), *Department of Defense Target Public Key Infrastructure Operational Requirements Document* (2001), and *DOD Key Recovery Policy for the Department of Defense Version 2.0* (2002).

Space Policy Directorate

The Space Policy Directorate (SPD) is part of ASD-C3I and is responsible for developing, coordinating, and implementing U.S. government and DOD space activities policy guidance while serving as the primary space policy contact within the Office of the Secretary of Defense.[106]

The SPD website (www.c3i.osd.mil/org/c3is/spacepol/) provides an organizational chart, an agency frequently asked questions (FAQ) link, and links to various U.S. government policy documents, international treaties, and DOD policy documents on appropriate uses of outer space. Examples of these materials are *Treaty on the Principles Governing the Activities of States in the Exploration and Use of Outer Space, Including the Moon and Other Celestial Bodies* (1967), *DOD Policy on the Use of Former Soviet Union Propulsion in Space Launch Vehicles* (1995), and *Memorandum of Agreement among DOD, Federal Aviation Administration, and National Aeronautics and Space Administration on Federal Interaction with Launch Site Operators* (1997).

Additional information on A3D-C3I programs is provided via www.defenselink.mil/nii/org/c3is/, including links to military command agencies such as the United States Space Command and the Air Force Command and Control Battlelab along with links to specific reports including *Information Superiority Investment Strategy* (1999) and *Unmanned Aerial Vehicles (UAV) Roadmap 2000–2025* (2001).

TriCare

TriCare is DOD's global health care system for active-duty and retired uniformed military service personnel and their families and replaced its predecessor program Civilian Health and Medical Program of the Uniformed Services (CHAMPUS).[107] Administered by the Office of the Secretary of Defense, TriCare provides a variety of health insurance options and levels of coverage for military personnel and their families.

Detailed information on TriCare programs and services can be found on its website (www.tricare.osd.mil/). Examples of available resources are news releases, beneficiary and provider information, assessments of TriCare management activity, toll-free information numbers, and locations of approved facilities. Numerous fact sheets and reports are accessible through the TriCare website with representative samples being *Tricare Stakeholders Reports* (1995–2002), *Tricare Cost and Workload Reports* (1995–2001), *TriCare Foreign Country Reports* (1998–2002), *Chartbook of Statistics* (1998–2002), and *TriCare Policy Manual* (2002).

These and other reports not only document the work and services performed by TriCare programs but also demonstrate the importance of health and benefits and the impact the quality of these services have on military personnel morale. Military morale, in turn, is an important consideration for policymakers implementing national security policies and for students and scholars studying national security policies.

Western Hemisphere Institute for Security Cooperation

Located at Georgia's Fort Benning, the Western Hemisphere Institute for Security Cooperation (WHINSEC) was created by the 2001 National Defense Authorization Act.[108] WHINSEC's institutional mission encompasses the following directives.

- Providing professional education and training to military, law enforcement, and civilians to support democratic principles of the Western Hemisphere.
- Building strong relationships among participating nations and helping ensure peace and stability in the hemisphere.
- Promoting democratic values, respecting human rights, and knowledge and understanding of U.S. customs and traditions.[109]

Further information about WHINSEC programs can be found on the website www.benning.army.mil/whinsec/. Accessible materials include descriptions of institute buildings; information about WHINSEC curriculum emphasis on human rights; information in Spanish on the institute's official journal, *El Hemispherico*; the text of a 2001 speech to students by Rep. Henry Hyde (R-Ill., 1975–), chairman of the House International Relations Committee (2001–); a description of WHINSEC's Occasional Papers series; and summaries of conference presentations.

No full text reports or student papers are available on WHINSEC's website. There are, however, detailed course descriptions, such as those for Civil Military Operations, Democratic Sustainment, Human Rights Instructor, International Operational Law, Counterdrug Operations, and Engineer Operations.

These courses help illustrate how WHINSEC seeks to impart principles of democracy and human rights to its students once they return to their native countries and help illustrate the importance DOD and other military entities place on providing U.S. and foreign military officers with high-quality education.

Notes

1. See U.S. Constitution, Article II, Section 2, Clause 1 for the president's designation as commander in chief; Article II, Section 1, Clause 1 for presidential executive powers; and Article II, Section 2, Clause 2 for presidential appointment powers.

2. For a one-volume history of the Department of Defense (DOD), see Roger R. Trask and Alfred Goldberg, *The Department of Defense, 1947–1997: Organization and Leaders* (Washington, D.C.: Office of the Secretary of Defense, Historical Office, 1997). For the text of key documentary materials in DOD's institutional formation and evolution, see Alice C. Cole and others, eds., *The Department of Defense: Documents on Establishment and Organization, 1944–1978* (Washington, D.C.: Office of the Secretary of Defense, Historical Office, 1979).

3. The history of the Office of the Secretary of Defense from its creation in 1947 until 1960 is exhaustively chronicled in an official four-volume work under the general editorship of Alfred Goldberg. See Steven L. Rearden, *History of the Office of the Secretary of Defense: The Formative Years, 1947–1950* (Washington, D.C.: Office of the Secretary of Defense, Historical Office, 1984); Doris M. Condit, *History of the Office of the Secretary of Defense: The Test of War, 1950–1953* (Washington, D.C.: Office of the Secretary of Defense, Historical Office, 1988); Richard M. Leighton, *History of the Office of the Secretary of Defense: Strategy, Money, and the New Look, 1953–1956* (Washington, D.C.: Office of the Secretary of Defense, Historical Office, 2001); and Robert J. Watson, *History of the Office of the Secretary of Defense: Into the Missile Age, 1956–1960* (Washington, D.C.: Office of the Secretary of Defense, Historical Office, 1997).

4. *U.S. Government Manual, 2003–2004* (Washington, D.C.: National Archives and Records Administration, 2003), 155.

5. U.S. Department of Defense, Office of the Assistant Secretary of Defense for Legislative Affairs, "About the Office of the Assistant Secretary of Defense for Legislative Affairs," 1 (www.defenselink.mil/la/aboutosdlamain.htm), accessed November 17, 2003.

6. U.S. Department of Defense, "Assistant Secretary of Defense for Public Affairs—OASD(PA)" (2001) (www.defenselink.mil/pubs/almanac/asdpa.html), accessed November 17, 2003.

7. U.S. Department of Defense, "Assistant to the Secretary of Defense for Intelligence Oversight" (n.d.), 2 (www.dtic.mil/atsdio/mission.html), accessed November 17, 2003.

8. U.S. Department of Defense, "Director of Administration and Management" (n.d.), 1 (www.defenselink.mil/odam), accessed November 17, 2003.

9. U.S. Department of Defense, "Defense Research and Engineering: Mission" (n.d.), 1 (www.defenselink.mil/ddre/aboutus/mission.htm), accessed November 17, 2003.

10. U.S. Department of Defense, Office of Director, Operational Test and Evaluation, "About DOT&E" (n.d.), 1 (www.dote.osd.mil/about.html), accessed November 17, 2003.

11. U.S. Department of Defense, Office of the Director, Program Analysis and Evaluation, "An Introduction to PA&E" (n.d.), 1 (www.pae.osd.mil/paeIntroduction.asp), accessed November 17, 2003.

12. U.S. Department of Defense, "Office of the Executive Secretary" (n.d.), 1 (www.defenselink.mil/execsec/about.html), accessed November 17, 2003.

13. U.S. Department of Defense, Department of Defense Inspector General, "Department of Defense Inspector General" (n.d.) (www.dodig.osd.mil/), accessed November 18, 2003.

14. Tony Mellor, ed., *Congressional Quarterly's Federal Staff Directory: The Executive Branch of the U.S. Government*, 30th ed. (Washington, D.C.: CQ Press, 1999), 179.

15. Mellor, *Congressional Quarterly's Federal Staff Directory*, 169.

16. Mellor, *Congressional Quarterly's Federal Staff Directory*, 182.

17. Mellor, *Congressional Quarterly's Federal Staff Directory*, 174.

18. Mellor, *Congressional Quarterly's Federal Staff Directory*, 176.

19. U.S. Department of Defense, Office of African Affairs, Assistant Secretary for International Security Affairs, "Mission" (n.d.), 1 (www.defenselink.mil/policy/isa/africa/mission.html), accessed November 17, 2003.

20. Information contained in statement on this agency's homepage (www.dtic.mil/dpmo/), accessed November 17, 2003.

21. Mellor, *Congressional Quarterly's Federal Staff Directory,* 211.

22. U.S. Department of Defense, Office of International Negotiations and Regional Affairs, "Our Mission" (n.d.), 1 (www.defenselink.mil/policy/isa/inra/), accessed November 17, 2003.

23. Mellor, *Congressional Quarterly's Federal Staff Directory,* 200.

24. U.S. Defense Advanced Research Projects Agency, "DARPA over the Years" (2001), 1 (www.darpa.mil/body/overtheyears.html), accessed November 17, 2003.

25. U.S. Defense Advanced Research Projects Agency, "DARPA Technical Offices" (2002), 1–3 (www.darpa.mil/body/darpaoff.html), accessed November 17, 2003.

26. U.S. Defense Commissary Agency, "Inside DCA" (n.d.), 1 (www.commissaries.com/insidedeca.htm), accessed November 17, 2003.

27. Mellor, *Congressional Quarterly's Federal Staff Directory,* 201.

28. U.S. Defense Contract Management Agency, "Welcome" (n.d.), 1 (www.dcma.mil/), accessed November 17, 2003.

29. Mellor, *Congressional Quarterly's Federal Staff Directory,* 202.

30. Mellor, *Congressional Quarterly's Federal Staff Directory,* 203.

31. U.S. Department of Defense, *Department of Defense Directive 5105.19* (1991), 1–2.

32. For a complete U.S. Defense Information Systems Agency (DISA) organizational chart including links to selected DISA component webpages,.see U.S. Defense Information Systems Agency, "DISA Organizational Structure" (n.d.), 1–2 (www.disa.mil/main/disaorga.html), accessed November 17, 2003.

33. For a historical overview, see U.S. Defense Logistics Agency, "History of the Defense Logistics Agency" (n.d.), 1, 4 (www.dla.mil/history/history.htm), accessed November 17, 2003. For additional examples of the historical role logistics have played in military operations, see David C. Rutenberg and James S. Allen, ed., *The Logistics of Waging War: American Logistics 1774–1985, Emphasizing the Development of Airpower* (Gunter Air Force Station, Ala.: Air Force Logistics Management Center, 1996); Roland G. Ruppenthal, *Logistics and the Broad-Front Strategy* (Washington, D.C: U.S. Army Center of Military History, 1990); Martin Van Creveld, *Supplying War: Logistics from Wallenstein to Patton* (New York: Cambridge University Press, 1980); and Charles R. Shrader, ed., *United States Army Logistics, 1775–1992: An Anthology,* 3 vols. (Washington, D.C.: U.S. Army Center of Military History, 1997).

34. U.S. Department of Defense, *Department of Defense Directive 5105.22* (1988), 1.

35. For recent media accounts on the Defense Policy Board, see Thomas E. Ricks, "Partisan Defense? Democrats Removal from Pentagon Boards Criticized," *Washington Post,* April 18, 2002, A19; Thomas E. Ricks, "Briefing Depicted Saudis as Enemies: Ultimatum Urged to Pentagon Board," *Washington Post,* August 6, 2002, A1; and U.S. Department of Defense, "News Transcript: Secretary Rumsfeld Town Hall Meeting," August 6, 2002, 6–7 (www.defenselink.mil/news/Aug2002/t08062002_t0806townhall.html), accessed November 17, 2003.

36. U.S. Defense Science Board, "The Defense Science Board Was Established in 1956 in Response to Recommendations of the Hoover Commission" (n.d.), 1–2 (www.acq.osd.mil/dsb/history.htm), accessed November 19, 2003. The Defense Science Board is part of the Office of Under Secretary of Defense for Acquisition, Technology, and Logistics.

37. Mellor, *Congressional Quarterly's Federal Staff Directory,* 211.

38. See U.S. Defense Security Service, "Our History" (2003), 1–3 (www.dss.mil/aboutdss/history.htm), accessed February 27, 2004; and *U.S. Government Manual,* 196.

39. U.S. Defense Security Service, "DSS," 1.

40. Lane E. Wallace, *The Story of the Defense Technical Information Center: 1945–1995* (Fort Belvoir, Va.: Defense Technical Information Center, 1995), 10–15.

41. Wallace, *The Story of the Defense Technical Information Center,* 15, 46.

42. U.S. Defense Technical Information Center, "Who We Are" (n.d.), 1 (www.dtic.mil/), accessed November 17, 2003.

43. U.S. Defense Threat Reduction Agency (DTRA), "Vienna Document 1994 of the Negotiations on Confidence and Security Building Measures" (1999), 2 (www.dtra.mil/news/his_mat/factsheets/nw_vdoc_94.html), accessed November 17, 2003. For a history of DTRA's predecessor agency, see U.S. Defense Special Weapons Agency, *Defense Special Weapons Agency, 1947– 1997: The First 50 Years of National Service* (Washington, D.C.: Defense Special Weapons Agency, 1996) (www.dtra.mil/news/his_mat/dswa/dswa2_tabcon.pdf), accessed November 17, 2003. For an official history of DTRA and its predecessors, see U.S. Defense Threat Reduction Agency, *Defense's Nuclear Agency 1947–1997* (Washington, D.C.: DTRA, 2002).

44. U.S. Defense Threat Reduction Agency, "About DTRA—Mission" (2001), 1 (www.dtra.mil/about/ab_mission.html), accessed November 17, 2003.

45. U.S. Defense Threat Reduction Agency, "About DTRA—Welcome" (2001), 1 (www.dtra.mil/about/ab_index.html), accessed November 17, 2003.

46. PL 81-216, "To Reorganize Fiscal Management in the National Military Establishment to Promote Economy and Efficiency, and for Other Purposes," 63 *U.S. Statutes at Large,* 578–592. Section 211 of this law (63 *U.S. Statutes of Large,* 582) contains the text of the statutory directions and the requirement that the Joint Chiefs of Staff (JCS) chairman receive Senate confirmation. The JCS has been the subject of extensive historical analysis. The official U.S. government history of the JCS, a seven-volume set, covers to 1960. See James F. Schnabel, *History of the Joint Chiefs of Staff: The Joint Chiefs of Staff and National Policy,* vol. 1: *1945–1947* (Washington, D.C.: Joint Chiefs of Staff, Historical Division, 1996); Kenneth W. Condit, *History of the Joint Chiefs of Staff: The Joint Chiefs of Staff and National Policy,* vol. 2: *1947–1949* (Washington, D.C.: Joint Chiefs of Staff, Historical Division, 1996); James F. Schnabel and Robert J. Watson, *History of the Joint Chiefs of Staff,* vol. 3: *1951–1953: The Korean War,* 2 vols. (Washington, D.C.: Joint Chiefs of Staff, Historical Division, 1998); Walter S. Poole, *History of the Joint Chiefs of Staff: The Joint Chiefs of Staff and National Policy,* vol. 4: *1950–1952* (Washington, D.C.: Joint Chiefs of Staff, Historical Division, 1998); Kenneth W. Condit, *History of the Joint Chiefs of Staff: The Joint Chiefs of Staff and National Policy,* vol. 5: *1955–1956* (Washington, D.C.: Joint Chiefs of Staff, Historical Division, 1986); and Byron R. Fairchild and Walter S. Poole, *History of the Joint Chiefs of Staff: The Joint Chiefs of Staff and National Policy,* vol. 6: *1957–1960* (Washington, D.C.: Joint Chiefs of Staff, Historical Division, 1992). Analyses of the JCS's historical evolution include Lawrence J. Korb, *The Joint Chiefs of Staff: The First Twenty-Five Years* (Bloomington: Indiana University Press, 1976); and Amy B. Zegart, *Flawed by Design: The Evolution of the CIA, JCS, and NSC* (Stanford, Calif.: Stanford University Press, 1999). For a biographical history of JCS chairmen, see U.S. Office of the Chairman of the Joint Chiefs of Staff, Joint History Office, *The Chairmanship of the Joint Chiefs of Staff 1949–1999* (Washington, D.C.: Joint Chiefs of Staff, Joint History Office, 2000).

47. PL 99-433, "Goldwater-Nichols Department of Defense Reorganization Act of 1986," 100 *U.S. Statutes at Large,* 992–1075.

48. U.S. Office of the Chairman of the Joint Chiefs of Staff, Joint History Office, *Chairman of the Joint Chiefs of Staff 1949–1999,* 39.

49. See U.S. Secretary of Defense, "Missile Defense Program Direction" (2002), 1–5 (www.defenselink.mil/news/Jan2002/d20020102mda.pdf), accessed November 17, 2003. For mention of the assistant to the secretary of defense for intelligence oversight's and Ballistic Missile Defense Organization's origins; see U.S. Secretary of Defense, *Harnessing the Power of Technology: The Road to Ballistic Missile Defense from 1983–2007* (2000), 3, 5, 29 (www.acq.osd.mil/bmdo/bmdolink/pdf/power.pdf), accessed November 17, 2003. For a

historical overview of U.S. missile defense programs, see Donald R. Baucom, *The Origins of SDI, 1944–1983* (Lawrence: University Press of Kansas, 1992).

50. U.S. Secretary of Defense, "Missile Defense Program Direction," 1.

51. For the text of the memo, see U.S. Department of Defense, Deputy Secretary of Defense, "Reintroduction of the Anthrax Vaccine Immunization Program (AVIP)" (2002), 1–2 (www.anthrax.osd.mil/media/pdf/resumptionpolicy.pdf), accessed November 17, 2003. For examples of congressional concern over this program, see U.S. Congress, House Committee on Armed Services, Subcommittee on Military Personnel, *Department of Defense Anthrax Vaccine Immunization Program (AVIP)*, 107th Cong., 1st sess., 2001; U.S. Congress, House Committee on Government Reform, *The Anthrax Vaccine Immunization Program—What Have We Learned?*, 107th Cong., 1st sess., 2001; U.S. Congress, House Committee on Government Reform, *The Department of Defense Anthrax Vaccine Immunization Program: Unproven Force Protection: Fourth Report by the Committee on Government Reform Together with Dissenting and Supplemental Views*, H Rept 106-556, 106th Cong., 2d sess., 2000; and U.S. General Accounting Office, *Medical Readiness: DOD Faces Challenges in Implementing Its Anthrax Vaccine Immunization Program* (Washington, D.C.: General Accounting Office, 1999).

52. See PL 103-335, "Making Appropriations for the Department of Defense for the Fiscal Year Ending September 30, 1995, and for Other Purposes," 108 *U.S. Statutes at Large*, 2599–2662; and Asia-Pacific Center for Security Studies, "History and Seal of the APCSS" (n.d.), 1 (www.apcss.org/History/hist.html), accessed November 17, 2003.

53. U.S. Department of Defense, Computer Emergency Response Team, "FTP Access Requirements" (n.d.), 1 (www.cert.mil/misc/access.htm), accessed November 17, 2003.

54. U.S. Defense Advisory Committee on Women in the Services, "About DACOWITS" (2002), 1 (www.dtic.mil/dacowits/tableabout_subpage.html), accessed November 17, 2003.

55. U.S. Department of Defense, "DuBois to Lead Defense Installations and Environment Office" (2001), 1 (www.defenselink.mil/news/Jun2001/b06082001_bt258-01.html), accessed November 17, 2003.

56. U.S. Defense Information Technology Testbed, "About the Defense/Digital Information Technology Testbed (DITT)" (n.d.), 1 (http://call-ditt.leavenworth.army.mil/docs/aboutDITT.htm), accessed November 17, 2003.

57. U.S. Defense Modeling and Simulation Office, "DMSO Role and Responsibilities" (2002), 1 (https://www.dmso.mil/public/roles/), accessed November 17, 2003.

58. See U.S. Department of Defense, Deployment Health Support Directorate, "DU Library: Depleted Uranium Information Page" (n.d.), 1 (http://deploymentlink.osd.mil/du_library), accessed November 17, 2003; and U.S. Department of Defense, Deployment Health Support Directorate, "Depleted Uranium" (n.d.), 1 (http://deploymentlink.osd.mil/du_library/intro/faqs/faq_17apr.shtml), accessed November 17, 2003.

59. U.S. Department of Defense, Office of the Deputy Under Secretary of Defense for Industrial Policy, "Our Mission . . ." (n.d.), 1 (www.acq.osd.mil/ip/), accessed November 17, 2003.

60. U.S. Department of Defense, Communications and Directives Directorate, Directives and Records Division "About DoD Issuances," 1.

61. U.S. Department of Defense, Statistical Information and Analysis Division, "Mission Statement" (n.d.), 1 (http://web1.whs.osd.mil/mmid/mmidfunc.htm), accessed November 17, 2003.

62. U.S. Department of Defense, Washington Headquarters Services, Executive Services and Communications Directorate, Directives and Records Division, "DOD Issuances and OSD Administrative Instructions" (n.d.), 1 (www.dtic.mil/whs/directives/), accessed November 17, 2003. For a detailed explanation of the different kinds of Department of Defense policy documents, see U.S. Department of Defense, Communications and Directives Directorate, Directives

and Records Division "About DoD Issuances" (n.d.), 1–2 (www.dtic.mil/whs/directives/general.html), accessed November 17, 2003.

63. George C. Marshall European Center for Security Studies, "History of the George C. Marshall Center" (2003), 1 (www.marshallcenter.org/site-graphic/lang-en/page-mc-about-1/xdocs/mc/factsheets/history/01-center.htm), accessed November 17, 2003.

64. U.S. Department of Defense, *DOD Directive 5200.34: George C. Marshall European Center for Security Studies* (1992), 1–2. For a biographical portrait and analysis of George C. Marshall, see Forrest C. Pogue, *George C. Marshall: Statesman, 1945–1959* (New York: Penguin Books, 1989). For Marshall's perspectives on various issues during his political and military careers, see Larry I. Bland, ed., *The Papers of George Catlett Marshall,* 4 vols. (Baltimore, Md.: Johns Hopkins University Press, 1981–1996).

65. George C. Marshall European Center for Security Studies, "FAO Program Overview" (2003), 1 (www.marshallcenter.org/site-text/lang-en/page-coll-fao-1/xdocs/fao/resource-menu-docs/01-fao-overview.htm), accessed November 17, 2003.

66. "Executive Order 12961: Presidential Advisory Committee on Veterans Illnesses," 60 *Federal Register,* 60, no. 104 (May 31, 1995), 28505–28508.

67. Persian Gulf War illnesses have received extensive coverage in governmental literature and been the subject of controversy among Gulf War veterans and federal policymakers. Examples of the literature are U.S. Presidential Advisory Committee on Gulf War Veterans Illnesses, *Presidential Advisory Committee on Gulf War Veterans Illnesses: Final Report* (Washington, D.C.: Government Printing Office, 1996); U.S. Congress, Senate Committee on Veterans Affairs, Special Investigation Unit on Gulf War Illnesses, *Report of the Special Investigation Unit on Gulf War Illnesses* (Washington, D.C.: Government Printing Office, 1998); and U.S. Congress, House Committee on Government Reform, Subcommittee on National Security, Veterans Affairs, and International Relations, *Gulf War Veterans Illnesses: The Current Research Agenda* (Washington, D.C.: Government Printing Office, 2000).

68. U.S. Department of Defense, Under Secretary of Defense for Acquisitions, Technology, and Logistics, Joint Total Asset Visibility, "History" (2001), 1 (www.defenselink.mil/acq/jtav/newhistory.htm), accessed November 17, 2003.

69. Joint Chiefs of Staff, *Joint Vision 2020* (2000), 1 (www.dtic.mil/jointvision/jv2020a.pdf), accessed November 17, 2003.

70. Joint Chiefs of Staff, *Joint Vision 2020,* 2.

71. National Defense University, *National Defense University Catalogue 1996–1998* (Washington, D.C.: National Defense University, 1996), 4.

72. National Defense University, "Mission and Vision of NDU" (n.d.) (www.ndu.edu/info/mission.cfm), accessed April 14, 2004.

73. Africa Center for Strategic Studies, "About the Africa Center" (2002), 1 (www.africacenter.org/Dev2 Go.web?Anchor-ACSS_about&rnd=18864), accessed November 17, 2003.

74. National Defense University, Center for Counterproliferation Research, "Our Mission" (2002), 1 (www.ndu.edu/centercounter/prolif_mission.htm), accessed November 17, 2003.

75. National Defense University, Center for Hemispheric Defense Studies, "The Center's Origin" (n.d.), 1 (www3.ndu.edu/chds/English/History/History.htm), accessed November 18, 2003.

76. PL 106-65, "An Act to Authorize Appropriations for Fiscal Year 2000 for Military Activities of the Department of Defense for Military Construction, and for Defense Activities of the Department of Energy, to Prescribe Personnel Strengths, for Such Fiscal Year for the Armed Forces, and for Other Purposes," 113 *U.S. Statutes at Large,* 512, 721, 779–782.

77. National Defense University, Center for the Study of Chinese Military Affairs, "Mission" (2000), 1 (www.ndu.edu/inss/China_Center/CSCMA_main.htm), accessed November 18, 2003.

78. National Defense University, Center for Technology and National Security Policy, "About CTNSP" (n.d.), 1 (www.ndu.edu/ctnsp/about.html), accessed November 18, 2003.

79. National Defense University, Industrial College of the Armed Forces, "History" (2003), 1 (www.ndu.edu/icaf/handbook2003/history.htm), accessed November 18, 2003.

80. National Defense University, Industrial College of the Armed Forces, "ICAF Mission" (n.d.), 1 (www.ndu.edu/icaf/mission/mission.htm), accessed November 18, 2003.

81. National Defense University, Information Resources Management University, "IRM College: Who We Are" (n.d.), 1 (www.ndu.edu/irmc/about.html), accessed November 18, 2003.

82. National Defense University, Institute for National Strategic Studies, "About INSS" (2002), 1 (www.ndu.edu/inss/aboutinss.html), accessed November 18, 2003.

83. National Defense University, Institute for National Strategic Studies, "About INSS," 2.

84. U.S. Defense Technical Information Center, Joint Electronic Library, "Mission Statement" (n.d.), 1 (www.dtic.mil/doctrine/mission_statement.htm), accessed November 17, 2003.

85. National Defense University, Joint Forces Staff College, "History" (2002), 1 (www.jfsc.ndu.edu/about/history.asp), accessed November 18, 2003.

86. National Defense University, Joint Forces Staff College, "Overview" (2000), 1 (www.jfsc.ndu.edu/about/overview.asp), accessed November 18, 2003.

87. National Defense University Library, "About NDU Library" (2002), 1 (www.ndu.edu/library/about.html), accessed November 18, 2003.

88. PL 102-183, "Intelligence Authorization Act for Fiscal Year 1992," 105 *U.S. Statutes at Large*, 1271.

89. National Defense University, National Security Education Program, "National Security Education Program: Developing the Nation's International Capacity" (2002), 2 (www.ndu.edu/nsep/), accessed November 18, 2003.

90. National Defense University, National Security Education Program, "National Security Education Program," 2–5.

91. National Defense University, National Strategic Gaming Center, "About the NGSC" (2002), 1 (www.ndu.edu/inss/nsgc_internet_site/), accessed November 18, 2003.

92. National Defense University, National War College, "History of the National War College" (n.d.), 1 (www.ndu.edu/nwc/history/), accessed November 18, 2003.

93. National Defense University, National War College, "Mission" (n.d.), 1 (www.ndu.edu/nwc/mission/), accessed November 18, 2003.

94. National Defense University, Near East South Asia Center for Strategic Studies, "History" (n.d.), 1 (www.ndu.edu/nesa/info/), accessed November 18, 2003.

95. National Defense University, Near East South Asia Center for Strategic Studies, "Mission Statement" (n.d.), 1 (www.ndu.edu/nesa/mission.html), accessed November 18, 2003.

96. National Defense University, School for National Security Executive Education, "Director's Message" (n.d.), 1 (www.ndu.edu/snsee/), accessed November 18, 2003.

97. Office of the Deputy Assistant to the Secretary of Defense for Chemical and Biological Defense Programs, "OSD CP CBD Mission Statement" (n.d.), 1 (www.acq.osd.mil/cp/mission.html), accessed November 18, 2003.

98. "Executive Order 12788: Defense Economic Adjustment Program," *Federal Register*, 57 (January 21, 1992), 2213–2215.

99. U.S. Department of Defense, Office of Economic Adjustment, "About the Office of Economic Adjustment" (n.d.), 1 (http://oea.osd.mil/), select "Profile," accessed November 18, 2003.

100. U.S. Secretary of Defense, *Defense Reform Initiative Report* (1997), 55 (www.defenselink.mil/pubs/dodreform/fullreport.pdf), accessed November 18, 2003.

101. Leighton, *History of the Office of Secretary of Defense*, vol. 3, 277.

102. Trask and Goldberg, *The Department of Defense*, 86.

103. For a biographical sketch of Marshall, see Mellor, *Congressional Quarterly's Federal Staff Directory,* 1276. Examples of media coverage received by Marshall and the Office of Net Assessment during 2001 and 2002 include John Barry and Evan Thomas, "The Pentagon's Guru," *Newsweek,* May 21, 2001, 41; Nicholas Lemann, "Dreaming about War," *New Yorker,* July 16, 2001, 32–38; Marty Kauchak, "FY02 Bush Defense Budget Delivered," *Armed Forces Journal International,* 138 (April 2001): 12; and Bill Keller, "The Fighting Next Time," *New York Times,* March 10, 2002, section 6, 32–44.

104. U.S. Department of Defense, Assistant Secretary of Defense for Command, Control, Communications, and Intelligence, "About the PKI PMO" (n.d.), 1 (www.c3i.osd.mil/org/sio/ia/pki/), accessed November 18, 2003.

105. U.S. Department of Defense, Assistant Secretary of Defense for Command, Control, Communications, and Intelligence, "About the PKI PMO."

106. U.S. Department of Defense, Space Policy Directorate, "Mission" (n.d.), 1 (www.c3i.osd.mil/org/c3is/spacepol/), accessed November 18, 2003.

107. See U.S. Office of the Secretary of Defense, "Tricare: The Basics," (2002), 1 (www.tricare.osd.mil/factsheet,cfm?id=1273), accessed November 18, 2003; and U.S. Army, *Tricare and More on the Quality of Life* (Washington, D.C.: U.S. Army, 1996), 2.

108. U.S. Army, Western Hemisphere Institute for Security Cooperation, "History of the Institute" (2001), 1 (www.benning.army.mil/whinsec2/about.asp?id=31), accessed November 17, 2003.

109. U.S. Army, Western Hemisphere Institute for Security Cooperation, "Mission" (2003), 1 (www.benning.army.mil/whinsec2/about.asp? id=13), accessed November 18, 2003.

CHAPTER 3

Other Executive Branch Agencies

Numerous executive branch agencies besides the Department of Defense possess national security policy responsibilities and produce national security–related information resources, such as the Department of Commerce, Department of Energy (DOE), Department of Health and Human Services (HHS), Department of Homeland Security (DHS), Department of Justice (DOJ), Department of State, Department of Transportation (DOT), Department of the Treasury, and Executive Office of the President (EOP). The authority to produce these resources comes from the Constitution as well as the continually broadening definition of national security policy stemming from the evolving international security environment and congressional mandates. Note that a 2002 law consolidated many agencies creating national security policy information resources into a single executive department—the Department of Homeland Security.[1]

Department of Commerce

The Department of Commerce and Labor was created in 1903 and was separated into the Department of Commerce and the Department of Labor in 1913. The Commerce Department's purpose is encouraging and promoting U.S. international trade, economic growth, and technological advancement.[2] Commerce Department agencies producing national security–related information include the Bureau of Industry and Security (BIS), Critical Infrastructure Assurance Office (CIAO), National Institute of Standards and Technology (NIST), National Technical Information Service (NTIS), and Office of Inspector General (OIG).

Bureau of Industry and Security

The Bureau of Export Administration was created within the Commerce Department in 1987.[3] It was renamed the Bureau of Industry and Security (BIS) in 2002.[4] BIS processes export license applications and enforces export control laws to ensure that commodities exported from the United States do not endanger national security, seeks to establish a strong U.S. defense industrial base, implements a national computer and encryption policy, investigates suspected U.S. export control law violations, implements preventive enforcement actions against such violations, and helps other countries strengthen their national export control systems to reduce the proliferation of weapons of mass destruction.[5]

A wide variety of resources reflecting the agency's broad institutional mandate can be found at www.bis.doc.gov/. Examples are general fact sheets on what commodity classifications are, export license requirements, listings of individuals and companies in violation of U.S. export control laws, information about industry inspections of suspected Chemical Weapons Convention violators, and the text of relevant federal export control regulations such as "Revisions and Clarifications to Encryption Controls in the Export Administration Regulations—Implementation of Changes in Category 5, Part 2 ('Information Security') of the Wassenaar Arrangement of List of Dual Use Goods and Other Technologies," which appeared in the June 6, 2002, issue of the *Federal Register*.

BIS's website and its "Electronic Freedom of Information Act" (EFOIA) section have the text of public comments on proposed regulations, letters to companies warning them that they may be violating export control laws, and information about ongoing studies such as those covering air delivery systems and shipbuilders supply bases. The full text of various reports also are available, such as *Foreign Policy Report to Congress* (2001 and 2002), *Efforts in Defense Trade: An Annual Report to Congress* (1996–2001), and industry-specific sectoral analysis reports including *The Effect on the National Security of Imports of Crude Oil and Refined Petroleum Products* (1999), *Technology Transfer to China* (1999), *National Security Assessment of the High Performance Explosives and High Performance Components Industries* (2001), and *The Effect of National Security: Investigation of Imports of Iron Ore and Semi-Finished Steel* (2001). BIS resources show how economics can affect national security policy.

Critical Infrastructure Assurance Office

Presidential Decision Directive 63, issued in May 1998, created the Critical Infrastructure Assurance Office to coordinate federal government critical infrastructure assurance initiatives.[6] This document offers the following description of critical infrastructures.

> Critical infrastructures are those physical and cyber-based systems essential to the minimum operations of the economy and government. They include, but are not limited to, telecommunications, energy, banking and finance, transportation, water systems and emergency services, both governmental and private.[7]

CIAO works with the public and private sectors to improve the security of the U.S. critical infrastructures. It produces a number of national security–related resources, most of which are accessible on its website (www.ciao.gov/). Such resources include congressional testimony by CIAO personnel, PowerPoint slides of

Project Matrix on CIAO's assistance to federal civilian agencies in prioritizing their critical infrastructure assurance programs, presidential executive orders, and publications such as *Vulnerability Assessment Framework 1.1* (1998), *Third Party Liability for Hacking* (2000), *Defending America's Cyberspace: National Plan for Information Systems Protection Version 1.0: An Invitation to Dialogue* (2000), and *Report of the President of the United States on the Status of Federal Critical Infrastructure Protection Activities* (2001).

In 2002 CIAO became part of the Department of Homeland Security's Information Analysis and Infrastructure Protection Directorate.[8]

National Institute of Standards and Technology

The National Bureau of Standards was established in 1901.[9] Its name was changed to the National Institute of Standards and Technology (NIST) in a 1988 law, which aimed to improve the overall international economic competitiveness of the United States.[10]

NIST works to strengthen the U.S. economy by developing and applying technology, measurements, and standards in areas as diverse as electronics, electrical and manufacturing engineering, chemical science and technology, materials science, building and fire research, and information technology.[11]

Work is performed by the Computer Security Resource Center (CSRC), Computer System Security and Privacy Advisory Board (CSSPAP), the Federal Information Systems Security Educators Association (FISSEA), and other subject-specific research and development centers within NIST, including areas of homeland security research such as safer structures, threat detection and protection, tools for law enforcement, emergency response, and biometrics. The results of much of NIST's cutting-edge national security–related technological research are publicly accessible through the website www.nist.gov/.

Examples of the rich variety of national security resources on NIST's website are an audio webcast in RealPlayer and Windows Media of a June 24, 2002, report of an investigation into the World Trade Center's collapse from the September 11, 2001, terrorist attacks; the complete text of articles from *Journal of Research of the National Institute of Standards and Technology* from 1995 to the present; and downloadable software packages such as Fire Dynamic Simulator and Multizone Airflow and Contaminant Transport Analysis Software.

Fire Dynamic Simulator is used to recreate building fires resulting in firefighter deaths and can predict fire behavior in high-rise buildings such as the World Trade Center. Multizone Airflow and Contaminant Transport Analysis Software enables prediction of building airflow and ventilation along with the dispersal of airborne contaminants and how much exposure building occupants will have to contaminants such as anthrax.

Specific national security policy publications accessible on NIST's website are *National Security Telecommunications and Information Systems Security Advisory Memorandum (NSTISSAM): COMPUSEC/1-99: Transition from the Trusted Computer Systems Evaluation Criteria to the International Common Criteria for Information*

Technology Security Evaluation (1999), *A Denial of Service Restraint Intrusion Detection Architecture* (2000), *Guidelines to Federal Organizations on Security Assurance and Acquisition/Use of Tested/Evaluated Products—Recommendations of the National Institute of Standards and Technology* (2000), *Common Biometric Exchange File Format* (2001), and *Computer System Security and Privacy Board Findings and Recommendations on Government Privacy Policy Setting and Management* (2002).

National Technical Information Service

The Publications Board was created in 1945 to manage the release of thousands of technical reports such as captured German documents and classified technical reports to U.S. industry after World War II. The Publications Board went through various name and organizational changes within the Commerce Department before being established as the National Technical Information Service (NTIS) in 1970. Its institutional purpose is simplifying and enhancing access to the numerous data files and scientific and technical reports produced by federal agencies and their contractors. NTIS receives no congressional appropriations and charges for all costs associated with collecting, abstracting, storing, reproducing, and selling the information it receives through sales to the public.[12]

The website www.ntis.gov/ provides detailed information about NTIS's institutional purpose, products, and services. It also includes information about ordering products and detailed searching capability. NTIS resources of interest to national security policy students and scholars include its Homeland Security Information Center (www.ntis.gov/hs/), searchable collection of military manuals, full-text access to selected government publications, and descriptions of the more than 2.5 million titles NTIS possesses.

Office of Inspector General

The Commerce Department's Office of Inspector General (OIG) was created by the Inspector General Act of 1978.[13] The mission of the Commerce Department OIG is promoting economy and efficiency and detecting and preventing waste, fraud, abuse, and mismanagement in the department's programs and operations.[14]

Many reports produced by the OIG on national security programs of Commerce Department agencies are accessible through the website www.oig.doc.gov/. Examples of these reports include OIG's semiannual report to Congress, which provides a broad overview of specific Commerce Department programs administered by agencies such as BIS and NIST. Two specific national security policy–related reports available on the website are *Improvements Are Needed in Programs Designed to Protect against the Transfer of Sensitive Technologies to Countries of Concern* (2000) and *Management of the Commerce Control List and Related Processes Should Be Improved* (2001). Such investigative and audit reports by federal inspectors general are worthwhile documents for probing managerial and administrative aspects of national security policy programs.

Department of Energy

The Department of Energy (DOE) is a major producer of national security policy information because of the role commodities such as petroleum and nuclear energy play in influencing national security policy and because of DOE's responsibility for producing and maintaining the U.S. nuclear weapons arsenal.[15] The 1977 Department of Energy Organization Act replaced the Energy Research and Development Administration and the Atomic Energy Commission with the Department of Energy. The hope was that the new cabinet department would create more centralized and efficient federal energy policies.[16]

DOE's influence is felt, not only from its Washington, D.C., headquarters, but also in various locations across the United States and globally as a result of the presence of a large number of laboratories, offices, and programs striving to fulfill DOE's responsibilities. Numerous DOE facilities are involved in national security policy–related research and policy formulation.

Argonne National Laboratory

Argonne National Laboratory (ANL) is the first U.S. national laboratory. It received its official charter in 1946. A significant development leading to its establishment was creation of the world's first controlled nuclear chain reaction by Enrico Fermi and his colleagues at the University of Chicago on December 2, 1942.[17] Located in Argonne, Illinois, and with a satellite facility near Idaho Falls, Idaho, the Argonne National Laboratory is operated for DOE by the University of Chicago. ANL has more than four thousand employees, including nearly fourteen hundred scientists and engineers. Its annual operating budget of more than $475 million supports approximately two hundred research projects in areas such as basic science, scientific facilities, energy resources, and environmental management.[18]

While ANL has never served as a nuclear weapons factory, its research and development program covers three major national security areas.[19]

1. Nuclear nonproliferation, treaty verification, arms control, and counterterrorism technology.
2. Domestic infrastructure assurance.
3. Chemical and biological counterterrorism science and technology.[20]

Many aspects of ANL's national security policy research are classified but substantive amounts can be accessed through the laboratory's website (www.anl.gov/). Examples are the quarterly periodical *Logos,* which provides information on ANL research activities from 1998 to the present; the newsletter *Tech Transfer Highlights,* which describes technological innovations and scientific advances at ANL from 1997 to the present; and the *ANL Guide to Exporting,* (2002), which describes procedures to prevent the unauthorized export of sensitive technologies and materials from the United States.

Additional worthwhile national security policy resources available on ANL's website include the following fact sheets: *Cutting-Edge Science and Technology Help Safeguard National Security* (2002), *Nuclear Nonproliferation, Treaty Verification, Arms Control, and Counterterrorism* (2002), *Homeland Infrastructure Assurance* (2002), *Argonne Provides Full Support against Chemical and Biological Terrorism* (2002), and *Nabbing Nuclear Smugglers* (2002).

Brookhaven National Laboratory

Brookhaven National Laboratory (BNL) was established in 1947 and is located in Upton, New York, on Long Island. Operated by Brookhaven Science Associates for DOE, BNL has more than three thousand scientists, engineers, technicians, and support staff and conducts research in nuclear and high-energy physics, physics, materials chemistry, environmental and energy research, nonproliferation, neurosciences and medical imaging, and structural biology.[21]

Further information about BNL programs can be found on the laboratory's website (www.bnl.gov/). National security–related work at BNL is performed by the U.S.-Russian Security Programs Division and the Safeguards and Arms Control Division. The Security Programs Division assists the DOE Office of International Materials Protections and Emergency Cooperation's Materials Protection, Control, and Accounting Program by working with Russia to consolidate nuclear materials in fewer locations to reduce their vulnerability to theft. The Safeguards and Arms Control division supports U.S. policies to reduce the proliferation and danger of biological, chemical, and nuclear weapons.[22]

Publicly accessible resources on BNL's website include the fact sheet *Counterterrorism Initiatives at Brookhaven* (2002), videos on the test of a cable vehicle barrier designed to prevent vehicle bombs from entering U.S. Air Force alert bombing parking areas and on the Murmansk Initiative in which the United States and Russia work together to prevent nuclear waste from being disposed of in the ocean, and information on BNL cooperation with the International Atomic Energy Agency safeguards program to ensure nuclear power plant safety.

Chemical and Biological Defense Program

Located at DOE's Pacific Northwest Laboratory (PNL) in Richland, Washington, the Chemical and Biological Defense Program provides general information about biological pathogens such as anthrax, botulism, and salmonella. It offers ways of detecting and responding to chemical and biological weapons assaults through its website (www.pnl.gov/chembio). Links to credible chemical and biological weapons resources such as the Centers for Disease Control and Prevention (CDC) are also provided on this site.

Closing the Circle—DOE Office of Environmental Management

The Office of Environmental Management provides information chronicling DOE's historical role in producing U.S. nuclear weapons and the often-serious environmental consequences evident in areas surrounding production facilities. Located at http://legacystory.apps.em.doe.gov/, accessible historical assessments of the environmental impact of nuclear weapons production include *Closing the Circle on the Splitting of the Atom* (1996) and *Linking Legacies: Connecting the Cold War Nuclear Weapons Production Processes to Their Environmental Consequences* (1997).

Directives, Regulations, Policies, and Standards

Like any other large organization, DOE makes extensive use of regulations and other documents to execute and implement its institutional mission. The website www.directives.doe.gov/ provides one-stop access to DOE departmental directives, orders, and related administrative documents. Some directives accessible online are *Order 5610.3: Joint Department of Energy/Department of Defense Nuclear Weapons System, Safety, Security, and Control Activities* (1990), *Order 5530.2: Nuclear Emergency Search Team* (1991), and *Order 5639.8A: Security of Foreign Intelligence Information and Sensitive Compartmented Information Facilities* (1993).

Other available DOE administrative materials are technical standards *STD 1104-96: Review and Approval of Nuclear Facility Safety Basis Documents (Documented Safety Analyses and Technical Safety Requirements)* (2002) and *STD 1105: Radiological Training for Tritium Facilities* (2002). Access is also provided to forms such as *DOE F 284: Nuclear Material Transfer Report* (1988) and *DOE F 471.1: Security Incident Notification Report* (1999).

Users can receive e-mail alerts of impending DOE regulatory changes and post comments on these proposed changes.

DOE Representative to the Defense Nuclear Facilities Safety Board

The DOE representative to the Defense Nuclear Facilities Safety Board (DNFSB) is responsible for issuing recommendations on safety and operational conditions at DOE's nuclear facilities. The mission of the departmental representative to DNFSB includes

- Representing the secretary of energy in ongoing interactions with the DNFSB;
- Advising the secretary and other DOE executives of DNFSB priorities, concerns, actions, and plans;
- Facilitating communication and cooperation between DOE and DNFSB; and
- Maintaining DOE's central repository of DNFSB communications and making this information available to DOE and DOE contractor personnel.[23]

The website www.deprep.org/ provides information on DOE's relationship with DNFSB. Resources include listings of DNFSB recommendations to DOE, assessments on DOE's follow-up to various DNFSB recommendations, and publications such as *Interface with the Defense Nuclear Facilities Safety Board* (2001) and *Clarification of the Term "Vital Safety System" under Implementation Plan for DNFSB Recommendation 2000-2* (2001).

Energy Information Administration

The Energy Information Administration (EIA) was created within DOE in 1977 to serve as a centralized national energy information resource.[24] EIA has produced reports, statistical compilations, presentations, and other materials to assist the nation's policymakers and U.S. citizens in their understanding of energy policy trends and developments and how these trends and developments can shape national energy policy, including the role energy plays in determining national security policy.

Resources accessible at EIA's website (www.eia.doe.gov/) include qualitative assessments of energy developments in the United States and other countries; analysis of activities in specific energy commodity sectors such as the oil, natural gas, electric, and nuclear power industries; and quantitative statistics documenting developments in these areas of energy activity. Examples are *International Energy Annual* (1993–2000); *International Petroleum Monthly* (1996–present); *Country Analysis Briefs*, which are regularly updated assessments of the energy situation in countries and areas such as the Caspian Sea region, Kazakhstan, Libya, Saudia Arabia, South China Sea, and Venezuela; *Measures of Oil Import Dependence* (1998); *Challenges of Electric Power Industry Restructuring for Fuel Suppliers* (1998); *Foreign Investment in U.S. Energy* (1999–2000); *World Oil Transit Chokepoints* (2001); *The Impact of U.S. Nuclear Generation on Greenhouse Gas Emissions* (2001); *Summary Analysis of Selected Transportation Fuel Issues Associated with Proposed Energy Legislation* (2002); *U.S. Imports from OPEC and the Persian Gulf* (most recent month); and *Energy Supply Security* (n.d.).

Environment, Safety, and Health Researchers Workstation

The Environment, Safety, and Health Researchers Workstation serves as a finding aid to locate records produced by DOE and its predecessor agencies—the Energy Research and Development Administration and the Atomic Energy Commission—on environmental, safety, and health aspects of U.S. nuclear energy and weapons research and production activities.

Information on the website http://tis.eh.doe.gov/workstation/ describes finding aids for relevant materials produced by DOE and its institutional components. Sample files are "Guide to Archival Collections Relating to Radioactive Fallout from Nuclear Weapons Testing," "History of the Atomic Energy Commission," and "Institutional Origins of the Department of Energy: The Office of Military Applications."

Idaho National Engineering and Environmental Laboratory

Located in Idaho Falls, Idaho, and managed for DOE by the Bechtel Corporation, the Idaho National Engineering and Environmental Laboratory (INEEL) has operated since 1949 in support of DOE missions in environment, energy, science, and national defense. Regarding national security policy, INEEL conducts research, development, and deployment in threat mitigation areas such as chemical demilitarization and operations, command and control, explosives, software engineering, and contraband materials detection in these fields.[25]

Detailed information on INEEL programs can be found at www.inel.gov/. National security–related resources available include the July 10, 2002, opening statement of INEEL director Billy Shipp on homeland security before the U.S. Senate Energy and Natural Resources Committee, *Plutonium at the Idaho National Engineering and Environmental Laboratory* (1999), issues of INEEL's national security division's newsletter *Need to Know* (October 2000–present), and the *INEEL Intelligence Newsletter* (July 2001–present).

Initiatives for Proliferation Prevention

Located at New Mexico's Los Alamos National Laboratory, Initiatives for Proliferation Prevention (IPP) is a nonproliferation program of DOE and the National Nuclear Security Administration (NNSA). IPP's purpose is increasing U.S. national security by working with nuclear weapons scientists, engineers, and technicians from the former Soviet Union to use their expertise to destroy nuclear and other weapons of mass destruction and develop peaceful and sustainable commercial activities.[26]

The website http://ipp.lanl.gov/ describes IPP's institutional mandate and lists program contacts at DOE facilities. The website also contains links to "Project Databases" and "Project Snapshots," which are restricted to DOE personnel.

International Nuclear Safety Program

Located at the Pacific Northwest National Laboratory in Richland, Washington, the International Nuclear Safety Program (INSP) seeks to improve safety at nuclear power plants designed by the former Soviet Union in various eastern European and Central Asian countries.[27] INSP seeks to improve safety and diminish risks at these facilities by improving physical operating conditions, installing safety equipment and developing improved safety procedures, establishing centers for training reactor personnel, conducting detailed safety assessments, developing appropriate institutional and regulatory structures, and dealing with the acute problems caused by the 1986 nuclear accident at Chernobyl.[28]

Detailed information on INSP programs and activities may be found at http://insp.pnl.gov/. Accessible materials include photos of nuclear facilities in former Soviet bloc countries, maps of their locations, and information on their ongoing operational conditions. Publications include *Activity Reports* (1996–present) *Proceedings: U.S-Ukraine Conference on Nuclear Trade Cooperation* (1998), *A Brief History of Nuclear Criticality Accidents in Russia: 1953–1997* (1999), *Soviet Designed Nuclear Power Plant Profiles* (2000), *2000 Status Report: Improving the Safety of Soviet-Designed Nuclear Power Plants* (2000), and reports and descriptions of INSP activities at the Chernobyl plant.

Kansas City Plant

Located in Kansas City, Missouri, the Kansas City Plant (KCP) is responsible for manufacturing non-nuclear mechanical, electronic, and engineered material components for U.S. nuclear weapons. KCP and the affiliated Kirtland facility in Albuquerque, New Mexico, produce materials such as high-energy laser ignition systems, microwave hybrid microcircuits, and related products whose sizes range from semi-tractor trailers to miniature electromechanical devices.[29]

KCP's origins date to 1949, when the Atomic Energy Commission opened the facility and asked the Bendix Corporation to manage it. In 1993 DOE designated KCP as the official site for producing all non-nuclear nuclear weapons components. The Honeywell Corporation assumed management of KCP in 1999.[30]

More about KCP operations can be found on its website (www.kcp.com/), including information on employment opportunities and upcoming activities. No national security policy–related publications were accessible on this site as of late March 2004.

Knolls Atomic Power Laboratory

The Knolls Atomic Power Laboratory (KAPL) is operated for DOE by the Lockheed Martin Company. KAPL is a research and development community responsible for supporting the U.S. Naval Nuclear Propulsion Program. Aspects of the program include developing advanced nuclear propulsion technology, providing technical support for the safe and dependable operation of existing naval reactors, and providing training to naval personnel operating this equipment on ships and submarines. KAPL's main facilities, located in Niskayuna and West Milton, New York, employ more than twenty-six hundred people. Additional KAPL personnel work at shipyards in Connecticut, Hawaii, New Hampshire, Virginia, and Washington State.[31]

Information on KAPL can be found on its website (www.kapl.gov/), including descriptions of training programs and career opportunities. No publications are accessible, but a description is available of KAPL's *Chart of the Nuclides,* which is a reference source on the nuclear characteristics of atomic elements and their isotopes. Information on ordering paper copies of this publication also is provided.

Lawrence Berkeley National Laboratory

The Lawrence Berkeley National Laboratory (LBNL) was founded in 1931 by Earnest Orlando Lawrence (1907–1958), the inventor of the cyclotron, which played a key role in advancing particle physics and in the early development of nuclear weapons.[32] Located in Berkeley, California, and operated jointly by DOE and the University of California—Berkeley, LBNL is a multiprogram lab conducting research in advanced materials, life sciences, detectors, and accelerators. It has approximately four thousand employees.[33]

Detailed information about LBNL activities can be found through its website (www.lbl.gov/). Accessible resources include descriptions of LBNL research in areas such as physics and engineering; the LBNL library's online catalog from 1989 to the present and information on obtaining reports featured in this catalog; the text of publications such as the journal *LBL Research Review* (1993–present), *LBL Biosafety Manual* (n.d.), and I>Bloodborne Pathogens Exposure Control Plan (n.d.); and information on employee radiation training courses. Another useful LBNL resource is "Advice for Safeguarding Buildings Against Chemical or Biological Attack" (http://securebuildings.lbl.gov/), which provides specific recommendations for defense against such assaults.

Lawrence Livermore National Laboratory

Located in Livermore, California, and operated by the University of California, the Lawrence Livermore National Laboratory (LLNL) was founded in September 1952 as a nuclear weapons design laboratory to encourage innovative design of the U.S. nuclear weapons arsenal. LLNL conducts state-of-the-art scientific research in disciplines as varied as energy, biomedicine, and environmental science. Regarding national security policy, its research focuses on areas such as nonproliferation, arms control, counterterrorism, bioagent detection, and surveillance of aging nuclear weapons and is conducted through laboratory divisions such as the Center for Global Security Research.[34]

Useful general information resources on LLNL's website (www.llnl.gov/) include *Creating the Laboratory's Future—A Strategy for Lawrence Livermore National Laboratory* (1997). In addition, numerous national security policy–related resources are available, including *Dealing with a Dangerous Surplus from the Cold War* (1997), *Forensic Seismology Supports the Comprehensive Test Ban Treaty* (1998), *Inspection Procedures for Compliance Monitoring of the Biological Weapons Convention* (1998), *Seismic Discrimination of the May 11, 1998, Indian Nuclear Test with Short-Period Regional Data from Station NIL (Nilore, Pakistan)* (1999), *Stockpile Stewardship and a Comprehensive Test Ban* (1999), *Simulating Warfare: It's No Video Game* (2000), *Uncovering Bioterrorism* (2000), *Preventing Nuclear Proliferation: The Post-Cold War Challenge* (2000), and *From Crisis to Transition: The State of Russian Science Based on Focus Groups with Nuclear Physicists* (2001).

Los Alamos National Laboratory

The Los Alamos National Laboratory (LANL) is located in Los Alamos, New Mexico. Its origins date back to April 15, 1943, when the University of California and the Manhattan Engineering District began to develop the atomic bomb in Los Alamos for the U.S. military. LANL became a key producer of the U.S. nuclear weapons arsenal in the ensuing decades.[35] LANL administers the Stockpile Stewardship Program to ensure the reliability of the U.S. nuclear weapons arsenal without nuclear testing; develops nuclear nonproliferation support technology; works to ensure nuclear materials security internationally; provides means for identifying and detecting nuclear, chemical, and biological weapons; responds to counterterrorism requirements; and develops cutting-edge science and technology applicable to national security requirements.[36]

The LANL website (www.lanl.gov/worldview/) has descriptions of LANL nuclear weapons design activities, institutional history, links to laboratory divisions and program offices such as those dealing with threat reduction and security safeguards, and access to selected publications including *China's Energy: A Forecast to 2015* (1996), *Modeling Cities: The Los Alamos Urban Security Initiative* (2000), and the inaugural issue of *Los Alamos Research Quarterly* (fall 2002) featuring articles on using small-scale laboratory experiments to corroborate computer simulations of nuclear weapons performance, how LANL biological laboratory researchers have developed tools enabling the use of molecular signatures to detect, identify, and trace biothreat agents, possible uses of sound as a diagnostic tool for chemical and biological threat reduction, and LANL personnel serving on the Nuclear Emergency Search Team (NEST) to try to prevent a nuclear weapons emergency within the United States.

National Nuclear Security Administration

The National Nuclear Security Administration (NNSA) was created by Congress in 1999 as part of DOE as a result of concerns over serious security lapses at DOE facilities such as LANL. NNSA was given responsibility for nuclear weapons development and defense nuclear nonproliferation and for ensuring the security of the U.S. nuclear weapons arsenal.[37]

Materials about NNSA and its mission can be found at www.nnsa.doe.gov/—for example, an organizational chart, the text of its organic statute; biographies of key NNSA officials; speeches by NNSA policymakers; congressional testimony; descriptions of activities in NNSA program areas such as nuclear nonproliferation, naval reactors, and overall DOE defense programs; and press releases such as an October 21, 2002, announcement of a completed security upgrade on a nuclear facility in Uzbekistan. Additional NNSA site contents include reports such as *Report to Congress on the Plan for Organizing the National Nuclear Security Administration* (2001) and *Report to Congress on the Organization and Operation of the National Nuclear Security Administration* (2002).

National Spent Nuclear Fuel Program

The National Spent Nuclear Fuel Program (NSNFP) is administered through DOE's Idaho National Engineering and Environmental Laboratory in Idaho Falls, Idaho. NSNFP responsibilities include the safe and efficient management of spent nuclear fuel with DOE and preparing this material for disposal. NSNFP works with relevant federal, state, and local officials and constituents in carrying out its disposal responsibilities, which involve materials production fuels, naval nuclear propulsion fuel, research reactor fuel, specialty fuels such as those used in the space program, and commercial nuclear power reactor fuels.[38]

The NSNFP website (http://nsnfp.inel.gov/) has descriptions of spent nuclear fuel, a chart describing the locating of spent nuclear fuel sites, and project summaries of lessons learned from spent nuclear fuel handling cases. Publications include fact sheets on spent nuclear fuel such as *Transportation Cask System* (2000), *Packaging*

Standard for Spent Nuclear Fuel (2000), *Materials Aging* (2000), and *Spent Nuclear Fuel Database* (2001). Reports and documents featured on the website are *Settlement Agreement on Spent Nuclear Fuel between the State of Idaho, Department of Energy, and the U.S. Navy* (1995) and *Accelerating Cleanup: Paths to Closure* (1998).

National Transportation Program

The National Transportation Program (NTP) consists of personnel from DOE offices in Washington, D.C., Albuquerque, New Mexico, and Idaho Falls, Idaho. NTP is responsible for coordinating transportation activities for all unclassified shipments of hazardous materials such as radioactive and mixed wastes; ensuring the safe, secure, and cost-effective transport services for DOE programs; and maintaining necessary tools and resources for carrying out these programs.[39] NTP ships materials by multiple transportation modes using commercial and private carriers. During federal fiscal year 1997 (October 1, 1996–September 30, 1997), 77 percent of this transportation was by air, 22 percent by motor, and 1 percent by rail. For this same fiscal year, DOE transported 430,000 shipments of non-defense-related materials—412,000 with nonhazardous materials and 18,000 with hazardous materials, of which 5,200 contained radioactive materials. DOE provides formal highway route notification of these shipments of controlled radioactive material quantities to the Nuclear Regulatory Commission, Department of Transportation, states, and tribal governments. DOE does not notify local governments of these shipments, though states may inform local officials on a need-to-know basis.[40]

Further details on NTP programs and activities may be found on the website www.ntp.doe.gov/. Examples of publicly accessible materials include transportation fact sheets such as *Radioactive Materials Shipping Regulations* (1999), *International Transportation of Radioactive Materials* (1999), and *DOE's Motor Carrier Evaluation Program* (2001). Available program reports include *Transportation Operations Manual* (1999), *Transportation Compliance Evaluation Assistance Program: Fiscal Year 2000 Annual Report* (2000), and *A Resource Handbook on DOE Transportation Risk Assessment* (2002).

Nevada Operations Office

The Nevada Operations Office is located in Las Vegas and is responsible for administering DOE activities in the state. Historically, the most important of these activities has been the Nevada Test Site (NTS). On December 18, 1950, President Harry S. Truman authorized establishing 680 square miles of the Nellis Air Force Gunnery and Bombing Range as a secure place to test the growing U.S. nuclear weapons arsenal. The range formally became NTS in 1955.[41]

NTS is located in a rural area sixty-five miles north of Las Vegas and is next to the Nellis Air Force range site.[42] NTS saw more than four decades as the continental proving ground for nuclear weapons testing until a moratorium on U.S. nuclear weapons testing was set in 1992. Current NTS activities, under DOE auspices, cover hazardous chemical spill testing, emergency response training, conventional weapons testing, waste management, and environmental technology studies.[43] Numerous resources on Nevada Operations Office and NTS are available at www.nv.doe.gov/. These resources include information on visiting NTS, how to order films of declassified nuclear weapons tests, RealPlayer video excerpts of some of these films, and information on the Las Vegas public reading facility provided under Freedom of Information Act provisions.

The principal value of the site is its fact sheets and reports chronicling historical and current activities at the NTS. Examples of the fact sheets include *Groundwater and the Nevada Test Site* (2000), *Big Explosives Experimental Facility* (2001), *Device Assembly Facility* (2001), *Overview of the Nevada Test Site* (2001), and *Stockpile Stewardship Program* (2001). The rich variety of reports includes *Radiological Effluents Released from U.S. Continental Tests: 1961 through 1992* (1996), *Position Paper on the Proper Characterization and Disposal of Sealed Radioactive Sources* (1997), *Origins of the Nevada Test Site* (2000), *United States Nuclear Tests: July 1945 through September 1992* (2000), *Atlas Relocation and Operation at the Nevada Test Site: Final Environmental Assessment* (2001), *Radiological Emergency Response Health and Safety Manual* (2001), *Nuclear Rocket Research* (2001), and *An Aerial Radiological Survey of Abandoned Uranium Mines in the Navajo Nation* (2001).

New Brunswick Laboratory

Located in Argonne, Illinois, the New Brunswick Laboratory (NBL) was established by the Atomic Energy Commission in 1949 in New Brunswick, New Jersey. NBL's initial purpose was providing the federal government with the ability to test uranium-containing materials for the U.S. atomic energy program. NBL was moved from New Jersey to the Argonne National Laboratory between 1975 and 1977. Its current mission is serving as the U.S. government's certification authority for nuclear reference materials and providing technical staff and laboratory resources to perform nuclear material measurements along with safeguards and nonproliferation functions to support multiple governmental program sponsors in these areas.[44]

A limited amount of NBL information is provided through its website (www.nbl.doe.gov/). Accessible material includes a mission statement and brief history, descriptions of NBL program areas such as its Nuclear Safeguards and Nonproliferation Support Program, and an online brochure request form. There is no access to reports, documents, or reference materials produced by NBL and its employees.

Nuclear Energy, Science, and Technology Office

The responsibilities of the Nuclear Energy, Science, and Technology Office include promoting nuclear energy and advancing nuclear science and engineering education within the United States.[45] A variety of resources on nuclear energy is accessible on the office's website (www.nuclear.gov/), including an organization chart, biographies of officials, congressional testimony, press releases, and information on program activities such as the Office of Isotopes for Medicine and Science and university programs.

Publicly accessible reports include *Nuclear Power in Space* (1978), *Low-Level Radioactive Waste Basics* (n.d.), *Nuclear Power Plant Safety Design and Planning: Understanding Radiation* (1986), *Strategic Plan 2000: America's Nuclear Technology Future* (2000), *The Future of University Nuclear Engineering Programs and University Research and Training Reactors* (2000), and *Technological Opportunities to Increase the Proliferation Resistance of Global Civilian Nuclear Power Systems* (2000).

Nuclear Explosion Monitoring, Research, and Engineering Program

DOE's Nuclear Explosion Monitoring, Research, and Engineering Program (NEMRE) is responsible for developing, demonstrating, and delivering technologies and systems to governmental agencies, such as the U.S. Air Force's Technical Applications Center, which is responsible for executing U.S. monitoring requirements and policies for detecting and describing nuclear explosions.[46] The website www.nemre.nn.doe.gov/nemre/ provides information on NEMRE's research areas including seismic monitoring, radionuclide monitoring, hydroacoustic monitoring, infrasound monitoring, automated data processsing, and space-based monitoring along with an overview of its institutional mission. Publicly accessible reports include *Nuclear Explosion Monitoring, Research, and Engineering Program Strategic Plan* (2002), *National Nuclear Security Administration Knowledge Base Core Table Schema Document* (2002), and *The Integration Process for Incorporating Nuclear Explosion Research Results into the National Nuclear Security Administration Knowledge Base* (2002).

Oak Ridge National Laboratory

Located in Oak Ridge, Tennessee, near Knoxville, the Oak Ridge National Laboratory (ORNL) was established in 1943 as part of the Manhattan Project to develop a way to produce and separate plutonium. ORNL subsequently became an important international center for nuclear energy research and affiliated research in the physical sciences. During the 1970s ORNL research moved into areas such as energy production, transmission, and conservation.[47]

In the early years of the twenty-first century, ORNL had grown to be an operation with a staff exceeding thirty-eight hundred and with nearly three thousand guest researchers spending two weeks or longer per year in residence. Its projected funding for federal fiscal year 2004 is expected to be over $1 billion. ORNL has been managed since April 2000 by a partnership between the University of Tennessee and the Battelle Corporation.[48]

Information on ORNL activities and research can be found at www.ornl.gov/. Regarding national security policy, ORNL's nuclear nonproliferation program is involved in reducing nuclear weapons proliferation risks by strengthening material protection, control, and accounting systems of nuclear weapons producers such as the former Soviet Union; safeguarding weapons and direct-use weapons; working with Russian nuclear institutes to upgrade their security and safeguards; conducting training and evaluations for the International Atomic Energy Agency (IAEA); and providing technical support to DOE in implementing IAEA safeguards in foreign countries and the United States.[49]

ORNL also conducts nonproliferation and arms control activities in the United States and overseas. Examples of these activities are designing, developing, and demonstrating arms control treaty verification systems; providing technical support to U.S. domestic nuclear export control agencies; securing U.S. nuclear technological assets and DOE high-risk assets; providing border security enhancements for export control of nuclear and affiliated materials and technologies; lending international technical support to multilateral export control regimes; and providing secure workplaces for classified information.[50]

National security–related publications produced by ORNL include *United States Transportation Plan for MOX (Mixed Oxide) Fuel Shipments under Project Parallex* (1999), *Quality Assurance Calculations to Support Use of HELIOS Version 1.6 for Plutonium Disposition Studies* (2001), and *Investigations and Recommendations on the Use of Existing Experiments in Criticality Safety Analysis of Nuclear Fuel Cycle Facilities for Weapons Grade Plutonium* (2002).

Another important component of ORNL is its Y-12 National Security Complex. This facility was built in 1944 under wartime secrecy, and its manufacturing capacities resulted in the creation of the first nuclear weapon. During subsequent decades, parts of all nuclear weapons in the U.S. arsenal were manufactured at Y-12.[51]

Although the United States is no longer producing nuclear weapons, Y-12's activities have involved participating in the Stockpile Stewardship Program, which is responsible for ensuring the reliability of the U.S. nuclear deterrent. A 2002 document listed the following as Y-12's primary missions.

- Dismantlement of retired weapons;
- Modification, repair, or replacement of secondaries as required;
- Surveillance of weapons through disassembly, inspection, and documentation of findings;
- Production of hardware to support laboratory tests required for stockpile certification;
- Management and storage of nuclear materials; and
- Stewardship of required technology, critical skills, and physical assets.[52]

Selected information about Y-12 operational activities can be found at www.y12.doe.gov/. Accessible materials include descriptions of NNSA activities at Y-12 and Y-12's highly enriched uranium facility, information on Y-12 programs such as the stockpile stewardship, nuclear materials management and storage, weapons dismantlement and disposal, and nuclear packaging systems. Additional Y-12 website contents include explanation of how Y-12's Center for International Threat Reduction (CITR) works to implement domestic and international programs to lessen the threat posed by weapons of mass destruction, U.S. interaction with IAEA programs and cooperative nuclear threat reduction activities with Russia, and CITR newsletters from 2000 to the present.

Office of Civilian Radioactive Waste Management

The Office of Civilian Radioactive Waste Management (OCRWM) was established by the Nuclear Waste Policy Act of 1982.[53] OCRWM responsibilities include developing and managing a system for disposing all spent nuclear fuel from commercial nuclear reactors and high-level radioactive waste from defense nuclear activities. The Nuclear Waste Policy Act Amendments of 1987 directed DOE to designate Yucca Mountain, Nevada, as a final repository for disposing of spent nuclear fuel and high-level radioactive waste.[54]

OCRWM's website (www.rw.doe.gov/) provides additional information about the office's activities such as a description of the nuclear waste management process, congressional testimony and public speeches by OCRWM officials, important regulatory activity engaged in by OCRWM, and links to information on federal nuclear waste regulation by agencies such as the Nuclear Regulatory Commission. Materials available on the website include fact sheets such as *Spent Nuclear Fuel* (n.d.) and *Transportation of Spent Nuclear Fuel* (n.d.). Available reports include OCRWM's *Annual Report to Congress* (1996–present), *Proceedings of the Conference on Geologic Repositories: Facing Common Challenges* (1999), *Allocating Nuclear Waste Disposal Costs for Civilian and Defense High-Level Wastes* (2002), *Total System Life Cycle Cost for Site Recommendation Letter Report* (2002), and OCRWM audit reports of various waste contractors at sites around the United States.

Office of Environmental Management

The Office of Environmental Management (EM) was created in 1989 to lessen the dangers caused by nuclear weapons production (for example, to the environment) and research (which, for instance, produces large amounts of contaminated waste, soil, and structures that will remain radioactive for millennia).[55]

EM's website (www.em.doe.gov/) contains information resources describing DOE's environmental recovery and remediation activities, such as descriptions of program offices dealing with long-term environmental stewardship, project management, health, safety, and security; the integration and disposition of contaminated materials; and an office organizational chart. Additional general reference materials include press releases, program budget information, engineering cost data and appraisals, listings of acronyms, a glossary defining environmental terms such as *National Priorities List* and *transuranic waste,* and descriptions of EM activities in states and territories.

Accessible reports include *Status Report on Paths to Closure* (2000), *Buried Transuranic Contaminated Waste Information for U.S. Department of Energy Facilities* (2000), *Savannah River Site Canyons Nuclear Material Identification Study* (2001), *Remotely Operated Vehicle (ROV) System for Horizontal Tanks* (2001), *Revision to the Record of Decision for the Department of Energy Waste Management Program: Treat-*

ment and Storage of Transuranic Waste* (2001), and *Guidance for Optimizing Ground Water Response Activities at Department of Energy Sites* (2002).

Office of Independent Oversight and Performance Assurance

The Office of Independent Oversight and Performance Assurance is responsible for independently evaluating the effectiveness of DOE's safeguards and security policies. Examples of these policies include protecting special nuclear material and classified and sensitive information and providing security for foreign visits to U.S. DOE facilities. The office is responsible for regularly evaluating and assessing DOE security programs and issuing reviews and recommendations to ensure corrective actions are taken when deficiencies are found.[56]

At www.oa.doe.gov/ are descriptions of the Office of Safeguards and Security Evaluations, Office of Cyber Security and Special Reviews, Office of Emergency Management Oversight, Office of Management and Information Resources, and Office of Environment, Safety, and Health Evaluations. Publicly accessible information resources include the newsletter *Inside Oversight* from April 2000 to the present, *Weekly Highlights* from December 10, 2001, to the present, and reports such as *FY 2000 Program Plan: Office of Safeguards and Security Evaluation* (1999), *Physical Security Systems Inspectors Guide* (2000), and *Inspectors Guide: Classified Matter Protection and Control* (2002). A listing of classified but publicly inaccessible reports is also provided.

Office of Inspector General

DOE's Office of Inspector General (OIG) was created as part of the Inspector General Act of 1978.[57] The OIG's mission includes looking for ways of reducing expenditures, enhancing DOE program operational efficiency, and returning money to DOE and the U.S. Treasury as a result of civil and criminal investigations.[58]

The website www.ig.doe.gov/ contains a hotline to allow reporting of legal or financial violations by DOE organizational entities or contractors, the testimony of OIG officials before Congress, an organizational chart, position requirements, and listings of current job openings. Numerous publications are accessible, including semiannual reports to Congress from 1995 to the present that describe OIG's overall activities.

The highlight of the website for those studying DOE's national security policy making is the full text of audit and inspection reports from 1995 to the present. Examples of these reports are *Audit of Department of Energy Site Safeguards and Security Plans* (1995), *Audit of Staffing Requirements for the Strategic Petroleum Reserve* (1995), *Audit of Alternatives to Testing at the Tonopah Test Range* (1998), *Inspection of Selected Issues Regarding the Department of Energy Accident Investigation Program* (1999), *Office of Defense Programs Robotics and Intelligent Machines Projects* (1999), *Summary Report on Inspection of Allegations Relating to Albuquerque Operations Office Security Survey Process and the Security Operations Self-Assessments at Los Alamos National Laboratory* (2000), *Management of the Nuclear Weapons Production*

Infrastructure (2000), *Inspection of Cyber Security Standards for Sensitive Personnel Information* (2001), *Accounting for Sealed Sources of Nuclear Materials Provided to Foreign Countries* (2002), and *Depleted Uranium Operations at the Y-12 National Security Complex* (2002).

Office of Policy and International Affairs

The assistant secretary for policy and international affairs, who heads the DOE Office of Policy and International Affairs (PI), serves as the chief policy adviser to the secretary of energy on domestic and international policy formulation and implementation. PI is responsible for delivering objective advice to DOE policymakers that is based upon empirically solid data and analysis as well as for developing and leading DOE's bilateral and multilateral scientific cooperation, investment, and trade activities with other nations and international organizations.[59]

Offices within the PI's organizational umbrella include the Office of Nuclear Materials Management Policy, which is responsible for assessing DOE national security policy management; the Office of Energy Emergencies, which serves as DOE's emergency preparedness and response coordinator; the Office of Electricity and Natural Gas Analysis, which provides economic analyses in areas such as electricity markets, global climate change, and environmental regulations affecting energy use and production; the Office of Newly Independent States, Russian, and Middle Eastern Affairs, which establishes U.S. energy policy objectives for these regions; and other entities that facilitate U.S. energy policy interaction internationally and domestically.[60]

Further information about PI program areas and information resources may be found on the website www.pi.energy.gov/. Accessible materials include congressional testimony and public speeches by the assistant secretary of energy for policy and international affairs; a listing of energy treaties and agreements among the United States, individual countries, and international governmental organizations; and descriptions of ongoing U.S. domestic and international energy policy initiatives.

Available reports are *Department of Energy Research and Development Portfolio: National Security* (2000), *A Strategic Approach to Integrating the Long-Term Management of Nuclear Materials* (2000), *Horizontal Market Power in Restructured Electricity Markets* (2000), *United States Department of Energy International Agreements Handbook* (2000), *Status Report to Congress on Current and Proposed Activities under the Clean Energy Technology Exports (CETE) Initiative* (2001), and *North America: The Energy Picture* (2002).

Office of Scientific and Technical Information

DOE's Office of Scientific and Technical Information (OSTI) is located in Oak Ridge, Tennessee. Its origins date back to the 1946 creation of the Atomic Energy Commission and the 1947 establishment of its Technical Information Program. OSTI became a major producer of scientific and technical information and, during the 1990s, became a leader in digitizing significant quantities of information produced by DOE employees and contractors.[61]

Information about OSTI and access to reports produced for it can be found through its website (www.osti.gov/). Three particularly noteworthy features on the website are DOE's "Information Bridge" (www.osti.gov/bridge/), "Eprint Network" (www.osti.gov/eprint/), and "Energy Citations" (www.osti.gov/energycitations/). "Information Bridge" provides access to full-text research and development reports on energy-related topics from 1995 to the present, "Eprint Network" provides pre-publication access to more than 340,000 scientific research articles and papers from U.S. and foreign sources, and "Energy Citations" provides citations and limited full-text access to reports from 1948 to the present produced by DOE and predecessor agencies such as the Atomic Energy Commission and the Energy Research and Development Administration.[62]

Some examples of the resources provided by OSTI are *Seismic Results from DOE's Nonproliferation Experiment: A Comparison of Chemical and Nuclear Explosions* (1995), *The Soviet Program for Peaceful Uses of Nuclear Explosions Revision 1* (1996), *Offsite Environmental Monitoring Report: Radiation Monitoring around United States Nuclear Test Areas, Calendar Year 1996* (1997), *Investigation of High Energy Density Matter for Science-Based Stockpile Stewardship* (1998), *Training Options for Countering Nuclear Smuggling* (1999), and *ENTNEA: A Concept for Enhancing Nuclear Transparency for Confidence Building in Northeast Asia* (1999).

Office of Site Closure

The Office of Site Closure (OSC) is part of DOE's Office of Environmental Management, which was established in 1989. OSC is responsible for closing defense nuclear facilities once environmental contaminants have been removed. It hopes to achieve this objective by 2006.[63]

Further information about OSC activities can be found on its website (http://apps.em.doe.gov/closure/), including a listing of sites that have been cleaned up and require closure, information on specific sites that have done work designing and constructing nuclear weapons parts and are being considered for closure, and press releases for 2000 and 2001. Accessible reports are *Memorandum of Agreement: Transfer of Responsibilities for the Mount Plant from Defense Programs to the Office of Environmental Management* (1995), *Draft Policy and Planning Guidelines for Community Transitional Activities* (1999), *Understanding, Communicating, and Achieving Site Closure* (2000), and *DOE's Office of Site Closure: Progress Towards 2006* (2001).

OpenNet

Secretary of Energy Hazel O'Leary announced on June 27, 1994, that numerous records pertaining to U.S. nuclear weapons testing and the multifaceted impacts of this testing would be declassified.[64] The mission of OpenNet is to declassify and publicly release all DOE information that no longer endangers national security, implement openness policies to foster greater governmental accountability and public trust in government, and support U.S. nonproliferation goals.[65]

OpenNet's website address is www.osti.gov/opennet/. Available materials include historical nuclear weapons test films from the Nevada Test Site, the "Human Radiation Experiment" database describing Atomic Energy Commission experiments involving human subjects, and links to documents describing the historic involvement of DOE and its predecessor agencies in nuclear weapons development and testing along with information on how to obtain paper copies of these materials.

Examples of resources accessible through the website are DOE's reports to Congress entitled *Inadvertent Releases of Restricted Data and Formerly Restricted Data under Executive Order 12958* (1999–present) and *Special Historical Records Review Plan* (2000).

Pacific Northwest Laboratory

The Pacific Northwest Laboratory (PNL) is located in Richland, Washington. Its origins date back to 1965, when the Battelle Corporation won a contract from the Atomic Energy Commission to perform research and development at the Hanford nuclear site in southeastern Washington State.[66] PNL's national security work helps promote U.S. government goals against the proliferation of weapons of mass destruction and their delivery systems. Approximately one-third of PNL's annual $600 million research and development budget is national security–related and is used to develop ways of diagnosing the life span of the U.S. Army's Abrams tank, create technologies for verifying Comprehensive Nuclear Test Ban Treaty compliance, help North Korea properly secure spent nuclear fuel in storage canisters, and train U.S. and foreign border enforcement officials.[67] PNL's website is accessible at www.pnl.gov/. National security–related resources include the laboratory's magazine *Breakthroughs,* descriptions of national security project areas such as high-tech crime fighting, remote sensing, pathogen detection, a personal security scanner, the Northwest National Security Analysis Team, the Information Security Resource Center, and the Pacific Northwest Center for Global Security. Available publications are *Debt Swapping as a Tool for Economic and Social Stabilization in Russia's Closed Nuclear Cities* (2000), *Economic Globalization and a Nuclear Renaissance* (2001), and *Reactive Behavior of K-Basin Spent Nuclear Fuel* (2002).

Pantex Plant

The Pantex Plant (PP), near Amarillo, Texas, is the only nuclear weapons assembly and disassembly plant in the United States. It is managed by BWXT Pantex contractors, the Army Corps of Engineers, and DOE's Sandia National Laboratories (SNL) and had approximately thirty-two hundred employees as of January 2001. PP was established in 1942 as the Pantex Army Ordance Plant.[68]

Pantex's core mission areas are seeing to nuclear weapons assembly and disassembly, evaluating the reliability of U.S. nuclear weapons, conducting high-explosive research and development, and overseeing interim plutonium pit storage.[69]

Further information about Pantex missions and community activities can be found on its website (www.pantex.com). Materials provided include documentation of public meetings with Pantex officials, Pantex activities in areas such as procurement and the environment, and issues of the *PanTexan* newsletter from 1998 to the present. Accessible documents are *Pantex Site Environmental Reports* (1995–2000), *Environmental Monitoring Quarterly Reports* (1998–present), and *Pantex Nuclear Weapons Facility Ambient Air Monitoring Annual 1999 Report* (2000).

Sandia National Laboratories

In Albuquerque, New Mexico, in 1945, an ordinance, design, testing, and assembly component of LANL was created. This entity, which would become the Sandia National Laboratories (SNL), was moved to Sandia Base in Albuquerque and renamed Sandia in 1948. Sandia and a supplemental facility in Livermore, California, were managed by AT&T from 1949 to 1993. DOE then transferred SNL management to Lockheed Martin. SNL has more than seventy-six hundred employees and manages $1.8 billion worth of work per year.[70]

SNL's national and homeland security activities include research in antiterror analysis tools for public health and other agencies, development of chemical-biological decontamination formulations for the army, assessment of building vulnerabilities to chemical-biological attacks, protection of critical infrastructure, detection of explosives at airports, development of bomb disabling robots, and training of U.S. bomb squads.[71]

SNL's website (www.sandia.gov/) provides information about laboratory programs. Accessible publications include the fact sheets *Energy Infrastructure Surety* (2001) and *Improved Air Transportation Safety* (2001). Noteworthy national security reports and periodicals produced by SNL are *Sandia Technology: A Quarterly Research and Development Journal* (1999–present), *Sandia Perspectives* and *Annual Reports* (1997–present), *Pursuing a New Nuclear Weapons Policy for the 21st Century* (2001), and *Capabilities of Sandia National Laboratories to Support the Recommendations of the President's Commission on Critical Infrastructure Protection* (n.d.).

Many SNL-produced materials are also accessible through the DOE Reading Room provided by the University of New Mexico's Zimmerman Library Government Information Department. Information on this service can be found at http://elibrary.unm.edu/doe/.

Savannah River Site

The Savannah River Site (SRS) is located on the Savannah River separating Georgia and South Carolina near Aiken, South Carolina. SRS was established in 1950 by the Atomic Energy Commission to produce plutonium and tritium for the U.S. nuclear weapons arsenal.[72] E. I. DuPont de Nemours and Company assumed design, construction, and management responsibilities in 1950 and continued these responsibilities until 1987, when it notified DOE of its desire to end its stewardship. Westinghouse Savannah River Company took over SRS site management responsibilities in 1989.[73]

Current SRS institutional responsibilities revolve around nuclear weapons stockpile stewardship and nuclear materials stewardship. Stockpile stewardship activities include ensuring the safe and reliable delivery, recycling, and management of tritium resources; contributing to the overall stockpile stewardship program; and assisting in developing alternatives to large-scale pit production capability in the event the United States resumes nuclear weapons testing. Nuclear materials stewardship activities encompass managing excess nuclear materials and include transporting, stabilizing, storing, and disposing of these materials in support of nuclear nonproliferation objectives. Key nuclear materials within this program are dismantled weapons components, weapons processing activity residues, spent nuclear fuel, and other nuclear environmental legacy materials.[74]

Numerous resources about SRS activities are available at www.srs.gov/. Materials include a historical chronology, news releases, business and employment opportunities, and descriptions of SRS program activities. The accessible historical and contemporary publications include *Radiolysis of Chloroform in the Intense Radiation Pulse from a Nuclear Explosion* (1967), *Plutonium Burning* (1968), *A Strong U.S Nuclear Enterprise Enhances Global Nuclear Proliferation Management* (2001), *Activities of the ANS [American Nuclear Society] Special Committee on Nonproliferation* (2001), *Safety Aspects of Receipt and Storage of Spent Nuclear Fuel at the Savannah River Site* (2001), *Proposed Savannah River Site Environmental Management Program Performance Management and Plan* (2002), and *Overview Defense Waste Processing Facility Operating Experience* (2002).

Additional materials may be found at the DOE Public Reading Room in the Gregg-Graniteville Library at the University of South Carolina—Aiken in Aiken, South Carolina. Contact the library's Government Documents Department for more information. The Government Documents Department of the Cooper Library at the University of South Carolina in Columbia, South Carolina, maintains a webpage (www.sc.edu/library/pubserv/gdsrs.html) describing its SRS materials holdings.

Strategic Petroleum Reserve

The Strategic Petroleum Reserve (SPR) was established by Congress in 1975 to decrease the vulnerability of the United States to severe energy supply disruption. It provides partial protection against limited and short-term interruptions in petroleum supplies.[75] SPR crude oil contents are located in salt caverns along the Louisiana and Texas coastline. These caverns have typical holdings of ten million barrels, are cylindrical in shape, possess diameters of two hundred feet, and are approximately two thousand feet high.[76]

The Project Management Office website, at www.spr.doe.gov/, has a description of SPR's fuel oil storage and job announcements. More detailed information can be found through DOE's Fossil Energy Petroleum Reserves website (www.fe.doe.gov/facilities/sprpmo/). Materials include a profile of the SPR and its storage sites, the reserve's current inventory, information on the Clinton administration's 2000 decision to tap into the reserve, and links to DOE resources on naval petroleum reserves and the Northeast Home Heating Oil Reserve.

SPR annual reports have been withdrawn for security reasons, but accessible SPR-related documents include fossil energy overviews of selected countries, *Advanced Power Assessment for Czech Lignites, Volume I* (1995), *Report to Congress on the Feasibility of Establishing a Heating Oil Component to the Strategic Petroleum Reserve* (1998), *Meeting the Challenges of the Nation's Growing Natural Gas Demand* (1999), *Commercial Potential of Natural Gas Storage in Lined Rock Caverns* (1999), *Strategic Petroleum Reserve Plan Amendment No. 6—Regional Distillate Reserve in the Northeast* (2000), and the quarterly *Natural Gas Imports and Exports*.

Yucca Mountain Project

The Yucca Mountain Project (YMP) is located in Nye County, Nevada, approximately one hundred miles northwest of Las Vegas. The Nuclear Waste Policy Act of 1982 formally established a national policy process to solve the problem of nuclear waste disposal. Following DOE reports issued in 1985, Hanford, Washington, Deaf Smith County, Texas, and Yucca Mountain were selected by President Ronald Reagan as candidate nuclear waste storage repositories. The Nuclear Waste Policy Act Amendments of 1987 directed DOE to study Yucca Mountain as the exclusive U.S. nuclear waste storage site.[77]

Congress approved Yucca Mountain as the U.S. nuclear waste repository in July 2002.[78] Yucca Mountain was selected because scientists believe that the rock at this locale will isolate the radioactive waste for thousands of years and pose the same or a decreased level of public risk as that caused by unmined uranium ore. Additional factors include Yucca Mountain's physical isolation from large population centers, its dry climate characterized by less than six inches of annual rainfall, and its very deep water table, which is eight hundred to one thousand feet below the level of other potential repositories.[79]

Numerous information resources about YMP operations and activities can be found at www.ymp.gov/. Available materials include historical overviews of U.S. nuclear waste policy; descriptions of YMP research areas and projects; a historical, a current, and a projected timeline of U.S. nuclear waste policy developments; and a virtual tour of YMP. Accessible YMP project fact sheets include *Viability Assessment of a Repository at Yucca Mountain* (1997), *What Is Nuclear Fuel and Waste?* (2000), *Managing Heat in a Repository at Yucca Mountain* (2000), *Germany's Radioactive Waste Management Program* (2001), and *Studying the Movement of Rock and Earthquakes* (2001).

A wide variety of technical reports is also accessible at www.ymp.gov/. Examples include regularly issued site characterization reports, *Final Environmental Impact Statement for a Geologic Repository for the Disposal of Spent Nuclear Fuel and High-Level Radioactive Waste at Yucca Mountain, Nye County, Nevada* (2002), *Yucca Mountain Igneous Consequences Peer Review Panel: Interim Report* (2002), *Yucca Mountain Site Suitability Evaluation* (2002), and *Site Environmental Report for Calendar Year 2001: Yucca Mountain Site Nye County, Nevada* (2002).

Environmental Protection Agency

The Environmental Protection Agency (EPA) has been responsible for directing federal environmental policy since its formation in 1970.[80] Information about EPA's overall operational scope and mission can be found on its website (www.epa.gov/).

The growing danger of weapons of mass destruction and the consequences of their destructive powers being used against the U.S. civilian population have increased EPA's role as a national security policy-making player. EPA has produced a number of national security–related resources that are publicly accessible in the "Counter-Terrorism" section of its website (www.epa.gov/ebtpages/emercounterterrorism.htm).

Subjects covered by these resources include accident investigation and prevention, contingency plans for responding to weapons of mass destruction disasters, consequence management, countermeasures, and poisoning. Some accessible publications are *EPA's Emergency Response Organizational Structure* (1998), *Overview: Counter-Terrorism Status Report* (1998), *EPA Capabilities: Responding to Nuclear-Biological-Chemical (NBC) Terrorism* (2000), *Environmental Protection Agency Radiological Emergency Response Plan* (2000), and *Local Emergency Planning Committees and Deliberate Releases: Addressing Terrorist Activities in the Local Emergency Plan* (2001).

Department of Health and Human Services

The Department of Health, Education, and Welfare in 1979 was split into the Department of Health and Human Services (HHS) and the Department of Education. HHS administers the U.S. government's health care programs and various social assistance programs.[81] The far-flung organizational missions of HHS are carried out by, for example, the Center for Medicare and Medicaid Services, Centers for Disease Control (CDC), National Institutes of Health (NIH), Public Health Service, and Substance Abuse and Mental Health Services Administration. HHS national security information resources include the CDC, the Food and Drug Administration (FDA), the Office of Inspector General, the National Institute of Allergy and Infectious Diseases (NIAID), the National Library of Medicine Biodefense and Bioterrorism, and the National Disaster Medical System (NDMS).

Centers for Disease Control Emergency Preparedness and Response

The Centers for Disease Control and Prevention, headquartered in Atlanta, Georgia, seeks to promote health and life quality by preventing and controlling disease, injury, and disability. CDC conducts research, implements prevention strategies, advocates safe and healthy environments, and works with public and private sector partners.[82] Overall information about CDC, including many information products, can be found on its website (www.cdc.gov/).

CDC's bioterrorism resources website (www.bt.cdc.gov/) is particularly informative for those studying national security policy. Available materials include descriptions of biological and chemical agents such as botulism toxin and cutaneous anthrax, bioterrorism funding information for states, webcasts, clinical testing and trials data, information on appropriate officials to contact in an emergency, and relevant articles from CDC journals *Emerging Infectious Diseases* and *Morbidity and Mortality Weekly Reports*.

Examples of accessible fact sheets and publications are *Bioterrorism Readiness Plan: A Template for Healthcare Facilities* (1999), *Facts about Anthrax* (2001), *Technical Information about Anthrax* (2001), *The Public Health Response to Biological and Chemical Terrorism: Interim Planning Guidance for State Public Health Officials* (2001), *Emergency Room Procedures in Chemical Hazard Emergencies: A Job Aid* (2002), *Dirty Bombs* (2002), *Nuclear Terrorism and Health Effects* (2002), *Sheltering in Place during a Radiation Emergency* (2002), and *Smallpox Response Plan and Guidelines* (2002).

Food and Drug Administration Counterterrorism

The Food and Drug Administration was established in 1931 as part of the U.S. Department of Agriculture (USDA).[83] FDA's institutional mission is protecting public health by ensuring that foods are safe, wholesome, sanitary, and properly labeled and by applying the same level of regulatory scrutiny to medicine and cosmetics.[84]

Information about FDA can be found at www.fda.gov/. The website maintains a counterterrorism information clearinghouse accessible at www.fda.gov/oc/opacom/ hottopics/ bioterrorism.html. It has FDA-produced information about bioterrorism as well as links to other U.S. government bioterrorism resources such as the USDA-sponsored www.foodsafety.gov/ site.

Examples of materials on the FDA bioterrorism site are news releases, descriptions of FDA enforcement actions, information on the Public Health Security and Bioterrorism Preparedness and Response Act of 2002, and publications such as *Approval of Cipro for Use after Exposure to Inhalational Anthrax* (2000), *Countering Bioterrorism: Frequently Asked Questions* (2001), *FDA Issues Cyber Letters to Web Sites Selling Unapproved Foreign Ciprofloxacin* (2001), *Frequently Asked Consumer Questions about Food Safety and Terrorism* (2001), and *Anthrax Vaccines: Efficacy Testing and Surrogate Markers of Immunity Workshop* (2002).

National Disaster Medical System

The National Disaster Medical System (NDMS) administers the National Disaster Medical System established by National Security Decision Directive 47 in July 1982. Within HHS, NDMS is responsible for managing and coordinating federal health, medical, and social services responses to major emergencies and federally declared disasters such as terrorism, major transportation accidents, technological disasters, and natural disasters.[85] The National Disaster Medical System is charged with establishing one integrated medical response for assisting state and local officials in dealing with the medical and health impact of major peacetime disasters while supporting the military and Veterans Health Administration medical systems in caring for U.S. military casualties in overseas operations who are brought back to the United States.[86]

The website http://ndms.dhhs.gov/ contains information about NDMS activities, such as a PowerPoint presentation describing its history and mission, forms, links to various state disaster medical assistance team websites, and documents such as *Federal Coordinating Center Guide* (1999).

National Institute of Allergy and Infectious Diseases

The National Institute of Allergy and Infectious Diseases (NIAID) is part of the National Institutes of Health. Since its beginnings in 1887, NIH has grown to become the premier U.S. medical and behavioral research center.[87] NIAID's origins also derive from 1887, and it received its present name in 1955. The institutional mission of NIAID is conducting and supporting research to enhance understanding of and ability to treat the infectious, immunologic, and allergic diseases that affect people internationally.[88]

NIAID research of interest to those studying national security policy can be found on its "Biodefense" web page (www.niaid.nih.gov/publications/bioterrorism.htm). Available materials include information on biodefense research funding opportunities, webcasts of NIAID-sponsored conferences on biodefense, and listings of priority areas in biodefense product development. Retrievable reports include *NIAID Strategic Plan for Biodefense Research* (2002), *NIAID Biodefense Research Agenda for Category A Agents* (2002), *NIAID Blue Ribbon Panel on Bioterrorism and Its Implications for Medical Research: Summary* (2002), and *Summary of the NIAID Expert Panel on Immunity and Biodefense* (2002).

National Library of Medicine Biodefense and Bioterrorism

The National Library of Medicine website (www.nlm.nih.gov/medlineplus/biodefenseandbioterrorism.html) provides access to information on medical aspects of biological warfare. Information is presented on anthrax, smallpox, plague, botulism, tularemia, and other biological disease. The website also describes the CDC's Strategic National Stockpile Program, which is intended to ensure an adequate amount of medicine, equipment, and supplies to respond to biological and chemical weapons attacks in the United States. The site has links to citations, abstracts, and some articles on medical aspects of biological warfare from the National Library of Medicine's *Medline* medical literature index.[89]

Office of Inspector General

The HHS Office of Inspector General is responsible for evaluating the performance of HHS programs for the secretary of health and human services and Congress and issuing reports containing recommendations to improve these programs.[90]

Information about the office's activities and reports can be found at http://oig.hhs.gov/. A limited number of national security–related reports are on the site, including *Child Support and the Military* (1993) and *Physical Security over Data Processing Operations at the Centers for Disease Control and Prevention* (1994). However,

HHS inspector general Janet Rehnquist informed a congressional committee on March 5, 2002, that the office was examining security controls at the CDC, FDA, National Institutes of Health, and university laboratories to see how these institutions were handling access to selected agents by restricted individuals. Rehnquist also mentioned that OIG was working with state and local health departments to assess their capacity and readiness to detect and respond to bioterrorist incidents.[91]

Department of Homeland Security

The Department of Homeland Security (DHS) was established in November 2002, in response to the September 11, 2001, terrorist attacks.[92] Its creation marked the largest reorganization of federal national security institutions since the 1947 National Security Act, which provided for the Department of Defense, Central Intelligence Agency, and National Security Council (NSC). DHS absorbed numerous agencies and offices from existing federal departments. For example, the Immigration and Naturalization Service (INS) was transferred from the Justice Department to DHS; the Coast Guard and Transportation Security Administration, from the Transportation Department; and the Customs Service, from the Treasury Department.[93]

DHS superseded the Office of Homeland Security, which operated from the Executive Office of the President. The website for the Office of Homeland Security was www.whitehouse.gov/deptofhomeland/; it was changed to www.dhs.gov in February 2003. Examples of accessible information resources are presidential homeland security budget priorities, policy documents, press releases, a listing of and links to state homeland security contact personnel and state agency websites, and descriptions of DHS jurisdiction over matters such as border and transportation security; chemical, biological, radiological, and nuclear countermeasures; emergency preparedness and response; and information analysis and infrastructure protection.

Animal and Plant Health Inspection Service

The Animal and Plant Health Inspection Service (APHIS) was established in 1971 through a USDA internal agency reorganization memorandum issued by the secretary of agriculture.[94] Its mission is protecting U.S. animal and plant resources from agricultural pests and diseases and from threats to the food supply, responding to other countries' animal and plant health import requirements, and protecting ecosystems from invasive pests and pathogens.[95] In 2003, DHS assumed from USDA responsibilities concerning agricultural import and entry inspection activities.[96]

The APHIS website (www.aphis.usda.gov/) contains fact sheets such as *Safeguarding U.S. Agriculture in the Global Environment* (2001), *Inland Inspection Program: Safeguarding American Agriculture against Invasive Species* (2001), *Anthrax—Clinical Signs and Diagnosis* (2001), and *Emergency Response: Foot-and-Mouth Disease and Other Foreign Animal Diseases* (2002). Additional website contents include information on plant protection and quarantine, invasive species, and various epidemiological trends.

> ### Department of Homeland Security
>
> The Department of Homeland Security (DHS) was established by the 2002 Homeland Security Act and came into existence on January 24, 2003. DHS is headed by the secretary of homeland security and is responsible for preventing terrorist attacks while permitting the free flow of people, goods, and commerce across national borders.
>
> The DHS organization includes the Border and Transportation Security Directorate (BTSD), Emergency Preparedness and Response Directorate (EPRD), Information Analysis and Infrastructure Protection Directorate (IAIPD), Management Directorate (MD), and Science and Technology Directorate (STD).
>
> BTSD is responsible for securing national borders and transportation systems and enforcing federal immigration laws. EPRD works to see that the United States is prepared for natural disasters or terrorist assaults by coordinating federal response and recovery strategies with first responders. IAIPD strives to identify and assess current and emerging threats to critical infrastructures such as computer networks. MD responsibilities encompass departmental budgets, human resources, facilities, equipment, and performance-measuring activities. STD seeks to organize national scientific and technological assets to prevent or mitigate terrorism against the United States and its allies and develop antiterrorism countermeasures.
>
> Also within the DHS organizational umbrella are agencies such as the U.S. Coast Guard and U.S. Secret Service.

Citizenship and Immigration Services

With creation of DHS, the Immigration and Naturalization Service (INS) was divided in two, and both were transferred to the new department. The Bureau of Citizenship and Immigration Services (BCIS) handles immigration services, and the Border and Transportation Security Directorate (BTSD) deals with immigration law enforcement.[97] INS was established in 1891 to facilitate the legal entry of visitors and immigrants; assist those seeking asylum, temporary, or permanent resident status; prevent the improper entry and receipt of benefits by illegal immigrants; apprehend and remove aliens who enter or remain illegally in the United States and whose presence is not in the public interest; and enforce sanctions against those acting or conspiring to subvert federal immigration laws including imposing sanctions against employers who knowingly hire unauthorized aliens to work.[98] Information about BCIS can be found at (http://uscis.gov/). Available materials include location and contact information for BCIS offices, recent relevant legal and regulatory developments, congressional testimony of BCIS officials, position openings and job application information, and information about the incorporation of INS into DHS. Specific resources are the *Triennial Comprehensive Report on Immigration* (1999 and 2002), *Statistical Yearbook of the Immigration and Naturalization Service* (1996–2002), the current *Monthly Statistical Report, Report on H-1B Petitions* for high-skill foreign workers (2000–present), *Report on Characteristics of Specialty Occupation Workers (H-1B)* (2000–2001), and information on the Student and Exchange Visitor Information System (SEVIS), which tracks and monitor nonimmigrant students in the United States.

U.S. Coast Guard

The U.S. Coast Guard (USCG) dates to 1790, when it was the Revenue Marine. It became known as the Coast Guard in 1915. The Coast Guard became part of the Department of Transportation in 1967 and was transferred to DHS in 2003.[99] The mission of USCG includes establishing and maintaining U.S. navigational aids such as lights, buoys, and marine radio beacons; developing and directing a national boating safety program; and administering statutes regulating the construction, maintenance, and operation of bridges and causeways across navigable U.S. waters.[100]

USCG is responsible for ensuring maritime homeland security by enforcing federal laws and international maritime agreements in areas such as smuggling and drug trafficking, enforcing rules and regulations concerning port safety and security, supervising cargo transfer operations, conducting harbor patrols, inspecting waterfront facilities, and serving as a branch of the U.S. Navy in wartime.[101]

Information on USCG operations and activities can be found at www.uscg.mil/. Available resources include speeches by USCG and DOT officials on the Coast Guard's homeland defense mission and publications such as *Coast Guard Migrant Interdictions* (1982–present), *Alien Migrant Interdiction* (1999), *Interagency Task Force Report on Coast Guard Roles and Missions* (1999), *The Drug Smuggling Problem in the Caribbean* (2000), *The Coast Guard at War* (2002), and *Guidelines for Port Security Committees and Port Security Plans Required for U.S. Ports* (2002).

U.S. Customs and Border Protection

The First Congress in 1789 established customs districts and authorized customs officers to collect duties on materials imported into the United States. A Bureau of Customs was established as a separate Treasury Department agency in 1927 and was redesignated as the U.S. Customs Service in 1973. In 2003 it was integrated into the Department of Homeland Security as U.S. Customs and Border Protection (CBP).[102]

CBP's mission includes enforcing customs and related laws, collecting revenue from imports, protecting Americans from international terrorism, intercepting and seizing contraband materials such as narcotics and other illegal drugs, enforcing Bank Secrecy Act requirements and export control laws, and intercepting illicit high-technology and weapons exports.[103]

Available at www.cbp.gov/ are news on CBP activities from various media sources, information on how to report smuggling, various forms, information on CBP enforcement activities, and drug interdiction and seizure statistics. Other resources include the web pages "Customs-Trade Partnership against Terrorism," "Container Security Initiative," and "Customs Electronic Bulletin Board" and numerous publications such as the serial *Customs Bulletin* (June 2000–present), which documents CBP decisions, rulings, and regulations on customs issues, *U.S. Import Requirements* (n.d.), *U.S. Customs Service Strategic Plan: Fiscal Years 2000–2005* (n.d.), and *Foreign Assembly of U.S. Components* (2001).

Federal Law Enforcement Training Center

The Federal Law Enforcement Training Center (FLETC), established in the Treasury Department in 1970, serves as an interagency training resource for more than seventy federal law enforcement organizations. It also conducts advanced programs in areas of common federal law enforcement needs such as antiterrorism, advanced law enforcement photography, marine law enforcement, international banking, money laundering, and highly advanced training programs for selected state, local, and international law enforcement officials.[104]

FLETC's website (www.fletc.gov/) provides information about its programs and activities. Materials available include publications such as *Training Programs Catalog 2001–2002* (2001) and information about the Advanced Law Enforcement Photography Training Program, Critical Incident Response Training Program, Critical Infrastructure Training Program, Land Transportation Antiterrorism Training Program, Seaport Security Antiterrorism Training Program, Small Craft Enforcement Training Program, Vehicle Ambush Countermeasures Training Program, and Weapons of Mass Destruction Training Program.

Office for Domestic Preparedness

The Office for Domestic Preparedness (ODP) was created by Congress in 1998 and placed within the Justice Department's Office of Justice Programs. It was transferred to DHS in 2003. ODP's purpose is enhancing the ability of state and local governments to respond to and alleviate the consequences of terrorist incidents in their jurisdictions. A key part of congressional intent in establishing this office as part of DHS was authorizing the attorney general to assist state and local public safety personnel in acquiring the specialized equipment and training essential to respond to and deal with terrorism involving weapons of mass destruction.[105]

Information resources on ODP's website (www.ojp.usdoj.gov/odp/) include press releases, training and technical assistance information, details about the equipment acquisition grants program, information and procedures for applying for available grants, and listings of state administering agencies and contact personnel. ODP publications include *Critical Incident Protocol: A Public and Private Partnership* (2000); *Fiscal Year 2001 Nunn-Lugar-Domenici Domestic Preparedness Equipment Program Guidelines and Application Kit* (2000), *State and Local Approaches Mass Casualty Decontamination: Massachusetts Rapid Response System* (2001); ODP's *Course Catalog* (2001), featuring courses such as Emergency Response to Terrorism: Basic Concepts, Public Works: Basic Concepts for Weapons of Mass Destruction (WMD) Incidents and bulletins such as *WMD Emergency Response Training Course (Live Agent);* Information Bulletin 51: State Assistance Plans (2002); *Information Bulletin 64: Crisis*

Information Management Software Features Comparison Report (2002); and *Emergency Responder Guidelines* (2002).

Plum Island Animal Disease Center

Located in the Atlantic Ocean between Long Island and Connecticut, the Plum Island Animal Disease Center (PIADC) was transferred from the U.S. Army to the Department of Agriculture in 1954 and was formally dedicated in 1956. Impetus for creating the center came from outbreaks of foot-and-mouth disease in Canada and Mexico in the years after World War II and from the desire of federal policymakers to prevent such incidents from occurring in the United States.[106]

Plum Island's mission is to

- Develop new strategies to prevent and control foreign or emerging animal disease epidemics; through a better understanding of the nature of infectious organisms; their pathogenesis in susceptible animals; the host immune responses; the development of novel vaccines; and the development and the improvement of diagnostic tests;
- Conduct diagnostic investigations of suspected cases of foreign or emerging animal diseases in the United States, or in countries abroad through cooperation with animal health international organizations;
- Test imported animals and animal products to assure they are free of foreign animal disease [FAD] agents;
- Assess risks involved in the importation of animals and animal products from countries where epidemic FAD occurs;
- Produce and maintain materials used in diagnostic tests for foreign animal disease;
- Test and evaluate vaccines for foreign animal diseases, and maintain the North American foot-and-mouth disease vaccine bank; and
- Train veterinarians and animal health professionals in the diagnosis and recognition of foreign animal diseases at PIADC and at other domestic and international locations.[107]

Plum Island's website (www.ars.usda.gov/plum/) contains information on center operations. Available materials include descriptions of foot-and-mouth disease research, African horse sickness research, African swine fever virus research, foreign animal diseases, and laboratory safety procedures.

U.S. Secret Service

The U.S. Secret Service was created in 1865, as part of the Department of the Treasury, to combat counterfeiting and is responsible for protecting the president and vice president and their immediate families, former presidents, distinguished foreign visitors to the United States, and official U.S. representatives performing special missions abroad. It also provides security at the White House, other presidential and vice presidential residences, and foreign diplomatic residences in the United States.[108]

The Secret Service's website (www.secretservice.gov/) provides an agency historical timeline; press releases; information about the Secret Service's protective, forensic, and investigative activities; and listings and contact information for agency field offices. In addition, access is provided to relevant studies produced by the Justice Department's National Institute of Justice such as *Threat Assessment: An Approach to Prevent Targeted Violence* (1995) and *Protective Intelligence Threat Assessment Investigations: A Guide for State and Local Law Enforcement Officials* (1998) along with the text of scholarly journal articles such as "Assassination in the United States: An Operational Study of Recent Assassins, Attackers, and Near-Lethal Approachers" (1999) and "Assessing Threats of Targeted Group Violence: Contributions from Social Psychology" (1999).

Transportation Security Administration

The Transportation Security Administration (TSA) was created in 2001 as a Department of Transportation agency in response to the September 11 terrorist attacks.[109] TSA, which is to provide passenger and cargo security at U.S. airports, became part of DHS on March 1, 2003.[110]

The website www.tsa.dot.gov/ provides numerous information resources about TSA's mission and operations. Available materials include lists of permitted and prohibited items for passenger air travel, travel preparation tips, employment opportunities, business contractor opportunities, listings of aviation security laws and regulations, press releases, and statements and speeches made by TSA officials.

Available documents produced by the Department of Transportation and the Federal Aviation Administration (FAA) include *Criminal Acts against Aviation* (1996–2001), excerpts from the 1997 White House Commission on Aviation Security report, *Report to Congress on Air Cargo Security* (1998), *Aviation Security Advisory Committee* meeting transcripts (1995–present), and updates on TSA progress in meeting congressionally mandated objectives.

■ Department of Justice

Established in 1870 and headed by the attorney general, the Department of Justice (DOJ) is responsible for enforcing U.S. laws and plays a key role in protecting against crime and subversion.[111] Overall access to DOJ resources and agencies can be found at www.usdoj.gov/.

Some Justice Department agencies with national security policy responsibilities such as INS and ODP were transferred to DHS in late 2002 or early 2003. Other national security–related entities remaining in DOJ include the Computer Crime and Intellectual Property Section (CCIPS), the Drug Enforcement Administration (DEA), the Executive Office for Immigration Review (EOIR), the Federal Bureau of Investigation (FBI), the Office of Inspector General, the National Drug Intelligence Center (NDIC), and the Office of Intelligence Policy and Review (OIPR).

Computer Crime and Intellectual Property Section

The Computer Crime and Intellectual Property Section (CCIPS) of DOJ produces and maintains the website www.cybercrime.gov. CCIPS responsibilities include focusing on computer and intellectual property crime, advising federal prosecutors and law enforcement agencies, commenting upon and proposing relevant legislation, coordinating initiatives combating international computer crime, and training law enforcement groups. Subjects of expertise possessed by CCIPS personnel include encryption, electronic privacy statutes, searching and seizing computers, e-commerce, hacker investigations, and intellectual property crimes.[112]

Available resources at www.cybercrime.gov/ include an introductory video from the attorney general, links to relevant federal computer crime statutes, summaries of recently prosecuted computer crime court cases, press releases, speeches and congressional testimony by CCIPS personnel, information on how to report Internet-related crimes, and details of international efforts to combat computer crime.

Examples of available reports are *The Electronic Frontier: The Challenge of Unlawful Conduct Involving the Use of the Internet* (2000), *Computer Records and the Federal Rules of Evidence* (2001), *Field Guidance on New Authorities That Relate to Computer Crime and Electronic Evidence Enacted in the USA Patriot Act of 2001* (2001), *It's Not Just Fun and "War Games"—Juveniles and Computer Crime* (2001), and *Searching and Seizing Computers and Obtaining Electronic Evidence in Criminal Investigations* (2002).

Counterespionage Section

Located within DOJ's Criminal Division, the Counterespionage Section (CS) is responsible for investigating and prosecuting cases covering national security, foreign relations, and the exporting of military and strategic commodities and technology. CS authorizes prosecution of criminal cases involving espionage, sabotage, neutrality, and atomic energy. It advises U.S. Attorney's Offices and investigative agencies on eighty-eight federal statutes affecting national security such as the Classified Information Procedures Act and the Foreign Agents Registration Act.[113]

The website www.usdoj.gov/criminal/iss.html provides information about ISS activities. Accessible resources include questions and answers about the Foreign Agents Registration Act and this statute's mandated *Semiannual Report* from 1997 to 2002.

Drug Enforcement Administration

The Drug Enforcement Administration (DEA), established in 1973, enforces federal narcotics and controlled substances laws and regulations. DEA investigates major narcotic violators operating at interstate and international levels; seizes assets originating in and intended for illegal drug trafficking; manages a national narcotics intelligence system; coordinates anti-drug enforcement activities with federal, state, and local law enforcement authorities; cooperates in anti-drug efforts with foreign counterpart agencies; and exchanges in training, scientific research, and information to support drug traffic control and prevention.[114]

DEA's website (www.dea.gov/) provides information about the agency's programs and activities. Materials include descriptions of major federal drug laws such as the Controlled Substances Act; listings of recent cases and major operations; detailed descriptions of DEA program areas such as foreign cooperative investigations, forensics, intelligence, money laundering, and the Southwest Border Initiative program; news releases; and speeches and congressional testimony by DEA officials.

DEA intelligence reports are particularly helpful for those wishing to study the national security implications of international drug trafficking. Reports accessible on the website include *Hong Kong's Changing Role in Drug Trafficking* (1999), *The Mexican Heroin Trade* (2000), *Price Dynamics of Southeast Asian Heroin* (2001), *The Drug Trade in the Caribbean: A Threat Assessment* (2002), *Afghanistan Country Brief* (2001), *Target America: Traffickers, Terrorists, and Your Kids: A National Symposium on Narco-Terrorism* (2001), *Pakistan Country Brief* (2002), *The Drug Trade in Colombia: A Threat Assessment* (2002), and *Drugs and Terrorism: A New Perspective* (2002).

Executive Office for Immigration Review

The Executive Office for Immigration Review (EOIR) was created in 1983 through an internal DOJ reorganization, which combined the Board of Immigration Appeals with the position of immigration judge, which had been under the jurisdiction of INS.[115] EOIR administers and interprets federal immigration laws and regulations by conducting immigration court proceedings, appellate reviews, and administrative hearings in individual cases. These responsibilities are carried out by the Board of Immigration Appeals, which hears appeals of decisions made by immigration judges, INS district directors, and other immigration officials; the Office of the Chief Immigration Judge, which is responsible for overseeing all U.S. immigration courts and proceedings; and the Office of the Chief Administrative Hearing Officer, which is responsible for taking care of cases involving employer sanctions, document fraud, and immigration-related employment discrimination.[116] Detailed information about EOIR activities can be found at www.usdoj.gov/eoir/. Available resources include the text of legal decisions, forms, employment opportunities, press releases, and listings of local immigration courts with the text of their operating procedures. Individual publications include *Asylum Statistics,* by nationality (fiscal years 1997–2001), *Classified Information in Immigration Court Proceedings* (1998), *Statistical Yearbook* (fiscal years 2000–2001), and *Board of Immigration Appeals Practice Manual* (2002).

Federal Bureau of Investigation

The Federal Bureau of Investigation was established in 1908 by the attorney general, who wanted DOJ investigations handled by in-house staff. The FBI is responsible for investigating violations of federal law except those explicitly assigned to other federal agencies by legislative or executive action. FBI responsibilities encompass various areas in criminal and civil law along with national security. Particular emphasis is placed on areas such as counterterrorism, counterintelligence, cybercrime, international and national organized crime, drug matters, and financial crimes. In addition,

> ## USA PATRIOT Act
>
> Enacted in October 2001, in the immediate aftermath of the September 11 terrorist attacks, the United and Strengthening America by Providing Appropriate Tools Required to Intercept and Obstruct Terrorism Act, or USA PATRIOT Act, sought to prevent such attacks.
>
> Areas covered by the USA PATRIOT Act were tracking and gathering communications during criminal investigations, foreign intelligence investigations, and money laundering. Examples of penal provisions within the statute are permitting law enforcement personnel to register, trap, and trace orders for electronic communications such as e-mail; permitting authorities to intercept communications to and from trespassers within a computer system; increasing the number of judges on the Foreign Intelligence Surveillance Act court from seven to eleven; permitting court-ordered access to any tangible item beyond business records; permitting the Treasury Department to issue regulations under which securities brokers and other financial advisers must report suspicious activity; imposing measures to combat foreign money laundering; establishing minimum customer identity standards and record-keeping requirements; encouraging financial industries and law enforcement agencies to share information on suspected money laundering and terrorist activities; and allowing the Justice Department to collect DNA (deoxyribonucleic acid) samples from prisoners convicted of any federal crime or terrorism.
>
> The USA PATRIOT Act has supporters who argue that it has been successful in deterring further terrorist attacks in the United States and critics who complain that it infringes on civil liberties. Controversy over this act and its provisions shows no signs of abating.

the FBI offers cooperative services to local, state, and foreign law enforcement agencies such as fingerprint identification, forensics, police training, and online communication and information services for the law enforcement communities.[117]

The FBI's website (www.fbi.gov/) contains information on the investigation into the 2001 anthrax attacks in the Washington, D.C., area, congressional testimony by the director and other FBI officials, press releases, bureau employment opportunities, and photos and biographical information on the most wanted terrorists. National security–related information resources include publications such as *Terrorism in the United States* (1996–1999), *CONPLAN: United States Government Interagency Domestic Terrorism Concept of Operations Plan* (2001), and *The 35 Groups on the U.S. State Department's Designated Foreign Terrorist Organization List* (2002).

An additional noteworthy feature of the FBI's website is its "Freedom of Information Act" (FOIA) section (http://foia.fbi.gov/), which has documents on historic criminal cases and investigations. Examples of documentary materials released in 1999 include espionage investigation reports on British Soviet spies Guy Burgess, Donald MacLean, and Kim Philby; similar material on U.S. Soviet spy Owen Lattimore; and information on the Bowtie investigation, which lead to the 1963 downfall of British defense minister John Profumo due to his relationship with a prostitute who was also involved with a Soviet naval attaché. FBI materials released in 2001on the 1983 downing of Korean Airlines Flight 007 are another example of the rich resources available on the FOIA website.

National Drug Intelligence Center

The National Drug Intelligence Center (NDIC) is located in Johnstown, Pennsylvania, and was created in 1993. The General Counterdrug Intelligence Plan, signed by President Clinton in 2000, designated NDIC as the principal center for strategic domestic counterdrug intelligence. Its missions include supporting national policymakers and law enforcement with strategic domestic drug intelligence, supporting intelligence community counterdrug efforts, and producing national, regional, and state drug threat assessments.[118]

Information about NDIC and its publications can be found at www.usdoj.gov/ndic/. On the site are *Heroin Distribution in Three Cities* (2000), *National Drug Threat Assessment 2002* (2001), *United States–Canada Border Drug Threat Assessment* (2001), *California Southern District Threat Assessment* (2001), *Hawaii Drug Threat Assessment* (2002), and *Intelligence Brief: National Drugs Threat Assessment: Marijuana Update* (2002).

Office of Inspector General

The Justice Department's Office of Inspector General (OIG) seeks to promote economy and efficiency within DOJ and enforces civil and criminal laws, regulations, and ethical standards by investigating individuals and organizations allegedly involved in financial, contractual, or criminal misconduct in administering DOJ programs and operations.[119]

Information on the OIG and access to the office's reports can be found at www.usdoj.gov/oig/. National security–related reports include *Border Patrol Drug Interdiction Activities on the Southwest Border* (1998); *Top Management Challenges in the Department of Justice* (2000–2002); *Status of IDENT/IAFIS Integration,* which deals with FBI and INS fingerprint identification systems (2001); *Departmental Critical Infrastructure Protection Planning for the Protection of Physical Infrastructure* (2001); *Follow-Up Report on the Border Patrol's Efforts to Improve Northern Border Security* (2002); *The Federal Bureau of Investigation's Control over Weapons and Laptop Computers* (2002); *A Review of the Federal Bureau of Investigation's Counterterrorism Program: Threat Assessment, Strategic Planning, and Resource Management* (2002); and *Review of the Office of International Affairs Role in the International Extradition of Fugitives* (2002).

Office of Intelligence Policy and Review

The Office of Intelligence Policy and Review (OIPR) advises the attorney general on U.S. national security activities. OIPR prepares and files applications for electronic surveillance and physical search under the 1978 Foreign Intelligence Surveillance

Act, provides national security law and policy advice to other government agencies, represents DOJ on interagency committees, comments on proposed legislation affecting intelligence, and advises the attorney general and agencies such as the CIA, DOD, and FBI on legal, regulatory, and procedural questions concerning domestic and foreign intelligence operations.[120]

OIPR's website (www.usdoj.gov/oipr/) contains information about the office's mission and links to its *Annual Foreign Intelligence Surveillance Act Report to Congress* (1996–2001) documenting the number of search applications it requested from the Foreign Intelligence Surveillance Court.

Office of International Affairs

The Office of International Affairs (OIA) advises and assists the attorney general and other senior DOJ officials on international criminal matters. OIA coordinates the extradition of international fugitives and international evidence gathering; collaborates with the State Department in negotiating international criminal treaties, conventions, and agreements; participates on various United Nations committees and other international organizations to resolve global law enforcement issues such as drug trafficking, organized crime, cybercrime, terrorism, and money laundering; and has exchange programs with selected foreign government law enforcement agencies.[121]

The website www.usdoj.gov/criminal/oia.html contains descriptions of OIA activities and of specific programs such as the Interagency International Fugitive Outlook program along with links to DOJ publications such as *Department of Justice Assessment of the Increased Risk of Terrorist or Other Criminal Activity Associated with Posting Off-Site Consequence Analysis Information on the Internet* (2000).

Department of State

The First Congress established the Department of Foreign Affairs on July 27, 1789. It was renamed the Department of State on September 15, 1789. The State Department's mission is advising the president in formulating and executing U.S. foreign policy and promoting long-term U.S. security and well-being in the international community. It carries out these responsibilities through ongoing interaction with the American public, Congress, and other U.S. government agencies; negotiating treaties and agreements with foreign countries and international governmental organizations; and representing the United States at the United Nations and in other international forums. Overall information about State Department programs can be found at www.state.gov/.[122]

Although traditionally associated with diplomacy, State Department activities also encompass the formulation and implementation of national security policy. These policies and the information resources describing them are produced by such State Department entities as the Bureau of Arms Control (BAC), Bureau of Diplomatic Security (BDS), Bureau of International Narcotics and Law Enforcement Affairs (INL), Bureau of Nonproliferation (BN), Bureau of Political-Military Affairs

(BPMA), Bureau of Verification and Compliance (BVC), coordinator for counterterrorism (CT), Historian's Office, Office of Inspector General, Directorate of Defense Trade Controls, and Office of War Crimes Issues (OWCI).

Bureau of Arms Control

The Bureau of Arms Control (BAC) maintains responsibility for formulating U.S. foreign policy concerning conventional, chemical and biological, and nuclear forces; supporting arms control negotiations; implementing existing arms control agreements; and advising the secretary of state on national security issues such as nuclear testing and missile defense.[123]

Further information about BAC can be found on its website (www.state.gov/t/ac/). Available information resources include speeches by the Undersecretary for arms control and international security and fact sheets such as *Missile Defense and Deterrence* (2001), *Chemical Weapons Convention State Parties and Signatories* (2002), *Parties and Signatories of the Biological Weapons Convention* (current as of November 17, 2003), and *Defending against Biological Terrorism* (2002). Further site content includes descriptions of the Office of Conventional Arms Control, Office of Chemical and Biological Weapons Conventions, Office of International Security Negotiations, Office of Strategic and Theater Defenses, Office of Strategic Negotiations and Implementation, Office of Strategic Transition, and Office of Public Affairs and Public Diplomacy.

BAC's website also includes the text of currently active bilateral and multilateral arms control agreements the United States adheres to, including the Nuclear Risk Reduction Centers Agreement (1988), Ballistic Missile Launch Notification Agreement (1988), Convention Forces in Europe Treaty (1990 and 1996), the Chemical Weapons Convention (2002), and U.S.-Russia Strategic Offensive Reduction Treaty (Moscow Treaty) (2002). Also posted are the text of arms control agreements the United States no longer adheres to, such as the Antiballistic Missile Treaty (1972), and an archive of Clinton administration arms control activities from 1997 to 2000 featuring reports such as *Adherence to and Compliance with Arms Control Agreements* (1996–1998) and *World Military Expenditures and Arms Transfers* (1996–1998).

Bureau of Diplomatic Security

Bureau of Diplomatic Security (BDS) responsibilities encompass providing security for personnel working in all U.S. diplomatic facilities around the world, the secretary of state, the U.S. ambassador to the United Nations, and foreign dignitaries other than heads of state who visit the United States as well as for more than ninety domestic State Department facilities. BDS is also responsible for investigating passport and visa fraud, conducting personnel security investigations, and assisting foreign embassies and consulates in the United States in providing security for their facilities and personnel. It has carried out such activities since its establishment in 1916 by Secretary of State Robert Lansing.[124]

The BDS website (www.state.gov/m/ds/) contains additional information about bureau programs and operations as well as a link to the Overseas Security Advisory Council website (www.ds-osac.org/). The council facilitates the exchange of security information between the U.S. government and private sector American companies operating abroad. Examples of publications on the BDS website are the annual *Political Violence against Americans* (1988–2002), *Emergency Planning Guidelines for American Business Abroad* (1994), *Issues in Global Crime* (1998), *Countering Terrorism: Security Suggestions for U.S. Business Representatives Abroad* (1999), and *Responding to a Chemical-Biological Threat in the U.S.* (2001).

Bureau of International Narcotics and Law Enforcement Affairs

The Bureau of International Narcotics and Law Enforcement Affairs (INL) advises the president, secretary of state, other State Department bureaus, and other U.S. government agencies on developing policies and programs to combat international narcotics and crime. INL's programs support State Department initiatives to reduce the entry of illegal drugs into the United States and to minimize the impact of international crime on the United States and its citizens. In addition, INL counternarcotic and anticrime programs assist the war on terrorism by facilitating the promotion of modernization and supporting operational activities by foreign criminal justice and law enforcement agencies responsible for counterterrorism activities.[125]

Available resources on the INL website (www.state.gov/g/inl/) include congressional budget requests and testimony by State Department officials, announcements of U.S. international drug policy developments, and press releases. Information resources include the following fact sheets: *Convention against Transnational Organized Crime and Supplementary Protocols* (2001), *Why Americans Should Care about Plan Colombia* (2001), and *The Nexus between Drug Trafficking and Terrorism* (2002). INL reports include the annual *International Narcotics Control Strategy* (1996–2001), *Peru Investigation Report: The April 20, 2001, Peruvian Shootdown Incident* (2001), *Aerial Eradication of Illicit Cocoa in Colombia* (2002), and *End-Use Monitoring Report 2001* (2002), which summarizes U.S. counterdrug support efforts under its International Narcotics Control Effort program.

Bureau of Nonproliferation

The Bureau of Nonproliferation (BN) provides leadership for U.S. efforts to prevent the spread of weapons of mass destruction such as nuclear, chemical, and biological weapons and their missile delivery systems; secure nuclear materials in the former Soviet Union; and promote nuclear safety and materials protection internationally. BN also leads U.S. efforts in promoting responsibility, transparency, and restraint in international conventional arms and sensitive dual-use technology transfers, provides primary interagency federal leadership on nonproliferation issues, leads major nonproliferation negotiations and discussions with other countries, and participates in all nonproliferation dialogues with the international community.[126]

The website www.state.gov/t/np/ contains speeches and congressional testimony by BN personnel, nonproliferation policy developments news, the text of major nonproliferation agreements the United States adheres to, and links to the office's website maintained during the Clinton administration. Numerous fact sheets on nonproliferation issues are provided, including *The Treaty on the Non-Proliferation of Nuclear Weapons: A Global Success* (2001), *African Nuclear Free Weapons Zone* (2001), *Export Controls on High Performance* (2001), *Missile Technology Control Regime* (2001), *Nuclear Suppliers Group* (2001), *Defending against Biological Terrorism* (2002), *Continuation of the National Emergency with Respect to Risk of Nuclear Proliferation Created by the Accumulation of Weapons—Usable Fissile Material in the Territory of the Russian Federation* (2002), and a General Accounting Office report *Nonproliferation: Strategy Needed to Strengthen Multilateral Export Control Regimes* (2002).

Bureau of Political-Military Affairs

Bureau of Political-Military Affairs (BPMA) responsibilities cover regional security policy, security assistance, arms transfers, confidence and security building measures, humanitarian demining programs, critical infrastructure protection, burden sharing, complex contingency operations, and contingency planning. BPMA advances U.S. national security objectives by managing bilateral political-military relations and formal security interactions with more than thirty countries, maintaining global access for U.S. military forces, controlling access to militarily critical technologies and promoting responsible U.S. defense trade by administering defense trade controls, informing Congress on defense burden-sharing issues, and working with other governmental and military agencies to coordinate responses to military options and deployment matters.[127]

Further information about BPMA activities can be found on its website (www.state.gov/t/pm/). Site contents include descriptions of BPMA component parts such as the Office of International Security Operations, Office of Contingency Planning and Peacekeeping, and Office of Mine Action Initiatives and Partnerships as well as speeches by BPMA officials, press releases, and an archive of BPMA activities from 1997 to 2000. Additional accessible resources include the following fact sheets: *The Inter-American Convention against the Illicit Manufacturing of and Trafficking in Firearms, Ammunition, Explosives, and Other Related Materials* (2002) and *United Nations Instrument for Reporting Military Expenditures* (2002). Reports available include *To Walk the Earth in Safety: The United States Commitment to Humanitarian Demining* (1999–2002), *Foreign Military Training and DOD Engagement Activities of Interest* (2000–2002), *Generic Political Reports Military Plan Format: Multilateral Complex Contingency Operation* (2001), *The U.S. Approach to Combatting the Spread of Small Arms* (2001), and *U.S. Humanitarian Mine Action in the Middle East: A Six-Year Progress Report* (2002).

Bureau of Verification and Compliance

The Bureau of Verification and Compliance (BVC) was created by Congress and began operations in 2000. BVC's mission is supporting the secretary of state and undersecretary of state for arms control and international security in identifying, negotiating, implementing, assessing compliance, and ensuring optimum verification of arms control and nonproliferation agreements and commitments.[128]

Further information about BVC activities can be found at www.state.gov/t/vc/. The site has the text of arms control treaties and information about the Foster Fellows Visiting Scholars Program, which provides opportunities for scholars in fields such as biology, engineering, history, and military operations analysis to work on arms control issues with the State Department. Accessible information resources include the November 1, 2002, speech of Under Secretary of State for Arms Control and International Security John Bolton, "The International Aspects of Terrorism and Weapons of Mass Destruction"; the current edition of *World Military Expenditures and Arms Transfers, 1999–2000* (2001); and archival materials such as *World Military Expenditures and Arms Transfers* (1996–1998), *Adherence to and Compliance with Arms Control Agreements* (1996–1998), and *Arms Control, Nonproliferation, and Disarmament Studies: Annual Report to Congress* (1998–1999).

Coordinator for Counterterrorism

The CT coordinates all U.S. government efforts to improve counterterrorism cooperation with foreign governments, chairs the Interagency Working Group on Counterterrorism and the State Department's terrorism task forces that coordinate responses to ongoing major international terrorist incidents, and develops and implements U.S. counterterrorism policy.[129]

The website www.state.gov/s/ct/ provides information about U.S. counterterrorism activities including announcements of significant U.S. and foreign policy actions, information on the Rewards for Justice program that seeks to capture international terrorists and war criminals, terrorism-related speeches by U.S. policymakers, and fact sheets such as *Comprehensive List of Terrorist Groups Identified under Executive Order 13224* (2001), *Foreign Emergency Support Team* (2002), *Foreign Terrorist Organizations* (2002), *Terrorist Interdiction Program* (2002), and *Yemen: The Economic Costs of Terrorism* (2002).

Reports produced under CT auspices include *America's Overseas Presence in the 21st Century* (1999), *Report of the Accountability Review Boards on the Embassy Bombings in Nairobi and Dar es Salaam on August 7, 1998* (1999), *Report on Foreign Terrorist Organizations* (1999 and 2001), *Patterns of Global Terrorism 2000 and 2001* (2001–2002), *The Global War on Terrorism: The First 100 Days* (2001), and *U.S. Report to the United Nations Counterterrorism Committee* (2001).

Directorate of Defense Trade Controls

Located within the State Department's Bureau of Political-Military Affairs, the Directorate of Defense Trade Controls (DDTC) is responsible for controlling the export and temporary import of defense articles and defense services covered by the United States Munition List (USML), which includes weapons categories as diverse as firearms, tanks and military vehicles, and nuclear weapons design and test equipment. DDTC's primary missions include making final decisions on license applications for defense trade exports and dealing with issues of defense trade compliance, enforcement, and reporting while also administering provisions of the Arms Export Control Act and International Traffic in Arms Regulations.[130]

The website www.pmdtc.org/ contains a variety of information about DDTC's activities, including announcements of new laws and regulations affecting international arms sales and defense products licensing and relevant registration forms. Publicly accessible information resources include *International Trafficking in Arms Regulations* from the U.S. government's *Code of Federal Regulations*, *Instructions for the Permanent Export of Firearms and Ammunition* (1999), *Commercial Communications Satellite Components, Systems, Parts, Accessories, and Associated Technical Data to U.S. Allies: Guidelines for Preparing License Applications for Exports* (2000), *Defense Trade Controls—List of Debarred Parties July 1988–March 2002* (2002), and *Country Embargo Reference Chart* (2002).

Historian's Office

The State Department's Historian's Office is responsible for preparing and publishing *Foreign Relations of the United States* (FRUS), which serves as the official documentary record of U.S. foreign policy. The Historian's Office also researches and writes historical studies on U.S. diplomacy for State Department and other federal policymakers as well as for the general public.[131]

The Historian's Office website (www.state.gov/r/pa/ho/) contains the text of some FRUS volumes as well as other works of interest to those studying U.S. national security policy. Accessible FRUS volumes include *1945–1950: Emergence of the Intelligence Establishment* (1996), *1961–1963: Volume XIV Berlin Crisis, 1961–1962* (1993), *1964–1968: Volume X National Security Policy* (2001), and *1964–1968: Volume XX Arab-Israeli Dispute, 1967–1968* (2001).

Additional national security–related information resources include *History of the Department of State during the Clinton Presidency, 1993–2001* (2001), *Significant Terrorist Incidents, 1961–2001: A Brief Chronology* (2001), and *The United States and the Global Coalition against Terrorism, September–December 2001: A Brief Chronology* (2001).

Office of Inspector General

The State Department's Office of Inspector General serves as an independent and objective evaluator of State Department operations and activities. It investigates fraud, waste, and mismanagement within these programs and reports them to the secretary of state and Congress while also striving to promote effective and cost-conscious State Department programs and operations.[132] Located at http://oig.state.gov/ is information about the Office of Audits, Office of Inspections, Office of Security and Intelligence Oversight, and Office of Investigations. Examples of publicly accessible reports on national security topics are *Protecting Classified Documents at State Department Headquarters* (1999), *Critical Infrastructure Protection: The Depart-*

ment Can Enhance Its International Leadership and Its Own Cybersecurity (2001), *Classified Connectivity Program: Problems and Challenges* (2002), and *Review of Non-Immigrant Visa Issuance Policies and Procedures* (2002).

Office of War Crimes

The Office of War Crimes Issues (OWCI) advises the secretary of state on U.S. attempts to address serious international human rights violations around the world. These violations include widespread atrocities such as crimes against humanity, genocide, and war crimes. OWCI coordinates U.S. support for international criminal tribunals for Rwanda and the former Yugoslavia and assists in creating and operating other courts or judicial systems for bringing offenders of international humanitarian law to justice.[133]

OWCI's website (www.state.gov/s/wci/) provides additional information about the office's activities. Accessible materials include press releases, speeches by OWCI personnel, and fact sheets such as *The International Criminal Court* (2002) and *War Crimes Wanted Poster* (2002). Available reports from OWCI's Clinton administration archival site include *Erasing History: Ethnic Cleansing in Kosovo* (1999) and *Ethnic Cleansing in Kosovo: An Accounting* (1999).

Department of Transportation

The Department of Transportation (DOT) was established in 1966. DOT's mission is coordinating and effectively administering federal transportation programs and developing national transportation policies and programs to produce fast, safe, convenient, and low-cost transportation.[134]

Departmental information on DOT can be found at its website (www.dot.gov/). Some national security–related sections of DOT, such as the Coast Guard, have been transferred to DHS. Other entities that remain under DOT jurisdiction are the Federal Aviation Administration, the Office of Inspector General, the Maritime Administration (MARAD), and the Office of Assistant Secretary for Aviation and International Affairs.

Federal Aviation Administration

The Federal Aviation Agency was established in 1958 and was incorporated into DOT under its present name, the Federal Aviation Administration (FAA), in 1967. Its responsibilities include assigning, maintaining, and enhancing safety and security in air traffic; regulating commerce in ways that promote safety and fulfill national defense requirements; controlling navigable airspace use and regulating civil and military operations in that airspace to enhance the safety and efficiency of those activities; developing and operating common air traffic control and navigation systems for civilian and military aircraft; assisting law enforcement agencies in enforcing laws on regulating controlled substances consistent with aviation safety concerns; and regulating U.S. commercial space transportation.[135]

The FAA's website (www.faa.gov/) includes speeches, congressional testimony, and information about regulatory and policy actions taken by the FAA. A number of reports and other materials relating to aviation security and international aviation are available, including publications from FAA's advisory circulars series such as *AC 108-3: Screening of Persons Carrying U.S. Classified Material* (1982), *AC 210-5B: Military Flying Activities* (1990), and *AC 431.35-1: Expected Casualty Calculation for Commercial Space Launch and Reentry Missions* (2000).

Maritime Administration

The Maritime Administration (MARAD) is responsible for developing and maintaining a well-balanced U.S. merchant marine to support U.S. domestic and foreign waterborne commerce, enabling the merchant marine to serve as a naval and military adjunct in wartime or national emergency, and ensuring that the United States has sufficient shipbuilding and repair facilities, efficient ports and intermodal land and water transport systems, and adequate reserve shipping capacity in national emergencies.[136]

Further details about MARAD programs and activities can be found at www.marad.dot.gov/. Through this site, users can access resources such as security advisories for U.S.-flagged vessels, mission descriptions for MARAD component parts, information on applying for port security grants, a listing of recent recipients of these grants and the amount of money they received, and statistics on the nature of cargo handled at individual U.S. ports. Specific publications include *U.S. Waterborne Commerce* (selected years), *Maritime Security Reports* (1995–2001), *National Port Readiness Network* (1997), *A Report to Congress on the Status of the Public Ports of the United States 1996–1997* (1998), *An Assessment of the U.S. Marine Transportation System* (1999), *U.S. Foreign Waterborne Traffic* (2000–2001), *MARAD Annual Report 2001* (2001), *Military Ships under Construction as of April 1, 2001* (2001), and *Reserve Fleet Manual* (2002).

Office of Assistant Secretary for Aviation and International Affairs

The Office of Assistant Secretary for Aviation and International Affairs is responsible for developing, reviewing, and coordinating international transportation policy, licensing U.S. and foreign carriers to serve in international air transportation, conducting carrier fitness evaluations for carriers serving in the United States, developing policies to support DOT in bilateral and multilateral aviation and maritime negotiations with foreign governments, developing policies on various international transportation issues, and arranging and coordinating agreements with foreign governments for exchanging current scientific and technical information.[137]

Detailed information about this office and its operations can be found on its website (http://ostpxweb.dot.gov/aviation/intro.htm). Materials cover a variety of resources on domestic aviation industry developments and competition along with similar data for international aviation. Representative samples include *Transatlantic Deregulation: The Alliance Network Effect* (2000), *U.S. International Air Passenger and Freight Statistics* (2000–2001), samples of bilateral and multilateral open skies agreements the United States has with foreign countries and international governmental organizations, lists of international aviation agreements the United States participates in, and materials on the domestic aviation industry and competition within that industry.

Office of Inspector General

DOT's inspector general is responsible for conducting and supervising audits and investigations of DOT programs and operations; preventing and detecting fraud, waste, and abuse in these programs; reviewing existing laws and regulations affecting DOT and making recommendations concerning them; and ensuring that Congress and the secretary of transportation are fully informed about problems involving DOT programs and operations.[138]

Available materials on the website www.oig.dot.gov/ include press releases, coverage of ongoing investigations, congressional testimony by OIG officials, and the text of recent semiannual reports to Congress. Examples of national security–related reports produced by OIG are *Federal Air Marshall Program* (1997), *Security for Passenger Terminals and Vessels, U.S. Coast Guard* (1998), *National Aviation Safety Inspection Program* (1999), *Head-Quarters Computer Network Security* (2000), *Operations Systems Center Computer Security and Controls, U.S. Coast Guard* (2001), and *Report on Information Security Program, Department of Transportation* (2002).

Department of the Treasury

The Department of the Treasury was created on September 2, 1789, and is the oldest of the federal executive departments. Its responsibilities cover a wide variety of domestic and international economic issues including formulating and recommending domestic and international financial, economic, and tax policy; managing the public debt; manufacturing coins and currency; and controlling assets of restricted countries, individuals, and organizations in the United States.[139] Overall access to Treasury Department resources is available at www.treas.gov/. Treasury Department entities with national security–related information resources are the Office of Enforcement (OE), Office of Foreign Assets Control (OFAC), and Office of Inspector General.

Office of Enforcement

The Office of Enforcement (OE), headed by the Treasury undersecretary for enforcement, is responsible for strengthening the Treasury Department's law and regulatory enforcement efforts. Areas covered by its institutional mission include counterterrorist financing, counterterrorism, money laundering and financial crimes, counterfeiting, drug interdiction, violent crime, economic sanctions, training, and tariff and trade enforcement.[140]

OE's website (www.treas.gov/offices/enforcement/) contains an organizational chart; links to the Executive Office for Asset Forfeiture, the Financial Crimes

Enforcement Network, and the Office of Foreign Assets Control; the text of Executive Order 13224, *Blocking Terrorist Property and Designation of Foreign Terrorist Organizations* (2001–present); information about the Terrorist Financing Rewards Program; and reports such as *National Money Laundering Strategy* (2001–2002).

Office of Foreign Assets Control

Located within the Treasury Department's Office of Enforcement, the Office of Foreign Assets Control (OFAC) was created in December 1950 by President Truman when he declared a national emergency under the Trading with the Enemy Act and blocked Chinese and North Korean assets subject to U.S. jurisdiction.[141] Over the ensuing half century, OFAC's responsibilities have increased. They currently entail administering and enforcing economic and trade sanctions as part of U.S. foreign and national security policy goals against selected foreign countries, terrorists, drug traffickers, and individuals and organizations involved in proliferating weapons of mass destruction. OFAC authority is derived from presidential wartime and national emergency powers and congressional legislation to impose transaction controls and freeze foreign assets under U.S. jurisdiction. Many of these sanctions are based on United Nations or other international mandates, possess multilateral scope, and include close cooperation with allied governments.[142]

OFAC's website (www.ustreas.gov/offices/enforcement/ofac/) provides detailed information about U.S. foreign sanctions policy. Examples of the resources provided are upcoming OFAC-sponsored workshops on foreign sanctions; an e-mail subscription service notifying users of changes in U.S. sanctions policies, laws, and regulations; forms; and the ability to comment on proposed regulations.

A number of documentary resources are provided, including *Iraq: What You Need to Know about the U.S. Embargo* (1999), *Guidance Payments for Iraqi-Origin Petroleum Pursuant to Licensed Purchase* (2000), *Nonproliferation: What You Need to Know about Treasury Restrictions* (2001), *Narcotics: What You Need to Know about U.S. Sanctions against Drug Traffickers* (2002), *Foreign Assets Control Regulations for the Financial Community* (2002), *Terrorist Assets Report Calendar Year 2001: Annual Report to the Congress on Assets in the United States of Terrorist Countries and International Terrorism Program Designees* (2002), *Specially Designated Nationals and Blocked Persons* (2003), *Terrorism: What You Need to Know about U.S. Sanctions* (2003), *U.S. Economic Sanctions: Concerns for Mariners* (2003).

Office of Inspector General

The Treasury Department's Office of Inspector General (OIG) was established in 1989 according to the Inspector General Act Amendments of 1988. OIG responsibilities include conducting and supervising audits and investigations of Treasury Department programs; promoting economy, efficiency, and effectiveness in these programs and operations; preventing and detecting fraud and abuse; and keeping the secretary of the Treasury and Congress informed about such problems and deficiencies.[143]

The website www.treas.gov/offices/inspector-general/ provides a description of OIG operations; a hotline for contacting the office to report abuse, fraud, or waste; congressional testimony; and position vacancy information. Numerous reports covering national security topics are available, including *Integrity Oversight Review of the United States Customs Service* (2000), *Money Laundering: Review of Financial Crimes Enforcement Network's Use of Artificial Intelligence to Combat Money Laundering* (2001), *Financial Management: Review of Assertions Included in the United States Secret Service's Fiscal Year 2001 Annual Report of Drug Control Funds* (2002), *Narcotics Interdiction: Remote Video Inspection System Deployment Goals Have Not Been Achieved* (2002), *Timeliness of Departmental Offices' Security Clearances Can Be Improved* (2002), and *Trade and Passenger Processing: Customs Personal Search Policies, Procedures, and Training Appear Reasonable* (2002).

Executive Office of the President

The president of the United States is authorized by the U.S. Constitution to be the commander in chief of the nation's armed forces.[144] Recent decades have seen presidential power on military and other issues exercised through the Executive Office of the President, which encompasses White House policy-making organs as diverse as the National Security Council, Office of Management and Budget (OMB), the Office of National Drug Control Policy (ONDCP), the Office of Science and Technology Policy (OSTP), the President's Critical Infrastructure Protection Board (PCIPB), and the White House Military Office (WHMO).[145] General information about presidential activities and policies can be found on the White House website (www.whitehouse.gov/) and information about Clinton administration activities and polices can be found at the Clinton Presidential Materials project website (www.clinton.archives.gov/) maintained by the National Archives and Records Administration.

Presidential Speeches, Proclamations, and Executive Orders

Presidential speeches, proclamations, and executive orders are important documents for those studying national security policy or other aspects of individual presidential administrations. Presidential speeches may be nationally televised addresses from the Oval Office or the annual State of the Union address before a joint session of Congress, the weekly Saturday morning radio address, comments made at a press conference, or remarks made at various locations before selected national or international audiences. Examples of national security–related addresses made by President George W. Bush that are available through the White House website are *President's Remarks at the United Nations General Assembly on Iraq* (2002) and *Remarks by the President at the Signing of H.R. 5005, The Homeland Security Act of 2002* (2002). Presidential speeches will include a transcript and perhaps RealAudio audio or video clips for listening or viewing. Presidential proclamations are announcements recognizing the historical and contemporary importance of individuals, organizations, and events and have no legal force. Besides appearing on the White House website, they run in the *Federal Register,* which is published every weekday by the National Archives and Records Administration. Recent presidential proclamations include *National Defense Transportation Day and National Transportation Week, 2001* (2001), *General Pulaski Memorial Day, 2002* (2002), and *National Employer Support of the Guard and Reserve Week, 2002* (2002).

Executive orders are presidential orders that have the force of law but do not require congressional approval. These orders are generally directed to executive branch agencies and are issued to implement the president's constitutional and statutory responsibilities for managing and leading the executive branch of the federal government.[146] Executive orders are also published in the *Federal Register* and are available on the White House website. Examples are *Executive Order on Terrorist Financing* (2001), *Afghanistan Combat Zone Executive Order* (2001), *Executive Order Further Amending Executive Order 10173, as Amended, Prescribing Regulations Relating to the Safeguarding of Vessels, Harbors, and Waterfront Facilities of the United States* (2002), and *Home Security Council Executive Order* (2002).

Other national security publications available on the White House website are *A Decade of Deception and Defiance: Saddam Hussein's Defiance of the United Nations* (2002), *National Strategy for Homeland Security* (2002), *Protecting Americans: Smallpox Vaccination Program* (2002), and *Rebuilding Afghanistan* (2002).

National Security Council Documents

Documents issued by the National Security Council (NSC) are key source materials for U.S. national security policy. These documents provide guidance to federal agencies and departments for executing and formulating national security policy.

The documents have gone by different names since the NSC was established in 1947. They were called National Security Action Memoranda (NSAM) during the Kennedy and Johnson administrations, National Security Decision Directives (NSDD) during the Reagan administration, and Presidential Decision Directives (PDD) during the Clinton administration. During the George W. Bush administration they were called National Security Presidential Directives (NSPD) and were supplemented by Homeland Security Presidential Directives (HSPD).

NSC documents are generally numbered by presidential administration. Many of the originals can be found at the National Archives or presidential libraries, which also may have them available on their websites. Some of this material may be found in the print *Federal Register* or its electronic version in "GPO Access." The Federation of American Scientists has listings and the text of many presidential national security documents accessible on its website (www.fas.org/irp/offdocs/direct.htm), including historically significant ones such as *NSC 68: United States Objectives and Programs* (1950), which outlined a proposed U.S. strategy for confronting the Union of Soviet Socialist Republics in the cold war.

National Security Council

The National Security Council (NSC) was created in 1947 by the National Security Act, which also established the Central Intelligence Agency and the Department of Defense.[147] NSC membership consists of the president, who also serves as NSC chair; the vice president; and the secretaries of defense, state, and Treasury. The chairman of the Joint Chiefs of Staff is the NSC's statutory military adviser, the director of Central Intelligence serves as the NSC's intelligence adviser, and the assistant to the president for national security affairs is also an NSC member. NSC and its professional staff serve as the president's primary forum for reviewing national security and foreign policy matters with senior presidential national security advisers and cabinet members. It advises and assists the president in executing U.S. national security policies and is the president's chief mechanism for coordinating these policies with various government agencies, which is done through documents such as National Security Decision Directives.[148]

NSC's website is accessible at www.whitehouse.gov/nsc/. Available information includes an organizational description, a biography of the national security adviser, and reports such as *History of the National Security Council, 1947–1997* (1997), *National Security Strategy of the United States of America* (2002), and *National Strategy to Combat Weapons of Mass Destruction* (2002). The Clinton administration's NSC website (http://clinton5.nara.gov/WH/EOP/NSC/html/NSC_Documents.html) provides access to a number of informative resources such as *The Clinton Administration's Policy on Critical Infrastructure Protection* (1998), *A National Security Strategy for a New Century* (1999), *National Plan for Information Systems Protection* (2000), and *International Crime Threat Assessment* (2000). Another noteworthy feature of the Clinton NSC website is listings of NSC meeting agenda topics arranged in chronological order from 1947 to 1992.

Office of Management and Budget

The Office of Management and Budget (OMB) was established within the EOP in 1939 as a result of a federal reorganization plan. OMB reviews, formulates, and coordinates management procedures and program goals among federal departments and agencies, controls administration of the federal budget, and provides the president with recommendations concerning budget proposals and pertinent legislative enactments. Besides preparing the budget, OMB assists the president by clearing and coordinating agency and departmental input on proposed legislation, developing regulatory reform and paperwork reduction proposals, assisting in preparing and approving proposed executive orders, planning and developing information systems to provide the president with program performance data, and improving the economy and efficiency of governmental programs and expenditures.[149]

Further information about OMB and its programs and responsibilities can be found at www.whitehouse.gov/omb/. Materials include an organization chart, information about governmental regulatory matters, statistical programs, guidelines and resolutions to follow regarding agency operations, information policy, information technology, and e-government from OMB's Office of Information and Regulatory Affairs, news releases, speeches by OMB officials, policy documents such as circulars, and various budget documents.

Numerous national security–related resources and data are provided by OMB. These materials can contain budgetary expenditures for individual agency programs such as weapons systems or various kinds of policy guidance. Budget expenditures are listed for the federal fiscal year, which runs from October 1 to September 30. Examples are *Budget of the U.S. Government: Fiscal Year 2005* (2004), with previous editions of this and related works dating back to fiscal year 1996 available at www.gpo.gov/usbudget/; *Analytical Perspective: Budget of the U.S. Government, Fiscal Year 2005* (2004); *Historical Tables: Budget of the U.S. Government, Fiscal Year 2005* (2004); *Fiscal Year 2001 Report to Congress on Federal Government Information Security Reform* (2001); *Annual Report to Congress on Combatting Terrorism* (2001–2002); *Report on Expenditures from the Emergency Response Fund* (2002–present), which covers emergency supplemental appropriations for recovery from the 2001 terrorist attacks; *OMB Final Sequestration Report to the President and Congress for Statistical Year 2003* (2002); *Memorandum 02-14: Additional Information Requirements for Overseas Combatting Terrorism and Homeland Security for the Fiscal Year 2004 Budget* (2002); and *Memorandum 03-04: Determination Orders for Organizing the Department of Homeland Security* (2003).

Office of National Drug Control Policy

The Office of National Drug Control Policy (ONDCP) was established by the National Narcotics Leadership Act of 1988, and its director is appointed by the president and subject to Senate confirmation. Responsibilities of the director and ONDCP include setting policies, objectives, priorities, and performance measurements for the U.S. drug control program; presenting a national drug control strategy; and advising the president on organization, management, budgetary, and personnel changes required for federal agencies involved in drug enforcement activities.[150]

ONDCP's website (www.whitehousedrugpolicy.gov/) provides information about the office's programs and a number of reports. Site contents include descriptions of the Office of Demand Reduction, Office of State and Local Affairs, and the deputy director for supply reduction; anti-drug media campaign information including video clips and a link to the www.theantidrug.com/ website featured in television public service advertisements; and overviews and descriptions of the effects of illicit drugs such as cocaine and heroin. A variety of information resources is available, including fact sheets and reports such as *Mission Accomplished: Advanced Technology Pursuit Boat Becomes Operational* (2001), *Measuring the Deterrent Effect of Enforcement Operations on Drug Smuggling, 1991–1999* (2001), *Counterdrug and Counterterror* (2002), *Training against Drugs and Terror* (2002), *National Drug Control Strategy* (2002), *Estimations of Cocaine Availability, 1996–2000* (2002), *U.S.-Colombia Initiative* (2002), *Breaking Heroin Sources of Supply* (2002), *International Money Laundering and Asset Forfeiture* (2002), *Bilateral Cooperation with Bolivia* (2002), and *Interdiction Operations* (2002).

ONDCP's website also provides links to drug policy reports produced by other U.S. government agencies, foreign governments, and international government organizations. These resources illustrate the impact of drug abuse and drug policy on local neighborhoods and communities as well as the foreign and national security policies of individual countries and the international community. ONDCP resources can also be used to investigate the periodic nexus between the drug trade and international terrorism.[151]

Office of Science and Technology Policy

The Office of Science and Technology Policy (OSTP) was established within EOP by the National Science and Technology, Policy, Organization, and Priorities Act of 1976. OSTP's purpose is providing the president with scientific, engineering, and technological analysis on major federal plans, policies, and programs. This advice can cover areas as diverse as national security, foreign relations, health, economics, and environmental science. OSTP also assists the president in providing coordinated leadership for federal research and development programs.[152]

OSTP's website (www.ostp.gov/) provides information about the President's Council of Advisors on Science and Technology (PCAST) and the National Science and Technology Council (NSTC), speeches and congressional testimony by the OSTP director, federal research and development budget request documents, and a calendar of upcoming events. Reports or other materials dealing with national security include *PCAST Letter on Critical Infrastructure Protection* (1998), *Improving Federal Laboratories to Meet the Challenges of the 21st Century* (1999), *National Research and Development Plan for Aviation Safety, Security, Efficiency, and Environmental Compatibility* (1999), and *Memorandum for Federal Mail Managers and First Responders to Federal Mail Centers: Purchase of Anthrax Detection Technologies* (2002).

President's Critical Infrastructure Protection Board

The President's Critical Infrastructure Protection Board (PCIPB) was established by Executive Order 13231 in October 2001, serves as the executive branch's focal point for cyberspace security, and continues Clinton administration initiatives in this area.[153] PCIPB responsibilities, according to the executive order, involve recommending policies and coordinating programs to protect critical information systems pertaining to U.S. infrastructure such as emergency readiness, communications, and the physical assets supporting such systems. PCIPB was also charged with cooperating with the private sector and local, state, and federal government agencies as it seeks to fulfill its objectives.[154] Its website (www.whitehouse.gov/pcipb/) contains the text of *The National Strategy to Secure Cyberspace* (2003) and *The National Strategy for the Physical Protection of Critical Infrastructure and Key Assets* (2003).

White House Military Office

The White House Military Office (WHMO) origins probably begin in 1942 with the establishment of Camp David as a presidential retreat in Maryland and the creation of the White House Communications Agency to ensure that the president has safe, secure, and reliable communications capabilities. Over subsequent decades a number of additional units and responsibilities have been added to WHMO duties, which can basically be summarized as providing the president with military support for domestic and international activities.[155]

Information about WHMO can be found at www.whitehouse.gov/whmo/. Although no publicly accessible WHMO activity reports are provided on this website, information is available about the activities of WHMO component organizations and services such as *Air Force One*, Camp David, the *Marine One* presidential helicopter, the White House Communications Agency, White House Medical Unit, and White House Transportation Agency.

Notes

1. PL 107-296, "To Establish the Department of Homeland Security, and for Other Purposes," 116 *U.S. Statutes at Large*, 2135–2232.

2. See *U.S. Government Manual, 2002–2003* (Washington, D.C.: National Archives and Records Administration, 2002), 134; and PL 57-87, "An Act to Establish the Department of Commerce and Labor," 32 *Statutes of the United States of America*, 825.

3. For the Bureau of Export Administration's organizational statement, see "Commerce Department Organization Order 10–16," *Federal Register*, 53 (June 7, 1988), 20881–20882.

4. U.S. Department of Commerce, Bureau of Industry and Security, "Commerce Department Renames Agency 'Bureau of Industry and Security,'" (April 18, 2002) (www.bis.doc.gov/news/2002/commercerenames agencybis.htm), accessed November 13, 2003.

5. *U.S. Government Manual, 2001–2002* (Washington, D.C.: National Archives and Records Administration, 2001), 137–138.

6. U.S. Critical Infrastructure Assurance Office, "About Us" (2002), 1 (www.ciao.gov/publicaffairs/about.html), accessed November 13, 2003.

7. U.S. Critical Infrastructure Assurance Office, "White Paper: The Clinton Administration's Policy on Critical Infrastructure Protection: Presidential Decision Directive 63" (1998), 1 (www.ciao.gov/publicaffairs/pdd63.html), accessed November 13, 2003.

8. U.S. Department of Homeland Security, Information Analysis and Infrastructure Protection Directorate, "The Critical Infrastructure Assurance Office Has Moved to the Department of Homeland Security" (2003), 1 (www.ciao.gov/), accessed November 13, 2003.

9. PL 56-735, "An Act to Establish the National Bureau of Standards," 31 *U.S. Statutes at Large*, 1449–1450.

10. PL 100-418, "To Enhance the Competitiveness of American Industry, and for Other Purposes," 102 *U.S. Statutes at Large*, 1427–1432.

11. *U.S. Government Manual, 2001–2002*, 150.

12. Joe Morehead, *Introduction to United States Government Information Sources*, 6th ed. (Englewood, Colo.: Libraries Unlimited, 1999), 374–375.

13. PL 95-452, "To Reorganize the Executive Branch of the Federal Government and Increase Its Economy and Efficiency by Establishing Offices of Inspector General within the Departments of Agriculture, Commerce, Housing and Urban Development, Interior, Labor, and Transportation, and within the Community Services Administration, the Environmental Protection Agency, the General Services Administration, the National Aeronautics and Space Administration, the Small Business Administration, and the Veterans Administration, and for Other Purposes," 92 *U.S. Statutes at Large*, 1101–1109.

14. U.S. Department of Commerce, Office of Inspector General, "Our Mission" (n.d.), 1 (www.oig.doc.gov/Mission/body_mission.html), accessed November 13, 2003. For a more detailed overview on the role played by governmental inspectors general and public access to their reports, see Thelma Friedes, "Inspector General Reports as Instruments of Government Accountability," *Government Information Quarterly*, 9 (1) (1992): 53–64.

15. For succinct historical background on the Department of Energy (DOE), see Terrence R. Fehner, *Department of Energy, 1977–1994: A Summary History* (Washington, D.C.: DOE, 1994). For an official historical view on the role of DOE and its predecessor agencies in developing the U.S. nuclear weapons arsenal, see Charles R. Loeber, *Building the Bomb: A History of the Nuclear Weapons Complex* (Albuquerque, N.M.: Sandia National Laboratories, 2002).

16. PL 95-91, "To Establish a Department of Energy in the Executive Branch by Reorganization of Energy Functions within the Federal Government in Order to Secure Effective Management to Assure a Coordinated National Energy Policy, and for Other Purposes," 91 *U.S. Statutes at Large*, 565.

17. U.S. Department of Energy, Argonne National Laboratory, "America's First National Laboratory" (n.d.), 1 (www.anl.gov/OPA/vtour/ovw.htm), accessed November 13, 2003. For a general history of Argonne, see Jack M. Holl, *Argonne National Laboratory, 1946–96* (Urbana: University of Illinois Press, 1997).

18. U.S. Department of Energy, Argonne National Laboratory, "America's First National Laboratory," 1–2.

19. U.S. Department of Energy, Argonne National Laboratory, "America's First National Laboratory," 1.

20. U.S. Department of Energy, Argonne National Laboratory, "Cutting-Edge Science and Technology Help Safeguard National Security" (2002), 1 (www.anl.gov/OPA/factsheets/e1-02.htm), accessed November 13, 2003.

21. U.S. Department of Energy, Brookhaven National Laboratory, "About Brookhaven" (2002), 1 (www.bnl.gov/bnlweb/about_BNL.htm), accessed November 13, 2003. For a history of the Brookhaven National Laboratory, see Robert P. Crease, *Making Physics: A Biography of Brookhaven National Laboratory, 1946–1972* (Chicago: University of Chicago Press, 1999).

22. Brooking National Laboratory, "Divisions" (2001), 1 (www.bnl.gov/nns/divisions.asp), accessed November 13, 2003.

23. U.S. Department of Energy, Departmental Representative to the Defense Nuclear Facilities Safety Board, "About Us: Mission and Functions" (n.d.), 1–2 (www.deprep.org/office/), accessed November 13, 2003.

24. PL 95-91, 572–74. For additional background on the Energy Information Administration and its publications, see Bert Chapman, "Serials of the Energy Information Administration," *Serials Review*, 19 (3) (1993): 53–62; and U.S. Congress, Joint Economic Committee, *Maintaining the Quality of Energy Statistics for Economic and Energy Analysis: Studies*, 97th Cong., 2d sess., 1982.

25. U.S. Department of Energy, Idaho National Engineering and Environmental Laboratory, "About the Idaho National Engineering and Environmental Laboratory" (2002), 1, 4 (www.inel.gov/about/), accessed November 13, 2003.

26. U.S. Department of Energy, Los Alamos National Laboratory (LANL), Initiatives for Proliferation Prevention, "Welcome to the Program" (n.d.), 1 (http://ipp.lanl.gov/ipp/ippext.nsf/Welcome?OpenPage), accessed November 13, 2003.

27. U.S. Department of Energy, Pacific Northwest National Laboratory, International Nuclear Safety Program, "Improving the Safety of Soviet-Designed Nuclear Power Plants—Overview" (1999), 1 (http://insp.pnl.gov/?info/brochure/progbroch98a), accessed November 13, 2003.

28. U.S. Department of Energy, Pacific Northwest National Laboratory, International Nuclear Safety Program, "Improving the Safety of Soviet-Designed Nuclear Power Plants."

29. U.S. Department of Energy, Kansas City Plant, "Products and Services" (n.d.), 1 (www.kcp.com/servlet/Content/about/products.ep), accessed November 13, 2003.

30. U.S. Department of Energy, Kansas City Plant, "History" (n.d.), 2 (www.kcp.com/servlet/Content/about/history.ep), accessed November 13, 2003.

31. U.S. Department of Energy, Knolls Atomic Power Laboratory, "Knolls Atomic Power Laboratory" (n.d.), 1 (www.kapl.gov/), accessed November 13, 2003.

32. For a portrait of Earnest Orlando Lawrence, see George B. Kauffman, "Lawrence, Earnest Orlando," in *American National Biography*, vol. 13, ed. John A. Garraty and Mark C. Carnes (New York: Oxford University Press, 1999), 279–282. For a portrait and analysis of the Lawrence Berkeley National Laboratory's historical origins and evolution, see J. L. Heilbron and Robert W. Seidel, *Lawrence and His Laboratory: A History of the Lawrence Berkeley Laboratory* (Urbana: University of Illinois Press, 1989).

33. U.S. Department of Energy, Lawrence Berkeley National Laboratory, "About Berkeley Lab" (n.d.), 1 (www.lbl.gov/LBL-PID/LBL-Overview.html), accessed November 13, 2003.

34. U.S. Department of Energy, Lawrence Livermore National Laboratory (LLNL), "About the Lab" (2002), 1 (www.llnl.gov/llnl/001index/02about-index.html), accessed November 13, 2003. Historical background on LLNL can be found at U.S. Department of Energy, Lawrence Livermore National Laboratory, "About the Lab: Laboratory History" (2002), 1 (www.llnl.gov/llnl/02about-llnl/history.html), accessed November 13, 2003; and Hugh Gusterson, *Nuclear Rites: A Weapons Laboratory at the End of the Cold War* (Berkeley, Calif.: University of California Press, 1996). Examples of congressional oversight of LLNL operations include U.S. Congress, House Committee on Science, Space, and Technology, Subcommittee on Investigations and Oversight, *Administration and Implementation of the Management and Operating Contract for the Lawrence Livermore National Laboratory and the Lawrence Berkeley Laboratory*, 102d Cong., 1st sess., 1991; and U.S. Congress, House Committee on Commerce, Subcommittee on Oversight and Investigations, *Results of Security Inspections at the Department of Energy's Lawrence Livermore National Laboratory*, 106th Cong., 2d sess., 2000.

35. U.S. Department of Energy, Los Alamos National Laboratory, "You Know What They're Doing Down in Los Alamos? UC's First Contract to Operate the Laboratory" (2001), 1 (www.lanl.gov/worldview/welcome/history/15_uc-contract.html), accessed November 13, 2003. For an examination of Los Alamos history, see Jo Ann Shroyer, *Secret Mesa: Inside Los Alamos National Laboratory* (New York: John Wiley and Sons, 1998). For coverage of the security failures at Los Alamos and other DOE facilities in the late 1990s, see U.S. Congress, House Committee on Armed Services, *Security Failures at Los Alamos National Laboratory*, 107th Cong., 1st sess., 2001; U.S. Congress, House Committee on Armed Services, Subcommittee on Military Procurement, *Results of the Department of Energy's Inspector General Inquiries into Specific Aspects of the Espionage Investigation at the Los Alamos National Laboratory*, 106th Cong., 2d sess., 2000; and U.S. Congress, Senate Select Committee on Intelligence, *Loss of National Security Information at the Los Alamos National Laboratory*, 107th Cong., 1st sess., 2001. The status of the University of California's stewardship of Los Alamos was uncertain following the late 2002 resignation of lab director John C. Browne, a letter sent from Energy Secretary Spencer Abraham to University of California system president Richard C. Atkinson warning that the university's association with LANL was in jeopardy, and DOE inspector general and congressional committee investigations of financial improprieties by LANL employees, as reported in Edward Walsh, "Los Alamos Lab Chief Quits Amid Criticism," *Washington Post*, January 3, 2003, A17. University of California president Robert Dynes announced in February 2004 that DOE would continue letting the university compete for the Los Alamos contract scheduled to expire September

30, 2005, according to University of California, *Lab Update,* no. 13 (February 27, 2004), 1 (www.universityofcalifornia.edu/news/losalamos/feb04_labupdate.pdf), accessed March 10, 2004.

36. U.S. Department of Energy, Los Alamos National Laboratory, "Message from the Director" (2001), 1–2 (www.lanl.gov/worldview/news/releases/archives/01-062.shtml), accessed November 13, 2003.

37. PL 106-65, "National Defense Authorization Act for Fiscal Year 2000," 113 *U.S. Statutes at Large,* 954–971. For a current description of the National Nuclear Security Administration's institutional mandate, see U.S. Department of Energy, National Nuclear Security Administration, "About NNSA" (n.d.), 1 (www.nnsa.doe.gov/about.asp), accessed November 13, 2003.

38. U.S. Department of Energy, National Spent Nuclear Fuel Program, "Mission of the National Spent Nuclear Fuel Program" (2000), 1–2 (http://nsnfp.inel.gov/mission.asp), accessed November 13, 2003.

39. U.S. Department of Energy, National Transportation Program, "Transportation of Radioactive Materials by DOE" (n.d.), 1–5 (http://www.ntp.doe.gov/question_answers.html), accessed November 13, 2003.

40. U.S. Department of Energy, National Transportation Program, "Transportation of Radioactive Materials by DOE," 2–3.

41. U.S. Department of Energy, Nevada Operations Office, "Overview of the Nevada Test Site" (2001), 1 (www.nv.doe.gov/news&pubs/dirpdfs/DOENV705_Overview.pdf), accessed November 13, 2003.

42. U.S. Department of Energy, Nevada Operations Office, "More about the Nevada Test Site" (2000), 1 (www.nv.doe.gov/nts/more.htm), accessed November 13, 2003.

43. U.S. Department of Energy, Nevada Operations Office, "Nevada Test Site" (2002), 1 (www.nv.doe.gov/nts/default.htm), accessed November 13, 2003. For an overview of environmental, safety, and health activities at the Nevada Test Site, see U.S. Department of Energy, *U.S. Department of Energy Environment, Safety, and Health Progress Assessment of the Nevada Test Site* (Washington, D.C.: DOE, 1992). For a historical overview of U.S. nuclear weapons testing, see A. Costandina Titus, *Bombs in the Backyard: Atomic Testing and American Politics* (Reno: University of Nevada Press, 1986). For a pictorial essay on the Nevada Test Site, see Peter Goin, *Nuclear Landscapes* (Baltimore, Md.: Johns Hopkins University Press, 1991).

44. U.S. Department of Energy, New Brunswick Laboratory, "Our Mission" (n.d.), 1 (www.nbl.doe.gov/mission/mission.htm), accessed November 13, 2003.

45. U.S. Department of Energy, Office of Nuclear Energy, Science, and Technology, "From the Director: Welcome" (n.d.), 1 (www.nuclear.gov/home/welcome1.html), accessed November 13, 2003.

46. U.S. Department of Energy, Nuclear Explosion Monitoring, Research and Engineering Program, "General Information" (2001), 1–2 (www.nemre.nn.doe.gov/nemre/general_info.htm), accessed November 13, 2003.

47. U.S. Department of Energy, Oak Ridge National Laboratory, "Oak Ridge National Laboratory Fact Sheet" (2002), 1 (www.ornl.gov/ornlhome/fact.pdf), accessed November 13, 2003. For a history of Oak Ridge National Laboratory and its operations, see Leland Johnson and Daniel Schaffer, *Oak Ridge National Laboratory: The First Fifty Years* (Knoxville: University of Tennessee Press, 1994).

48. U.S. Department of Energy, "Department of Energy FY 2005 Congressional Budget Request: Laboratory Table" (2003), 6 (www.mbe.doe.gov/budget/05budget/content/labtable/labtable.pdf), accessed March 8, 2004.

49. U.S. Department of Energy, Oak Ridge National Laboratory, "Nuclear Nonproliferation Program" (n.d.), 1–3 (http://ntr.ornl.gov/programs.html), accessed November 13, 2003.

50. U.S. Department of Energy, Oak Ridge National Laboratory, "Nuclear Science and Technology Division: Mission and Vision" (2002), 1 (www.ornl.gov/sci/nuclear_science_technology/), accessed November 13, 2003.

51. U.S. Department of Energy, Y-12 National Security Complex, "Y-12 Defense Programs" (2002), 1 (www.y12.doe.gov/bwxt/y12/y12-defense.html), accessed November 13, 2003.

52. U.S. Department of Energy, "Today at the Y-12 National Security Complex" (2002), 1 (www.y12.doe.gov/bwxt/y12/y12-today.html), accessed November 13, 2003.

53. PL 97-425, "An Act to Provide for the Development of Repositories for the Disposal of High-Level Radioactive Waste and Spent Nuclear Fuel, to Establish a Program of Research, Development, and Demonstration Regarding the Disposal of High-Level Radioactive Waste, and Spent Nuclear Fuel, and for Other Purposes," 96 *U.S. Statutes at Large,* 2201.

54. U.S. Department of Energy, Office of Civilian Radioactive Waste Management, "Office of Civilian Radioactive Waste Management" (n.d.), 1 (www.rw.doe.gov/), accessed November 13, 2003.

55. U.S. Department of Energy, Office of Environmental Management, "Learn about the Environmental Management Program" (2002), 1 (www.em.doe.gov/learn.html), accessed November 13, 2003.

56. U.S. Department of Energy, Office of Independent Oversight and Performance Assurance, "Mission and Functions" (n.d.), 1 (www.oa.doe.gov/sase/mission.html), accessed November 14, 2003.

57. PL 95-452, 1101–1109.

58. U.S. Department of Energy, Office of Inspector General, "Welcome to the OIG Web Site" (n.d.), 1 (www.ig.doe.gov/), accessed November 13, 2003.

59. U.S. Department of Energy, Office of Policy and International Affairs, "Office of Policy and International Affairs" (n.d.), 1 (www.pi.energy.gov/orgsummaries.html), accessed November 13, 2003.

60. U.S. Department of Energy, Office of Policy and International Affairs, "Office of Policy and International Affairs," 2–5.

61. U.S. Department of Energy, Office of Scientific and Technical Information, "Short History of OSTI" (n.d.), 1–3 (www.osti.gov/osthist.html), accessed November 13, 2003.

62. U.S. Department of Energy, Office of Scientific and Technical Information, "Short History of OSTI," 2–3.

63. See James J. Fiore and others, *DOE's Office of Site Closure: Progress toward 2006* (Washington, D.C.: Office of Site Closure, 2001), 1–2 (http://apps.em.doe.gov/closure/Documents/Publications/speakers_Papers/fiore-wm01-jan18.pdf), accessed November 13, 2003; and U.S. Department of Energy, Office of Environmental Management, "Site Closure Vision" (n.d.), 1 (http://apps.em.doe.gov/closure/vision.cfm), accessed November 13, 2003.

64. U.S. Department of Energy, Office of Scientific and Technical Information, "Documents Provided at the Secretary's June 27, 1994, Press Conference" (n.d.), 1 (www.osti.gov/html/osti/opennet/document/fulltext.html), accessed November 13, 2003.

65. U.S. Department of Energy, Office of Scientific and Technical Information, "Office of Nuclear and National Security Information Mission Statement" (n.d.), 1 (www.osti.gov/opennet/odmissio.html), accessed November 13, 2003.

66. U.S. Department of Energy, Pacific Northwest Laboratory, "History" (2002), 1 (www.pnl.gov/main/welcome/history.html), accessed November 13, 2003. For a polemical and undocumented sociocultural perspective on working at Pacific Northwest Laboratory, see Paul Rogat Loeb, *Nuclear Culture: Living and Working in the World's Largest Atomic Complex* (Philadelphia: New Society, 1986).

67. U.S. Department of Energy, Pacific Northwest Laboratory, "National Security" (2002), 1 (www.pnl.gov/main/sectors/national.html), accessed November 13. 2003.

68. See U.S. Department of Energy, Pantex Plant, "Pantex Plant: General Description" (n.d.), 1 (www.pantex.com/ds/pxgeng.htm), accessed November 13, 2003. For background on Pantex, see A. G. Mojtabai, *Blessed Assurance at Home with the Bomb in Amarillo, Texas* (Albuquerque: University of New Mexico Press, 1986), 47. For a managerial appraisal of Pantex operations, see W. R. Peters, *Weapons Evaluation Test Laboratory at Pantex: Testing and Data Handling Capabilities of Sandia National Laboratories at the Pantex Plant* (Washington, D.C.: DOE, 1993).

69. U.S. Department of Energy, Pantex Plant, "Mission Statement" (n.d.), 1–2 (www.pantex.com/ds/pxgend1.htm), accessed November 13, 2003.

70. See U.S. Department of Energy, Sandia National Laboratories, "About Sandia: History" (2002), 1 (www.sandia.gov/about/history/), accessed November 13, 2003; and U.S. Department of Energy, Sandia National Laboratories, "About Sandia: President's Welcome" (2002), 1 (www.sandia.gov/about/welcome/), accessed November 13, 2003. For historical coverage of the Sandia National Laboratories, see Leland Johnson, *Sandia National Laboratories: A History of Exceptional Service in the National Interest* (Albuquerque, N.M.: Sandia National Laboratories, 1997). For one DOE assessment of the laboratories' management practices, see U.S. Department of Energy, Office of Environment, Safety, and Health, *Tiger Team Assessment of the Sandia National Laboratories* (Washington, D.C.: DOE, 1991).

71. U.S. Department of Energy, Sandia National Laboratories, "Capabilities: Homeland Security" (2002), 1 (www.sandia.gov/capabilities/homeland-security/links.html), accessed November 13, 2003.

72. U.S. Department of Energy, Savannah River Site (SRS), "Inside Savannah River" (2002), 1 (http://sro.srs.gov/inside1.htm), accessed November 13, 2003. For an overall history of SRS, see William P. Bebbington, *History of DuPont at the Savannah River Plant* (Wilmington, Del.: E. I. DuPont de Nemours and Co., 1990). For congressional investigations of SRS management problems during the 1980s, see U.S. Congress, House Committee on Armed Services, Subcommittee on Procurement and Military Nuclear Systems, *P–Reactor Operations at Savannah River*, 100th Cong., 2d sess., 1988; and U.S. Congress, Senate Committee on Armed Services, Subcommittee on Strategic Forces and Nuclear Deterrence, *Reactors at the Savannah River Plant*, 100th Cong., 2d sess., 1988.

73. U.S. Department of Energy, Savannah River Site, "Historical Highlights @ SRS" (2002), 1–3 (www.srs.gov/general/about/hilits.htm), accessed November 13, 2003.

74. U.S. Department of Energy, Savannah River Site, "Inside Savannah River," 1–2.

75. PL 94-163, "To Increase Domestic Energy Supplies and Availability; to Restrain Energy Demand; to Prepare for Energy Emergencies; and for Other Purposes," 89 *U.S. Statutes at Large*, 881–890. For examples of literature examining various Strategic Petroleum Reserve operational aspects, see U.S. Department of Energy, *Technical Safety Appraisal of the Strategic Petroleum Reserve, West Hackberry, Big Hill, New Orleans* (Washington, D.C.: DOE, 1989); U.S. Congress, House Committee on Commerce, Subcommittee on Energy and Power, *Strategic Petroleum Reserve: A Closer Look at the Drawdown*, 106th Cong., 2d sess., 2000; and U.S. Congress, Senate Committee on Energy and Natural Resources, *Strategic Petroleum Reserve: Hearing before the Committee on Energy and Natural Resources, United States Senate, One Hundred Sixth Congress, Second Session, to Conduct Oversight on the Department of Energy's Recent Decision to Release 30 Million Barrels of Crude Oil from the Strategic Petroleum Reserve and the Bid Process Used to Reward Contracts Regarding Same*, 107th Cong., 1st sess., 2001.

76. U.S. Department of Energy, Office of Fossil Energy, Strategic Petroleum Reserve,

"Strategic Petroleum Reserve: Crude Oil Assays" (2003), 1 (www.spr.doe.gov/reports/Crude_Oil_Assays.htm), accessed November 13, 2003.

77. U.S. Department of Energy, Yucca Mountain Project, "History of Nuclear Waste Program" (n.d.), 1 (www.ocrwm.doe.gov/about/history.shtml), accessed November 13, 2003. For additional background information on Yucca Mountain and nuclear waste disposal in the United States, see U.S. Department of Energy, Yucca Mountain Site Characterization Project, *Why Are Scientists Studying Yucca Mountain?* (Las Vegas, Nev., and Washington, D.C.: Yucca Mountain Site Characterization Project and Government Printing Office, 1995); U.S. Department of Energy, Office of Civilian Radioactive Waste Management, *Yucca Mountain Preliminary Site Suitability Evaluation* (Las Vegas, Nev.: U.S. Department of Energy, Office of Civilian Radioactive Waste Management, 2001); James Flynn and others, *One Hundred Centuries of Solitude: Redirecting America's High-Level Nuclear Waste Policy* (Boulder, Colo.: Westview Press, 1995); and Gerald Jacob, *Site Unseen: The Politics of Siting a Nuclear Waste Repository* (Pittsburgh: University of Pittsburgh Press, 1990).

78. U.S. Department of Energy, "Abraham Praises U.S. Senate Approval of Yucca Mountain" (July 9, 2002), 1 (www.energy.gov/engine/content.do?PUBLIC_ID=12990&BT_CODE=PR_PRESSRELEASES&TT_CODE=PRESSRELEASE), accessed November 13, 2003.

79. U.S. Department of Energy, Yucca Mountain Project, "Why Yucca Mountain?" (n.d.), 1 (www.ocwr.doe.gov/ymp/about/why.shtml), accessed November 13, 2003.

80. See Tony Mellor, ed., *Congressional Quarterly's Federal Staff Directory: The Executive Branch of the U.S. Government,* 30th ed. (Washington, D.C.: CQ Press, 1999), 887; and U.S. Environmental Protection Agency, *The Guardian: Origins of the EPA* (Washington, D.C.: U.S. Environmental Protection Agency, 1992).

81. PL 96-88, "To Establish a Department of Education and for Other Purposes," 93 *U.S. Statutes at Large,* 695.

82. U.S. Department of Health and Human Services, Centers for Disease Control and Prevention (CDC), "About CDC" (2002), 1 (www.cdc.gov/aboutcdc.htm#mission), accessed November 13, 2003. For a history of the CDC, see Elizabeth W. Etheridge, *Sentinel for Health: A History of the Centers for Disease Control* (Berkeley: University of California Press, 1992).

83. PL 71-272, "An Act Making Appropriations for the Department of Agriculture for the Fiscal Year Ending June 30, 1931, and for Other Purposes," 46 *U.S. Statutes at Large,* 422–423. For coverage of the Food and Drug Administration's institutional origins, see Oscar Edward Anderson, *The Health of a Nation: Harvey W. Wiley and the Fight for Pure Food* (Chicago: University of Chicago Press, 1958).

84. U.S. Department of Health and Human Services, Food and Drug Administration, "FDA's Mission" (1998), 1 (www.fda.gov/opacom/morechoices/mission.html), accessed November 13, 2003.

85. For introductory background on the National Disaster Medical System (NDMS) institutional mandate, see the NDMS homepage (http://ndms.dhhs.gov/), accessed November 14, 2003.

86. See OEMS homepage (http://ndms.dhhs.gov/).

87. For a brief overview of the mission of the National Institutes of Health (NIH), see U.S. Department of Health and Human Services, National Institutes of Health, "The NIH Almanac" (2002), 1 www.nih.gov/about/almanac/), accessed November 13, 2003. For an NIH institutional history, see Victoria Angela Harden, *Inventing the NIH: Federal Biomedical Research Policy, 1887–1937* (Baltimore, Md.: Johns Hopkins University Press, 1986).

88. U.S. Department of Health and Human Services, National Institute of Allergy and Infectious Diseases, "Overview" (2002), 1 (www.niaid.nih.gov/facts/overview.htm), accessed November 11, 2003.

89. U.S. Centers for Disease Control and Prevention, National Center for Environmental Health, "Strategic National Stockpile" (2003), 1–4 (www.bt.cdc.gov/stockpile/), accessed November 11, 2003.

90. U.S. Department of Health and Human Services, Office of Inspector General, "OIG Mission" (n.d.), 1 (http://oig.hhs.gov/organization/OIGmission.html), accessed November 13, 2003.

91. U.S. Department of Health and Human Services, Office of Inspector General, "Department of Health and Human Services Office of Inspector General Fiscal Year 2003 Budget Request" (2002), 3 (http://oig.hhs.gov/testimony/docs/2002/020305fin.pdf), accessed November 13, 2003.

92. P.L. 107–296, "An Act to Establish the Department of Homeland Security, and for Other Purposes," 116 *U.S. Statutes at Large*, 2135–2321.

93. For the text of the Department of Homeland Security's institutional organization, see President of the United States, *Department of Homeland Security Reorganization Plan* (2002), 1–16 (www.whitehouse.gov/news/releases/2002/11/reorganization_plan.pdf), accessed November 13, 2003.

94. U.S. Animal and Plant Health Inspection Service, "A 25-Year Retrospective of the Animal and Plant Health Inspection Service" (1997), 3 (www.aphis.usda.gov/oa/pubs/aphis_25yrretro.html), accessed March 9, 2004.

95. U.S. Department of Agriculture, Animal and Plant Health Inspection Service, "Welcome to the Animal and Plant Health Inspection Service Website!" (n.d.), 1 (www.aphis.usda.gov/lpa/about/welcome.html), accessed November 13, 2003.

96. President of the United States, *Department of Homeland Security Reorganization Plan*, 4.

97. President of the United States, *Department of Homeland Security Reorganization Plan*, 2–3.

98. *U.S. Government Manual, 2002–2003*, 268.

99. *U.S. Government Manual, 2002–2003*, 309. See Paul A. Powers, *They That Go Down to the Sea: A Bicentennial Pictorial History of the United States Coast Guard* (Springfield, Va.: U.S. Coast Guard Chief Petty Officers Association, 1990). For historical overviews of Coast Guard operations, see *Record of Movements: Vessels of the United States Coast Guard: 1790–December 31, 1933* (Washington, D.C.: U.S. Coast Guard, Office of the Assistant Commandant, 1989).

100. *U.S. Government Manual, 2002–2003*, 310.

101. *U.S. Government Manual, 2002–2003*, 310–311.

102. *U.S. Government Manual, 2002–2003*, 340. For histories of the U.S. Customs Service, see Carl E. Prince and Mollie Keller, *The U.S. Customs Service: A Bicentennial History* (Washington, D.C.: Department of the Treasury, U.S. Customs Service, 1989); and U.S. Customs Service, *U.S. Customs Service: Protectors of Independence since 1789* (Washington, D.C.: Department of the Treasury, U.S. Customs Service, 1998).

103. *U.S. Government Manual, 2002–2003*, 340–341.

104. *U.S. Government Manual, 2002–2003*, 342.

105. U.S. Department of Justice, Office of Justice Programs, Office for Domestic Preparedness, "About ODP" (2002), 1 (www.ojp.usdoj.gov/odp/about/overview.htm), accessed November 13, 2003.

106. U.S. Department of Agriculture, Agricultural Research Service, "USDA Research at the Plum Island Animal Disease Center" (1995), 1–3 (www.ars.usda.gov/plum/forum1295.htm), accessed November 13, 2003.

107. U.S. Department of Agriculture, Agricultural Research Service, "Mission at Plum Island" (n.d.), 1–2 (www.ars.usda.gov/plum/USDAmission.html), accessed November 13, 2003.

108. *U.S. Government Manual, 2002–2003*, 345. For historical overviews of the U.S. Secret Service, see Marcia Roberts, *Moments in History* (Washington, D.C.: Department of the Treasury, U.S. Secret Service, 1990); and Philip H. Melanson, *Secret Service: The Hidden History of an*

Enigmatic Agency (New York: Carroll and Graf Publishers, 2002). For a timeline of Secret Service history including the agency's 1901 assumption of presidential protection responsibilities following the assassination of President William McKinley, see U.S. Secret Service, "Secret Service History—Timeline" (2002), 1 (www.secretservice.gov/history.shtml), accessed November 13, 2003.

109. PL 107-71, "To Improve Aviation Security, and for Other Purposes," 115 *U.S. Statutes at Large,* 597–647.

110. President of the United States, *Department of Homeland Security Reorganization Plan,* 3–4.

111. *U.S. Government Manual, 2002–2003,* 258.

112. U.S. Department of Justice, Computer Crime and Intellectual Property Section, "What Does CCIPS Do?" (2002), 1 (www.cybercrime.gov/ccips.html), accessed November 13, 2003.

113. U.S. Department of Justice, Criminal Division, "Counterespionage Section" (n.d.), 1 (www.usdoj.gov/criminal/iss.html), accessed November 13, 2003.

114. *U.S. Government Manual, 2002–2003,* 269. For evaluations of Drug Enforcement Administration activities, see U.S. Congress, House Committee on Government Reform, *The Drug Enforcement Administration: Were Criminal Investigations Swayed by Political Considerations?,* 107th Cong., 1st sess., 2001; and U.S. General Accounting Office, *Seized Drugs and Weapons: DEA Needs to Improve Certain Physical Safeguards and Strengthen Accountability* (Washington, D.C.: U.S. General Accounting Office, 1999.

115. U.S. Department of Justice, Executive Office for Immigration Review, "Background Information" (n.d.), 1 (www.usdoj.gov/eoir/background.htm), accessed November 13, 2003.

116. U.S. Department of Justice, Executive Office for Immigration Review, "Responsibilities" (n.d.), 1 (www.usdoj.gov/eoir/responsibilities.htm), accessed November 13, 2003.

117. For succinct overviews of the Federal Bureau of Investigation (FBI), see *U.S. Government Manual, 2002–2003,* 266; and U.S. Department of Justice, Federal Bureau of Investigation, *FBI Facts and Figures: A Compendium of General Information about the Federal Bureau of Investigation* (Washington, D.C.: FBI, 1996).

118. U.S. Department of Justice, National Drug Intelligence Center, "About NDIC" (n.d.), 1–4 (www.usdoj.gov/ndic/tri1.htm), accessed November 13, 2003.

119. U.S. Department of Justice, Office of the Inspector General, "Introduction" (n.d.), 1 (www.usdoj.gov/oig/igintro.htm), accessed November 13, 2003.

120. U.S. Department of Justice, Office of Intelligence Policy and Review, "Office of Intelligence Policy and Review" (2002), 1 (www. usdoj.gov/oipr/), accessed November 13, 2003.

121. U.S. Department of Justice, Criminal Division, Office of International Affairs, "Office of International Affairs" (n.d.), 1 (www.usdoj.gov/criminal/oia.html), accessed November 13, 2003.

122. *U.S. Government Manual, 2002–2003,* 289. For historical background, see Elmer Plischke, *U.S. Department of State: A Reference History* (Westport, Conn.: Greenwood Press, 1999); and David F. Trask, *A Short History of the U.S. Department of State, 1781–1981* (Washington, D.C.: U.S. Department of State, Bureau of Public Affairs, 1981).

123. U.S. Department of State, Bureau of Arms Control, "Bureau of Arms Control" (n.d.), 1 (www.state.gov/t/ac/), accessed November 13, 2003.

124. For the historical origins of diplomatic security, see U.S. Department of State, Bureau of Diplomatic Security, "Overview: Keeping American Diplomacy Safe" (n.d.), 1 (www.state.gov/m/ds/about/overview/), accessed November 13, 2003; and U.S. Department of State, Bureau of Diplomatic Security, "A Brief History" (n.d.), 1 (http://www.state.gov/m/ds/about/history/), accessed November 13, 2003.

125. U.S. Department of State, Bureau of International Narcotics and Law Enforcement Affairs, "Bureau of International Narcotics and Law Enforcement" (n.d.), 1 (www.state.gov/g/inl/), accessed November 13, 2003.

126. U.S. Department of State, Bureau of Nonproliferation, "Bureau of Nonproliferation" (n.d.), 1 (www.state.gov/t/np/), accessed November 13, 2003.

127. U.S. Department of State, Bureau of Political-Military Affairs, "Bureau of Political-Military Affairs," (n.d.), 1 (www.state.gov/t/pm/), accessed November 13, 2003.

128. U.S. Department of State, Bureau of Verification and Compliance, "Bureau of Verification and Compliance" (n.d.), 1 (www.state.gov/t/vc/), accessed November 13, 2003.

129. U.S. Department of State, Counterterrorism Office, "Counterterrorism Office" (n.d.), 1 (www.state.gov/s/ct/), accessed November 13, 2003.

130. U.S. Department of State, Office of Defense Trade Controls, "Defense Trade Controls—Who We Are" (n.d.), 1 (www.pmdtc.org/whoweare.htm), accessed November 13, 2003.

131. U.S. Department of State, Office of the Historian, "Office of the Historian" (n.d.), 1 (www.state.gov/r/pa/ho/), accessed November 13, 2003.

132. U.S. Department of State, Office of Inspector General, "OIG's Mission" (n.d.), 1 (http://oig.state.gov/about/), accessed November 13, 2003.

133. U.S. Department of State, Office of War Crimes Issues, "Office of War Crimes Issues" (n.d.), 1 (www.state.gov/s/wci/), accessed November 13, 2003.

134. *U.S. Government Manual, 2002–2003,* 306. For additional background on the Department of Transportation (DOT), see U.S. Department of Transportation, Bureau of Transportation Statistics, *The Changing Face of Transportation* (Washington, DC: U.S. Department of Transportation, Bureau of Transportation Statistics, 2000); and Donald Robert Whitnah, *U.S. Department of Transportation: A Reference History* (Westport, Conn.: Greenwood Press, 1998).

135. *U.S. Government Manual, 2002–2003,* 312.

136. U.S. Department of Transportation, Maritime Administration, "MARAD's Mission" (n.d.), 1 (www.marad.dot.gov/Offices/mission.html), accessed November 13, 2003.

137. *U.S. Government Manual, 2002–2003,* 306, 308.

138. U.S. Department of Transportation, Office of Inspector General. *Semiannual Report to Congress: April 1, 2001–September 30, 2001* (Washington, D.C.: DOT, 2001), 5.

139. *U.S. Government Manual, 2002–2003,* 336. For additional background on the Treasury Department and its operations, see Gene and Clare Gurney, *The United States Treasury: A Pictorial History* (New York: Crown, 1978); and U.S. Congress, House Committee on Ways and Means, Subcommittee on Oversight, *Department of the Treasury's Efforts to Address Money Laundering,* 104th Cong., 1st. sess., 1995.

140. U.S. Department of the Treasury, Office of Enforcement, "Mission" (n.d.), 1 (www.treas.gov/offices/enforcement/), accessed November 13, 2003.

141. U.S. Department of the Treasury, Office of Foreign Assets Control, "Frequently Asked Questions" (2002), 2 (www.treas.gov/offices/enforcement/ofac/faq/), accessed November 13, 2003.

142. U.S. Department of the Treasury, Office of Foreign Assets Control, "Mission" (n.d.), 1 (www.ustreas.gov/offices/enforcement/ ofac/), accessed November 13, 2003.

143. U.S. Department of the Treasury, Office of the Inspector General, "Mission" (n.d.), 1 (www.treas.gov/offices/inspector-general/), accessed November 13, 2003.

144. United States Constitution, Article II, Section 2, Clause 1.

145. The exercise and analysis of presidential power are the subjects of an enormous and continually growing body of scholarly assessment. See, for example, Lyn Ragsdale and John J. Theis III, "The Institutionalization of the American Presidency, 1924–1992," *American Journal of*

Political Science, 41 (4) (1996): 1280–1318; Peri Arnold, *Making the Managerial Presidency: Comprehensive Reorganization Planning, 1905–1980* (Princeton, N.J.: Princeton University Press, 1986); Michael A. Genovese, *The Power of the American Presidency: 1789–2000* (New York: Oxford University Press, 2001); Forrest McDonald, *The American Presidency: An Intellectual History* (Lawrence: University Press of Kansas, 1994); and Sidney M. Milkis, *The American Presidency: Origins and Development, 1776–1990* (Washington, D.C.: CQ Press, 1990).

146. U.S. National Archives and Records Administration, Office of the Federal Register, *The Federal Register: What It Is and How to Use It* (Washington, D.C.: Government Printing Office, 1992), 32.

147. PL 80-253, "To Promote the National Security by Providing for a Secretary of Defense; for a National Military Establishment; for a Department of the Army, a Department of the Navy, and a Department of the Air Force; and for the Coordination of the Activities of the National Military Establishment with Other Departments, and Agencies of the Government Concerned with the National Security," 61 *U.S. Statutes at Large*, 495–499. For additional historical background and reviews of National Security Council activities, see U.S. Department of State, Office of the Historian, *History of the National Security Council, 1947–1997* (Washington, D.C.: U.S. Department of State, Office of the Historian, 1997) (www.whitehouse.gov/nsc/history.html), accessed November 13, 2003; U.S. Central Intelligence Agency, *Organizational History of the National Security Council during the Truman and Eisenhower Administrations* (Washington, D.C.: National Security Council, 1988); Bromley K. Smith, *Organizational History of the National Security Council during the Kennedy and Johnson Administrations* (Washington, D.C.: Central Intelligence Agency, 1988); and Mark M. Lowenthal, *The National Security Council: An Organizational History* (Washington, D.C.: Library of Congress, Congressional Research Service, 1978). For a nongovernmental perspective, see John Prados, *Keepers of the Keys: A History of the National Security Council from Truman to Bush* (New York: Morrow, 1991).

148. U.S. National Security Council, "Establishment of the National Security Council" (n.d.) (www.whitehouse.gov/nsc/), accessed November 13, 2003.

149. *U.S. Government Manual, 2002–2003*, 96, 98. For further background and analysis of the Office of Management and Budget, see U.S. Congress, Senate Committee on Governmental Affairs, *Office of Management and Budget: Evolving Roles and Future Issues*, 99th Cong., 2d sess., 1986; Richard Rose, *Managing Presidential Objectives* (New York: Free Press, 1976); Larry Berman, *The Office of Management and Budget and the Presidency, 1921–1979* (Princeton, N.J.: Princeton University Press, 1979); and Frederick C. Mosher, *A Tale of Two Agencies: A Comparative Analysis of the General Accounting Office and the Office of Management and Budget* (Baton Rouge: Louisiana State University Press, 1984).

150. *U.S. Government Manual, 2002–2003*, 99.

151. For a recent example of congressional exploration of this connection, see U.S. Congress, House Committee on International Relations, *International Global Terrorism: Its Links with Illicit Drugs as Illustrated by the IRA and Other Groups in Colombia*, 107th, 2d sess., 2002.

152. *U.S. Government Manual, 2002–2003*, 101. An extensive body of literature exists analyzing and documenting the complex and sometimes contentious relationship between the scientific research community and the federal government. For example, see Daryl E. Chubin, *Peerless Science: Peer Review and U.S. Science Policy* (Albany: State University of New York Press, 1990); Hugh Davis Graham and Nancy Diamond, *The Rise of American Research Universities: Elites and Challengers in the Postwar Era* (Baltimore, Md.: Johns Hopkins University Press, 1997); Alfred K. Mann, *For Better or for Worse: The Marriage of Science and Government in the United States* (New York: Columbia University Press, 2000); and Gregg Herken, *Cardinal Choices: Presidential Science Advising from the Atomic Bomb to SDI* (Stanford, Calif.: Stanford University Press, 2000).

153. U.S. President's Critical Infrastructure Protection Board, *National Strategy to Secure Cyberspace* (Washington, D.C.: President's Critical Infrastructure Protection Board, 2003), 2 (www.whitehouse.gov/pcipb/cyberspace_strategy.pdf), accessed November 13, 2003.

154. President of the United States, "Executive Order on Critical Infrastructure Protection" (2002), 1–2 (www.whitehouse.gov/news/releases/2001/10/20011016-12.html), accessed November 13, 2003.

155. U.S. White House Military Office, "History of White House Military Office" (n.d.), 1 (www.whitehouse.gov/whmo/history.html), accessed November 13, 2003.

CHAPTER 4

Military Agencies

Military publications are particularly valuable sources of national security policy information. These publications are produced by unified combatant commands of the armed forces; individual armed service branches such as the U.S. Air Force (USAF), U.S. Army, U.S. Marine Corps (USMC), and U.S. Navy (USN); and units and organizations that are part of the armed forces. Attributes of these information resources include descriptions of weapons systems, photographs, audio and video clips, statements of military doctrine and strategy, analysis of military issues and international security trends, budgetary figures, statistical analysis, medical treatments for exposure to deadly toxins and scientific research findings.

A surprising amount of material produced by the U.S. military is available in print format in federal depository libraries and on armed services websites. Some information was removed from the sites for security reasons following the September 11, 2001, terrorist attacks.[1] While websites are listed below for several military agencies, some information is not publicly accessible and is restricted to users in the .gov or .mil domains. Furthermore, "https" are listed as the means of accessing some of these websites instead of "www" because military agencies use Secure Socket Layering (SSL) to provide enhanced security for their websites. In some cases, users must take a few additional anonymous registration steps to ensure that their computers have the requisite SSL protection before accessing these sites.

■ Unified Combatant Commands

Unified combatant commands are assigned operational control of the U.S. combat forces. An individual command consists of forces from two or more armed services, has a large and ongoing mission, and is geographically organized. Such a command is part of the national chain of command running from the president to the secretary of defense and on to the unified commander. The commander receives orders and other communications from the president or secretary of defense, which are transmitted through the chairman of the Joint Chiefs of Staff.[2]

As of early 2004, nine unified commands were scattered around the globe: Central Command (CENTCOM), European Command (USEUCOM), Joint Forces Com-

> ## Military Acronyms
>
> Military science uses a variety of acronyms to describe organizational units, weapons systems, strategies, planning documents, and other subjects. Examples of military acronyms include
>
> - AAIFF—Air-to-Air Identification Friend or Foe
> - CFE—Conventional Forces Europe; Communications Front-End
> - JSTARS—Joint Surveillance and Target Attack Radar System
> - MCR—Military Command Region
> - NAVSPAWAR—Naval Space and Warfare Systems Command
>
> Links to military acronyms glossaries are provided by the Indiana University-Purdue University Indianapolis University Library website at www.ulib.iupui.edu/subjectareas/gov/military.html.

mand (USJFCOM), Northern Command (NORTHCOM), Pacific Command (PACOM), Southern Command (SOUTHCOM), Special Operations Command (SOCOM), Strategic Command (STRATCOM), and Transportation Command (TRANSCOM). A Unified Command Plan was created in 2002 to better coordinate these commands.

Central Command

Located at MacDill Air Force Base in Tampa, Florida, Central Command (CENTCOM) consists of military personnel whose areas of responsibility stretch from Central Asia to the Horn of Africa. Activated on January 1, 1983, CENTCOM seeks to enhance regional stability and demonstrate a commitment to regional security. These objectives are obtained through combat training exercises such as the biennial Bright Star exercises with Egyptian military forces, assorted humanitarian and security assistance programs, and combining training and education opportunities for military members in countries within this region.[3]

CENTCOM's website (www.centcom.mil/) includes a January 2003 Pentagon slide briefing on Saddam Hussein's potential destruction of Iraqi oil fields, press releases, information on Operation Enduring Freedom (Afghanistan) and Operation Iraqi Freedom, Operation Anaconda battle video clips from Afghanistan, and speeches and press briefings by the CENTCOM commander.

European Command

European Command (USEUCOM) was established in 1952 and given responsibility for twelve European and Mediterranean–area countries plus the then-divided city of Berlin.[4] During the subsequent five decades USEUCOM's area of coverage expanded to encompass most of Africa, as well as Europe. Its jurisdiction now contains ninety-one countries, eighty thousand miles of coastline, and more than fourteen million square miles stretching from Norway to South Africa.[5] USEUCOM, located in Stuttgart, Germany, maintains a website (www.eucom.mil/) describing its activities and including links to resources on the countries in its area of influence. Specific publications that are publicly accessible are *Staff Memorandum 55-1: HQ USEUCOM Battle Staff Operations* (1997), *Directive 40-5: International Intelligence Contacts and Arrangements* (2000), *Security Awareness* (2001), *Directory of United States Armed Forces Contracting Activities in Europe and Africa* (2002), *2002 United States European Command Strategy of Readiness and Engagement* (2002), and *FY 2003 US EUCOM Posture Statement* (2002).

Joint Forces Command

Located in Norfolk, Virginia, Joint Forces Command (USJFCOM) plays a key role serving as the transformation laboratory of the U.S. military to develop and test concepts and promote the training of military leaders and forces to assist U.S. joint warfighting capabilities.[6] The Atlantic Command was established in 1947 with responsibility for the geographic area surrounding the Atlantic Ocean and changed its name to the Joint Forces Command in October 1999 to stress its leadership role in the transformation of U.S. military forces.[7]

The website www.jfcom.mil/ provides information on the historical origins and ongoing evolution of USJFCOM, news releases, publications such as *Joint Forces Command Glossary* (n.d.), and information about USJFCOM initiatives such as global command and control system-integrated intelligence and mergers, operational net assessment tools, theater medical information planning, joint automated single guard solution, and unattended ground sensory support to special reconnaissance.

Northern Command

Located at Peterson Air Force Base in Colorado Springs, Colorado, Northern Command (NORTHCOM) is responsible for protecting the air, land, and sea approaches to the United States, Canada, Mexico, and surrounding water (extending out five hundred miles and including the Gulf of Mexico, Puerto Rico, and the U.S. Virgin Islands) from military attack.[8] NORTHCOM's origins date to 1946. Its existing mission and form were established on October 1, 2002.[9]

NORTHCOM's website (www.northcom.mil) contains resources about the command's activities such as supporting first responders in the event of a natural or human disaster within the United States and material about its homeland security activities. NORTHCOM also encompasses the North American Aerospace Defense Command (NORAD), a joint U.S.-Canadian effort to protect the North American continent from hostile military action, and NORAD's Cheyenne Mountain Operations Center (www.cheyennemountain.af.mil/).

Pacific Command

Located in Honolulu, Hawaii, Pacific Command (PACOM) was established on January 1, 1947, and is the oldest and largest of the U.S. unified commands.[10] Its area of responsibility covers over half of the world's surface (the west coast of the U.S. mainland to Africa's east coast, the Arctic, and the Antarctic), forty-three countries, twenty territories and possessions, ten U.S. territories, and the armed forces of China, Russia, India, North Korea, and South Korea. Overall PACOM mission responsibilities are to increase security and promote peaceful economic development in the Asia-Pacific region.[11]

The website www.pacom.mil/ has biographical information on key PACOM personnel, descriptions of military exercises with allied Asia-Pacific countries such as the Philippines, news releases from 1999 to the present, speeches by PACOM leaders, and terrorist threat information for U.S. military personnel in Asia-Pacific countries. Available publications include the periodical *Asia-Pacific Defense Forum* (1999–present) and *Asia-Pacific Economic Update* (2000 and 2002).

Southern Command

Located in Miami, Florida, Southern Command (SOUTHCOM) dates to 1903, when U.S. Marines first arrived in Panama to protect the Panama Railroad connecting the Atlantic and Pacific Oceans while providing security for construction of the Panama Canal. SOUTHCOM on January 6, 1963, received its current nomenclature, reflecting its command responsibility for U.S. military activities in Central and South America.[12] SOUTHCOM responsibilities also encompass the Gulf of Mexico, the Caribbean Sea and its island countries, and a small portion of the Atlantic Ocean.[13]

SOUTHCOM's website (www.southcom.mil/) provides further information about the command's institutional mandate and has news releases, departmental component descriptions, hurricane preparation tips, and publications such as the newspaper *Southern Star* (1999–present) and *US SOUTHCOM's Theater Strategy* (2002).

Special Operations Command

Special Operations Command (SOCOM) was created by a 1987 statute to rectify what were seen as deficiencies in the ability of the United States to conduct special operations and engage in low-intensity conflict.[14] The same law established the Office of the Assistant Secretary of Defense for Special Operations and Low-Intensity Conflict as a resource and policy fulcrum for the special operations and low-intensity conflict activities of the Department of Defense (DOD). SOCOM membership is drawn from all armed services branches. Its primary missions are combating terrorism, counterproliferation, special reconnaissance, psychological operations, and unconventional warfare. SOCOM's 2000 posture statement describes the mission of U.S. special forces.

Special operations are characterized by the use of small units in direct and indirect military actions focused on strategic and operational objectives. These actions require units with combinations of specialized personnel, equipment, training, and tactics that go beyond the routine capabilities of conventional military forces.[15]

SOCOM's website (www.socom.mil/) contains limited information about SOCOM activities with a primary emphasis on procurement and opportunities for businesses. Additional material on SOCOM can be obtained from the 1998 and 2000 posture statements available at www.defenselink.mil/pubs/sof/ and from the DOD Comptroller's Office report *FY 2002 Budget Estimate United States Special Operations Command (USSOCOM)* (2002). Some additional information on SOCOM may be obtained from annual congressional committee hearings on the DOD budget request.

Strategic Command

Strategic Command (STRATCOM) is located at Offutt Air Force Base, in Nebraska. It serves as the command and control center for U.S. strategic forces and oversees military space operations, computer networks, information operations, strategic warning and intelligence assessments, and global strategic planning. STRATCOM responsibilities also encompass early warning and defense against long-range conventional attacks, missile strikes, and defensive measures against proliferating weapons of mass destruction.[16]

The U.S. Air Force's Strategic Air Command was set up in March 1946 at Offut, where its bomber forces served as the foundation of the U.S. emerging nuclear deterrent against the Union of Soviet Socialist Republics' increasing nuclear arsenal. STRATCOM replaced the Strategic Air Command on June 1, 1992, following the Soviet Union's collapse. This new organization brought the planning, targeting, and wartime employment of U.S. strategic forces under a single commander while daily force training, maintenance, and equipment responsibilities stayed with the air force and navy. A separate Space Command force also existed at this time; it merged into STRATCOM on October 1, 2002.[17]

STRATCOM's website (www.stratcom.mil/) provides biographical portraits of STRATCOM leadership personnel and fact sheets about various STRATCOM operational attributes such as *Airborne Command Post* (n.d.), *B-2 Bomber* (n.d.), *Computer Network Operations* (n.d.), *Military Space Forces* (n.d.), *National Airborne Operations Center* (n.d.), and *RC-135 Reconnaissance Aircraft* (n.d.)

Transportation Command

The U.S. Transportation Command (TRANSCOM) system, created in 1987, is located at Scott Air Force Base in Illinois. Its responsibilities are coordinating the military's human and transportation assets to enable the projection and sustaining of U.S. military forces for as long as necessary to fulfill their missions. Components of TRANSCOM include the Air Mobility Command, which serves as TRANSCOM's air component; the Military Sealift Command, which provides effectual sea transportation internationally; and Military Traffic Management Command, which is the overland lift component and traffic manager for TRANSCOM.[18]

The website www.transcom.mil/ contains additional information about TRANSCOM's mission and operations. Available materials include photos of TRANSCOM at work, biographical portraits of key TRANSCOM personnel, fact sheets on equipment such as the C-5 Galaxy cargo plane, descriptions of organizational entities such as Military Traffic Management Command, and press releases. Accessible publications include *Voluntary Intermodal Sealift Agreement and the Sealift Mobilization Programs* (1998), *Transportation for a New Millennium, Strategic Guidance FY 2002,* and *Understanding the Defense Transportation System* (2002).

Unified Command Plan

The website www.defenselink.mil/specials/unifiedcommand/ contains the Unified Command Plan, which was last revised on October 1, 2002. Information provided on the website includes media briefings and presentations on plan characteristics, maps of geographic areas covered by unified commands, links to command websites, and news releases with updated information on events affecting individual commands.

U.S. Air Force

The U.S. Air Force (USAF) was established by the 1947 National Security Act and is a military department within the Department of Defense. USAF is headed by the secretary of the air force and operates under the secretary of defense's authority, direction, and control. The secretary of the air force is concerned with the organization, training, logistical assistance, administration, research and development, and other activities of the USAF as directed by the president and secretary of defense. USAF's overall mission is defending the United States by controlling and exploiting air and space.[19]

AF News: The Air Force News Agency

Located at Kelly Air Force Base in San Antonio, Texas, the Air Force News Agency (AF News) began in 1978 as the Air Force Information and News Center. Its mission was communicating prompt and factual information to air force personnel. This mission has expanded to providing news and entertainment to air force personnel domestically and internationally and providing the American public with news and information about U.S. Air Force activities.[20]

The website www.afnews.af.mil/ has information about AF News activities, including details about the Air Force News Service, Army and Air Force Hometown News Service, Air Force Broadcasting Service, and Communications and Information Systems Directorate. It has audio and video webcasts as well as publications such as *Airman Magazine* (1995–present).

Air Force Link

The Air Force Link website (www.af.mil/) serves as a one-stop access point to all USAF resources including secretary of the air force headquarters in Washington, D.C., and to individual USAF units and organizational components. It also provides information on senior USAF leadership, news releases, and data regarding USAF's budget.

A noteworthy resource of Air Force Link is its special studies section (www.af.mil/library/studies.asp), which has policy documents and research studies on various aspects of air force strategic thought and planning. Examples of publicly accessible resources are *The Aerospace Force: Defending America in the 21st Century* (n.d.), the interactive study *Air Force 2025* (1996), *Control of the Air: The Enduring Requirement* (1999), *Air Force Posture Statement* (1999–2002), and *U.S. Air Force White Paper on Long-Range Strike Aircraft* (2001).

Air Combat Command

The Air Combat Command (ACC), headquartered at Langley Air Force Base, Virginia, is responsible for providing aerial combat forces to the unified combatant commands. ACC offers battle management, bomber, command, control, communications, and intelligence systems; reconnaissance; and rescue and theater airlift aircraft to the air force. ACC maintains responsibility for organizing, training, supplying, and maintaining combat-ready forces for rapid deployment and use and takes steps to ensure that strategic air defense forces are capable of fulfilling peacetime air control and wartime air defense requirements to implement national policies on a global scale.[21]

Further materials about ACC mission and activities can be found on its website (www2.acc.af.mil/). Available resources include news releases, a map of air force bases with links to pertinent websites, publications such as the periodical *Airman* (1995–present), and fact sheets on air force weapons systems such as the A-10/OA-10 Thunderbolt II plane, the E-8 Joint Stars battle management aircraft, F-117A Nighthawk Stealth fighter/bomber, AIM-9 Sidewinder air-to-air missile, and RQ-1 Predator Unmanned Aerial Vehicle.

Air Command and Staff College

The Air Command and Staff College (ACSC) is part of Air University at Maxwell Air Force Base, Alabama. ACSC serves as the air force's intermediate professional military school and is responsible for preparing field-grade military officers from all services, international officers, and civilians to take positions with increased responsibility in the military and other government offices. ACSC's curriculum is focused on teaching the requisite skills for aerospace operations to support joint military campaigns. The U.S. Army's Air Corps Tactical School was located at Maxwell from 1931 to 1942 and became known as ACSC in 1954.[22]

ACSC's website (www.acsc.maxwell.af.mil/) contains listings of ACSC graduates from 1995 to 2001, the *Air Command and Staff College AY-2004 Student Guide* (2003), and information on specific courses such as Air and Space Operations, Airpower Studies, National Planning Systems, and National and International Security Studies.

Air National Guard

The Air National Guard (ANG) is a reserve component of the air force. It was officially established on September 18, 1947, although twenty-nine National Guard aviation observation squadrons existed between World War I and World War II.[23] Information about ANG can be found on its website (www.ang.af.mil/). Examples of accessible resources are an organizational synopsis, recruiting information, listings of career opportunities, and links to individual ANG unit websites.

Air University

Air University (AU) is located at Maxwell Air Force Base, Alabama. Since its 1946 establishment, its purpose has been conducting professional military, graduate, and continuing education for officers, enlisted personnel, and civilians to prepare them for leadership, command, staff, and management responsibilities. Besides its instructional missions, AU conducts research in aerospace education, leadership, and management while playing a key role in developing and testing air force doctrine, concepts, and strategy. These instructional and research missions are carried out by the Air War College; Air Command and Staff College; College of Aerospace Doctrine, Research, and Education; School of Advanced Air and Space Studies; and Air University Press.[24]

General information about Air University and its component parts can be found through its website (www.au.af.mil/). Available information includes course descriptions and publication listings for selected AU faculty. The highlight of AU's website is the full-text access provided to many research publications produced by students and faculty at AU entities. Some AU student papers go back to 1992 and include *High Power Radio Frequency Weapons: A Potential Counter to U.S. Stealth and Cruise Missile Technology* (1999), *The B-52: Can It Fly Until 2050?* (2000), *No Fly Zones: Costs, Benefits, and Conditions* (2001), and *The Central Asian Republics after September 11, 2001: How Should the U.S. Alter Its Engagement Strategy* (2002).

Other research resources are the scholarly journal *Air and Space Power Journal* (1987–present) and reports such as *Unmanned Aerial Vehicles: Implications for Military Operations* (2000), *Assessment of the Emerging Biocruise Threat* (2000), *Computer Networks and Information Warfare: Implications for Military Operations* (2000), *Space-Based Global Strike: Understanding Strategic and Military Implications* (2001), *Infrared Systems for Tactical Aviation: An Evolution in Military Affairs?* (2002), and *The Gathering Biological Warfare Storm* (2002).

AU's publishing arm, Air University Press (http://aupress.au.af.mil/), produces a significant output of scholarly material on aerospace theory and doctrine. Accessible publications include *Does the United States Need Space-Based Weapons?* (1999), *U.S.-Led Cooperative Theater Missile Defense in Northeast Asia: Challenges and Issues* (2000), *Identifying and Mitigating the Risks of Cockpit Automation* (2001), *China in Space: Civilian and Military Developments* (2001), *The Long Search for a Surgical Strike: Precision Munitions and the Revolution in Military Affairs* (2001), *Employee Warriors and the Future of the American Fighting Force* (2002), and *The Politics of Coercion: Toward a Theory of Coercive Airpower for Post-Cold War Conflict* (2002).

Air Force Academy

The U.S. Air Force Academy (USAFA) is located in Colorado Springs, Colorado, and is responsible for providing undergraduate education to enable the development of aerospace officers with the knowledge, discipline, and motivation to lead the U.S. Air Force.[25] Since its congressionally authorized creation in 1954, the academy has grown to its present cadet strength of four thousand, which has included women since 1976.[26]

On USAFA's website (www.usafa.af.mil/) is information on obtaining service academy appointments, a virtual tour, descriptions of course curriculum and physical training, recreational activity, publications such as the current *Air Force Academy* catalog and the journal *Airman-Scholar* (1997–2001), and links to USAFA component parts such as the Institute for National Security Studies.

Air Force Academy Institute for National Security Studies

The Air Force Academy's Institute for National Security Studies (INSS) was created in 1992 as part of a collaborative effort between the USAFA dean of faculty and the Policy Division of the Division of the Nuclear and Counterproliferation Directorate of USAF headquarters. The INSS mission is promoting national security research for DOD within the military academic community while supporting the air force national security education program. INSS sponsored more than $1.3 million in research at military and civilian universities during its initial six years of operation.[27]

The website www.usafa.af.mil/inss/ provides information about INSS activities and access to numerous reports produced under institute auspices. Available materials include annual reports, agendas of selected conference proceedings, and the text of books such as *The Terrorism Threat and United States Government Response: Operational and Organizational Factors* (2001), *Controlling Non-Strategic Nuclear Weapons: Obstacles and Opportunities* (2001), and *Milestones in Strategic Arms Control, 1945–2000: United States Air Forces Roles and Doctrines* (2002).

A valuable feature of the website is the complete text of the INSS occasional papers series on national security and international political topics from 1994 to the present. Examples include *Water: The Hydraulic Parameter of Conflict in the Middle East and North Africa* (2000), *Aerospace Power in Urban Warfare: Beware the Hornet's Nest* (2001), *United States Military Space: Into the Twenty-first Century* (2002), *Squaring the Circle: Cooperative Security and Military Operations* (2002), *Tactical Nuclear Weapons: Debunking the Mythology* (2002), *View from the East: Arab Perceptions of*

United States Presence and Policy (2003), and *Arms Control without Arms Control: The Failure of the Biological Weapons Convention Protocol and a New Paradigm for Fighting the Threat of Biological Weapons* (2003).

Air Force Audit Agency

The Air Force Audit Agency (AFAA) was established in 1948 as the 1030th Air Force Auditor General Group and became part of the Office of Secretary of the Air Force with staff supervision from the assistant secretary of the air force (financial management) in 1978. AFAA's mission is providing air force management with independent, objective, and high-quality audit services focusing on reviewing and promoting economical programs, fostering operational efficiency, assessing and improving financial management, and enhancing the accuracy of financial reporting.[28]

AFAA's website (www.afaa.hq.af.mil/) provides further information about agency activities including employment opportunities, listings of U.S. and international office locations, descriptions of audit services, instructions for making Freedom of Information Act requests for AFAA reports, and *Air Force Audit Agency Strategic Plan Fiscal Years 2003–2007: Vision for the Future* (2002).

Air Force Command and Control and Intelligence, Surveillance, and Reconnaissance Center

Located at Langley Air Force Base, Virginia, the Air Force Command and Control and Intelligence, Surveillance, and Reconnaissance Center (AFC2ISRC) was created during the late 1990s and formally began operations on December 31, 1998.[29] AFC2ISRC seeks to augment air force information distribution by bringing together diverse systems into an integrated command and control battle information system that fulfills warfighter needs and reduces duplicative efforts.[30] AFC2ISRC's website (www.afc2isrc.af.mil/) contains an organizational chart; center history; a video clip on program activities; information on AFC2ISRC components such as the Air Force Experimentation Office and the Air Force Command and Control Battlelab; descriptions of projects such as Joint Expeditionary Force Experiment 2004, B-52 Close Air Support Enhancement, Video Imaging Capacity Enhancement, and Federated Assessment and Targeting Enhancements; and the fact sheet *Advanced Process and Technology Experiment 2001* (2001).

Air Force Communications Agency

The Air Force Communications Agency (AFCA) is located at Scott Air Force Base, in Illinois. It originated in 1938 as the Army Airways Communication System.[31] AFCA's mission is providing U.S. Air Force warfighters with optimum capability to execute the voice, data, video, and information services necessary to achieve command and control of air and space. It seeks to promote service-wide communications, information planning, optimum use of air force communications resources, testing, and training and to implement information warfare capabilities.[32]

AFCA's website (www.usaf.com/orgs/3.htm) has an image library; agency leadership biographies; historical background information; fact sheets such as *Military Affairs Radio System* (2002), *Hammer Adaptive Communications Element* (2002), and *Technology and Interoperability Facility* (2002); issues of the periodical *Intercom* from 2001 to the present; a listing of members of AFCA's Communications Hall of Fame; and descriptions of AFCA organizational components.

Air Force Doctrine Center

The Air Force Doctrine Center (AFDC) stores U.S. Air Force statements on various military operations, which cover strategic and tactical aspects of service missions. Located at www.e-publishing.af.mil/pubs/unit.asp?unit=AFDC, representative samples of these documents are *Airspace Control in the Combat Zone* (1998), *Multiservice Procedures for the Theater Air-Ground System* (1998), *Air Mobility Support* (1999), *Intelligence, Surveillance, and Reconnaissance Operations* (1999), *Air Warfare* (2000), *Military Operations Other Than War* (2000), *Space Operations* (2001), and *Health Service Support in Nuclear, Biological, and Chemical Environments* (2002).

Air Force Flight Test Center

Located at Edwards Air Force Base, California, the Air Force Flight Test Center (AFFTC) started as a bombing test range in 1933. During World War II, Edwards became a bomber training base. In subsequent years, flight test milestones—such as Chuck Yeager's breaking of the sound barrier in 1947—took place at the base.[33]

AFFTC's website (www.edwards.af.mil/) provides a variety of information resources on historical flight test operations. Materials available include information on the base's annual open house; news releases; descriptions of historical and contemporary planes tested at AFFTC such as the X-15 Envelope, YB-40 Flying Wing bomber, and the F-22 Raptor fighter; information on the Air Force Test Pilot School; descriptions of unmanned aerial vehicles; and contracting information. A number of operational publications are also available, such as *Aircrew Operations* (2000), *AFFTC Priorities* (2000), and *Weapons Range Management Aircraft Gun Harmonization Range* (2002).

Air Force Historical Research Agency

The Air Force Historical Research Agency (AFHRA), at Maxwell Air Force Base, Alabama, serves as the repository for the U.S. Air Force's historical documents. The collection, which began in Washington, D.C., moved to Maxwell in 1949. AFHRA provides research facilities for professional military education centers, faculty, visiting scholars, and the general public. More than 90 percent of AFHRA's pre-1955 holdings are declassified and publicly accessible.[34] AFHRA's website (www.maxwell.af.mil/au/afhra/) provides access to the personal papers of noteworthy air force personnel such as Henry "Hap" Arnold and Curtis Lemay, listings of historical studies, details of U.S. Air Force unit historical manuscript holdings, information on historic and contemporary air force heraldry, photo albums, and the digitized text of publications such as *Army Air Forces Statistical Digest: World War II* (1946) and *USAF Wartime Aerial Victory Credits* (2000), which documents U.S. military aviation combat triumphs from World War I through 1999.

Air Force History Support Office

Located at Washington, D.C.'s Bolling Air Force Base, the Air Force History Support Office (AFHSO) provides historical information, analysis, and perspective to U.S. Air Force leaders and their staffs in supporting their planning, policy formulation, and decision making. AFHSO has a reference staff of historians, librarians, and volunteers to respond to information requests from private organizations, government agencies, and the general public.[35]

AFHSO's website (www.airforcehistory.hq.af.mil/) provides further information about the office's mission. Materials available include information about finding missing aircrew reports, American military personnel buried overseas, how to research air force personnel records, and information on individual aircraft. A listing of AFHSO publications is also provided, including full-text access to *The Emerging Shield: The Air Force and the Evolution of Continental Air Defense, 1945–1960* (1991), *Case Studies in Strategic Bombardment* (1998), *The Air Force Role in Developing International Outer Space Law* (1999), and *Control of the Air: The Enduring Requirement* (1999).

Air Force Information Warfare Center

The Air Force Information Warfare Center (AFIWC) is responsible for developing information warfare capabilities to meet military requirements for aerospace and joint force operations, exploring and demonstrating information warfare capabilities, testing weapons, creating tactics, and assessing the vulnerabilities of air force units and systems for offensive and defensive information warfare operations.[36] AFIWC is located at Lackland Air Force Base in San Antonio, Texas.

AFIWC is part of the Air Intelligence Agency at Lackland. Its origins derive from the July 1, 1953, activation of the 6901st Special Communications Center. The 6901st was redesignated the Air Force Electronic Warfare Center on July 1, 1975, and its technical expertise would play critical roles in the command and control success experienced during Operation Desert Storm. Policymakers thus realized that command and control warfare could also encompass the total information spectrum and be implemented as information warfare. Consequently, AFIWC was created on September 10, 1993, and incorporated technical skills from the Air Force Cryptologic Support Center's Securities Directorate into its mission.[37]

The website http://afiwcweb.lackland.af.mil/ contains descriptions of AFIWC component parts such as the Mission Systems Division; Plans, Requirements, and Resource Division; Operations Support Division; and Requirements and Solutions Analysis Branch. Also publicly accessible are requirements for entering into cooperative research and development agreements with AFIWC, links to air force information warfare battlelabs, and the publication *Air Force Information Warfare Definitions and Corresponding Validated Requirements* (n.d.).

Air Force Institute of Technology

The Air Force Institute of Technology (AFIT), at Wright-Patterson Air Force Base in Dayton, Ohio, is part of Air University. AFIT serves as the U.S. Air Force's graduate engineering and management school and its technical professional continuing education institution.[38] Its origins go back to the 1919 establishment of the Air School of Application at McCook Field in Dayton. AFIT received its current name in 1947, when the U.S. Air Force became a separate armed service branch. The institute has provided educational services to more than 266,000 DOD personnel during its more than eight decades of existence.[39]

AFIT's website (www.afit.edu/) provides information about the institute's multifaceted programs. Available resources include descriptions the School of Systems and Logistics and the Civil Engineer and Services School, the course curriculum, a list of the distance learning programs, a virtual tour, and publications such as *Graduate Catalog* from 1996–1997 to the present, *Instruction 31-102: Real Property Security* (1996), *Instruction 10-206: Operational Reporting* (1998), and *Instruction 31-101: Information Security* (2001).

Air Force Office of Scientific Research

The Air Force Office of Scientific Research (AFOSR) is located in Washington, D.C., and has various locations internationally. AFOSR was established in 1951 in the headquarters of the Air Research and Development Command. Its creation came from the realization that an intimate association exists among science, technology, and air force operations. AFOSR has sponsored cutting-edge scientific research to assist the air force in its operational planning.[40]

The website www.afosr.af.mil/ has descriptions of AFOSR directorates including Aerospace and Materials Science, Air Vehicles, Mathematics and Space Sciences, and Physics and Electronics; the newsletter *Research Highlights* (1995–present); and fact sheets such as *High-Powered Semiconductor Laser Development* (1998), *Starfire Optical Range* (2001), and *A Brief History of the Airborne Laser* (2002).

The Scientific Advisory Board (SAB), part of AFOSR, promotes the exchange of scientific and technical information between the U.S. Air Force and the U.S. scientific community that can enhance air force service missions.[41] SAB's website (https://www.sab.hq.af.mil/) provides information about SAB activities such as listings of current studies and the text of some board recommendations from 1994 to 2003, including *Global Air Navigation Systems* (1997), *A Space Roadmap for the 21st Century Aerospace Force* (1998), *Ensuring Successful Implementation of Commercial Off-the-Shelf Systems in Air Force Systems* (1999), and *Technology Options to Leverage Aerospace Power in Operations Other Than Conventional War (OOTCW)* (1999).

Air Force Research Laboratory

The Air Force Research Laboratory (AFRL) employs around fifty-four hundred individuals—a mixture of military and civilian personnel—at Ohio's Wright Patterson

Air Force Base. It is responsible for the U.S. Air Force's science and technology budget. AFRL's overall mission is providing leadership in the discovery, development, and integration of affordable warfighting technologies for U.S. aerospace forces.[42]

AFRL's website (www.afrl.af.mil/) provides access to various descriptions of laboratory work including the fact sheets *Air Force Independent Research and Development Program* (1998) and *Air Force Small Business Innovation Research* (1999), AFRL newsletters (1999–present), AFRL monthly accomplishment reports (2001–present), and the report *Air Force Research Laboratory's Contingency Support to Operation Allied Force* (n.d.).

Air Force Safety Center

The Air Force Safety Center (AFSC), at Kirtland Air Force Base, New Mexico, develops, tests, and evaluates Air Force aviation, ground, and nuclear weapons; enhances combat readiness; promotes safety awareness; and develops and directs safety and operational risk management. In the 1950s, AFSC was part of the U.S. Air Force's Office of Inspector General. The Air Force Safety and Inspection Center was activated on December 31, 1971, and air force safety operations were consolidated at Kirtland on January 1, 1996.[43]

The website http://afsafety.af.mil/ provides descriptions of AFSC and its respective divisions including the Aviation Safety Division, Ground Safety Division, Safety Issues Directorate, and Weapons, Space, and Nuclear Safety Division. Publicly accessible information resources include various Air Force safety and accident statistics, periodicals such as *Flying Safety* (1997–present) and *Road and Rec: The Air Force Journal of Occupational, Recreational, and Driving Safety* (1997–present), and publications such as *Aircraft Flight Line-Ground Operations and Activities* (1998), *Nuclear Weapons and Systems Surety* (1999), *Safety Rules for U.S. Strike Aircraft* (2000), *USAF Safety Deployment and Contingency Pamphlet* (2001), and *Nuclear Safety Review and Launch Approval for Space or Missile Use of Radioactive Material and Nuclear Systems* (2002).

Air Force Senior Leadership

The website (www.af.mil/lib/afchain.shtml) has photos and biographical information on leading U.S. Air Force personnel including the secretary of the air force, the air force chief of staff, air force historian, legislative liaison, and command heads of, for example, the Air Force Material Command and U.S. Air Forces Command.

Air Force Space Command

Air Force Space Command (AFSC) is headquartered at Peterson Air Force Base in Colorado and has numerous domestic and international locations. AFSC's mission is protecting the United States against military attacks originating in areas stretching from the earth's surface to geosynchronous orbit 22,300 miles above the earth. Satellites play a crucial role in executing AFSC responsibilities, which have been carried out since its official formation in 1982.[44]

A variety of publicly accessible resources on AFSC activities are accessible through its website (www.peterson.af.mil/hqafspc/). These materials include news releases; links to AFSC units; program fact sheets such as *Space Warfare Center* (n.d.), *Atlas II Launch Vehicle* (2002), *NAVSTAR Global Positioning System* (2002), and *Space and Missile Systems Center* (2003); and publications such as *2002 Performance Plan* (n.d.) and *Strategic Master Plan FY04 and Beyond* (2002).

Deputy Undersecretary of the Air Force—International Affairs

The deputy undersecretary of the air force—international affairs, operating from the Pentagon, is responsible for promoting U.S. Air Force security objectives with other countries through foreign military sales, education and training, and cooperative research and development agreements with U.S. government, foreign, and industry partners.[45]

The website www.safia.hq.af.mil/ provides information about the Foreign Area Officer Program and descriptions of activities in areas such as technology transfer and foreign arms sales.

Space and Missile Systems Center

The Space and Missile Systems Center (SMSC) is located on Los Angeles Air Force Base, in California. Its mission is producing high-quality space and missile products to meet the needs of U.S. aerospace warriors.[46]

SMSC's website (www.losangeles.af.mil/) contains news releases, program-specific information dealing with space launches and satellite launch and control, various fact sheets, and the full text of publications including *Historical Overview: Space and Missile Systems Center 1954–1995* (1996–1997), *Origins of the USAF Space Program: 1945–1956* (1997 reprint), and *Defense Dissemination Program Office Record of Achievement* (1998).

U.S. Army

The Continental Congress on June 14, 1775, established the American Continental Army; the First Congress on August 7, 1789, created the Department of War; the 1947 National Security Act established the Department of the Army headed by the secretary of the Army.[47]

The U.S. Army's mission is organizing, training, and supplying active and reserve land forces to defend the United States while administering environmental protection programs, improving waterway navigation, combating flood and beach erosion, and providing military assistance to federal, state, and local government agencies including natural disaster relief assistance.[48]

The Army's website (www.army.mil/) includes news releases, information about service-wide activities, and links to domestic and international U.S. Army websites.

Aberdeen Proving Ground

Aberdeen Proving Ground (APG) was established on October 20, 1917, and occupies more than 72,500 acres in Harford County, Maryland. APG employs more than seventy-five hundred civilians and thirty-nine hundred military personnel and serves as a center for laboratory research, army material testing, and military training. Organizational components include the U.S. Army's Soldier and Biological Chemical Command; Medical Research Institute of Chemical Defense; and Ordnance Center.[49]

Information about APG activities can be found at www.apg.army.mil/. Accessible resource include a "What's New" page, news releases, public affairs personnel contact information, and publications such as *Environmental Assessment: Prescribed Burns at Aberdeen and Edgewood Area Test Ranges for Air Monitoring of Range Fire Emissions* (1999) and *Environmental Testing for Ballistics Testing of Tent and Foam for Use in Removal Actions at Aberdeen Proving Ground* (n.d.).

American, British, Canadian, and Australian Armies Program

The American, British, Canadian, and Australian Armies Program (ABCA) started in 1947, when American and British military leaders agreed that World War II levels of cooperation between their two countries and selected British commonwealth countries should continue. Formal agreement took place in 1949 between the United States, Great Britain, and Canada. Australia joined the agreement in 1963. ABCA's mission is promoting enhanced interoperability among these armies through cooperation, collaboration, and standardization to effectively integrate their military capabilities in coalition operations.[50]

ABCA's website (http://abca.hqda.pentagon.mil/) contains information about cooperation among these armies, listings of exercises they have participated in, and assorted publications including *Coalition Airspace Control Manual* (2000), *Digitization Interoperability Plan* (2001), *Coalition Medical Interoperability Handbook* (n.d.), and *Intelligence Handbook* (n.d.).

Armor School

The Armor School is part of the Armor Center located at Fort Knox, Kentucky. The center's mission is preparing mounted force warriors for the full spectrum of contemporary combat operations and forging future mounted forces by providing power projection capability and superior training.[51]

The Armor School's website (http://knox.www.army.mil/school/) provides listings of courses such as M1A2 Tank Commander Certification and Armor Captain Career Preparation, links to Armor Center component organizations such as the University of Mounted Warfare, the journal *Armor* (1995–present), and publications such as *Installation Anti-Terrorism/Force Protection Program* (2001), *Fort Knox Information Security Program* (2002), and *Policy Memo 1-03 M1 Series (Abrams) Tank Security* (2003).

Army Chemical School

Located at Fort Leonard Wood in Pulaski County, Missouri, the Army Chemical School (ACS) is responsible for protecting army forces and allowing them to thwart nuclear, biological, and chemical (NBC) threats. In carrying out these mandates, ACS seeks to develop doctrine, equipment, and training capabilities for NBC defense. ACS also provides the army with smoke, obscurant, and flame capabilities in its operations.[52]

ACS' website (www.wood.army.mil/usacmls/) provides student information, descriptions of courses including Biological Defense and NBC Reconnaissance, tables of contents for the journal *Army Chemical Review* from 2001 to 2003 (security reasons precluding full-text publication), the text of some doctrinal draft documents such as *Obscuration Targeting* (2000), and the full text of *Chemical Vision 2010* (1999) and *Proceedings of Worldwide Chemical Conference XIX* (2002).

Army Leadership

The website www.army.mil/leaders/ offers biographical data about leading Army Department officials such as the secretary of the army, army chief of staff, undersecretary of the army, and vice chief of staff of the army.

Army Mountain Warfare School

The Army Mountain Warfare School (AMWS) is devoted to developing and conducting basic and advanced mountain warfare training and cold weather tactical skills for army forces and to training mountain search and rescue teams.[53] AMWS is in Jericho, Vermont.

AMWS' website (www.benning.army.mil/AMWS/) has summer and winter course descriptions, selected training photos, and the *Army Mountain Warfare School Information Letter* (2002) welcoming incoming students and specifying school requirements.

Army National Guard

The Army National Guard (ANG) consists primarily of civilians serving in the military on a part-time basis. State governors may command the guard for local and statewide emergencies, and the president may dispatch ANG for federal missions around the world.[54]

The website www.arng.army.mil/ provides information on the guard's history and missions. Resources include references to the National Guard in the U.S. Constitution, recruitment information, local National Guard unit listings, and publications such as *National Guard Posture Statements* (fiscal years 1997–2004) and *Annual Financial Report* (fiscal years 1998–2003).

Army Newspapers

Army newspapers produced on bases in the United States and globally can be useful for gathering local reactions to important military and international events such as the 2003 deployment of many U.S. forces for combat operations against Iraq. The website www4.army.mil/ocpa/resources/armynewspapers.php provides access to numerous newspapers produced at Army bases. Holdings will vary for these newspapers. Examples of the titles and their place of origin are *Army Flier* (Fort Rucker, Alabama), *Cannoneer* (Fort Sill, Oklahoma), *Georgia Guardsman* (Georgia National Guard, Atlanta, Georgia), *Kwajalein Hourglass* (Marshall Islands), *Pentagram* (Fort Myer, Virginia), *Scout* (Fort Huachuca, Arizona), and *Tower Times* (Army Corps of Engineers, Rock Island, Illinois).

Army Research Institute for the Behavioral and Social Sciences

Experimental psychologists at Harvard University in 1917 met to discuss how psychology and scientific method application could enhance national defense. The secretary of war created a Committee on Classification of Personnel in the Army in August 1917, and that committee was responsible for many scientific personnel management achievements. The committee would become the Army Research Institute for the Behavioral and Social Sciences (ARI). This organization, in Alexandria, Virginia, would go on to produce data and studies to enhance army training and leadership capabilities.[55]

ARI's mission includes providing new technology to meet army personnel and training challenges, conducting studies and analyses to address short-term issues and respond to emerging trends affecting army operations, and providing technical assistance on vital issues affecting the army in areas as such as organization, personnel, and emerging technologies.[56]

Further information about ARI and access to many of its information resources is available at www.ari.army.mil/. Materials include information on recently produced products, topics of ongoing research, and research reports. Examples of publicly available research reports are *How to Support Families during Overseas Deployments: A Sourcebook for Service Providers* (1996), *Plan for Combat Operations (Battlefield Function 18) as Accomplished by a Forward Support Battalion Volume 1: Function Analysis* (1998), *Papers from the 1998 Infantry Situation Awareness Workshop* (1999), *Structured Stimulation-Based Training Program for a Digitized Force: Approach, Design, and Functional Requirements Volume 1* (1999), *The Virtual Sandtable: Intelligent Tutoring for Field Artillery Training* (2001), *Distance Learning: The Soldier's Perspective* (2002), and *Web-Based Collaborative Learning: An Assessment of a Question-Generation Approach* (2003).

Army Research Laboratory

The Army Research Laboratory (ARL) is part of the U.S. Army's Material Command and was activated in 1992 from existing army scientific and technical research capabilities. Its headquarters are at the White Sands Missile Range, in New Mexico, and it has outposts at several other continental U.S. locations. ARL serves as the army's primary laboratory for combat material. It collaborates with industry and academic partners to produce programs and equipment that provide soldiers in the field with technological and analytical support to ensure their success in land operations.[57]

ARL's web page at www.arl.army.mil/ has information on internship and contractor opportunities and press releases. Detailed descriptions are also provided of research performed by organizational entities including the Weapons and Materials Research Directorate, Sensors and Electron Devices Directorate, Computational and Information Sciences Directorate, Survivability and Lethality Directorate, and Vehicle Technology Directorate. Technical reports from 1999 to the present are a highlight of the website, with representative samples including *XLCB: A New Closed-Bomb Data Acquisition and Reduction Program* (2001), *Estimates of the Electromagnetic Radiation from Detonation of Conventional Explosives* (2001), *A Computational Study to Determine the Critical Velocity Required to Initiate Explosively Loaded Munitions* (2002), *Critical Velocity of Electromagnetic Rail Gun in Response to Projectile Movement* (2002), and *The Effects of Physical Exertion on Cognitive Performance* (2002).

Army Science Board

The Army Science Board (ASB) was created in 1977 and serves as the Department of the Army's senior scientific advisory organization. It advises and makes recommendations to the secretary of the army, chief of staff of the army, the ASA(ALT), army staff, and major army commanders on relevant scientific and technological members. Its membership consists of accomplished individuals from the private sector, academia, and government agencies other than DOD representing diverse disciplinary perspectives.[58]

ASB's website (https://webportal.saalt.army.mil/sard-asb/) contains a description of board activities and links to such studies as *Battlefield Visualization* (1998), *Enabling Rapid and Decisive Strategic Maneuver* (1999), *Adapting Future Wireless Technologies* (2002), and *Human Robot Interface Issues* (2002).

Army War College

The U.S. Army War College (USAWC) is located in Carlisle Barracks, Pennsylvania, and serves as the army's graduate educational institution. The area's involvement in military history goes back to before 1794, when President George Washington made an unsuccessful recommendation for it to become the site of a federal military academy. USAWC was established in 1903 in Washington, D.C., and its early graduates included John J. Pershing, Dwight D. Eisenhower, and Omar Bradley. The college was moved to Carlisle Barracks in 1951 and has grown to include divisions such as the Strategic Studies Institute established in 1954, the Military History Institute established in 1967, and the Center for Strategic Leadership established in 1994 to provide state-of-the-art war-gaming training.[59] USAWC's website (www.carlisle.army.mil/) is a treasure trove of national security–related information. Examples of publications from the Center for Strategic Leadership are *Environmental Security and Preventative Defense* (1997), *The Day After: The Army in Post-Conflict Iraq* (2002), *Responding to Terror: A Report of the U.S. Army War College Consequence Management Symposium* (2002), and *Planning Considerations for International Involvement in the Israeli-Palestinian Conflict* (2003).

Peacekeeping Institute publications include *Hurricane Mitch after Action Review Conference Report* (1999) and *SFOR Lessons Learned in Creating a Secure Environment with Respect for the Rule of Law Based on a Study of Bosnia* (2000). USAWC's quarterly scholarly journal *Parameters* from 1996 to the present is also accessible.

Publications from USAWC's Strategic Studies Institute are available from 1993 to the present and include substantive works such as *Army Professionalism, the Military Ethic, and Officership in the 21st Century* (1999), *Generations Apart: Xers and Boomers in the Officer Corps* (2000), *Colombia's Paramilitaries: Criminals or Political Force?* (2002), *China's Growing Military Power: Perspectives on Security, Ballistic Missiles, and Conventional Capabilities* (2002), *South Asia in 2020: Future Strategic Balances and Alliances* (2002), and *Reconstructing Iraq: Insights, Challenges, and Missions for Military Forces in a Post-Conflict Scenario* (2003).

While not browsable by publication data, USAWC student research papers can be searched by keywords and cover numerous national security–related topics. Examples include *The Role of the Corps of Engineers in Homeland Security* (2002), *DOD and the Biological Weapons Domestic Response Plan: Does It Contribute?* (2002), *Information Operations and Asymmetric Warfare: Are We Ready?* (2002), *Army Vision 2010: Integrating Measurement and Signature Intelligence* (2002), *Defeating Militant Islamic Extremists* (2002), and *Islamism and Terrorism in Algeria* (2002). These papers are also available on the Defense Technical Information Center's Scientific and Technical Information Network (STINET) website (http://stinet.dtic.mil/) from September 1998 on.[60]

Assistant Secretary of the Army (Acquisition, Logistics, and Technology)

The assistant secretary of the army (acquisition, logistics, and technology), also known as ASA(ALT), is responsible for carrying out the army's acquisition functions and acquisition management systems, overseeing the army's logistics management function and operations, reviewing security assistance portions of the Army International Affairs Plan, executing army research and development functions, directing the Army Science Board (ASB), ensuring weapons systems production readiness, overseeing the army's industrial base and preparedness programs, and supporting Department of the Army space and strategic acquisition programs.[61]

The ASA(ALT) website (https://webportal.saalt.army.mil/) provides information on directorates dealing with research and technology, defense exports and cooperation, and integrated logistics support along with a mission statement and contracting information. Publicly accessible publications include the periodicals *Army Logistician* (1969–present) and *Army Acquisition, Logistics, and Technology Magazine* (1995–present) and documents such as *Army Equipping Policy* (1999), *Defense Acquisition Deskbook* (2002), the current edition of the annually published *United States Army Weapons Systems,* and *Army Economic Analysis: A Brief Tutorial* (n.d.).

Center for Army Lessons Learned

The Center for Army Lessons Learned (CALL) was established at Fort Leavenworth, Kansas, in 1985 to document warfighting lessons learned at the National Training Center in California and from military operations such as Operation Urgent Fury (Grenada, 1983). CALL consists of organizations such as the Actual Operations Branch, Combat Training Center Branch, Information Systems Division, and Research Division that seek to distill and disseminate information gained from training and combat to all army units to enhance their future performance.[62]

CALL's website (http://call.army.mil/) provides access to a rich and textured variety of U.S. Army training–related resources. Examples include descriptions of CALL programs and publications such as *Operation Enduring Freedom: Tactics, Techniques, and Procedures Handbook No. 2-8* (2002) and resources from CALL's Foreign Military Studies Office, which studies and analyzes trends and developments in foreign militaries and transnational security and has on its website (http://fmso.leavenworth.army.mil/) publications such as *Behind the Great Firewall of China: A Look at Revolution in Military Affairs (RMA)/Information Warfare (IW) Theory from 1996–1998* (1998), *Information Technology: U.S./Russian Perspectives and Potential for Military-Political Cooperation* (1999), and *Tectonic Shifts and Putin's Russia in the New Security Environment* (2002).

Center for Military History

The importance of documenting U.S. military history is reflected in Congress's 1864 authorization for the War Department to collect Civil War military records, which resulted in the publication of the *Official Records of the War of the Rebellion* between 1880 and 1901. The Center for Military History (CMH), so named in 1973, since March 1989 has served as a field operating agency under the Office of the Army Chief of Staff, publishing and documenting the army's activities and operations.[63]

CMH's website (www.army.mil/cmh-pg/) provides downloadable artwork and photographs, screensavers, research guidance, publication lists, and the full text of individual historical studies such as *United States Army in the Korean War—Policy and Direction: The First Year* (1992), *The Whirlwind War: The United States Army in Operations Desert Shield and Desert Storm* (1995), and *United States Army in World War II: The Employment of Negro Troops* (2000).

Central Identification Laboratory

The Central Identification Laboratory (CILHI), at Hickam Air Force Base in Hawaii, is responsible for searching for, recovering, and identifying the remains of U.S. military personnel unaccounted for during World II, the Korean and Vietnam Wars, and the cold war.[64]

The website www.cilhi.army.mil/ provides information about CILHI programs including historical information about its establishment, repatriation photographs, descriptions of forensic laboratory work, and press releases.

Command and General Staff College

The School of Application for Cavalry and Infantry was established on January 6, 1882, became the Command and General Staff College (CSGC) in 1947, and received congressional authorization in 1974 to award the master of military science degree to its graduates.[65] CGSC, at Fort Leavenworth, Kansas, aims to educate leaders in professional military values and practices, serve as the primary agent for the U.S. Army's Leadership Development Program, develop army doctrinal guidance, and promote and support the growth of military art and science.[66]

CGSC's website (www.cgsc.army.mil/) provides information about the college and its educational philosophy, accreditation, upcoming class schedules, the online catalog for its Combined Arms Research Library, and component organizations such as the Combat Studies Institute, School for Advanced Military Studies, School for Command Preparation, and Schools of Combined Arms and Staff Services.

Publicly accessible publications include the journal *Military Review* (1922–present) and reports such as *Studies in Battle Command* (1995), *Sharp Corners: Urban Operations at Century's End* (2001), and *Envisioning Future War* (n.d.).

Corps of Engineers

The U.S. Army Corps of Engineers (USACE) was formally established in 1779 and reestablished in 1802 when the U.S. Military Academy (USMA) was created to train military engineers.[67] USACE provides engineering, construction management, and environmental services in peace and wartime. Examples of its responsibilities and activities are navigation, flood damage reduction, army and air force facility construction, force protection, military contingency support, and strategic mobility.[68]

The website www.usace.army.mil/ has USACE organizational information covering the Washington headquarters and various regional offices, leadership biographies, and employment information. General and technical publications are accessible, such as *Engineering and Design: Explosives Storage Magazines* (1995), *Grounding and Bonding in Command, Control, Computers, Intelligence, Surveillance, and Reconnaissance Facilities* (2002), *Use of Geogrids in Pavement Construction* (2003), and *Conceptual Site Models for Ordnance and Explosives and Hazardous, Toxic, and Radioactive Waste Products* (2003).

Field Artillery School

Located at Fort Sill, Oklahoma, the Field Artillery School (FAS) is responsible for preparing soldiers and Marines for war and other operations by instructing and training them in the tactics, techniques, and procedures for using artillery fire support systems to execute military objectives. The army in 1907 reorganized its artillery forces, and Fort Sill was selected as the best location for artillery training because fifteen thousand acres of land were available for target practice and provided topographic diversity to facilitate divergent types of tactical training.[69]

The FAS website (http://sill-www.army.mil/TNGCMD/tc.htm) provides further information about command activities. It has descriptions of the Directorate of Training and Doctrine and the Depth and Simultaneous Attack Battle Lab, PowerPoint presentations of FAS activities, course descriptions, an overview of combat training, and descriptions of individual artillery support systems such as the lightweight towed 105 millimeter (mm) howitzer and the M270 multiple launch rocket system.

Also available are the professional journal *Field Artillery* (2000–present) and army artillery doctrinal field manuals (FMs) such as *FM 6-20: Fire Support in the Airland Battle* (1988) and *FM 3-09.31: Tactics, Techniques, and Procedures for Fire Support for the Combined Army Commander* (2002).

General Dennis J. Reimer Training and Doctrine Digital Library

The General Dennis J. Reimer Training and Doctrine Digital Library (www.adtdl.army.mil/) is named for the U.S. Army's chief of staff from 1995 to 1999 and provides one-stop access to approved army training and doctrinal materials. Although some resources are restricted to users in the .mil domain, a number of administrative and training resources and doctrinal publications are publicly accessible. Particularly noteworthy for those studying national security policy are the field manuals, which provide information on theoretical and operational aspects of various army battlefield endeavors. Examples include *FM 1-112: Attack Helicopter Operations* (1997), *FM 20-3: Camouflage, Concealment, and Decoys* (1999), *FM 3-34.230: Topographic Operations* (2000), *FM 4-30.13: Ammunition Handbook: Tactics, Techniques, and Procedures for Munitions Handlers* (2001), *FM 3-11.21: Multiservice Tactics, Techniques, and Procedures for Nuclear, Biological and Chemical Aspects of Consequence Management* (2001), and *FM 3-3.07: Stability and Support Operations* (2003).

Human Resources Command

The Human Resources Command (HRC) began in 1973 as the United States Military Personnel Center and received its present name in 2003. Its mission is managing the careers of army personnel and civilian employees from its Alexandria, Virginia, headquarters.[70]

HRC's website (https://www.hrc.army.mil/) provides information about obtaining personnel records, resources for enlisted personnel and officers, retiree services, descriptions of individual units such as the Casualty and Memorial Affairs Operations Center, and publications such as *Army Regulation 290-5: Army National Cemeteries* (1980), *Army Regulation 190-8: Enemy Prisoners of War, Related Personnel, Civilian Internees, and Detainees* (1997), and *Army Regulation 600-85: Army Substance Abuse Program* (2001).

Infantry School

The U.S. Army's Infantry School (IS), at Fort Benning, Georgia, trains and develops infantry leaders, develops and integrates infantry doctrine, and provides doctrinal and combined arms expertise for the army.[71] The IS website (www.infantry.army.mil/) provides information about school programs and units such as the Basic Combat Training Brigade, Combined Arms and Tactics Directorate, and Army Rangers. It also offers course information. Available publications include the table of contents and the full text of some articles from *Infantry Magazine* (1982–present) along with links to army doctrinal publications on infantry from the Reimer Digital Library such as *FM 7-20: The Infantry Battalion* (1992), *FM 23-10: Sniper Training and Deployment* (1994), and *FM 3-25.26: Map Reader and Land Navigation* (2001).

Medical Research Institute of Chemical Defense

The U.S. Army Medical Research Institute of Chemical Defense (USAMRICD) is located at Aberdeen Proving Ground, Maryland. USAMRICD is part of the Army's Medical Research and Material Command, and its mission is developing medical countermeasures for chemical warfare agents and training medical personnel to manage chemical casualties. USAMRICD's origins derive from Army Medical Department elements responsible for defending against chemical weapons used in World War I. A Medical Research Division was organized at Edgewood Arsenal in October 1922, became the U.S. Army Biomedical Laboratory in the early 1960s, and gained its present name in 1981.[72] USAMRICD's website (http://usamricd.apgea.army.mil/) provides descriptions of its training activities, links to chemical weapons medical websites, bibliographic citations to publications by its staff from 1980 to 2003, and the text of reports such as *Technical Bulletin 296: Assay Techniques for Detection of Exposure to Sulfur Mustard, Cholinesterase Inhibitors, Sarin, Soman, GF, and Cyanide* (1996), *USAMRICD's Medical Management of Biological Casualties Handbook* (2001), and *Standard Operating Procedure for Obtaining, Handling, and Shipment of Biomedical Samples* (n.d.).

U.S. Military Academy

The U.S. Military Academy (USMA) was founded on March 16, 1802. The members of its current cadet corps of four thousand are nominated by members of Congress or the Department of the Army. USMA's mission is providing undergraduate education and training for aspiring army officers who are commissioned as second lieutenants upon graduation from this West Point, New York, facility.[73]

USMA's website (www.usma.edu/) provides information about the academy's history, curriculum, and activities. Descriptions are provided for courses such as

History of Asian Warfare, History of Middle Eastern Warfare, War and Its Theorists, and Grand Strategy in the 20th Century. Links are also provided to the History Department's digital map library, to information on obtaining nominations to USMA, and to USMA research centers including the Enhanced Performance Center, Information Technology and Operations Center, and Mechanical Engineering Research Center.

National Simulation Center

The National Simulation Center, in Fort Leavenworth, Kansas, promotes modeling and simulation capabilities within live, virtual, and constructive training environments, to support U.S. Army combat readiness.[74] The center's website (www.leavenworth.army.mil/nsc/) contains brief descriptions of component parts such as the Constructive Directorate, Logistics Directorate, Operations Directorate, and Virtual Directorate as well as some downloadable PowerPoint presentations. Most material is not publicly accessible for security reasons.

Office of Army International Affairs

Army International Affairs (AIA) prepares the Army International Affairs Plan, which serves as the political-military staff for the chief of staff of the army; represents the army in international policy matters; and oversees the development, coordination, and policy implementation for army involvement with international organizations. AIA also is responsible for establishing multinational force compatibility, promoting democracy and human rights, participating in peacekeeping, and providing humanitarian and civil-military emergency planning assistance.[75]

AIA's website (http://international.army.mil/) provides additional information about office activities including an organizational chart, biographical portraits of office personnel, office function descriptions, and the document *Army International Affairs Policy* (2000).

Official Department of the Army Publications and Forms

Administrative publications, forms, and technical manuals are essential in the effective operation of any organization. The website www.army.mil/usapa/ has Department of the Army publications and forms, broken down into categories such as technical and equipment, engineering, and administrative. Many are in PDF format. Examples are *Form NBC 3: Immediate Warning of Predicted Contamination and Hazard Areas* (1992), *Technical Manual MIL-PRF-63033: Performance Specification Manuals, Technical: Demilitarization of Surplus Military Items, Preparation of* (1997), and *Form 85-R: Scorecard for M249, M60/M240B Machine Guns* (2002).

Ordnance Corps

Headquartered at Aberdeen Proving Ground, Maryland, and other locations, the Ordnance Corps (OC) was established by Congress on May 14, 1812, in preparation for war with Great Britain.[76] OC's mission is supporting the development, production, acquisition, and sustaining of weapon systems and providing explosive ordnance disposal to ensure combat superiority for the U.S. Army.[77]

OC's website (www.goordnance.apg.army.mil/) has corps leader biographies, career information, links to the Ordnance Museum website, publications such as the most recent issue of *Ordnance Reports,* and training materials such as *Prepare the AH-64 (Apache Helicopter) for Operation/Movement* (2001) and *Repair the Launch Tube* (2003).

Soldier and Biological Chemical Command

Soldier and Biological Chemical Command (SBCCOM) is located at eight stockpile locations across the United States, including Edgewood, Maryland; Newport, Indiana; and Tooele, Utah. Its responsibilities include supporting research, development, and preparedness in issues involving chemical and biological weapons. SBCCOM activities encompass emergency preparedness and response; safe and secure chemical weapons storage; developing partnerships with communities, industries, and government agencies to develop chemical and biological defense systems to produce maximum protection for the United States; monitoring compliance with the Chemical Weapons Convention; and providing direct support for chemical weapons demilitarization.[78]

The U.S. Army Ordnance Department on October 16, 1917, authorized the first U.S. chemical shell filling plant, which was located in Gunpowder Neck, Maryland. A Chemical Warfare Service was formally established by the War Department on June 28, 1918. U.S. chemical warfare programs went through various policy developments, such as the 1969 suspension of U.S. chemical weapons production, and institutional incarnations, such as the October 1, 1998, creation of SBCCOM, as the military's principal chemical weapons authority.[79]

Detailed information resources about SBCCOM and its activities are provided on its website (www.sbccom.army.mil/), including an October 9, 2003, notice on agency reorganization. Other available resources pertain to contracting information, clothing and individual equipment, rations and field feeding, obscuration and decontamination, military operations in urban terrain, materials testing and analysis, homeland defense, and modeling and simulation.

Numerous publications are also accessible, such as the most recent issues of *CB Quarterly* and *e-Catalyst* (2000–present) and reference materials such as *Biological and Chemical Agent Quick Reference Tables* (2002). Numerous research reports are also provided, including *Chemical and Biological Defense Plan Annual Report* (1998), *History of Chemical and Biological Detectors, Alarms, and Warning Systems* (2000), *Edgewood Chemical Biological Center Annual Report* (2000), *Acute Care Center: A Mass Casualty Care Strategy for Biological Terrorism Incidents* (2001), *Guidelines for Use of Personal Protective Equipment by Law Enforcement Personnel during a Terrorist Chemical Agent Incident* (2001), *Guidelines for Cold Weather Mass Decontamination during a Terrorist Chemical Agent Incident* (2002), *The Advantages of Using a Negative Pressure Respirator Hood* (2002), *and History of the Army's Protective Mask* (n.d.).

Space and Missile Defense Command

Headquartered in Huntsville, Alabama, the Space and Missile Defense Command (SMDC) was established in August 1992, when the U.S. Army Space Command and U.S. Army Missile Defense Command were combined. The U.S. Army's role in space, however, dates back into the early 1960s, and its accomplishments include the first intercepts of intercontinental ballistic missiles (1962) and orbiting satellites (1963), development of directed energy weapons including lasers and particle beams, and cutting-edge simulations creating virtual reality tactical and strategic battlefields.[80] SMDC's mission involves being the army's service component to U.S. STRATCOM along with commanding and controlling army space forces, integrated missile defense, and computer network operations.[81]

Various information resources are provided on SMDC's website (www.smdc.army.mil/). These include an acronym glossary, press releases, and fact sheets such as *Atmospheric Interceptor Technology* (n.d.), *Battlefield Ordnance Awareness* (n.d.), *Low-Earth Orbit Position and Reporting Device* (n.d.), and *Space and Missile Defense Battle Lab* (n.d.). Additional publications include the periodicals *The Eagle* (1998–present), *The Kwajalein Hour Glass* (1999–present), and *Army Space Journal* (2001–present).

Training and Doctrine Command

The Training and Doctrine Command (TRADOC) is responsible for training and setting U.S. Army standards and requirements for combat developments. TRADOC was established in July 1973 during a period of turbulence and changing priorities in U.S. defense policies. During the 1970s and 1980s it executed sustained reforms in training, weapons, equipment, force modernization, and army doctrine, which drastically transformed the army's ability to meet international security needs.[82] TRADOC is at Fort Monroe in Virginia.

TRADOC's website (www.tradoc.army.mil/) provides a link to the Reimer Digital Library, a listing of new resources, historical publications such as *Prepare the Army for War: A Historical Overview of the Army Training and Doctrine Command 1973–1998* (1998), and numerous administrative publications such as *Pamphlet 52505: Force XXI Operations* (1994), *Pamphlet 525-80: Army Aviation Warfighting Concept of Operation* (1998), *Regulation 525-13: Force Protection Program* (1997), *Regulations 95-5: Aviation Flight Operations* (2000), and *Regulation 350-50-3: Battle Command Training Program* (2002).

U.S. Marine Corps

The Continental Congress established the U.S. Marine Corps (USMC) on November 10, 1775. As part of the Navy Department, USMC personnel are congressionally mandated to fight on land, air, and sea, although their primary purpose is serving as a maritime force focused on moving forces from sea to fight on land. Training focuses on Marines being first responders to attacks on the United States and its interests, acting against political violence on Americans overseas, providing disaster relief and humanitarian assistance, and evacuating Americans from foreign countries.[83]

USMC's website (www.usmc.mil/) provides information about Marine Corps history, news releases, biographies of key corps personnel, and links to other sites and resources.

Headquarters

The website www.hqmc.usmc.mil/ serves as a gateway to various USMC component agencies. It provides recruiting information, biographical portraits of the Marine Corps commandant and other major USMC officials, links to the websites of individual units such as Camp Pendleton and the 11th Marine Expeditionary Unit, and access to publications such as *Marines Online* magazine (1996–present), *Marine Corps Strategy 21* (2000), and *Expeditionary Maneuver Warfare* (2001).

Plans, Policies, and Operations Department

The Plans, Policies, and Operations Department (PP&O) serves as the focal point for USMC's interface with other military services, the Joint Chiefs of Staff, and unified commanders in chief and allied and foreign defense agencies. It is responsible for coordinating the structure and deployment of USMC forces.[84]

PP&O's website (http://hqinet001.hqmc.usmc.mil/pp&o/) provides links to component organization such as the Operations Division, Strategy and Plans Division, Security Division, Strategic Initiatives Group, and Joint Non-Lethal Weapons Directorate; descriptions of their work; and biographies of key PP&O personnel.

Chemical Biological Incident Response Force

Located in Indian Head, Maryland, the Chemical Biological Incident Response Force (CBIRF) was created in 1996 and provided support for events such as the 1996 Summer Olympics in Atlanta, Georgia; the 1998 State of the Union address; and the North Atlantic Treaty Organization fiftieth anniversary summit in Washington, D.C., in 1999. CBIRF's purpose is assisting local, state, and federal agencies and designated military commanders in situations that feature biological, chemical, high-yield explosives, nuclear, or radiological terrorist incidents. It provides agent detection and identification capabilities, casualty search, rescue and personnel decontamination, and emergency care of those affected by such incidents.[85]

The website www.lejeune.usmc.mil/4thmeb/cbirf.htm has information about CBIRF's background, personnel strength, and organization.

History and Museums Division

The purpose of the History and Museums Division (HMD) is collecting, recording, preserving, and publicizing USMC's overall operational and institutional experience, providing ways of using history to assist in command decision making, and educating and training Marines.[86] HMD's website (http://hqinet001.hqmc.usmc.mil/HD/) provides various resources on Marine Corps history including a "What's New" section, descriptions of corps customs and traditions including an audio clip of the "Marines' Hymn," biographies of historically significant Marines such as John Lejeune, art history images, and a listing of USMC historical publications from 1920 to the present.

Installations and Logistics Departments

Headed by the deputy commandant, installations and logistics, the Installations and Logistics Departments (I&LD) is responsible for increasing Marine Air Ground Task Force (MAGTF) lethal effectiveness by providing support through modern logistics processes, implementing proven technology and best practices, and developing appropriate performance standards.[87]

The website www.hqmc.usmc.mil/ilweb.nsf contains descriptions of I&LD offices, contracting information, and reports including *United States Marine Corps Campaign Plan* (2001) and *United States Marine Corps Logistics Plan* (2002).

Logistics Command

USMC's Logistics Command (LOGCOM) is located in Albany, Georgia; Barstow, California; and Jacksonville, Florida. Its purpose is providing life cycle management of USMC ground weapons systems, equipment, ammunition, and information systems to ensure their operational readiness.[88]

The website www.matcom.usmc.mil/ provides information about LOGCOM operations including news releases, the text of relevant directives, contractor information, and the ability to contact LOGCOM's waste, fraud, and abuse hotline.

Manpower and Reserve Affairs

The Manpower and Reserve Affairs Department (MRA) assists USMC's commandant by planning, directing, coordinating, and supervising active and reserve forces.[89]

MRA's website (www.manpower.usmc.mil/) features information about USMC policies in areas such as reserve affairs, manpower management, personnel plans, personal and family readiness, and financial management. The website also has biographies of key MRA personnel.

Marine Air Ground Task Force Staff and Training Program

Located in Quantico, Virginia, the Marine Air Ground Task Force Staff and Training Program is responsible for providing training in joint and combined force warfighting skills to enhance the warfighting skills of senior commanders and their staffs.[90]

The website www.mstp.quantico.usmc.mil/ provides information about MAGTF sections such as exercise design and ground combat element, course descriptions, and links to publications such as *Marine Corps Order 1500.53A: Marine Air-Ground Task Force Staff Training Program* (2002), *Pamphlet 6-0.2: Guide to U.S. Marine Corps Command and Control Systems* (1998), *Pamphlet 2-0.2: Intelligence Preparation of the Battlespace* (2001), and *Pamphlet 6-0.2: Force Protection* (2002).

Marine Aviation

The Department of Aviation, at the Pentagon, assists the corps commandant in planning and coordinating matters concerning the organization, equipment, manpower, support, and training for USMC aviation units and facilities.[91]

The website http://hqinet001.hqmc.usmc.mil/AVN/ provides information about corps aviation activities. Available resources include descriptions of Department of Aviation entities such as the Aviation Command and Control Branch, Aviation Logistics Support Branch, and Aviation Weapons Branch. Also posted are photographs and descriptions of aircraft used in USMC aviation programs such as the AH-1W Super Cobra helicopter, the EA-6B Prowler Airborne Electronic Warfare support plane, and the FA-18D Hornet jet fighter. Accessible documents include *Aviation Implementation Plan* (n.d.) and *Aviation Campaign Plan* (2002).

Marine Corps Combat Development Command

The Marine Corps Combat Development Command (MCCDC) is located at the Marine Corps Base in Quantico, Virginia. Its mission is developing USMC warfighting concepts and determining relevant requirement capabilities in areas such as doctrine, organization, equipment, training, and support facilities so the Marines are able to field combat-ready forces.[92]

MCCDC's website (https://www.mccdc.usmc.mil/) provides biographies of command leaders and descriptions of component organizations including the Command and Control Integration Division, Capability Assessment Branch, Studies and Analysis Division, and Future Warfighting Division. Numerous MCCDC resources are publicly accessible, including the PowerPoint presentation "Marine Corps Warfighting Concepts in the 21st Century" (n.d.) and the research documents *Operational Maneuver from the Sea* (1996), *A Concept for Operations in a Riverine Environment* (1997), *A Concept for Future Military Operations on Urban Terrain* (1997), *A Concept for Antiarmor Operations* (1998), *The MAGTF in Sustained Operations Ashore* (1998), and *MAGTF Aviation and Operational Maneuver from the Sea* (1999).

Marine Corps Doctrine Division

The USMC Doctrine Division coordinates, develops, maintains, and publishes service doctrinal materials; coordinates corps contributions to joint and multiservice military doctrine; and participates in matters concerning standardization, terminology, and other combat development system processes.[93]

The publications on the website https://www.doctrine.usmc.mil/ cover warfighting, intelligence operations, training, and ground and aerial combat. It also has Navy doctrinal publications.

Samples of these resources are DOD orders affecting USMC and Marine Corps Doctrinal Publications (MCDP) such as *MCDP1: Warfighting* (1997) and *MCDP3: Expeditionary Operations* (1998). Other corps operational and theoretical resources are *Tactical Fundamentals of Helicopter-Borne Operations* (1991), *Reconnaissance Reports Guide* (1998), *Religious Ministry Support in the U.S. Marine Corps (2001), Multiservice Procedures for Theater Missile Defense Intelligence Preparation of the Battlespace* (2001), and *Artillery Operations* (2002).

Marine Corps Institute

The Marine Corps Institute (MCI), in Washington, D.C., facilitates education and training for individual Marines focusing on improving performance, enhancing professional military education, and providing promotion opportunities. These programs and activities have been under way since MCI's establishment in 1920.[94]

MCI's website (https://www.mci.usmc.mil/) provides information about institute courses such as Fundamentals of Marine Corps Leadership, Terrorism Awareness for Marines, Operations against Guerilla Units, and Military Operations in Urban Terrain. It also includes issues of the newsletter *Hotline* (April 2000–present) and the reports *Afghanistan: An Introduction to the Country and People* (2004) and *Iraq: An Introduction to the Country and People* (2004).

Marine Corps Systems Command

The Marine Corps Systems Command (MCSC), located at Quantico, Virginia, is charged with serving as USMC's means for equipping its operational forces. It provides quality systems and equipment in a timely and consistent manner, manages systems and equipment during their life cycles, and employs efficient and innovative business practices.[95]

MCSC's website (www.marcorsyscom.usmc.mil/) contains information about services provided, an exhaustive acronym glossary, contracting opportunities, news releases, and PowerPoint presentations about MCSC activities.

Marine Corps University

The Marine Corps University (MCU) was founded on August 1, 1989, by an order from Gen. Alfred Gray, the USMC commandant. However, Marine Corps higher educational efforts date back to the 1891 establishment of the School of Application in Washington, D.C.[96] MCU, in Quantico, Virginia, develops, delivers, and evaluates professional military education for Marines by focusing on leadership and core competencies through resident and distance education programs to enable students to meet current and future operational challenges.[97]

MCU's website (www.mcu.usmc.mil/) provides biographies of the university president and civilian and military faculty members; a recommended readings list for students to facilitate classroom discussion; information about university entities such as Command and Control Systems School, Expeditionary Warfare School, Law of Warfare Program, and Marine Corps War College; information on MCU course curriculum such as Foundations of the Operational Art, Operational Planning, and Future War; monthly MCU newsletters (2001–present); and the current *University Catalog*.

Marine Corps Warfighting Laboratory

The Marine Corps Warfighting Laboratory (MCWL) was established in 1995 in Quantico, Virginia, and is part of the Marine Corps Combat Development Plan. MCWL's mission is improving contemporary and future naval expeditionary warfare capabilities over the total conflict spectrum for USMC operating forces.[98]

MCWL's website (www.mcwl.quantico.usmc.mil/) provides further information about laboratory activities. It covers MCWL divisions such as the Center for Emerging Threats and Capabilities, Experiment Plans Division, Experiment Operations Division, and Office of Science and Technology Integration. Fact sheets on laboratory research are provided including *Dismounted Combat Identification* (n.d.), *Command and Control Integration* (2002), and *M3M .50 Caliber Machine Gun* (2002). Examples of accessible research reports include *When Devils Walk the Earth: The Mentality and Roots of Terrorism, and How to Respond* (2001), *Child Soldiers: Implications for U.S. Forces* (2002), and *Matrix Warfare: The New Face of Competition and Conflict in the 21st Century* (2002).

Programs and Resources Department

The Programs and Resources Department (P&R) is the primary staff agency of USMC's commandant for developing and defending corps requirements, policies, and programs. It formulates the polices and principles enabling effective control and oversight of all USMC financial and budgetary operations.[99]

P&R's website (http://hqinet001.hqmc.usmc.mil/p&r/) provides further information about departmental activities. Accessible materials include coverage of activities performed by P&R's three divisions: Programs, Fiscal, and Special Operations; listings of key personnel; a description of USMC's budget preparation process; and the annual publication *Marine Corps Concepts and Programs* (2000–2004).

Safety Division

The Safety Division (SD) is charged with enhancing Marine Corps readiness by educating and equipping Marines, sailors, and civilians to manage risks and reduce mishaps. SD has been performing these responsibilities since its July 1993 formation from other USMC entities.[100] SD's website (www.hqmc.usmc.mil/safety.nsf/)

provides information on corps safety programs including flight mishap statistics from fiscal year 1990 to the present, ground fatality statistics from fiscal year 1988 to the present, aircraft breakdown statistics, the current year of *Monthly Fatality and Accident Summary,* and *Marine Corps Safety Strategic Plan* (n.d.).

Training and Education Command

The Marine Corps Training and Education Command (TECOM) is responsible for developing, coordinating, carrying out, and evaluating educational and training materials, plans, and programs to ensure that Marines are able to meet the challenges of existing and potential operational environments.[101]

TECOM's website (www.tecom.usmc.mil/) provides information about key personnel, curriculum development and distance learning programs, information on the Marine Corps Mountain Warfare Training Center, and the text of training materials including *Training and Readiness Manual for Assault Amphibian Vehicles* (1999), *Infantry Training and Readiness Manual* (2002), *Marine Corps Physical Fitness Test and Body Composition Program Manual* (2002), and *System for Marine Combat Water Survival Training* (2002).

U.S. Navy

The Continental Congress on October 13, 1775, established the Continental Navy of the American Revolution. A Department of the Navy and the Office of Secretary of Navy were established by statute on April 30, 1798, and the National Security Act Amendments of 1949 established the modern Department of the Navy in the Department of Defense. The U.S. Navy's mission is protecting the United States by effectively prosecuting sea war including seizing or defending naval bases, supporting all U.S. military forces, and maintaining freedom of the seas.[102]

Navy information resources are produced by a variety of entities including the chief of naval operations (CNO), Naval Historical Center (NHC), Naval War College (NWC), and Office of Naval Research (ONR). Many resources are accessible through the Navy's gateway website (www.navy.mil/).

Chief of Naval Operations

The chief of naval operations (CNO) is the Navy Department's senior military officer and a four-star admiral who reports to the secretary of the navy. The CNO's responsibilities include commanding, deploying resources, and enhancing the operating efficiency of naval forces and shore activities.

The CNO also serves on the Joint Chiefs of Staff, is recognized as the key adviser to the president and secretary of the navy on naval military operations, and directs a staff of officers referred to as the Office of the Chief of Naval Operations (OPNAV).[103]

On the website http://chinfo.navy.mil/navpalib/cno/ are a biography of the current CNO, news articles, congressional testimony, an article "Sea Power 21: Projecting Decisive Joint Capabilities" (2002), and the reports *Top Five Priorities—A Status Report on CNO Guidance for 2002* (2002), and *Achieving Sea Power 21!: CNO's Guidance for 2003* (2003).

FOIA Online

Accessible at http://foia.navy.mil/ are Navy documents released under the Electronic Freedom of Information Act (EFOIA) and links to Marine Corps and U.S. Navy EFOIA sites. Links to EFOIA resources are from agencies such as Office of the General Counsel and the U.S. Atlantic Fleet. Available documents include *Naval Discharge Review Board Dockets* (1997–2002) and *Annual Consumer Report on the Quality of Tap Water Naval Air Station Fallon (NV) Public Water System* (2002).

Military Sealift Command

The Military Sealift Command (MSC) is responsible for supplying ocean transportation equipment, fuel, supplies, and ammunition to support U.S. forces internationally during peacetime and war. MSC is the sea transportation unit of TRANSCOM. The Military Sea Transportation Service was, in 1949, the sole managerial agency for DOD ocean transport requirements. It became the Military Sealift Command in 1970.[104]

Information on MSC's services can be found on its website (www.msc.navy.mil/). Available resources include descriptions of command ships, discussion of engineering issues facing MSC, press releases, and fact sheets such as *Fast Sealift Ships* (2001), *Underway Replenishment Oilers* (2001), and *Ammunition Ships* (2002). Accessible reports are *Operations Security Plan* (2000), *Year in Review Annual Report* (2001–2002), and *Military Sealift Command Mission Capability Assessment* (2002).

U.S. Naval Academy

The U.S. Naval Academy (USNA), located in Annapolis, Maryland, was founded in 1845 by Secretary of the Navy George Bancroft. Its serves as the U.S. Navy's undergraduate naval educational institution and strives to promote the moral, mental, and physical education of its student body, known as midshipmen.[105]

USNA's website (www.nadn.navy.mil/) provides information resources on the academy's mission. It includes a demographic profile of the first year's class (plebes), descriptions of departmental research activity from 1997 to 2000, links to the USNA's library web page, and descriptions of research centers such as the Center for the Study of Professional Military Ethics and Center for Teaching and Learning. Additional content includes descriptions for curricular offerings such as Ship Structures, Coastal Engineering, Analytical Applications in Ship Design, American Naval Heritage, Recent Military and Naval History, and Information Technology, National Security, and International Relations. Other website contents include the current year *Catalog;* a lecture by former Vietnam War prisoner of war Admiral James Stockdale, "Stockdale on Stoicism I: The Stoic Warrior's Triad: Tranquility, Fearlessness, and Freedom" (1995); and *Autonomous Underwater Vehicle Team 2002 Journal Paper* (2002).

Naval Aerospace Medical Research Laboratory

Located in Pensacola, Florida, the Naval Aerospace Medical Research Laboratory (NAMRL) has been conducting research and development in aviation medicine since 1939 to improve the health, safety, and readiness of U.S. Navy and Marine Corps personnel. NAMRL's programs focus on research in areas such as spatial orientation, human performance, and aeromedical standards.[106] The laboratory's website (www.namrl.navy.mil/) contains a biography of the current commanding officer and descriptions of current projects areas including the Impact Acceleration Injury Database, Night Vision Acuity Tester, and Tactile Situation Awareness System.

Naval Air Systems Command

Headquartered at Patuxent River, Maryland, and with other facilities in the continental United States, the Naval Air Systems Command (NAVAIR) is responsible for coordinating and using naval aviation and associated technologies to fulfill U.S. national security objectives.[107] NAVAIR's website (www.navair.navy.mil/) contains resources such as news releases, contracting opportunities, and information on naval aircraft systems including the V-22 Osprey air transport craft, the F-18 Hornet strike fighter, and unmanned aerial vehicles. It also provides links to various NAVAIR-affiliated organizations, including the Weapons and Systems Development Energetics Test Ranges in China Lake, California (www.nawcwpns.navy.mil./), the Support Equipment Aircraft Launch and Recovery Equipment facility in Lakehurst, New Jersey (www.lakehurst.navy.mil/), and the Training Systems Instructional Systems facility in Orlando, Florida (www.ntsc.navy.mil/).

Naval Cost Analysis Division

The Naval Cost Analysis Division (NCAD) guides, directs, and strengthens cost analysis within the Navy Department; prepares credible cost estimates of the resources needed to develop, purchase, and operate military systems; advises the secretary of the navy and chief of naval operations on weapons system cost estimates; and conducts economic analyses of naval weapons and information systems.[108] NCAD is in Washington, D.C.

The website www.ncca.navy.mil/ has descriptions of naval programs that NCAD analyzes, descriptions of methodologies used to make estimates, a searchable library of reports produced, and descriptions of NCAD components such as the Cost Research and Operations Division, Economic Studies Division, Platform Program Support Division, and Cost Analysis Tools Division. Accessible information resources include charts such as "Ship Life Cycle Cost Profile" (n.d.) and "Aircraft Total Ownership/Life Cycle Cost Composition" (n.d.) and documents such as *Policy*

Manual (2001) and *Strategic Business Plan* (2001). NCAD's website does not include the text of its major analytical reports.

Naval Facilities Engineering Command

The Naval Facilities Engineering Command (NAVFAC) is responsible for planning, designing, and constructing shore facilities for naval activities around the world. Its annual business activities exceed $8 billion, and its sixteen thousand civilian and military employees provide services such as base development, planning, and design; base realignment and closure; and military operations and contingency engineering at field components in the United States and Europe.[109]

The website www.navfac.navy.mil/ has information about NAVFAC's work, contracting information, and publications including *Inspection of Shore Facilities* (1993), *Pavement Design for Airfields* (2001), *Design: General Building Requirements* (2002), and *Strategic Plan 2003–2009*.

Naval Historical Center

President John Adams in 1800 set up the Navy Department Library. This evolved into the Naval Historical Center (NHC), which has grown to encompass a museum, art gallery, research library, archives, and research and writing programs. NHC, in Washington, D.C., preserves, analyzes, and interprets the U.S. Navy's historical experience for itself and the American public.[110]

NHC's website (www.history.navy.mil/) provides further information about the center's programs and activities. Examples of available materials are listings of navy and Marine personnel killed and wounded in combat or terrorist incidents from the 1790s to the present, listings of U.S. libraries with naval history manuscript collections, an annotated bibliography of recommended naval history works encompassing government and nongovernment resources, historical paintings and photographs, online exhibits such as "Alaska during the Pacific War," NHC visitors information, and reports on historical topics including underwater archaeology.

Naval Medicine Online

Naval Medicine Online (NMO) is responsible for providing high-quality and economical health care to active-duty and retired Navy and Marine Corps personnel and their families while supporting ongoing naval operational requirements.[111] NMO dates from August 31, 1842, when it was created as part of a Navy Department reorganization; its modern incarnation dates from the August 4, 1989, termination of the Naval Medical Command and NMO's reactivation.[112]

NMO's website (http://navalmedicine.med.navy.mil/) provides information about bureau activities including the text of directives and forms, news releases, leadership biographies, links to worldwide naval medical facility websites, and the text of publications such as *Radiation Health Protection Manual* (2001).

U.S. Naval Observatory

The U.S. Naval Observatory (USNO) is located in Washington, D.C., and was established in 1830 as the Depot of Charts and Instruments with responsibility for caring for naval chronometers, charts, and navigational equipment. Its current responsibilities include determining the positions and motions of celestial entities; observing motions of the earth; keeping track of the precise time; providing astronomical and timing data needed by the U.S. Navy and other DOD entities for navigation, precise positioning, and command, control, and communications; making this data available to other government agencies and the general public; and conducting relevant research on these subjects.[113]

USNO's website (www.usno.navy.mil/) has descriptions of USNO departments covering astrometry; astronomical applications; earth orientation; the Flagstaff, Arizona, facility; and library collections and services. Additional features include descriptions of USNO's master clock, which serves as the U.S. government's official timekeeper; the ability to search for and calculate the moonrise and sunrise for U.S. and foreign locales; information about USNO research activity; and details about USNO publications including the annual *Air Almanac, Astronomical Almanac,* and *Nautical Almanac,* which are produced in collaboration with the United Kingdom's Her Majesty's Nautical Almanac Office. The full text of these three publications is not on the USNO website, although supplemental update information is accessible.

Naval Postgraduate School

The modern incarnation of the Naval Postgraduate School (NPS) dates from a 1945 law making it a fully accredited graduate institution. NPS moved to its present campus, in Monterey, California, in 1951.[114] NPS consists of approximately fifteen hundred students representing officers from U.S. military services and nearly thirty countries. Enrollees also include selected U.S. government employees. Students pursue master's and doctoral degrees in subjects as diverse as national security affairs, aeronautical engineering, meteorology and physical oceanography, information technology management, and applied physics in ways appropriate to Navy and DOD research interests and requirements.[115]

The NPS website (www.nps.navy.mil/) contains news releases, information about NPS faculty, school policies and procedures, and links to NPS pedagogical and research centers such as the Center for Autonomous Underwater Vehicle Research, Center for Civil-Military Relations, Center for Contemporary Conflict, Center for Information Systems Security Studies and Research, and Center on Terrorism and Irregular Warfare.

Descriptions, and some syllabi, are provided for NPS curricular offerings including Aerospace System Dynamics, Aerodynamic Analysis, Helicopter Stability and Control, U.S. Foreign Policy in the Middle East, and Government and Security in China.

A number of research reports produced by NPS faculty, and in some cases students, are also accessible on the NPS website. Examples include *The Democratic Con-*

trol of the Mongolian Armed Forces: The State Ih Hural (2000), The Future of Armed Resistance: Cyberterror? Mass Destruction? (2000), Application of Formation Control for Multi-Vehicle Robotic Minesweeping (2001), Defense Budgets and Civilian Oversight (2001), A Cautionary Note Regarding the Data Integrity Capacity of Certain Secure Systems (2001), The Information Revolution in Military Affairs: Prospects for Asia (2002), Germany, Japan, and the "De-Baathification" of Iraq (2003), and Post-War Iraq: Prospects and Problems (2003).

Naval Research Laboratory

The Naval Research Laboratory (NRL) is located in Washington, D.C., and in other locations nationwide. It began operations in 1923.[116] NRL conducts multidisciplinary research in scientific and technological development in fields such as maritime applications of materials technology, atmospheric and space sciences, and other programs assisting naval operations within the Office of Naval Research.[117]

Additional information about NRL and its programs can be acquired through its website (www.nrl.navy.mil/). Resources describe the work performed by NRL's organizational entities including the Naval Center for Space Science and Nanoscience Institute, news releases, contracting opportunities, and publications such as the biennially published journal NRL Review and reference volumes such as NRL Factbook (2001) and Naval Research Laboratory's Major Facilities (2001).

Naval Sea Systems Command

The Naval Sea Systems Command (NAVSEA) is headquartered at the Washington Navy Yard in Washington, D.C., and has operations at other domestic and international facilities. NAVSEA responsibilities are to build, engineer, and support U.S. naval ship and combat systems and to manage more than 130 acquisition programs and a nearly $20 billion budget.[118]

NAVSEA's website (www.navsea.navy.mil/) contains information about command history, a searchable ship availability database that includes the shipyards producing a ship, contracting information, Quicktime videos describing command activities, descriptions of NAVSEA research in areas such as compassed and stabilized altitude heading systems and gaskets for watertight closures, and links to NAVSEA component organizations such as the Naval Surface Warfare Center and Naval Undersea Warfare Center.

Naval Surface Warfare Center

The Naval Surface Warfare Center (NSWC) is headquartered in Washington, D.C., and has divisions around the United States. Its mission, as part of NAVSEA, is providing research, development, testing, evaluation, and engineering to support technical aspects of naval surface ships and their offensive and defensive systems involved in naval surface warfare.[119]

NSWC's website www.nswcdc.navy.mil/ provides information about center activities including links to center divisions at Carderock, Maryland; Crane, Indiana; Corona, California; and elsewhere. Information provided by these facilities includes descriptions of their research areas, contracting opportunities, contact information, employment opportunities, statistics, and selected reports such as *Impact Assessment of Crane Division of Naval Surface Warfare Center, Naval Sea System Command: A Report to the Southern Indiana Business Alliance* (2000).

Naval Treaty Implementation Program

The Naval Treaty Implementation Program (NTIP), under the auspices of the Department of the Navy, formulates plans and procedures to ensure compliance with nonstrategic international treaties and agreements. Its personnel consists of senior military and civilians with expertise in treaty implementation and compliance planning and in policy and preparation for treaty verification assignments.[120]

NTIP's website (www.nawcwpns.navy.mil/~treaty/) provides information on program activities including an overview of arms control treaties and agreements such as the Mine Ban Treaty, Sea Bed Arms Control Treaty, Transparency in Armaments Agreement, and Strategic Arms Reduction Talks (START) Treaty implementation and the naval importance of these treaties. Accessible publications include the current issue of the *Treaty Times* newsletter and *DOD Directive 2060.1: Implementation of, and Compliance with, Arms Control Agreements* (2001).

Naval Undersea Warfare Center

The Naval Undersea Warfare Center (NUWC) is located in Newport, Rhode Island, and Keyport, Washington. It is part of NAVSEA. Formally established on January 2, 1992, NUWC serves as the U.S. Navy's chief research, development, test and evaluation, and engineering and fleet support organization for submarines, independent underwater systems, and offensive and defensive weapons systems involved with underseas warfare.[121]

NUWC's website (www.nuwc.navy.mil/) contains information about Rhode Island naval history, links to the Newport and Keyport division homepages, and descriptions of work performed by NUWC divisions such as the Atlantic Undersea Test and Evaluation Center, the Underwater Sound Reference Division, and the Undersea Vehicles Group. Available publications include NUWC's *Strategic Plan* (1998) and *NUWC Year in Review* (2000).

Naval Vessel Register

The Naval Vessel Register (NVR) is an official inventory of ships and service craft in U.S. Navy custody or title. Its origins date to the 1880s, and it is maintained by NAVSEA's Shipbuilding Support Office in collaboration with CNO's Logistics, Support Maintenance, and Modernization division. It is maintained and updated weekly in electronic format only. More than sixty-five hundred unique record transactions are processed annually and augmented with official documentation. NVR includes a current listing of available ships and service craft, those under construction, and those assigned to MSC. Information provided in NVR includes ship class, fleet assignment, vessel name, age, homeport, planning yard, hull and machinery descriptors, builder, key construction dates, battle actions, and status condition.[122]

NVR's website (www.nvr.navy.mil/) has a list of currently active ships, such as the aircraft carrier USS *John Stennis* and nuclear submarine USS *Dallas*, and of defunct naval ships, such as the battleship USS *Iowa* and the tank landing ship *Vernon County*.

Naval War College

Located in Newport, Rhode Island, the Naval War College (NWC) provides graduate education for naval officers. Since its 1884 establishment, NWC's purpose has been to enhance the professional capabilities of its students to make sound decisions in combat, staff, and management positions in naval, joint, and combined environments; provide solid understanding of military strategy and operational art; instill joint attitudes and perspectives; and serve as a research and gaming center to develop advanced strategic, warfighting and campaign concepts for future deployment of maritime, joint, and combined forces.[123]

NWC and its activities are discussed at www.nwc.navy.mil/. Detailed descriptions, including some curricular materials, are provided about NWC units including the Center for Naval Warfare Studies, Strategic Research Department, Decision Strategies Department, War Gaming Department, International Law Department, Naval War College Press, and Strategic Studies Group. News releases are available along with information about library resources, speeches by distinguished visitors, and information on NWC's museum.

Noteworthy publications accessible on the website are articles from NWC's scholarly journal *Naval War College Review* (autumn 1996–present) and reports such as *Theater Ballistic Missile Defense from the Sea: Issues for the Maritime Component Commander* (1998), *International Environmental Law and Naval War: The Effect of Marine Safety and Pollution Conventions during International Armed Conflict* (2000), *Asia and the Pacific: U.S. Strategic Traditions and Regional Realities* (2001), and *Case Studies in Policy Making and Implementation* (2002).

Navy International Programs Office

The Navy International Programs Office (NIPO) provides assistance to U.S. allies with the guidance of U.S. laws, DOD policy, and congressional direction. NIPO programs encompass foreign military sales, leases, defense article grants, cooperative programs, protecting key technologies, granting release authority for transferable technologies, and education and training.[124]

NIPO's website (https://www.nipo.navy.mil/) contains an organizational chart; information on the Export License Division, International Agreements Division, and Security Assistance Directorate; PowerPoint slides on various topics; and links to governmental security assistance agency websites such as the Defense Security Cooperation Agency. Publications include NIPO's current newsletter, *Data Exchange*

Guidelines for Technical Project Officers (1997), *Department of the Navy Strategic Plan for International Programs 1999–2003* (1998), and *Security Assistance Strategic Plan 2001–2003* (2001).

Navy Personnel Research, Studies, and Technology

Navy Personnel Research, Studies, and Technology (NPRST), in Millington, Tennessee, serves as the navy's manpower and personnel research laboratory. Institutional foci stress researching, developing, and confirming new technologies, methods, and management processes to enhance the readiness, performance, retention, and life quality of navy and USMC personnel.[125]

The website www.nprst.navy.mil/ provides organizational charts; a listing of NPRST components such as the Navy Personnel Readiness and Community Support Department and the Personnel Progression, Performance, and Security Department; and descriptions of ongoing research areas such as the retention measurement and monitoring system and e-commerce technology for personnel distribution and assignment. Accessible research reports include *Virtual Environment Training for Engineering: Material Readiness Assessment* (1998), *Assessment of USMC Quality of Life Program Contributions to Readiness, Performance, and Retention, Volume 11: Pilot Test Results* (1999), and *A Progress Check on the Navy Values Community: Report on the 1998 Navy Core Values Survey* (1999).

Navy Warfare Development Command

The Navy Warfare Development Command (NWDC) has been tapped to introduce new ideas to fleet operations, conduct dialogues exploring the merits of these ideas, collaboratively develop projects to implement these ideas, and keep the navy informed and involved as the fleet recognizes warfighting benefits that can be gained from these new ideas.[126] NWDC is in Newport, Rhode Island.

NWDC's website (www.nwdc.navy.mil/) provides additional information about command activities. Descriptions of NWDC's Maritime Battle Center, Operations Department, and Doctrine Department are provided along with details on past and future conferences sponsored by NWDC. Publicly accessible publications include the draft concept paper *High Speed Vessel: Adaptability, Modularity, and Flexibility for the Joint Force* (n.d.), *Naval Doctrine Publication 1: Naval Warfare* (1994), *Naval Doctrinal Publication 6: Naval Command and Control* (1995), *Naval Mission Essential Task List Development Handbook* (2000), and *Naval Doctrinal Publication 4: Naval Logistics* (2001).

Network Centric Innovation Center

The Network Centric Innovation Center (NCIC) is located in San Diego, California, and was founded in 1999. NCIC is devoted to creating, discovering, and promoting solutions that will benefit the U.S. Navy in network centric warfare. In fulfilling its mission, NCIC works closely with other navy components and the private sector to develop the best practices in this field to meet naval operational requirements.[127]

NCIC's website (www.ncic.navy.mil/) provides further information about center activities and work. Website contents include monthly activity listings (July 2001–present) and PowerPoint presentations including "Navy-Marine Corps Intranet Progress Report" (2002), "Building a Secure Windows Platform for Trustworthy Computing" (2002), and "Fleet Innovation" (2002).

Office of Naval Research

The Office of Naval Research (ONR) coordinates, executes, and promotes U.S. Navy and Marine Corps science and technology programs in partnership with schools, universities, government laboratories, and nonprofit and for profit organizations. ONR, in Washington, D.C., also provides technical advice to the CNO and secretary of the navy and works with industry to improve technological manufacturing processes.[128] The office began operations in 1946.

The website www.onr.navy.mil/ has ONR job opportunity listings; descriptions of ONR departments such as Expeditionary Warfare, Information Electronics, and Surveillance and Ocean, Atmosphere, and Space; contracting information; and press releases. Other ONR-produced materials include fact sheets such as *Battlespace Preparation Autonomous Underwater Vehicle* (n.d.), *A Future Naval Capability: Autonomous Operations* (n.d.), *Littoral Antisubmarine Warfare* (n.d.), *Semi-Autonomous Hydrographic Reconnaissance Vehicle* (n.d.), and *Warfighter Protection* (n.d.) and reports including *Amphibious Counter-Mine and Counter-Obstacle Requirements in Support of Operational Maneuver from the Sea* (n.d.).

Space and Naval Warfare Systems Command

Space and Naval Warfare Systems Command (SPAWAR) was established in 1966 to support the U.S. Navy and Marine Corps electronic systems; equipment; and command, control, and communications. Headquartered in San Diego, California, since 1997 and augmented by facilities in other U.S. locations, SPAWAR has more than eight thousand employees and seeks to give warfighters knowledge superiority by supporting effective and integrated command, control, and communications; computer intelligence; surveillance and reconnaissance; information technology; and space systems capabilities.[129]

SPAWAR's website (www.spawar.navy.mil/) provides an organizational chart, biographies of command leaders, news releases, an Excel spreadsheet of active SPAWAR contracts, the manual *Acquisition Program Structure Guide* (2002), and the following fact sheets: *Ultra High Frequency Follow-On Program* (1999), *Advanced Buoyant Cable Antenna Program* (2001), and *Naval Space Surveillance System* (2002).

Surface Warfare Directorate

The Surface Warfare Directorate (SWD) is part of the CNO's office. Its responsibilities include determining force levels, shipboard and related support requirements, and major program characteristics involving cruisers, destroyers, logistics, and auxiliary ships. These missions are augmented by the need to enhance readiness, safety, survivability, and training for surface warfare operations; to execute Navy shipbuilding and conversion programs; and to carry out the surface warfare missions of assured access and support for maneuver warfare, theater air dominance, maritime dominance, and joint command, control, computers, information surveillance, and reconnaissance in naval surface operations.[130]

The web page http://chinfo.navy.mil/navpalib/cno/n76/ describes SWD missions and features an organizational chart, ship descriptions, mine warfare information, descriptions of various weapons systems including the Advanced Gun System, Advanced Tomahawk Weapons Control System, and Naval Fires Control System. Access is also provided to publications such as *Surface Warfare Commanders Conference Report* (2001–2002) and the magazine *Surface Warfare* (2002–present).

Notes

1. U.S. Government Printing Office, "About the Federal Depository Library Program (FDLP)" (2003), 1 (www.gpoaccess.gov/fdlp.html), accessed November 24, 2003.

2. U.S. Department of Defense, *Defense Almanac* (Washington, D.C.: Department of Defense, n.d.), 1 (www.defenselink.mil/pubs/almanac/almanac/organization/Combatant_Commands.html), accessed November 11, 2003.

3. U.S. Central Command, "About Centcom" (n.d.), 1–2 (www.centcom.mil/aboutus/centcom.htm), accessed November 11, 2003.

4. U.S. European Command, "Unified Command Plan Changes in USEUCOM since 1952" (n.d.), 1 (www.eucom.mil/AOR/history.htm), accessed November 11, 2003.

5. U.S. European Command, "2002 U.S. European Command Strategy of Readiness and Enlargement" (n.d.), 1 (www.eucom.mil/Command/Strategy/strategic-environment.htm), accessed November 11, 2003.

6. U.S. Joint Forces Command, "About Us" (n.d.), 1 (www.jfcom.mil/about/about1.htm), accessed November 11, 2003.

7. U.S. Joint Forces Command, "In the Beginning" (n.d.), 1 (www.jfcom.mil/about/History/abthist1.htm), accessed November 11, 2003; and U.S. Joint Forces Command, "New Name, Future Focus" (n.d.), 1 (www.jfcom.mil/about/History/abthist6.htm), accessed November 11, 2003.

8. U.S. Northern Command, "Who We Are" (n.d.), 1 (www.northcom.mil/index.cfm?fuseaction=s.whoweare&section=4), accessed November 11, 2003. For a historical overview of U.S. homeland defense, see Stetson Conn, Rose C. Engelman, and Byron Fairchild, *Guarding the United States and Its Outposts* (Washington, D.C.: U.S. Army Center for Military History, 2000).

9. U.S. Northern Command, "Who We Are—Mission" (n.d.), 1 (www.northcom.mil/index.cfm?fuseaction=s.who_mission), accessed November 11, 2003.

10. U.S. Pacific Command, "About U.S. Pacific Command" (n.d.), 1 (www.pacom.mil/about/history.shtml), accessed November 11, 2003.

11. U.S. Pacific Command, "About U.S. Pacific Command" (n.d.), 1–2 (www.pacom.mil/about/pacom.shtml), accessed November 11, 2003.

12. U.S. Southern Command, "U.S. Southern Command History" (n.d.), 1–2 (www.southcom.mil/pa/Facts/History.htm), accessed November 11, 2003.

13. U.S. Southern Command, "U.S. Southern Command Profile" (n.d.), 1 (www.southcom.mil/pa/Facts/Profile.htm), accessed November 11, 2003.

14. See U.S. Special Operations Command, *Special Operations Posture Statement 2000* (Washington, D.C.: U.S. Special Operations Command, 2000), 1 (www.defenselink.mil/pubs/

sof/organize.pdf), accessed November 11, 2003; and PL 99-661, "To Authorize Appropriations for Fiscal Year 1987 for Military Activities of the Department of Defense, for Military Construction, and for Defense Activities, of the Department of Energy, to Prescribe Personnel Strength for Such Fiscal Year for the Armed Forces, to Improve the Defense Acquisition Process, and for Other Purposes," 100 *U.S. Statutes at Large,* 3816, 3983–3986.

15. U.S. Special Operations Command, *Special Operations Posture Statement 2000,* 4.

16. U.S. Strategic Command, "USSTRATCOM Headquarters" (n.d), 1 (www.stratcom.mil/), accessed November 11, 2003.

17. U.S. Strategic Command, "Fact File: U.S. Strategic Command History," 1–2 (www.stratcom.mil/factsheetshtml/history.htm), accessed November 11, 2003. For additional historical background, see Harry R. Borowski, *A Hollow Threat: Strategic Air Power and Containment Before Korea* (Westport, Conn.: Greenwood Press, 1982); and J. C. Hopkins and Sheldon A. Goldberg, *The Development of Strategic Air Command, 1946–1986: The Fortieth Anniversary History* (Offutt Air Force Base, Nebraska: Headquarters Strategic Air Command, Office of the Historian, 1986).

18. U.S. Transportation Command (TRANSCOM), Office of Public Affairs, "United States Transportation Command" (n.d.), 1 (www.transcom.mil/history/summary.htm), accessed November 11, 2003. For succinct and detailed historical overviews of TRANSCOM, see U.S. Transportation Command, "United States Transportation Command: A Short History" (2002), 1–2 (www.transcom.mil/history/history.html), accessed November 11, 2003; and James K. Matthews and Cora J. Holt, *So Many, So Much, So Far, So Fast: United States Transportation Command and Strategic Deployment for Operation Desert Shield/Desert Storm* (Washington, D.C.: Joint History Office, Office of the Chairman of the Joint Chiefs of Staff and U.S. Transportation Command, Research Center, 1999).

19. *U.S. Government Manual, 2002–2003* (Washington, D.C.: National Archives and Records Administration, 2002), 167. For official histories of the U.S. Air Force, see Stephen L. McFarland, *A Concise History of the United States Air Force* (Washington, D.C.: Air Force History and Museums Program, 1998); and Warren A. Trest, *Air Force Roles and Missions: A History* (Washington, D.C.: Air Force History and Museums Program, 1998). For coverage on historical air force doctrine and strategic thinking, see Robert Frank Futrell, *Ideas, Concepts, and Doctrine: Basic Thinking in the United States Air Force,* 2 vols. (Maxwell Air Force Base, Ala.: Air University Press, 1989).

20. AFNEWS: The Air Force News Agency, "History of AFNEWS", (n.d.), 1 (www.afnews.af.mil/about/history.htm), accessed November 11, 2003.

21. U.S. Air Force, Air Combat Command, "Air Combat Command Mission" (2002), 1 (www2.acc.af.mil/library/mission/), accessed November 11, 2003.

22. U.S. Air Force, Air Command and Staff College, "About ACSC" (2002), 1 (http://www.acsc.maxwell.af.mil/About/about.htm), accessed November 11, 2003.

23. U.S. Air National Guard, "Forging the Air National Guard" (2003), 1 (www.ang.af.mil/history/forging.asp), accessed November 11, 2003.

24. See U.S. Air University, "Welcome to the Air University (AU) Home Page" (2003), 3 (www.au.af.mil/about_max_gun.html), accessed November 11, 2003; U.S. Air University, "Air University: Home of Air Force Professional Military Education" (2002), 1–2 (www.au.af.mil/au/facts.html), accessed November 11, 2003; and Jerome A. Ennels, *A Short History of Air University, 1946–2001* (Maxwell Air Force Base, Ala.: Air University Office of History, 2001).

25. U.S. Air Force Academy, "Mission and Vision" (n.d.), 1 (www.usafa.af.mil/misvis/), accessed November 11, 2003.

26. U.S. Air Force Academy, "Academy History" (2001), 1–2 (www.usafa.af.mil/pa/factsheets/history.htm), accessed November 11, 2003. See PL 83-325, "To Provide for the Establishment of

a United States Air Force Academy, and for Other Purposes," 68 *U.S. Statutes at Large,* 47–49. For additional historical background, see U.S. Air Force Academy, *The United States Air Force Academy's First Twenty-five Years: Some Perceptions* (Colorado Springs, Colo.: U.S. Air Force Academy, 1979); and John P. Lovell, *Neither Athens Nor Sparta? The American Service Academies in Transition* (Bloomington: Indiana University Press, 1979).

27. U.S. Air Force Academy, Institute for National Security Studies, "USAF Institute for National Security Studies" (n.d.), 1 (www.usafa.af.mil/inss/longdesc.htm), accessed November 6, 2003.

28. See U.S. Air Force Audit Agency, "AFAA History" (2002), 1 (www.afaa.hq.af.mil/organization/history.htm), accessed November 11, 2003; and U.S. Air Force Audit Agency, "Our Mission" (2000), 1 (www.afaa.hq.af.mil/index2.shtml), accessed November 11, 2003.

29. U.S. Air Force Command and Control and Intelligence, Surveillance, and Reconnaissance Center, "AFC2ISRC History" (n.d.), 1 (www.afc2isrc.af.mil/History.asp), accessed November 11, 2003.

30. U.S. Air Force Command and Control and Intelligence, Surveillance, and Reconnaissance Center, "AFC2ISRC Mission": (n.d.), 1 (www.afc2isrc.af.mil/Mission.asp), accessed November 11, 2003.

31. U.S. Air Force Communications Agency, "The Air Force Communications and Information History Office Online" (n.d.), 1 (https://public.afca.scott.af.mil/public/history/), accessed November 11, 2003. For an official history of the Air Force Communications Agency, see Larry R. Morrison, *Flares to Satellites: A Brief History of Air Force Communications* (Scott Air Force Base, Ill.: U.S. Air Force Communications Agency, Office of History, 1997).

32. U.S. Air Force Communications Agency, "About AFCA Communications and Information" (n.d.), 1 (http://public.afca.af.mil/about.htm), accessed March 12, 2004.

33. U.S. Air Force Flight Test Center, "About Edwards—History" (2002), 1 (www.edwards.af.mil/history/), accessed November 11, 2003. For a historical overview, see Steve Pace, *Edwards Air Force Base Experiment Flight Test Center* (Osceola, Wis.: Motorbooks International, 1994).

34. U.S. Air Force Historical Research Agency, "About the Agency" (2002), 1 (www.maxwell.af.mil/au/afhra/about.html), accessed November 11, 2003.

35. U.S. Air Force History Support Office, "The AFHSO Research and Analysis Division" (n.d.), 1 (www.airforcehistory.hq.af.mil/AboutAFHSO/aboutHOR.htm), accessed November 11, 2003.

36. U.S. Air Force Information Warfare Center, "Mission" (n.d.), 1 (http://afiwcweb.lackland.af.mil/organization/mission.cfm), accessed November 11, 2003.

37. U.S. Air Force Information Warfare Center, "History of AFIWC" (n.d.), 1 (http://afiwcweb.lackland.af.mil/organization/history.cfm), accessed November 11, 2003.

38. U.S. Air Force Institute of Technology, "What Is AFIT?" (n.d.), 1 (www.afit.edu/about/what_is_afit.cfm/), accessed November 11, 2003.

39. U.S. Air Force Institute of Technology, "AFIT History" (n.d.), 1–2 (www.afit.edu/about/history.cfm), accessed November 11, 2003. For additional historical background on U.S. Air Force scientific research efforts in the Dayton, Ohio, area, see James F. Aldridge, *Wright from the Start: The Contributions of Dayton's Science and Engineering Community to American Air Power in the Twentieth Century* (Wright-Patterson Air Force Base, Ohio: Air Force Material Command, Aeronautical Systems Center, History Office, 1997).

40. U.S. Air Force Office of Scientific Research, "The History of AFOSR" (n.d.), 1–3 (www.afosr.af.mil/afrhistory.htm), accessed November 11, 2003. For a history of U.S. Air Force scientific research efforts, see Dwayne A. Day, *Lightning Rod: A History of the Air Force Chief Scientist's Office* (Washington, D.C.: U.S. Air Force, Chief Scientist's Office, 2000).

41. U.S. Air Force, Scientific Advisory Board, "Mission" (n.d.), 1 (https://www.sab.hq.af.mil/mission/), accessed November 11, 2003.

42. U.S. Air Force Research Laboratory, "Fact Sheet: Air Force Research Laboratory" (n.d.), 1 (www.afrl.af.mil/factsht/afrlfactsheet.htm), accessed November 11, 2003.

43. U.S. Air Force Safety Center, "Mission" (n.d.), 1–2 (http://safety.kirtland.af.mil/AFSC/organization.html), accessed November 11, 2003.

44. U.S. Air Force Space Command, "Almanac" (n.d.), 2 (www.peterson.af.mil/hqafspc/library/almanac/pg2/almanac_2.htm), accessed November 11, 2003. For a managerial perspective on one aspect of Air Force Space Command operations, see U.S. General Accounting Office, *Defense Computers: U.S. Space Command's Management of Its Year 2000 Operational Testing* (Washington, D.C.: General Accounting Office, 1999). For historical origins, see U.S. Air Force Space Command, "The Heritage of Air Force Space Command" (n.d.), 1–7 (www.spacecom.af.mil/hqafspc/history/heritage.htm), accessed November 11, 2003.

45. U.S. Air Force, Deputy Under Secretary of the Air Force—International Affairs, "Vision—Mission" (n.d.), 1 (www.safia.hq.af.mil/ia/internet/CoreInit2.htm), accessed November 11, 2003.

46. U.S. Air Force, Space and Missile Systems Center, "Our Mission" (n.d.), 1 (www.losangeles.af.mil/mission.htm), accessed November 11, 2003.

47. See *U.S. Government Manual,* 174; and PL 1-7, "An Act to Establish an Executive Department, to Be Denominated the Department of War," 1 *U.S. Statutes at Large,* 49–50. Additional historical background is provided by David W. Hogan Jr., *225 Years of Service: The U.S. Army, 1775– 2000* (Washington, D.C.: U.S. Army Center of Military History, 2000); and Russell F. Weigley, *History of the United States Army* (Bloomington: Indiana University Press), 1984.

48. *U.S. Government Manual.*

49. U.S. Army, Aberdeen Proving Ground, "Aberdeen Proving Ground" (n.d.), 1 (www.apg.army.mil/aberdeen_proving_ground.htm), accessed November 11, 2003.

50. Australian, British, Canadian, and Australian Armies Program, "ABCA: Introduction to the Program" (n.d.), 1 (http://abca.hqda.pentagon.mil/Introduction/background.html), accessed October 30, 2003.

51. U.S. Army, Armor Center, "Our Mission" (n.d.), 1 (www.knox.army.mil/center/mission.htm), accessed November 11, 2003.

52. U.S. Army Chemical School, "Mission" (n.d.), 1 (www.wood.army.mil/usacmls/mission.htm), accessed November 11, 2003.

53. U.S. Army, Mountain Warfare School, "Welcome" (n.d.), 1 (www.benning.army.mil/AMWS/), accessed November 11, 2003.

54. U.S. Army National Guard, "About Us" (n.d.), 1 (www.arng.army.mil/About_Us/), accessed November 11, 2003. For a historical overview, see Michael D. Doubler, *Civilian in Peace, Soldier in War: The Army National Guard, 1636–2000* (Lawrence: University Press of Kansas, 2003).

55. U.S. Army Research Institute for the Behavioral and Social Sciences, "ARI: A Brief History" (n.d.), 1 (www-ari.army.mil/history.htm), accessed November 11, 2003. For an organizational history, see Joseph Zeidner and Arthur J. Drucker, *Behavioral Science in the Army: A Corporate History of the Army Research Institute* (Washington, D.C.: U.S. Army Research Institute for the Behavioral and Social Sciences, 1987).

56. U.S. Army Research Institute for the Behavioral and Social Sciences, "ARI Mission" (n.d.), 1 (www.ari.army.mil/about/mission.htm), accessed November 11, 2003.

57. U.S. Army Research Laboratory, *The Genealogy of ARL* (Adelphi, Md.: U.S. Army Research Laboratory, 1997), inside cover, 1.

58. U.S. Army Science Board, "The Army Science Board" (n.d.), 1 (https://webportal.saalt.army.mil/sard-asb/Descript.htm), accessed November 12, 2003.

59. PL 57-132, "An Act Making Appropriations for the Support of the Army for the Fiscal Year Ending June Thirtieth, Nineteen Hundred and Four," 32 *U.S. Statutes at Large,* 927; U.S. Army War College, "History" (n.d.), 5, 12 (www.carlisle.army.mil/history.htm), accessed November 11, 2003; Harry P. Ball, *Of Responsible Command: A History of the United States Army War College* (Carlisle Barracks, Pa.: Alumni Association of the United States Army War College, 1994); and Judith Hicks Stiehm, *U.S. Army War College: Military Education in a Democracy* (Philadelphia: Temple University Press, 2002).

60. Reference librarian, U.S. Army War College, telephone conversation with author, March 10, 2003.

61. U.S. Department of the Army, "Assistant Secretary of the Army for Acquisition, Logistics, and Technology: Missions, Functions, and Responsibilities" (n.d.), 1–2 (https://webportal.saalt.army.mil/mission.cfm), accessed November 12, 2003.

62. See U.S. Army, Center for Army Lessons Learned, "History of the Army's Lessons Learned System," in *A Guide to the Services and Gateway of the Center for Army Lessons Learned: Handbook 97-13* (Fort Leavenworth, Kan.: Center for Army Lessons Learned, 1997) (http://call.army.mil/products/handbook/97-13/history.htm); and U.S. Army, Center for Army Lessons Learned, "Introduction to CALL," in *A Guide to the Services and Gateway of the Center for Army Lessons Learned: Handbook 97-13* (Fort Leavenworth, Kan.: Center for Army Lessons Learned, 1997) (http://call.army.mil/products/handbook/97-13/intro.htm).

63. Terrence J. Gough, *The U.S. Army Center of Military History: A Brief History* (Washington, D.C.: U.S. Army Center of Military History, 1996), 1, 3–4 (www.army.mil/cmh-pg/reference/History/gough.htm), accessed November 11, 2003.

64. U.S. Army, Central Identification Laboratory, Hawaii, "Mission and History" (n.d.), 1 (www.cilhi.army.mil/eBrochure.htm), accessed November 11, 2003.

65. U.S. Army, Command and General Staff College, "History and Chronology" (2002), 6–7 (www.cgsc.army.mil/history.asp), accessed November 12, 2003. For an overall history, see Boyd L. Dastrup, *The U.S. Army Command and General Staff College: A Centennial History* (Manhattan, Kan.: Sunflower University Press, 1982).

66. U.S. Army, Command and General Staff College, "About the Command and General Staff College" (2002), 1 (www.cgsc.army.mil/about.asp), accessed November 12, 2003.

67. For historical overviews, see U.S. Army Corps of Engineers, *The History of the U.S. Army Corps of Engineers* (Washington, D.C.: U.S. Army Corps of Engineers, 1986), 3–4; and Todd A. Shallat, *Structures in the Stream: Water, Science, and the Rise of the U.S. Army Corps of Engineers* (Austin: University of Texas Press, 1994).

68. *U.S. Government Manual,* 177.

69. U.S. Army, Field Artillery School, "Homepage" (2003), 2–3 (http://sill-www.army.mil/TNGCMD/tc.htm), accessed November 12, 2003. For the command's role in the 1991 Persian Gulf War, see Boyd L. Dastrup, *The Come-as-You-Are War: Fort Sill and Operations Desert Shield and Desert Storm* (Fort Sill, Okla.: U.S. Army Field Artillery Center, 1997). For an overview of the role played by artillery in the U.S. Army, see Janice E. McKenney, *Field Artillery: Regular Army and Army Reserve* (Washington, D.C.: U.S. Army Center of Military History, 1992).

70. U.S. Army, Human Resources Command, "About the U.S. Army Human Resources Command" (2003), 1 (https://www.hrc.army.mil/AboutUs.asp), accessed November 12, 2003. For relevant historical background, see U.S. Army, Center of Military History, *The Personnel Replacement System in the United States Army* (Washington, D.C.: U.S. Army, Center of Military History, 1988); and John C. Sparrow, *History of Personnel Demobilization in the United States Army* (Washington, D.C.: U.S. Army, Center of Military History, 1994).

71. U.S. Army Infantry, "Combined Arms and Tactics Directorate (CATD) Mission" (2003), 1 (www.infantry.army.mil/CATD/hq/mission.htm), accessed November 12, 2003. For additional

historical background on the infantry's role in the U.S. Army, see Kenneth Finlayson, *An Uncertain Trumpet: The Evolution of U.S. Army Infantry Doctrine, 1919–1941* (Westport, Conn.: Greenwood, 2001); Charles T. Lanham, *Infantry in Battle,* 2nd ed. (Washington, D.C.: U.S. Army Center for Military History, 1934, 1996); and Scott R. McMichael, *A Historical Perspective on Light Infantry* (Fort Leavenworth, Kan.: U.S. Army Command and General Staff College, Combat Studies Institute, 1991).

72. U.S. Army Medical Research Institute of Chemical Defense, "Mission" (n.d.), 1 (http://usamricd.apgea.army.mil/), accessed November 12, 2003. For a historical summary, see U.S. Army Medical Research Institute of Chemical Defense, "Our Past and Present" (n.d.), 1 (http://usamrid.apgea.army.mil/history/history.asp), accessed November 12, 2003. For a topical overview of military chemical weapons medical practice, see Richard A. Rettig, *Military Use of Drugs Not Yet Approved by the FDA for CW/BW Defense: Lessons from the Gulf War* (Santa Monica, Calif.: RAND Corporation, 1999) (www.rand.org/publications/MR/MR1018.9/), accessed November 12, 2003.

73. See U.S. Military Academy, "About the Academy" (n.d.), 1–2 (www.usma.edu/about.asp), accessed November 12, 2003; and U.S. Military Academy, "USMA Mission" (n.d.), 1 (www.usma.edu/mission.asp), accessed November 12, 2003. For an overall history, see Theodore J. Crackel, *West Point: A Bicentennial History* (Lawrence: University Press of Kansas, 2002).

74. National Simulation Center, "Mission" (n.d.), 1 (www.leavenworth.army.mil/famsim/), accessed November 12, 2003.

75. U.S. Army, Office of Army International Affairs, "Army International Affairs Organization and Functions," (2003), 1 (http://international.army.mil/AboutAIA/AIAorg.htm), accessed March 15, 2004.

76. PL 12-83, "An Act for the Better Regulation of Ordnance," 2 *U.S. Statutes at Large,* 732–734. For a historical overview, see Keir B. Sterling, *Serving the Line with Excellence: The Development of the U.S. Army Ordnance Corps* (Aberdeen Proving Ground, Md.: U.S. Army Ordnance Center and School, 1987).

77. U.S. Army Ordnance Corps, "Mission" (1998), 1 (www.goordance.apg.army.mil/odmission.htm), accessed November 12, 2003.

78. U.S. Army, Soldier and Biological Chemical Command, "U.S. Army Soldier and Biological Chemical Command [SBCCOM]" (2002), 1–2 (www.sbccom.army.mil/about/sbccom.htm), accessed November 12, 2003.

79. Jeffrey K. Smart, "History of the U.S. Army Soldier and Biological Chemical Command" (n.d.), 1, 3, 5 (www.sbccom.army.mil/about/historySBCCOM.pdf), accessed November 12, 2003.

80. U.S. Army, Space and Missile Defense Command, *Strategic Plan 2002* (Huntsville, Ala.: U.S. Army, Space and Missile Defense Command, 2002), 4 (www.smdc.army.mil/MAIN/StratPlan.pdf), accessed November 12, 2003. For additional discussion of the army's role in space, see Leslie Lewis, *The Army's Role in Space: Strategies for Achieving Future Objectives* (Santa Monica, Calif.: RAND Corporation, 1997).

81. U.S. Army, Space and Missile Defense Command, "USASMDC: The U.S. Army Service Component to the U.S. Strategic Command" (n.d.), 1 (www.smdc.army.mil/FactSheets/SMDCFACT.pdf), accessed November 12, 2003.

82. See U.S. Army, Training and Doctrine Command, "Mission" (n.d.), 1 (www.tradoc.army.mil/mission2.htm), accessed November 12, 2003; and Anne W. Chapman and others, *Prepare the Army for War: A Historical Overview of the Army Training and Doctrine Command: 1973–1998* (Fort Monroe, Va.: U.S. Army, Training and Doctrine Command, Military History Office, 1998), 1 (www.tradoc.army.mil/historian/pubs/TRADOC25/chap1.htm), accessed November 12, 2003. For more historical background, see Susan Canedy and others, *TRADOC*

Support to Operations Desert Shield and Desert Storm: A Preliminary Study (Fort Monroe, Va.: U.S. Army. Training and Doctrine Command, Office of the Command Historian, 1992); Anne W. Chapman, *The Army's Training Revolution, 1973–1990: An Overview* (Fort Monroe, Va: U.S. Army, Training and Doctrine Command, Office of the Command Historian, 1991); and William E. Dupuy, *Changing an Army: An Oral History of General William E. DePuy, USA Retired* (Washington, D.C., and Carlisle Barracks, Pa.: U.S. Army Center of Military History and U.S. Military History Institute, 1988).

83. *U.S. Government Manual,* 190. Examples of U.S. Marine Corps histories are Allen R. Millett, *Semper Fidelis: The History of the United States Marine Corps* (New York: Macmillan Publishing Company, 1980); and Kenneth J. Clifford, *Progress and Purpose: A Developmental History of the United States Marine Corps, 1900–1970* (Washington, D.C.: U.S. Marine Corps, History and Museums Division, 1973).

84. U.S. Marine Corps, Plans, Policies, and Operations Department, "PP&O Mission/Functions" (n.d.), 1 (http://hqinet001.hqmc.usmc.mil/pp&o/), accessed November 12, 2003.

85. U.S. Marine Corps, *USMC Concepts and Issues 2000: Leading the Pack in a New Era* (Washington, D.C.: U.S. Marine Corps, 2000), 46; and U.S. Marines Corps, 4th Marine Expeditionary Brigade (Anti-Terrorism), "Chemical Biological Incident Response Force" (n.d.), 1 (www.lejeune.usmc.mil/4thmeb/cbirf.htm), accessed November 12, 2003.

86. U.S. Marine Corps, History and Museums Division, "Mission" (n.d.), 1 (http://hqinet001.hqmc.usmc.mil/HD/Contents/Mission.htm), accessed November 12, 2003.

87. U.S. Marine Corps, Installations and Logistics Department, "Installations and Logistics Department" (2003), 1 (www.hqmc.usmc.mil/ilweb.nsf/Header?OpenPage&BaseTarget=Info), accessed November 12, 2003.

88. U.S. Marine Corps, Logistics Command, "MCLB Barstow History" (2000), 1 (https://www.bam.usmc.mil/history.htm), accessed November 12, 2003.

89. U.S. Marine Corps, Manpower and Reserve Affairs, "Manpower and Reserve Affairs Home" (n.d.), 1 (www.manpower.usmc.mil/), accessed November 12, 2003.

90. U.S. Marine Corps, Marine Air Ground Staff Training Program, "Mission" (n.d.), 1 (www.mstp.quantico.usmc.mil/), accessed November 12, 2003.

91. U.S. Marine Corps, Headquarters Marine Department of Aviation, "Marine Aviation Implementation Plan" (n.d.), 1 (http://hqinet001.hqmc.usmc.mil/AVN/aip.htm), accessed November 12, 2003.

92. U.S. Marine Corps, Marine Corps Combat Development Command, "Mission" (2003), 1 (https://www.mccdc.usmc.mil/), accessed November 12, 2003.

93. U.S. Marine Corps, Marine Corps Doctrine Division, "Welcome to Our Home Page" (n.d.), 1 (https://www.doctrine.usmc.mil/), accessed November 12, 2003.

94. See U.S. Marine Corps, Marine Corps Institute, "MCI Mission Statement" (n.d.), 1 (www.mci.usmc.mil/misc/mission_statement.asp), accessed November 12, 2003; and U.S. Marine Corps, "History of MCI" (n.d.), 1–2, (www.mci.usmc.mil/aboutmci/history.asp), accessed November 12, 2003.

95. U.S. Marine Corps, Marine Corps Systems, "Marine Corps Systems Command MCSC" (2003), 1–2 (www.marcorsyscom.usmc.mil/vision/missionvision.asp), accessed November 12, 2003.

96. U.S. Marine Corps, Marine Corps University, "History" (n.d.), 1 (www.mcu.usmc.mil/mcu/History/about.htm), accessed November 12, 2003.

97. U.S. Marine Corps, Marine Corps University, "Our Mission" (n.d.), 1 (www.mcu.usmc.mil/) accessed November 12, 2003.

98. U.S. Marine Corps, Marine Corps Warfighting Laboratory, "Marine Corps Warfighting Laboratory" (n.d.), 1 (www.mcwl.quantico.usmc.mil/), accessed November 12, 2003.

99. U.S. Marine Corps, Programs and Resources Department, "Programs and Resources Department Mission" (2003), 1 (http://hqinet001.hqmc.usmc.mil/p&r/main/mission.htm), accessed November 12, 2003.

100. U.S. Marine Corps, Safety Division, "Safety Division Mission Statement" (n.d.), 1 (www.hqmc.usmc.mil/safety.nsf/), accessed November 12, 2003.

101. U.S. Marine Corps, Training and Education Command, "Our Mission" (n.d.), 1 (www.tecom.usmc.mil/), accessed November 12, 2003.

102. *U.S. Government Manual,* 185, 187. For a history of the U.S. Navy, see Stephen Howarth, *To Shining Sea: A History of the United States Navy, 1775–1991* (New York: Random House, 1991).

103. U.S. Navy, Chief of Naval Operations, "Responsibilities of the Chief of Naval Operations" (n.d.), 1 (http://chinfo.navy.mil/navpalib/people/cno/cno-resp.html), accessed November 12, 2003. For institutional historical background, see Thomas Hone, *Power and Change: The Administrative History of the Office of the Chief of Naval Operations, 1946–1986* (Washington, D.C.: Department of the Navy, Naval Historical Center, 1989).

104. U.S. Navy, Military Sealift Command, "MSC Mission" (n.d.), 1 (www.msc.navy.mil/N00P/ mission.htm), accessed November 12, 2003. For historical and evaluative appraisals, see James K. Matthews and others, ed., *United States Transportation Command the National Defense Reserve Fleet and the Ready Reserve Force: A Chronology* (Washington, D.C., and Scott Air Force Base, Ill.: United States Transportation Command Research Center, 1999); and U.S. General Accounting Office, *Strategic Mobility: Later Deliveries of Large, Medium Speed Roll-On/Off Ships* (Washington, D.C.: General Accounting Office, 1997).

105. U.S. Naval Academy, "About USNA" (n.d.), 1 (www.nadn.navy.mil/about.htm), accessed November 12, 2003. See also Jack Sweetman, *The U.S. Naval Academy: An Illustrated History* (Annapolis, Md.: Naval Institute Press, 1995.)

106. U.S. Navy, Naval Aerospace Medical Research Laboratory, "Homepage" (2003), 1 (www.namrl.navy.mil/), accessed November 12, 2003.

107. U.S. Navy, Naval Air Systems Command, "About NAVAIR" (n.d.), 1 (www.navair.navy.mil/index.cfm?fuseaction=about.default), accessed November 12, 2003.

108. U.S. Navy, Naval Cost Analysis Division, "NCAD Mission" (n.d.), 1 (www.ncca.navy.mil/about/mission.cfm), accessed November 12, 2003.

109. U.S. Navy, Naval Facilities Engineering Command, "NAVFAC Facts" (2000), 1 (www.navfac.navy.mil/facts.htm), accessed November 12, 2003.

110. U.S. Navy, Naval Historical Center, "Origins of the Naval Historical Center" (2002), 1–2 (www.history.navy.mil/ branches/origin.htm), accessed November 12, 2003.

111. U.S. Navy, Naval Medicine Online, "About Navy Medicine" (n.d.), 1 (http://navymedicine.med.navy.mil/nav_about_us.asp), accessed November 12, 2003.

112. U.S. Navy, Naval Medicine Online, "Naval Medicine" (n.d.), 2, 6 (http://navymedicine.med.navy.mil/med09h/bumed_history.cfm), accessed November 12, 2003. See also Harold D. Langley, *A History of Medicine in the Early U.S. Navy* (Baltimore, Md.: Johns Hopkins University Press, 1995).

113. For historical background, see Steven J. Dick, *Sky and Ocean Joined: The U.S. Naval Observatory, 1830–2000* (New York: Cambridge University Press, 2003). For a mission synopsis, see U.S. Naval Observatory, "The Mission of the Naval Observatory" (Washington, D.C.: U.S. Naval Observatory (n.d.), 1 (www.usno.navy.mil/mission.shtml), accessed November 12, 2003.

114. U.S. Navy, Naval Postgraduate School, "A Short History of the Naval Postgraduate School" (2001), 1 (www.nps.navy.mil/PAO/history/history.htm), accessed November 12, 2003.

115. U.S. Navy, Naval Postgraduate School, "NPS at a Glance" (2001), 1–2 (www.nps.navy.mil/PAO/at_a_glance.htm), accessed November 12, 2003.

116. U.S. Navy, Naval Research Laboratory, "History" (n.d.), 1 (www.nrl.navy.mil/content.php?P=HISTORY), accessed November 12, 2003. For additional historical background, see Ivan Amato, *Pushing the Horizon: Seventy-five Years of High Stakes Science and Technology at the Naval Research Laboratory* (Washington, D.C.: U.S. Naval Research Laboratory, 1998); and U.S. Naval Research Laboratory, *Highlights of NRL's First 75 Years, 1923–1998* (Washington, D.C.: U.S. Naval Research Laboratory, Technical Information Division, 1999).

117. U.S. Navy, Naval Research Laboratory, "Mission: We Are the Navy's Corporate Laboratory" (n.d.), 1–2 (www.nrl.navy.mil/content.php?P=MISSION), accessed November 12, 2003.

118. U.S. Navy, Naval Sea Systems Command, "About NAVSEA" (n.d.), 1 (www.navsea.navy.mil/aboutnavsea.asp), accessed November 12, 2003.

119. U.S. Navy, Naval Surface Warfare Center, "The Nation's Center of Excellence for Surface Warfare" (n.d.), 1 (www.nswcdc.navy.mil/), accessed November 12, 2003.

120. U.S. Navy, Naval Treaty Implementation Program, "Naval Treaty Implementation Program" (n.d.) (www.nawcwpns.navy.mil/~treaty/progovw.html), accessed November 12, 2003. For additional background on naval arms control treaty activities, see Michael Krepon and Dan Caldwell, eds., *The Politics of Arms Control Treaty Ratification* (New York: St. Martin's Press, 1991); and Emily O. Goldman, *Sunken Treaties: Naval Arms Control between the Wars* (University Park: Pennsylvania State University Press, 1994).

121. U.S. Navy, Naval Undersea Warfare Center, "NUWC Overview" (n.d.), 1 (www.nuwc.navy.mil/hq/overview/verview.html), accessed November 12, 2003. For a history of the Naval Undersea Warfare Center's predecessor organization between 1970 and 1991, see John Merrill and Lionel D. Wyld, *Meeting the Submarine Challenge: A Short History of the Naval Underwater Systems Center* (Washington, D.C.: Department of the Navy, 1997).

122. U.S. Navy, Naval Vessel Register, "History: Naval Vessel Register" (n.d.), 1 (www.nvr.navy.mil/nvrhist), accessed November 12, 2003. For a print counterpart, see Navy Department, Naval History Division, Office of the Chief of Naval Operations, *Dictionary of American Naval Fighting Ships* (Washington, D.C.: Government Printing Office, 1959–1981 and 1991–).

123. U.S. Navy War College, "NWC Mission" (n.d.), 1 (www.nwc.navy.mil/aboutnwc/mission.htm), accessed November 12, 2003. For further historical background, see Ronald H. Spector, *Professors of War: The Naval War College and the Development of the Naval Profession* (Newport, R.I.: Naval War College Press, 1977); and John B. Hattendorf and others, *Sailors and Scholars: The Centennial History of the U.S. Naval War College* (Newport, R.I.: Naval War College Press, 1984).

124. U.S. Navy International Programs Office, "Mission" (n.d.), 1 (https://www.nipo.navy.mil/mission.cfm), accessed November 12, 2003.

125. U.S. Navy Personnel Research, Studies, and Technology, "Navy Personnel Research, Studies, and Technology" (n.d.), 1 (https://www.nprst.navy.mil/), accessed November 12, 2003.

126. U.S. Navy Warfare Development Command, "NWDC Organization" (n.d.), 1 (www.nwdc.navy.mil/Organization.asp), accessed November 12, 2003.

127. U.S. Navy, Network Centric Innovation Center, "What Is NCIC?" (n.d.), 1 (www.ncic.navy.mil/whoisNCIC.asp), accessed November 12, 2003.

128. For the origins of the Office of Naval Research (ONR), see U.S. Navy, Office of Naval Research, "Homepage" (n.d.), 1 (www.onr.navy.mil/), accessed November 12, 2003. For ONR's mission, see U.S. Navy, Office of Naval Research, "About ONR" (2003), 1 (www.onr.navy.mil/onr/), accessed November 12, 2003. For historical review and analysis, see Harvey M. Sapolsky, *Science and the Navy: The History of the Office of Naval Research* (Princeton, N.J.: Princeton University Press, 1990).

129. U.S. Navy, Space and Naval Warfare Systems Command, "About SPAWAR" (n.d.), 1 (http://enterprise.spawar.navy.mil/about.cfm), accessed November 12, 2003.

130. U.S. Navy, Surface Warfare Directorate, "Surface Warfare: What We Do" (2003), 1 (http://chinfo.navy.mil/navpalib/cno/n76/n76do.html), accessed November 12, 2003.

CHAPTER 5

Independent Agencies

In addition to executive departments, individual armed services branches, and other cabinet-level entities, many independent federal government agencies play important roles in formulating and implementing national security policy and producing national security information. Congress created these agencies for public policy or political reasons. Their institutional mandates do not directly cover national security but have national security policy-making interests, such as environmental protection, draft registration enforcement, and the competitive status of U.S. industries involved in producing commodities and resources with national security implications such as steel, computer software, and electronics.

■ Chemical Safety and Hazard Investigation Board

The Chemical Safety and Hazard Investigation Board was created by the Clean Air Act Amendments of 1990 but did not receive funding until 1998.[1] A scientific investigative, not regulatory, agency, the board studies chemical accidents to determine their causes and recommends ways to prevent their occurrence.[2] Increased interest in the board's activities has coincided with growing concern over possible terrorist uses of chemical weapons.

Information resources available on the board's website (www.chemsafety.gov/) include links to other federal government chemical incident data sources produced by the Environmental Protection Agency (EPA), the U.S. Coast Guard, Occupational Safety and Health Administration (OSHA), Department of Transportation, and U.S. Fire Administration. Also accessible are the board's five-year strategic plan; information about the Chemical Incident Reports Center, which provides news reports on chemical accidents; selected investigative reports such as *Propane Tank Explosion: Honig Brothers Feather Creek Farm, Albert City, Iowa—April 9, 1998* (1998) and *Refinery Fire Incident: Tosco Avon Refinery, Martinez, California—February 23, 1999* (2001); periodicals such as *Safety Bulletin;* information on reporting chemical incidents; and press releases.

Defense Nuclear Facilities Safety Board

In response to concerns over safety conditions at the Department of Energy (DOE) defense nuclear facilities such as Hanford Plant in Washington, Rocky Flats Depot in Colorado, Savannah River Site in South Carolina, and Pantex in Texas, Congress in 1988 established the Defense Nuclear Facilities Safety Board (DNFSB).[3] Its responsibilities include overseeing operational and safety issues at DOE defense nuclear facilities, investigating events or practices at these facilities that may jeopardize public health and safety, and issuing recommendations to the secretary of energy on measures needed to produce facility operational enhancements and public safety.[4]

DNFSB's website can be found at www.dnfsb.gov. DNSFB has performed inspections of DOE defense nuclear facilities and issued recommendations to improve the quality of their operations. Some of these recommendations are available on the website, such as *Prioritization for Stabilizing Nuclear Materials* (2000) and *High-Level Waste Management at the Savannah River Site* (2001).

Also accessible are DNFSB reports, including its annual reports to Congress from 1991 to 2004, staff reports relating to individual DOE defense nuclear sites such as *Electrical Instrumentation and Control Systems at Hanford's Plutonium Finishing Plant* (2002), technical reports such as *Safe Handling of Insensitive High Explosive Weapon Subassemblies at the Pantex Plant* (1999), *Status of Emergency Management at Defense Nuclear Facilities of the Department of Energy* (1999), *Criticality Safety of Department of Energy Defense Nuclear Facilities* (2001), and *Fire Protection of Defense Nuclear Facilities* (2001).

The website also has a Windows Media webcast of the board's August 15, 2001, public meeting; employment information; the text of its enabling legislation; agency customer service policies; and information about its public reading room in Washington, D.C.

Federal Emergency Management Agency

The Federal Emergency Management Agency (FEMA) was created by a 1979 executive order to consolidate federal agencies dealing with emergency-related programs.[5] FEMA formerly reported directly to the White House and is probably best known for providing federal funding assistance after natural and human-caused disasters. Its institutional responsibilities focusing on national security include coordinating responses to and recovery from major natural disasters or human-caused emergencies, fostering emergency management planning, dealing with hazardous materials, securing the safety of dams, planning for emergencies at commercial nuclear power plants and U.S. Army chemical stockpile sites, ensuring federal government continuity during national security responses, and coordinating the federal response to major terrorist incidents.[6]

FEMA produces a variety of publications on national security–related issues in addition to its publications dealing with natural disaster response and preparedness. Examples of publications produced by FEMA and affiliated agencies such as the U.S.

Fire Administration include *The World Trade Center Bombing: Report and Analysis* (1993), *Model State Dam Safety Program* (1998), *Federal Response Plan* (1999), *Transport of Radioactive Materials: Questions and Answers about Incident Response* (2000), and *World Trade Center Building Performance Study* (2002). These and other relevant information resources can be found on FEMA's website (www.fema.gov).

FEMA became part of the Department of Homeland Security in March 2003.[7]

Federal Maritime Commission

Established in 1961 by federal Reorganization Plan No. 7, the Federal Maritime Commission (FMC) regulates U.S. waterborne foreign commerce.[8] Specific responsibilities under this broad jurisdictional mandate include assuring that U.S. foreign trade has access to all nations on equitable terms and protecting against unauthorized and illicit activity in U.S. waterborne commerce. FMC conducts surveillance over steamship conferences and common carriers by water, reviews agreements between individuals subject to 1984 Shipping Act provisions encouraging an economically sound and efficient U.S. flag liner fleet capable of meeting national security needs, enforces provisions prohibiting various discriminatory acts and practices against U.S. shippers and carriers, and ensures that sufficient financial responsibility levels are maintained to indemnify passengers affected by discriminatory acts or practices.[9]

FMC publications describe the commission's activities and how they can affect national security policy. Examples of recent publications are FMC's *Annual Report*, *Decisions of the Federal Maritime Commission* (1996–present), *Possible Discriminatory Treatment of U.S. and Third Flag Carriers Serving the Brazil Trades* (1997), *Shipping Restrictions, Requirements, and Practices of the People's Republic of China* (2000), *The Impact of the Ocean Shipping Reform Act of 1998* (2001), and *Port Restrictions and Requirements in the United States/Japan Trade* (2001). These and other information resources such as regulatory forms are available on FMC's website (www.fmc.gov).

General Services Administration

The General Services Administration (GSA) was established by the 1949 Federal Property and Administrative Services Act.[10] GSA is responsible for providing for the economic and efficient management of government property and records including building construction and operation.[11]

GSA may initially appear to be a property management agency. However, within its organizational umbrella are the Federal Protective Service, which provides law enforcement and security to more than eight thousand federally owned and leased buildings and to nearly one million federal employees and building visitors, and the Federal Computer Incident Response Center, which ensures the federal government is able to endure and recover from attacks against its information resources and critical information infrastructure.[12]

Examples of national security–related information resources produced by GSA include its annual reports to Congress beginning in fiscal year 1997, *Chemical/*

Biological Threat Checklist (n.d.), *Making Federal Buildings Safe* (2001), *Briefing on Irradiated Mail* (2002), *Guidelines for Opening Irradiated Mail* (2002), and *Mail Center Manager's Security Guide* (2002). These and other relevant materials can be found on GSA's website (www.gsa.gov).

U.S. Institute of Peace

The U.S. Institute of Peace (USIP) was established in 1984 as an independent nonpartisan institution. It advocates for the prevention, peaceful resolution, and management of international conflict. USIP carries out various education and training programs as it fulfills its objectives.[13]

The website www.usip.org/ features summaries of institute-sponsored events (1996–present), listings and biographies of USIP specialists, information on institute library holdings, and the *Peace Watch* newsletter (1996–present). Accessible reports include *Preventing Genocide in Burundi* (1998), *Mistrust and the Korean Peninsula: Dangers of Miscalculation* (1998), *NATO at Fifty: New Challenges, Future Uncertainties* (1999), *AIDS and Violent Conflict in Africa* (2001), *From Revolutionary Internationalism to Conservative Nationalism: The Chinese Military's Discourse on National Security and Identity in the Post-Mao Era* (2001), *The Israeli Military and Israel's Palestinian Policy: From Oslo to the Al Aqsa Intifada* (2002), *Islamic Perspectives on Peace and Violence* (2002), and *Boundary Disputes in Latin America* (2003).

U.S. International Trade Commission

The U.S. International Trade Commission (ITC) was created in 1916 as the U.S. Tariff Commission, acquiring its current name from the 1974 Trade Act.[14] ITC is responsible for investigating the customs laws of the United States and other countries; studying import product volumes as compared with domestic production and consumption; and examining the conditions, causes, and impacts of foreign industry competition on U.S. industries and related matters affecting international trade competition between U.S. products and foreign products imported into the United States.[15] These multiple responsibilities are carried out by ITC offices covering industries, investigations, operations, tariff affairs and trade agreements, and unfair import investigations and ITC divisions focusing on commodities such as minerals, metals, machinery, energy, chemicals, services, electronics, and transportation.[16]

ITC reports focus on how specific U.S. industries producing strategically important commodities such as steel, software, or electronics may have their international economic competitiveness injured by the practices of foreign companies and foreign governments. ITC publications on subjects with national security economics implications include studies under Section 332 of the 1930 Tariff Act examining competitive conditions between U.S. and foreign industries, such as *The Economic Impact of U.S. Sanctions with Respect to Cuba* (2001) and *Competitive Assessment of the U.S. Large Civil Aircraft Aerostructures Industry* (2001).[17]

Another ITC report, available at www.usitc.gov/, is *Steel: Section 201 Investigation—Certain Steel Products, U.S. Imports of Products Indicated in a Request Letter of*

June 22, 2001 (2001–2002). It received considerable publicity and resulted in the George W. Bush administration imposing tariffs on steel imports from various countries in March 2002. Also accessible are working papers such as "Factors Affecting U.S. Trade and Shipments of Information Technology Products: Computer Equipment, Telecommunications Equipment, and Semiconductors" (2002), the journal *Industry, Trade, and Technology Review,* and information about ongoing ITC investigations.[18] The website also has a link to the Electronic Document On-Line System (EDIS).

National Academy of Sciences

The National Academy of Sciences (NAS) was established by Congress in 1863 to "investigate, examine, and report on any subject of science or art" when requested to by a government agency.[19] NAS was created to advise the U.S. government on scientific and technological matters and has expanded from its initial authorization to include the National Research Council, National Academy of Engineering, and Institute of Medicine, which together employ nearly eleven hundred people. NAS is a private organization and does not receive direct federal appropriations. However, financial support for its research projects comes from individual federal agency appropriations.[20]

NAS publications on national security deal with various scientific and technological issues such as cybersecurity, explosive identification, and nuclear proliferation. Examples of NAS national security publications, available at www.nap.edu/, are *Research Required to Support Comprehensive Nuclear Test Ban Treaty Monitoring* (1997), *Proliferation Concerns: Assessing U.S. Efforts to Help Contain Nuclear and Other Dangerous Materials and Technologies in the Former Soviet Union* (1997), *Black and Smokeless Powders: Technologies for Finding Bombs and the Bomb Makers* (1998), *Containing the Threat from Illegal Bombings: An Integrated National Strategy for Marking, Tagging, Rendering Inert, and Licensing Explosives and Their Precursors* (1998), *Improving Civilian Medical Response to Chemical or Biological Terrorist Incidents: Interim Report on Capabilities* (1998), *Assessment of Technologies Deployed to Improve Aviation Security: First Report* (1999), *Protecting Nuclear Weapons Material in Russia* (1999), *Summary of Discussions at a Planning Meeting on Cyber-Security and the Insider Threat to Classified Information* (2000), *Firepower in the Lab: Automation in the Fight against Infectious Diseases and Bioterrorism* (2001), *Cybersecurity Today and Tomorrow: Pay Now or Pay Later* (2002), and *Biological Threats and Terrorism: Assessing the Science and Response Capabilities: Workshop Summary* (2002).

National Archives and Records Administration

Created in 1934, the National Archives and Records Administration (NARA) establishes policies and procedures for managing and maintaining U.S. government records.[21] It became an independent agency in 1984.[22] NARA assists federal agencies in chronicling and documenting their activities; acquires, arranges, describes, preserves, and provides access to key documents produced by all three governmental branches; manages the presidential library system; publishes federal laws, regulations, and presidential and other public documents; and assists the Information Security Oversight Office in managing federal classification and declassification policies.[23]

NARA acts as a steward of records produced by national security policy-making agencies. While significant volumes of these records are accessible to qualified researchers at www.archives.gov/, some are inaccessible for periods of time because they contain sensitive materials, which, if declassified prematurely, could compromise national security or ongoing operations affecting national security.

As of the mid-1990s, the agency's holdings consisted of 1.7 million cubic feet of textual records, nearly 300,000 microfilm rolls, 2.2 million maps and charts, 2.8 million architectural and engineering plans, 9.2 million aerial photographs, 123,000 motion picture reels, 33,000 video recordings, 178,000 sound recordings, 7,000 computer data sets, and 7.4 million still pictures. The records are kept in NARA's Washington, D.C., headquarters and auxiliary facilities in College Park, Maryland, and other locations across the United States.[24]

NARA records are arranged numerically by record group (RG). Examples include "Records of the Army Air Force" (RG18, 1903–1964), "Records of the United States Coast Guard" (RG 26, 1785–1988), "Records of the Office of the Chief of Naval Operations" (RG 38, 1875–1985), "Records of United States Senate Committees Relating to Defense" (RG 46.5, 1816–1988), "Records of Naval Districts and Shore Establishments" (RG 181, 1784–1981), "Records of the U.S. Joint Chiefs of Staff" (RG 218, 1941–1978), "Records of the President's Commission on an All-Volunteer Armed Force" (RG 220.15.2, 1969–1979), "Records of the United States Strategic Bombing Survey" (RG 243, 1928–1947), "Records of the Central Intelligence Agency" (RG 263, primarily 1947–1974), and "Records of the National Security Council" (RG 273, 1947–1969).[25] Examples of NARA-produced reference manuals on the website are *Records Management in the U.S. Army Corps of Engineers, Department of the Army: A NARA Evaluation* (1995), *Records of the German Naval High Command 1935–1945: Guides to Microfilmed Records of the German Navy, 1850–1945* (1999), and *Records of Military Agencies Relating to African Americans from the Post-World War I Period to the Korean War* (2000).

NARA's website also provides access to information about the agency's collection holdings, public exhibits, and archival record-keeping policies and procedures. NARA's National Archives Information Locator (NAIL) and its subsequent replacement, the Archival Research Catalog (ARC), provides searchable access to many NARA resources, including some digitized resources, at www.archives.gov/research_room/arc/.[26]

Information Security Oversight Office

Reporting to the president and receiving guidance from the National Security Council (NSC), the Information Security Oversight Office (ISOO) has policy oversight of the federal government's security clearance system and the National Industrial Security Program. ISOO's authority is derived from 1993 Executive Order 12829 and 1995 Executive Order 12958 dealing with the National Industrial Security Program and classified national security information.[27] ISOO develops and implements directives and instructions on classifying and declassifying government information; maintains liaisons with agency counterparts and conducts on-site inspections to ensure agency compliance with federal security classification procedures; collects, analyzes, and reports relevant statistical data to the president; and recommends security classification changes to the president through the NSC.[28]

Three oversight groups within ISOO execute institutional responsibilities: the Classification Management Committee (CMC), the Interagency Security Classification Appeals Panel (ISCAP), and the National Industrial Security Program Policy Advisory Committee (NISPPAC). CMC coordinates, formulates, and evaluates classification and declassification management policy and assists federal agencies on classification management policy and procedural issues.[29]

ISCAP decides on appeals by authorized individuals filing classification challenges under Section 1.9 of Executive Order 12958; approves, denies, or amends agency exemptions from mandatory declassification under Section 3.4(d) of Executive Order 12958; and decides on compulsory declassification review appeals by those whose declassification requests under Section 3.6 of Executive Order 12958 were denied at the agency level.[30]

NISPPAC's mandate is providing advice on National Industrial Security Program (NISP) policy matters under Section 103 of Executive Order 12829, recommending changes to NISP, and serving as a forum for discussing disputed policy issues as they affect participating government agencies and nongovernmental contractors, licensees, and grantees.[31]

ISOO and its entities produce numerous information resources explaining their activities and executing their respective missions. These publications, on the ISOO website (www.archives.gov/isoo/), include the text of the 1993 and 1995 executive orders; the directive "Safeguarding National Security Information," found in Title 32, Part 2004 of the *Code of Federal Regulations; Classified Information Nondisclosure Agreement (Standard Form 312) Briefing Booklet* (2001); and *Marking Booklet: Executive Order 12958 Classified National Security Information* (2001).

Presidential Libraries

Presidential libraries and records are important and sometimes controversial sources for researching national security policy.[32] The presidential library system began in 1939, when President Franklin D. Roosevelt (FDR) donated his personal papers to the federal government; he pledged a portion of his Hyde Park, New York, estate to the United States to house the collection; and his friends formed a nonprofit corporation to raise funds to construct a library and museum facility. Roosevelt asked NARA to assume custody of his papers and to administer the library, which was dedicated on June 30, 1941.[33]

Three laws are responsible for creating and maintaining the presidential library system, which includes libraries and archives for every president since Herbert Hoover. The Presidential Libraries Act of 1955 formally established the presidential libraries system, placed it under NARA control, ensured the availability of presidential papers to the American public, and required private or nonfederal public funding to build the libraries.[34]

Despite the language of the law, presidents and many scholars believed that papers created by the president and his staff remained their personal property even after the president left office.[35] Opposition to this viewpoint and controversy over President Richard M. Nixon's refusal to turn over his presidential papers to the National Archives led to passage of the Presidential Records Act of 1978.[36] This statute firmly established the principle that presidential records documenting the president's constitutional, statutory, and ceremonial duties are U.S. government property and that custody of these records is transferred from the president to the archivist of the United States after the president leaves office, effective January 20, 1981. Presidents were given the power, under this statute, to impose public access restrictions on the records for up to twelve years on records dealing with national security, appointments, trade secrets, and financial, medical, and personnel matters.[37]

The growing proliferation of presidential libraries and accompanying increases in facility maintenance costs—from $63,745 in 1955 to $15,734,000 in 1985—resulted in passage of the 1986 Presidential Libraries Act.[38] The act required the archivist of the United States to ensure that a nonfederally provided endowment equal to 20 percent of a library's cost be available before the library can become a presidential library, that income from this endowment be allocated to paying for ongoing library operational and maintenance costs, and that this endowment be the sole funding source for any presidential library desirous of expanding beyond the federal facility limit of seventy thousand square feet for a president elected after January 20, 1985.[39]

In 2001 President George W. Bush issued Executive Order 13233, giving former presidents expanded authority to block the release of presidential papers beyond the requirements provided for in the 1978 Presidential Records Act.[40] Historical organizations and libraries opposed the White House move. Legislation was introduced in both the 107th and 108th Congresses to nullify the executive order.[41] As of early 2004, none of the legislation had advanced beyond committee consideration.

Despite the controversy over Executive Order 13233, presidential libraries are excellent resources for researchers who want to learn more about national security policy decisions and actions from the Hoover to the Clinton administration. The growth of the Internet, the declassification of significant quantities of government information resources, and the placement of some of these resources on presidential library websites allow expanded access for those unable to travel to a presidential library.

Franklin Delano Roosevelt Presidential Library and Museum

Located in Hyde Park, New York, the library contains resources documenting FDR's presidency (1933–1945), which coincided with the Great Depression and World War II. Digitized resources on national security issues include about thirteen thousand documents covering subjects such as military correspondence on the war with Germany, diplomatic correspondence between the United States and the United Kingdom, White House safe files featuring military correspondence to FDR, and correspondence to FDR from U.S. Vatican envoy Myron Taylor documenting his conversations with Pope Pius XII.

Examples of resources available on the FDR library website (www.fdrlibrary.marist.edu) are a July 16, 1941, intelligence report on British naval operations against Germany; a February 8, 1942, letter from Gen. Douglas MacArthur to Gen. George C. Marshall, army chief of staff, on the military situation in the Philippines; and a September 5, 1944, list of recommendations by Secretary of War Harry Stimson on Germany's future treatment.

Truman Presidential Museum and Library

Located in Independence, Missouri, the Truman library contains material documenting the developments in U.S. national security policy—including the cold war—occurring during Harry S. Truman's presidency (1945–1953). At the library and on its website (www.trumanlibrary.org) are documents chronicling the decision to drop atomic bombs on Japan, U.S. entry into the North Atlantic Treaty Organization (NATO), U.S. actions during the Berlin Airlift, recognition of Israel as a sovereign nation, U.S. actions during the Korean War, and other national security policy activities.

Documents on the Berlin Airlift available on the website include the Central Intelligence Agency (CIA) report *Effect of Soviet Restrictions on the U.S. Position in Berlin* (1948), National Security Council memorandum "Possible Soviet Interruption to the Berlin Airlift" (1948), and a draft of a top-secret historical analysis done by the State Department Division of Historical Policy Research, "The Berlin Crisis" (1949).

Accessible materials regarding World War II include the minutes of a June 18, 1945, White House meeting on testing the atomic bomb; the U.S. Strategic Bombing Survey (USSBS) report *The Effects of the Atomic Bombings of Hiroshima and Nagasaki* (1946); and the USSBS report *Japan's Struggle to End the War* (1946). Available Korean War documents include the State Department's June 24, 1950, telegram to Truman informing him that North Korean forces had invaded South Korea; transcript of a June 25, 1950, meeting between the Pentagon and MacArthur's Far East Command discussing the status of North Korea's military and how South Korea was responding to the northern invasion; and a July 31, 1950, message to MacArthur from the Joint Chiefs of Staff describing placement of atomic bomb parts on Guam for possible use against North Korea.

The website also has audio files of selected Truman speeches or interviews that are accessible with the RealPlayer plug-in. Examples include Truman's May 8, 1945, broadcast to the American people announcing Germany's surrender and a 1951 interview in which Truman announces his reasons for firing MacArthur as commander of American military forces in Korea.

Dwight D. Eisenhower Library and Museum

This Abilene, Kansas, facility provides information about Dwight D. Eisenhower's presidency (1953–1961) and other aspects of his life and career. The Eisenhower administration dealt with the 1956 crushing of the Hungarian revolution by the Union of Soviet Socialist Republics, the 1956 Anglo-French attempt to seize control of the Suez Canal, the 1957 *Sputnik* satellite launch by the Soviet Union, the 1960 U-2 spy plane incident with the Soviet Union, and other national security issues. Although the Eisenhower library website (www.eisenhower.utexas.edu/) does not contain as many full-text resources as those for some other presidential libraries, available documents include the October 16, 1957, memorandum of a conference on American science education and *Sputnik* attended by Eisenhower and his science advisers; summary of an October 11, 1957, NSC meeting on the implications of the launching of *Sputnik* for U.S. security and the intercontinental ballistic missile and intermediate-range ballistic missile programs; and the memorandum of a February 6, 1958, conference on the progress of U.S. missile programs attended by Eisenhower and his science advisers.

Digitized documents on the U-2 spy plane incident are also accessible, such as a May 5, 1960, State Department statement; Eisenhower's November 24, 1954, presidential authorization to produce thirty U-2 aircraft; a May 10, 1960, telegram from the American Embassy in Moscow to the secretary of state providing a translation of Soviet reaction to the U-2's downing; and the May 26, 1960, memorandum of a conversation between Eisenhower and bipartisan congressional leaders on the U-2 incident and related intelligence and espionage issues.

John F. Kennedy Library and Museum

The John F. Kennedy (JFK) library is located in Boston, Massachusetts, and provides information about the thirty-fifth president's life, political career, and tenure in office (1961–1963). Its website (www.jfklibrary.org/) includes audio excerpts of selected speeches and meetings, including an extract of an October 18, 1962, meeting between President John F. Kennedy and his national security advisers on possible military responses to the unfolding Cuban Missile Crisis.

The website contains more than two hundred National Security Action Memorandums (NSAM), which are summaries of Kennedy administration national security policy decisions. Because some of the NSAM have been reproduced from copies on onion-skinned paper, their viewing quality and resolution are not ideal. Accessible examples include *Development of Counterguerrilla Forces* (NSAM 2, 1961), *Forces in Vietnam* (NSAM 12, 1961), *Improving the Security of Nuclear Weapons in NATO* (NSAM 26, 1961), *Military Planning for a Possible Berlin Crisis* (NSAM 41, 1961), *Guidance on U.S. Nuclear Assistance to France* (NSAM 148, 1962), *Cuba* (NSAM 181, 1962), *A Separate Arms Control Measure for Outer Space* (NSAM 192, 1962), *Underground Nuclear Tests* (NSAM 210, 1962), *Australian Procurement of French Mirage Aircraft and Possible Future Military Purchases by Australia from the United States* (NSAM 242, 1963), *High Yield Nuclear Weapons* (NSAM 245, 1963), *Test Ban Agreement* (NSAM 254, 1963), and *Cooperation with the USSR on Outer Space Matters* (NSAM 271, 1963).

Also on the website are the complete text of the State Department's *Foreign Relations of the United States* documentary series, with individual volumes on the Cuban

Missile Crisis and its aftermath, and Kennedy's correspondence with Soviet leader Nikita Krushchev.

Lyndon Baines Johnson Library and Museum

Situated in the heart of Austin, Texas, on the University of Texas campus, the library documents the presidency of Lyndon B. Johnson (LBJ) (1963–1969). The LBJ library website (www.lbjlib.utexas.edu/) contains *Vietnam* (NSAM 274, 1963), *Guidelines for Discussions on the Nuclear Defense of the Atlantic Alliance* (NSAM 322, 1964), *Intensified and Expanded Psychological Operation Activities in Vietnam* (NSAM 330, 1965), *U.S. Intelligence Facilities in Pakistan* (NSAM 337, 1965), *Indian Nuclear Weapons Problem* (NSAM 351, 1966), and *Intelligence Information Handling System* (NSAM 368, 1968).

The library website also has transcripts of interviews done with individuals who were political allies of Johnson or served in the Johnson administration. Particularly noteworthy are those for Secretary of Defense Robert S. McNamara, national security adviser Walt Rostow, Secretary of State Dean Rusk, and William E. Colby, who would become CIA director.

The library's holding include recordings of telephone conversations Johnson had with colleagues and governmental officials. The website provides links to these conversations on the Cable Satellite Public Affairs Network (C-SPAN) website (www.cspan.org/lbj/) in RealPlayer format. Examples include a December 27, 1965, conversation between Johnson and General Maxwell Taylor on domestic political concerns over Vietnam; an August 19, 1965, conversation between Johnson and national security adviser McGeorge Bundy; an August 2, 1965, conversation between Johnson and Dean Rusk on various Vietnam-related matters; a July 26, 1965, conversation with Senate Armed Services Committee chair Richard B. Russell (D-Ga.) on dealing with surface to air missile sites in North Vietnam; and an August 18, 1965, conversation with former president Eisenhower on Vietnam and other issues.

Nixon Presidential Materials Staff

Nixon's presidential papers are stored as part of the Nixon Presidential Materials Staff in NARA's College Park, Maryland, facility. The website www.archives.gov/nixon/ features detailed finding aids for information about Nixon's presidency (1969–1974) and information on when new materials become publicly available. However, no links are provided for digitized versions of Nixon presidential documents, including those dealing with national security policy issues. Resources on Nixon's career before and after the presidency may be found at the privately supported Richard Nixon Library in Yorba Linda, California. The website www.nixonfoundation.org/ contains information about events at the library and the full text of Nixon administration volumes of *Public Papers of the President,* which contain speeches Nixon made as president along with proclamations and executive orders that may cover national security–related issues.

Gerald R. Ford Library and Museum

Located at the University of Michigan in Ann Arbor, Michigan, the Ford library preserves the archival record of Gerald R. Ford's presidency (1974–1977). A separate museum in Grand Rapids, Michigan, provides more publicly accessible information on Ford's life and political career. The Ford library website (www.ford.utexas.edu/) has compiled digitized national security policy documents on issues such as the fall of South Vietnam, nuclear arms control, and Cuban military activity in Africa. The website also contains National Security Council meeting minutes from 1974 to 1977, with only a small portion being inaccessible because of redacted (marked out) material. Examples of meeting minutes that are accessible in hypertext markup language (HTML) and Portable Document Format (PDF) are *Leaks of Classified Documents: Strategic Arms Limitation Talks (SALT)* (October 7, 1974), *Seizure of American Ship Mayaguez by the Cambodians* (May 12-15, 1975), *Lebanon, Cubans in Southern Africa* (1976), *U.S. Defense Policy and Military Posture* (1976), and *Semi-Annual Review of the Intelligence Community* (1977). Meeting participants are noted, and they include Secretary of State Henry Kissinger, White House chief of staff Donald H. Rumsfeld, and national security adviser Brent Scowcroft.

Ford administration National Security Study Memoranda (NSSM) and National Security Decision Memoranda (NSDM) also are accessible on the website. The NSSM direct the National Security Council to study a particular issue; NSDM reflect Ford administration policy decisions and actions.[42] Posted are *U.S. Security Assistance to the Republic of China* (NSSM 212, 1974), *National Security Aspects of Releasing Safeguard Procedures and Data on Nuclear Materials* (NSSM 216, 1975), *Review of the Management of Classified National Security Information* (NSSM 229, 1975), *U.S. Policy toward the Persian Gulf* (NSSM 238, 1976), *National Defense Policy and Military Posture* (NSSM 246, 1976); *Turkish Opium Production* (NSDM 267, 1974), *Instructions for the Mutual and Balanced Force Reduction Talks, Vienna* (NSDM 269, 1974), *Ratification of the Geneva Protocol of 1925 on Gas Warfare* (NSDM 281, 1974), *U.S. Military Supply Policy to Pakistan and India* (NSDM 289, 1975), *Instructions for the SALT Talks in Geneva* (NSDM 301, 1975), *Panama Canal Treaty Negotiations* (NSDM 302, 1975), *Underground Nuclear Test Program for the Second Half of FY 1976 and the Transition Quarter (ANVIL II)* (NSDM 319, 1976), *U.S. Policy toward Thailand* (NSDM 327, 1976), *U.S. Port Security Program* (NSDM 340, 1976), and *Navy Shipbuilding Program* (NSDM 344, 1977).

Additional noteworthy materials provided on the Ford library website are national security and foreign affairs conversation memoranda involving President Ford, national security policymakers from his administration, foreign leaders, and congressional delegations. Examples include a January 4, 1975, conversation between Ford and former CIA director Richard Helms on the CIA's domestic activities; an April 15, 1975, meeting between Ford and Kissinger on Vietnam; a July 5, 1975, meeting between Ford, Kissinger, and Indonesian president Mohamed Suharto; and a December 10, 1975, meeting on a presidential trip to the Far East with the Republican congressional leadership.

Jimmy Carter Library and Museum

Jimmy Carter's presidential library is located in Atlanta, Georgia, and provides information about the thirty-ninth president's life, political career, and tenure in office (1977–1981). Digitally accessible national security policy–related resources on the library's website (www.jimmycarterlibrary.org/) include a personnel directory of NSC staff during the Carter administration. A report on the failed 1980 Iran hostage rescue mission prepared for White House counsel Lloyd Cutler by a Joint Chiefs of Staff–commissioned review group is accessible through NARA's NAIL service. Additional digitally accessible resources include Carter's Presidential Directives (PDs) for the NSC and correspondence between Carter and other individuals regarding the Panama Canal Treaty. Despite some redacted material, available resources include *Southern Africa* (PD 5, 1977), *Nuclear Nonproliferation* (PD 8, 1977), *U.S.-USSR Talks on Conventional Arms Restraint* (PD 36, 1978), *U.S.-China Scientific and Technological Relationships* (PD 43, 1978), *Ballistic Missile Submarine Commitments to NATO* (PD 48, 1979), *National Security Telecommunications Policy* (PD 53, 1979), *Nuclear Weapons Employment Policy* (PD 59, 1980), and *Modifications in U.S. National Strategy* (PD 62, 1981).

Accessible documents regarding the Panama Canal Treaty include a July 5, 1977, letter to Carter from American Legion national commander William J. Rogers; a September 7, 1977, memo to Press Secretary Jody Powell from NSC Latin America specialist Robert A. Pastor; an October 4, 1977, memo from Assistant Secretary of State for Public Affairs Hodding Carter III to Secretary of State Cyrus Vance; and a April 26, 1978, letter from Carter to various senators.

Ronald W. Reagan Presidential Library and Museum

The library is located in Simi Valley, California, and contains documentary material on Ronald Reagan's presidency (1981–1989). A limited amount of foreign policy–related materials have been digitized and are accessible at www.reagan.utexas.edu/. Featured on the website are finding aids for records on various individuals and organizations serving during Reagan's presidency that are at least partially open for research. Examples include State Department ambassador at large for counterterrorism Robert Oakley (1986–1988), national security advisers John Poindexter and Colin L. Powell, White House Situation Room staff support (1985–1989), and National Security Planning Group (1981–1987).

A detailed listing of Reagan administration National Security Decision Directives (NSDDs) includes those that have been at least partially declassified and are available at the Reagan library. Examples are *U.S. National Security Strategy* (NSDD 32, 1982), *Next Steps in Lebanon* (NSDD 64, 1982), *Nuclear Capable Missile Technology Transfer Policy* (NSDD 70, 1982), *U.S. Relations with the USSR* (NSDD 75, 1983), *Central America: Promoting Democracy, Economic Improvement, and Peace* (NSDD 124, 1984), and *Acting against Libyan Support of International Terrorism* (NSDD 205, 1986).

The website also features *Public Papers of the President,* which is browsable by month and contains Reagan's speeches, proclamations, and executive orders.

George Bush Presidential Library and Museum

Located on the campus of Texas A&M University in College Station, Texas, the library chronicles the career of George H. W. Bush, who served as president from 1989 to 1993. A number of digitized and partially declassified national security policy resources are accessible via the Bush library website (http://bushlibrary.tamu.edu/).

These resources include *Public Papers of the President,* which is browsable by month, and finding aids fashioned from Freedom of Information Act (FOIA) requests on subjects such as immigration from Mexico and Central America, the Persian Gulf War, the NATO heads of state summit (November 7–8, 1991), Operation Just Cause (Panama), and the Strategic Petroleum Reserve.

Some National Security Reviews (NSRs) and National Security Directives (NSDs) are also accessible on the website: *Review of U.S. Arms Control Policies* (NSR 14, 1989), *Counterintelligence and Security Counter-Measures* (NSR 18, 1989), *Intelligence Capabilities 1992–2005* (NSR 29, 1991), *Organization of the National Security Council System* (NSD 1, 1989), *U.S. Policy toward Nicaragua and Nicaraguan Resistance* (NSD 8, 1989), *Cocaine Trafficking* (NSD 13, 1989), *Organizing to Manage On-Site Inspection for Arms Control* (NSD 41, 1990), *Interagency Review and Disposition of Export Control Licenses Issued by Department of Commerce* (NSD 53, 1990), *Responding to Iraqi Aggression in the Gulf* (NSD 54, 1991), *U.S. Port Security Program* (NSD 57, 1991), *Civil Defense* (NSD 66, 1992), and *American Policy toward Sub-Saharan Africa in the 1990s* (NSD 75, 1992).

William Clinton Presidential Materials Project

The Clinton library is under construction in Little Rock, Arkansas. However, NARA has compiled the Clinton Presidential Materials Project website (http://clinton.archives.gov/). Because the Clinton administration was the first to make public use of the Internet and to establish a White House website, the Clinton Presidential Materials Project website contains all versions of the Clinton White House website. NSC reports on the website include *The Clinton Administration's Policy on Managing Complex Contingency Operations* (1997), *The Clinton Administration's Policy on Critical Infrastructure Protection* (1998), *International Crime Control Strategy* (1998), *National Security Strategy Report* (1999), *National Plan for Information Systems Protection* (2000), and *International Crime Threat Assessment* (2000).

Also accessible are presidential speeches, proclamations, and executive orders as chronicled in *Public Papers of the President,* the President's Foreign Intelligence Advisory Board report *Science at Its Best, Security at Its Worst* on security conditions at DOE laboratories, and White House press secretary briefings from the "Virtual Library" section of the Clinton White House websites.

Nuclear Regulatory Commission

The Nuclear Regulatory Commission (NRC) was created by a 1974 law that established the Energy Research and Development Administration (a forerunner of the

Department of Energy) and shut down the Atomic Energy Commission, which had been responsible for nuclear energy research and development.[43] NRC licenses the construction, operation, and closure of commercial nuclear facilities; licenses the possessing, handling, processing, use, and export of nuclear material; licenses nuclear power and nonpower test and research reactors; inspects licensed nuclear facilities and their activities; investigates nuclear incidents and allegations concerning NRC-regulated matters; collects, analyzes, and disseminates information about the operational safety of these reactors; and develops strong working relationships with states concerning reactor operations and nuclear material safety.[44] NRC's responsibilities are executed by its component parts such as the Office of Nuclear Security and Incident Response, Office of Investigations, Office of Nuclear Reactor Regulation, Office of Nuclear Material Safety and Safeguards, Office of International Programs, Advisory Committee on Reactor Safeguards, and Advisory Committee on Nuclear Waste and other NRC entities including regional offices in Philadelphia, Atlanta, Chicago, and Arlington, Texas.[45]

NRC provides public access to numerous information resources through its website (www.nrc.gov/) and the Agencywide Documents Access and Management System (ADAMS). Examples of NRC or NRC contractor publications with national security relevance are *Briefing on Electric Grid Reliability* (1997), *U.S. Nuclear Materials Management and Safeguard System* (n.d.), *Reactor Oversight Process* (2000), *Spent Nuclear Fuel Transportation Package Performance Study Issues Report* (2001), *National Report for the Convention on Nuclear Safety* (2001), *Nuclear Energy Security Issues in the Post-September 11 World: Physical Security, Safety, Reliability of Supply* (2001), *Criteria for Preparation and Evaluation of Radiological Emergency Response Plans and Preparedness in Support of Nuclear Power Plants: Final Report* (2002), and *Withholding Sensitive Homeland Security Information from the Public* (2002).

Nuclear Waste Technical Review Board

Established in 1987, the Nuclear Waste Technical Review Board (NWTRB) reviews DOE's scientific and technical management and disposal of U.S. commercial spent nuclear fuel.[46] Its eleven members are recognized experts in science and engineering, recommended by NAS, and appointed by the president. NWTRB is particularly concerned with nuclear waste management and disposal activities as they pertain to Yucca Mountain, Nevada, which DOE designated as the final repository for U.S. nuclear waste, and with packaging and transporting commercial spent nuclear fuel and high-level defense nuclear waste.[47]

Documentation of NWTRB activities is provided at www.nwtrb.gov/. Accessible materials include *Nuclear Waste Management in the United States: The Nuclear Waste Technical Review Board's Perspective* (1996), *Moving beyond the Yucca Mountain Viability Assessment* (1999), NWTRB annual reports to Congress and the secretary of energy from 1990 to the present, and reports on DOE's scientific and technological investigations of Yucca Mountain.

Additional website contents are NWTRB strategic plans, correspondence with DOE officials and members of Congress, the opening statements of board members in testimony before congressional oversight committees, press releases, transcripts of board meetings in Washington, D.C., and Nevada, and board member biographies. Ongoing controversy over Secretary of Energy Spencer Abraham's February 14, 2002, decision to designate Yucca Mountain as the U.S. permanent nuclear waste repository site makes NWTRB reports of continuing relevance and germane to those concerned with nuclear waste's possible influence on homeland security.[48]

Selective Service System

Established in 1948, the Selective Service System (SSS) is responsible for carrying out the registration of male U.S. citizens and all males in the United States between the ages of eighteen and twenty-six for possible military service, unless such individuals are already active armed forces members or nonimmigrant aliens.[49]

Resources available on the agency's website (www.sss.gov/) include a list of SSS directors, press releases, how to obtain information on individual registrants, an online registration form, how a possible military draft today would differ from the Vietnam War era draft, SSS annual reports to Congress from 1996 to 2001, the *Register* newsletter from 1998 to the present, *Calendar Year 2001 Selective State by State Registration Compliance Report Card* (2002), a draft registration booklet, and the PowerPoint presentation "Teacher's Guide to the Selective Service" (2000).

Notes

1. PL 101-549, "To Amend the Clean Air Act to Provide for Attainment and Maintenance of Health Protective National Ambient Air Quality Standards, and for Other Purposes," 104 *U.S. Statutes at Large*, 2565–2574.

2. U.S. Chemical Safety and Hazard Investigation Board, "CSB Mission and History" (n.d.), 1 (www.chemsafety.gov/mission_history/index.cfm?ID=1), accessed November 6, 2003.

3. PL 100-456, "To Authorize Appropriations for Fiscal Year 1989 for Military Activities of the Department of Defense, for Military Construction, and for Defense Activities of the Department of Energy, to Prescribe Personnel Strengths, for Such Fiscal Year for the Armed Forces, and for Other Purposes," 102 *U.S. Statutes at Large*, 1918.

4. *U.S. Government Manual, 2001–2002* (Washington, D.C.: National Archives and Records Administration, 2001), 382. For an in-depth analysis of the Defense Nuclear Facilities Safety Board's initial years of operation, see Bert Chapman, "The Defense Nuclear Facility Safety Board's First Decade," *Journal of Government Information*, 27 (3) (2000): 345–383.

5. "Executive Order 12127: Federal Emergency Management Agency," *Federal Register*, 44 (April 3, 1979), 19367–19368.

6. *U.S. Government Manual*, 409.

7. U.S. Federal Emergency Management Agency, "About FEMA: FEMA History" (2003), 1 (www.fema.gov/about/history.shtm), accessed November 6, 2003.

8. "Reorganization Plan No. 7 of 1961," 75 *U.S. Statutes at Large*, 840–843.

9. *U.S. Government Manual*, 418. For 1984 Shipping Act provisions, see 40 USC app. 1701, *U.S. Code* (Washington, D.C.: Government Printing Office, 1994), 1348.

10. PL 81-152, "To Simplify the Procurement, Utilization, and Disposal of Government Property, to Reorganize Certain Agencies of the Government, and for Other Purposes," 63 *U.S. Statutes at Large*, 377–403.

11. *U.S. Government Manual,* 437–438.

12. U.S. General Services Administration, "GSA Administrator Commends Bush's Homeland Security Proposal" (2002), 1–2 (www.gsa.gov/Portal/gsa/ep/contentView.do?contentType=GSA_BASIC&contented=9501&contentType-GSA_BASIC), accessed November 6, 2003.

13. See PL 98-525, "Department of Defense Authorization Act 1985," 98 *U.S. Statutes at Large,* 2649–2660; and U.S. Institute of Peace, "About Us" (n.d.), 1 (www.usip.org/aboutus/), accessed October 16, 2003.

14. *U.S. Government Manual,* 546.

15. *U.S. Government Manual,* 546.

16. *U.S. Government Manual,* 546.

17. U.S. International Trade Commission, "General Factfinding Reports" (2002), 1 (www.usitc.gov/332s/332index.htm), accessed November 6, 2003.

18. For the text, see "Proclamation 7529: To Facilitate Positive Adjustment to Competition from Imports of Certain Steel Products," *Federal Register,* 67 (March 7, 2002), 10551–10592.

19. PL 37-326, "An Act to Incorporate the National Academy of Sciences," 12 *U.S. Statutes at Large,* 806–807.

20. U.S. National Academy of Sciences, "Organization of the National Academies" (2002), 1–4 (www.nas.edu/about/faq1.html), accessed November 6, 2003. For a historical overview, see Rexmund Canning Cochrane, *The National Academy of Sciences: The First Hundred Years, 1863–1963* (Washington, D.C.: National Academy of Sciences, 1978). For a critique of the academy's role in providing scientific expertise in the public policy arena, see Stephen Hilgartner, *Science on State: Expert Advice as Public Drama* (Stanford, Calif.: Stanford University Press, 2000).

21. PL 73-432, "To Establish a National Archives of the United States Government and for Other Purposes," 48 *U.S. Statutes at Large,* 1122–1124. For historical overviews, see Timothy Walch, ed., *Guardian of Heritage: Essays on the History of the National Archives* (Washington, D.C.: National Archives and Records Administration, 1985).

22. PL 98-497, "To Establish the National Archives and Records Administration, and for Other Purposes," 98 *U.S. Statutes at Large,* 2280–2295.

23. *U.S. Government Manual,* 453–54.

24. Robert B. Matchette and others, comp., *Guide to Federal Records in the National Archives of the United States,* vol. 1 (Washington, D.C.: National Archives and Records Administration, 1995): xi–xv.

25. For detailed annotations on the kind of records that are available, see Matchette and others, *Guide to Federal Records in the National Archives of the United States,* 1:18-1–18-8 (Army Air Force); 1:26-1–26-12 (U.S. Coast Guard); 1:38-1–38-7 (Office of the Chief of Naval Operations); 1:46-2–46-3 (U.S. Senate Committees Relating to Defense); 2:181-1–181-13 (naval districts and shore establishments); 2:218-1–218-2 (Joint Chiefs of Staff); 2:220–24 (President's Commission on an All-Volunteer Armed Force); 2:243-1–243-2 (U.S. Strategic Bombing Survey); 2:263-1–263-2 (Central Intelligence Agency); and 2:273-1–273-2 (National Security Council).

26. U.S. National Archives and Records Administration, "About ARC" (n.d.), 1 (www.archives.gov/research_room/arc/), accessed November 6, 2003.

27. "Executive Order 12829: National Industrial Security Program," *Federal Register,* 58 (January 8, 1993), 3479–3483; and "Executive Order 12958: Classified National Security Information," *Federal Register,* 60 (April 20, 1995), 19825–19843.

28. U.S. National Archives and Records Administration, Information Security Oversight Office, "Mission and Functions" (n.d.), 1) (www.archives.gov/isoo/about_isoo/mission_and_functions.html), accessed November 6, 2003. For coverage of recent developments in gov-

ernmental security classification, see Harold C. Relyea, "Security Classification Reviews and the Search for Reform," *Government Information Quarterly,* 16 (1) (1999): 5–27.

29. U.S. National Archives and Records Administration, "Classification Management Committee" (n.d.), 1 (www.archives.gov/isoo/oversight_groups/cmc.html), accessed November 6, 2003.

30. U.S. National Archives and Records Administration, "Interagency Security Classification Appeals Panel" (n.d.), 1 (www.archives.gov/isoo/oversight_groups/iscap.html), accessed November 6, 2003.

31. U.S. National Archives and Records Administration, "National Industrial Security Policy Program Advisory Committee" (n.d.), 1 (www.archives.gov/isoo/oversight_groups/nisppac.html), accessed November 6, 2003.

32. For a historical overview of presidential libraries and analysis of issues confronting these facilities, see Richard J. Cox, "America's Pyramids: Presidents and Their Libraries," *Government Information Quarterly,* 19 (1) (2002): 45–75.

33. U.S. National Archives and Records Administration, "A Brief History" (n.d.), 1–2 (www.archives.gov/presidential_libraries/about/history.html), accessed November 6, 2003.

34. PL 84-373, "To Provide for the Acceptance and Maintenance of Presidential Libraries, and for Other Purposes," 69 *U.S. Statutes at Large,* 695–697.

35. U.S. National Archives and Records Administration, "A Brief History" (n.d.), 1–2 (www.archives.gov/presidential_libraries/about/history.html), accessed November 6, 2003.

36. For how Richard M. Nixon's refusal to turn over his presidential records to the National Archives and Records Administration resulted in legal intervention into presidential records access and helped contribute to passage of the 1978 Presidential Records Act, see Don W. Wilson, "Presidential Records: Evidence for Historians or Ammunition for Prosecutors," *Government Information Quarterly,* 14 (4) (1997): 339–342. See also PL 95-951, "To Amend Title 44 to Insure the Preservation of and Public Access to the Official Records of the President, and for Other Purposes," 92 *U.S. Statutes at Large,* 2523–2528.

37. U.S. National Archives and Records Administration, "A Brief History" (n.d.), 1–2 (www.archives.gov/presidential_libraries/about/history.html), accessed November 6, 2003. For coverage of access restrictions presidents can impose on their papers, see Cox, "America's Pyramids: Presidents and Their Libraries," 52.

38. U.S. Congress, Senate Committee on Governmental Affairs, *Presidential Libraries Act of 1985: Report to Accompany H.R. 1349,* S Rept 99-257 (Serial 13672), 99th Cong., 2d sess., 1986, 2.

39. PL 99-323, "Presidential Libraries Act of 1986," 100 *U.S. Statutes at Large,* 495–498. For enumeration of future presidential library financing conditions, see U.S. Congress, Senate Committee on Governmental Affairs, "Presidential Libraries Act of 1985," 2–3.

40. "Executive Order 13233: Further Implementation of the Presidential Records Act," *Federal Register,* 68 (November 5, 2001), 56025–56029.

41. HR 4187 was introduced in the 107th Congress; HR 1493 and S 1517, in the 108th Congress.

42. U.S. National Archives and Records Administration, Gerald R. Ford Library and Museum, "The National Security Council System and the Use of National Security Decision Memorandums and Study Memoranda" (1998), 1 (www.ford.utexas.edu/library/document/nsdmnssm/backgrou.htm), accessed November 6, 2003.

43. PL 93-438, "An Act to Reorganize and Consolidate Certain Functions of the Federal Government in a New Energy Research and Development Administration and in a New Nuclear Regulatory Commission in Order to Promote More Efficient Management of Such Functions," 88 *U.S. Statutes at Large,* 1233–1254.

44. *U.S. Government Manual,* 488–489. For additional historical background on the Nuclear Regulatory Commission and U.S. government nuclear power regulation, see J. Samuel Walker, *A Short History of Nuclear Regulation, 1946–1999* (Washington, D.C.: Nuclear Regulatory Commission, 2000); George T. Mazuzan and J. Samuel Walker, *Controlling the Atom: The Beginnings of Nuclear Regulation, 1946–1962* (Berkeley, Calif.: University of California Press, 1984); and J. Samuel Walker, *Containing the Atom: Nuclear Regulation in a Changing Environment, 1963–1971* (Berkeley, Calif.: University of California Press, 1992).

45. U.S. Nuclear Regulatory Commission, "Nuclear Regulatory Commission Organization Chart" (2002) (www. nrc.gov/who-we-are/organization/nrcorg.pdf), accessed November 6, 2003.

46. PL 100- 203, "Nuclear Waste Policy Amendments Act of 1987," 101 *U.S. Statutes at Large,* 1330-27–1330-251, 1330–253, 1330–255.

47. U.S. Nuclear Waste Technical Review Board, "What Is the Nuclear Waste Technical Review Board?" (1999), 1 (www.nwtrb.gov/nwtrb.pdf), accessed November 6, 2003.

48. For the text of Spencer Abraham's announcement, see U.S. Department of Energy, "Secretary Abraham Recommends Yucca Mountain Site to President Bush Citing 'Sound Science' and 'Compelling National Interests' " (2002), 1–3 (www.energy.gov/engine/content.do?PUBLIC_ID=12962&BT_CODE=PR_PRESSRELEAS ES&TT_CODE=PRESSRELEASE), accessed November 10, 2003. Information on Yucca Mountain projects and activities can be found at www.ymp.gov/. For opposition to Yucca Mountain's designation, see State of Nevada, Agency for Nuclear Projects (www.state.gov/nucwaste/), accessed November 6, 2003; Sen. Harry Reid (D-Nev.) website (www.senate.gov/~reid/), accessed November 10, 2003; and Sen. John Ensign (R-Nev.) website (www.senate.gov/~ensign/), accessed November 10, 2003.

49. PL 80-759, "To Provide for the Common Defense by Increasing the Strength of the Armed Forces of the United States, Including the Reserve Components Thereof, and for Other Purposes," 62 *U.S. Statutes at Large,* 604–644; and *U.S. Government Manual,* 518.

CHAPTER 6

Intelligence Agencies

Intelligence agencies are important producers of national security policy information. The secretive nature of their work and the need to keep it under wraps, to protect the individuals and technologies required to obtain information, means that a long time passes before much intelligence information is publicly accessible. Nevertheless, a large amount of intelligence information is available in paper and electronic formats. Some intelligence agencies such as the Central Intelligence Agency (CIA) have broad statutory responsibilities for the amount of intelligence they collect and analyze. Other agencies such as the National Security Agency (NSA) have more restricted institutional mandates.

Central Intelligence Agency

The Central Intelligence Agency is the largest U.S. government intelligence agency and a prolific producer of national security policy information. The 1947 National Security Act provided for the CIA.[1] This act created a centralized U.S. intelligence agency whose functions included coordinating governmental foreign intelligence activities, collecting foreign intelligence information outside the United States by all means necessary, giving this information timely evaluation and interpretation, disseminating national intelligence to the president and appropriate governmental departments and agencies, protecting the sources and methods used in gathering this intelligence, formulating and promoting integrated security policies and procedures to protect classified information, and carrying out other intelligence-related functions.[2] The CIA has achieved successes, endured failures, and weathered controversies throughout its history.[3]

The vast majority of information produced by the CIA since its establishment is not publicly accessible. However, declassification initiatives of the 1990s resulted in the release of significant quantities of national security policy information by the CIA and its component parts.[4] Publications, such as the annual *World Factbook* and *Chiefs of State and Cabinet Members of Foreign Governments,* have been distributed in print format to federal depository libraries for many years. Other publications are distributed through the CIA's website (www.odci.gov/). Examples include *Director of*

> ## Intelligence Community
>
> The Intelligence Community (IC) consists of U.S. executive branch agencies that work individually and collectively to conduct intelligence operations necessary for U.S. foreign policy and national security. Headed by the director of central intelligence, the IC consists of the Central Intelligence Agency, Defense Intelligence Agency, National Security Agency, intelligence-gathering units at cabinet level agencies such as the Departments of State and Energy, and armed services intelligence organizations.
>
> The IC's contemporary institutional structure was initially defined by Executive Order 12333 issued by President Ronald Reagan on December 4, 1981. It received statutory definition in the Intelligence Authorization Act signed by President George H. W. Bush on October 24, 1992.

Central Intelligence Annual Report for the United States Intelligence Community (1997–present), *CIA Inspector General Report of Investigation: Improper Handling of Classified Information by John M. Deutsch* (2000), *National Intelligence Estimate: The Global Infectious Disease Threat and Its Implications for the United States* (2000), *Long-Term Global Demographic Trends: Reshaping the Geopolitical Landscape* (2001), *Foreign Missile Developments and the Ballistic Missile Threat through 2015* (2001), *Unclassified Report to Congress on the Acquisition of Technology Relating to Weapons of Mass Destruction and Advanced Conventional Munitions* (2002), and *Annual Report to Congress on the Safety and Security of Russian Nuclear Facilities and Military Forces* (2002).

Directorate of Intelligence

The CIA's Directorate of Intelligence (DI) is the agency's analytical arm and is charged with providing timely, accurate, and objective intelligence analysis on national security threats and foreign policy issues facing the United States.[5] DI has offices dealing with analysis of developments in global regions such as Russia, Europe, Latin America, Asia and the Pacific, South Asia, and Africa, along with sections providing analysis of issues such as nonproliferation and narcotics.[6] Publicly accessible DI publications include *Analytic Toolkit* (1995–1997), *International Terrorism in 1997: A Statistical View* (1998), *Kosovo: History of a Balkan Hotspot* (1998), and *Heroin Movement Worldwide* (2000). The DI's website (www.odci.gov/cia/di/) provides links to these and other DI resources.

Directorate of Science and Technology

The Directorate of Science and Technology (DS&T) addresses national intelligence operations with technology and tradecraft. It works to fulfill national intelligence requirements in areas such as information technology, open-media acquisition and

> **Central Intelligence Agency**
>
> The Central Intelligence Agency (CIA) is the most important U.S. intelligence agency. An independent agency, the CIA collects information on foreign intelligence and conducts counterintelligence activities and operations relevant to national security as directed by the president for the president, National Security Council, and officials directing and implementing U.S. national security policy. The CIA is accountable to the American public through the two congressional oversight committees. It cooperates with other foreign government intelligence agencies when prudent and is legally prohibited from gathering information about individual Americans unless reason exists that they are involved in espionage or terrorist activities.

dissemination, technical collection and support, satellite technologies, and research and development to support open and clandestine intelligence gathering.[7]

The DS&T came into being in 1963 as a result of efforts to merge various agencies' scientific and technological entities.[8] A preponderance of its work is classified, but the directorate's website (www.odci.gov/cia/dst/) does contain information about its activities, employment opportunities, and some publications about historical work done by DS&T and its predecessor agencies. Significant information on the Corona satellite program of the 1950s and 1960s is featured, as well as the publication *Between the Sun and Earth: The First NRO Reconnaissance Eye in Space* (1997) and links to declassified Corona photography on the U.S. Geological Survey's web page.

Center for the Study of Intelligence

The Center for the Study of Intelligence (CSI) promotes the scholarly study of intelligence for research and historical purposes to enhance public understanding of intelligence operations and analysis. CSI holds conferences in which academic specialists participate, and it publishes works on the CIA and the history of intelligence.[8]

CSI produces *Studies in Intelligence,* which is the CIA's principal historical research journal of intelligence operations and activities and is available at many federal depository libraries. The journal is accessible on CSI's website (www.odci.gov/csi/), as are numerous publications such as *Sherman Kent and the Board of National Estimates: Collected Essays* (1994), *Corona: America's First Satellite Program* (1995), *CIA Assessments of the Soviet Union: The Record versus the Charges* (1996), *Intentions and Capabilities: Estimates on Soviet Strategic Forces, 1950–1983* (1996), *CIA Briefings of Presidential Candidates* (1996), *Sharing Secrets with Lawmakers: Congress as a User of Intelligence* (1997), *Intelligence in the War of Independence* (1997), *The CIA and the U-2 Program: 1954–1974* (1998), *On the Front Lines of the Cold War: Documents on the Intelligence War in Berlin* (1999), *At Cold War's End: U.S. Intelligence on the Soviet*

> **Intelligence Acronyms**
>
> The often-secretive world of intelligence is a large producer of acronyms used to describe intelligence analysis and operations. Examples of intelligence acronyms include
>
> - CCJ2—U.S. Central Command Intelligence Directorate
> - CESM—Cryptologic Electronic Warfare Support Measures
> - IMINT—Imagery Intelligence
> - NIE—National Intelligence Estimate
> - NRO—National Reconnaissance Office
>
> National Defense University's Joint Military Intelligence College has published *Defense and Intelligence Abbreviations and Acronyms* to help researchers understand intelligence acronyms. It is accessible at www.dia.mil/Public/Foia/abbrev_acron.pdf.

Union and Eastern Europe, 1989–1991 (1999), *The Office of Strategic Services: America's First Intelligence Agency* (2000), *Central Intelligence: Origin and Evolution* (2001), and *U.S. Intelligence and the Polish Crisis, 1980–1981* (2001).

Electronic Freedom of Information Act

The Electronic Freedom of Information Act (EFOIA) section of the agency provides access to CIA products declassified under the Freedom of Information Act (FOIA). It collects frequently requested records on important and controversial CIA operations. It has, for example, declassified documents on the Bay of Pigs, American prisoners of war (POW) and missing in action (MIA) from the Vietnam War, the 1954 overthrow of Guatemala's Arbenz regime, human rights in Latin America, the Julius and Ethel Rosenberg atomic spy case, Soviet military intelligence official Lt. Colonel Oleg Penkowsky who provided valuable information to the United States during the Cuban Missile Crisis, and Francis Gary Powers and the U-2 aircraft.

Accessible on the EFOIA website (www.foia.cia.gov/) are *CIA Inspector General Report of the CIA's Internal Probe of Bay of Pigs Affair* (1996), the National Security Council briefing *Sino-Soviet Campaign in Latin America* (1959), *Viet Cong Prisoner of War Camps in Cambodia* (1969), *U.S. Prisoners of War at Viet Cong Military Region Tri-Thien-Hue Detention Camp* (1970), *Operation PBSuccess: The United States and Guatemala 1952–1954* (1994), *CIA and Guatemala Assassination Proposals 1952–1954* (1995), *Untitled: The Rosenbergs Rented an Apartment at 65 Morton Street* (1953), *Supporters of Communist Pro-Rosenberg Campaign* (1955), and *Untitled Blank Admitted Soviet Agent Testified before the Committee on Un-American Activities* (1966).

A "Special Collections" section of the FOIA website is acessible at www.foia.cia.gov/special_collections.asp. It contains DI reports on the former Soviet Union, which were declassified and released for a March 2001 conference at Princeton University. Examples include *Atomic Defense in the USSR* (1954), *Paramilitary*

Activity in the USSR and the Satellites (1954), *Soviet Machinery Offered to Britain* (1963), *Soviet Antitank Guided Missile Systems Now Deployed in Cuba, East Germany, and Iraq* (1963), *Soviet Oil Exports* (1975), *USSR: Production and Consumption of Oil, Gas, and Primary Energy* (1975), and *The Soviet Bloc Aluminum Industry* (1984). Print copies of many of these reports are deposited at the National Archives and Records Administration (NARA), and the "Special Collections" website has information on accessing these print resources.

National Intelligence Council

The National Intelligence Council (NIC) produces reports on national security policy issues involving collaboration between the intelligence community and functional experts from other government agencies, academia, and the private sector. NIC has national intelligence officers covering subjects and geographic regions such as Africa, conventional military issues, East Asia, economics and global issues, Europe, Latin America, Near East and South Asia, Russia and Eurasia, science and technology, strategic and nuclear programs, and warning about potential national security crisis areas.

Numerous NIC-produced reports are available at www.odci.gov/nic/, including *The Environmental Outlook in Russia* (1999), *Transformations in Global Defense Markets and Industries: Implications for the Future of Warfare* (2000), *The Future of the Information Revolution in Latin America* (2001), *Global Trends 2015: A Dialogue about the Future with Nongovernment Experts* (2001), *Impact of the War on Terror on Certain Aspects of U.S. Policy in the Middle East* (2001), *Growing Global Migration and Its Implications for the United States* (2001), and *North Korea's Engagement—Perspectives, Outlook, and Implications* (2001).

NIC areas of research include the future of military conflict; the nation-state's evolving authority; changes in the nature and sources of military power; implications of growing interactions among information technology, biotechnology, materials technology, and nanotechnology for the United States and the world; energy geopolitics; and global education.[10]

Foreign Broadcast Information Center

The Foreign Broadcast Monitoring Service was established in 1941 under the jurisdiction of the Federal Communications Commission. During World War II, it became part of the Military Intelligence Division of the War Department's General Staff. In 1947 it was transferred to the CIA and became the Foreign Broadcast Information Center (FBIS). FBIS monitors, records, transcribes, and analyzes foreign broadcasts for the U.S. intelligence community.[11]

FBIS translates these broadcasts, and many of its transcriptions can be found in federal depository libraries nationwide. Online the material is available on the World Wide Web through the Commerce Department's National Technical Information Service's (NTIS) World News Connection (WNC). Because this information is produced from copyrighted news sources, individuals and organizations must pay to

> ### National Intelligence Estimates
>
> National Intelligence Estimates (NIEs) are documents from the director of central intelligence that are written appraisals of national security issues. The documents can cover strengths, weaknesses, and likely policy actions foreign nations may take that are important to U.S. national interests. NIEs are prepared by members of the Central Intelligence Agency's National Intelligence Council with assistance from specialists outside the intelligence community.
>
> NIEs tend to be measured in their key assumptions, can include alternative scenarios, incorporate dissenting views, and include information about which the intelligence community is uncertain. Controversy arose in 2003 over the CIA's October 2002 NIE concerning Iraq's weapons of mass destruction program and whether information in this document was used inaccurately by the Bush administration as justification for going to war with Iraq.
>
> NIEs are eventually declassified, can appear in publications issued by the CIA or other organizations, and are valuable historical source materials. A caveat, however, is that NIEs are estimates based on the best information available to intelligence analysts and policymakers at a given time. They are subject to revision depending upon subsequent information that may corroborate or disprove the assumptions upon which the original estimates were based.

subscribe to WNC. Examples of national security policy news reports translated by FBIS for WNC are *Colombia: Strong Guerrilla Paramilitary Presence in Medellin* and *Colombia: Air Force Reports 40 FARC Believed Dead in Bombing* from Bogota's *El Espectador*, *Kazakhstan Expands Cooperation with NATO* from Moscow Interfax, *Russian Defense Minister against Joining NATO as Military Organization* from Moscow's ITAR-TASS news service, *Du Tiehuan Leads Chinese Military Delegation to Zambia for Goodwill Visit* from Beijing's *Xinhua* news service, and *ZTS: Joint Chinese, Russian–U.S. Mediation Efforts Will Avert Indo-Pakistani War* from Hong Kong's *Zhongguo Tongxun Sue*.

Information on World News Connection content and subscriptions can be found at its website (http://wnc.fedworld.gov/) hosted by NTIS.

Defense Intelligence Agency

Concern arose over duplicative intelligence gathering by the military services after World War II. Various initiatives during the Eisenhower and Kennedy administrations sought to rectify this situation, but it took a February 1961 recommendation from Secretary of Defense Robert McNamara to the Joint Chiefs of Staff (JCS) to begin the process of developing a unified Defense Intelligence Agency (DIA). The JCS completed a DIA conceptual plan by July 1961 and published it in Department of Defense Directive 5105.21. The agency was formally created on October 1, 1961.[12]

> ### President's Daily Brief
>
> The President's Daily Brief (PDB) is a compilation of intelligence information presented to the president each morning by an individual or group from the Central Intelligence Agency (CIA). It may contain information about ongoing intelligence operations or noteworthy intelligence trends or developments of interest to the president and members of his administration. Materials presented in the PDB and the PDB's format will vary depending on the president's wishes and the needs of presidential national security advisers. The PDB can involve intelligence community members orally briefing the president. The president or his national security advisers can ask oral questions or present written questions to the briefers, which are then answered in a timely manner.
>
> PDBs are classified, and presidential administrations have strongly resisted declassifying them. However, the George W. Bush administration in April 2004 declassified and released to the National Commission on Terrorist Attacks Upon the United States the August 6, 2001, PDB describing Osama bin Laden's desire to launch terrorist attacks in the United States.

DIA reports to the secretary of defense through the JCS.[13] The agency's institutional mandate and responsibilities were expressed in Executive Order 12333 issued by President Ronald Reagan on December 4, 1981.

1. Collection, production, or through tasking and coordination, provision of military and military-related intelligence for the Secretary of Defense, the Joint Chiefs of Staff, other defense components, and, as appropriate, non-Defense sources;
2. Collection and provision of military intelligence for national foreign intelligence and counterintelligence products;
3. Coordination of Department of Defense intelligence collection requirements;
4. Management of the defense attaché system; and
5. Provision of foreign intelligence and counterintelligence staff support as directed by the Joint Chiefs of Staff.[14]

DIA and its components, including the Joint Military Intelligence College, have produced works publicly accessible at federal depository libraries or on the Internet. Examples include *North Korea: The Foundations for Military Strength* (1991), *A Selective Bibliography on Imagery Reconnaissance and Related Matters* (1993), *Intelligence Training Courses* (1993), *Intelligence for Multilateral Decision and Action* (1997), and *Intelligence Essentials for Everyone* (1999).

The website www.dia.mil/ has information about DIA's history, mission, and recruitment efforts. The "Freedom of Information Act (FOIA)" section of its website contains additional information resources.

Military Intelligence Agencies

Individual U.S. armed services have intelligence agencies that perform operations and analyses meeting their respective mission requirements.

Air Force Intelligence—Air Intelligence Agency

The U.S. Air Force Security Service (USAFSS) was established on October 20, 1948.[15] Air force intelligence operations went through varying degrees of changes before a single centralized Air Intelligence Agency (AIA) was created on October 1, 1993, under the command of the U.S. Air Force assistant chief of staff, intelligence.[16]

According to its mission statement, AIA "conducts full spectrum information operations for the U.S. Air Force and the nation. . . . Air Intelligence Agency gains, exploits, defends and attacks information to ensure air, space, and information superiority for war-fighters, national decision-makers and modernization forces."[17] AIA organizational entities include the National Air Intelligence Center at Wright-Patterson Air Force Base (AFB) in Dayton, Ohio; the Air Force Information Warfare Center at Lackland AFB in San Antonio, Texas; the 67th Information Operations Wing at Lackland, AFB; the 70th Intelligence Wing at Fort Meade, Maryland; and the Joint Information Operations Center at Lackland AFB.[18]

The National Air Intelligence Center is the primary producer of foreign aerospace intelligence in the Department of Defense (DOD). It analyzes foreign aerospace weapons systems to determine their performance characteristics, capabilities, vulnerabilities, and intentions. Center personnel have been involved in U.S. weapons treaty negotiation and verification agreements. Primary activities of the Air Force Information Warfare Center are to develop, maintain, and deploy information warfare capabilities to support military operations, campaign planning, and acquisitions and testing. It also provides technical expertise for computer and communications security.[19]

Responsibilities of the 67th Information Operations Wing include assisting air force entities in developing concepts, exercises, and employment of AIA forces in support of contingency, low-intensity conflict, counterdrug, and special operations activities. The 70th Intelligence Wing provides national decisionmakers, tactical theater commanders, and warfighters of all armed services with tailored and timely information. It plans and directs the integration of its components into theater or localized exercises, tests and validates wartime capabilities, and assists commanders in refining their product and service requirements. The Joint Information Operations Center assists in planning, coordinating, and executing information operations along with supporting the integration of operations security, psychological operations, military deception, and electronic warfare and destruction during the planning and execution of military operations.[20]

AIA's website (http://aia.lackland.af.mil/) contains information on the agency's historical development, its contemporary mission and organizational structure, press information, and agency career opportunities. Publicly accessible materials include *Airborne Maintenance Standardization and Evaluation Program* (1996), *Standardization, Evaluation, and Quality Assurance for U.S. Air Force Imagery Production Facili-*

ties (1997), *Air Force Information Warfare Center Mission Directive* (1998), *Headquarters Air Intelligence Agency Networks Infrastructure and Computer Systems Management* (1999), and *Air Intelligence Agency Inspection System Guidance, Procedures, and Responsibilities* (2000).

Army Intelligence

A Division of Military Information was established in 1885 within the Military Reservations Division, Miscellaneous Branch of the Army's Adjutant Generals Office.[21] Formal recognition of intelligence as a distinct professional discipline within the U.S. Army did not occur until 1962, when the Army Intelligence and Security Branch was created. The Military Intelligence Corps incorporating all military intelligence and personnel into a single regiment in 1987.[22]

Army Intelligence School

The Army Intelligence School is responsible for training army intelligence personnel and has been located at Fort Huachuca in Arizona since 1971.[23] Its website (http://usaic.hua.army.mil/) requires an Internet Explorer browser and the Macromedia Flash plug-in. Site contents include descriptions of intelligence positions such as imagery analyst and cryptologic analyst and the current number of legally authorized positions.

The website also has information on courses offered at the school and biographical portraits of significant military intelligence figures such as modern military intelligence pioneer Arthur L. Wagner, aerial reconnaissance pathfinder George M. Goddard, and World War II Southeast Asian theatre commander Gen. Joseph Stilwell. Other features include articles from the *Military Intelligence Professional Bulletin* and descriptions of Army Intelligence School courses including Intelligence in Combating Terrorism, Intelligence Officer Basic Course, Ground Surveillance Radar Operator, and Military Information Systems Security Monitor. Links to individual intelligence unit homepages such as the 112th Military Intelligence Brigade and 306th Military Intelligence Battalion are also provided.

Army Intelligence and Security Command

The Army Intelligence and Security Command (INSCOM) was organized on January 1, 1977, to provide the U.S. Army with a single organization for conducting multidisciplinary intelligence, security operations, and electronic warfare above the corps level and to produce completed intelligence customized to the army's requirements.[24] INSCOM is located at Fort Belvoir, Virginia. Its mission statement describes the multiple areas of intelligence operations falling within its jurisdiction.

> Charged with providing the warfighter the seamless intelligence needed to understand the battlefield and to focus and leverage combat power, INSCOM collects intelligence information in all intelligence disciplines. INSCOM also conducts a wide

range of production activities, ranging from intelligence preparation of the battlefield to situation development, SIGINT analysis, imagery exploitation, and science and technology intelligence production. INSCOM also has major responsibilities in the areas of counterintelligence and force protection, electronic warfare and information warfare, and support to force modernization and training.[25]

A limited number of information resources are provided on INSCOM's publicly accessible website (www.inscom.army.mil/). These include *INSCOM Insight: The Intelligence Newsletter,* the current issue of *INSCOM Journal,* an INSCOM historical overview, INSCOM's mission statement, functional descriptions of INSCOM personnel such as the chief information officer and inspector general, and links to INSCOM field unit web pages including the "Joint Surveillance Target Attack Radar System (JSTARS)."

Army Department—Deputy Chief of Staff

The Office of the Deputy Chief of Staff of the Secretary of the Army (G-2) for Intelligence is responsible for formulating policy, planning, programming, budgeting, managing, supervising staff, evaluating, and conducting intelligence oversight activities for the Army Department. In addition, it coordinates overall army imagery intelligence, signals intelligence (SIGINT), human intelligence, measurement and signature intelligence, and counterintelligence and security countermeasures.[26]

Its website (www.dami.army.pentagon.mil/) contains a March 6, 2002, briefing for the Cable News Network on Operation Anaconda against al Qaeda in Afghanistan, the text of recruitment policy documents, and PowerPoint presentations from an April 2002 conference on asymmetrical warfare such as "Domestic Urban Terrorism: Avoiding a Maginot Defense" and "Asymmetric Warfare: Impact on U.S. Industry, Society, and the Army."

Additional website contents include presentations on the Army Intelligence Master Plan, army intelligence transformation planning, presentations from a February 2002 conference sponsored by G-2's Counterintelligence, Foreign Disclosure, and Security Directorate on foreign disclosure and civilian defense intelligence information, a *Military Attaché Guide* from the Foreign Liaison Directorate detailing proper U.S. Army relationships with foreign government military attachés stationed in the United States, and G-2 organizational charts. Furthermore, the website has selected Army intelligence regulations such as *Industrial Security Program (AR 380-49)* (1982) and *Personnel Security Program (AR 380-6)* (1988).

Marine Corps Intelligence Department

Commandant James L. Jones established the Marine Corps Intelligence Department on April 27, 2000, to continue U.S. Marine Corps (USMC) progress in intelligence capabilities, doctrine, and training.[27] The Marine Corps Intelligence Department is the USMC commandant's intelligence staff officer and its director serves as the corps intelligence chief on joint intelligence matters, participates in electronic warfare policy formulation, and sponsors research, development, and projects studying intelligence, cryptology, and ground electronic warfare.[28]

Also under the jurisdiction of the USMC Intelligence Department are the USMC Headquarters; Reserve Intelligence Detachment, which provides trained and qualified individuals with intelligence-related expertise to augment DOD or other governmental time-sensitive intelligence operational activities; the Intelligence Programs and Budget Branch, which carries out USMC Headquarters resource planning, programming, and budgeting responsibilities for the director of intelligence such as preparing intelligence budget briefs for the commandant's annual congressional testimony; the Intelligence Plans and Policy Division, which executes USMC Headquarters oversight for intelligence resource planning, programming, geospatial, cryptologic, and electronic warfare programs; the Imagery and Geospatial Plans and Policy Branch, which develops and coordinates USMC imagery and geospatial intelligence programs; and the Intelligence Plans and Policy/Tactical Exploitation of National Capabilities Program, which provides intelligence support to operating USMC forces and coordinates the development of selected intelligence planning documents.[29]

The Signals Intelligence and Science Commands Plans and Policy Branch covers USMC involvement in DOD cryptologic activities, signals intelligence, and information systems security monitoring and serves the director of intelligence as a resource contact on electronic warfare, intelligence support to information, and intelligence systems architectural issues. The Counterintelligence/Human Intelligence Plans and Policy Branch develops and implements USMC counterintelligence and human resource intelligence policy. The Intelligence Estimates Branch compiles and disseminates completed intelligence to the commandant and staff officers while liaising with the Joint Chiefs of Staff and other U.S. intelligence agencies. The Intelligence Operations and Personnel Resource Branch manages corps intelligence personnel structure, training, and career development programs and The Special Security Office/Special Intelligence Communications Branch manages various intelligence branch communications security programs.[30]

The website http://hqinet001.hqmc.usmc.mil/DirInt/ provides information such as biographies of key officials, an organizational chart, and component mission descriptions.

Naval Intelligence

U.S. Navy intelligence operations and analysis are performed by the Office of Naval Intelligence (ONI) and the Naval Criminal Investigative Service (NCIS).

Office of Naval Intelligence

The Office of Naval Intelligence (ONI) is the U.S. Navy's principal intelligence agency. Secretary of the Navy William H. Hunt on March 23, 1882, issued General Order 292 establishing ONI in the Navy's Bureau of Navigation "for the purpose of collecting and recording such information as may be useful to the Department in time of war, as well as peace." ONI would not receive official recognition until 1899, when Congress granted it fiscal year 1900 funding for employing five clerks, one translator, one assistant draftsman, and a laborer.[31] William E. Chandler, Hunt's successor as secretary of the navy, in a July 25, 1882, letter to ONI's first director, Lt. Theodorus B. M. Mason, provided specifics regarding the office's purpose. ONI was to collect information on the cruising fleets and war material of foreign navies, defensive armaments in foreign ports, transport facilities of foreign governments, foreign coastal and port facilities for landing men and supplies, routes followed by foreign shipping lines, global facilities for obtaining coal and supplies, U.S. coastal defenses, and enhancement of the professional development of U.S. naval officers.[32]

Located at the National Maritime Intelligence Center (NMIC) in Suitland, Maryland, ONI is the oldest continually operating U.S. intelligence agency. It remains committed to keeping naval leaders and national civilian policymakers informed with essential warfighting information to ensure the navy's triumph over any foreign naval force desirous of challenging U.S. interests. The NMIC also supports the U.S. Coast Guard Intelligence Coordination Center and Naval Information Warfare Activity.[33]

ONI publications include *A Century of U.S. Naval Intelligence* (1996), which provides detailed coverage of the office's historical and institutional development, and the regularly updated *ONI Military Information Handbook,* which contains information about working at ONI. The website www.nmic.navy.mil/ has information on ONI's history and current mission, employment opportunities, and a link to the Navy's Freedom of Information Act website.

Naval Criminal Investigative Service

The Naval Criminal Investigative Service (NCIS) is an international federal law enforcement agency charged with protecting and serving U.S. Navy and Marine Corps personnel and their families and providing counterintelligence, criminal investigation, and law enforcement services for these armed service branches. NCIS has approximately 1,600 employees, including 850 civilian special agents, stationed in over 150 locations around the world including some ships and aircraft carriers. Some of these employees are law enforcement professionals who are investigators, crime laboratory technicians, technical information specialists, and security specialists.[34]

NCIS was established in 1915 as part of ONI to investigate espionage and sabotage in light of the outbreak of World War I. The personnel structure of NCIS was made up of military officers, but this began to change after World War II as civilians became more numerous in NCIS rankings. This augmented civilian influence was most reflected in 1992, when the current NCIS organizational structure was established and a civilian director was appointed with reporting responsibilities to the secretary of the navy through the navy general counsel.[35]

Resources on the NCIS website (www.ncis.navy.mil/) include information about the service's criminal investigations activities with descriptions of its general crimes investigations, counterdrug programs, economic crimes, the cold case squad (which investigates inactive or unsolved homicides), criminal intelligence, and agency technical services activities such as forensic science, hidden cameras, photography, armored vehicles, secure police communications, and polygraph examinations.[36] Also accessible are biographical information on the agency's director, a pamphlet on protecting personal computers while traveling, links to headquarters and field office websites, information on the NCIS security clearance adjudication process, photographs and biographical information about missing and fugitive naval personnel, anthrax handling guidance, and information on careers within NCIS.

National Geospatial Intelligence Agency

The National Geospatial Intelligence Agency (NGA) was created on November 24, 2003, when the 2004 Defense Authorization Act was signed into law. NGA replaced the Defense Mapping Agency (DMA), which had been established in 1972 and had predecessor agencies within the military. DMA was replaced in 1996 by the National Imagery and Mapping Agency (NIMA).[37] NGA's purpose is providing timely, relevant, and accurate geospatial intelligence to support national security to the White House, Congress, military commanders, law enforcement officials, and civil leaders.[38]

NGA, NIMA, and DMA publications, including maps, atlases, and charts, are available in many federal depository libraries. Examples of these publications include *Digitizing the Future* (1990), *Military Specifications: Gridded Airfield Photographs* (1994), *Photo Interpretation Student Handbook* (1996), *Performance Specification Tactical Ocean Data—Level O* (1998), and *Performance Specification Digital Topographic Data* (1999).

The website www.nima.mil/ provides information about NIMA activities and links to the agency's publications. The growing importance of imagery, imagery intelligence, and geospatial data in cartographic intelligence gathering and analysis are reflected in NIMA's 2002 strategic planning document.[39]

National Security Agency

The National Security Agency (NSA), created in 1952, serves as the premier U.S. cryptologic organization. Its institutional mission is providing U.S. policymakers and warfighters with intelligence information gathered from code-breaking operations and protecting U.S. signals and information systems from being exploited by U.S. adversaries.[40]

The NSA's highly sensitive work prevents it from being a major producer of publicly accessible information. However, the amount of NSA information released to the public in recent years has increased. Examples include *External Team Report: A Management Review for the Director NSA* (1999) and *New Enterprise Team (NETeam) Recommendations: The Director's Work Plan for Change* (1999). Many publications are accessible through the agency's website (www.nsa.gov/).

More significant are recently released materials on historical operations involving NSA and predecessor U.S. government cryptological agencies. *OpenDoor,* NSA's declassification initiative, provides information about declassified cryptological materials. It can be found at the National Archives and Records Administration on

NSA's website (www.nsa.gov/programs/opendoor/). The website also contains the full text of documents and photographs of various historic operations that NSA and its predecessors have conducted.

NSA has released a monographic series, *Project Venona*, detailing its involvement with tracking Soviet espionage in the United States during and immediately after World War II.[41] *Monograph #2: The 1942–43 New York-Moscow KGB Messages* (1995) is an example of a *Project Venona* monograph accessible through the NSA website.

The website also commemorates U.S. cryptological and signals intelligence operations during the Korean War. Representative publications are *NSA Korean War 1950–1953 Commemoration* (2000), *The Korean War: The SIGINT Background* (2000), and *The Start of the Digital Revolution: SIGSALY Secure Digital Voice Communications in World War II* (n.d.).

Information about the Cuban Missile Crisis is available on the NSA website. Other useful contemporary and publicly accessible material produced by NSA deals with information security and desirable security measures for computer systems.

National Counterintelligence Executive

The National Counterintelligence Council (NACIC) was established in 1994 by Presidential Decision Directive/NSC-24. Consisting of counterintelligence and security professionals from various federal departments and agencies, NACIC worked with government agencies and the private sector to compile intelligence and open-source reporting on secret targeting of U.S. industry and technologies by foreign intelligence services. It devised methods for protecting the security of U.S. trade secrets or threats against U.S. business personnel.[42]

NACIC was reorganized in 2001 by Presidential Decision Directive 75, which changed its name to the National Counterintelligence Executive (NCIX). This directive tasked NCIX with providing the U.S. government with policy-driven leadership to enhance U.S. counterintelligence capabilities and to produce coherent programs and strategies.

> NCIX will accomplish these objectives through the identification of the nation's most critical assets (tangible and intangible), production of strategic CI [counterintelligence] analysis, development of a national threat assessment, formulation of a national CI strategy, creation of an integrated CI budget, and an agenda of program reviews and evaluations. This approach will require direct interaction with policymakers and the private sector and the adoption of a new philosophy that embraces cooperation, coordination, and collaboration among the intelligence, law enforcement, security, and CI communities.[43]

Publicly accessible NCIX resources are provided through the agency's website (www.ncix.gov) or through the NACIC website (www. nacic.gov). Examples of information resources found on NCIX's website are updates on the trial involving the Four Pillars Enterprise Company, which was convicted of conspiring and attempting to steal a trade secret as part of the first case tried under the Economic Espionage Act of 1996.

NCIX's website includes the complete text of the *Annual Report to Congress on Foreign Economic Collection and Industrial Espionage* (1995–2003), a *Be Alert* brochure on foreign intelligence collection of trade secrets and how to respond to such activity, other resources on counteracting foreign intelligence industrial espionage, and information on ordering the video *Insider Betrayal: Protecting Trade Industry Secrets*.

National Reconnaissance Office

The National Reconnaissance Office (NRO) conducts satellite surveillance for U.S. intelligence agency and military operations. Its origins date back to 1961.[44] However, its existence was kept from the public until it was declassified by the deputy secretary of defense as recommended by the director of central intelligence on September 18, 1992.[45]

NRO's mission is ensuring that the U.S. possesses the technology and space-borne assets needed to achieve global information superiority. It is accomplished through the research, development, acquisition, and operation of national intelligence satellites. NRO resources collect intelligence in support of functions such as indications and warnings, monitoring arms control agreements and military exercises, and keeping track of natural disasters or other environmental occurrences.[46]

The highly sensitive nature of the work prevents immediate public release of NRO-produced information. In recent years, however, significant historical NRO operational material has been declassified. For example, President Bill Clinton on February 22, 1995, issued an executive order permitting the public release of satellite photo imagery from NRO's Corona program from August 1960 to May 1972.[47] Within eighteen months of the order, the photographs were transferred to the National Archives and Records Administration and the U.S. Geological Survey.[48] Some Corona imagery can be found on NRO's website (www.nro.gov), including a 1962 satellite photo of a Soviet intercontinental ballistic missile launch complex, a 1967 photo of a Soviet nuclear launch site at Chelyabinsk, and a photo of the Chinese nuclear weapons Lop Nor test site four days after a nuclear weapons test.

The website also features a book with pictures and biographical information about NRO directors, Corona program information accompanied by video and audio clips in Windows Media software, announcements of new NRO developments, press releases from 1995 to the present, NRO director speeches before professional organizations and opening statements at congressional committee hearings, and video of a 1996 NRO satellite launch from California's Vandenburg Air Force Base. NRO's "Freedom of Information Act (FOIA)" web pages have a list of individuals requesting NRO FOIA records and the nature of the records they requested.

Department of Energy Intelligence Agencies

The U.S. Department of Energy (DOE), responsible for managing the U.S. nuclear weapons arsenal, has three entities that carry out intelligence and counterintelligence–related activities: Office of Intelligence, Office of Counterintelligence, and Office of Security.

The Office of Intelligence seeks to make efficient use of federal intelligence resources to support information gathering on global nuclear weapons development, nonproliferation, and nuclear and other forms of energy production and consumption. The Office of Counterintelligence develops and implements counterintelligence programs to identify, neutralize, and deter foreign governmental or industrial intelligence activities directed at DOE programs, personnel, facilities, technologies, and classified or sensitive information. Both of these agencies were reconfigured in 1998 as a result of Presidential Decision Directive 61.[49] Neither has a publicly accessible website and, consequently, their publication output is restrained.[50]

The Office of Security manages security operations of DOE facilities in the Washington, D.C., area; develops policies to protect national security and other critical assets entrusted to DOE; establishes and maintains direct communication with federal, state, and local law enforcement entities on interpreting domestic threat information; ensures the proper training of DOE information and security personnel; develops policies and procedures to guide foreign visits and assignments to DOE laboratories and facilities; and makes sure that all documents prepared at DOE headquarters are properly analyzed to reflect the categories of printed information they contain.[51]

The responsibilities of the Office of Security are carried out by its individual units, including the Security Policy Staff; the Office of Headquarters Security Operations; the Office of Foreign Visits, Assignments, and Travel; and the Office of Classified and Controlled Information Review. The Office of Plutonium and Special Materials Inventory maintains current, reliable, and complete information on DOE materials subject to special control and accounting procedures on domestic inventory and on inventory transferred to foreign countries.[52]

The Security Office's website (www.so.doe.gov/) contains information about office operations and activities. It also has the text of relevant statutory and regulatory documents on DOE security policies such as *Employee Polygraph Protection* (1994) as spelled out in Title 29 of the *United States Code;* the Privacy Act of 1974 describing the privacy rights of federal agency employees; Executive Order 12968, *Access to Classified Information* (1995); Executive Order 12958, *Classified National Security Information* (1995); and DOE's *Polygraph Examination Regulation* from the December 17, 1999, *Federal Register.* Also on the website are recent *Federal Register* notices concerning eligibility criteria for access to classified information or special nuclear materials and the opening statement of Security Office director Joseph Mahaley on DOE responses to terrorist threats at a December 5, 2001, hearing of the House Budget Committee.

Department of State Bureau of Intelligence and Research

The Department of State Bureau of Intelligence and Research coordinates the activities of U.S. intelligence agencies to ensure that their overseas operations remain consistent with U.S. foreign policy objectives and interests. It organizes seminars on subjects relevant to intelligence community policymakers and monitors and analyzes foreign public and media opinion.[53] The bureau also analyzes geographic and international boundary issues.[54]

Publicly accessible information resources on the bureau's website (www. state.gov/s/inr/) include a "Geographic Learning Site" on international geography issues for K–12 students; *Arms and Conflict in Africa* (2001); information about Title 7 discretionary grant programs—provided for in the 1983 Soviet-Eastern Europe Research and Training Act—which seek to build expertise on Russia, Eurasia, and Central and Eastern Europe for advanced research, language, and graduate training; and a listing of fiscal year 2001–2003 Title 7 grant recipients.

Department of Transportation Office of Intelligence and Security

The 1990 Aviation Security Act established the Office of Intelligence and Security (OIS) within the Department of Transportation (DOT).[55] OIS advises the secretary of transportation on domestic and international intelligence and security matters, coordinates the development and implementation of long-term strategic plans for programs affecting the security of cargo and the traveling public, and serves as the DOT's key instrument of intelligence and security policy.[56]

The website www.dot.gov/ost/ois/ contains information about the office's institutional mission, links to relevant U.S. government and private sector transportation security organization websites, a "Research and Development" section with links to a summary of the OIS strategic plan and the Federal Aviation Administration's Technical Center, a "Documents/Product Library" (which is under development as of April 2004), and a link containing information about a June 2002 National Cargo Security Council conference.

National Cyber Security Division

The Justice Department and Federal Bureau of Investigation (FBI) on February 26, 1998, established the National Infrastructure Protection Center (NIPC) in response to recommendations from the President's Commission on Critical Infrastructure Protection. NIPC's creation was influenced by increasing governmental experience grappling with illegal intrusions into government and private sector computer systems.[57] IPC on June 6, 2003, became the National Cyber Security Division (NCSD) in the Department of Homeland Security Information Analysis and Infrastructure Protection Directorate.[58]

NCSD, like its predecessors, is a joint government and private sector partnership consisting of participants from federal, state, and local government agencies. It serves as the federal government's central means for assessing and responding to threats or attacks against critical national infrastructures such as telecommunications, energy, banking and finance, water systems, government operations, and emergency services.[59] Presidential Decision Directives (PDDs) 62 and 63, issued May 22, 1998, addressed this entity's institutional mandate. PDD 62 stressed the growing unconventional security threats the United States faced from cyberterrorism and chemical, radiological, and biological weapons. It sought to create a systematic approach to defend against them. PDD 63 emphasized protecting U.S. critical infrastructures from physical and cyberattacks that could originate from foreign governments, foreign or domestic terrorist organizations, and foreign or domestic criminal organizations.[60]

Numerous information resources may be found on NCSD's website at www.nipc.gov/. Available publications include *Cybernotes,* a bimonthly newsletter on computer security issues such as viruses and bugs (1999–present); *Highlights,* a monthly newsletter for policymakers on computer network security matters for 2001–2002; and *Information Bulletins* (2002) with titles such as "Hijacked Tractor-Trailer Transporting Sodium Cyanide Found in Mexico with Missing Cargo" and "Identifying Indications of Terrorist Truck Bombs." Assessments of computer security problems posted on NCSD's website for 2001 and beyond include *Multiple Vulnerabilities in Microsoft Internet Explorer—All Versions, Code Red Reminder and Clarification,* and *Anna Kournikova Also Known as "VBS/SST" VBS Virus.* Computer security advisories posted for 2002 include *Update Universal Plug and Play Vulnerabilities, Multiple Remote Vulnerabilities in Microsoft's Internet Information Services (IIS), Daily Reports* (2003–present, *Continuing Threats to Home Users* (2004), and *Vulnerability in Microsoft Outlook 2002* (2004).

Other materials on the website are information on NIPC's resource-sharing activities with the electric industry; information on and the text of computer security statutes; press releases on agency activities; general security guides such as *Trust But Verify: A Guide to Using E-mail Correspondence* (2001), *Cyber Protests Related to the War on Terrorism: The Current Threat* (2001), *Password Protection 101* (2001), and *Cyber Protests: The Threat to the U.S. Information Infrastructure* (2001); and information on major computer crime investigations and criminals such as the "I Love You" virus and "Mafiaboy" and Brian West. An incident report form for reporting computer or network security attacks is provided as are links to relevant government and private sector computer and network security resources.

President's Foreign Intelligence Advisory Board

President Dwight D. Eisenhower's 1956 Executive Order 10656 established the President's Board of Consultants on Foreign Intelligence Activities.[61] It became the President's Foreign Intelligence Advisory Board (PFIAB) during the Kennedy administration and has served all presidents since then except Jimmy Carter. It has sixteen members who are not government employees.[62]

PFIAB offers the president expert and objective advice on U.S. foreign intelligence conduct. Through its Intelligence Oversight Board, PFIAB members meet with intelligence policymakers, receive substantive briefings, and visit intelligence facilities.[63] Through these efforts PFIAB strives to identify weaknesses in intelligence collection, analysis, and reporting; eliminate unnecessary functional duplication; and ensure that major programs are responsive to policymakers' needs and that intelligence technology is of the highest quality.[64]

The highly sensitive nature of its work prevents public accessibility to much PFIAB work. However, in 1999 PFIAB permitted public release of *Science at Its Best, Security at Its Worst: A Report on Security Problems at the U.S. Department of Energy.* The current PFIAB website (www.whitehouse.gov/pfiab/) provides background information and a listing of all PFIAB chairs. The Rudman Report—named for the sitting PFIAB chair, former senator Warren B. Rudman (R-N.H., 1890–1993), and its appendix were posted on PFIAB's website and made available to federal depository libraries. An archived electronic version of the Rudman Report and its appendix can be found on the Clinton Presidential Materials Project website at http://clinton2.nara.gov/WH/EOP/pfiab/pfiab_report.pdf and http://clinton2.nara.gov/WH/EOP/pfiab/appendix.pdf.

Notes

1. PL 80-253, "To Promote the National Security by Providing for a Secretary of Defense; for a National Military Establishment; for a Department of the Army, a Department of the Navy, and a Department of the Air Force; and for the Coordination of the Activities of the National Military Establishment with Other Departments, and Agencies of the Government Concerned with the National Security," 61 *U.S. Statutes at Large,* 495–499.

2. U.S. Department of State, *Foreign Relations of the United States, 1945–1950: Emergence of the Intelligence Establishment,* C. Thomas Thorne Jr., David S. Patterson, and Glenn W. LaFantasie, eds. (Washington, D.C.: Government Printing Office, 1996), 545. This volume provides valuable documentary coverage on the origins of the Central Intelligence Agency (CIA) and the modern intelligence community.

3. For examples of substantive and credible assessments of the CIA's origins and development, see John Ranelagh, *The Agency: The Rise and Decline of the CIA from Wild Bill Donovan to William Casey* (New York: Simon and Schuster, 1986); Arthur B. Darling, *The Central Intelligence Agency: An Instrument of Government to 1950* (University Park: Pennsylvania State University Press, 1990); Loch Johnson, *America's Secret Power: The CIA in a Democratic Society* (New York: Oxford University Press, 1989); and David F. Rudgers, *Creating the Secret State: The Origins of the Central Intelligence Agency, 1943–1947* (Lawrence: University Press of Kansas, 2000).

4. For coverage of these developments, see Christopher Andrew, *For the President's Eyes Only: Secret Intelligence and the American Presidency from Washington to Bush* (New York: HarperCollins, 1995), 535. For a critical assessment of what one analyst regards as excessive intelligence declassification, see Thomas Patrick Carroll, "The Case against Intelligence Openness," *International Journal of Intelligence and Counterintelligence,* 14 (4) (2001): 559–574.

5. U.S. Central Intelligence Agency, Directorate of Intelligence, "About The DI: Organization" (n.d.), 1 (www.odci.gov/cia/di/mission_section.html), accessed November 5, 2003.

6. U.S. Central Intelligence Agency, "Directorate of Intelligence Organizational Components" (n.d.), 1 (www.odci.gov/cia/di/org/_chart_section.html), accessed November 5, 2003.

7. U.S. Central Intelligence Agency, Directorate of Science and Technology, "Who Are We?" (2002), 1 (www.odci.gov/cia/dst/about.html), accessed November 5, 2003.

8. Jeffrey T. Richelson, *The Wizards of Langley: Inside the CIA's Directorate of Science and Technology* (Boulder, Colo.: Westview Press, 2001): 293.

9. U.S. Central Intelligence Agency, Center for the Study of Intelligence, "About CSI" (n.d.), 1 (www.odci.gov/csi/about.html), accessed November 5, 2003.

10. U.S. Central Intelligence Agency, National Intelligence Council, "Research Supported by the NIC" (n.d.), 1 (www.odci.gov/nic/NIC_researchsupported.htm), accessed March 23, 2004.

11. Robert B. Matchette and others, comp., *Guide to Federal Records in the National Archives of the United States,* Vol. II: *Record Groups 171–515* (Washington, D.C.: National Archives and Records Administration, 1995), 262–1.

12. U.S. Defense Intelligence Agency, "DIA History: 40 Years of History" (2002), 1 (www.dia.mil/History/40years/intro.html), accessed November 5, 2003.

13. U.S. Defense Intelligence Agency, "DIA History."

14. "United States Intelligence Activities," *Federal Register,* 46 (December 8, 1981), 59947.

15. U.S. Air Intelligence Agency, "History Retrospective: 1940s" (2002), 1 (http://aia.lackland.af.mil/homepages/ho/40s-2.cfm), accessed November 6, 2003. For additional historical background, see Dennis F. Casey and Gabriel G. Marshall, *USAFSS to AIA: A Brief History of the Air Intelligence Agency and Its Predecessor Organizations* (San Antonio, Texas: Air Intelligence Agency History Office, 2000).

16. U.S. Air Intelligence Agency, "History Retrospective 1990s (2002), 3 (http://aia.lackland.af.mil/homepage/ho/90s-2.cfm), accessed November 6, 2003.

17. U.S. Air Intelligence Agency, "Mission and Vision" (2002), 1 (http://aia.lackland.af.mil/homepages/pa/missionvision.cfm), accessed November 6, 2003.

18. U.S. Air Intelligence Agency, "About AIA Fact Sheet" (2001), 1–3 (http://aia.lackland.af.mil/homepages/pa/fact_sheets/aiafact.cfm), accessed November 6, 2003.

19. U.S. Air Intelligence Agency, "About AIA Fact Sheet," 1–2.

20. U.S. Air Intelligence Agency, "About AIA Fact Sheet," 2–3.

21. John Patrick Finnegan, *Military Intelligence* (Washington, D.C.: Center of Military History United States Army, 1998), 7.

22. Finnegan, *Military Intelligence,* foreword.

23. Finnegan, *Military Intelligence,* 161.

24. U.S. Army Intelligence and Security Command, "INSCOM Mission" (2003), 1 (www.inscom.army.mil/mission.asp), accessed November 6, 2003.

25. U.S. Army Intelligence and Security Command, "INSCOM Mission."

26. U.S. Army Department, Deputy Chief of Staff G-2, "G-2 Vision and Mission" (n.d.), 1 (www.dami.army.pentagon.mil/vision-mission.asp), accessed November 6, 2003.

27. U.S. Marine Corps, "All Marine Messages (ALMAR) 021/00" (2000) (www.usmc.mil/almars/almar2000.nsf), accessed November 6, 2003.

28. U.S. Marine Corps Intelligence Department, "Mission and Functions" (n.d.), 1 (http://hqinet001.hqmc.usmc.mil/DirInt/mission.html), accessed November 6, 2003.

29. U.S. Marine Corps Intelligence Department, "Organization" (n.d) 1 (http://hqinet001.hqmc.usmc.mil/DirInt/organizational_chart.html), accessed November 6, 2003.

30. U.S. Marine Corps Intelligence Department, "Organization."

31. Wyman H. Packard, *A Century of U.S. Naval Intelligence* (Washington, D.C.: Department of the Navy, Office of Naval Intelligence and Naval Historical Center, 1996), 2, 9.

32. Packard, *A Century of U.S. Naval Intelligence.* 3. For a contemporary synopsis of the Office of Naval Intelligence's mission and activities, see Office of Naval Intelligence, "Our Mission" (n.d.), 1–2 (www.nmic.navy.mil/mission.htm), accessed November 6, 2003.

33. Office of Naval Intelligence, "Our History" (n.d.), 3–4 (www.nmic.navy.mil/history.htm), accessed November 6, 2003.

34. See U.S. Naval Criminal Investigative Service, "About NCIS" (n.d.), 1 (www.ncis.navy.mil/aboutNCIS.html), accessed November 6, 2003; and *U.S. Government Manual, 2001–2002* (Washington, D.C.: National Archives and Records Administration, 2001), 186.

35. U.S. Naval Criminal Investigative Service, "NCIS History" (n.d.), 1–3 (www.ncis.navy.mil/aboutNCIS/history.html), accessed November 6, 2003.

36. U.S. Naval Criminal Investigative Service, "General Crimes" (2003), 1–2 (www.ncis.navy.mil/activities/GenCrim/GenCrim.html), accessed November 6, 2003.

37. See National Geospatial Intelligence Agency, "NGA History" (n.d.), 1–2 (www.nga.mil/StaticFiles/OCR/nga_history.pdf), accessed April 15, 2004; and PL 104-201, "To Authorize

Appropriations for Fiscal Year 1997 for Military Activities of the Department of Defense, for Military Construction, and for Defense Activities of the Department of Energy, to Prescribe Personnel Strengths for Such Fiscal Year for the Armed Forces, and for Other Purposes," 110 *U.S. Statutes at Large*, 2421, 2678–2688. For Defense Mapping Agency (DMA) statutory codification, see 10 U.S.C. 2791; and for its 1972 authorization, see Donna Batten, ed., *Guide to U.S. Government Publications* (Farmington Hills, Mich.: Gale Group, 2000), 228. For information on National Imagery and Mapping Agency and DMA publications, see Joe Morehead, *Introduction to United States Government Information Sources*, 6th ed. (Englewood, Colo.: Libraries Unlimited, 1999), 410–411. For coverage of the roles played by maps in library collections, see Mary Lynette Larsgaard, *Map Librarianship: An Introduction*, 3rd ed. (Englewood, Colo.: Libraries Unlimited, 1998).

38. U.S. National Imagery and Mapping Agency, "NIMA Statement of Strategic Intent January 2002" (2002), I–ii. (www.nima.mil/ast/fm/aca/strategicintent.pdf), accessed November 5, 2003.

39. U.S. National Imagery and Mapping Agency, "NIMA Statement of Strategic Intent January 2002," ii.

40. See *U.S. Government Manual*, 200–201. For statutory information on the National Security Agency (NSA), see PL 86-36, "To Provide Certain Administrative Authorities for the National Security Agency, and for Other Purposes," 73 *U.S. Statutes at Large*, 63–64. For a historical portrait of the NSA, see James Bamford, *Body of Secrets: Anatomy of the Ultra-Secret National Security Agency from the Cold War through the Dawn of a New Century* (New York: Doubleday, 2001).

41. For a summary and analysis of the historical and operational significance of *Project Venona*, see John Earl Haynes and Harvey Klehr, *Venona: Decoding Soviet Espionage in America* (New Haven, Conn.: Yale University Press, 1999).

42. U.S. Counterintelligence Executive, "What Is the NACIC" (1995), 2–3 (www.ncix.gov/nacic/news/1995/nov95.htm), accessed November 6, 2003.

43. U.S. Counterintelligence Executive, "About NCIX" (2001), 1 (www.nacic.gov/info/about.html), accessed November 6, 2003.

44. For historical background on the National Reconnaissance Office (NRO), see Dwayne A. Day, John M. Logsdon, and Brian Latell, eds. *Eye in the Sky: The Story of the Corona Spy Satellites* (Washington, D.C.: Smithsonian Institution Press, 1998), 147; and Jeffrey T. Richelson, "Undercover in Outer Space: The Creation and Evolution of the National Reconnaissance Office, 1960–1963," *International Journal of Intelligence and Counterintelligence*, 13 (3) (2000): 301–344.

45. U.S. National Reconnaissance Office, "Who We Are" (n.d.), 1 (www.nro.gov/index1.html), accessed November 6, 2003. For additional NRO historical background, see U.S. National Commission for the Review of the National Reconnaissance Office, *Report of the National Commission for the Review of the National Reconnaissance Office* (Washington, D.C.: National Reconnaissance Commission, 2000), 115–120.

46. U.S. National Reconnaissance Office, "Who We Are" (n.d.), 1 (www.nro.gov/index1.html), accessed March 23, 2004.

47. "Executive Order 12951: Release of Imagery Acquired by Space-Based National Intelligence Reconnaissance Systems," *Federal Register* 60, no. 39 (February 28, 1995), 10789–10790.

48. "Release of Imagery Acquired by Space-Based National Intelligence Reconnaissance Systems." For detailed historical overviews of Corona, see Kevin C. Ruffner, ed., *Eye in the Sky: The Story of the Corona Spy Satellites* (Washington, D.C.: Central Intelligence Agency, Center for the Study of Intelligence, 1995); and Kevin C. Ruffner, ed., *Corona: America's First Satellite Program* (Washington, D.C.: Central Intelligence Agency, Center for the Study of Intelligence, 1995).

49. For the directive's declassified text, see U.S. Department of Energy, Office of Security, "Counterintelligence Capabilities" (1998), 1–2 (www.so.doe.gov/documents/pdd61.pdf), accessed November 6, 2003.

50. *U.S. Government Manual,* 215.

51. U.S. Department of Energy, Office of Security, "About the Office of Security" (n.d.), 1–2 (www.so.doe.gov/index.cfm?fuseaction=home.aboutSO), accessed November 6, 2003.

52. For a Office of Security organizational chart, see U.S. Department of Energy, Office of Security, "Programs" (n.d.), 1 (www.so.doe.gov/index.cfm?fuseaction= home.programs), accessed November 6, 2003.. For a description of the Office of Plutonium, Uranium, and Special Materials Inventory responsibilities, see U.S. Department of Energy, Office of Security, "Office of Plutonium, Uranium, and Special Materials Inventory (SO-62)" (n.d.), 1 (www.so.doe.gov/index.cfm?fuseaction=home.SO62), accessed November 6, 2003.

53. *U.S. Government Manual,* 297.

54. U.S. Department of State, "Bureau of Intelligence and Research" (n.d.), 1 (www.state.gov/s/inr), accessed November 6, 2003.

55. PL 101-604, "An Act to Promote and Strengthen Aviation Security, and for Other Purposes," 104 *U.S. Statutes at Large,* 3066–3068.

56. *U.S. Government Manual,* 311, 313.

57. U.S. Federal Bureau of Investigation, "History of the FBI: The Rise of a Wired World (1993–2001)," 2 (www.fbi.gov/libref/historic/history/wiredworld.htm), accessed November 6, 2003.

58. U.S. Computer Emergency Readiness Team, "Ridge Creates New Division to Combat Cyber Threats" (2003), 1–2 (www.us-cert.gov/press_room/ncsd-announced.html), accessed March 22, 2004.

59. U.S. Federal Bureau of Investigation, "Congressional Statement before the Senate Judiciary Subcommittee on Technology, Terrorism, and Government Information, June 10, 1998" (1998), 1–7 (www.fbi.gov/congress/congress98/vatis0610.htm), accessed November 6, 2003.

60. U.S. Federal Bureau of Investigation, "Congressional Statement before the Senate Judiciary Subcommittee on Technology, Terrorism, and Government Information."

61. "Executive Order 10656: Establishing the President's Board of Consultants on Foreign Intelligence Activities," *Federal Register,* 21, no. 26 (February 8, 1956), 859.

62. President's Foreign Intelligence Advisory Board (PFIAB), "President's Foreign Intelligence Advisory Board" (2001), 1–2 (www.whitehouse.gov/pfiab/), accessed November 6, 2003. For a listing of all PFIAB chairs, see President's Foreign Intelligence Advisory Board, "PFIAB Chairpersons" (n.d.), 1 (www.whitehouse.gov/pfiab/chairpersons.html), accessed November 6, 2003.

63. President's Foreign Intelligence Advisory Board, "President's Foreign Intelligence Advisory Board," 1–2. For the establishment and mandate of the President's Intelligence Oversight Board, see "Executive Order 12334: President's Intelligence Oversight Board," *Federal Register,* 46, no. 235 (December 8, 1981), 59955–59956.

64. President's Foreign Intelligence Advisory Board, "President's Foreign Intelligence Advisory Board," 1–2.

CHAPTER 7

Congress and Congressional Support Agencies

The work of executive branch government agencies that are major producers of national security policy information—executive departments such as the Department of Defense (DOD), independent agencies such as the Defense Nuclear Facilities Safety Board, and intelligence agencies such as the Central Intelligence Agency (CIA)—must be approved and funded by Congress according to constitutional requirements.[1] Consequently, to gain a complete understanding of the factors shaping the formulation of U.S. national security policy, one must understand and use the materials produced by the U.S. Congress and congressional support agencies. Individual members of the House of Representatives and Senate, congressional committees and task forces, and congressional support agencies such as the Congressional Research Service (CRS) of the Library of Congress generate information on national security policy as well as other public policy issues.

Congressional Bills and Resolutions

During each biennial congressional session, thousands of bills and numerous resolutions are introduced by representatives and senators on a variety of subjects. Bills and joint resolutions have the force of law and require presidential approval; concurrent and simple resolutions do not have legal force and do not require presidential approval. Most bills and resolutions die upon final adjournment of Congress, without having completed the legislative process. Members often change the language contained in bills and resolutions as they make their way through Congress. As a result, different versions of the legislation are under consideration at different points in the legislative process.[2] Locating and retrieving these different versions became easier in the mid-1990s, when Internet resources such as "GPO Access" (www.gpoaccess.gov/) and the Library of Congress's "Thomas" (http://thomas.loc.gov/) became available.

A bill is designated by HR or S (referring to the chamber into which it was introduced—the House of Representatives or Senate) and is numbered sequentially upon introduction. For instance, S 1534, the Department of National Homeland Security Act of 2001, was the 1,534th bill introduced in the Senate in the 107th Congress.[3] The first page of the printed bill has the Congress and session, the bill number, the purpose of the bill, the chamber into which it was introduced, the date of introduction, the name of the member(s) introducing the bill, notes if the bill was read on the floor and how many times, and the congressional committee(s) the bill was referred to for further consideration. The first page then says in all capital letters and boldface type "A BILL" and states the general purpose of the bill. The provisions of the bill follow, such as what sections of the *United States Code* will be changed, how much money is to be allocated, what the criminal penalties would be for violations, which departments and agencies will have the authority to carry out the bill's provisions, where the specific facilities are and how many personnel would be required to implement the provisions, and what reports administering agencies would have to file with Congress. Legislation varies in length from one or two paragraphs to several hundred or thousands of pages long.

The changes made in bills as they go through the legislative process generally are in wording or program funding levels. Online resources, such as "GPO Access" and "Thomas," indicate where the changes originated by the use of abbreviations: (ih), for introduced in the House, and (is), for introduced in the Senate.

If a piece of legislation dies and the substance of it is to be reconsidered in a subsequent Congress, it must be reintroduced and will likely be assigned a new number. Copies of historic congressional bills may be available on microfiche at specific federal depository libraries. Other good sources for obtaining copies of these bills are the Library of Congress Law Library and the U.S. House and Senate Libraries.[4]

Congressional Committee Hearings

Once a bill is introduced, it is referred to a congressional committee having jurisdiction over the subject area covered by the legislation or a subcommittee of that committee. Most national security policy legislation is reviewed by the House and Senate Armed Services Committees. Because national security policy crosses the jurisdictional boundaries of many committees, those dealing with foreign relations, energy, intelligence, and judiciary also may conduct hearings on the legislation.

Supporters and opponents of the legislation testify during congressional committee hearings. Witnesses include subject experts from other government agencies, the military, and research institutes; academic scholars; business or labor leaders; and average citizens. Most hearings are open to the public and announced in advance through press releases or on the committee's web page.

Witnesses answer questions submitted by committee members and may submit reports or other material that will be included in the transcript of the committee's hearings. Depending on the nature of the subject, the questioning between some committee members and witnesses can become contentious as can the debate between committee members. Transcripts of most hearings, which could run for hundreds or thousands of pages, are distributed to many federal depository libraries

> ## Congressional Oversight of National Security Policy
>
> Congress plays an important role in overseeing American national security policy. Article I, Section 8 of the U.S. Constitution gives Congress power to provide for the common defense, borrow money, declare war, fund military programs, and issue legal and regulatory guidance for those programs.
>
> Congressional oversight of national security policy is primarily conducted by the House and Senate Armed Services Committees and their subcommittees. Representatives and senators serving on these committees benefit from the professional expertise of committee staff members and their personal office staffs in writing legislation affecting all aspects of U.S. military activity and in conducting oversight of federal military programs. Members can acquire high degrees of substantive knowledge about U.S. military programs during their committee service.
>
> Congressional national security program oversight is also provided by, for example, the Appropriations Committees and the House Government Reform Committee. Additional congressional national security review is facilitated by materials produced by congressional support organizations such as the Congressional Budget Office (CBO), Congressional Research Service (CRS), and General Accounting Office (GAO).
>
> CBO publications analyze budgetary aspects of national security programs. CRS publications provide nonpartisan analysis of national security policy such as combat deaths in Iraq and the performance of individual weapons systems. GAO publications analyze the financial performance of programs such as military health benefits and ballistic missile contractor performance.

in paper format or on microfiche within a few months. Some transcripts are now accessible through "GPO Access" or on congressional committee websites before their publication in paper format. Many congressional committee websites will feature opening statements made in hearings by members and witnesses within twenty-four hours of their appearance, if such statements are submitted electronically to the committee. C-SPAN, the Cable Satellite Public Affairs Network, televises many congressional committee hearings and includes a webcast archive of some hearings on its website (www.cspan.org/).

After considering the information gathered from hearings and making modifications to the bill, committee members decide whether to approve or reject the proposed legislation. While much legislation dies in committee, many bills are approved and moved to the floor for full chamber consideration. In these cases, the committee often files a report on the legislation being considered.[5]

Congressional Committee Reports

Congressional committees generally will file reports on bills they want to become law. However, on occasion, a committee will file an adverse report on a piece of proposed legislation (or send a bill to the floor without recommendation). Committee reports are important documents because in them members express what the proposed legislation is intended to accomplish.

A committee report begins by stating that the chair of the committee files the report for the consideration of the full House or Senate. The report goes on to specify, for example, what has occurred during the bill's consideration, the legal requirements of the bill and penalties for violations, the proposed funding levels, the location of particular facilities required to carry out the legislation's provisions, and the Congressional Budget Office estimations of the legislation's costs. The report can include other pertinent information such as descriptions of committee roll-call votes taken on the bill.

Many committee reports are approved without dissent by committee members. Some reports, however, include the signed dissents from representatives or senators stating their individual or collective reasons for not supporting the committee action. Some reports may also include the comments of committee members who agree with the overall content of the report but wish to emphasize different issues in their appraisals of the report's significance.

In the normal course of events, the full House or Senate considers on the floor the version of the bill that was reported from its respective committee. The legislation is debated and sometimes modified. If each version of the legislation passed in the House and the Senate is identical, it is ready to be sent to the president for his signature or veto. If the two versions have any differences, and they cannot be reconciled informally, the legislation goes to conference.

When this happens, the leadership of the House and Senate appoints a conference committee to attempt to resolve differences in the two versions of the bill. The conference committee consists of representatives and senators, often selected members of the committees that reported the legislation. If the conference committee members are successful, they file a conference committee report, which must be approved by the full House and Senate before the legislation can be sent to the president. If the legislation becomes law, the conference committee report is regarded as the authoritative legislative history document for the bill. (Some legal scholars and judges have voiced their opposition to this view of conference committee reports, however, as they are not law. Others argue that ignoring the report can lead to misinterpretation of the law.) If the conference committee members are unsuccessful, the bill is likely to die for that particular congressional session.[6]

Congressional committee reports, including those coming out of conference committees, are numbered by Congress and in the order issued. For instance, House Report 107-194 was the 194th committee report produced by a House committee during the 107th Congress. Besides reports on legislation, the House and Senate file reports on relevant topics; they are known as House or Senate documents. Senate committees also file reports on proposed international treaties. (The Constitution stipulates that the Senate must ratify treaties the U.S. government proposes to enter into with foreign governments or international government organizations.)

Congressional documents and reports have been available online at "GPO Access" and "Thomas" since 1995. Earlier documents and reports can be found in many federal depository libraries.

Legislative Calendars

Congressional committee calendars are published annually or biennially by committees and describe legislation considered during a given year or congressional session. They list bills by number and include the sponsor and cosponsors. Committee calendars also contain information about the status of legislation. Besides the committee calendars, the full House and Senate publish calendars each day they are in session, indicating what legislation was considered on the House or Senate floor during the daily legislative session.

Committee Activity Reports

Each oversight committee issues a report on its legislative activities for each Congress. The report contains a roster of the committee and subcommittees membership; a list of the federal programs and agencies the committee has jurisdiction over; a history of the committee; the bills considered by the committee; the legislation on which reports were filed; the dates and topics of committee hearings and the witnesses who testified; the nominations and confirmations of heads of federal agencies; military promotions (for Senate oversight committees); the committee rules and procedures; and the names of committee staff members. Examples of these reports are *Survey of Activities of the Permanent Select Committee on Intelligence, During the 106th Congress,* House Report 106-1054 (2001), and *Report on the Activities of the Committee on Armed Services United States Senate 106th Congress First and Second Sessions,* Senate Report 107-32 (2001).

Floor Debate

Since 1873, the *Congressional Record* has served as the official record of floor debates in the U.S. Congress. Contrary to popular belief, it is not a verbatim record, as members can edit their remarks before publication. Besides floor debates, the *Congressional Record* has the text of proposed legislation and amendments, states when committee reports have been filed, lists the cosponsors of bills and resolutions, reports on the status of nominations, and contains all the recorded vote tallies taken on the floor. The Extensions of Remarks section has the text of speeches made by members on the House floor after the conclusion of daily business or are inserted into the *Record* by these representatives without having delivered them.

The *Congressional Record* has been available on "GPO Access" since 1995 and "Thomas" since 1989. Many depository libraries also carry the publication. The U.S. Government Printing Office publishes an index to the *Congressional Record,* which makes it possible to search, for example, for when a representative or senator made a speech on a particular piece of legislation or for when the legislation was introduced. Commercial databases such as Lexis-Nexis's *Congressional Universe* also incorporate search capabilities for the *Congressional Record* and other congressional documents.

Congressional National Security Committees

Numerous congressional committees and subcommittees have jurisdiction over national security issues and programs. The House and Senate Armed Services Committees have primary jurisdiction, but the multidisciplinary nature of U.S. national security policy brings in other committees and subcommittees.

House Appropriations Committee

The large and powerful House Appropriations Committee, created in 1865, is responsible for authorizing expenditures for all federal programs and consisted of sixty-five members during the 108th Congress (2003–2005).[7] Appropriations subcommittees having oversight responsibilities for national security issues are Defense, Energy and Water Development, Foreign Operations, and Military Construction. The Subcommittee on Defense has jurisdiction over the Department of Defense, all armed services branches except military construction, defense agencies, the Central Intelligence Agency, and intelligence community staff. The Subcommittee on Energy and Water Development covers many areas of the Department of Energy, the Army Corps of Engineers within the Department of Defense, the Defense Nuclear Facilities Safety Board, the Nuclear Regulatory Commission, and the Nuclear Waste Technical Review Board.[8]

The Subcommittee on Foreign Operations, Export Financing, and Related Programs has jurisdiction over national security foreign assistance programs such as the Department of State's nonproliferation, antiterrorism, and demining programs; the Foreign Military Financing Program; international military education and training; the Military Assistance Program; and the Special Defense Acquisition Fund. The Subcommittee on Military Construction oversees military construction for active and reserve forces, defense agencies, military family housing, DOD's Base Closure Account, the North Atlantic Treaty Organization (NATO) Security Investment Program, and other related programs.[9]

Examples of Appropriations Committee publications on national security policy include the annual appropriations hearings such as *Military Construction Appropriations for 2003: Parts 1–5* (2003) and investigations on defense-related topics such as military force readiness, the U.S. Air Force's F-22 fighter plane program, the army's main battle tank upgrade programs, DOD's chemical weapons demilitarization programs, and DOD's defense health program. Some information resources are accessible on the committee's website (www.house.gov/appropriations/).[10]

House Armed Services Committee

The House Armed Services Committee was established on January 2, 1947, when separate committees on military and naval affairs—which had been established in 1882—were merged.[11] Armed Services' jurisdiction encompasses ammunition depots, forts, and arsenals; the common defense; the use, conservation, and development of naval petroleum reserves; DOD; the army, navy, and air force; interoceanic canals; the Merchant Marine Academy and state maritime academies; military applications of nuclear energy; tactical intelligence and DOD-related intelligence activities; national security aspects of the merchant marine fleet; armed forces members' privileges and benefits such as pay, promotion, and retirement; scientific research and development benefiting the armed services; the Selective Service System; the size and composition of the armed service branches; soldiers' and sailors' homes; strategic and critical materials essential for national defense; international arms control and disarmament; and military dependents' education.[12]

During the 108th Congress (2003–2005), the House Armed Services Committee consisted of sixty-one members and had five subcommittees.[13] The Subcommittee on Military Installations and Facilities has jurisdiction over military construction, real estate acquisitions and disposals, housing support, and base closure. The Subcommittee on Military Personnel has jurisdiction over military forces and authorized personnel strengths, integrating active and reserve forces, military personnel policy, and compensation and benefits. The Subcommittee on Military Procurement is responsible for the annual authorization for procuring military weapons systems and components and military applications of nuclear energy. The Subcommittee on Military Readiness oversees annual operation and maintenance budget authorizations and military readiness and preparedness. The Subcommittee on Military Research and Development is responsible for military research and development.[14]

The Armed Services Committee chair appoints investigative panels to investigate matters falling within the jurisdiction of more than one subcommittee. They report to the full committee.[15] Four panels were part of the Armed Services Committee for the 107th Congress (2001–2003): Special Oversight Panel on Terrorism, Special Oversight Panel on Department of Energy Reorganization, Merchant Marine Panel, and Morale, Welfare, and Recreation Panel.[16] Examples of House Armed Services Committee national security policy publications are *Hearings on National Defense Authorization for Fiscal Year 2000—H.R. 1401 and Oversight of Previously Authorized Programs* (1999), *Security against Terrorism on U.S. Military Bases* (2001), *Department of Energy Budget Request (Defense Programs) for Fiscal Year 2001 and Related Matters* (2001), and *Department of Defense Anthrax Vaccine Immunization Program (AVIP)* (2001). Many current and recent historical resources can be found on the committee's website (www. house.gov/hasc/).

House Budget Committee

The 1974 Congressional Budget and Impoundment Control Act established the House Budget Committee, which had forty-three members in the 108th Congress. The committee considers measures setting U.S. government budget levels, modifying the congressional budget process, and concerning the establishment, extension, and enforcement of special controls over the federal budget including off-budget federal agencies.[17]

Recent national security policy publications issued by the committee are *The Clinton Defense Plan: Shipshape or Treading Water?* (1999) and *Defense Department Budget Priorities for Fiscal Year 2002* (2001). The committee's reports on annual federal budget authorizations contain information on defense spending and defense policy programs. In addition, the committee's website (www.house.gov/budget/) provides information about hearings and the budgetary perspectives of committee Democrats and Republicans.

House Energy and Commerce Committee

The House Energy and Commerce Committee covers subjects as diverse as biomedical research, consumer protection, national energy policy, Department of Energy management, domestic nuclear energy regulation, telecommunications, and public health.[18] Established in 1795, the committee has oversight authority so extensive that former chairman (1981–1995) John D. Dingell (D-Mich.) once said that it covered "everything that moves, is sold, or is burned."[19] The panel had fifty-seven members in the 108th Congress.

The Energy and Power Subcommittee and the Oversight and Investigations Subcommittee deal most directly with national security policy issues. They are particularly concerned with Energy Department matters.

Examples of recent national security policy–related hearings conducted by Energy and Commerce and its subcommittees are *Bioterrorism and Proposals to Combat Bioterrorism* (2002), *Protecting America's Critical Infrastructure: How Secure Are Government Computer Systems?* (2001), *The Rudman Report: Science at Its Best, Security at Its Worst* (1999), and *Internet Posting of Chemical "Worst Case" Scenarios: A Roadmap for Terrorists* (1999). Some of these resources are accessible on the committee's website (http://energycommerce.house.gov/).

House Government Reform Committee

The House Government Reform Committee dates to 1816.[20] In 1927, eleven committees covering government departmental expenditures were consolidated, forming the modern incarnation of the panel.[21] The committee's forty-four members oversee the federal civil service; District of Columbia governance; the overall economy, efficiency, and management of governmental operations and activities; public information and records; relationships among federal, state, and local governments; and executive branch governmental reorganizations.[22]

The National Security, Veterans Affairs, and International Relations Subcommittee and the Technology and Procurement Policy Subcommittees are the key producers of national security policy information. Their areas of jurisdiction include foreign and domestic antiterrorism efforts. Examples of recent hearings conducted by the Subcommittee on National Security are *Combatting Terrorism: Assessing Threats, Risk Management, and Establishing Priorities* (2001), *F-22 Cost Controls: Will Product Cost Savings Materialize?* (2001), *National Missile Defense: Test Failures and Technology Development* (2001), and *Anthrax Vaccine Adverse Reactions* (2000). Recent Subcommittee on Technology and Procurement Policy hearings on national security issues include *Helping Federal Agencies Meet Their Homeland Security Missions: How Private Sector Policies Can Be Applied to Public Sector Problems* (2002) and *Battling*

Bioterrorism: Why Timely Information-Sharing between Local, State, and Federal Governments Is the Key to Protecting Public Health (2002).

Hearings, reports, and witness opening statements can be found on the committee's website (www.house.gov/reform).

House Permanent Select Intelligence Committee

The House Permanent Select Committee on Intelligence was created in 1977 to "oversee and make continuing studies of the intelligence and intelligence-related activities and programs of the United States Government and to submit to the House appropriate proposals for legislation and report to the House concerning such intelligence and intelligence-related activities and programs."[23] Committee oversight responsibilities cover the National Foreign Intelligence Program and include intelligence-related activities of the Central Intelligence Agency, the Department of Defense, Defense Intelligence Agency, National Security Agency, National Reconnaissance Office, National Imagery and Mapping Agency, the armed services, Department of State, Department of the Treasury, Department of Energy, and the Federal Bureau of Investigation.[24]

During the 108th Congress, the committee had twenty members and four subcommittees: Subcommittee on Terrorism and Homeland Security; Subcommittee on Human Intelligence, Analysis, and Counterintelligence; Subcommittee on Technical and Tactical Intelligence; and Subcommittee on Intelligence Policy and National Security.[25] Although the sensitive nature of its deliberations partially limits its publication output, this committee still produces significant documentation of its oversight activities. Examples of recent hearings are *Record of Proceedings on H.R. 3829, the Intelligence Community Whistleblower Protection Act* (1999), *Domestic Preparedness and Emergency Response to Terrorist Attacks* (2001), and *Protecting the Homeland from Asymmetric/Unconventional Threats* (2001). The website http://intelligence.house.gov/ provides information about the committee's activities (2001–present), and www.access.gpo.gov/congress/house/house22.html has information about committee activities for the 105th Congress (1997–1999).

House International Relations Committee

On November 29, 1775, the Continental Congress created a committee, put under Pennsylvania delegate Benjamin Franklin's leadership, to contact and correspond with friends of the American Revolution. It was formally designated a standing committee by the House of Representatives in 1822.[26]

The House International Relations Committee oversees State Department programs and operations. Within this broad mandate, the committee is responsible for meeting with foreign political leaders, overseeing international security issues such as peacekeeping operations, addressing the security threats posed by rogue regimes that seek weapons of mass destruction, reviewing conventional military force and nuclear weapons treaties, dealing with terrorism and intelligence issues affecting foreign policy operations, and shaping U.S. policies toward other countries.[27]

In collaboration with the Senate Foreign Relations Committee and with the assistance of the Congressional Research Service at the Library of Congress, the committee produces *Legislation on Foreign Relations,* a five-volume set that describes existing foreign relations laws, treaties, and executive agreements and orders and is updated for each Congress.[28] Recent International Relations Committee hearings include *Post-1999 U.S. Security and Counter-Drug Interests in Panama* (1999), *European Common Foreign, Security, and Defense Policies: Implications for the United States and the Atlantic Alliance* (1999), *Munitions List Export Licensing Issues* (2000), *The ILSA (Iran/Libya Sanctions Act) Extension Act of 2001* (2001), *Al Qaeda and the Global Reach of Terrorism* (2001), *The U.S. Diplomatic Efforts in the War against Terrorism* (2001), and *Meeting with the President of Pakistan, H. E. General Pervez Musharraf* (2002).

The committee's website (www.house.gov/international_relations/) contains the transcripts of committee hearings, witness opening statements, and webcasts of hearings.

House Judiciary Committee

The House Judiciary Committee was established in 1813.[29] Its jurisdictional responsibilities include areas of law as diverse as federal judicial proceedings, bankruptcy, espionage, counterfeiting, civil liberties, constitutional amendments, immigration and naturalization, intellectual property, and subversive activities affecting U.S. internal security.[30]

The historical importance of the House Judiciary Committee as a congressional oversight panel in the areas of immigration, internal security, and civil liberties make it a significant information resource for national security policy studies. In addition, as the events of September 11, 2001, and subsequent U.S. government policy responses such as freezing the financial assets of al Qaeda supporters and trying alleged terrorists in military courts show, an increasing nexus exists between legal activity and national security policy.

The House Judiciary Committee had thirty-seven members in the 108th Congress. The Subcommittee on Immigration and Claims and the Subcommittee on Crime, Terrorism, and Homeland Security are particularly concerned with national security policies. Examples of recent Immigration and Claims Subcommittee hearings are *Law Enforcement Problems at the Border between the United States and Canada Focusing on the Issues of Drug Smuggling, Illegal Immigration, and Terrorism* (1999), *Using Information Technology to Secure America's Borders: INS Problems with Planning and Implementation* (2001), *A Review of Department of Justice Immigration Detention Policies* (2001), and *The INS' March 2002 Notification of Approval of Change of Status for Pilot Training for Terrorist Hijackers Mohammed Atta and Marwan Al-Shehhi* (2002).

Recent hearings conducted by the Crime, Terrorism, and Homeland Security Subcommittee include *Breaches of Security at Federal Agencies and Airports* (2000), *Threat Posed by the Convergence of Organized Crime, Drug Trafficking, and Terrorism* (2000), *Legislative Hearing and Markup on H.R. 3275, Implementation Legislation for the International Convention for the Suppression of the Financing of Terrorism* (2001), and *Markup of H.R. 3482, the Cyber Security Enhancement Act of 2001* (2002).

The website www.house.gov/judiciary provides information on committee and subcommittee activities and deliberations.

House Select Committee on Homeland Security

Created in 2003, the House Select Committee on Homeland Security has jurisdiction over matters covering the Homeland Security Act of 2002 (PL 107-296).[31] Consisting of fifty members during the 108th Congress, the committee has five subcommittees: Subcommittee on Infrastructure and Border Security; Subcommittee on Rules; Subcommittee on Emergency Preparedness and Response; Subcommittee on Cybersecurity, Science, and Research and Development; and Subcommittee on Intelligence and Counterterrorism.

The committee's website (http://hsc.house.gov/) features information on committee activities, including the text of witness opening statements from 2003 hearings.

Senate Appropriations Committee

Originating in 1867, the Senate Appropriations Committee is responsible for preparing annual federal agency appropriations bills, although its role has traditionally been considered less significant than that played by the House Appropriations Committee.[32]

With twenty-nine members during the 108th Congress, the Senate Appropriations Committee has four subcommittees covering national security policy programs.[33] The Subcommittee on Defense has jurisdiction over the Ballistic Missile Defense Organization, CIA, DOD and the military, and NATO. The Subcommittee on Energy and Water Development reviews the Department of Energy's defense nuclear programs and the Nuclear Regulatory Commission. The Subcommittee on Foreign Operations, Export Financing, and Related Programs scrutinizes the State Department's antiterrorism programs and the Defense Department's international military education and training programs. The Subcommittee on Military Construction covers agencies such as the Defense Logistics Agency and all military construction activities.[34]

The committee's principal publications are annual reviews of federal department and program budget requests. Recently conducted hearings include *Kosovo Operations Supplemental Appropriations for FY 1999* (1999), *Bioterrorism—Domestic Weapons of Mass Destruction* (1999), and *Homeland Defense* (2002). Additional information on Senate Appropriations Committee activities and hearings can be obtained from its website (www.senate.gov/~appropriations).

Senate Armed Services Committee

The Senate Armed Services Committee, like its House counterpart, was created as a result of the 1946 Legislative Reorganization Act. The law combined existing committees on military and naval affairs.[35] Areas falling within the panel's jurisdiction are aeronautical and space activities associated with weapons systems development or military operations; DOD and the armed services; military research and development; national security aspects of nuclear energy; military personnel pay, promotion, and benefits; the Selective Service System; strategic and critical materials essential for national defense; and military promotions.[36]

The Senate Armed Services Committee consisted of twenty-five members during the 108th Congress.[37] Its six subcommittees had jurisdiction over national security–related areas, including airland forces, emerging threats and capabilities, personnel, readiness and management support, seapower, and strategic forces. The Subcommittee on Airland Forces oversees the army, the air force (except strategic and airlift forces), and the National Guard. The Subcommittee on Emerging Threats and Capabilities has jurisdiction over antiproliferation and antiterrorism programs, information warfare, and drug interdiction. The Subcommittee on Personnel examines military personnel force levels and personnel issues. The Subcommittee on Readiness and Management Support reviews military readiness and training, logistical issues, and conventional weapons infrastructure. The Subcommittee on Seapower reviews naval and Marine Corps programs, special operations forces, sealift, and airlift. The Subcommittee on Strategic Forces scrutinizes nuclear forces, national intelligence programs, ballistic missile defense, Energy Department nuclear programs, and chemical and biological weapons.[38] Recent hearings, reflecting the wide variety of national security policy subjects falling within the committee's jurisdiction, include *Emerging Threats and Capabilities* (1999), *National Security Implications of Export Controls* (2000), *U.S. Strategic Nuclear Force Requirements* (2000), *Department of Energy Laboratories Security Failures at Los Alamos* (2000), and *To Receive Testimony on the Department of Defense's Quadrennial Defense Review* (2001).

The committee's website (www.senate.gov/~armed_services/) is a helpful information resource for coverage of current and recent historical committee activities.

Senate Budget Committee

The Senate Budget Committee oversees federal budget programs, outlays, and issues.[39] Examples of recent national security hearings are *Public Pension Programs in Europe, NATO Enlargement, European Union Expansion, and EMU: Policy Implications and Debate* (1998), *Budgeting for Defense: Maintaining Today's Force* (2000), and *The President's FY2003 Budget Request: Winning the War, Transformation, and Reform Issues* (2002). The panel was established in 1974 and had twenty-three members in the 108th Congress.[40]

The committee's website (www.senate.gov/~budget/) has member and witness opening statements, hearings webcasts, and budgetary charts. The budgetary interests and priorities of Democratic and Republican committee members also are presented.

Senate Energy and Natural Resources Committee

Created in 1977 as part of a plan to reorganize Senate committees, the Senate Energy and Natural Resources Committee reviews policy concerning coal production, distribution, and use; energy; energy regulation and conservation; energy research and development; naval petroleum reserves in Alaska; and nonmilitary uses of nuclear energy.[41]

During the 108th Congress, committee membership numbered twenty-three.[42] The panel had four subcommittees: Subcommittee on Energy Research, Development, Production and Regulation; Subcommittee on Forests and Public Land Management; Subcommittee on National Parks, Historic Preservation, and Recreation; and Subcommittee on Water and Power.[43]

The committee issued 193 reports and conducted 153 oversight hearings in the 106th Congress.[44] Examples of national security policy hearings conducted by the Energy and Natural Resources Committee and its subcommittees include *Nuclear Waste Storage and Disposal Policy* (1999), *Chinese Espionage* (1999), and *National Energy Security Act* (2000). The website www.senate.gov/~energy/ provides additional information on committee activities and the panel's position on issues as diverse as national energy policy, nuclear waste, and proposals to drill for oil in the Arctic National Wildlife Refuge.

Senate Foreign Relations Committee

The Senate Foreign Relations Committee, like that of the House International Relations Committee, is concerned with overseeing U.S. foreign policy and State Department operations. However, its oversight responsibilities are more expansive as a result of the Senate's constitutional mandate to advise and consent to presidential nominations and ratify treaties with foreign governments.[45] The committee, which was established in 1816, had nineteen members in the 108th Congress.[46] The Foreign Relations Committee had seven subcommittees in the 108th Congress: Subcommittee on African Affairs; Subcommittee on East Asian and Pacific Affairs; Subcommittee on European Affairs; Subcommittee on International Economic Policy, Export, and Trade Promotion; Subcommittee on International Operations; Subcommittee on Near Eastern and South Asian Affairs; and Subcommittee on Western Hemisphere, Peace Corps, Narcotics, and Terrorism. The subcommittees cover topics as diverse as U.S. foreign assistance programs, international crime control, intellectual property, technology transfer, international monetary policy, security assistance programs and policies, and U.S. relations with international governmental organizations such as the World Bank and World Trade Organization.[47]

The Foreign Relations Committee produces treaty documents, reports on bills and nominations, hearings, and prints. Studies of foreign policy–related issues, published as committee prints, are prepared by committee members, the committee's professional staff, or the Congressional Research Service. Examples of recent prints are *Legislation on Foreign Relations*, which is published in collaboration with the House International Relations Committee every two years, *U.S. Defense Policy toward Taiwan: In Need of an Overhaul* (2001), and *Strategies for Homeland Defense* (2001). Recently published committee hearings include *Fiscal Year 2000 Foreign Affairs Budget and Embassy Security for a New Millennium* (1999), *Final Review of the Comprehensive Nuclear Test Ban Treaty (Treaty Doc. 105-28)* (2000), and *Department of Energy Non-Proliferation Programs with Russia* (2001).

The committee's web site (www.senate.gov/~foreign/) provides information about hearings, witness opening statements, and other resources including Democratic and Republican members' perspectives on issues falling within the committee's purview.

Senate Governmental Affairs Committee

The Committee on Expenditures in Executive Departments was set up in 1842.[48] Its contemporary structure was fashioned in 1977 as a result of Senate committee reorganizations. At that time, it was known as the Committee on Government Operations, which was changed to the Committee on Governmental Affairs.[49] The panel's broad jurisdictional mandate is examining the management of federal government agencies and programs. Consequently, the committee has oversight responsibilities for agencies such as the National Archives and Records Administration, Bureau of the Census, Department of Homeland Security, and U.S. Postal Service, along with federal programs as diverse as the federal civil service, District of Columbia municipal affairs, organization and management of U.S. nuclear export policy, government information policy, and federal employee classification, compensation, and benefits.[50]

During the 108th Congress, the Governmental Affairs Committee consisted of seventeen members.[51] Its three subcommittees were the Subcommittee on Oversight of Government Management, Restructuring, and the District of Columbia; the Permanent Subcommittee on Investigations; and the Subcommittee on International Security, Proliferation, and Federal Services.

The Subcommittee on International Security is an important producer of national security policy information. Recent committee prints include *The Proliferation Primer* (1998), which deals with nuclear proliferation, and *Stubborn Things: A Decade of Facts about Ballistic Missile Defense: A Report by Senator Thad Cochran* (2000). The subcommittee also conducts a large number of hearings, such as *Safety and Reliability of the U.S. Nuclear Deterrent* (1997), *The Comprehensive Test Ban Treaty and Nuclear Nonproliferation* (1998), *The Future of the ABM Treaty* (2000), *Iran's Ballistic Missiles and Weapons of Mass Destruction Programs* (2001), and *Critical Skills for National Security and the Homeland Security Federal Workforce Act* (2002).

The committee's home page (www.senate.gov/~gov_affairs/) provides information about committee activities including webcasts of selected hearings.

Senate Select Committee on Intelligence

The Senate Select Committee on Intelligence was established in 1976 to strengthen congressional oversight of U.S. intelligence agency programs and operations.[52] The committee's 2001 activities report stated:

> The Committee's charge is to ensure that the Intelligence Community provides the accurate and timely intelligence necessary to identify and monitor threats to the national security to support the executive and legislative branches in their decisions on national security matters, ensure that U.S. military commanders have the intelligence support to allow them to prevail swiftly and decisively on the battlefield, and to

ensure that all intelligence activities and programs conform with the Constitution and laws of the United States of America.[53]

Consisting of seventeen members during the 108th Congress, the Senate Select Committee on Intelligence conducts oversight hearings on intelligence-related subjects like its House committee counterpart. However, it has the additional responsibility of confirming presidential nominations to key intelligence policy-making positions, such as the director of central intelligence.[54] The sensitive nature of many of its deliberations limits the public distribution of much of its work but a significant amount is publicly accessible.

Examples include committee prints such as *Report on Impacts to U.S. National Security of Advanced Satellite Technology Exports to the People's Republic of China (PRC), and Report on PRC's Efforts to Influence U.S. Policy* (1999) and hearings such as *Department of Energy Counterintelligence, Intelligence, and National Security Reorganization* (2000), *The President's Foreign Intelligence Advisory Board's Report to the President: Science at Its Best, Security at Its Worst: A Report on Security Problems at the U.S. Department of Energy* (2000), *Loss of National Security Information at the Los Alamos National Laboratory* (2001), and *Current and Projected Security Threats to the United States* (2001).

The committee's website is at http://intelligence.senate.gov/, and the U.S. Government Printing Office website (www.access.gpo.gov/congress/senate/senate23.html) has selected committee publications from 1997 to the present.

Senate Judiciary Committee

The Senate Judiciary Committee, which began operation in 1816, covers bankruptcy, mutiny and espionage, federal courts and judges, immigration and naturalization, criminal and civil judicial proceedings, and other subjects.[55] The committee had nineteen members during the 108th Congress.[56] Its six subcommittees were the Subcommittee on Administrative Oversight and the Courts; Subcommittee on Antitrust, Competition, Business, and Consumer Rights; Subcommittee on the Constitution; Subcommittee on Crime and Drugs; Subcommittee on Immigration; and Subcommittee on Technology, Terrorism, and Government Information.

The Subcommittee on Technology is an important and prolific producer of documents on national security policy issues. Examples include *Biological Weapons: The Threat Posed by Terrorists* (1998), *Homeland Defense: Exploring the Hart-Rudman Report* (2002), and *Domestic Response Capabilities for Terrorism Involving Weapons of Mass Destruction* (2002). The full Judiciary Committee issued *Reforming the FBI in the 21st Century: The Lessons of the Hanssen Espionage Case* (2002).

The committee maintains a website at www.senate.gov/~judiciary/.

Senate Caucus on International Narcotics Control

The United States Commission on International Narcotics Control was established in 1985, and its name was changed to the United States Senate Caucus on International Narcotics Control later that year.[57] Consisting of seven members during the

108th Congress, the caucus was created to oversee and encourage governmental and private programs seeking to expand international cooperation against drug abuse and trafficking. The caucus also promotes greater international compliance with narcotics control treaties and narcotics eradication programs.[58]

The caucus conducts hearings and issues reports on various aspects of U.S. narcotics control policies and the intersection of those policies with national security policy issues. Examples include *U.S. Anti-Drug Interdiction Efforts and the Western Hemisphere Drug Elimination Act* (1998), *Drug Control: Update on United States-Mexican Counternarcotics Efforts* (1999), *The Continued Threat of Corruption to U.S. Border Law Enforcement Agencies* (1999), *Colombia: Counter-Insurgency vs. Counter-Narcotics* (2000), *A Review of the President's Annual Certification Process* (2000), and *Plan Colombia: An Initial Assessment* (2001).

The website http://drugcaucus.senate.gov provides links to committee hearings, members' speeches, and other information resources.

Commission on Security and Cooperation in Europe

The Commission on Security and Cooperation in Europe (CSCE) was established in 1976 to monitor and support compliance with the Helsinki Final Act's human rights and humanitarian cooperation requirements between Western and Eastern Europe and adherence to Organization for Security and Cooperation in Europe (OSCE) requirements.[59]

Nine representatives, nine senators, and three people from the executive branch made up CSCE in the 108th Congress.[60] CSCE members and staff hold regular hearings and issue reports on European political and security issues and how they impact U.S. foreign and national security policies. Examples include *Accountability for War Crimes: Progress and Prospects* (1999), *The Chechen Crisis and Its Implications for Russian Democracy* (2000), and *Moldova: Are the Russian Troops Really Leaving?* (2001). Hearings, press releases, issues of the *CSCE Digest* newsletter, and relevant European security links may be found on CSCE's website (www.csce.gov/).

Congressional Support Agencies

Congressional support agencies offer additional assistance to Congress in conducting legislative oversight of public policy issues—including national security—beyond that provided by the professional staffs of representatives, senators, and committees.

Congressional Budget Office

The Congressional Budget Office (CBO) was formed in 1974 by the Congressional Budget and Impoundment Control Act, which gave Congress effective control over the federal budgetary process.[61] CBO formally began operations in February 1975 under the leadership of Alice Rivlin. Its institutional mandate was providing economic and budgetary information to Congress in support of the budget and legislative processes.[62]

CBO estimates the costs of pending legislation, offers annual federal budget surplus and deficit projections, and analyzes annual presidential budget proposals. CBO representatives routinely testify at congressional committee hearings.[63]

Recent examples of CBO publications on national security policy include *A Look at Tomorrow's Tactical Air Forces* (1997), *Moving U.S. Forces: Options for Strategic Mobility* (1997), *Budget Options for National Defense* (2000), *Budgeting for Naval Forces: Structuring Tomorrow's Navy at Today's Funding Level* (2000), and *Increasing the Mission Capability of the Attack Submarine Force* (2002). CBO's website (www.cbo.gov) provides access to many of its recent reports and the text of correspondence between CBO analysts and members of Congress on the budgetary implications of current or proposed federal programs.

General Accounting Office

The General Accounting Office (GAO), created in 1921, audits federal agencies' handling of government funds and evaluates the performance of government programs for Congress.[64] GAO "blue book" reports analyze government programs in areas as diverse as education, environmental policy, governmental management, international relations, and national security. They are compiled primarily at the request of congressional committee and subcommittee chairpersons and ranking members, although GAO may respond to requests from individual members of Congress.

GAO published 1,163 reports during federal fiscal year 1999.[65] For fiscal year 2002, GAO had 3,200 employees located at its headquarters in Washington, D.C., and in regional offices in Atlanta, Boston, Chicago, Los Angeles, and other locales; had a budget of $432 million; and produced $37 billion in federal government expenditure savings. That same year, GAO representatives testified before Congress 216 times.[66]

The testimony of GAO officials before congressional oversight committees can produce valuable information about government program performance without the depth of detail contained in blue book reports. Examples of congressional testimony are *Homeland Security: Key Elements of a Risk Management Approach* (2001), *Homeland Security: Progress Made; More Direction and Partnership Sought* (2001), and *Combating Terrorism: Intergovernmental Cooperation in the Development of a National Strategy to Enhance State and Local Preparedness* (2002).

GAO reports on national security policy include *Defense Trade: Identifying Foreign Acquisitions Affecting National Security Can Be Improved* (2000), *Nuclear Nonproliferation: Security of Russia's Nuclear Material Improving; Further Enhancements Needed* (2001), *Information Security: Challenges to Improving DOD's Incident Response Capabilities* (2001), *European Security: U.S. and European Contributions to Foster Stability and Security in Europe* (2001), and *Missile Defense: Review of Allegations about an Early National Missile Defense Flight Test* (2002).

Blue book reports and testimony are arranged by fiscal year and then listed in numerical order. For example, report number GAO-02-125 was the 125th report issued by GAO during fiscal year 2002. Congressional testimony statements have the letter *T* following their classification number. For instance, the statement GAO-02-550T was the 550th congressional testimony statement made by a GAO official during fiscal year 2002.

GAO's website (www.gao.gov/) has current and recent reports and testimony. The site also contains the agency's correspondence with executive branch and congressional officials.

Library of Congress—Congressional Research Service

The Congressional Research Service, part of the Library of Congress, is Congress's in-house research arm. Originally created as the Legislative Research Service in a 1914 law, it evolved from a compiler of legislative statutes to a supplier of objective analysis of issues.[67] The 1970 Legislative Reorganization Act changed the name of the Legislative Research Service to the Congressional Research Service.[68]

The primary objectives of CRS are giving Congress the most effective and efficient service, responding as quickly as possible to congressional needs, and discharging its responsibilities to Congress.[69] The practical effect of these directives is that CRS products are restricted to congressional members and their staff, even though these resources are financed by tax dollars. Some members of Congress have moved to make CRS products publicly accessible on the Internet.[70] CRS information traditionally was obtained through requests to congressional offices or through fee-based commercial service providers such as Pennyhill Press and University Publications of America. Its accessibility experienced significant growth because of the proliferation of Internet websites. A number of governmental and nonprofit organizations provide varying levels of access to CRS publications, which include short reports of less than six pages, long reports of greater than six pages, issue briefs, and annual appropriations reports for various departments and agencies.

CRS reports on national security policy are prepared by its Foreign Affairs, Defense, and Trade Division, which employs nearly eighty staff members and sixty-five policy analysts.[71] Examples of government websites with significant collections of CRS reports on national security policy and other topics are the State Department's Foreign Press Center (http://fpc.state.gov/c4763.htm) and the U.S. Embassy in Rome, Italy (www.usembassy.it/policy/crs.htm). Nonprofit organizations that have posted CRS reports include the National Council for Science and the Environment's National Library for the Environment (http://cnie.org/NLE/CRS/), which has a strong collection of CRS natural resources policy reports, and the Federation of American Scientists (www.fas.org/man/crs).

CRS national security policy reports available through these websites are *Airborne Intelligence, Surveillance, and Reconnaissance (ISR): The U-2 Aircraft and Global Hawk UAV Programs* (2000), *China: Possible Missile Technology Transfers from U.S. Satellite Export Policy—Actions and Chronology* (2002), *Cyberwarfare* (2001), *Intelligence and Law Enforcement: Countering Transnational Threats to the U.S.* (2001), *Nunn-Lugar Cooperative Threat Reduction Programs: Issues for Congress* (2002), and *Iraq: U.S. Efforts to Change the Regime* (2002).

Office of Technology Assessment

The Office of Technology Assessment (OTA) was created in 1972 to provide Congress with timely analysis of scientific issues, which it felt was not being provided by other federal agencies or by existing congressional support systems. Some of the functions of OTA, as stated in its authorizing statute, were:

Identifying existing or probable impacts of technology
Determining cause and effect relationships
Identifying alternative technological methods for implementing specific programs
Identifying alternative programs for achieving required goals
Making estimates and comparisons of alternative programs and methods
Presenting findings of analyses to appropriate legislative authorities
Undertaking additional associated activities as directed by appropriate legislative authorities[72]

OTA produced reports on scientific and technological issues until it ceased operation in 1995.[73] Publications produced by OTA on aspects of national security policy include *Other Approaches to Civil-Military Integration: The Chinese and Japanese Arms Industries* (1995), *Arming Our Allies: Cooperation and Competition in Defense Technology* (1990), *American Military Power: Future Needs, Future Choices* (1991), *Ballistic Missile Defense Technologies* (1985), and *Virtual Reality and Technologies for Combat Simulation* (1994).

OTA reports are still accessible in many federal depository libraries. A complete electronic archive of these reports is also accessible through the *OTA Legacy* CD-ROM published by the U.S. Government Printing Office and through a website at Princeton University's Woodrow Wilson School of Advanced International Affairs (www.wws.princeton.edu:80/~ota/). Some members of Congress in 2001 attempted to reconstitute OTA.[74]

Notes

1. See U.S. Constitution, Article I, Section 8, Clause 1 for congressional power to provide for the common defense; Article I, Section 8, Clause 2 for congressional borrowing authority; and Article I, Section 8, Clauses 11–18 for congressional war declaration authority, military funding authority, and military legal and regulatory authority.

2. For information on researching the legislative histories of congressional bills and resolutions, see Jerrold Zwirn, *Congressional Publications and Proceedings: Research on Legislation, Budgets, and Treaties,* 2nd ed. (Englewood, Colo.: Libraries Unlimited, 1988), 143–171.

3. U.S. Congress, Senate, "S. 1534: To Establish the Department of National Homeland Security," 107th Cong., 1st sess., October 11, 2001.

4. For a description of Library of Congress congressional bill collections, see Library of Congress, "United States Congressional Publications Collection" (2000), 1 (http://lcweb.loc.gov/spcoll/248.html), accessed November 5, 2003.For a description of the U.S. Senate Library and its

holdings, see U.S. Senate, *United States Senate Library,* Senate Publication 106-26, 106th Cong., 2d sess., 2000. For coverage of commercial online providers of congressional bills, see Joe Morehead, *Introduction to United States Government Information Sources,* 6th ed. (Englewood, Colo.: Libraries Unlimited, 1999), 110.

5. See Morehead, *Introduction to United States Government Information Sources,* 101–132, 147–152. For additional coverage of congressional documentation, see Bernard D. Reams, comp., *Federal Legislative Histories: An Annotated Bibliography and Index to Officially Published Sources* (Westport, Conn.: Greenwood Press, 1994). See also Lexis-Nexis Academic and Library Solutions, *Congressional Information Service (CIS) Index* (Bethesda, Md.: Lexis-Nexis Academic and Library Solutions, 1970–present), which indexes numerous congressional publications including the names of committee hearing witnesses.

6. Zwirn, *Congressional Publications and Proceedings,* 54–55, 57.

7. U.S. Congress, House Committee on Appropriations, "Report of Committee Activities, One Hundred Sixth Congress: January 6, 1999, through December 15, 2000, Pursuant to Clause 1(d) of Rule XI," H Rept 106-1039 107th Cong., 1st sess., 2001, 1, 25; and U.S. Congress, House Committee on Appropriations, "About the Committee: Full Committee" (n.d.), 1–2 (http://appropriations.house.gov/index.cfm?FuseAction=AboutTheCommitteeMemberList&SubcommitteeId=18), accessed March 25, 2004. For congressional committee originating dates, see *Congressional Quarterly's Guide to Congress,* 5th ed. (Washington, D.C.: CQ Press, 2000), 540. For historical documentation of the beginning and ending dates of U.S. congressional committees, see Walter Stubbs, comp., *Congressional Committees, 1789–1982: A Checklist* (Westport, Conn.: Greenwood Press, 1985).

8. U.S. Congress, House Committee on Appropriations, "Report of Committee Activities," 33–34.

9. U.S. Congress, House Committee on Appropriations, "Report of Committee Activities," 35–38.

10. U.S. Congress, House Committee on Appropriations, "Report of Committee Activities," 14.

11. U.S. Congress, House Committee on Armed Services, *Report of the Activities of the Committee on Armed Services for the 106th Congress,* H Rept 106-1043, 107th Cong., 1st sess., 2001, 1. For analysis of how congressional politics affects defense spending, see Barry S. Rundquist and Thomas M. Carsey, *Congress and Defense Spending: The Distributive Politics of Military Procurement* (Norman: University of Oklahoma Press, 2002).

12. U.S. Congress, House Committee on Armed Services, *Report of the Activities of the Committee on Armed Services for the 106th Congress,* 3.

13. For a listing of committee members updated to February 28, 2003, see U.S. Congress, House Committee on Armed Services, "About the Committee" (20023), 1–2 (www.house.gov/hasc/about/members.html), accessed November 5, 2003.

14. U.S. Congress, House Committee on Armed Services, *Report of the Activities of the Committee on Armed Services for the 106th Congress,* 5. For a listing of 107th Congress House Armed Services Committee subcommittee membership, see U.S. Congress, House Committee on Armed Services, "Subcommittees" (n.d.), 1–4 (www.house.gov/hasc/subcommittees.html), accessed November 5, 2003.

15. U.S. Congress, House Committee on Armed Services, *Report of the Activities of the Committee on Armed Services for the 106th Congress,* 5.

16. See House Armed Services Committee, "Panel Memberships" (2002), 1–3 (www.house.gov/hasc/about/panels.html), accessed November 5, 2003.

17. Joel D. Treese, ed., *Congressional Quarterly's Congressional Staff Directory: Members, Committees, Staffs, Biographies: 2003 Fall,* 68th ed. (Washington, D.C.: CQ Press, 2003), 688–689.

18. U.S. Congress, House Committee on Commerce, *Report of the Committee on Commerce for the One Hundred Sixth Congress,* H Rept 106-1047, 107th Cong., 1st sess., 2001, 1. (This committee was known as the Commerce Committee from 1995 to 2001. Its name was changed back to the Committee on Energy and Commerce at the beginning of the 107th Congress.)

19. *Congress A to Z: CQ's Ready Reference Encyclopedia of American Government,* 2nd ed. (Washington, D.C.: Congressional Quarterly, 1993), 118–119.

20. *Congress A to Z,* 162.

21. U.S. Congress, House Committee on Government Reform, *Activities of the House Committee on Government Reform, One Hundred Sixth Congress, First and Second Sessions, 1999–2000 (Pursuant to House Rule XI, I(d)),* H Rept 106-1053, 107th Cong., 1st sess., 2001, 9.

22. U.S. Congress, House Committee on Government Reform, *Activities of the House Committee on Government Reform,* 2.

23. U.S. Congress, House Permanent Select Committee on Intelligence, *Survey of Activities of the Permanent Select Committee on Intelligence during the 106th Congress,* H Rept 106-1054, 107th Cong., 1st sess., 2001, 1. For a brief overview of the congressional intelligence committees' early years, see *Congress A to Z,* 192–193. For historical coverage of congressional intelligence oversight activities, see Frank John Smist, *Congress Oversees the United States Intelligence Community, 1947–1989* (Knoxville: University of Tennessee Press, 1990).

24. U.S. Congress, House Permanent Select Committee on Intelligence, *Survey of the Activities of the Permanent Select Committee on Intelligence during the 106th Congress,* 2.

25. U.S. Congress, House Permanent Select Committee on Intelligence, "Committee Membership" (n.d.), 1 (http://intelligence.house.gov/committee_membership.htm), accessed November 5, 2003.

26. U.S. Congress, House Committee on International Relations, *Legislative Review Activities of the Committee on International Relations, One Hundred Sixth Congress: A Report Filed Pursuant to Section 136 of the Legislative Reorganization Act of 1946 (2 U.S.C. 190d), as Amended by Section 118 of the Legislative Reorganization Act of 1970 (Public Law 91-510), as Amended by Public Law 92-136,* H Rept 106-1049, 107th Cong., 1st sess., 2001, 91.

27. U.S. Congress, House Committee on International Relations, *Legislative Review Activities of the Committee on International Relations,* 6–15.

28. U.S. Congress, House Committee on International Relations, *Legislative Review Activities of the Committee on International Relations,* 15–16.

29. *Congressional Quarterly's Guide to Congress,* 452.

30. U.S. Congress, House Committee on the Judiciary, *Report on the Activities of the Committee on the Judiciary of the House of Representatives during the One Hundred Sixth Congress Pursuant to Clause 1(d) Rule XI of the Rules of the House of Representatives,* H Rept 106-1048, 107th Cong., 1st sess., 2001, 1–2.

31. Treese, *Congressional Quarterly's Congressional Staff Directory: 2003 Fall,* 737.

32. *Congressional Quarterly's Guide to Congress,* 452; and *Congress A to Z,* 20–21.

33. U.S. Congress, Senate Committee on Appropriations, "Membership" (n.d.), 1–7 (http://appropriations.senate.gov/members/members.htm/), accessed November 5, 2003.

34. Joel D. Treese, ed., *Congressional Quarterly's Congressional Staff Directory: Members, Committees, Staffs, Biographies: 2001 Spring,* 60th ed. (Washington, D.C.: Congressional Quarterly, 2001), 139–140, 142.

35. U.S. Congress, Senate Committee on Armed Services, *Report on the Activities of the Committee on Armed Services, 106th Congress First and Second Sessions,* S Rept 107-32, 107th Cong., 1st sess., 2001, 1.

36. U.S. Congress, Senate Committee on Armed Services, *Report on the Activities of the Committee on Armed Services,* 1–2.

37. U.S. Congress, Senate Armed Services Committee, "Members" (n.d.), 1 (www.senate.gov/~armed_services/members.htm), accessed November 5, 2003.

38. *Congressional Quarterly's Congressional Staff Directory: 2001 Spring,* 144–146.

39. See *Congressional Quarterly's Guide to Congress,* 452; and *Congressional Quarterly's Congressional Staff Directory: 2001 Spring,* 148.

40. For listings of committee numbers, see U.S. Congress, Senate Committee on the Budget, "Democratic Members" (n.d.), 1 (http://budget.senate.gov/democratic/democrats.html), accessed on March 25, 2004; and U.S. Congress, Senate Committee on the Budget, "Republican Members" (n.d.), 1 (www.senate.gov/~budget/democratic/republican.html), accessed March 25, 2003.

41. U.S. Congress, Senate Committee on Energy and Natural Resources, *History, Jurisdiction, and a Summary of Activities of the Committee on Energy and Natural Resources during the 106th Congress,* S Rept 107-135, 107th Cong., 2d sess., 2002, vii.

42. U.S. Congress, Senate Committee on Natural Resources, "Members" (n.d.), 1 (www.senate.gov/~energy/about/about_members.html), accessed November 5, 2003.

43. *Congressional Quarterly's Congressional Staff Directory: 2001 Spring,* 153–155.

44. U.S. Congress, Senate Committee on Energy and Natural Resources, *History, Jurisdiction, and a Summary of Activities of the Committee on Energy and Natural Resources during the 106th Congress,* 3.

45. See U.S. Constitution, Article II, Section 2, Clause 2 for the Senate's power to ratify treaties and confirm presidential nominations; and *Congressional Quarterly's Congressional Staff Directory: 2001 Spring,* 158.

46. *Congressional Quarterly's Guide to Congress,* 452. For a listing of Democratic and Republican committee members, see U.S. Congress, Senate Committee on Foreign Relations, "108th Congress Committee Members" (n.d.), 1 (http://foreign.senate.gov/committee), accessed November 5, 2003.

47. *Congressional Quarterly's Congressional Staff Directory: 2001 Spring,* 158–161.

48. *Congress A to Z,* 161.

49. U.S. Congress, Senate Committee on Governmental Affairs, *Activities of the Committee on Governmental Affairs: Report of the Committee on Governmental Affairs, United States Senate, and Its Subcommittees for the One Hundred Sixth Congress,* S Rept 107-20, 107th Cong., 1st sess., 2001, 11–12.

50. U.S. Congress, Senate Committee on Governmental Affairs, *Activities of the Committee on Governmental Affairs,* 12.

51. U.S. Congress, Senate Governmental Affairs Committee, "Membership" (www.senate.gov/~gov_affairs/index.cfm?Fuseaction-About.Membership), accessesd January 9, 2004.

52. U.S. Congress, Senate Select Committee on Intelligence, *Committee Activities: Special Report of the Select Committee on Intelligence, United States Senate, January 6, 1999, to December 15, 2000,* S Rept 107-51, 107th Cong., 1st sess., 2001, 1.

53. U.S. Congress, Senate Select Committee on Intelligence, *Committee Activities,* 1–2.

54. U.S. Congress, Senate Select Committee on Intelligence, "Members" (n.d.), 1 (http://intelligence.senate.gov/members.htm), accessed November 5, 2003.

55. *Congressional Quarterly's Guide to Congress,* 452; and U.S. Congress, Senate Committee on the Judiciary, "Legislative Jurisdiction" (n.d.), 1 (www.senate.gov/~judiciary/jurisdiction.cfm), accessed November 5, 2003.

56. U.S. Congress, Senate Committee on the Judiciary, "Members" (n.d.), 1 (www.senate.gov/~judiciary/members.cfm), accessed November 5, 2003.

57. U.S. Congress, Senate Caucus on International Narcotics Control, "About the Caucus" (n.d.), 1–2 (http://drugcaucus.senate.gov/about.html), accessed November 5, 2003

58. U.S. Congress, Senate Caucus on International Narcotics Control, "About the Caucus," 2.

59. PL 94-304, "To Establish a Commission on Security and Cooperation in Europe," 90 *U.S. Statutes at Large,* 661–662.

60. PL 94-304. See also U.S. Congress, Commission on Security and Cooperation in Europe, "Commissioners" (2001), 1 (www.csce.gov/commissioners.cfm), accessed November 5, 2003.

61. PL 93-344, "To Establish a New Congressional Budget Process; to Establish Committees on the Budget in Each House; to Establish a Congressional Budget Office; to Establish a Procedure Providing Congressional Control Over the Impoundment of Funds by the Executive Branch; and for Other Purposes," 88 *U.S. Statutes at Large,* 297–298, 302–305.

62. U.S. Congressional Budget Office, *A Profile of the Congressional Budget Office* (Washington, D.C.: Congressional Budget Office, 1990), 1.

63. U.S. Congressional Budget Office, *A Profile of the Congressional Budget Office,* 1–10.

64. PL 67-13, "An Act to Provide a National Budget System and an Independent Audit of Government Activities, and for Other Purposes," 42 *U.S. Statutes at Large,* 20, 23–27. For coverage of the General Accounting Office's origins and evolution, see Roger R. Trask, *GAO History: 1921–1991* (Washington, D.C.: General Accounting Office, 1991); and Roger R. Trask, *Defender of the Public Interest: The General Accounting Office, 1921–1966* (Washington, D.C.: General Accounting Office, 1996).

65. U.S. General Accounting Office, "About GAO Reports" (2003), 1–2 (www.gao.gov/about/aboutrpt.html), accessed November 5, 2003.

66. U.S. General Accounting Office, "GAO at a Glance" (n.d.), 1 (www.gao.gov/about/gglance.html), accessed November 5, 2003.

67. PL 63-127, "An Act Making Appropriations for the Legislative, Executive, and Judicial Expenses of the Government for the Fiscal Year Ending June Thirtieth, Nineteen Hundred and Fifteen, and for Other Purposes," 38 *U.S. Statutes at Large,* 454, 462–463.

68. For early historical information on the Congressional Research Service, see James D. Carroll, "Policy Analysis for Congress: A Review of the Congressional Research Service," in U.S. Congress, Commission on the Operation of the Senate, *Congressional Support Agencies: A Compilation of Papers* (Washington, D.C.: Government Printing Office, 1976), 4–5; and PL 91-510, "An Act to Improve the Operation of the Legislative Branch of the Federal Government, and for Other Purposes," 84 *U.S. Statutes at Large,* 1140–1203.

69. 2 U.S.C. 166(b), *United States Code* (2000 edition).

70. Sens. John McCain (R-Ariz.) and Patrick J. Leahy (D-Vt.) in 2001 introduced S Res 21, "Directing the Sergeant-at-Arms to Provide Internet Access to Certain Congressional Documents, Including Certain Congressional Research Service Publications, Senate Lobbying and Gift Report Filings, and Senate and Joint Committee Documents."

71. Library of Congress, Congressional Research Service, "CRS Employment Opportunities: Foreign Affairs, Defense, and Trade Division" (2003), 1–4 (www.loc.gov/crsinfo/divwork/fdtwork.html), accessed November 5, 2003. The website also describes the work done by the division's various components, including the Defense Resources Section and Military Forces and Trade Reduction Section.

72. PL 92-484, "To Establish an Office of Technology Assessment for the Congress as an Aid in the Identification and Consideration of Existing and Probable Impacts of Technological Application; to Amend the National Science Foundation Act of 1950; and for other Purposes," 86 *U.S. Statutes at Large,* 797–798.

73. Providing for the closure of the Office of Technology Assessment (OTA) is PL 104-53, "Making Appropriations for the Legislative Branch for the Fiscal Year Ending September 30,

1996, and for Other Purposes," 109 *U.S. Statutes at Large,* 526. See also Hon. Amo Houghton, "In Memoriam: The Office of Technology Assessment, 1972–1995," *Congressional Record,* daily ed., 104th Cong., 1st sess., September 28, 1995, E1868–1870.

74. U.S. Congress, House of Representatives, "H.R. 2148: To Reestablish the Office of Technology Assessment," 107th Cong., 1st sess., June 13, 2001, introduced by Rep. Rush Holt (D-N.J.).

CHAPTER 8

Commissions and Advisory Organizations

U.S. government commissions and advisory organizations serve as valuable national security policy information resources. These organizations may be appointed by the president or Congress to research a public policy issue and prepare reports containing recommendations for resolving problems. Governmental commissions and advisory organizations generally have limited life spans of one or two years. Members are experts from federal, state, and local governments and recognized authorities from academe, businesses, and nonprofit organizations.[1]

Most commission and advisory organization reports are available in many federal depository libraries and, since the mid-1990s, on the Internet.[2] Numerous governmental commission reports have examined national security–related issues. These reports often are popularly known by the name of the commission leader(s) instead of by the officially authorized name of the commission. For instance, the U.S. Commission on National Security/21st Century, which existed from 1998 to 2001, was known as the Hart-Rudman Commission after its chairs: former senators Gary Hart (D-Colo., 1975–1987) and Warren B. Rudman (R-N.H., 1980–1993). For research purposes, however, the author is "United States Commission on National Security/21st Century," not "Hart-Rudman Commission."

Ronald Reagan Administration

National security issues such as the cold war, Mideast terrorism, pro-Soviet subversion in Central America, and technological change confronted the Reagan administration, Congress, and those involved in national security policy-making in the 1980s. A number of commissions and advisory bodies examined these issues and made recommendations.[3]

Commission on Integrated Long-Term Strategy

The Commission on Integrated Long-Term Strategy, a combined National Security Council and Department of Defense (DOD) group, worked from October 1986 to January 1988 examining national security issues that were expected to emerge over the next two decades. These issues included the role of advanced technology in military systems, the posture of the United States in global regional conflicts, and the interrelationship between offensive and defensive military systems near the Union of Soviet Socialist Republics.[4]

Reports produced by the commission and affiliated working groups includ the primary report *Discriminate Deterrence* (1988) and supplemental findings in *Commitment to Freedom: Security Assistance as a U.S. Policy Instrument in the Third World* (1988), *Extended-Range Smart Conventional Weapon Systems* (1988), and *The Future Security Environment* (1988).

Commission on Merchant Marine and Defense

Established by PL 98-525 on October 19, 1984, the Commission on Merchant Marine and Defense formally came into existence on December 5, 1986, when its members were sworn in following Senate confirmation. The commission was charged with studying transportation problems involving cargo and personnel for national defense purposes in war or national emergencies, the ability of the U.S. merchant marine to fulfill these transportation needs, and the adequacy of the U.S. shipbuilding industry to meet naval and merchant ship construction requirements in wartime or national emergencies.[5]

Commission work and activities continued through 1988. Publications produced by the commission include public meeting transcripts and *First Report of the Commission on Merchant Marine and Defense: Findings of Fact and Conclusions* (1987), *Second Report of the Commission on Merchant Marine and Defense: Recommendations* (1987), *Third Report of the Commission on Merchant Marine and Defense: Findings of Fact and Conclusions* (1988), and *Third Report of the Commission on Merchant Marine and Defense: Appendices* (1988).

Military Manpower Task Force

The Military Manpower Task Force was formed by President Reagan on May 27, 1981, and was headed by Secretary of Defense Caspar W. Weinberger. The task force was charged with examining the status of the military's all-volunteer force and reviewing its manpower capabilities, analyzing the U.S. ability to sustain its forces with requisite capabilities through 1987, identifying shortcomings detracting from those capabilities, and developing and recommending solutions to rectify these deficiencies.[6]

A Report to the President on the Status and Prospects of the All-Volunteer Task Force (1982) gave a favorable appraisal of the all-volunteer force's performance. Report contents covered educational and demographic characteristics of military personnel, reenlistment rates, military compensation, educational benefits, and issues to consider if military conscription were introduced again.

National Advisory Committee on Oceans and the Atmosphere

The National Advisory Committee on Oceans and the Atmosphere (NACOA) was established on August 16, 1971, to review the progress of federal marine and atmospheric science service programs and advise the secretary of commerce on how to fulfill the institutional mandate of the National Oceanic and Atmospheric Administration. Congress discontinued funding for NACOA in the mid-1980s.[7]

The committee issued numerous reports on oceanic and atmospheric policy. Those of greatest national security policy relevance include *U.S. Coast Guard: Status, Problems, and Potential* (1983), *Marine Transportation in the United States: Constraints and Opportunities: National Ocean Goals and Objectives for the 1980s* (1983), and *Shipping, Shipyards, and Sealift: Issues of National Security and Federal Support* (1985).

National Bipartisan Commission on Central America (Kissinger Commission)

The National Bipartisan Commission on Central America, established on July 19, 1983, recommended long-term policy options for Central America, which was being buffeted by civil war in countries such as El Salvador, Guatemala, and Nicaragua. The commission was chaired by former secretary of state Henry Kissinger (1973–1977) and was known as the Kissinger Commission.[8]

The commission issued the *Report of the National Bipartisan Commission on Central America* (1984) and *Appendix to the Report of the National Bipartisan Commission on Central America* (1984). The main report presents recommendations and an assessment of key Central American historical, political, economic, human rights, and security issues. The appendix includes the commission's charter; descriptive assessments of individual Central American countries; the text of papers submitted by commission consultants covering topics such as social development, U.S. security policy issues, regional diplomatic options, and Soviet power in Central America and the Caribbean; a history of U.S. Latin American economic assistance programs; and the testimony of selected witnesses appearing before the commission.

President's Blue Ribbon Commission on Defense Management (Packard Commission)

The President's Blue Ribbon Commission on Defense Management was set up to review the sufficiency of the defense acquisition process and defense industrial base, assess the adequacy of the secretary of defense's authority in military department oversight, review the procedures for developing and deploying military systems and new technologies in a timely manner, and recommend ways of improving the effectiveness and stability of defense resource allocation.[9] Known as the Packard Commission, it was chaired by Hewlett-Packard Corporation president David Packard.

During its 1985–1986 life span, the Packard Commission issued reports and made recommendations to improve the defense acquisition and management process. The commission issued *A Quest for Excellence: Final Report to the President* (1986) and an accompanying *Appendix* (1986) and the supplemental volumes *The Legal Structure of Defense Organization: Memorandum* (1986), *National Security Planning and Budgeting* (1986), *An Interim Report to the President* (1986), *A Formula for Action: A Report to the President on Defense Acquisition* (1986), and *Conduct and Accountability* (1986).

President's Commission on Strategic Forces (Scowcroft Commission)

The President's Commission on Strategic Forces was created in 1983 and charged with reviewing strategic modernization plans for U.S. intercontinental ballistic missiles with particular emphasis on the proposed deployment of the MX missile. Chaired by Ford administration (and later George H. W. Bush administration) national security adviser Brent Scowcroft, the Scowcroft Commission issued the *Report of the President's Commission on Strategic Forces* (1983), which called for the United States to build and deploy the MX missile, develop a single warhead missile, continue its strategic modernization program, and pursue international arms control agreements to promote nuclear arms reduction and stability.[10]

President's Private Sector Survey on Cost Control (Grace Commission)

The President's Private Sector Survey on Cost Control in the Federal Government was established by executive order on June 30, 1982.[11] Headed by W. R. Grace and Company chairman J. Peter Grace, the Grace Commission conducted a private sector survey on federal government cost and control and issued recommendations to the president and other executive branch agency heads on ways of reducing costs and enhancing efficiencies in federal government operations. The Grace Commission terminated on January 31, 1984.[12]

Grace Commission works pertaining to national security policy and recommendations for enhancing the cost-effectiveness and managerial quality of these programs include *Report on the Department of the Air Force* (1983), *Report on the Department of the Army* (1983), *Report on the Department of Energy, the Federal Energy Regulatory Commission, and the Nuclear Regulatory Commission* (1983), *Report on the Department of the Navy* (1983), and *Report on the Office of the Secretary of Defense* (1983).

President's Special Review Board (Tower Commission)

The President's Special Review Board (Tower Commission), chaired by former senator John Tower (R-Texas, 1961–1985) during its 1986–1987 operations, reviewed National Security Council operations in light of revelations of the role it played in selling weapons to Iran and transferring the proceeds of these sales to military forces fighting Nicaragua's Sandanista regime.[13] *Report of the President's Special Review Board* (1987) was the sole public document produced by the Tower Commission.

George H. W. Bush Administration

The George H. W. Bush administration confronted significant national security policy issues during its tenure from 1989 to 1993. These included the collapse of the Soviet Union and its eastern European satellites, German reunification, Iraq's 1990 seizure of Kuwait and the 1991 initiation of Operation Desert Storm to expel Iraqi forces from Kuwait, concerns over aviation security and terrorism, professional military education trends, military intervention in Panama, China's Tiananmen Square massacre, and the emergence of social issues in military policy making such as whether women should serve in combat roles in the armed services.[14]

Defense Conversion Commission

The Defense Conversion Commission, under the jurisdiction of the Department of Defense, was established in 1992 to consider the economic impact on the United States of reducing military personnel and defense spending and the potential for strengthening or establishing federal programs for retraining military personnel and DOD's civilian workforce in nondefense employment. The commission was also directed to examine the possibility of cooperative efforts between governmental and defense-related companies to assist these enterprises in converting to commercial activities.[15] *Adjusting to the Drawdown* (1992) is the commission's principal report, and it contains commission recommendations for lessening the negative economic impact of reduced defense spending on local economies. The report also provides overviews of defense industry policies and programs, discussion of workforce assistance programs, and related materials.

House Armed Services Committee Panel on Military Education

The Panel on Military Education of the House Armed Services Committee was chaired by Rep. Ike Skelton (D-Mo.). The Skelton Panel was established in 1987 during implementation of the 1986 Goldwater-Nichols Department of Defense Reorganization Act, which sought to instill joint interservice perspectives among military leaders. House Armed Services Committee chair Rep. Les Aspin (D-Wis.) stated:

> The Panel on Military Education should review Department of Defense Plans for implementing the joint professional military education requirements of the Goldwater-Nichols Act with a view toward assuring that this education provides the proper linkage between the Service competent officer and the competent joint officer. The panel should also assess the ability of the current Department of Defense military education system to develop professional military strategists, joint warfighters, and tacticians.[16]

The panel in 1989 issued its *Report*, which described how the study was conducted, offered an overview of professional military education, expressed the need to promote an expanded role for joint education among military officers, and analyzed the current quality of professional military education. Panel recommendations included establishing a framework for DOD schools specifying and relating the key educational objectives of each professional military educational level, allowing the hiring of more civilian faculty to enhance faculty quality at military educational institutions, converting National Defense University's National War College to a National Center for Strategic Studies to serve as a research and educational institution, making national military strategy the chief focus at senior service colleges such as the Army War College, implementing a substantive capstone course that includes studying national security and military strategy, and requiring intermediate- and senior-level students in these institutions to complete regular essay examinations and write papers and reports subject to thorough faculty review, critique, and grading.[17]

President's Commission on Aviation Security and Terrorism

The President's Commission on Aviation Security and Terrorism was established in August 1989 in response to the December 21, 1988, bombing of Pan American Airways Flight 103, which resulted in many American fatalities. The commission studied and evaluated practices and policy options for preventing aviation terrorist attacks, examined existing aviation security procedures, reviewed terrorist response options, and investigated procedures, policies, and laws concerning the families of terrorism victims.[18]

The *Report of the President's Commission on Aviation Security and Terrorism* (1990) recommended transferring the lead negotiating role in aviation security from U.S. carriers to the State Department, having the Federal Aviation Administration (FAA) seek the assistance of the Federal Bureau of Investigation (FBI) in assessing current and potential threats to the U.S. domestic air transportation system, requiring Congress to impose criminal record checks for all airport employees, sharing international terrorism reporting information received by U.S. law enforcement officials with U.S. intelligence community members and the FAA, developing procedures for notifying the traveling public of possible terrorist threats, advising State Department personnel to be sensitive to the emotional needs posed by tragedies such as Pan Am 103, and improving U.S. human intelligence gathering on terrorism in concert with other countries.[19]

President's Commission on Catastrophic Nuclear Accidents

The President's Commission on Catastrophic Nuclear Accidents was established by Congress in 1988 to develop appropriate means of fully compensating victims of catastrophic nuclear accidents beyond the $7.3 billion permitted by the Price-Anderson statute.[20]

The *Report to the Congress from the Presidential Commission on Catastrophic Nuclear Accidents* (1990) contains the transcript of commission hearings, documentary resources, and a detailed bibliography. The commission recommended resolving claims from such accidents though administrative procedures designed to expedite case resolution, compensating wrongful death claims at a predetermined amount, and compensating pecuniary and nonpecuniary claims stemming from the latent health effects of such accidents.[21]

President's Council of Advisors on Science and Technology

The President's Council of Advisors on Science and Technology (PCAST) is part of the Office of Science and Technology Policy (OSTP) within the Executive Office of the President. A PCAST panel prepared the report *Science, Technology, and National Security,* which was released in December 1992. Report contents discuss various scientific and technological developments affecting national security such as U.S. political stability and military dominance, the growing proliferation of weapons of mass destruction and delivery systems, and inefficient government methods of creating, applying, and procuring sophisticated technologies. The report identified six key areas for presidential focus: exploiting advanced science and technology to gather and interpret vital intelligence, staving off the proliferation of advanced conventional weapons and weapons of mass destruction, rearranging governmental approaches to applying technology and acquiring cutting-edge defense and intelligence systems, attracting and retaining technically qualified people for key national security positions, providing new emphasis on exploring defensive technologies to defend against proliferation threats, and developing presidential strategic planning for maintaining U.S. scientific and technological superiority.[22]

Presidential Commission on the Assignment of Women in the Armed Forces

Established by Congress on December 5, 1991, the Presidential Commission on the Assignment of Women in the Armed Forces evaluated laws and policies restricting the assignments of servicewomen.[23] The *Report to the President* (1992) included literature research, surveys of foreign military policies concerning women in combat, and the text of existing U.S. laws and regulations on women in combat. Commission recommendations often reflected the divided nature of the panel's membership. The commission suggested that DOD establish a policy to ensure that no one who is best qualified for an assignment be denied on the basis of gender, that military services retain gender-specific physical fitness tests and standards, that these services adopt specific requirements for assignments requiring muscular strength or endurance and cardiovascular capacity, that DOD review policies allowing single parents to be deployed on overseas operations without considering the impact on their children, and that women be excluded from direct land combat units and positions.[24]

Bill Clinton Administration

The Clinton administration assumed office in 1993 facing a dramatically different international security environment as a result of the Soviet Union's collapse, which heralded the cold war's conclusion. These events, however, did not mean the end of global national security interests and responsibilities for the United States. The administration had to deal with internecine strife in the Balkans; genocidal strife in Rwanda; the rise of Osama bin Laden's al Qaeda terrorist network; controversy over a proposal to allow homosexuals to openly serve in the military; the increasing and controversial use of U.S. military forces for peacekeeping in, for example, Somalia, Haiti, and Bosnia; and the impact of the Internet on military operations.[25]

Many of the government commissions established during the Clinton administration used the Internet to disseminate government information. However, the permanence of these websites is uncertain once the commission's statutory life span expires. In some cases, other governmental agencies maintain commission websites; in other cases, nonprofit organizations such as the Federation of American Scientists or academic institutions such as the University of North Texas Library take on the task. Consequently, the websites cited for some of the following commissions may not include .gov or .mil in their URL.

Advisory Committee on Human Radiation Experiments

Members of the Advisory Committee on Human Radiation Experiments were drawn from the Departments of Energy, Health and Human Services, Justice, and Veterans Affairs and were supported with professional staff. Established by President Clinton on January 15, 1994, the committee reported on experiments conducted on human subjects by predecessor agencies of the Department of Energy. Subjects had been intentionally exposed to ionizing radiation beyond dosages occurring during normal medical procedures.[26]

The *Advisory Committee on Human Radiation Experiments: Final Report* (1995) and two supplemental volumes found that the U.S. government sponsored several thousand human radiation experiments between 1944 and 1974, that these experiments contributed to medical advances and public health while also causing significant harm to many individuals, that the government did not have comprehensive policies requiring individual consent to being research subjects until 1974, and that some military personnel were used in experiments related to atomic weapons testing.[27] Committee recommendations were that the government should deliver apologies and financial compensation to the subjects or next of kin of human radiation experiments when governmental efforts had been made to keep the experiments secret from these individuals, their families, or the general public; that Congress should consider amending 1990 Radiation Exposure Compensation Act provisions to include populations environmentally exposed to radiation from nuclear weapons program development; that ethics should be the central feature when scientists conduct human subjects research; and that historical records of these experiments should be declassified and made publicly accessible.[28]

Advisory Panel to Assess Domestic Response Capabilities for Terrorism Involving Weapons of Mass Destruction (Gilmore Commission)

The Advisory Panel to Assess Domestic Response Capabilities for Terrorism Involving Weapons of Mass Destruction (Gilmore Commission), chaired by former governor James Gilmore (R-Va., 1998–2002), was provided for in the National Defense Authorization Act for fiscal year 1999. Panel responsibilities were to assess federal agency efforts to enhance domestic preparedness for incidents involving weapons of mass destruction; review the progress of federal training programs for local emergency responses to such incidents; determine deficiencies in these local programs such as unfunded communications, equipment, and planning requirements; recommend strategies for effectively coordinating with federal agency weapons of mass destruction response efforts; and stipulate proper state and local government roles in funding effective local response capabilities.[29]

The *First Annual Report to the President and Congress: Assessing the Threat* (1999) recommended that officials involved in protecting civil liberties should be in place at all governmental levels, that a true national strategy to combat terrorist incidents must be developed in concert with state and local officials and law enforcement and emergency response personnel, that strategies must include conventional high-explosive or fabricated weapons such as those used in the 1995 bombing of the Alfred P. Murrah Federal Building in Oklahoma City, that Congress should form a joint oversight committee to more efficiently review programs and appropriate funding to state and local governments, and that incident response equipment providers engage in more research and development to meet local responder requirements.[30]

Subsequent reports produced by the Gilmore Commission, which operated until 2003, were *Second Annual Report to the President and Congress: Toward a National Strategy for Combating Terrorism* (2000), *Third Annual Report to the President and Congress: For Ray Downey* (2001), and *Fourth Annual Report to the President and Congress: Implementing the National Strategy* (2002). The commission's website, hosted by the RAND Corporation at www.rand.org/nsrd/terrpanel/, contains the text of all annual reports, meeting minutes, listings of commission members, and public contact information.

U.S. Commission on National Security/21st Century (Hart-Rudman Commission)

The U.S. Commission on National Security, or the Hart-Rudman Commission, was chartered in 1998 by the secretary of defense with White House and congressional endorsement to examine emerging international security developments, devise an appropriate U.S. national security strategy for this emerging environment, assess existing national security institutions for their relevance and effectiveness, and recommend necessary changes to these institutions.[31] The commission was cochaired by former senators Gary Hart and Warren B. Rudman.

Commission reports include *New World Coming: American Security in the 21st*

Century, Supporting Research and Analysis (1999), *Seeking a National Strategy: A Concert for Preserving Security and Promoting Freedom* (2000), *Road Map for National Security: Addendum on Structure and Process Analyses* (2001), and *Road Map for National Security: Imperative for Change* (2001).

The commission recommended creating a National Homeland Security Agency to handle homeland security responsibilities, having the National Intelligence Council include homeland security and asymmetric threats as areas of analysis, doubling the federal science and technology research and development budget by 2010, making the secretary of Treasury a member of the National Security Council, having Congress and the secretary of defense move the Quadrennial Defense Review to the second year of a presidential term, having the National Security Council play a key role in determining intelligence priorities in its interactions with the director of central intelligence, and directing congressional and executive branch leaders to build programs that encourage government personnel to acquire national security and foreign policy expertise.[32]

The commission's website (www.nssg.gov/) contains the text of reports and other materials.

Commission on Protecting and Reducing Government Secrecy

The Commission on Protecting and Reducing Government Secrecy was created in 1994 and cochaired by Sen. Daniel Patrick Moynihan (D-N.Y.) and Rep. Larry Combest (R-Texas). It examined the implications of extensive government information classification, made recommendations to reduce the amount of information that is classified, strengthened the protection of legitimately classified information, and put forth recommendations regarding the granting of security clearances.[33] The *Report of the Commission on Protecting and Reducing Government Secrecy* (1997) contained an overview of issues involved in protecting secrets and reducing secrecy, provided a rethinking of the information classification process, discussed trying to strike a balance between prudent declassification and public access to government information, considered improving the personnel security process, and addressed information security in a technology-driven age.

Commission recommendations were to enact legislation stating the principles on which federal information classification and declassification should be based, require agencies requesting that information be classified to provide detailed rationales for such decisions, direct agencies to restructure their records management and declassification programs to facilitate maximum access to records likely to be of greatest public interest, and develop an information systems security career path throughout the federal government.[34]

Internet access to the commission's report is provided at www.access.gpo.gov/congress/commissions/secrecy/.

Commission on Roles and Capabilities of the U.S. Intelligence Community (Brown-Rudman Commission)

The Intelligence Authorization Act for Fiscal Year 1995 provided for the creation of the Commission on Roles and Capabilities of the U.S. Intelligence Community. The commission reviewed the usefulness and appropriateness of U.S. intelligence activities in the post–cold war world.[35] The commission, known as the Brown-Rudman Commission, was chaired by former defense secretary Harold Brown (1977–1981) and former New Hampshire senator Warren B. Rudman.

Preparing for the 21st Century: An Appraisal of U.S. Intelligence (1996) addressed the need for the United States to maintain an intelligence capability, the need for a coordinated response to global crime, the necessity of improving intelligence analysis, the rebuilding of the intelligence community, the role of space reconnaissance and technical collection management, and the need for government agencies and the public to exercise effective oversight and accountability over federal intelligence agencies.

The commission recommended that the United States maintain a strong intelligence capability, policy makers become more involved in how intelligence capabilities are used, the United States retain a covert action capability to achieve selected policy objectives, the budget process be substantially realigned and the overall intelligence budget be made public, intelligence analysts' skills and expertise be depended upon more, and regular infusions of new members be placed on congressional intelligence oversight committees.[36]

The commission's report can be viewed at www.access.gpo.gov/intelligence/int/.

Commission on Roles and Missions of the Armed Forces

Established in November 1993 under the auspices of the Department of Defense, the Commission on Roles and Missions of the Armed Forces was charged with reviewing the usefulness and appropriateness of existing military force roles, missions, and functions for the post–cold war era; evaluating and reporting on alternative allocations of these roles, missions, and functions; and making recommendations for changes in how they are defined and distributed by DOD.[37]

Directions for Defense (1995) provides an overview of the commission's work, offers the commission's vision of joint force operations, expresses the need for effective and responsive support for all military force activities, and cites the importance of improved management and direction in DOD operations. The commission's recommendations sought to strengthen unified operations by enhancing the joint structures responsible for planning and performing missions, focus DOD's infrastructure on effectively supporting unified military capabilities, and enhance DOD's decision-making processes so they have a departmental mission focus.[38]

Commission to Assess the Organization of the Federal Government to Combat the Proliferation of Weapons of Mass Destruction (Deutch-Specter Commission)

Created in 1998, the Commission to Assess the Organization of the Federal Government to Combat the Proliferation of Weapons of Mass Destruction was cochaired by former Central Intelligence Agency (CIA) director John Deutch (1995–1996) and Sen. Arlen Specter (R-Pa.). Its mandate was to thoroughly study the federal government's organizational ability to combat the proliferation of weapons of mass destruction. Congress specifically asked the Deutch-Specter Commission to assess the effectiveness of U.S. cooperation with foreign governments on nonproliferation matters with particular emphasis on cooperation between the United States and foreign intelligence communities, between federal departments and agencies and their foreign counterparts, and between the federal government and international governmental organizations.[39]

The commission released its report and an annex volume: *Combating Proliferation of Weapons of Mass Destruction* (1999). Provided were listings of nonproliferation activities performed by the National Security Council, State Department, Department of Defense (DOD), Commerce Department, and intelligence community; descriptions of the role of export controls in combating proliferation; and recommendations for government agencies to improve their nonproliferation activities.

The commission recommended that Congress consolidate the proliferation-related reports it requires from the executive branch, the Office of Management and Budget create a separate proliferation budget item in the president's budget, U.S. export control and enforcement efforts target end-users, discipline in the U.S. export control system be enhanced, the State Department create country-specific strategies for nonproliferation efforts, the secretary of defense establish a senior position for proliferation issues, Department of Energy (DOE) consolidate its nonproliferation efforts under one assistant secretary of energy, and the director of central intelligence ensure the presence of integrated collection planning against priority proliferation targets.[40]

An Internet version of the report is accessible through the Federation of American Scientists website at www.fas.org/spp/starwars/program/deutch/.

Commission to Assess U.S. National Security Space Management and Organization

As provided for in the National Defense Authorization Act for fiscal year 2000, the Commission to Assess U.S. National Security Space Management and Organization was directed to examine which military space assets could be exploited to support U.S. military operations, existing interagency coordination processes concerning national security space asset operations, relationships between intelligence and nonintelligence aspects of national security space, how military space issues are discussed in professional military education, and the potential costs and benefits of establishing a military branch dedicated to national security space missions or similar entities or officials within DOD.[41]

Report of the Commission to Assess United States National Security Space Management and Organization was released in 2001. Its findings focused on the existing role space plays in national security operations, organizations affecting U.S. national security space activities, the management of these activities, and possible ways of improving military space management activities. Commission recommendations included establishing space activity as a fundamental U.S. national interest, encouraging DOD to develop and deploy space systems to deter attack and defend U.S. earth and space interests, recognizing the important roles played by commercial and civilian space sectors in domestic and international economic affairs and national security, and developing a cohort of military and space professionals within DOD, the intelligence community, and other governmental branches.[42] The commission's report can be found at www.defenselink.mil/pubs/space20010111.html.

Defense Base Closure and Realignment Commission

The Defense Base Closure and Realignment Commission, created in 1990, was charged with making recommendations to DOD on military bases to close or realign in light of a perceived decline in defense requirements after the cold war. The commission recommended three rounds of closings between 1990 and 1995 and issued three reports.[43]

The final commission report, *Defense Base Closure and Realignment Commission Report to the President* (1995), described the local political and economic pain that defense base closure or realignment can cause, discussed assistance efforts that individual federal agencies can provide to communities facing base closure or realignment, and listed the names of the 132 bases recommended for closure or realignment and provided detailed justifications explaining commission decision-making rationales for these actions.[44]

The report can be found as House Document 104-96 in the U.S. Government Printing Office's "GPO Access" service accessible at www.gpoaccess.gov/.

IC21: The Intelligence Community in the 21st Century

IC21: The Intelligence Community in the 21st Century contains the results of a 1995–1996 study conducted by the professional staff of the House of Representatives Permanent Select Committee on Intelligence. The report, issued in 1996, contained an overview of possible restructuring required within the intelligence community to meet twenty-first century intelligence and national security requirements.

The report was compiled by House Intelligence Committee members and staff; witnesses from intelligence agencies such as the Air Intelligence Agency, National Security Agency (NSA), and Office of Naval Intelligence; and seven who had served as CIA director. The report addressed intelligence community management, signals intelligence, imagery intelligence, measurement and signatures intelligence, clandestine activities, and congressional oversight. Historical background on intelligence agency reform is also provided by the Congressional Research Service report *Proposals for Intelligence Reorganization, 1949–1996* (1996).

IC21 recommendations included that the director of central intelligence serve at the president's pleasure and exercise direct control over clandestine operations, the CIA director be given expanded personnel authority over all federal foreign intelligence agencies, the CIA's role be reinforced as the key all-source analytical agency, the House of Representatives make its intelligence committee a standing committee whose members are appointed by the Speaker, and the Clandestine Service's military component consist of military operations officers having viable career tracks in their specialized area with personal and professional qualifications equal to their civilian counterparts.[45]

The report can be found at ww1.access.gpo.gov/congress/house/intel/ic21/.

Interagency Commission on Crime and Security in U.S. Seaports

An April 27, 1999, presidential memorandum directed the Interagency Commission on Crime and Security in U.S. Seaports to analyze the nature and extent of serious crime and the overall security in U.S. seaports; review the missions and authorities of federal agencies with port security responsibilities; assess the quality of port security coordination efforts among federal, state, and local government agencies; and issue recommendations for improving the responses of these authorities to seaport crime.[46]

Commission findings were released in *Report of the Interagency Commission on Crime and Security in U.S. Seaports* (2000). Report contents discussed the divergent authorities and the roles they play in maintaining seaport security, U.S. seaport security practices, the threat posed by terrorism, the role of intelligence and information management in port security, and international implications of port security problems.

Recommendations proposed by the commission included strengthening interagency, intergovernmental, and private sector efforts to address seaport crime threats including terrorism; modifying existing federal agency databases to ensure ready collection and retrievability of seaport crime information; preparing annual interagency crime threat assessments for seaports with international trade; creating a structure for discussing, evaluating, and proposing seaport security solutions emphasizing emerging technologies; and encouraging agencies to develop specific collection requirements for foreign intelligence agencies tracking illicit merchandise movement through seaports that have national security threat potential such as drug trafficking and proliferating weapons of mass destruction.[47] The report is available on the Security Management Online website (www.securitymanagement.com/library/seaport1200.pdf).

National Commission for the Review of the National Reconnaissance Office

The National Commission for the Review of the National Reconnaissance Office was directed to review the National Reconnaissance Office's (NRO) roles and mission, organizational structure, technical skills, contractor relationships, commercial imagery use, launch vehicles acquisition and services, acquisition authorities, and relationships with other federal agencies.[48] The commission was established in 1999.

The NRO at the Crossroads was issued in November 2000 and presented a number of recommendations to enhance the quality of NRO's space-based intelligence-gathering activities. The recommendations included requiring the secretary of defense and director of central intelligence to determine proper roles for the NRO, National Security Agency (NSA), and the National Imagery and Mapping Agency in tasking, processing, exploitation, and dissemination activities; ensuring that the secretary and director have a common understanding of NRO's current and future capabilities and application of its technology to meet the needs of mission partners and customers; establishing an Office of Space Reconnaissance directed by the NRO director to enhance NRO's ability to use the best space technology to handle intelligence problems; and having the two offices work closely together to achieve appropriate balance between NRO systems strategic and technical requirements. The commission also stressed the need for the president, secretary of defense, and director of central intelligence to develop a clear national strategy to fully utilize the U.S. commercial satellite industry.[49]

Internet access to the commission's report is provided through the Federation of American Scientists website at www.fas.org/irp/nro/commission/.

National Commission on Terrorism (Bremer Commission)

The National Commission on Terrorism was established in October 1998. Chaired by former U.S. ambassador at large for counterterrorism L. Paul Bremer, the Bremer Commission examined international terrorism issues directed at the United States. Specific topics addressed by the commission were reviewing laws, regulations, policies, and practices on counterterrorism relating to the prevention and punishment of anti-American terrorism; assessing the effectiveness of existing U.S. counterterrorism laws, regulations, and directives; determining if terrorist organizations have established a Western Hemisphere infrastructure; examining if executive branch attempts to coordinate counterterrorism activities with local, state, and foreign agencies have been effective; assessing executive branch efforts to prevent nuclear, chemical, and biological terrorism; and recommending changes to U.S. counterterrorism policy to prevent and punish international terrorism directed at the United States.[50] *Countering the Changing Threat of International Terrorism Pursuant to Public Law 105-277* (2000) contained numerous recommendations to improve the quality of U.S. counterterrorism policy. For example, the FBI should use its full authority to investigate suspected terrorist groups or individuals; the FBI should establish a cadre of reports officers to distill and disseminate terrorism-related information once it is collected; Iran and Syria should remain on the list of state terrorism sponsors until they stop such support; senior government agency officials involved in responding to catastrophic terrorist threats should be required to participate in annual national exercises to test their capabilities and coordination; the president should establish comprehensive, coordinated, and long-term catastrophic terrorism research and development efforts; and Congress should develop mechanisms to review the president's counterterrorism budget.[51]

The Bremer Commission report is accessible at w3.access.gpo.gov/nct/ and as House Document 106-250 in the U.S. Government Printing Office's "GPO Access" website (www.gpoaccess.gov/).

National Partnership for Reinventing Government/National Performance Review

The National Partnership for Reinventing Government, also known as the National Performance Review (NPR), was established on March 3, 1993, and directed by Vice President Al Gore. NPR issued numerous reports on ways to improve the managerial and operating efficiency of federal agencies and departments.[52] Many reports dealing with national security–related agencies were released during 1993 under the general title *From Red Tape to Results: Creating a Government That Works Better and Costs Less*. Specific reports covering national security–oriented agencies and programs were *Department of Defense* (1993), *Department of Energy* (1993), *Federal Emergency Management Agency* (1993), and *Intelligence Community* (1993).

Examples of NPR national security recommendations include establishing a unified budget for DOD, having the Federal Emergency Management Agency develop an anticipatory and customer-driven response to disasters, and requiring the intelligence community to reassess information collection practices to meet analytical challenges caused by gaps in open-source information.[53]

An archive of NPR's activities, recommendations, and reports is available through the CyberCemetery website (http://govinfo.library.unt.edu/npr/) hosted by the University of North Texas Library's Government Documents Department.

President's Advisory Committee on Gulf War Veterans Illnesses

A May 26, 1995, executive order established the President's Advisory Committee on Gulf War Veterans Illnesses to review research on possible biological and chemical contamination Operation Desert Storm veterans may have been exposed to and to evaluate the performance of governmental programs responding to these illnesses.[54]

The committee's *Final Report* (1996) included an overview of the government's responses to these illnesses and listings of risk factors from these illnesses such as exposures to pesticides and biological warfare agents. Report recommendations included advocating that research on these illnesses should emphasize causes and methods of preventing and treating musculoskeletal conditions and that DOD and the Department of Veterans Affairs should perform long-term mortality studies to investigate cancer rates among Gulf War veterans.[55]

The report can be found at www.gwvi.ncr.gov/toc-f.html.

President's Commission on Critical Infrastructure Protection

The President's Commission on Critical Infrastructure Protection (PCCIP) was established by executive order in July 1996. PCCIP examined vulnerabilities to U.S. economic and national security that are present in critical infrastructures such as telecommunications; electrical power and water supply systems; banking and finance; emergency medical, police, and fire services; and computer systems. The commission recommended comprehensive legal, regulatory, policy, and implementation changes to protect these critical infrastructures.[56]

PCCIP issued its report, *Critical Foundations: Protecting America's Infrastructures*, in October 1997. The report found that U.S. vulnerabilities to critical infrastructure attacks are increasing and that the costs of making an effective attack will continue falling. The commission called for relying more on industry-government partnerships instead of legislation and regulations; having governmental facilities be the first to adopt best practices and improved security planning; providing local responders with additional federal funding for improving the detection, identification, and management of chemical, biological, and radiological incidents; and the president to establish an national infrastructure assurance office within the National Security Council.[57]

The report can be found at http://permanent.access.gpo.gov/lps15260/PCCIP_Report.pdf.

White House Commission on Aviation Safety and Security (Gore Commission)

The White House Commission on Aviation Safety and Security was established on August 22, 1996, and chaired by Vice President Al Gore. The Gore Commission was charged with developing and recommending a strategy to improve domestic and international aviation safety and security.[58] *Final Report to President Clinton: White House Commission on Aviation Safety and Security* (1997) presents commission assessments of ways to improve aviation safety, enhance air traffic control safety and efficiency, improve traveler security, and respond to aviation disasters. Recommendations proposed by the commission included rewriting federal aviation regulations in plain English and making them performance-based, enacting legislation to protect aviation industry employees reporting safety or security violations, securing access to airport-controlled areas and ensuring the physical security of aircraft, and having the U.S. government ensure that family members of international aviation disaster victims receive just compensation and equitable treatment from federal laws and international treaties.[59]

The report can accessed at www.airportnet.org/depts/regulatory/gorefinal.htm, which is hosted by an airport managers trade association.

George W. Bush Administration

Bush administration national security policies and priorities were fundamentally altered by the September 11, 2001, al Qaeda terrorist attacks in which airplanes were flown into the World Trade Center in New York City and into the Pentagon. In the opening salvo of the war against terrorism, President George W. Bush took U.S. military action in Afghanistan, which harbored al Qaeda and its leader, Osama bin Laden. In March 2003, Bush launched a war against Iraq, to remove Saddam Hussein's Baathist regime.[60]

Commission on the Future of the U.S. Aerospace Industry

The Defense Authorization Act for fiscal year 2001 provided for the Commission on the Future of the U.S. Aerospace Industry. Chaired by former representative Robert S. Walker (R-Pa., 1977–1997), the commission was directed to study the adequacy of the federal government's aerospace research, development, and procurement budget; determine whether the existing system for controlling the export of aerospace goods, services, and technologies struck a proper balance between protecting national security and ensuring unrestricted global marketplace access; assess the quality of U.S. and international trade laws and policies for maintaining the U.S. aerospace industry's competitive position; review the status of the U.S. space launch infrastructure; and assess the sufficiency of programs supporting aerospace science and engineering higher education programs.[61]

The commission released its *Final Report* (2002) after nearly two years of work. General report content featured overviews of the roles played by the aerospace industry in air transportation, space, and national security. Additional content discussed the government's role in facilitating the industry's development or regression, information on the international commercial aerospace market, and descriptions of the aerospace industry workforce and research developments.

The commission recommended that the federal government make expediting runway and airport development national priorities, the National Aeronautics and Space Administration and DOD develop and support future launch capability requirements, a U.S. military industrial base policy be developed, barriers to defense procurement of commercial aerospace products and services be removed, a government-wide management structure be created to establish a national aerospace policy, a federal interagency task force be set up to develop a national aerospace workforce strategy to raise public awareness of this industry's importance and opportunities, and federal spending on basic aerospace research be substantially increased.[62]

The commission's website (http://permanent.access.gpo.gov/lps43534/AeroCommissionFinalReport.pdf) provides access to the *Final Report,* interim reports, information about individual commissioners, and meeting minutes and agendas.

National Commission on Terrorist Attacks Upon the United States

Established in November 2002, the National Commission on Terrorist Attacks Upon the United States was to investigate the September 11, 2001, terrorist attacks. In its organic statute, the commission was charged with evaluating and reporting on evidence developed by government agencies concerning facts and circumstances prompting these attacks, reviewing the investigations and conclusions of congressional and other governmental investigations into these attacks, accounting for U.S. preparedness and immediate response to these events, and reporting to the president and Congress findings and recommendations for measures to prevent future terrorist attacks.[63]

The commission was still conducting its investigation and had not released a final report as of early 2004. The commission's website (www.911commission.gov/) contained a list of commission members, two interim reports, statements made by witnesses at public hearings, and webcasts of these hearings.

U.S.-China Economic and Security Review Commission

Provided for in the Defense Authorization Act for fiscal year 2001, the U.S.-China Economic and Security Review Commission monitored, investigated, and reported to Congress on the national security implications of the United States and China's bilateral trade and economic ties. The commission was directed to prepare a report whose contents were to include the portion of Sino-U.S. goods and service trade that

China dedicates to military systems or systems that could be used militarily, whether Chinese acquisition of military or dual-use technologies contributes to proliferating weapons of mass destruction, analysis of writings or statements by Chinese officials concerning military competition with the United States or its Asian allies, possible effects of Chinese financial transactions on U.S. national security interests, whether China's trade surplus with the U.S. enhances China's military budget, and an overall appraisal of whether security challenges presented by China to the United States are increasing or decreasing from previous years.[64]

The commission released its initial findings in *The National Security Implications of the Economic Relationship between the United States and China* in July 2002. Accompanying volumes to this report include *Documentary Annex* (2002) containing a variety of papers prepared for the commission and *Compilation of Hearings Held Before the U.S-China Security Review Commission* (2002) featuring the transcripts of eight hearings and one technical briefing held by the commission during 2001–2002.

Numerous recommendations were made by the commission in its primary report. These recommendations include having the U.S. government expand its collection, translation, and analysis of open-source Chinese language materials and making them widely available through increased funding; having the president designate an executive branch agency to coordinate compiling a database of all official government-to-government and federal government–funded programs with China; creating a federally mandated corporate reporting system to gather data to provide expanded understanding of Sino-U.S. trade and investment relationships; prohibiting satellite launch cooperation with China until it implements a commitment to restrict proliferation of weapons of mass destruction and technologies to other countries and organizations; continuing DOD dialogue with Taiwan on security-related issues; and having DOD and the FBI jointly review Chinese targeting of sensitive U.S. defense technologies and taking the required steps to deny Chinese access to and purchaseof these resources.[65]

The U.S.-China Economic and Security Review Commission remained an active organization as of early 2004. Its website (www.uscc.gov/) provides information about commission members, hearing transcripts, annual reports, papers written for the commission, and translations of selected Chinese military writings.

Notes

1. Works evaluating presidential commissions include David Flitner, *The Politics of Presidential Commissions* (Dobbs Ferry, N.Y.: Transnational Publications, 1986); David F. Linowes, *Creating Public Policy: The Chairman's Memoirs of Four Presidential Commissions* (Westport, Conn.: Praeger, 1998); Terrence R. Tutchings, *Rhetoric and Reality: Presidential Commissions and the Making of Public Policy* (Boulder, Colo.: Westview Press, 1979); and Thomas R. Wolanin, *Presidential Advisory Commissions: Truman to Nixon* (Madison: University of Wisconsin Press, 1975.)

2. Bibliographic reference guides to these works include Bernard A. Bernier Jr. and Karen A. Wood, comps., *Popular Names of U.S. Government Reports: A Catalog*, 4th ed. (Washington, D.C.: Library of Congress, 1984); and Steven D. Zink, *Guide to Presidential Advisory Commissions, 1973–1984* (Alexandria, Va.: Chadwyck-Healy, 1987). For congressional commissions,

essential resources are the biennially published U.S. Government Printing Office, *United States Congressional Serial Set Catalog* (Washington, D.C.: Government Printing Office, 1981–present); and U.S. Congress, House Committee on Armed Services, *Defense Acquisition: Major U.S. Commission Reports (1949–1988), Volume 1,* 100th Cong., 2d sess., 1988.

3. Examples of Reagan administration national security policy appraisals include William P. Snyder and James Brown, eds., *Defense Policy in the Reagan Administration* (Washington, D.C.: National Defense University Press, 1988); Michael M. Boll, *National Security Planning: Roosevelt through Reagan* (Lexington: University Press of Kentucky, 1988); and Jay Winik, *On the Brink: The Dramatic Behind-the-Scenes Saga of the Reagan Era and the Men and Women Who Won the Cold War* (New York: Simon and Schuster, 1996).

4. U.S. Commission on Integrated Long Term Strategy, *Discriminate Deterrence: Report of the Commission on Integrated Long-Term Strategy* (Washington, D.C.: Department of Defense, 1988). For congressional response to the commission's report, see U.S. Congress, House Committee on Armed Services, Defense Burdensharing Panel, *Defense Burdensharing: The Costs, Benefits and Future of U.S. Alliances,* 101st Cong., 1st sess., 1989.

5. U.S. Commission on Merchant Marine and Defense, *Second Report of the Commission on Merchant Marine and Defense: Recommendations* (Washington, D.C.: Government Printing Office, 1987), 1. For further historical background on U.S. merchant marine activities, see Andrew Gibson and Arthur Donovan, *The Abandoned Ocean: A History of United States Maritime Policy* (Columbia: University of South Carolina Press, 2000).

6. U.S. Military Manpower Task Force, *A Report to the President on the Status and Prospects of the All-Volunteer Task Force,* rev. ed. (Washington, D.C.: U.S. Military Manpower Task Force, 1982), xiii. Additional background on the all-volunteer force is provided by William Bowman and others, eds., *The All-Volunteer Force after a Decade: Retrospect and Prospect* (Washington, D.C.: Pergamon-Brassey's, 1986); and Robert K. Griffith, *The U.S. Army's Transition to the All-Volunteer Force, 1968–1974* (Washington, D.C.: U.S. Army Center of Military History, 1996).

7. PL 92-125, "To Establish the National Advisory Committee on the Oceans and Atmosphere," 85 *U.S. Statutes at Large,* 344–345. For discontinuation of National Advisory Committee on Oceans and the Atmosphere funding, see e-mail message from Thomas Kitsos, executive director, U.S. Commission on Ocean Policy, to author, April 14, 2003.

8. "Executive Order 12433: National Bipartisan Commission on Central America," *Federal Register,* 48, no. 141 (July 21, 1983), 33227–33228.

9. "Executive Order 12526: President's Blue Ribbon Commission on Defense Management," *Federal Register,* 50, no. 138 (July 18, 1985), 29203–29204. For congressional response to Packard Commission findings, see U.S. Congress, House Committee on Armed Services, Investigations Subcommittee, *Department of Defense Implementation of the Packard Commission Report of 1986* 101st Cong., 2d sess., 1990.

10. Zink, *Guide to Presidential Advisory Commissions,* 491. For congressional reactions, see U.S. Senate Appropriations Committee, *S. Con. Res. 26: A Resolution to Approve Funding for the MX Missile* 98th Cong., 1st sess., 1983); and U.S. Congress, Senate Committee on Foreign Relations, *President's Commission on Strategic Forces,* 98th Cong., 1st sess., 1983.

11. "Executive Order 12369: President's Private Sector Survey on Cost Control," *Federal Register,* 47, no. 128 (July 2, 1982), 28899–28900.

12. For appraisals of the Grace Commission, see Zink, *Guide to Presidential Advisory Commissions,* 456–459; U.S. Congress, House Committee on Armed Services, Grace Commission Panel, *Recommendations of the Grace Commission* (Washington, D.C.: Government Printing Office, 1987); Charles H. Levine, ed., *The Unfinished Agenda for Civil Service Reform: Implications of the Grace Commission Report* (Washington, D.C.: Brookings Institution, 1985); and Randall

Fitzgerald and Gerald Lipson, *Porkbarrel: The Unexpurgated Grace Commission Story of Congressional Profligacy* (Washington, D.C.: Cato Institute, 1984).

13. "Executive Order 12575: President's Special Review Board," *Federal Register,* 51, no. 232 (December 3, 1986), 43718–43719. For information about the Iran-contra affair, see Lawrence E. Walsh, *Final Report of the Independent Counsel for Iran/Contra Matters* (Washington, D.C.: U.S. Court of Appeals for the District of Columbia Circuit, Division for the Purpose of Appointing Independent Counsel, 1993); U.S. Congress, Senate Select Committee on Intelligence, *Were Relevant Documents Withheld from the Congressional Committees Investigating the Iran-Contra Affair?,* S Print 101-44, 101st Cong., 1st sess., 1989; Harold Hongju Koh, *The National Security Constitution: Sharing Power after the Iran-Contra Affair* (New Haven, Conn.: Yale University Press, 1990); and David P. Thelen, *Becoming Citizens in the Age of Television: How Americans Challenged the Media and Seized Political Initiative during the Iran-Contra Debate* (Chicago: University of Chicago Press, 1996).

14. Examples of works on George H. W. Bush administration national security policy issues include George Bush and Brent Scowcroft, *A World Transformed* (New York: Knopf, 1998); and Philip Zelikow and Condoleezza Rice, *Germany Unified and Europe Transformed: A Study in Statecraft* (Cambridge, Mass.: Harvard University Press, 1995).

15. For the commission's charter, see U.S. Defense Conversion Commission, *Adjusting to the Drawdown: Report of the Defense Conversion Commission* (Washington, D.C.: Department of Defense, 1992), 85.

16. U.S. Congress, House Committee on Armed Services, *Report of the Panel on Military Education of the One Hundredth Congress,* 101st Cong., 1st sess., 1989), v, 11. For background reference, see U.S. Congress, House Committee on Armed Services, Panel on Military Education, *Professional Military Education,* 101st Cong., 2d sess., 1990.

17. U.S. Congress, House Committee on Armed Services, *Report of the Panel on Military Education of the One Hundredth Congress,* 2–7.

18. "Executive Order 12686 of August 4, 1989: President's Commission on Aviation Security and Terrorism," *Federal Register,* 54, no. 152 (August 9, 1989), 32629–32630.

19. U.S. President's Commission on Aviation Security and Terrorism, *Report of the President's Commission on Aviation Security and Terrorism* (Washington, D.C.: Government Printing Office, 1990), 121, 123, and 125.

20. PL 100-408, "Price-Anderson Amendments Act of 1988," 102 *U.S. Statutes at Large,* 1074–1075.

21. U.S. Presidential Commission on Catastrophic Nuclear Accidents, *Report to the Congress from the Presidential Commission on Catastrophic Nuclear Accidents,* vol. 1 (Washington, D.C.: U.S. Presidential Commission on Catastrophic Nuclear Accidents, 1990), 5–10.

22. President's Council of Advisors on Science and Technology, *Science, Technology, and National Security* (Washington, DC: President's Council of Advisors on Science and Technology, 1992), v–vi.

23. U.S. Presidential Commission on the Assignment of Women in the Armed Forces, *Presidential Commission on the Assignment of Women in the Armed Forces: Report to the President* (Washington, D.C.: U.S. Presidential Commission on the Assignment of Women in the Armed Forces, 1992), A-2.

24. U.S. Presidential Commission on the Assignment of Women in the Armed Forces, *Presidential Commission on the Assignment of Women in the Armed Forces: Report to the President,* 1, 5, 7, 15, 24.

25. Some assessments of Clinton administration national security policies are Frederick H. Fleitz, *Peacekeeping Fiascoes of the 1990s: Causes, Solutions, and U.S. Interests* (Westport, Conn.:

Praeger, 2002); Bill Gertz, *Betrayal: How the Clinton Administration Undermined American Security* (Washington, D.C.: Regnery Publications, 1999); and Ryan C. Hendrickson, *The Clinton Wars: The Constitution, Congress, and War Powers* (Nashville: Vanderbilt University Press, 2002).

26. "Executive Order 12891 of January 15, 1994: Advisory Committee on Human Radiation Experiments," *Federal Register,* 59, no. 13 (January 20, 1994), 2935–2937.

27. United States, Advisory Committee on Human Radiation Experiments, *Advisory Committee on Human Radiation Experiments: Final Report* (Washington, D.C.: Government Printing Office, 1995): 777–800.

28. United States, Advisory Committee on Human Radiation Experiments, *Advisory Committee on Human Radiation Experiments: Final Report,* 801–846.

29. PL 105-261, "Strom Thurmond National Defense Authorization Act for Fiscal Year 1999," 112 *U.S. Statutes at Large,* 2169.

30. U.S. Advisory Panel to Assess Domestic Response Capabilities Involving Weapons of Mass Destruction, *First Annual Report to the President and Congress: Assessing the Threat* (Washington, D.C.: U.S. Advisory Panel to Assess Domestic Response Capabilities Involving Weapons of Mass Destruction, 1999), 54–57, 60.

31. U.S. Commission on National Security/21st Century, *New World Coming: American Security in the 21st Century: Supporting Research and Analysis* (Washington, D.C.: U.S. Commission on National Security/21st Century, 1999), iv, vi.

32. U.S. Commission on National Security/21st Century, *Road Map for National Security: Imperative for Change* (Washington, D.C.: U.S. Commission on National Security/21st Century, 2001), 14, 22, 31, 52, 69, 84, 112.

33. PL 103-236, "Foreign Relations Authorization Act, Fiscal Years 1994 and 1995," 108 *U.S. Statutes at Large,* 525–529. An accompanying overview on governmental secrecy is Daniel P. Moynihan, *Secrecy: The American Experience* (New Haven, Conn.: Yale University Press, 1998).

34. U.S. Commission on Protecting and Reducing Government Secrecy, *Report of the Commission on Protecting and Reducing Government Secrecy* (Washington, D.C.: Government Printing Office, 1997).

35. PL 103-359, "Intelligence Authorization Act for Fiscal Year 1995," 108 *U.S. Statutes at Large,* 3456–3461.

36. U.S. Commission on the Roles and Capabilities of the U.S. Intelligence Community, *Preparing for the 21st Century: An Appraisal of U.S. Intelligence* (Washington, D.C.: Government Printing Office, 1996), xv–xxv.

37. PL 103-160, "National Defense Authorization Act for Fiscal Year 1994," 107 *U.S. Statutes at Large,* 1738–1739.

38. U.S. Commission on Roles and Missions of the Armed Forces, *Directions for Defense* (Washington, D.C.: U.S. Commission on Roles and Missions of the Armed Forces, 1995), 1-9, 1-10.

39. PL 104-293, "Intelligence Authorization Act for Fiscal Year 1997," 110 *U.S. Statutes at Large,* 3471.

40. U.S. Commission to Assess the Organization of the Federal Government to Combat the Proliferation of Weapons of Mass Destruction, *Combating Proliferation of Weapons of Mass Destruction* (Washington, D.C.: U.S. Commission to Assess the Organization of the Federal Government to Combat the Proliferation of Weapons of Mass Destruction, 1999.)

41. PL 106-65, "National Defense Authorization Act for Fiscal Year 2000," 113 *U.S. Statutes at Large,* 81.

42. U.S. Commission to Assess United States National Security Space Management and Organization, *Report of the Commission to Assess United States National Security Space Management and Organization* (Washington, D.C.: U.S. Commission to Assess United States National Secu-

rity Space Management and Organization, 2001), xxx. For congressional review of this report, see U.S. Congress, Senate Committee on Armed Services, Subcommittee on Strategic Forces, *Report of the Commission to Assess United States National Security Space Management and Organization,* 107th Cong., 2d sess., 2002.

43. PL 101-510, "Defense Base Closure and Realignment Commission Act of 1990," 104 *U.S. Statutes at Large,* 1812.

44. For these detailed explanations, see U.S. Defense Base Closure and Realignment Commission, *Defense Base Closure and Realignment Commission Report to the President* (Washington, D.C.: U.S. Defense Base Closure and Realignment Commission, 1995): 1-1–1-125.

45. U.S. Congress, House Permanent Select Committee on Intelligence, *IC21: Intelligence Community in the 21st Century* (Washington, D.C.: Government Printing Office, 1996), 11, 13, 17, 30, 41.

46. U.S. Interagency Commission on Crime and Security in U.S. Seaports, *Report of the Interagency Commission on Crime and Security in U.S. Seaports* (Washington, D.C.: U.S. Interagency Commission on Crime and Security in U.S. Seaports, 2000), 176–178.

47. U.S. Interagency Commission on Crime and Security in U.S. Seaports, *Report of the Interagency Commission on Crime and Security in U.S. Seaports* xi–xii, xv, xvii.

48. PL 106-120, "Intelligence Authorization Act for Fiscal Year 2000," 113 *U.S. Statutes at Large,* 1621.

49. U.S. National Commission for the Review of the National Reconnaissance Office, *The NRO at the Crossroads* (Washington, D.C.: U.S. National Commission for the Review of the National Reconnaissance Office, 2000), 7–10, 12, 18. The commission's report can also be found in U.S. Congress, Senate Committee on Armed Services, Subcommittee on Strategic Forces, *Report of the National Commission for the Review of the National Reconnaissance Office and the Report of the Independent Commission on the National Imagery and Mapping Agency,* 107th Cong., 2d sess., 2002, 43–228.

50. PL 105-277, "Making Omnibus Consolidated and Emergency Appropriations for the Fiscal Year Ending September 30, 1999, and for Other Purposes," 112 *U.S. Statutes at Large,* 2681-10–2681-13.

51. U.S. National Commission on Terrorism, *Countering the Changing Threat of International Terrorism Pursuant to Public Law 105-277* (Washington, D.C.: U.S. National Commission on Terrorism, 2000), iv–v.

52. "Remarks Announcing the National Performance Review," *Public Papers of the Presidents of the United States: William J. Clinton 1993,* vol. 1 (Washington, D.C.: Government Printing Office, 1994), 233–235. For a critique of the National Performance Review, see Byron York, "Big Al's Big Scam," *American Spectator,* 29 (February 1996): 38–43.

53. U.S. National Performance Review, *From Red Tape to Results: Creating a Government That Works Better and Costs Less: Department of Defense* (Washington, D.C.: Government Printing Office, 1993), 47–48; U.S. National Performance Review, *Federal Emergency Management Agency* (Washington, D.C.: Government Printing Office, 1993), 9–11; and U.S. National Performance Review, *Intelligence Community* (Washington, D.C.: Government Printing Office, 1993), 13.

54. "Presidential Advisory Committee on Gulf War Veterans Illnesses—Executive Order 12961," *Federal Register,* 60, no. 104 (May 31, 1995), 28505–28507.

55. U.S. Presidential Advisory Committee on Gulf War Veterans Illnesses, *Final Report* (Washington, D.C.: U.S. Presidential Advisory Commission on Gulf War Veterans Illnesses, 1996), 92, 126.

56. "Executive Order 13010 of July 15, 1996: Critical Infrastructure Protection," *Federal Register,* 61, no. 138 (July 17, 1996), 37347–37348.

57. U.S. Commission on Critical Infrastructure Protection, *Critical Foundations: Protecting America's Infrastructures* (Washington, D.C.: U.S. Commission on Critical Infrastructure Protection, 1997), x, 23, 43, 51.

58. "Executive Order 13015 of August 22, 1996: White House Commission on Aviation Safety and Security," *Federal Register,* 61, no. 167 (August 27, 1996), 43937.

59. U.S. White House Commission on Aviation Safety and Security, *Final Report to President Clinton* (Washington, D.C.: U.S. White House Commission on Aviation Safety and Security, 1997), 11, 15, 27, 47.

60. Early assessments of the war against terrorism and its policy-making significance include Bob Woodward, *Bush at War* (New York: Simon and Schuster, 2002); Brian Michael Jenkins, *Countering Al Qaeda: An Appreciation of the Situation and Suggestions for Strategy* (Santa Monica, Calif.: RAND Corporation, 2002); Victor Davis Hanson, *An Autumn of War: What America Learned from September 11 and the War on Terrorism* (New York: Anchor Books, 2002); and Richard A. Clarke, *Against All Enemies: Inside America's War on Terror* (New York: Simon and Schuster, 2004).

61. PL 106-398, "Floyd D. Spence National Defense Authorization Act for Fiscal Year 2001," 114 *U.S. Statutes at Large,* 1654A-300–1643A-302.

62. U.S. Commission on the Future of the United States Aerospace Industry, *Final Report* (Washington, D.C.: U.S. Commission on the Future of the United States Aerospace Industry, 2002), viii–ix, xi–xii, xvi, xviii.

63. PL 107-306, "Intelligence Authorization Act for Fiscal Year 2003," 116 *U.S. Statutes at Large,* 2408.

64. PL 106-398, 1654A-334, 1654A-336–1654A-337.

65. U.S. China-Security Review Commission, *Report to Congress: The National Security Implications of the Economic Relationship between the United States and China* (Washington, D.C.: U.S. China-Security Review Commission, 2002), 4–5, 7–9.

CHAPTER 9

Legal and Regulatory Resources

Studying national security policy requires familiarity with the legal and regulatory information resources sculpting the U.S. national security policy process. Laws implement congressional intent for areas of national security policy as diverse as military personnel pay, weapons systems purchases, officer promotions, and weapons sales to foreign countries. Federal regulations instruct agencies on how they are to carry out congressionally mandated policies and programs. These regulations provide specific technical and operational guidance on topics such as administering defense contracts, providing defense contractors with technical specifications for fighter planes, and environmental standards for military bases. Court cases determine the constitutionality of governmental policies such as wiretapping and polygraph examinations, the amount of money payable in lawsuits, and which criminal penalties can be administered in cases ranging from military courts-martial to espionage.

U.S. Laws

Once laws are enacted, they are sent to the National Archives Office of the Federal Register where they are published in slip or pamphlet format. Slip laws are arranged in numerical order according to Congress. For instance, Public Law 108-3 was the third public law enacted by the 108th Congress (2003–2005). Slip laws range in length from a paragraph to hundreds or even thousands of pages. They contain the complete text of individual laws and their requirements such as how much money is to be spent on a particular weapons system, the criminal penalties for arson on a military base, and other matters including the law's legislative history, which can be important for tracking congressional intent.[1]

Paper copies of slip laws are available in most federal depository libraries and are reproduced commercially in print and electronic formats by publishers such as Congressional Quarterly, West Publishing, and LexisNexis. Free electronic access to slip laws from 1995 to the present (104th Congress on) is provided through the U.S. Government Printing Office's "GPO Access" service (www.gpoaccess.gov/).

U.S. Statutes at Large

Following their publication as slip laws, U.S. laws are eventually bound into *U.S. Statutes at Large,* also published by the National Archives. This publication contains the text of slip laws arranged in numerical order by Congress. Usually one or more years lag between publication of the slip laws and their compilation in *U.S. Statutes at Large.* Additional features include a subject index, an individual name index for access to private laws, and a popular names index—available since 1991—that indexes laws known by popular names (for example, Brady Bill) as well as by their official legal title.[2] A citation, for example, to 113 *Stat* 887 refers to volume 113, page 887 of *U.S. Statutes at Large.*

The "GPO Access" website (www.gpo access.gov/) has the text of public laws. Paper copies of public laws can be found in most federal depository libraries.

United States Code

The *United States Code* or *U.S. Code* is the most important of U.S. federal legal publications. Published by the House of Representatives Office of Law Revision Counsel, it contains the complete text of U.S. laws in a consolidated and codified format. The *U.S. Code* is published cumulatively every six years, with 2000 being the most complete cumulative edition, and updated annually.

It is divided into fifty titles or topical areas covering the complete text of U.S. laws, their amendments, and references to laws that have been repealed or superseded.

Posse Comitatus Act

The Posse Comitatus Act was enacted by Congress in 1878 with the trauma of the Civil War and Reconstruction serving as important contextual backdrops to its creation. Its purpose was prohibiting use of the U.S. Army for civilian law enforcement purposes including apprehending civilian criminals. This statute has remained in force, and it now also covers the U.S. Air Force.

Courts have determined that Posse Comitatus does not apply in cases such as indirect military involvement in civil law enforcement, the enforcement of civil law for civilians on military installations, when the National Guard has been activated, extraordinary circumstances in which the president exerts constitutional authority to maintain order, and conduct or actions Congress has exempted from being subject to Posse Comitatus provisions.

Controversy is ongoing over the statute's relevance. A 2003 U.S. Army War College study, accessible at http://purl.access.gpo.gov/GPO/LPS37253, argues that Posse Comitatus should be repealed because it restricts the flexibility of the U.S. government to respond to enemies with the ability to cause catastrophic damage and because such events will make it essential for the military to assist civil authorities. However, Section 780 of the 2002 Homeland Security Act asserts that Posse Comitatus has worked well in limiting the law enforcement use of the armed forces.

Each of these titles has different breakdowns by chapter and section, which further classify and explain sections of individual laws.[3]

The *U.S. Code* has a multivolume subject and a popular names index. Sections of this publication regarding national security policy include Title 10 and its appendix covering U.S. armed forces and Title 50 and its appendix covering war and national defense. For instance, Title 10, Chapter 131 of the *U.S. Code* (cited as 10 USC 131) covers the duties and responsibilities of the Office of the Secretary of Defense and Title 50, Chapter 216 (50 USC 216) allows the secretary of the Treasury to prohibit transportation of property used in insurrection against the U.S. government.

Paper copies of the *U.S. Code* are in most federal depository libraries, and commercial versions are produced by legal publishers such as Westlaw and LexisNexis. Free online access to the *U.S. Code* is provided by "GPO Access" and on the House of Representatives Office of Law Revision Counsel website (http://uscode.house.gov/).

Federal Court System

Cases are heard in the federal civilian court system that can affect national security policy making in areas such as wiretaps, search warrants, defense contracts, and espionage. A separate military court system covers military law cases.

The U.S. federal court system is authorized by the U.S. Constitution, which places judicial power in the U.S. Supreme Court and any lesser courts Congress authorizes.[4] The federal court system has grown considerably and is divided into three court levels: district, appellate or circuit, and the U.S. Supreme Court. The federal court system now consists of ninety-four district courts with 649 judges, thirteen appellate courts with 179 judges, and the U.S. Supreme Court with nine justices.[5] Federal court judges are appointed by the president for lifetime terms and are subject to U.S. Senate confirmation. The U.S. court system is administered by the Administrative Office of the U.S. Courts, which was created by Congress in 1939.[6] The office's website (www.uscourts.gov/) contains information about the federal court system including statistical information about the number of cases heard, court forms, publications such as *Wiretap Reports* (1997–present), news releases, and links to all district and appellate court websites.

Information on individual federal court websites includes local forms and procedures and court opinions in many of the cases heard by those courts. The scope and quality of these court websites varies, but they can contain useful information on national security–related cases, particularly in cases heard by the Washington, D.C., district and appellate courts. Federal court opinions are also available through online commercial service providers such as LexisNexis and Westlaw and in commercial print resources such as *Federal Reporter* and *Federal Supplement,* which may be available in many academic research libraries.

U.S. Supreme Court

The U.S. Supreme Court is the highest-ranking judicial entity in the United States and the final court of appeals for U.S. federal cases. Its nine justices are appointed by the president to lifetime appointments subject to Senate confirmation. The Supreme Court hears only a limited number of cases and declines to hear or review the vast majority of cases brought before it. The Supreme Court has the power of judicial review, which gives it the authority to strike down local, state, or federal laws it considers unconstitutional.[7]

Supreme Court opinions first appear in pamphlet format and are known as slip opinions. They will contain a brief description of the facts of the case, a summary of the Court's ruling in the case, and the text of the Court's opinion. The first opinion will be the ruling of the Court's majority in which the justices explain their ruling and the rationale behind it. In concurring opinions, justices agree with the majority's decision but wish to emphasize different points of constitutional law or doctrine. Justices who disagree with the Court's decision explain the reasons for their disagreement in dissenting opinions. In some cases, justices file opinions in which they agree or concur with parts of the Court's decision while disagreeing with other parts of the decision. The language used by justices in individual opinions can be contentious, depending on how controversial the case was and the zeal with which individual justices express their opinions in writing. This variety of opinions can also occur in lower federal court cases.[8]

After publication in slip format, Supreme Court slip opinions cumulate into softbound and then hardbound collections known as *United States Reports*. These reports are numbered consecutively from the beginnings of the Supreme Court in 1789 and now surpass five hundred volumes. For instance, 508 U.S. 224 refers to the Supreme Court case found in volume 508 on page 224 of *United States Reports*. Supreme Court opinions are also published commercially in publications such as *United States Supreme Court Reports Lawyers Edition* and *Supreme Court Reporter* published by LexisNexis and Westlaw.

The Supreme Court's website (www.supremecourtus.gov/) contains opinions and rulings from 2000 to the present and other useful information. Commercial publishers such as LexisNexis and Westlaw provide fee-based access to Supreme Court opinions through services they provide to many law school and academic libraries. These services also include access to briefs, which are written arguments presented to the Court in individual cases by interested individuals or organizations explaining how they think the Supreme Court should rule on particular cases. One free commercial resource providing access to Supreme Court briefs from 1999 to the present is accessible through the FindLaw service at http://supreme.lp.findlaw.com/supreme_court/briefs/.

Foreign Intelligence Surveillance Court

The Foreign Intelligence Surveillance Court (FISC) was created by Congress in 1978 as part of the Foreign Intelligence Surveillance Act (FISA) to regulate the collection of foreign intelligence information about foreign powers or agents in the United States. According to the law, the attorney general must obtain the approval of FISC judges for information requests involving applications for electronic surveillance, physical searches, and demands for other records. FISC consists of eleven federal district court judges who are appointed by the chief justice of the United States. The judges review attorney general requests presented by attorneys from the Justice Department's Office of Intelligence Policy and Review.[9]

FISC hearings are conducted in secret, and its records and findings are also kept secret. The motivating factor for the attorney general to request FISA search warrants is not probable cause according to Fourth Amendment protections but probable cause that the target is a foreign power or an agent of that power.[10]

Because of its secretive nature, the FISC does not possess a website. In a departure for the court, the November 2002 FISC decision upholding terrorist surveillance provisions established in the 2001 USA PATRIOT Act was published.[11] This ruling may be found on the Justice Department website at www.usdoj.gov/ag/fisaappealdecision.pdf. The ruling and accompanying analysis of its significance may be found on the news site of the legal Internet resource Findlaw (http://news.findlaw.com/).

In an attempt to provide further public visibility to FISC, Sens. Patrick J. Leahy (D-Vt.), Charles E. Grassley (R-Iowa), and Arlen Specter (R-Pa.) introduced the Domestic Surveillance Oversight Act of 2003. The legislation would require the attorney general to issue an annual report detailing the total number of individuals targeted for FISA searches, the number of times the attorney general permitted information from such searches to be used in criminal proceedings, and the number of FISA requests made to libraries or educational institutions.[12]

Foreign Intelligence Surveillance Act Annual Reports to Congress from 1996 to the present are available on the Justice Department's Freedom of Information Act website at www.justice.gov/04foia/readingrooms/oipr_records.htm.

Freedom of Information Act and Electronic Freedom of Information Act

Enacted in 1966, the Freedom of Information Act (FOIA) formally took effect on July 4, 1967, and established a clear statutory right of public access to federal executive branch information.[13] FOIA provisions require agencies to publish in the *Federal Register* information on agency organization and office addresses, procedural rules, substantive rules, policy statements, an index of documents they produce, and procedures for providing public access to this information.[14] FOIA has undergone revisions and amendments since its enactment, and the 1996 passage of the Electronic Freedom of Information Act (EFOIA) extended FOIA's obligations to provide public access to government records in electronic format given the increased influence of computerized record compilation and storage in federal agency operations.[15]

Both FOIA and EFOIA have established procedures for how individuals can request records from executive branch agencies including cabinet departments, military departments, government corporations and government-controlled corporations, and independent regulatory agencies. FOIA and EFOIA do not apply to elected federal officials such as the president, vice president, members of Congress, the federal judiciary, private companies, individuals receiving federal contracts or grants, private organizations, or state and local governments.[16]

Exempt from FOIA and EFOIA is information classified for foreign policy or national security reasons, about agency personnel practices, exempt under other laws, with trade secrets or about confidential business practices, with internal government communications about the federal policy-making process, about personal privacy, about law information processes or investigations, and about financial institutions or geological information.[17]

Individuals and organizations making requests for government records have to follow stipulated procedures and pay fees to facilitate agency processing of these requests. They can appeal denials of their requests. Agencies responding to requests also must follow procedures for locating such information and making timely responses to those requesting FOIA or EFOIA information.[18]

The Justice Department's Office of Information and Privacy website (www.usdoj.gov/oip/oip.html) serves as a gateway to information about FOIA and EFOIA. It provides access to the Justice Department's biennially published *Freedom of Information Act Guide and Privacy Act Overview* (2002) and the periodicals *FOIA Update* (1979–2000) and *FOIA Post* (2001–present), which provide information about ongoing agency FOIA activities and related litigation; information about FOIA and EFOIA reading rooms maintained by federal agencies covered by these statutes; links to federal agency FOIA response reports; and links to federal agency EFOIA websites featuring numerous reports and documentation.

Examples of federal national security agency FOIA websites are the Central Intelligence Agency (www.foia.cia.gov/), Defense Threat Reduction Agency (www.dtra.mil/foia/foia.html), Department of Energy (www.ma.mbe.doe.gov/execsec/foia.htm), and Federal Bureau of Investigation (http://foia.fbi.gov/).

Military Law

The U.S. military has an extensive legal system covering, for example, disciplinary matters affecting individual soldiers, rules of military engagement, legal matters affecting military operations in foreign countries, the proper treatment of captured enemy military personnel and of U.S. military personnel captured by foreign militaries, and the proper role of U.S. military personnel in domestic legal matters.[19]

The military law and legal weblinks provided by the Ira C. Eaker College for Professional Development at Air War College (www.au.af.mil/au/awc/awcgate/awc-law.htm) offer an introduction to military law issues.

Uniform Code of Military Justice

The Uniform Code of Military Justice (UCMJ) serves as the principal codification of military criminal law and is applicable to all U.S. military personnel. Its contents include general provisions, procedures for apprehending and restraining U.S. or foreign military personnel suspected of legal offenses, nonjudicial punishments that may be administered to such suspects, courts-martial description and jurisdiction, pretrial and trial procedures for courts-martial, sentencing, post-trial procedure and review, penalty administration, and the role played by the Court of Military Appeals. An online version of UCMJ is accessible through Air University's website at

> ### Courts-Martial
>
> Courts-martial are trials for offenses of military law committed by military personnel. Military law is made up of the statues and regulations governing military establishments that are issued under the president's constitutional powers and the authority of military commanders. Its overall purpose is promoting justice, maintaining order and discipline within the armed forces, promoting military establishment efficiency and effectiveness, and strengthening U.S. national security.
>
> More information on courts-martial and the procedures and legal protections involved in trying military cases can be found in *Manual for Courts-Martial, United States* (2000), which is accessible on the Navy Judge Advocate General's website (www.jag.navy.mil/documents/mcm2000.pdf).

www.au.af.mil/au/awc/awcgate/ucmj.htm, and an online version of the Department of Defense (DOD) *Manual for Courts-Martial United States* (2000) can be found through the U.S. Navy's Judge Advocates General (JAG) site at www.jag.navy.mil/documents/mcm2000.pdf.[20]

U.S. Court of Appeals for the Armed Forces

The U.S. Court of Appeals for the Armed Forces serves as the final appellate tribunal for reviewing military court-martial convictions, although the U.S. Supreme Court may review some of this court's decisions. The contemporary incarnation of the court was shaped in 1950. It consists of five civilian judges appointed for fifteen-year terms by the president and subject to Senate confirmation. Court judges are required to work jointly with a senior uniformed lawyer from each armed service, the Coast Guard's chief counsel, and two members of the public appointed by the secretary of defense. The court also must make an annual comprehensive survey, report to Congress on UCMJ developments, and recommend any UCMJ improvements it considers necessary.[21]

The website www.armfor.uscourts.gov/ has information about court operations. Examples of accessible resources are historical material, a description of the court's jurisdiction including its organizational placement within DOD, listings of current and past court judges, the text of court case opinions from 1996 to the present, *Annual Reports* from fiscal years 1997 to the present, court rules, and announcements of upcoming UCMJ code committee public meetings.[22]

Judge Advocates General

Judge Advocates General (JAGs) are important players in military legal proceedings. The contemporary structure of the position dates from a 1956 law revising U.S. military statutes in Titles 10 and 32 of the *U.S. Code*. This legislation created JAGs for each of the armed services and designated them as the chief legal officers for the services. The system as established continues to the present.[23]

JAGs are charged with receiving, revising, and recording court of inquiry and military commission proceedings; managing judge advocate assignments and making frequent field inspections to supervise military justice administration; recruiting and selecting officers and officer candidates for JAG duty; designating or withdrawing officers as judge advocates; and modifying or setting aside court-martial verdicts or sentences in certain restricted circumstances. JAGS in individual armed services also possess direct supervisory authority over their services' legal personnel, provide legal advice to other service personnel and officials, and administer legal programs within their individual services.[24]

Air Force Judge Advocate General's Department

The Air Force Judge Advocate General's Department is located at Maxwell Air Force Base in Alabama. Its website (http://hqja.jag.af.mil/) features biographical portraits of the air force judge advocate general and deputy judge advocate general and recruiting information for active-duty and reserve force personnel interested in becoming JAGs.

A reading room provides fact sheets such as *The Air Force Court of Criminal Appeals* (1998), *The Civilian Attorney* (2000), and *Judge Advocate General's Department* (2000). Information is also provided on the U.S. Air Force's JAG school along with course material, the text of UCMJ, and articles from the scholarly journal *Air Force Law Review* (1994–present) such as "The Imposition of Martial Law in the United States" (2000) and "On the Chopping Block: Cluster Munitions and the Law of War" (2001).

Army Judge Advocate General's Corps

Located in Washington, D.C., Fort Huachuca in Arizona, South Korea, and Germany, the Army Judge Advocate General's Corps provides legal services for U.S. Army personnel. Its website (www.jagcnet.army.mil/) contains a biography of the army's judge advocate general, listings of position openings, and information about the U.S. Army's JAG School in Charlottesville, Virginia. Material from the JAG School includes departmental descriptions and information on individual courses such as Law for Legal Noncommissioned Officers; Court Reporter Course; Advanced Topics in the Law of War; Current Issues in National Security Law; Law of War, Space, and Sea; and Environmental Law Practice in the Military.

Full-text access is provided to many Army JAG School publications including articles from the scholarly journals *Army Lawyer* (1971–present) and *Military Law Review* (1958–present) along with course-related materials including *Law of War Research Materials* (2001), *Operational Law Handbook* (2003), *26th Criminal Law New Developments Course Deskbook* (2003), and *27th Administrative Law for Military Installations Course Deskbook* (2003).

> ## Law of War
>
> The Law of War is a compendium of U.S. and international legal standards governing war's legal conduct. General principles of these legal provisions seek to motivate enemies to observe the same rules of war, provide advance notice of warfare's accepted limits, protect against unnecessary suffering and maintain certain fundamental human rights, reduce confusion and facilitate the identification of human rights violations, and assist in restoring peace.
>
> Three major documentary and statutory collections govern international Law of War: the 1907 Hague Convention, the 1949 Geneva Conventions, and 1977 Protocols to the 1949 Geneva Convention. The 1998 Department of Defense Directive 5100.77 and Title 10 Sections 801-940 of the *United States Code* also provide documentary and statutory foundation for the U.S. Law of War program activities.
>
> The 2000 *Law of War Deskbook,* produced by the U.S. Army's Judge Advocate General School's International and Operational Law Department, is accessible at www.au.af.mil/au/awc/awcgate/law/low-workbook.pdf.

The Center for Law and Military Operations (CLAMO), created at the direction of the secretary of the army in 1988, examines legal issues arising during military operations and develops training and resource strategies for analyzing these issues. CLAMO serves as the central repository within the U.S. Army's JAG Corps for materials relevant to legal support for domestic and foreign military operations, supports JAGs by analyzing data and information and developing lessons learned throughout military legal disciplines, integrates lessons gained from operations and army combat training centers, and sponsors conferences and symposia beneficial to operational lawyers.[25]

CLAMO's website (www.jagcnet.army.mil/CLAMO) has a variety of informative resources, although some materials are not publicly accessible. Examples of available publications are *The Law of Belligerent Occupation* (1944), the memorandum *Executive Order 12333 and Assassination* (1989), *Law of War Workshop Deskbook* (2000), *Rules of Engagement (ROE) Handbook for Judge Advocates* (2000), *Modern War, Modern Law, and Army Doctrine: Are We In Step for the 21st Century?* (2002), *Deployed Marine Air-Ground Task Force (MAGTF) Judge Advocate Handbook* (2002), *Iraq Penal Code* (2003), *Requested Legal Review of the Massive Ordnance Air Blast (MOAB) Weapon* (2003), and *Sorting the Wolves from the Sheep: Enemy Prisoner of War Operations during Operation Just Cause* (2003).

Marine Corps Commandant Staff Judge Advocate

The Marine Corps Staff Judge Advocate (SJA) provides legal advice to the U.S. Marine Corps (USMC) commandant; supervises and manages the Military Law, Operational Law Branch, and other elements of the Corps Judge Advocate Division; and provides administrative support to USMC's chief defense counsel.[26]

SJA's website (http://sja.hqmc.usmc.mil/) contains some publicly accessible information, such as legal advisories for corps members and their families, an organizational chart, information on SJA divisions such as the Judge Advocate Support Division and Operational Law Branch, photographs of past and present USMC SJAs, and personnel contact information.

Accessible legal forms include *General Court Martial: Memorandum of Pre-Trial Agreement* (n.d.) and *General Court Martial: Results of Trial* (n.d.). Legal reference publications include *DOD Directive 5100.77: DOD Law of War Program* (1998), *Prosecuting Urinalysis Cases: A Guide for Trial Counsel* (2000), *Judge Advocate Newsletter* (2001–present), *Administrative Separation of Marines Following a Court Martial* (2002), and *The Judge Advocate's Handbook for Litigating National Security Cases: Prosecuting, Defending, and Adjudicating National Security Cases* (n.d.).

Navy Judge Advocate General

The Navy Judge Advocate General (NJAG) is part of the Office of the Secretary of the Navy, and its mission is providing legal and policy advice to the secretary of the navy and advising and assisting the chief of naval operations in developing and implementing naval legal services and policies.[27]

NJAG's website (www.jag.navy.mil/) has an organizational chart; descriptions of NJAG component activities including the Inspector General, Assistant Judge Advocate (Civil Law), Admiralty and Maritime Law Division, National Security Litigation and Intelligence Law; the locations of domestic and international naval legal and trial service offices; and NJAG career opportunities and requirements.

Publicly accessible documents include *Manual for Courts-Martial, United States* (2000), *Navy-Marine Corps Court of Criminal Appeals Opinions* (2000–present), *Digest of Opinions* (2000–present), and *United States Navy-Marine Corps Court of Criminal Appeals Rules of Practice and Procedure* (n.d.).

Other Military Legal Affairs Resources

Military legal resources and services are not restricted to those provided by individual armed services JAG corps. The individual armed services and DOD also retain general counsel offices that are responsible for providing civilian legal advice to their respective services and offices.

Air Force General Counsel

The Air Force General Counsel (AFGC) is responsible for providing controlling legal opinions for the U.S. Air Force and its oversight responsibilities, guiding and directing the legal advice provided by the air force's civilian and military attorneys, working closely with air force JAG personnel, and enabling air force leadership and personnel to have the legal assistance required to accomplish service missions.[28]

AFGC's website (www.safgc.hq.af.mil/) contains an organizational chart and descriptions of the legal activities carried out by its component parts covering areas such as acquisition, contractor responsibility, installations and environmental law, international affairs, military affairs and national security, personnel policy, and security classification issues.

Army General Counsel

The Army General Counsel (AGC) serves as the secretary of the army's legal counsel and the Department of the Army's chief legal official. AGC responsibilities include coordinating legal and policy advice to U.S. Army offices, determining the department's position on legal questions or procedures, providing legal clearance on legislative proposals relevant to the army, providing professional guidance and oversight to those representing the department, protecting the Department of the Army's interests in litigation or other legal proceedings, and serving as the army's designated agency ethics authority.[29]

AGC's website (www.hqda.army.mil/ogc/) has a biography of the general counsel, an organizational chart, and descriptions of AGC organizational entities and their responsibilities in areas such as acquisition, civil works and environment, ethics and fiscal, and operations and personnel. Publicly available information resources include *Fiscal Law Course Outline* (2002), *Overview of Office of General Counsel Ethics Responsibilities* (2002), *Receipt of Gifts from Prohibited Sources* (2002), and *Restrictions on Contact with Defense Contractors* (2002).

Coast Guard Legal Program

The Coast Guard Legal Program (CGLP) provides legal advice and support to those carrying out Coast Guard functions to ensure that these activities comply with the spirit and letter of federal law.[30]

CGLP's website (www.uscg.mil/legal/) serves as a gateway to a rich variety of sources. These include information about the Coast Guard's incorporation into the Department of Homeland Security, career opportunities, and information on the Coast Guard Hearings Office, which is responsible for adjudicating Coast Guard civil penalty cases.

Publications accessible on the website include *Law Bulletin* (1933–1968), *Commandant Decisions* (1949–present), the text of *Coast Guard Court of Criminal Appeals Opinions* (fiscal year 1997–present), *Military Justice Manual* (2000), *Highlights of Coast Guard Legal Practice* (2002), some Coast Guard commandant civil penalty appeal decisions, and the text of proposed and adopted Department of Homeland Security regulations.

Defense Institute of International Legal Studies

The Defense Institute of International Legal Studies (DIILS) was created in 1992, is part of the Defense Security Cooperation Agency, and is based in Newport, Rhode

Island. Its mission is providing expertise in military law–related topics and conducting domestic and international programs on military law for civilian and military audiences.[31]

The website www.dsca.osd.mil/diils/ provides information about DIILS activities including descriptions of courses such as International Law of Military Operations and Peacekeeping for Decision Makers, the current issue of the *Legal News* newsletter, publications such as *Model Maritime Service Code* (1995) and *Mobile Education and Resident Programs 2003–2004* (2003), and PowerPoint slides describing the Law of War.

Defense Legal Services Agency

The Defense Legal Services Agency (DLSA) is part of DOD's Office of the General Counsel. DLSA responsibilities include providing legal advice and services for defense agencies, DOD field activities, and other assigned organizations; providing technical support and assistance for DOD legislative programs; serving as a centralized legislative document reference and distribution center for DOD and maintaining departmental historical legislative files; coordinating DOD ethical conduct programs; and administering DOD's Security Clearance Review Program.[32] The website www.defenselink.mil/dodgc/ contains DLSA's mission statement and links to organizational components, such as the Standards of Conduct Office, Legislative Reference Service, and Defense Office of Hearings and Appeals, which describe institutional responsibilities, show organizational charts, review defense-related legislation, contain DOD congressional testimony, and list federal ethical statutes and regulations. Examples of publicly accessible publications produced by DLSA entities are *Industrial Security Clearance Decisions* (1996–present), *Overview: Industrial Security Program* (1997), *Adjudicative Desk Reference*, *Advisories* from the Standards of Conduct Office (1997–present), *Employees Guide to Standards of Conduct* (2002), and *Post-Government Service Employment Restrictions (Rules Affecting Your New Job after DOD)* (2002).

Military Commissions

The September 11, 2001, terrorist attacks set in motion a number of diplomatic, financial, legal, and military responses by the United States. A key legal step taken by the U.S. government was a November 13, 2001, military order issued by President George W. Bush establishing special military courts to try the perpetrators of the attacks.[33]

DOD's Office of the General Counsel (OGC) worked on developing procedures for trying terrorists and released these procedures on May 2, 2003. Accessible on DOD's Defenselink website at www.dtic.mil/whs/directives/corres/mco.htm, the procedures are contained in eight documents: *Guidance on Military Commission Instructions* (2003), *Crimes and Elements for Trials by Military Commission* (2003), *Responsibilities of the Chief Prosecutor, Prosecutors, and Assistant Prosecutors* (2003), *Responsibilities of the Chief Defense Counsel, Detailed Defense Counsel, and Civilian*

> ## Military Commission Trials
>
> Military commission trials differ from courts-martials. They are established during wartime and are special war courts existing only during war or the aftermath of armed conflict. These tribunals are created by Congress or the president and have a narrow focus limited to war crimes and war-related offenses.
>
> Those participating in these proceedings, whether judges, prosecutors, or defense counsel, have military expertise making them suited to address such offenses. Military commission trials may be held at any geographic location, unlike courts-martial, and this permits better protection for classified and sensitive information to ensure the safety of those participating in the process.
>
> The U.S. Supreme Court upheld the constitutionality of military commissions in its 1942 ruling *Ex parte Quirin*, which involved the trial of German saboteurs caught in the United States. George W. Bush on November 13, 2001, issued a military order establishing these tribunals to try al Qaeda and allied terrorists involved in terrorist attacks against the United States. Although controversy over the establishment of these commission has emerged in some legal circles, no trials of terrorists had been conducted under these tribunals as of April 2004.
>
> Articles with historical background on military commissions are available in the March 2002 and November 2003 issues of *The Army Lawyer*, which are accessible at http://purl.access.gpo.gov/GPO/LPS31585.

Defense Counsel (2003), *Qualifications of Civilian Defense Counsel* (2003), *Reporting Relationships for Military Commission Personnel* (2003), *Sentencing* (2003), and *Administrative Procedures* (2003).

Navy General Counsel

The Navy General Counsel (NGC) provides legal advice and guidance to the U.S. Navy and Marine Corps to enable these services to fulfill their warfighting missions.[34]

The website http://ogc.navy.mil/ provides historical information about NGC activities, descriptions of OGC practice areas such as intellectual property law, biographies of OGC leaders, and domestic and international office locations. Naval ethical information resources are provided including *Ethics Counselor's Deskbook* (2002) along with sample motions and briefs presented during litigation in which OGC participated.

Office of the General Counsel

The general counsel serves as DOD's principal legal officer and is appointed by the president subject to Senate confirmation. This individual provides legal policy, oversight, and direction for DOD. Other OGC responsibilities include giving legal advice to the secretary and deputy secretary of defense on all DOD services, coordinating appeals on FOIA denial requests, developing DOD's legislative program and formulating DOD positions on legislation and presidential executive orders, and serving as chief counsel for DOD in international negotiations conducted by DOD components.[35]

The website www.defenselink.mil/dodgc/ includes descriptions of the job responsibilities performed by OGC's deputy general counsels for international affairs, fiscal issues, inspector general, intelligence, acquisitions and logistics, legal counsel, personnel and health policy, and environment and installations. Also accessible is the text of *DOD Directive 5500.17: Roles and Responsibilities of the Joint Service Committee on Military Justice* (2002).

U.S. Government Documents Regulatory Issues

Current U.S. regulatory structure stems from the Federal Register Act (1934), which established the Office of the Federal Register within the National Archives as a centralized repository for filing and promulgating federal regulations created by New Deal agencies, and the Administrative Procedure Act (1946), which established a public right to participate in the federal rule-making process by commenting on proposed agency regulations.[36]

Federal regulations are the formal procedures established by agencies to administer and enforce laws and generally contain more detailed and precise standards than the provisions contained in their organic statutes.[37] The National Archives Office of the Federal Register produces three major publications that constitute the corpus of federal regulatory publications: *Federal Register, Code of Federal Regulations,* and *Lists of Sections Affected*.

Federal Register

The *Federal Register* is published five times a week (Monday–Friday) and includes rules and regulations that have been adopted by federal agencies, proposed rules and regulations from federal agencies, presidential documents such as proclamations and executive orders, notices of public government agency meetings and grant availability, and editorial corrections of documents in previous *Federal Register* editions.[38]

A national security–related document published in the *Federal Register* is "Security Zone: Port Valdez and Valdez Narrows, AK." It describes why the Coast Guard wants to take the actions described in the document, how long the rule will be in effect, and the name and contact information of the official(s) responsible for enforcing the regulation. The document's citation is 68 *FR* 26490, which refers to volume 68, page 26490 of the May 16, 2003, issue of the *Federal Register*.

An example of a proposed federal agency rule is the Coast Guard's 2003 proposal to establish a permanent security zone in the waters next to National City Marine Terminal in San Diego Harbor, San Diego, California. The proposal contains the reasons that it should be implemented, provides information on where to send comments on the proposal, and states that such comments must reach the Coast Guard by a stipulated date.

Presidential documents such as proclamations and executive orders reflect how the president prescribes conduct for executive branch agencies. Proclamations generally tend to have more symbolic value. Proclamation 7660, *National Former Prisoner of War Recognition Day, 2003,* for example, declared April 9, 2003, as a day to commemorate former prisoners of war. Executive orders have the force of law and do not require congressional enactment. For example, Executive Order 13301 of May 14, 2003, increased the number of members on a governmental advisory board from four to five. Executive orders may be modified, revised, or terminated by later executive orders. Executive orders, like proclamations, are numbered consecutively from the *Federal Register's* 1936 establishment. Presidential authority to issue these proclamations and executive orders is derived from the president's constitutional authority as commander in chief of the armed forces and from existing legislation.[39]

The *Federal Register* also runs agency notices of public meetings. Each announcement includes date, time, and location along with the name and phone number of a contact from the organization.

A subsidiary publication of the *Federal Register* is the *Unified Agenda.* Produced twice a year (generally April and October), it lists regulatory activities agencies anticipate they will engage in over the next six months.

The *Federal Register* and *Unified Agenda,* along with other federal legal, legislative, and regulatory information resources, are electronically accessible on the U.S. Government Printing Office's "GPO Access" service at www.gpoaccess.gov/fr/ and www.gpoaccess.gov/ua/. The *Federal Register* is searchable from 1994 to the present and browsable from 1998 to the present. The *Unified Agenda* is searchable from 1994 to the present and browsable from October 2002 to the present.

An additional federal website (www.regulations.gov/) facilitates easy access to public participation in the federal regulatory process by providing a drop-down menu of the most recent proposed federal agency regulations to appear in the *Federal Register.*

Many U.S. federal depository libraries have extensive paper or microform holdings of the *Federal Register, Unified Agenda,* and other federal government regulatory publications.

Code of Federal Regulations

As the *U.S. Code* serves as the codification of U.S. laws, the *Code of Federal Regulations* (CFR) serves as the codification of federal regulations and rules published in the *Federal Register.* The CFR consists of fifty titles representing broad areas of federal regulation covering 214 paper volumes as of 2004. Each CFR is updated annually and on a rotating quarterly basis. For instance, Titles 1 through 16 are updated as of January 1, Titles 17 through 27 as of April 1, Titles 28 through 41 as of July 1, and Titles 42 through 50 as of October 1.[40]

Titles 3 and 32 cover presidential documents such as executive orders and national defense. (Title 6, covering homeland security, was introduced in 2004.) For example, CIA information declassification and downgrading policy is found at 32 CFR 1902.13, which refers to Title 32, Part 1902.13 of the CFR. Subparts a and b of

32 CFR 1902.13 are listed as "reserved," which means that they are being set aside for future regulatory information that might be covered by the CIA's information declassification and downgrading policy. The CFR entry ends with a citation from the *Federal Register* telling when the regulation was first adopted.

The CFR is electronically accessible through "GPO Access" at www.gpoaccess.gov/cfr/ and browsable and searchable from 1996 to the present. In addition, some federal agencies post their regulations from the CFR for more manageable browsing. See, for example, the Bureau of Industry and Security website (http://w3.access.gpo.gov/bis/). U.S. depository libraries will also keep the current year's CFR volumes, and law school libraries may keep significant or comprehensive CFR collections. Many of these libraries will also retain annual and cumulative volumes of CFR Title 3 because they contain the text of presidential executive orders, proclamations, and related edicts.

Lists of Sections Affected

The *Lists of Sections Affected* (LSA) is published monthly and updates regulations between their appearance in the annual CFR volumes and their appearance in the *Federal Register*. Because the CFR is updated throughout the year, four LSA monthly issues are needed to keep track of all annual regulatory changes in particular CFR citations. The December LSA is the annual reference issue for CFR Titles 1-16; the March LSA, Titles 17 through 27; the June LSA, Titles 28 through 41; and the September LSA, Titles 42 through 50.[41]

For example, page 12 of the April 2003 LSA covers changes in presidential executive orders from Title 3 of the CFR between January 1 and April 30, 2003. It says that Executive Order 13122 is being amended by Executive Order 13284, which appears on page 4075 of the 2003 *Federal Register*.

Another example is from page 47 of the April 2003 LSA covering the regulations concerning the titles of Navy commanders. These regulations may be found at 32 CFR 700.701(a). The April 2003 LSA issue notes that 32 CFR 700.701(a) was revised and that this regulatory revision appeared on page 2697 of the 2003 *Federal Register*. This section of the LSA covers thirty-two CFR regulatory changes between July 1, 2002, and April 30, 2003, with page numbers for changes appearing in the 2002 *Federal Register* highlighted in boldface.

Online access to LSA is provided through "GPO Access" at www.gpoaccess.gov/lsa/, which is browsable and searchable from 1997 to the present and is accompanied by a compilation from 1986 to 2000.

Notes

1. Joe Morehead, *Introduction to United States Government Information Sources*, 6th ed. (Englewood, Colo.: Libraries Unlimited, 1999), 137.

2. Morehead, *Introduction to United States Government Information Sources*.

3. Morehead, *Introduction to United States Government Information Sources*, 139; and U.S. Congress, Law Revision Counsel of the House of Representatives, *U.S. Code*, vol. 1 (Washington, D.C.: Government Printing Office, 2001), vii.

4. For an explanation of the constitutional origins of federal civilian judicial power, see U.S. Constitution, Article III, Sections 1–3. For additional historical background and contemporary insight on issues affecting the federal court system, see Russell R. Wheeler and Cynthia Harrison, *Creating the Federal Judicial System,* 2nd ed. (Washington, D.C.: Federal Judicial Center, 1994); and Richard A. Posner, *The Federal Courts: Challenge and Reform* (Cambridge, Mass.: Harvard University Press, 1996).

5. Wheeler and Harrison, *Creating the Federal Judicial System,* 23, 26.

6. See Administrative Office of U.S. Courts, "Federal Judiciary Frequently Asked Questions" (n.d.), 1 (www.uscourts.gov/faq.html), accessed October 30, 2003; and Wheeler and Harrison, *Creating the Federal Judicial System,* 23.

7. Morehead, *Introduction to United States Government Information Sources,* 267–268. A wide variety of literature and analysis has been made of U.S. Supreme Court history and rulings. Examples include Bernard Schwartz, *A History of the Supreme Court* (New York: Oxford University Press, 1993); and Forrest Maltzman and others, *Crafting Law on the Supreme Court: The Collegial Game* (New York: Cambridge University Press, 2000).

8. For a review of Supreme Court practices and procedures, see U.S. Supreme Court, "Rules of the Supreme Court of the United States" (2003) (www.supremecourtus.gov/ctrules/rulesofthecourt.pdf), accessed October 30, 2003.

9. For the organic statute and purpose, see PL 95-511, "Foreign Intelligence Surveillance Act of 1978," 92 *U.S. Statutes at Large,* 1783–1798; and Lee S. Strickland, "Civil Liberties vs. Intelligence Collection: The Secret Foreign Intelligence Surveillance Act Court Speaks in Public," *Government Information Quarterly,* 20 (1) (2003): 2.

10. Strickland, "Civil Liberties vs. Intelligence Collection," 2. Background on Justice Department counterintelligence programs and the Federal Intelligence Surveillance Court can be found in U.S. General Accounting Office, *FBI Intelligence Investigations: Coordination within Justice on Counterintelligence Criminal Matters Is Limited* (Washington, D.C.: General Accounting Office, 2001). Additional insight into court workings can be found in "An Interview with Judge Royce C. Lamberth," *The Third Branch: Newsletter of the Federal Courts,* 34 (6) (June 2002): 1–3 (www.uscourts.gov/ttb/june02ttb/interview.html), accessed October 30, 2003.

11. The text can be found in United States Foreign Intelligence Surveillance Court of Review, "In Re: Sealed Case 02-2001: On Motions for Review of Orders of the United States Foreign Intelligence Surveillance Court (Nos. 02-662 and 02-968)" (2002), 1–56 (www.usdoj.gov/ag/fisaappealdecision.pdf), accessed October 30, 2003.

12. U.S. Congress, Senate, "S. 436: Domestic Surveillance Oversight Act of 2003," 108th Cong., 1st sess., February 25, 2003.

13. For the organic statute, see PL 89-554, "Freedom of Information Act," 80 *U.S. Statutes at Large,* 383. See also U.S. Department of Justice, *Freedom of Information Act Guide and Privacy Act Overview* (Washington, D.C.: Government Printing Office, 2002), 5.

14. U.S. Congress, House Committee on Government Reform, *A Citizen's Guide on Using the Freedom of Information Act and the Privacy Act of 1974 to Request Government Records* (Washington, D.C.: Government Printing Office, 2002), 7–9.

15. PL 104- 231, "Electronic Freedom of Information Act Amendments," 110 *U.S. Statutes at Large,* 3048–3054.

16. U.S. Congress, House Committee on Government Reform, *A Citizen's Guide on Using the Freedom of Information Act and the Privacy Act of 1974 to Request Government Records,* 6.

17. U.S. Congress, House Committee on Government Reform, *A Citizen's Guide on Using the Freedom of Information Act and the Privacy Act of 1974 to Request Government Records,* 15–19.

18. U.S. Congress, House Committee on Government Reform, *A Citizen's Guide on Using the Freedom of Information Act and the Privacy Act of 1974 to Request Government Records,* 19–33.

19. For historical background and overall military legal reference sources, see Richard H. Kohn, ed., *The United States Military under the Constitution of the United States, 1789–1989* (New York: New York University Press, 1991); Jack L. Rives, Richard A. Gittins, and Kirk L. Davies, eds.,*The Military Commander and the Law* (Maxwell Air Force Base, Ala.: AFJAGS Press, 1996); U.S. Congress, House Committee on Armed Services, *Compilation of Defense-Related Federal Laws (Other Than Title 10, United States Code): As Amended through December 31, 2000* (Washington, D.C.: Government Printing Office, 2001); U.S. Department of Defense, *Manual for Courts-Martial, United States* (Washington, D.C.: Government Printing Office, 2002); and Michael J. Davidson, *A Guide to Military Criminal Law* (Annapolis, Md.: Naval Institute Press, 1999).

20. U.S. Air Force, Air University, Air War College, "Uniform Code of Military Justice" (n.d.), 1 (www.au.af.mil/au/awcgate/ucmj.htm), accessed October 30, 2003.

21. For the organic act, see PL 81-506, "To Unify, Consolidate, Revise, and Codify the Articles of War, the Articles for the Government of the Navy, and the Disciplinary Laws of the Coast Guard, and to Enact and Establish a Uniform Code of Military Justice," 64 *U.S. Statutes at Large,* 107–149. For the mission and responsibilities of the United States Court of Appeals for the Armed Forces, see *U.S. Government Manual, 2002–2003* (Washington, D.C.: National Archives and Records Administration, 2002), 75. For historical background, see Jonathan Lurie, *Military Justice: The U.S. Court of Appeals for the Armed Forces, 1775–1980* (Lawrence: University Press of Kansas, 2001). Additional background on the military justice system is provided by William T. Generous Jr., *Swords and Scales: The Development of the Uniform Code of Military Justice* (Port Washington, N.Y.: Kennikat Press, 1973); and S. Sidney Ulmer, *Military Justice and the Right to Counsel* (Lexington: University Press of Kentucky, 1970).

22. U.S. Court of Military Appeals, "Establishment" (n.d.), 1–2 (www.armfor.uscourts.gov/Establis.htm), accessed October 30, 2003.

23. For the text of Judge Advocate General organic statutes for the individual armed services, see PL 84-1028, "To Revise, Codify, and Enact into Law, Title 10 of the United States Code, Entitled 'Armed Forces,' and Title 32 of the United States Code, Entitled 'National Guard,'" 70A *U.S. Statutes at Large,* 164, 290, 495. For historical background, see Frederic L. Borch, *Judge Advocates in Combat: Army Lawyers in Military Operations from Vietnam to Haiti* (Washington, D.C.: U.S. Army Office of the Judge Advocate General and Center of Military History, 2001).

24. U.S. Air Force, Judge Advocate General, "Fact Sheet #2: The Judge Advocate General" (1998), 1–3 (http://afls14.jag.af.mil/dscgi/ds.py/Get/File-7564/r_02.htm), accessed October 30, 2003.

25. U.S. Army, Judge Advocate General's School, Center for Law and Military Operations, "The Center for Law and Military Operations" (n.d.), 1 (www.jagcnet.army.mil/CLAMO/), accessed October 30, 2003.

26. U.S. Marine Corps, Staff Judge Advocate to the Commandant of the United States Marine Corps, "Organization" (n.d.), 1 (http://sja.hqmc.usmc.mil/SJAOrg.htm), accessed October 30, 2003.

27. U.S. Navy, Judge Advocate General, "OJAG Mission" (n.d.), 1 (www.jag.navy.mil/AboutUS/Mission3.html), accessed October 30, 2003. For historical background, see Jay M. Siegel, *Origins of the Navy Judge Advocate General's Corps: A History of Legal Administration in the United States Navy, 1775 to 1967* (Washington, D.C.: U.S. Navy Judge Advocate General's Corps, 1997).

28. U.S. Air Force, General Counsel of the Air Force, "Mission and Role of the Office of the General Counsel" (n.d.), 1 (www.safgc.hq.af.mil/), accessed October 30, 2003.

29. U.S. Army, Office of the General Counsel, "Mission and Functions" (n.d.), 1–2 (www.hqda.army.mil/ogc/mis.htm), accessed October 30, 2003.

30. U.S. Coast Guard, "Mission" (2003), 1 (www.uscg.mil/legal/), accessed October 30, 2003.

31. U.S. Defense Institute of International Legal Studies, "Mission" (n.d.), 1 (www.dsca.osd.mil/diils/), accessed October 30, 2003.

32. U.S. Department of Defense, "Defense Legal Services Agency" (2003), 2 (www.defenselink.mil/dodgc/), accessed October 30, 2003.

33. For the text of this order, see "Military Order of November 13, 2001," *Federal Register*, 66, no. 222 (November 16, 2001), 57833–57836. For additional background on war crimes trials and military commissions, see Eugene Davidson, comp., *The Trial of the Germans: An Account of the Twenty-Two Defendants before the International Military Tribunal at Nuremberg* (Columbia: University of Missouri Press, 1997); Howard Ball, *Prosecuting War Crimes and Genocide: The Twentieth-Century Experience* (Lawrence: University Press of Kansas, 1999); Gary Jonathan Bass, *Stay the Hand of Vengeance: The Politics of War Crimes Tribunals* (Princeton, N.J.: Princeton University Press, 2000); and Howard Ball, *War Crimes and Justice: A Reference Handbook* (Santa Barbara, Calif.: ABC-CLIO, 2002).

34. U.S. Department of the Navy, Office of the General Counsel, "Purpose, Mission, and Vision" (2001), 1 (http://ogc.navy.mil/ogcwww/ogcmission.asp), accessed October 30, 2003.

35. U.S. Department of Defense, "Defense Legal Services Agency," 1.

36. For the original text of these statutes, see PL 74-220, "To Provide for the Custody of Federal Proclamations, Orders, Regulations, Notices, and Documents, and for the Prompt and Uniform Printing and Distribution Thereof," 49 *U.S. Statutes at Large*, 500–503; and PL 79-404, "Administrative Procedure Act," 60 *U.S. Statutes at Large*, 237–244. For an explanation of these statutes' key provisions, see U.S. National Archives and Records Administration, Office of the Federal Register, *The Federal Register: What It Is and How to Use It* (Washington, D.C.: National Archives and Records Administration, 1992), 1. For assessments of the federal regulatory process and the diversity of conflicting perspectives it generates, see Stanley A. Reigel, *Administrative Law: The Law of Government Agencies* (Ann Arbor, Mich.: Ann Arbor Science, 1982); David Schoenbrod, *Power without Responsibility: How Congress Abuses the People through Delegation* (New Haven, Conn.: Yale University Press, 1993); Bruce Alan Williams and Albert R. Matheny, *Democracy, Dialogue, and Environmental Disputes: The Contested Languages of Social Regulation* (New Haven, Conn.: Yale University Press, 1995); and U.S. Congress, Senate Committee on Governmental Affairs, Subcommittee on Oversight of Government Management and the District of Columbia, *Federal Regulations: Balancing Rights, Reason, and Responsibility*, 104th Cong., 1st sess., 1995.

37. Morehead, *Introduction to United States Government Information Sources*, 221.

38. Morehead, *Introduction to United States Government Information Sources*, 224.

39. Morehead, *Introduction to United States Government Information Sources*, 176–177.

40. U.S. Government Printing Office, "Code of Federal Regulations: About" (n.d.), 1 (www.gpoaccess.gov/cfr/about.html), accessed October 30, 2003.

41. U.S. Government Printing Office, "About the LSA (List of CFR Sections Affected)" (n.d.), 1–2 (www.gpoaccess.gov/lsa/about.html), accessed October 30, 2003.

CHAPTER 10

Research Institutions and Think Tanks in Washington, D.C.

A multitude of research organizations (often called think tanks) in the Washington, D.C., area, throughout the United States, and in countries around the world produce national security policy information.[1] Government departments and agencies hire these institutions to conduct research or design projects. Experts from such organizations are invited to testify before congressional committees to support or oppose policy proposals or to appear on media outlets to discuss pending legislation. The research institutions are funded by individual, nonprofit, governmental, and commercial sources representing various ideological or philosophical viewpoints.

■ American Enterprise Institute for Public Policy Research

The American Enterprise Institute for Public Policy Research (AEI) is an ideologically conservative institution founded in 1943. It has a staff of 125 and an annual budget of $12 million. It conducts research on foreign and defense policy, social and political studies, and domestic and international economic policy.[2]

AEI's website (www.aei.org/) provides information about organizational components such as the Joint Center for Regulatory Studies, news releases, and biographical information about affiliated scholars specializing in national security policy.

Access is provided to commentaries written by AEI scholars such as *A Better Way to Build a Missile Defense* (2000), *Losing the Intelligence War Overseas* (2002), *Toward a Global Cavalry: Overseas Rebasing and Defense Transformation* (2003), and *Lessons of Operation Iraqi Freedom* (2003). Additional publications include issues of the newsletter *National Security Outlook* (December 2002–present) and selected articles from the periodical *The American Enterprise* (2002–present).

The website also provides access to summaries of books published by AEI Press. Excerpts are available from *Over the Line: North Korea's Negotiating Strategy* (1999), *Study of Revenge: The First World Trade Center Attack and Saddam Hussein's War against America* (2002), *Safeguarding Defense, Technology, Enabling Commerce* (2002), and *Cuba: The Morning After* (2003).

ANSER Institute for Homeland Security

Created in 1999, the Advancing National Strategies and Enabling Results (ANSER) Institute for Homeland Security is a nonprofit public service research organization that seeks to examine the new national security challenges presented by homeland security issues such as crisis management, consequence management, deterrence, and preemption.[3]

The ANSER Institute's website (www.homelandsecurity.org/) has information about institute programs including biographies of key personnel, links to state homeland security agency office resources, and PowerPoint presentations. Accessible publications include *Weekly Homeland Security Newsletter* (2002–present), the *Journal of Homeland Security* (2000–present), and reports such as *ANSER Summary and Analysis: A Quick Look at the Proposed Department of Homeland Security* (2002), *The Down and Dirty on Dirty Bombs* (2002), and *The National Strategy for Homeland Security: Finding the Paths among the Trees* (2002).

Arms Control Association

The Arms Control Association (ACA) was founded in 1971 and features a staff of nine, an $800,000 annual budget, and fifteen hundred members. ACA conducts research on what it sees as effective arms control and disarmament policies and provides information on its research for the media and to U.S. government officials.[4]

Its website (www.armscontrol.org/) lists members of the ACA Board of Directors, summaries of media events (1999–present), the text of news releases (2001–present), and the full text of major international arms control agreements such as the Chemical Weapons Convention and Comprehensive Nuclear Test Ban Treaty. Articles from ACA's periodical *Arms Control Today* are provided from 1997 to the present as well as the text of numerous fact sheets on arms control topics including *India's Draft Nuclear Doctrine* (1999), *Current U.S. Strategic Nuclear Forces* (2002), *Chronology of U.S.-North Korean Nuclear and Missile Diplomacy* (2003), and *New Nuclear Policies, New Weapons, New Dangers* (2003).

Atlantic Council of the United States

The Atlantic Council of the United States (ACUS) was formed in 1961 on the recommendation of former secretaries of state Dean Acheson (1949–1953) and Christian Herter (1959–1961) and others who wanted a consolidation of U.S. citizens groups supporting the Atlantic Alliance of the United States, Canada, and various Western European nations. The purpose of ACUS is promoting U.S. leadership and participation in international affairs by discussing and debating crucial international issues in a nonpartisan manner and conducting educational and exchange programs so future American leaders will appreciate the value of U.S. engagement in international affairs.[5]

The website www.acus.org/ contains biographies of key staffers, information on the origins and development of ACUS, and selected audio and video webcasts. Accessible publications include *Atlantic Council Newsletter* (1999–present) and policy papers such as *Russian Policy towards the Baltics: What the West Can Expect and What It Could Do* (1999), *The Bulgarian Defence Industry* (2001), *Permanent Alliance? NATO's Prague Summit and Beyond* (2001), *New Capabilities: Transforming NATO Forces* (2002), *Elusive Partnership: U.S. and European Policies in the Near East and the Gulf* (2002), *U.S.-Libyan Relations: Toward Cautious Reengagement* (2003), *Missile Defense in Asia* (2003), and *Globalization of Defense Industries: China* (2003).

British-American Security Information Council

The British-American Security Information Council (BASIC), with offices in Washington, D.C., and London, England, describes itself as a liberal-progressive independent analysis and advocacy organization examining world security issues, nuclear policies, military strategies, weapons, and disarmament.[6]

BASIC's website (www.basicint.org/) has the text of the newsletter *Basic Reports* (1995–present) and reports and commentaries such as *Bunker Busters: Washington's Drive for New Nuclear Weapons* (2002), *The Republican Victory in the U.S. Congress: What It Will Mean for Nuclear Weapons and Missile Defense Policies* (2002), *European Governments Official Position on Missile Defence* (2003), *U.S. Chemical 'Non-Lethal' Weapons in Iraq: A Violation of the Chemical Weapons Convention?* (2003), *The Crisis in North Korea* (2003), and *NATO's Angry Sponsors: The View from Capitol Hill* (2003).

Brookings Institution

The Brookings Institution (BI) was founded in 1916 and serves as a nonpartisan research and educational center specializing in economics, government policy, and foreign policy. It has a staff of 250 and a $31 million annual budget. It is widely regarded as a leading think tank in shaping public policy research.[7]

BI's website (www.brookings.edu/) has news releases (March 2000–present), links to the web pages of organizational components such as the Center for Northeast Asian Policy Studies and the Saban Center for Middle East Policy, biographical information on national security policy scholars who are on staff, and speeches, writings, and RealPlayer video clips by these and other Brookings scholars.

Accessible publications include articles from recent issues of the periodical *Brookings Review*, lists and descriptions of books by BI scholars in the institution's bookstore, and the text of articles and reports on national security issues. Examples of such resources are *America and Iran: From Containment to Coexistence* (2001), *Reducing Collateral Damage to Indo-Pakistani Relations from the War on Terrorism* (2002), *The Bush National Security Strategy: An Evaluation* (2002), *Reflections on Homeland Security and American Federalism* (2002), *A "Master Plan" to Deal with North Korea* (2003), *French Lessons: The Importance of the Judicial System in Fighting Terrorism* (2003), *Building the New Iraq: The Role of Intervening Forces* (2003), and *Protecting the American Homeland: One Year On* (2003).

Carnegie Endowment for International Peace

Founded in 1910 by the noted industrialist Andrew Carnegie, the Carnegie Endowment for International Peace (CEIP) conducts research, discussion, publication, and educational programs in international affairs, U.S. foreign policy, and a variety of military, political, and economic issues while seeking to advance international cooperation.[8]

CEIP's website (www.ceip.org/) contains information and webcasts of endowment-sponsored events, biographical information on CEIP national security policy scholars, and links to descriptions of books published by the endowment. Access is provided to working papers and other endowment publications including *The Rise and Fall of START II: The Russian Perspective* (1999), *Drug Trafficking on the Great Silk Road: The Security Environment in Central Asia* (2000), *Enhancing Nuclear Security in the Counter Terrorism Struggle: India and Pakistan as a New Region for Cooperation* (2002), *Verifying North Korean Nuclear Disarmament: A Technical Analysis* (2003), and *From Victory to Success: Afterwar Policy in Iraq* (2003).

Cato Institute

Founded in 1977 and with a staff of one hundred and a $13 million annual budget, the Cato Institute (CI) presents research products consistent with a libertarian perspective on governmental issues focusing on limited government, individual liberty, and peace.[9]

CI's website (www.cato.org/) features descriptions of upcoming institute-sponsored conferences, news releases, biographies of national security policy experts who are part of CI's staff, and RealPlayer webcasts of media appearances by these and other CI personnel. In addition, descriptions are provided of books produced by CI analysts including *Tripwire: Korea and U.S. Foreign Policy in a Changed World* (1996), *China's Future: Constructive Partner or Emerging Threat?* (2000), *Exiting the Balkan Thicket* (2002), and *Bad Neighbor Policy: Washington's Futile War on Drugs in Latin America* (2003).

A number of full-text resources are also accessible: the newsletter *Policy Report* (1993–present), articles from the scholarly *CATO Journal* (1981–present), and policy reports and analyses including *Reducing a Common Danger: Improving Russia's Early Warning System* (2001), *Old Folly in a New Disguise: Nation Building to Combat Terrorism* (2002), *Joint Strike Fighter: Can a Multiservice Fighter Program Succeed?* (2002), *The China-Taiwan Military Balance: Implications for the United States* (2003), *After Victory: Toward a New Military Posture in the Persian Gulf* (2003), and *Casualties of War: Transatlantic Relations and the Future of NATO in the Wake of the Second Gulf War* (2003).

Center for Defense Information

The Center for Defense Information (CDI) was founded in 1972, has a staff of twenty-five, and operates with an annual budget of $2.1 million. With a leftist perspective, the think tank advocates that the United States rid itself of excessive defense strength, eliminate wasteful defense spending, avoid nuclear war, and try to limit military influence on domestic and foreign policies.[10]

CDI's website (www.cdi.org/) features transcripts of television programs on which its staff have appeared, a "What's New" section, and information about current staffers. Examples of accessible CDI-produced reports are *Military Reconnaissance Satellites* (2001), *Drawing the Line: The Path to Controlling Weapons in Space* (2002), *The Unfettered Missile Defense Agency (MDA)* (2003), *Cuban Biotechnology: A First-Hand Report* (2003), and *Stand-Off with North Korea: War Scenarios and Consequences* (2003).

Center for Security Policy

The Center for Security Policy (CSP) is a conservative-oriented institution founded in 1988, possesses a staff of four, and has an annual budget of $850,000. Its mission is serving the government's executive and legislative branches, press, industry, and public by exchanging information on foreign and national security policy issues while developing strategies to assist policy makers dealing with these matters.[11]

The website www.centerforsecuritypolicy.org/ has information on CSP's staff and board, on providing financial support, and on center-sponsored events. Publications ranging from journalistic op-eds to reports from the late 1980s to the present are available, including *"Loose Lips": U.S. Capabilities Vital to War on Terror Being Jeopardized by Dangerous Disclosures* (2002), *Invasion: Will the New Homeland Security Department Address the Crisis in U.S. Immigration Policy?* (2002), *Mixed Signals on Proliferation* (2003), and *Wishful Thinking about Islamist Terror* (2003).

Center for Strategic and Budgetary Assessments

The Center for Strategic and Budgetary Assessments (CSBA) was founded in 1983, has a staff of seven, and operates on a $500,000 annual budget.[12] Its mission is providing independent information for the U.S. government, media, and interested parties on the link between budgeting and defense strategies to promote a more efficient and effective U.S. defense policy in the midst of ongoing military technological transformation.[13]

CSBA's website (www.csbaonline.org/) contains information about organizational activities, a "What's New" page, institutional mission statement, staff directory, and the texts of various publications. The publications include *Options for U.S. Fighter Modernization* (1999), *Three Myths about DOD's Weapons Modernization Requirements* (2001), *The Military Use of Space: A Diagnostic Assessment* (2001), *The Military-Technical Revolution: A Preliminary Assessment* (2002), *Potential Cost of a War with Iraq and Its Post-War Occupation* (2003), and *Analysis of the FY2004 Defense Budget Request* (2003).

Center for Strategic and International Studies

The Center for Strategic and International Studies (CSIS) was born as an adjunct of Georgetown University in 1962. Its 190 staffers conduct nonpartisan research and issue publications dealing with new and emerging challenges to national and international security from strategic and interdisciplinary perspectives.[14]

The website www.csis.org/ features biographical information about CSIS scholars; a topical index of experts; descriptions of program areas such as homeland security, Middle East energy and security, Russia and Eurasia, and South Asia; press releases (1997–present); descriptions of CSIS-sponsored events (1999–present), some of which feature transcripts and webcasts; and congressional testimony by CSIS personnel (1998–present).

Also accessible are publications on global national security topics, including the periodicals *Policy Papers and the Americas* (1999–present), *South Asia Monitor* (1998–present), *Washington Quarterly* (1999–present), and *Turkey Update* (1996–present). The full text of numerous reports published since 1998 are provided, including *The New Balance of Gulf Arms* (1999), *Weapons of Mass Destruction in Iran and Iraq* (2000), *The Lasting Challenge: A Strategy for Counter-Terrorism and Asymmetric Warfare* (2001), *A Blueprint for U.S. Policy toward a Unified Korea* (2002), *Protecting against the Spread of Nuclear, Biological, and Chemical Weapons* (2003), and *Iraq's Post-Conflict Reconstruction: A Field Review and Recommendations* (2003).

Chemical and Biological Arms Control Institute

The Chemical and Biological Arms Control Institute (CBACI) began operations in 1993 with a focus on the elimination of chemical and biological weapons. It alerts governmental, industry, scientific community, and media leaders of the problems involved with these weapons by preparing research analyses and conducting educational and training programs.[15]

CBACI's website (www.cbaci.org/) features information on its training activities, staff biographies, and descriptions of program areas such as biotechnology, health and safety, nonproliferation, and terrorism. Accessible publications include the bimonthly periodical *Dispatch* (July 1997–present), a listing of articles written by CBACI personnel (1997–present), and information on ordering paper copies of institute reports. Accessible papers and reports include *Agricultural Biological Warfare: An Overview* (2000), *Bioterrorism in the United States: Threat, Preparedness, and Response* (2000), *Contagion and Conflict: Health as a Global Security Challenge* (2000), *Deterring Terrorism with CRBN Weapons: Developing a Conceptual Framework* (2001), *Pretoria's Shadow: The HIV/AIDS Pandemic and National Security in Southern Africa* (2002), *What Should We Know? Whom Do We Tell? Leveraging Communication and Information to Counter Terrorism and Its Consequences* (2002), and *Reducing the Biological Weapons Threat: New Thinking New Approaches* (2003).

Federation of American Scientists

The Federation of American Scientists (FAS) was founded in 1945, has twenty-five hundred members, supports a professional office staff of eighteen, and functions with a $3 million annual budget. The federation's focus is on increasing the relevance of scientific issues and providing what it considers science-based perspectives on public policy issues.[16]

The FAS website (www.fas.org/) has press releases (1997–present); web pages such as "Arms Sales Monitoring Project," "China Nuclear Forces Guide," "Cruise Missiles: Special Weapons Primer," and "Intelligence Resource Program"; and newsletters and periodicals including *Arms Sales Monitor* (1991–present), *Public Interest Report* (1993–present), and *Secrecy News* (September 2000–present).

The website also has reprints of government documents, including some removed from issuing agency websites, such as *Report of the Commission to Assess the Ballistic Missile Threat to the United States: Executive Summary* (1998), *National Missile Defense Deployment Readiness Review* (2000), *Military Transformation: Intelligence, Surveillance, and Reconnaissance* (2002), and *Homeland Security: Protecting Airliners from Terrorist Missiles* (2003).

Global Security

Global Security seeks to reduce reliance on nuclear weapons and the chance that they will be used, promote conventional U.S. forces toward dealing with post–cold war threats, improve the U.S. intelligence community's response to emerging security threats, reduce the need to use military force, and use space technology to increase international peace and security.[17]

Global Security's website (www.globalsecurity.org/) contains news coverage of topics such as the August 2003 electric blackout in the northeastern United States, maps and satellite imagery and photographs of global security hotspots such as the Persian Gulf and Iraq, information on the order of battle for U.S. forces sent to Liberia as peacekeepers in August 2003, the 2003 legal document indicting former Liberian president Charles Taylor for war crimes, links to national security–related reports such as the Justice Department inspector general's report on the Federal Bureau of Investigation's handling of the Robert Hanssen espionage case and the Central Intelligence Agency's National Intelligence Estimate of Iraqi weapons of mass destruction, national security news stories from U.S. and foreign media outlets, and reports such as *Liberia: Civil War and Regional Conflict* (2003).

Henry L. Stimson Center

Named for the U.S. secretary of state from 1929 to 1933, the Henry L. Stimson Center (HLSC) was founded in 1989. It serves as a nonprofit and nonpartisan institution devoted to enhancing international peace and security through a combination of analytical research and public outreach.[18]

HLSC's website (www.stimson.org/) contains press releases (October 1998–present), listings and descriptions of previous and upcoming center-sponsored events, and biographies of board of directors members. Accessible publications include the periodical *Quarterly Update on East Asian Security* (2002–present) and reports from 1991 to the present such as *Nuclear Risk Reduction Measures in Southern Asia* (1998), *Toxic Archipelago: Preventing Proliferation from the Former Soviet Chemical and Biological Weapons Complexes* (1999), *Taiwan and U.S.-PRC Relations* (2001), *Pakistan and India: Can Nuclear Risk Reduction Centers (NRRCs) Help*

Strengthen Peace? (2002), *Foreign High-Tech R&D in China: Risks, Rewards, and Implications for U.S.-China Relations* (2003), and *Space Assurance or Space Dominance? The Case against Weaponizing Space* (2003).

■ Heritage Foundation

The Heritage Foundation (HF) was founded in 1973 and has become one of the leading U.S. conservative think tanks. Its mission is developing and promoting conservative policies in free enterprise, limited government, traditional values, and a strong national defense.[19]

HF's website (www.heritage.org/) describes the foundation's work and research. Accessible resources include information about organizational components such as the Kathryn and Shelby Cullom Davis Center for International Studies, biographies of on-staff scholars, and news releases (1999–present). National security reports dating back to 1991 are also accessible, including *Improving Security at the Department of Energy's Weapons Laboratories* (1999), *The Importance of Vieques Island for Military Readiness* (2001), *Defending the American Homeland* (2002), *Securing America's Airports and Waterways: The Role of the U.S. Department of Transportation* (2002), *The Vital Role of Alliances in the Global War on Terrorism* (2002), *Road Map to Peace Requires an End to Palestinian Terrorism, Not Just a Cease-Fire* (2003), *Preventing a Crisis in U.S.-Russian Relations Over Moscow's Nuclear Technology Exports* (2003), and *The U.S. Role in Peace Operations: Past, Perspective, and Prescriptions for the Future* (2003).

■ Institute for Defense Analyses

In 1947 Secretary of Defense James Forrestal established a Weapons System Evaluation Group to provide technical analyses of military weapons systems and programs. From these beginnings evolved the Institute for Defense Analyses (IDA), which became a federally funded research and development center advising the Office of the Secretary of Defense, defense agencies, and the military's Joint Chiefs of Staff and unified commands on national security issues requiring scientific and technical expertise. To preserve institutional autonomy, IDA does not work directly for individual military departments, private industry, or foreign governments.[20]

IDA's website (www.ida.org/) provides information about the institute's divisions and work areas, listings of corporate officers and institutional trustees, and links to project websites including "Virtual Emergency Response Team's Virtual Cities," "Virtual Training Repository," and "Defense Science Study Group." Descriptions are also provided of ongoing research projects such as Joint Strike Fighter Alternatives, Future Long-Range Interdiction Aircraft, Acquisition of Antiarmor Munitions, Ballistic Imaging for Combat Identification, Assessment of Unmanned Aerial Vehicles, and Missile Defense Interoperability Standards.

The IDA website also provides access to some research reports including *Benchmarks for Submerged Structure Response to Underwater Explosions* (1999), *Network Centric Warfare: Developing and Leveraging Information Superiority* (2000), *American*

Primacy and the Major Power Concert: A Critique of the 2002 National Security Strategy (2002), and *Tripolar Stability: The Future of Nuclear Relations among the United States, Russia, and China* (2002).

Institute for Policy Studies

The Institute for Policy Studies (IPS) is an ideologically leftist institution. It was founded in 1963 and presents its vision on how to promote democracy, justice, human rights, and diversity in the United States and internationally.[21]

The website www.ips-dc.org/ includes biographical information on institute staff, links to various IPS project websites including "Foreign Policy in Focus and Nuclear Policy," and selected reports including *The War on Drugs: Addicted to Failure* (1998), *The Legacy of Depleted Uranium in the United States* (2003), *What Next for Pax Americana?* (2003), *Fearful Symmetry: Washington and Pyongyang* (2003), and *Nuclear Weapons Threats Abroad: Bush's Football in Dirty Game* (2003).

Jewish Institute for National Security Affairs

The Jewish Institute for National Security Affairs (JINSA) was founded in 1973 and has more than seventeen thousand members. Its institutional mission is educating Americans about the importance of effective military capabilities to defend vital interests and informing the U.S. foreign and defense policy communities of the crucial role that Israel plays in strengthening democracy in the Mediterranean and Middle East.[22]

JINSA's website (www.jinsa.org/) features biographies of the institute's board of directors, information about programs and lecture series it offers, a roster of professional staffers, and reports and issue commentaries such as *Who Is a "Terrorist" and Why?* (2002), *Material Breach? Send the Inspectors Home* (2002), *U.S.-Israel Strategic Relations in 2002: Counter-Terrorism, Missile Defense, and High-Tech Research Remain Priorities* (2002), *Israeli-Made Arms Commonplace in U.S. Arsenal* (2003), *Nuclear Smuggling: A First Step to Nuclear Terrorism* (2003), and *Uses of Intelligence* (2003).

National Institute for Public Policy

The National Institute for Public Policy (NIPP), located in Fairfax, Virginia, was founded in 1981 and has a staff of twenty. Its organizational purpose is examining rapidly changing foreign policy and international security issues including the effectiveness of deterrence after the cold war, the ability of the United States and its allies to counter the proliferation of weapons of mass destruction, and the future of the North Atlantic Treaty Organization (NATO) and other U.S.-allied security compacts.[23]

NIPP's website (www.nipp.org/) has biographies of professional staff members, descriptions of programs such as National Security Reform in the Republic of Georgia, and the text of articles written by NIPP staffers for periodicals such as *Arms Control Today*, *Defense News*, and *Washington Quarterly*. The website also has reports, including *Rationale and Requirements for U.S. Nuclear Forces and Arms Control; Volume 1: Executive Report* (2001), *Evolving Russian Perspectives on Missile Defense: The Emerging Accommodation* (2002), *Understanding "Asymmetric" Threats to the United States*, (2002), *European Perspectives on U.S. Ballistic Missile Defense* (2002), *Why the United States Rejected the Protocol to the Biological and Toxin Weapons Convention* (2002), and *Strategic Offensive Forces and the Nuclear Posture Review's "New Triad"* (2003).

National Security Archive

The National Security Archive (NSA) is a nonprofit research institution affiliated with George Washington University. It was founded in 1985 by journalists and scholars and receives nearly $1.8 million annual revenue from publication sales and from support by private organizations such as the Carnegie Foundation, Ford Foundation, and John D. and Catherine T. MacArthur Foundation. NSA's purpose is serving as a research institute on international affairs and maintaining an archive of declassified U.S. government documents obtained through the Freedom of Information Act (FOIA).[24]

NSA's website (www.gwu.edu/~nsarchiv/) contains information about the archive's documentary collections, daily operating hours and researcher visiting procedures, news releases (May 1997–present), information about subscription services NSA offers such as the Digital National Security Archive, and descriptions and sample documents from microfiche collections available for purchase such as *U.S. Espionage and Intelligence: Organization, Operations, and Management, 1947–1996* (1997), *U.S. Nuclear History: Nuclear Arms and Politics in the Missile Age, 1955–1968* (1997), and *China and the U.S.: From Hostility to Engagement, 1960–1998* (1999).

The Electronic Briefing Books series is accessible at www.gwu.edu/~nsarchiv/NSAEBB/. The series includes narrative summaries and the text of U.S. government documents from significant foreign and national security policy developments in recent decades, all reflecting the scope of the U.S. interests. Titles available in this continually growing series and their year of publication include *The Revolution of 1989: New Documents from Soviet/East Europe Archives Reveal Why There Was No Crackdown* (1999), *U.S. Satellite Imagery, 1960–1999* (1999), *The Chinese Nuclear Weapons Program: Problems of Intelligence Collection and Analysis, 1964–1972* (2000), *Operation Desert Storm: Ten Years After* (2001), *Conflicting Missions: Secret Cuban Documents on History of Africa Involvement* (2002), *The Making of the Limited Test Ban Treaty, 1958–1963* (2003), and *North Korea and Nuclear Weapons: The Declassified U.S. Record* (2003).

Nuclear Control Institute

The Nuclear Control Institute (NCI), founded in 1981, serves as an independent research and advocacy group focusing on nuclear nonproliferation. NCI seeks to promote strategies that will stop the spread of nuclear weapons and reduce their growth in number.[25]

NCI's website (www.nci.org/) includes links to global news stories on nuclear weapons, information on NIC organizational activities including conferences, and staff biographies. Some full-text reports are also provided including *Disposal of Weapons Plutonium in the U.S. and Russia: Issues and Options for the G-8* (2000), *Radiological Sabotage and Nuclear Power Plants: A Moving Target Set* (2000), and *A Reevaluation of Physical Protection Standards for Irradiated HEU (Highly Enriched Uranium) Fuel* (2002).

Potomac Institute for Policy Studies

The Potomac Institute for Policy Studies (PI) is an independent nonprofit public policy research institute. It promotes discussion on key scientific and technological issues facing society with a particular focus on national security issues such as terrorism, asymmetric warfare, emerging national security threats and opportunities, national health policies with national security implications, and science and technology forecasting.[26]

A variety of information resources can be found on PI's website (www.potomacinstitute.org/). These include a calendar of current year events; press releases (1996–present); descriptions of organizational components such as the International Center for Terrorism Studies, National Security Health Policy Center, and National Center for Unconventional Thought, with links to their websites; the text of the *Update* newsletter (2001–present); and links to descriptions and Amazon.com order sites for books written by institute personnel including *Terrorism and Medical Responses: U.S. Lessons and Policy Options* (2001) and *Combating Terrorism: Strategies of Ten Countries* (2002).

Access is also provided to a number of reports including *MARITECH Program Impacts on Global Competitiveness of the U.S. Shipbuilding and Navy Ship Construction* (1998), *Antipersonnel Landmine Alternatives: Organic Real Time Battlefield Shaping* (1999), *Out of the Box and into the Future: A Dialogue between Warfighters and Scientists on Far-Future Wars* (2000), *Department of Defense Science and Technology Invigoration* (2002), *What Is to Be Done? Emerging Perspectives on Public Responses to Bioterrorism* (2002), and *Rational Steps in the Information Technology, National Security, and Privacy Debate* (2003).

Russian American Nuclear Security Advisory Council

The Russian American Nuclear Security Advisory Council (RANSAC) is an independent nongovernmental research organization founded in 1997. Its mission is supporting the cooperative threat reduction agenda between the United States, Russia, and other former Soviet states while addressing global proliferation dangers. Key RANSAC emphases include reducing Russia's weapons of mass destruction complex, ensuring the security of such materials and technologies at the nuclear weapons production facilities, and transferring surplus workers at these facilities to peaceful careers, limiting fissile material production and use, and disposing excess weapons and materials.[27]

Additional information on RANSAC activities can be found at www.ransac.org/, including descriptions of institutional accomplishments and links to U.S. and Russian government documents such as arms control treaties and congressional committee hearings dealing with cooperative threat budget matters. Available research reports include *Renewing the Partnership: Recommendations for Accelerated Action to Secure Nuclear Material in the Former Soviet Union* (2000), *Accomplishments of Selected Threat Reduction and Nonproliferation Programs in Russia, By Agency* (2003), and *Strategies for Russian Nuclear Complex Downsizing and Redirection: Options for New Directions* (2003).

Terrorism Research Center

The Terrorism Research Center (TRC) began operations in 1996 and is an independent institution committed to researching terrorism, information warfare and security, critical infrastructure protection, and low-intensity political violence. TRC maintains an international network of terrorism and information warfare experts from industry, government, and academe and produces independent studies.[28]

Further information about TRC activities can be found at www.terrorism.com/. Accessible materials include links to terrorism-related news stories; profiles of terrorist organizations and attacks; listings of media outlets for which TRC personnel have provided commentary such as the Canadian Broadcasting Corporation, the *Economist*, and the *New York Times;* and organizations whose work TRC has supported including the Metro Boston Transit Authority, Federal Bureau of Investigation, Joint Chiefs of Staff, National Academies of Science, and British Ministry of Defence.

TRC offers some fee-based subscription services including terrorism advisories for countries around the world and special consultative reports on terrorism, information warfare, and other topics. Information about acquiring these services is provided on the website.

Examples of accessible TRC publications are *Chemical and Biological Terrorism: Can You Trust Your Umbrella?* (2000), *State-Sponsored WMD Terrorism: A Growing Threat?* (2000), and *Cyberterrorism and Private Corporations: New Threat Models and Risk Management Implications* (2002).

Wisconsin Project on Nuclear Arms Control

The Wisconsin Project on Nuclear Arms Control (WPNAC) was founded in 1986 by University of Wisconsin–Madison law professor Gary Milhollin in an effort to reduce the international proliferation of weapons of mass destruction including nuclear weapons. WPNAC is now located in Washington, D.C.[29]

The project's website (www.wisconsinproject.org/) features newspaper and periodical articles written by Milhollin and other project members (1990–present), congressional testimony (1992–present), and information on the *Risk Report* CD-ROM featuring unclassified information on international companies suspected of providing parts and technology to countries suspected of building weapons of mass destruction. Also available are reports such as *U.S. Exports to China 1988–1998:*

Fueling Proliferation (1999) and a link to the Iraqwatch.org website, which has information about Iraq's attempts to acquire weapons of mass destruction weapons and links to United Nations documents, U.S. government documents, and government documents from, for example, France, Russia, Ukraine, and the United Kingdom describing their views on how to deal with Iraq's efforts to acquire such weapons.

Woodrow Wilson International Center for Scholars

The Woodrow Wilson International Center for Scholars (WWICS) was established by Congress in 1968 as the official national memorial to Woodrow Wilson, the twenty-eighth president of the United States. It has a staff of ninety-five and a $15 million annual budget.[30] WWICS's purpose is serving as a nonpartisan center for advanced study of public policy issues and providing a neutral forum for serious and informed dialogue while taking broad and historical perspectives.[31]

The WWICS website (http://wwics.si.edu/) has descriptions of center-sponsored events (1998–present), biographies of institute fellows and scholars, descriptions of books written by WWICS fellows and scholars for the Woodrow Wilson Institution Press and other publishers, links to institutional project websites such as the "Conflict Prevention Project" and "Environmental Change and Security Project," and articles from the current issue of the periodical *Wilson Quarterly*. Accessible reports include *When the Cold War Did Not End: The Soviet Peace Offensive of 1953 and the American Response* (2000), *Uzbekistan and the Challenges of Creating a Regional Security System within Central Asia* (2001), *U.S. Policy toward the Former Yugoslavia* (2002), *Poverty, Terrorism, and National Security* (2003), and *Winning the Peace: Women's Role in Post-Conflict Iraq* (2003).

Notes

1. A variety of literature exists on the role of think tanks and whether they are a positive or negative influence on public policy. See, for example, Donald E. Abelson, *American Think-Tanks and Their Role in U.S. Foreign Policy* (Houndsmills, United Kingdom, and New York: Macmillan Press and St. Martin's Press, 1996); David M. Ricci, *The Transformation of American Politics: The New Washington and the Rise of Think Tanks* (New Haven, Conn.: Yale University Press, 1993); Ron Theodore Robin, *The Making of the Cold War Enemy: Culture and Politics in the Military-Industrial Complex* (Princeton, N.J.: Princeton University Press, 2001); and James Allen Smith, *The Idea Brokers: Think Tanks and the Rise of the New Policy Elite* (New York: Free Press, 1991).

2. "Associations Unlimited: The American Enterprise Institute" (2003) (www.galenet.com/servlet/AU), accessed August 12, 2003.

3. ANSER Institute for Homeland Security, "About the Institute" (2003), 1 (www.homelandsecurity.org/about.cfm), accessed September 10, 2003.

4. Arms Control Association, "About ACA: Mission" (2004), 1 (www.armscontrol.org/about.asp), accessed August 12, 2004.

5. Atlantic Council of the United States, "Mission and History" (n.d.), 1–2 (www.acus.org/history.html), accessed August 12, 2003.

6. British-American Security Information Council, "About Basic" (n.d.), 1 (www.basicint.org/about.htm), accessed August 12, 2003.

7. "Associations Unlimited: Brookings Institution" (2004) (www.galenet.com/servlet/AU), accessed April 1, 2004. Additional background on Brookings is provided by Donald T. Critchlow, *The Brookings Institution, 1916–1952: Expertise and the Public Interest in a Democratic Society* (Dekalb, Ill.: Northern Illinois University Press, 1985); and James Allen Smith, *Brookings at Seventy-Five* (Washington, D.C.: Brookings Institution, 1991).

8. "Associations Unlimited: Carnegie Endowment for International Peace" (2004) (www.galenet.com/servlet/AU), accessed April 1, 2004. Additional history provided by Larry L. Fabian, *Andrew Carnegie's Peace Endowment: The Tycoon, the President, and Their Bargain of 1910* (Washington, D.C.: Carnegie Endowment for International Peace, 1985).

9. "Associations Unlimited: Cato Institute" (2004) (www.galenet.com/servlet/AU), accessed April 1, 2004.

10. "Associations Unlimited: Center for Defense Information" (2004) (www.galenet.com/servlet/AU), accessed April 1, 2004.

11. "Associations Unlimited: Center for Security Policy" (2004) (www.galenet.com/servlet/AU), accessed April 1, 2004.

12. "Associations Unlimited: Center for Strategic and Budgetary Assessments" (2004) (www.galenet.com/servlet/AU), accessed April 1, 2004.

13. Center for Strategic and Budgetary Assessments, "CSBA Mission Statement" (n.d.), 1 (www.csbaonline.org/6About_Us/1Mission_Statement/Mission_Statement.htm), accessed August 15, 2003.

14. See James Allen Smith, *Strategic Calling: The Center for Strategic and International Studies, 1962–1992* (Washington, D.C.: Center for Strategic and International Studies, 1993), 1. For the founding date and an institutional history, see "CSIS at a Glance" (2003), 1 (www.csis.org/about/), accessed August 15, 2003.

15. Chemical and Biological Arms Control Institute, "The CBACI Commitment" (n.d.), 1 (www.cbaci.org/commitment.htm), accessed August 15, 2003.

16. For the origins of the Federation of American Scientists, see Donald A. Strickland, *Scientists in Politics: The American Scientists Movements, 1945–46* (West Lafayette, Ind.: Purdue University Studies, 1968). See also "Associations Unlimited: Federation of American Scientists" (2004) (www.galenet.com/servlet/AU), accessed April 1, 2004.

17. Global Security, "Mission" (n.d.), 1 (www.globalsecurity.org/org/overview/mission.htm), accessed August 18, 2003.

18. Henry L. Stimson Center, "General Information" (2002), 1 (www.stimson.org/about/), accessed August 27, 2003.

19. Heritage Foundation, "About the Heritage Foundation" (2003), 1 (www.heritage.org/about/about/), accessed August 19, 2003. For an institutional history, see Lee Edwards, *The Power of Ideas: The Heritage Foundation at 25 Years* (Ottawa, Ill.: Jameson Books, 1997).

20. Institute for Defense Analyses, "About IDA" (n.d.), 1 (www.ida.org/IDAnew/Welcome/history.htm), accessed August 27, 2003.

21. Institute for Policy Studies, "Organizational Overview" (n.d.), 1 (www.ips-dc.org/overview.htm), accessed August 19, 2003. For a highly critical assessment, see S. Steven Powell, *Covert Cadre: Inside the Institute for Policy Studies* (Ottawa, Ill.: Green Hill Publishers, 1987).

22. Jewish Institute for National Security Affairs, "JINSA Has a Two-Fold Mandate" (2003), 1–2 (www.jinsa.org/about/about.html), accessed August 20, 2003.

23. "Associations Unlimited: National Institute for Public Policy" (2004) (www.galenet.com/servlet/AU), accessed April 1, 2004.

24. National Security Archive, "About the Archive" (n.d.), 1–2 (www.gwu.edu/~nsarchiv/nsa/the_archive.html), accessed August 20, 2003.

25. Nuclear Control Institute, "About NCI" (2003), 1 (www.nci.org/new/about-nci.htm), accessed August 22, 2003.

26. Potomac Institute for Policy Studies, "Who We Are" (2002), 1 (www.potomacinstitute.org/who/), accessed August 22, 2003.

27. Russian American Nuclear Security Council, "Mission" (2003), 1 (www.ransac.org/About%20Ransac/), accessed September 10, 2003).

28. Terrorism Research Center, "About the Terrorism Research Center" (2003), 1 (www.terrorism.com/modules.php?op=modload&name=About&file=index), accessed August 22, 2003.

29. Wisconsin Project on Nuclear Arms Control, "About Us" (2002), 1 (www.wisconsinproject.org/aboutus.html), accessed August 22, 2003. For additional background information, see www.wisconsinproject.org/aboutus.html#profiles.

30. "Associations Unlimited: Woodrow Wilson International Center for Scholars" (2004), (www.galenet.com/servlet/AU), accessed April 1, 2004.

31. Woodrow Wilson International Center for Scholars, "About the Wilson Center" (2002), 1 (http://wwwics.si.edu/index.cfm?fuseaction=director.welcome), accessed August 27, 2003.

CHAPTER 11

Research Institutions and Think Tanks outside Washington, D.C.

A number of important national security–oriented think tanks and information services are located outside the Washington, D.C., area. Some of these organizations are part of universities with faculty members conducting research in national security policy to advance scholarship in the field or gain access to federal or commercial research contracts. Other organizations seek to provide tangible commercial benefits for their parent institutions, local facilities of government national security agencies such as the Department of Defense (DOD) or the Department of Energy (DOE), or neighboring defense industry businesses that have benefited from federal defense contracts earmarked for their agency, business, or university by politically astute and authoritative representatives and senators.[1]

■ Belfer Center for Science and International Affairs

The Belfer Center for Science and International Affairs (BCSIA) is part of the John F. Kennedy School of Government at Harvard University in Cambridge, Massachusetts. BCSIA "conducts research and disseminates knowledge in international security areas stressing the intersection of science, technology, environmental policy, and international affairs."[2]

BCSIA's website (http://bcsia.ksg.harvard.edu/) has biographical information about center faculty; descriptions of institutional programs regarding, for example, international security and science, technology, and public policy; recent news releases; and announcements and descriptions of upcoming events.

Publications produced by BCSIA personnel include the journal *International Security,* which is published by Massachusetts Institute of Technology (MIT) Press, with tables of contents, abstracts, and selected articles (2002–present) and a description of the monographic book series BCSIA Studies in International Affairs also published by MIT Press. Numerous publications by BCSIA scholars ranging from magazine articles to reports are also accessible, including *Prospects for U.S.-Russian Nonproliferation Cooperation under Bush and Putin* (2002), *Can Saddam Be Contained? History Says Yes* (2002), *Preventing Inadvertent War: Problems and Prospects for Sino-American Crisis Management* (2002), *A Changing Guard: The U.S. National Guard and Homeland Defense* (2003), *Nuclear Conflicts of the Twenty-first Century* (2003), *Russia: Grasping Reality of Nuclear Terror* (2003), and *U.S. Security and Military Cooperation with the Countries of the South Caucasus: Successes and Shortcomings* (2003).

Center for Civilian Biodefense Strategies

The Center for Civilian Biodefense Strategies (CCBS) is part of the Bloomberg School of Public Health at Johns Hopkins University in Baltimore, Maryland. CCBS works to prevent the development or use of biological weapons; decrease human suffering should such prevention efforts fail; provide independent critical analysis for governmental, national security, bioscience, medical, and public health policy makers; develop scenarios to help policy makers recognize the challenges involved in bioterrorism preparedness and response; and promote responsible uses of bioscience and biotechnology within the scientific community.[3]

The center's website (www.hopkins-biodefense.org/) provides biographical information about CCBS personnel, announcements of upcoming events, and fact sheets and articles about biological warfare agents such as anthrax, botulism, plague, smallpox, tularemia, and viral hemorrhagic fevers from publications such as *Journal of the American Medical Association (JAMA)*.

CCBS publications include all issues of its quarterly newsletter *Biodefense Quarterly* (1999–present), the congressional testimony of center personnel (1999–present), a recommended readings list, listings of articles written by CCBS personnel accompanied by links to some of these articles, and links to recommended government and academic biodefense websites.

Center for Global Peace and Conflict Studies

The Center for Global Peace and Conflict Studies (CGPACS) is a multidisciplinary program at the University of California–Irvine. It aims to expand scholarly, student, and public understanding of international conflict and cooperation. CGPACS has formed working groups on religion, ethics, and security; international environmental cooperation; international governance; and security and peace building. These groups host conferences and produce research products as part of their missions.[4]

Further information about CGPACS can be found on its website (http://hypatia.ss.uci.edu/gpacs/cgpacs.html), including events hosted, faculty biographies, descriptions of books written by center personnel, and the text of working papers such as "Humanitarian Intervention: The Early Years" (2000), "The Moral Basis of Humanitarian Intervention" (2000), and " 'Open Skies' for the 21st Century: A New Approach to Missile Defense and the Global Public Good" (2002).

Center for Infectious Disease Research and Policy

Located at the University of Minnesota–Minneapolis, the Center for Infectious Disease Research and Policy (CIDRAP) seeks to reduce illness and death from infectious diseases by engaging in interdisciplinary research and promoting the adoption of scientifically grounded best practices by medical professionals, public policy makers, and the public.[5]

CIDRAP's website (www.cidrap.umn.edu/cidrap/) includes links to websites about bioterrorism, anthrax, botulism, biosecurity, and chemical terrorism. Each of these websites features the text of pertinent laws and policies as well as writings by medical professionals and professional medical or public health organizations. The center's website features summaries of CIDRAP-sponsored meetings on topics such as enhancing food system biosecurity and bioterrorism and food safety.

Center for International Security and Cooperation

The Center for International Security and Cooperation (CISAC) is part of Stanford University's Institute of International Studies, which is a multidisciplinary entity focusing on research and training issues involving international security. CISAC originated from Stanford's interest in exploring concerns about international arms competition in the aftermath of World War II. Following the 1970 creation of Stanford's Arms Control and Disarmament Program, the university became one of the first U.S. academic institutions to allocate faculty and resources to study critical cold war issues and the unprecedented ability of the United States and Union of Soviet Socialist Republics to destroy each other.[6]

CISAC's website (http://cisac.stanford.edu/) has descriptions of ongoing research in areas such as chemical and biological weapons issues, ethnic conflict in the former Soviet Union, and strengthening security and stability in Asia; course descriptions; fellowship program information; a link to a nuclear terrorism website; and the newsletter *Monitor* (1999–present).

The website also has numerous reports including *China's Security Dilemma to the Year 2010* (1997), *High-Performance Computing, National Security Applications, and Export Control Policy at the Close of the 20th Century* (1998), *Chinese Perspectives on the South Asian Nuclear Tests* (1999), *The Geopolitics of Energy Development in the Caspian Region: Regional Cooperation or Conflict* (1999), *Communicating Nuclear Risk: Informing the Public about the Risks and Realities of Nuclear Terrorism* (2002), *People's Liberation Army Air Force (PLAAF): Shifting Airpower Balance and Challenges to India's Security* (2002), *Container Security Report* (2003), and *Effectiveness of Nuclear Weapons against Buried Biological Agents* (2003).

Center for International Trade and Security

The Center for International Trade and Security (CITS) is located at the University of Georgia. Established in 1987 as the Center for East-West Policy, CITS conducts research on political, economic, and security issues; international trade and technology transfer; and the relationship these issues have with terrorism, weapons of mass destruction, and U.S. preparedness.[7]

The CITS website (www.uga.edu/cits/) contains staff biographies; issues of *Export Control Newsletter* (2002–present); export control evaluations for countries such as China, Russia, Ukraine, and the United States; and an export control database featuring links to U.S. Bureau of Industry and Security and Office of Foreign Assets Control information resources. Additional CITS site content includes links to international nonproliferation regimes such as the Australia Group and Missile Technology Control Regime, descriptions of relevant University of Georgia classes and course syllabi, and citations to articles by CITS staff.

Center for Nonproliferation Studies

Located in Monterey, California, the Center for Nonproliferation Studies (CNS) is part of the Monterey Institute of International Studies. CNS was established in 1989, and its full-time staff includes more than sixty-five specialists and graduate research assistants in offices in Monterey, Washington, D.C., and Almaty, Kazakhstan. The center's mission is preventing the spread of weapons of mass destruction by training nonproliferation specialists and disseminating timely information and analysis.[8]

The CNS website (http://cns.miis.edu/) features staff biographies; listings and descriptions of organizational program areas such as the Newly Independent States (NIS) Nonproliferation Program, Proliferation Research and Assessment Program, and East Asia Nonproliferation Program with links to program websites; recent press releases; congressional testimony by CNS personnel; and links to resources about chemical and biological weapons and missiles as well as resources about the Middle East and Africa, NIS and Europe, and South Asia.

Numerous publications are also available through the CNS website, including articles from the scholarly journal *Nonproliferation Review* (1993–present) and the monthly newsletter *NIS Export Control Newsletter* (January 2003–present) and reports such as *Former Soviet Biological Weapons Facilities in Kazakhstan: Past, Present, and Future* (1999), *A History of Ballistic Missile Development in the DPRK [North Korea]* (2000), *Ballistic Missile Defense and Northeast Asian Security: Views from Washington, Beijing, and Tokyo* (2001), *The Chemical Weapons Convention Implementation Challenges and Solutions* (2001), *After 9/11: Preventing Mass Destruction Terrorism and Weapons Proliferation* (2002), *Future Security in Space: Commercial, Military, and Arms Control Trade-Offs* (2002), and *New Challenges in Missile Proliferation, Missile Defense, and Space Security* (2003). The Inventory of International Nonproliferation Organizations and Regimes website is accessible at http://cns.miis.edu/pubs/inven.

Columbia International Affairs Online

Columbia International Affairs Online (CIAO) is a subscription service that has been produced since 1991 by Columbia University Press. CIAO offers a wide range of international affairs scholarship, such as university research institute papers, resources from nongovernmental organizations, foundation-funded research projects, conference proceedings, books, journals, and policy briefs.[9]

Information about subscribing to CIAO can be obtained through its website (www.ciaonet.org/), and the service is available in many university libraries. The website has listings of editorial advisory board members; resources produced by organizations such as Africa Policy Information Center, Austrian National Defence Academy, Center for Strategic and International Studies, and International Security Studies (Yale University); and articles from journals such as *International Security, National Interest,* and *Strategic Analysis.*

CIAO subscribers also have access to reports and books from participating organizations including *The Second Nuclear Age* (1999), *Civil-Military Relations in Southeast Europe: A Survey of the National Perspectives and of the Adaptation Process to the Partnership for Peace Standards* (2001), *Violent Peace: Militarized Interstate Bargaining in Latin America* (2001), *An Indian Assault on Terrorism: The Military Option* (2002), *China's Rise and the U.S. Army: Leaning Forward* (2002), and *Iraq's Oil Tomorrow* (2003).

Declassified Documents Reference System

The Declassified Documents Reference System (DDRS) is a subscription service providing access to more than 500,000 pages of declassified documentary material covering the cold war, Vietnam War, and subsequent historical events. It contains documents from U.S. government agencies such as the Federal Bureau of Investigation, State Department, and White House, and it features materials such as cabinet meeting minutes, Central Intelligence Agency intelligence studies and reports, National Security Council policy statements, and presidential conferences.[10]

A number of larger academic research libraries subscribe to DDRS, which is produced by the Thomson and Gale subsidiary Primary Source Media. Information on subscribing to the service can be obtained by accessing www.galegroup.com/.

East-West Center

Located in Honolulu, Hawaii, the East-West Center (EWC) was founded in 1960, has a staff of 160, and operates with a $20 million annual budget. Its mission is serving as a national research and education organization to promote U.S.-Asia-Pacific relations and understanding through mutual research, study, and training and building an Asia-Pacific community with the United States as a valued partner.[11]

EWC's website (www.eastwestcenter.org/) provides information about center-sponsored events, biographies of the center's scholars, fellowship application forms, and the text of publications including *Democratic America in Northeast Asia: U.S. Strategy, Theater Missile Defense, and Allied Defense Relationships* (2002), *Changing Korean Perceptions of the Post-Cold War Era and the U.S.-ROK Alliance* (2003), and *Coast Guards: New Forces for Regional Order and Stability* (2003).

Foreign Policy Research Institute

The Foreign Policy Research Institute (FPRI) is located in Philadelphia, Pennsylvania, and was founded in 1955. Its institutional mission is ensuring that scholarly research affects policy developments advantageous to U.S. national interests. FPRI conducts research on the war on terrorism, South Asian nuclear proliferation, U.S. relations with countries such as China and Russia, the impact of religion and ethnicity in international politics, and how Western cultural identity affects the United States and Atlantic Alliance in their international relations.[12]

The website www.fpri.org/ has listings of FPRI-sponsored events (2002–present), information on named lecture series and the text of addresses, audio webcasts of selected presentations such as a March 4, 2003, address on Iraq by Kenneth Pollack, and descriptions of FPRI institutional components including the Defense Task Force, Ethnic Conflict Program, and Middle East Program.

Accessible publications include the periodical *Peacefacts: A Briefing on the Middle East Peace Process* (1995–present), table of contents from the scholarly journal *Orbis* (2002–present), and the text of FPRI's Bulletin commentary series (1995–present) with representative samples being *Why Nukes Still Trump: Deterrence and Security in the 21st Century* (2000), *Teaching Geography and Geopolitics* (2002), *What Our Children Should Learn about 9/11/2001* (2002), *The Spirit of the Antiwar Movement* (2003), *A Korea Peace Initiative* (2003), and *The Blackout and the Question of Homeland Security* (2003).

Hoover Institution on War, Revolution, and Peace

The Hoover Institution on War, Revolution, and Peace (HI) is located at Stanford University in California. Founded in 1919 by Herbert Hoover (U.S. president, 1929–1933), HI began as a specialized collection of documents focusing on the causes and impact of World War I. The institution grew to be one of the world's most comprehensive libraries and archives on twentieth-century political, economic, and social change. Beginning in the late 1940s, HI began recruiting scholars to use its documentary holdings, and the institution has evolved into a major research center focusing on domestic and international political developments and the role played by free markets in contributing to free societies.[13]

The website www-hoover.stanford.edu/ has descriptions of the institution's research programs in international rivalries and global cooperation, national security, and the Richard M. Scaife Initiative on the End of Communism. Accessible periodicals include selected articles from *Hoover Digest* (1996–present), the journal *Policy Review* (1995–present), and *China Leadership Monitor* (2002–present). Examples of national security books and reports are *Using Power and Diplomacy to Deal With Rogue States* (1999), *The Transnational Dimension of Cyber Crime and Terrorism* (2001), *War and Lack of Governance in Colombia: Narcos, Guerillas, and U.S. Policy* (2001), and *Our Brave New World: Essays on the Impact of September 11* (2002).

Hudson Institute

The Hudson Institute was founded in Croton-on-Hudson, New York, in 1961 by Herman Kahn, a noted futurist thinker and author of works such as *On Thermonuclear War*. Initially focusing on military issues, the institute shifted its emphasis to domestic social and economic issues. The institute moved its headquarters to Indianapolis in 1984 and retains a major office in Washington, D.C., and other U.S. locations. Currently the Hudson Institute is focused on serving as an innovative research and ideas source on a variety of public policy issues.[14]

Information about the Hudson Institute and its work can be accessed at www.hudson.org/. Material available includes descriptions of organizational components such as the Center for Central European and Eurasian Studies, Center for Middle East Policy, and National Security Studies program; information on past and upcoming events; press releases (2000–present); biographies of resident scholars; and speeches, congressional testimony, and op-eds by institute personnel.

Accessible publications include the institute's *Annual Report* (1999–present), selected articles from *American Outlook* (2002–present), and reports such as *An Alternative Strategy for the War on Terrorism* (2002) and *Oil, Terrorism, and the Problem of Saudi Arabia* (2002).

Institute for Foreign Policy Analysis

The Institute for Foreign Policy Analysis (IFPA) is affiliated with the Fletcher School of Law and Diplomacy at Tufts University and is located in Cambridge, Massachusetts. Founded in 1976, IFPA is an independent and nonpartisan research organization specializing in national security, foreign policy, political economy, and governmental–industrial relations issues.[15]

IFPA's website (www.ifpa.org/) features information about institutional activities including events such as the October 8, 2002, workshop "Missile Defense and Counterproliferation Planning on the Korean Peninsula: Exploring U.S. and ROK Responses and Options" and biographies of key staff. Descriptions are also provided of IFPA research projects such as "Planning for Long-Term U.S. Military Engagement in Central Asia," "Homeland Defense and Consequence Management," and "Northeast Asia after Korean Unification: Preparing the Japan-U.S. Alliance."

Accessible publications include the periodical *Security Issues in the Middle East* (2000–2002) and several reports including *Assessing the Cruise Missile Puzzle: How Great a Defense Challenge?* (2000), *Meeting the Homeland Security Challenge: Maritime and Other Critical Dimensions* (2002), *Homeland Security and Special Operations: Sorting-Out Procedures, Capabilities, and Operational Issues* (2002), *Northeast Asian Security after Korean Reconciliation/Reunification: Preparing the U.S.-Japan Alliance* (2002), and *Strategic and Operational Implications of NATO Enlargement in the Baltic Region* (2002).

John M. Olin Institute for Strategic Studies

Established in 1989, the John M. Olin Institute for Strategic Studies (JOISS) is part of Harvard University's Weatherhead Center for International Affairs, in Cambridge, Massachusetts. The institute conducts research on security and strategy to clarify security problems facing the United States and its allies. It seeks to educate and prepare national security and strategy scholars for employment in academe, research institutes, and government.[16]

The JOISS website www.wcfia.harvard.edu/olin/ has institute fellowship information, biographies of affiliated scholars, listings of current and alumni fellows, and papers from a November 2002 conference on the study of religion and terrorism. Publications provided include the institute's *Annual Report* (1999/2000–present), links to Weatherhead Center working papers (1993–present), and research papers such as *Swords into Stilettos: The Battle between Hedgers and Transformers for the Soul of DOD* (2000), *Multilateral Conflict Regulation: The Case of Kosovo* (2000), *Indivisible Territory and Ethnic War* (2001), and *Religion in the New Global War* (2002).

Johns Hopkins Center for Strategic and Advanced International Studies

The Johns Hopkins Center for Strategic and Advanced International Studies (SAIS) has its main facility in Baltimore, Maryland, and satellite facilities in Washington, D.C., Bologna, Italy, and Nanjing, China. SAIS was established during World War II to prepare future governmental leaders to cope with the new global responsibilities that the conflict's aftermath would thrust upon the United States. It became a part of Johns Hopkins University in 1950 and conducts graduate programs in international relations. SAIS offers a one-year master of international public policy degree program for mid-career business and government professionals from the United States and other countries.[17]

The SAIS website (www.sais-jhu.edu/) has institute press releases (1997–present), academic program descriptions, webcasts of selected events, and biographies of SAIS scholars. Accessible publications include the periodical *SAIS Reports* (2000–present), the scholarly journal *SAIS Review* (1995–present) with a link provided by Johns Hopkins University Press's Project Muse service, and research reports including *Japan's Military Capability in 2015* (1998), *Posing Problems without Catching Up: China's Rise and the Challenge for American Security* (2000), *The European Intifada: Demons Old and New* (2002), and *The Geopolitics of Hydropolitics: Negotiations Over Water in the Middle East and North Africa* (2003).

MIT Security Studies Program

Located in Cambridge, Massachusetts, the Security Studies Program (SSP) serves as a graduate research and education program affiliated with the Center for International Studies of the Massachusetts Institute of Technology. SSP offers curriculum focusing on grand strategy, technology, arms control, and bureaucratic political issues. Its faculty consists of engineers and natural and social scientists who strive to educate future scholars and national security policy makers.[18] Detailed information about SSP research and programs can be found at its website (http://mit.edu/ssp/). Access is provided to biographies of affiliated faculty and their research interests; information about guest lecture seminars; descriptions of courses including Defense Politics, Innovation in Military Organizations, and Technology and Policy of Weapons Systems; and course handouts and syllabi.

Retrievable publications include SSP's *Annual Report* (1998/1999–present), the research journal *Breakthroughs* (2000–present), and research reports and working papers including *Antisubmarine Warfare after the Cold War* (1997), *Urban Warfare: Options, Problems, and the Future* (1999), *Assuring Access and Projecting Power: The Navy in the New Security Environment* (2001), *The Helicopter Innovation in United States Army Aviation* (2001), *The Future of the Trident Force* (2002), *National Security Space Policy in the U.S. and Europe: Trends and Choices* (2002), and *The Political Science of Agent Orange* (2002).

National Bureau of Asian Research

Located in Seattle, Washington, the National Bureau of Asian Research (NBAR) is a nonpartisan and nonprofit organization conducting detailed and policy research on Asia, which it seeks to communicate to American and Asian policy makers.[19]

The website www.nbr.org/ has listings and biographies of members of the NBAR Board of Directors and Board of Advisers, information on NBAR-sponsored events (1990–present), links to Asian studies research organization websites, and information on organizational components such as the Center for Asian Security Studies, Eurasia Policy Studies, and Southeast Asian Studies.

Examples of accessible reports on national security topics include *Asian Reactions to U.S. Missile Defense* (2000), *Russia and Global Security: Approaches to Nuclear Arms Control and Nonproliferation* (2001), *The China-India-U.S. Triangle: Strategic Relations in the Post-Cold War Era* (2002), *Strategic Asia 2002–2003: Asian Aftershocks* (2002), and *NBR Analysis: Perspectives on the Future of the Korean Peninsula* (2003)

Nautilus Institute

The Nautilus Institute (NI) was founded in 1982, has a staff of twelve, and is located in Berkeley, California.[20] Its efforts are concentrated on solving problems in three areas: global climate change, the threat of nuclear war and global insecurity, and global economic activity surpassing ethical governance.[21]

NI's website (www.nautilus.org/) has links to institute programs, such as Energy, Security, and Environment and the Global Peace and Security Program, and links to government and other research institute reports on national security issues, such as nuclear nonproliferation. The website offers the ability to receive e-mail about NI events, and it has donor listings. Accessible reports include *The Changing Situation of the Korean Peninsula and Its Impact on Future Security* (n.d.), *The Matrix of Deterrence: U.S. Strategic Command Force Structure Studies* (2001), *Al-Qaeda's Nuclear Program: through the Window of Seized Documents* (2002), *Nuclear Free Zone on the*

Korean Peninsula: A Russian View (n.d.), Assessment of the North Korean Missile Threat (2003), and Plutonium Pineapples: Avoiding Awful Choices Over North Korean Nuclear Forces (2003).

Pacific Institute Studies in Development, Environment, and Security

The Pacific Institute Studies in Development, Environment, and Security (PISDES) is an independent nonprofit research organization founded in 1987 and based in Oakland, California. It describes its institutional mission as conducting public policy research and analysis in environmental policy, sustainable development, and international security with a particular emphasis on what it sees as connections between environmental policy and national security.[22]

PISDES's website (www.pacinst.org/) features information on institute programs such as Environment and Security and Water and Sustainability, press releases (1999–present), a "What's New" page, biographies of selected staff and board members, and information on supporting the institute's work. Examples of PISDES reports are *A New Vigilance: Identifying and Reducing the Risks of Environmental Terrorism* (2001) and *Fire and Water: An Examination of the Technologies, Institutions, and Social Issues in Arms Control and Transboundary Water-Resources Agreements* (2002).

Program in Arms Control, Disarmament, and International Security

The Program in Arms Control, Disarmament, and International Security (PACDIS) is an interdisciplinary research, teaching, and public service program located at the University of Illinois at Urbana-Champaign. Inaugurated in 1978, its primary interests encompass energy uses of technology and security; South Asia, Eastern Europe, and Russia; military history; and human rights. Funded by federal agencies, Illinois state government, and the private sector, PACDIS organizes seminars and conferences and produces publications featuring faculty and student research.[23]

The website www.acdis.uiuc.edu/ features information about the PACDIS research library holdings, links to South Asian national security research institute websites, descriptions of courses such as International War and Peace, faculty biographies and research interests, and descriptions of ongoing research activity. Accessible publications include the newsletter *Swords and Ploughshares* (fall 2002–present) and reports such as *End of Nuclear Testing* (1996), *Economic and Political Prospects of Nuclear Pakistan* (2003), and *Civil-Military Relations in Pakistan: The Case of the Recent Military Intervention (October 12, 1999) and Its Implications for Pakistan's Security Milieu* (2003).

Program on Science and Global Security

A part of Princeton University's Woodrow Wilson School of Public and International Affairs in Princeton, New Jersey, the Program on Science and Global Security (PSGS) was established in 1975. Its institutional mission is striving to provide a technical foundation for nuclear arms control, disarmament, and nonproliferation policy initiatives and informing U.S. and foreign scientists, along with their publics and governments, about nuclear arms control, disarmament, and assorted nonproliferation policy options.[24]

The PSGS website (www.princeton.edu/~globsec/) features Wilson School press releases (2001–present), descriptions of available courses such as Topics in International Relations: Protecting against Weapons of Mass Destruction, and links to websites of organizations supporting the program's work such as the Federation of American Scientists and the Ford Foundation. Accessible publications include articles from the scholarly journal *Science and International Security* (1989–2002) and tables of contents for more recent issues and reports including a reprint of the U.S. government publication *The Effects of Nuclear Weapons* (1977) and PSGS-produced works such as *The Application of Commercial Observation Satellite Imagery for the Verification of Declared and Undeclared Plutonium Production Reactors* (1999), *Conversion and Job Creation in Russia's Closed Nuclear Cities* (2000), *A Nuclear Tiger by the Tail: Some Problems of Command and Control in South Asia* (2001), and *Elementary Aspects of Noncompliance in the World of Arms Control and Nonproliferation* (2002).

Project on Defense Alternatives

The Project on Defense Alternatives (PDA) is located in Cambridge, Massachusetts, and was founded in 1991. Its institutional objectives are to adapt national and international security policies to what it sees as post–cold war era challenges and opportunities. It focuses on issues such as ensuring reliable and cost-effective defenses against aggression; (promoting military structures it contends will reduce international tensions, promote crisis stability, or decrease arms races; allowing significant military spending and armed force size reductions; promoting arms control and gradual international relations demilitarization; and placing increased reliance on collective security and global peacekeeping agencies.[25]

PDA's website (www.comw.org/pda/) has listings and biographies of advisory board and staff members and descriptions of research program areas including "The New Warfare" and the "New Calculus of War and Terrorism, World Order, and Cooperative Security." Links are provided to special topics such as "War Report," covering U.S. military operations in Afghanistan and Iraq; "Revolution in Military Affairs (RMA) Debate"; "Chinese Military Power"; and "Defense Strategy Review."

Full-text reports and commentaries are also available including *Building Confidence into the Security of Southern Africa* (1996), *Dealing with Uncertainty: The New Logic of American Military Planning* (1998), *German Defense Planning in a Crucial Phase* (2001), *Civilian Casualties in the 2003 Iraq War: A Compendium of Accounts and Reports* (2003), and *9/11 and the Meaning of Military Transformation* (2003).

RAND Corporation

The RAND Corporation began operations in December 1945 as Project RAND, a venture involving the Army Air Force and Douglas Aircraft Company.[26] Beginning in

May 1946, it issued the *Preliminary Design of an Experimental World-Circling Spaceship,* which sought to describe the potential design, performance, and use of man-made satellites. On May 14, 1948, RAND was incorporated as a nonprofit corporation in California and declared its institutional mission as being: "To further and promote scientific, educational, and charitable purposes, all the public welfare and security of the United States of America."[27] It is located in Santa Monica, California, and has offices in Washington, D.C., and other locations.

RAND has grown to become an arguably preeminent player in shaping national security policy research as well as performing public policy–oriented research in various social science disciplines. RAND has benefited from close relationships with and support from many U.S. government agencies—and especially the U.S. Air Force. The corporation is independent and nonprofit and seeks to present objective, nonpartisan, and rigorous research to address societal problems including those dealing with national and international security.[28]

RAND's website (www.rand.org/) has press releases (1995–present); lists of governmental, corporate, and academic supporters of the corporation's work; descriptions and website links for organizational components such as the Arroyo Center, which conducts research for the U.S. Army, the National Security Research Division, and its subdivisions the Center for Asia-Pacific Policy, Center for Middle East Public Policy, and Center for Russia and Eurasia; Project Air Force; and the International Security and Defense Policy Center. The website also has congressional testimony of RAND personnel (1999–present) and listings of RAND scholars arranged by name and subject specialty.

Examples of accessible publications are the journal *Rand Review* and its predecessor *RAND Research Review* (1993–present), reference publications such as *Selected RAND Abstracts: A Guide to RAND Publications* (1998–present), the text of selected RAND classics such as *Security Controls for Computer Systems: Report of Defense Science Board Task Force on Computer Security* (1979), and writings by influential strategist Albert Wohlstetter such as *Defending a Strategic Force after 1960* (1954).

RAND Corporation Arroyo Center publications accessible online include *Agility by a Different Measure: Creating a More Flexible U.S. Army* (2000), *Lightning Over Water: Assessing Options for Future Light Forces* (2000), *Keeping Military Pay Competitive: The Outlook for Civilian Wage Growth and Its Consequences* (2001), *Future Air and Missile Threats* (2002), *Improving Communications In Urban Warfare* (2002), and *Managing the Army's Arsenals and Ammunition Plants* (2003).

Center for Asia-Pacific Policy publications include *Taiwan's National Security, Defense Policy, and Weapons Procurement Processes* (1999), *Patterns in China's Use of Force: Evidence from History and Doctrinal Writings* (2000), *India's Emerging Nuclear Posture: Between Recessed Deterrent and Ready Arsenal* (2001), *Australian Foreign and Defense Policy in the Wake of the 1999/2000 East Timor Intervention* (2001), *The South Korean Debate Over Policies toward North Korea: Issues and Implications* (2002), *Terrorism and Asymmetric Conflict in Southwest Asia* (2002), *The Military and Democracy in Indonesia: Challenges, Politics, and Power* (2002), *Faultlines of Conflict in Central Asia and the South Caucasus: Implications for the U.S. Army* (2003), and *The Information Revolution in Asia* (2003).

Center for Middle East Public Policy resources include *Confronting Iraq: U.S. Pol-*

icy and the Use of Force since the Gulf War (2000), *The Future of NATO's Mediterranean Initiative: Evolution and Next Steps* (2000), *Iran's Security Policy in the Post-Revolutionary Era* (2001), *The Middle East in the Shadow of Afghanistan and Iraq* (2003), *A New Persian Gulf Security System* (2003), and *Turkish Foreign Policy in an Age of Uncertainty* (2003).

Center for Russia and Eurasia publications include *U.S. and Russian Policymaking with Respect to the Use of Force* (1996), *Conflict and Consensus in the Ethno-Political and Center Periphery Relations in Russia* (1998), *Ukraine and the Caspian: An Opportunity for the United States* (2000), *Assessing Russia's Decline: Trends and Implications for the United States and U.S. Air Force* (2002), *Russia and the Information Revolution* (2002), and *Beyond the Nuclear Shadow: A Phased Approach for Improving Nuclear Safety and U.S.-Russian Relations* (2003).

Project Air Force publications include *Airbase Vulnerability to Conventional Cruise Missile and Ballistic Missile Attacks: Technologies, Scenarios, and U.S. Air Force Responses* (1999), *Air Power as a Coercive Instrument* (1999), *NATO and Caspian Security: A Mission Too Far* (1999), *Supporting Expeditionary Aerospace Forces: An Operational Architecture for Combat Support, Execution, Planning, and Control* (2002), *Space Weapons Earth Wars* (2002), *Strategic Appraisal: United States Air and Space Power in the 21st Century* (2002), and *Mastering the Ultimate High Ground: Next Steps in the Military Uses of Space* (2003).

RAND's website contains information about ordering paper copies of its reports and lists academic and research libraries carrying RAND publications.

Ridgway Center for International Security Studies

Located at the University of Pittsburgh in Pittsburgh, Pennsylvania, the Ridgway Center for International Security Studies (RCISS) was established in 1988 as part of the university's Graduate School of Public and International Affairs. Named after U.S. Army General Matthew Ridgway, RCISS seeks to examine new security challenges facing the United States and the international community by training emerging policy analysts and scholars in international security. Key RCISS areas of emphasis are the growth of transnational criminal organizations involved in drug and weapons trafficking and people smuggling, proliferation of weapons of mass destruction, and regional conflicts stemming from declining state legitimacy, increased ethnic tensions, and traditional power and insecurity factors.[29] The website www.gspia.pitt.edu/ridgway/ features listings of RCISS faculty and their research interests, links to military and other national security–oriented websites and selected older publications including *Nuclear Terrorism: Sensational or Serious* (1995), *The National Guard in Disaster Relief Operations Hurricane Iniki: A Case Study* (1996), *Questions of How Much: U.S. National Defense Strategies, Budgets, and Force Structure 1940–1998* (1998), and *Please Impeach My Commander in Chief: Article 88 and the U.S. Military* (1999).

Stratfor

Stratfor is an Austin, Texas-based commercial global intelligence firm founded in 1997 that provides clients with geopolitical analysis along with country- and industry-oriented forecasts to assess possible risks and opportunities for their activities and missions.[30]

The website www.stratfor.com/ includes descriptions of research and data-gathering methodology Stratfor uses, biographies of organizational leaders, references to Stratfor analysis in print and electronic media, details about receiving the free *Stratfor Weekly* e-mail intelligence analysis, and subscription information.

Examples of free analyses accessible during September 2003 on Stratfor's website were *Iraqi Governing Council: A Window of Opportunity for the U.S.* (2003), *The Boomerang Effect: U.S. Aid Suspension and the Andes Drug War* (2003), and *Trouble in Uganda Could Threaten U.S. Relations with Sudan* (2003).

Triangle Institute for Security Studies

Established in 1958, the Triangle Institute for Security Studies (TISS) is an interdisciplinary research organization consisting of individuals and organizations at Duke University, North Carolina State University, and the University of North Carolina–Chapel Hill. TISS members are interested in national and international security issues involving the safety of individuals, groups, peoples, and nations. Its funding is derived from its parent institutions, private organizations such as the Ford Foundation, and governmental sources such as the Army War College. TISS is governed by a seven-member executive committee and conducts research and public outreach.[31]

The TISS website (www.duke.edu/web/tiss/) has listings of selected conferences and seminars, *Newsletter* issues (1995–present), an upcoming events calendar, and information about organizational research activities such as the study of war and civil-military relations. Additional information resources include summaries of past conferences and the table of contents of the book produced by the institute's civil-military relations study project, *Soldiers and Civilians: The Civil-Military Gap and American National Security*, published by MIT Press in 2001.

Notes

1. Works examining this and related phenomena from a variety of methodological and ideological perspectives are available. See, for example, John L. Boies, *Buying for Armageddon: Business, Society, and Military Spending since the Cuban Missile Crisis* (New Brunswick, N.J.: Rutgers University Press, 1994); James N. Dertouzos, *Defense Spending, Aerospace, and the California Economy* (Santa Monica, Calif.: RAND Corporation, 1993); Gregory M. Hooks, *Forging the Military-Industrial Complex: World War II's Battle of the Potomac* (Urbana: University of Illinois Press, 1991); Ann Markusen and others, *The Rise of the Gunbelt: The Military Remapping of Industrial America* (New York: Oxford University Press, 1991); Ann Markusen and others, *The Political Economy of Military Spending in the United States* (New York: Routledge, 1992); United States Congress, House Committee on Small Business, *Pentagon's Procurement Policies and Programs with Respect to Small Business*, 107th Cong., 2d sess., 2002; and U.S. Congress, Office of Technology Assessment, *A History of the Department of Defense Federally Funded Research and Development Centers*, 104th Cong., 1st sess., 1995.

2. Belfer Center for Science and International Affairs, "About BCSIA" (2003), 1 (www.bcsia.ksg.harvard.edu/about.cfm?program=CORE&pb_id=5), accessed August 27, 2003.

3. Center for Civilian Biodefense Strategies, "Mission" (2002), 1 (www.hopkins-biodefense.org/pages/center/mission.html), accessed August 28, 2003.

4. Center for Global Peace and Conflict Studies, "About CGPACS" (2002), 1 (http://hypatia.ss.uci.edu/gpacs/cgpacs.html), accessed August 29, 2003.

5. Center for Infectious Disease Research and Policy, "Mission and Activities" (2003), 1 (www.cidrap.umn.edu/cidrap/center/mission/), accessed August 29, 2003.

6. Center for International Security and Cooperation, "About CISAC" (n.d.), 1 (http://cisac.stanford.edu/about/), accessed August 29, 2003.

7. Center for International Trade and Security, "History" (2003), 1–2 (www.uga.edu/cits/about/history.htm), accessed September 3, 2003.

8. Center for Nonproliferation Studies, "About CNS" (2003), 1 (http://cns.miis.edu/cns/), accessed September 3, 2003.

9. Columbia International Affairs Online, "About CIAO" (n.d.), 1 (www.ciaonet.org/admin/about.html), accessed September 3, 2003.

10. Gale Group, "Declassifed Documents Reference System" (n.d.), 1 (www.gale.com/pdf/facts/ddrs.pdf), accessed September 3, 2003.

11. "Associations Unlimited: East-West Center," (n.d.) (www.galenet.com/servlet/ AU), accessed September 3, 2003.

12. Foreign Policy Research Institute, "About FPRI" (2003), 1 (www.fpri.org/about/), accessed September 3, 2003.

13. Hoover Institution, "Our History" (n.d.), 1 (www-hoover.stanford.edu/Main/brochure/history.html), accessed September 4, 2003.

14. Hudson Institute, "History" (2003), 1 (www.hudson.org/learn/index.cfm?fuseaction=history), accessed September 4, 2003; and Hudson Institute, "Mission Statement" (2003), 1 (www.hudson.org/learn/index.cfm?fuseaction=mission_statement), accessed September 4, 2003. For a biographical portrait of Herman Kahn, see Sharon Ghamari-Tabrizi, *American National Biography*, vol. 12 (New York: Oxford University Press, 1999), 336–339.

15. Institute for Foreign Policy Analysis, "About IFPA" (n.d.), 1 (www.ifpa.org/about/about.htm), accessed September 4, 2003.

16. John M. Olin Institute for Strategic Studies, "Homepage" (2002), 1 (www.wcfia.harvard.edu/olin/), accessed September 5, 2003.

17. Paul H. Nitze School of Advanced International Studies, "About SAIS" (2001), 1–2 (www.sais.jhu.edu/general/), accessed September 5, 2003.

18. Massachusetts Institute of Technology, Security Studies Program, "Welcome to the MIT Security Studies Program" (2003), 1 (http://mit.edu/ssp/), accessed September 8, 2003.

19. National Bureau of Asian Research, "Homepage" (2003), 1–2 (www.nbr.org/), accessed September 9, 2003.

20. "Associations Unlimited: Nautilus Institute" (n.d.) (www.galenet.com/servlet/AU), accessed September 9, 2003.

21. Nautilus Institute, "About the Nautilus Institute" (2001), 1 (www.nautilus.org/admin/about.html), accessed September 9, 2003.

22. Pacific Institute Studies in Development, Environment, and Security, "Overview" (n.d.), 1 (www.pacinst.org/overview.html), accessed September 9, 2003.

23. Program in Arms Control, Disarmament, and International Security, "Program Information" (2003), 1 (www.acdis.uiuc.edu/), accessed September 10, 2003.

24. Program on Science and Global Security, "S&GS Welcome" (n.d.), 1 (www.princeton.edu/~globsec/), accessed September 10, 2003.

25. Project on Defense Alternatives, "Mission Statement" (n.d.), 1 (www.comw.org/pda/about.html), accessed September 10, 2003.

26. RAND Corporation, "RAND's History: 50 Years of Service to the Nation" (2003), 2 (www.rand.org/history/), accessed September 12, 2003. For more detailed coverage of RAND's origins, see Martin J. Collins, *Cold War Laboratory: RAND, the Air Force, and the American State, 1945–1950* (Washington, D.C.: Smithsonian Institution Press, 2002).

27. RAND Corporation, "RAND's History," 2.

28. RAND Corporation, "RAND's History," 1–5; and Collins, *Cold War Laboratory,* 29–68.

29. Matthew B. Ridgway Center for International Security Studies, "About the Center" (n.d.), 1 (www.gspia.pitt.edu/ridgway/home/about/vision.asp), accessed September 12, 2003.

30. Stratfor, "About Us: Who We Are" (2003), 1 (www.stratfor.com/corp/Corporate.neo?s=ABO), accessed September 12, 2003.

31. Triangle Institute for Security Studies, "About TISS" (2003), 1 (www.duke.edu/web/tiss/about/about.html), accessed September 12, 2003.

CHAPTER 12

Foreign and International Government Organizations

Foreign governments and research institutions produce valuable national security information resources representing various political perspectives and research methodologies. They can influence international security trends and developments.

Unlike the United States, the three British Commonwealth countries of Australia, Canada, and the United Kingdom are parliamentary democracies, which means no separation of powers between the federal executive and legislative branches of government. For instance, the British prime minister holds a seat and represents a constituency in the lower house of the British Parliament, the House of Commons, while the U.S. president does not have a seat in the U.S. House of Representatives or Senate.[1] Like the United States, however, these three major English-speaking governments produce significant quantities of publicly accessible national security information, most of which is freely available on government agency websites. Public access is only partially diminished by the Official Secrets Acts in countries such as the United Kingdom that set guidelines for when specific forms of sensitive national security information may be declassified and publicly released. Australia, Canada, and the United Kingdom have many national security–related interests, and a variety of complex historical factors have shaped their perceptions of what are vital national security interests. Sometimes these perceptions are compatible with U.S. national security policy and sometimes they diverge. Generally, as of the early twenty-first century, their perspectives are more globally oriented, while the United States is focused on being militarily preeminent.

Freely available Internet resources also are produced by countries such as India, New Zealand, Singapore, and South Africa as well as by international governmental organizations such as the North Atlantic Treaty Organization (NATO), Organization for Security and Cooperation in Europe (OSCE), and the United Nations (UN).

Australia

Australian government publications focus on the country's close military cooperation with the United States, for example, in Operation Enduring Freedom (Afghanistan) and Operation Iraqi Freedom. The publications present Australia's perspectives on regionally significant strategic issues such as turmoil in neighboring Indonesia and on the importance of international sea-lane security.[2]

Department of Defence

Australia's Department of Defence is responsible for defending Australia and its national interests.[3] The department's website (www.defence.gov.au/) contains a biography of the sitting defense minister, ministerial media releases and speeches from 1998 to the present, links to Australian armed forces websites, and defense policy documents.

Examples of these resources include *Defence Annual Report* (1997-98–present), *Australian Defence Force Journal* (1997–present), *Defence and Industry Strategic Policy Statement* (1998), *Report to the Minister of Defence on the Collins Class Submarine and Related Matters* (1999), *Defence 2000: Our Future Defense Force* (2000), and *Australia's National Security: A Defence Update* (2003).

Royal Australian Air Force

The Royal Australian Air Force (RAAF) was established in 1921, and its members have seen action in World War II, the Korea War, the Vietnam War, and international peacekeeping operations.[4] The website www.defence.gov.au/raaf/ provides information about RAAF's leadership and operations including biographies, pictures of RAAF planes such as the F-111 fighter, training information, and a map with the location of RAAF bases.

Aerospace Centre

The RAAF's Aerospace Centre was established in 1989 at RAAF Base Fairbairn, in New South Wales. Its institutional mission is promoting understanding of air power's proper application within the Australian Defence Force (ADF). The centre develops and revises force doctrine and incorporates that doctrine into RAAF training and interaction with Australian society.[5]

The Aerospace Centre's website (www.defence.gov.au/RAAF/aerospace/) contains RAAF historical information, announcements of upcoming conferences, and publications such as *Royal Australian Air Force Air Power Manual* (1998), *A History of Attacks on Air Bases* (1999), *Kosovo Targeting—A Bureaucratic and Legal Nightmare: The Implications for US/Australian Interoperability* (2001), and *Space Operations: An Australian Perspective* (2001).

Royal Australian Army

The Royal Australian Army (RAA) was established on March 1, 1901, when 28,923 colonial soldiers were transferred from the British military to the new Australian Army. The troops were administered by individual Australian states until the October 22, 1903, Defence Act.[6]

The RAA's website (www.defence.gov.au/army/) contains press releases, salary rates, videos of Australian troops at work, regimental and historical information, and biographies of leading army officers. Publications include *Army Environmental Achievements* (1997), *Technical Regulation of Army Material Manual* (2002), and *The Fundamentals of Land Warfare* (2002).

Land Warfare Studies Centre

The Land Warfare Studies Centre (LWSC) is located in Canberra. Its mission is to promote wider understanding and appreciation of land warfare, provide an institutional and applied research focus to land warfare, and enhance professional and intellectual debate within the Australian Army.[7]

LWCS's website (www.defense.gov.au/army/LWSC/) provides reports and working papers such as "The Capacity of the Australian Army to Conduct and Sustain Land Force Operations" (1999), *From Desert Storm to East Timor: Australia, the Asia-Pacific, and "New Age" Coalition Operations* (2000), "From Legend to Learning: Gallipoli and the Military Revolution of World War I" (2000), "A Capability of First Resort: Amphibious Operations and Australian Defence Policy 1901–2001" (2002), "Information Operations during Operation Stabilise in East Timor" (2002), and "Australian Army Cooperation with the Land Forces of the United States: Problems of the Junior Partner" (2003).

Royal Australian Navy

The Royal Australian Navy (RAN) is responsible for fighting and winning in maritime environments as part of a joint or combined force, maintaining Australian sovereignty, and contributing to regional security.[8]

RAN's website (www.navy.gov.au/) includes leadership biographies, a virtual fleet tour, information on individual ships, recruiting information, information about RAN participation in Operation Falconer against Iraq, and documents such as *Report of the Board of Inquiry into the Fire in the HMAS Westralia on 5 May 1998* (1998).

Sea Power Centre

RAN's Sea Power Centre is located in Canberra and is responsible for promoting the study, discussion, and awareness of maritime issues and maritime strategy.[9] The

Seapower Centre's website (www.navy.gov.au/spc/) provides information about center activities and the text of many publications including *Australian Maritime Doctrine* (2000), *Struggling for a Solution: The RAN and the Acquisition of a Surface to Air Missile Capability* (2000), *The Development of Naval Strategy in the Asia-Pacific Region 1500–2000* (2000), and *Maritime Strategy and Defence of the Archipelagic Inner Arc* (2001).

Australian Intelligence Agencies

Australia's intelligence agencies perform intelligence operations in and analysis regarding areas of particular interest to Australian national security such as Southeast Asia. Some of their resources are publicly accessible through agency websites.[10]

Australian Secret Intelligence Service

The Australian Secret Intelligence Service (ASIS) serves as Australia's foreign intelligence collection agency. Its focus is obtaining and disseminating information on the capabilities, intentions, and activities of individuals and organizations outside of Australia that may impact national interests. It reports on defense, international relations, economics, international peacekeeping, and weapons proliferation threats. It is not a police or law enforcement agency and is legally prohibited from planning or executing paramilitary operations.[11]

ASIS was formed in 1952 but was not publicly acknowledged until 1977. It reports to the foreign minister and collects intelligence for needs determined by other federal departments. ASIS is governed by the 2001 Intelligence Services Act and reports to a parliamentary joint committee, which oversees other Australian intelligence agencies.[12]

The website www.asis.gov.au/ has descriptions of ASIS missions, employment requirements including selected forms, links to other Australian intelligence agency websites, and the text of publications such as *Intelligence Services Act* (2001) and *Rules to Protect the Privacy of Australians* (2001).

Australian Security Intelligence Organisation

The Australian Security Intelligence Organisation (ASIO) was formed in 1949 in a memorandum from Prime Minister Ben Chifley to the director-general of security.[13] Its institutional mandate is gathering information and producing intelligence to warn the Australian government of activities or situations endangering Australian national security. ASIO focuses on espionage, terrorism, politically motivated violence, and foreign interference. It reports to the attorney general.[14]

The website www.asio.gov.au/ has descriptions of ASIO's work providing security at the 2000 Sydney Olympics and 2002 Commonwealth Heads of Government meeting in Queensland, an overview of ASIO's 2001–2002 activities, employment information and requirements, and publications such as *ASIO Now: A Snapshot of*

Australia's Security Intelligence Organisation (2000), *Annual Report to Parliament* (1995-1996–present), and *Corporate Plan 2002–2006* (n.d.).

Defence Intelligence Organisation

The Defence Intelligence Organisation (DIO) is responsible for providing intelligence assessments to support governmental decision making and the planning and conduct of Australian military force operations. DIO analysis focuses on the Asia-Pacific region and covers strategic, military, political, economic, and technical areas.[15]

DIO's website (www.defence.gov.au/dio/) has listings of Australian support for international peacekeeping operations, job information, and *Defence Economic Trends in the Asia-Pacific* (2000–2001).

Defence Signals Directorate

The Defence Signals Directorate (DSD) is Australia's national signals intelligence and information security agency. Its key responsibilities are collecting foreign signals intelligence and providing information security for the Australian government and defense forces.[16]

DSD's website (www.dsd.gov.au/) provides career information, organizational history and descriptions, information on Australian supercomputers, computer security advisories, and the handbook *Australian Communications—Electronic Security Instruction 33* (n.d.).

Inspector General of Intelligence and Security

The Inspector General of Intelligence and Security (IGIS) is an independent agency that is part of the prime minister's institutional portfolio. Established by parliamentary statute in 1986, IGIS provides independent evaluation of Australian intelligence agencies and ensures that these agencies legally conduct their activities, adhere to ministerial guidelines and directives, and respect human rights.[17]

The website www.igis.gov.au/ includes the text of authorizing legislation, press releases, recruiting information, and publications such as *Annual Reports* (1986-1987–present) and *Bali Terror Attack of 12 October 2002* (2002).

Office of National Assessments

The Office of National Assessments (ONA) is an independent agency reporting directly to the prime minister. It provides analytical assessments of international political, strategic, and economic issues to assist the prime minister and other policymakers in policy formulation and planning. Reports are compiled from intelligence and open source material.[18]

ONA's website (www.ona.gov.au/) has an organizational chart, recruiting information, and publications such as the current budget statement and *ONA Corporate Plan for 2003–2006* (2001). Access is not provided to any ONA analytical reports.

Australian National Audit Office

The Australian National Audit Office (ANAO) provides audit services and independent analysis of governmental program performance for the Australian Parliament.[19]

The website www.anao.gov.au/ provides a variety of information resources describing ANAO's activities and the full text of its audit reports from 1995 to the present. Examples of national security–related reports are *Management of Australian Defence Force Deployments to East Timor* (2002), *Australian Defence Force Fuel Management* (2002), *Aviation Security in Australia* (2003), *Defence Ordnance Safety and Suitability for Service* (2003), and *Navy Operational Readiness* (2003).

Australian Parliament

Australia's Parliament is a bicameral legislature consisting of a House of Representatives and a Senate. Its membership includes sitting government ministers and is an important source for national security policy-making deliberations, debate, and decision making. Its website (www.aph.gov.au/) is a rich information resource for Australian national security policy and other aspects of Australian governmental activity.[20]

Examples of resources found on the website are the text of Australian laws, the text of bills from 1996 to the present, live webcasts when Parliament is in session, the browsable text of House and Senate debates known as *Hansard* from 1981 to the present, descriptions of parliamentary activities and committees, and listings of papers presented to Parliament from 1996 to the present.

Australian parliamentary committees conduct oversight of Australian national security programs and policies, and their webpages contain useful information.

Joint Standing Committee on Foreign Affairs, Defence, and Trade

The Joint Standing Committee on Foreign Affairs, Defence, and Trade (JFADT) reviews and reports on matters dealing with foreign affairs, defense, and trade that are referred to Parliament by the relevant departments or are brought up by the committee itself.[21]

JFADT's webpage (www.aph.gov.au/house/committee/jfadt/) has a list of committee members, hearing transcripts, and the text of reports from 1997 to the present including *Funding Australia's Defence* (1998), *Visit to Defence Establishments in Northern Australia* (1999), *From Phantom to Force: Towards a More Efficient and Effective Army* (2001), *Rough Justice? An Investigation into Allegations of Brutality in the Army's Parachute Battalion* (2001), *Visit to Australian Forces Deployed to the International Coalition against Terrorism* (2002), and *Review of Defence Annual Report 2001–2002* (2003).

Parliamentary Joint Committee on ASIO, ASIS, and DSD

The Parliamentary Joint Committee on ASIO, ASIS, and DSD (PJCAAD) is responsible for reviewing the expenditures of these intelligence agencies, their intelligence-gathering activities and operations, and legislation regarding these agencies.[22]

PJCAAD's website (www.aph.gov.au/house/committee/pjcaad/) has a roster of committee members, historical information, hearing transcripts, and the text of reports from 1998 to the present. Examples of these reports are *A Watching Brief: The Nature, Scope, and Appropriateness of ASIO's Reporting Activities* (2000), *An Advisory Report on the Australian Security Intelligence Organisation Amendment (Terrorism) Bill* (2002), and *Annual Report 2001–2002* (2002).

Parliamentary Library

The Australian Parliamentary Library and its website (www.aph.gov.au/library/) provide a number of services for Australian parliamentarians and the public about Australian governmental polices including those covering national security policy. The library's research papers are available from 1996 to the present. Examples of national security reports are *The Australian-Indonesian Security Agreement—Issues and Implications* (1996), *Thinking about the Unthinkable: Australian Vulnerabilities to High-Tech Risks* (1998), *Military Threats versus Security Problems: Australia's Emerging Strategic Environment* (1999), *Pressures on Defence Policy: The Defence Budget Crisis* (2000), *China and Taiwan: From Flashpoint to Redefining One China* (2000), *Internal Conflict in Indonesia: Causes, Symptoms, and Sustainable Resolution* (2001), and *India-U.S. Relations in a Changing Strategic Environment* (2002).

Canada

Canada is the northern neighbor of the United States and a NATO ally. As a bilingual nation, speaking English and French, Canada has been active in the Commonwealth of Nations consisting of former British colonies and in La Francophonie consisting of former French colonies. Canada is a part of the North American Aerospace Defense Command (NORAD) with the United States but has struggled to retain what it sees as some independence from U.S. national security policies. For instance, Canadian troops participated in Operation Enduring Freedom (Afghanistan) but not in Operation Iraqi Freedom. The Canadian military has sought to make a name for itself by participating in international peacekeeping operations around the world.[23]

Publications produced by Canadian government agencies on national security policy often reflect the divergent strains in Canadian thinking reflecting concerns over the country's willingness and ability to defend national sovereignty in the Arctic, the overall quality of its military forces, international military trends, and other subjects.

Department of National Defence

Canada's Department of National Defence (DND) and Canada's military (known as Canadian Forces) are responsible for protecting Canada's interest and values, defending North America in concert with the United States, and contributing to international peace and security.[24]

DND's website and the websites of the unified Canadian Forces are at www.dnd.ca/. Site contents include biographies of key officials, news releases, information about ongoing operations, and job requirements. Accessible reports and policy documents include *1994 Defence Policy White Paper* (1994), *Report on Plans and Priorities* (1999-2000–present), *In Service of the Nation: Canada's Citizen Soldiers for the 21st Century* (2000), *Annual Report of the Communications Security Establishment Commissioner 2001–2002* (2002), and *Board of Inquiry—Tarnak Farm* (2002), which was the report covering the 2002 friendly fire incident near Kandahar, Afghanistan, where four Canadian soldiers were killed by accidental U.S. F-16 fighter fire.

DND's website also has articles from the professional military journal *Canadian Military Journal* from 2000 to the present. Examples include "Asymmetric Warfare and the Use of Special Operations Forces in North American Law Enforcement" (2001), "Bosnia Revisited: A Recent National Commander's Perspective" (2002), and "Surveillance and Canadian Maritime Domestic Security" (2003).

DND Directorate of History and Heritage

DND's Directorate of History and Heritage (DHH) seeks to safeguard and publicize Canada's military history and heritage and to reinforce Canadian Forces identity.[25] DHH derives from a September 1, 1996, consolidation of functions within DND.

DHH's website (www.forces.gc.ca/hr/dhh/) provides links to Canadian military historical documents including accounts of Canadian participation in Operation Overlord. Accessible full-text publications include *Canadian Expeditionary Force, 1914–1919: Official History of the Canadian Army in the First World War* (1964), *Aerodrome of Democracy: Canada and the British Commonwealth Air Training Plan, 1939–1945* (1983), and *Canadian Military History since the 17th Century: Proceedings of the Canadian Military History Conference, Ottawa, 5–9 May 2000* (2001).

Canadian Forces—Air Force

Although organizationally part of the unified Canadian Forces, Canada's Air Force retains a separate identity. Its mission is creating and maintaining combat-ready air forces to meet Canadian defense objectives.[26]

The website www.airforce.dnd.ca/ provides details about the air force's organizational structure; information on individual units such as the 4th Wing based in Cold Lake, Alberta; historical background; news releases from 2001 to the present; and information on the Snowbirds aerobatic team. Accessible documents include *Defence Planning Guidance 2001 and the Air Force* (2000), *Chief of the Air Staff Planning Guidance* (2001), and *Out of the Sun: Aerospace Doctrine for the Canadian Forces* (2002).

Canadian Forces—Army

The Canadian Army, consisting of 19,500 active and 15,500 reserve forces, is responsible for defending Canada and North America. It also serves in peacekeeping missions in areas such as Afghanistan, East Timor, and Kosovo.[27]

The army's website (www.army.forces.gc.ca/) has descriptions of where Canadian Forces are deployed internationally, news releases, army leadership biographies, individual unit descriptions, and documents such as *The Army Strategy* (2002).

Canadian Forces—Navy

The Canadian Navy defends Canada's naval and maritime interests and engages in a variety of operational activities.[28] Further information about the Canadian Navy and its activities can be found at www.navy.dnd.ca/. Examples of accessible resources include news releases, career information, virtual tours and vessel descriptions for ships such as the frigate HMCS *Halifax* and submarine HMCS *Victoria,* and historical information focusing predominately on World War II.

Canadian Intelligence Agencies

Canada's intelligence agencies play an important role in Canadian national security policy. They also cooperate with U.S. and other allied intelligence agencies.

Canadian Security Intelligence Service

The Canadian Security Intelligence Service (CSIS) was created by parliamentary statute in 1984. Its institutional mission is collecting, analyzing, and retaining information on intelligence or other activities that may threaten Canadian security and providing security assessments for federal agencies except for those already conducted by the Royal Canadian Mounted Police (RCMP).[29]

The website www.csis-scrs.gc.ca/ contains the CSIS organic statute, an organizational chart, historical review of Canadian intelligence activities, employment opportunities, news releases, and a "What's New" page. Publicly accessible publications include annual *Public Reports* (1991–present), *Transnational Criminal Activity: A Global Context* (2000), *HIV-AIDS and the Security Sector in Africa: A Threat to Canada* (2001), and *Nuclear Weapons Proliferation* (2002).

Inspector General Canadian Security Intelligence Service

The Inspector General Canadian Security Intelligence Service (IGIS) was established in 1984 to monitor and review CSIS activities and provide advice to Canada's solicitor general on CSIS-related matters.[30]

IGIS's website (www.sgc.gc.ca/igcsis/index_e.asp) describes organizational activities and contains the publication *A Strategic Perspective for the Inspector General of CSIS* (2002).

Royal Canadian Mounted Police Criminal Intelligence Program

The Royal Canadian Mounted Police serves as Canada's principal law enforcement agency.[31] Its Criminal Intelligence Program manages criminal information and intelligence that allows the RCMP to detect and prevent crime with national security implications for Canada.[32]

The Criminal Intelligence Program website (www.rcmp.ca/crimint/ci_main_e.htm) provides descriptions of program activities and reports such as *Hackers: A Canadian Police Perspective* (2001), *Narcoterrorism and Canada* (2001), *Link between Al Qaida and the Diamond Industry* (2002), and *Marihuana Cultivation in Canada: Evolution and Current Trends* (2002).

Security Intelligence Review Committee

The Security Intelligence Review Committee (SIRC) serves as an external review mechanism for CSIS and as a tribunal to investigate complaints about CSIS. It reports to the solicitor general. Besides its investigative powers, SIRC since 1984 has been responsible for making recommendations on security clearance complaints involving federal employees or individuals providing goods or services to the federal government.[33]

SIRC's website (www.sirc-csars.gc.ca/) includes organizational background information, lists of present and past members, and procedures for filing complaints about CSIS. Accessible publications include *Annual Report* to the solicitor general (1984–1985 to the present) and title listings of reports prepared by SIRC. Most of these reports are classified as top secret or secret.

Solicitor General Public Safety

Canada's solicitor general is effectively Canada's preeminent law enforcement official having jurisdiction over the RCMP and CSIS. The solicitor general is accountable to Parliament.[34]

The main website is at www.sgc.gc.ca/. The public safety website (www.safecanada.ca/) provides links to Canadian government intelligence agencies and national and homeland security resources on topics such as border security, arms control, weapons of mass destruction, and military issues from CSIS and DND reports. The website also contains publications such as *The Canadian Security and Intelligence Community: Helping Keep Canada and Canadians Safe and Secure* (2001).

Canadian Parliament

Canada's Parliament is a bicameral legislature consisting of a House of Commons and a Senate. Numerous committees play important roles in national security policy formulation.[35] The Parliament's website (www.parl.gc.ca/) provides access to proposed bills, the transcript of debates from the House of Commons *Hansard* (1994–present) and Senate *Hansard* (1996–present), information about members of

Parliament, and links to committee web pages. Many Canadian parliamentary debates and committee hearings are webcast by Canada's Political Channel (CPAC) at www.cpac.ca/ and on the Parliament's website.

House of Commons Standing Committee on National Defence and Veterans Affairs

The House of Commons Standing Committee on National Defence and Veterans Affairs conducts oversight of Canada's defense budget and military forces. Its website (www.parl.gc.ca/InfoCom/CommitteeMain.asp?Language=E&CommitteeID= 3281&Joint=O) has a membership roster, hearing transcripts from 1995 to the present, and the text of reports including *Moving Forward: A Strategic Plan for Quality of Life Improvements in the Canadian Forces* (1998), *State of Readiness of the Canadian Forces: Response to the Terrorist Threat* (2001), and *Facing Our Responsibilities: The State of Readiness of the Canadian Forces* (2002).

Parliamentary Library

Canada's Parliamentary Library is responsible for giving members of Parliament comprehensive and reliable research and analysis on public policy issues in a timely fashion to support its legislative functions. The library also seeks to inform the public about Canada's Parliament.[36]

The Parliamentary Library website (www.parl.gc.ca/common/Library.asp?= Language=E&Parl=37&Ses=2) provides information about Canadian parliamentary activities, the text of reports such as *Arms Control and Disarmament* (1999), and reports analyzing specific legislation such as *Bill C-17: The Public Safety Act* (2002).

Office of Auditor General

The Office of Auditor General (OAG) is an independent office serving Parliament and Canadians. OAG conducts independent audits and studies of governmental programs to ensure that they are working effectively and making efficient use of their financial resources. OAG has carried out these responsibilities since 1878.[37]

OAG's website (www.oag-bvg.gc.ca/) provides news releases, organizational information and career information, and the text of statements made by OAG personnel and the auditor general to parliamentary committees. The website has annual reports to Parliament from 1981 to the present, Quicktime video excerpts from some of these reports, and coverage of national security–oriented agency programs and operations from these annual reports such as *Other Audit Observations—National Defence—Secret Commissions/ Kickbacks for Refueling Military Vehicles* (1999), *Status Report—Chapter 4—National Defence—NATO Flying Training in Canada* (2002), *Chapter 8—National Defence—Military Satellite Communication System Is Unused and Placed in Storage* (2002), and *Chapter 3—Canada's Strategy to Combat Money Laundering* (2003).

United Kingdom

The United Kingdom, during the British Empire's heyday, held dominion over nearly 25 percent of the world's territory and population. Although this imperial era is past, British global security influence remains significant because of its nuclear weapons arsenal, membership in the North Atlantic Treaty Organization, and close security cooperation with the United States. For example, the British military actively participated in Operation Enduring Freedom and Operation Iraqi Freedom, and the British government regularly consults with the United States on international security issues.[38]

Prime Minister's Office

The prime minister is the most powerful official in the British government and serves as the de facto commander in chief of British military forces. Although Parliament is consulted and partially involved in decisions to use British military forces, that power is essentially consolidated with the prime minister and his or her cabinet colleagues.[39]

Information about the activities of the sitting prime minister can be found at www.pmo.gov.uk/. Accessible are descriptions of the Prime Minister's Office, the text of speeches by Prime Minister Tony Blair from 1997 to the present, a separate archive of Blair speeches on Iraq, biographies of cabinet members, descriptions of the British legislative process, press briefings, and RealPlayer or Windows Media webcasts of the prime minister's responses to questions from House of Commons members from January 12, 2000, to the present. Additional site content includes policy documents such as *Iraq's Weapons of Mass Destruction: The Assessment of the British Government* (2002) and *Iraq: Its Infrastructure of Concealment, Deception, and Intimidation* (2003).

Cabinet Office—Intelligence Security Committee

The Cabinet Office is responsible for executing governmental business and coordinating security, intelligence, and civil contingencies issues to protect the United Kingdom against subversive challenges.[40] Further information about the Cabinet Office and its operations can be found on its website (www.cabinet-office.gov.uk/).

The Cabinet Office's Intelligence Security Committee was established in 1994 and provides parliamentary oversight of the Secret Intelligence Service (MI-6), the Government Communications Headquarters (GCHQ), and the Security Service (MI-5). The committee has nine members from multiple political parties and from both the House of Commons and the House of Lords. The members are appointed by the prime minister in consultation with the opposition leader. The committee reports annually to the prime minister on its work and periodically makes special reports to the prime minister. Despite the deletion of sensitive material, a significant portion of committee analysis can be found on its website (www.cabinet-office.gov.uk/intelligence/).[41]

Examples of publicly accessible works include the committee's *Annual Report* (1997-1998–present) and the *Government Response* to these reports, *National Intelli-*

gence Machinery (2000), *The Mitrokhin Inquiry Report* (2000), *Inquiry into Intelligence, Assessments, and Advice Prior to the Terrorist Bombings on Bali 12 October 2002* (2002), and *Intelligence Oversight* (2002).

Home Office

The Home Office (HO) serves as Britain's primary law enforcement agency and is responsible for internal affairs in England and Wales as well as dealing with national security issues such as immigration, passports, drug trafficking, and terrorism.[42]

HO's website (www.homeoffice.gov.uk/) has listings of outlawed terrorist groups; precautions individuals can take against terrorism when they are at home, at work, or traveling; British antiterrorism laws; and steps being taken to secure critical infrastructures such as communications and utilities.

Also available on the website are research reports and statistics from 1992 including *Business as Usual: Maximising Business Resilience to Terrorist Bombings* (1999), *Counter-Terrorist Action since September 2002* (2002), *Airport Security* (2002), and *The Decontamination of People Exposed to Chemical, Biological, Radiological, or Nuclear (CBRN) Substances or Material: Strategic National Guidance* (2003).

Ministry of Defence

The British Ministry of Defence (MOD) is responsible for defending the United Kingdom, its overseas territories, people, and interests and for strengthening international peace security.[43] MOD's modern institutional structure dates from 1964 and 1971 amalgamations of various British military institutions, although governmental administrative military agencies date from the 1546 creation of a Navy Board by King Henry VIII and the initial 1666 establishment of the War Office to cover land forces.[44]

MOD's website (www.mod.uk/) provides access to a variety of information resources on British military and defense policies. Materials available include information on key MOD officials, careers in the ministry's civil service and armed forces, and descriptions of component organizations such as the Defence Academy and Defence Scientific Advisory Council and links to their websites. Access is also provided to several MOD publications and reports including *Kosovo: Lessons from the Crisis* (2000), *Defence Acquisition* (2001), *Women in the Armed Forces* (2002), *Defence Industrial Policy* (2002), *The Government's Expenditure Plans 2003/2004–2005/2006* (2003), and *Operations in Iraq: First Reflections* (2003).

Royal Air Force

The Royal Air Force (RAF) was formed on April 1, 1918, from existing British military aerial activities.[45] The website www.raf.mod.uk/ contains materials about the RAF's history, mission, and activities. Website highlights include information on component organizations, base locations, career information, selected pictures and RealPlayer video webcasts, and publications including *British Air Power Doctrine*

(1999), *NATO Air-to-Air Refueling Document* (2000), and the scholarly journal *Air Power Review* (2000–present).

Royal Army

The Royal Army (RA) provides the land forces for the United Kingdom. Its organization is structured around its regiments, which are often geographic in origin and exert considerable influence on army operations.[46] The RA's website (www.army.mod.uk/) includes press releases from July 2001 to the present; career information; listings of international locations where British Army troops are stationed; the web pages of individual divisions and regiments such as the 1st UK Armored Division, Coldstream Guards, Queen's Dragoon Guards, and Scots Guards; descriptions of ongoing operations such as Veritas (Afghanistan) and Telic (Iraq); biographies of Operation Telic leaders; and pictures and descriptions of equipment including a sniper rifle, Chemical Agent Monitor—Level 3, and the Challenger main battle tank.

Policy documents and reports are also available including *Values and Standards of the British Army* (2000), *Military Courts Guide* (2002), and *Army Continuous Attitude Survey Questions* (n.d.).

Royal Navy

The Royal Navy (RN) is responsible for creating and maintaining an environment so British foreign policy and trade can grow. The RN maintains a force capable of deploying rapidly and sustaining operations to assert and protect British national interests.[47]

The RN's website (www.royal-navy.mod.uk/) has career information, descriptions of organizational components such as the fleet air arm and submarines, information on single vessels such as the aircraft carrier HMS *Invincible,* descriptions of ongoing naval activities and exercises, and interactive multimedia features such as "Do You Have the Strength of Mind to Become a Royal Marines Commando?" Access is also provided to press releases from 1999 to the present and reports such as *The Future Navy* (2000) and *Naval Strategic Plan: The Next Fifteen Years* (2001).

British Intelligence Agencies

British intelligence agencies are responsible for providing government officials with information about existing or emerging threats to United Kingdom interests. These agencies have complicated and sometimes controversial histories. The degree of information they produce about their work can vary.[48]

Government Communications Headquarters

Government Communications Headquarters (GCHQ) reports to the foreign secretary. Its institutional responsibilities cover signals intelligence (SIGINT) and information assurance. GCHQ's SIGINT activities help support governmental decision making in national security, military operations, and law enforcement and are crucial assets against terrorism and in preventing serious crime. Its information assurance functions strive to ensure the security of government communication and information systems from hackers and to assist officials responsible for securing critical infrastructures such as power and water from interference or sabotage.[49] GCHQ's website (www.gchq.gov.uk/) provides some information about agency activities including historical information regarding British signals intelligence, the names and accomplishments of important individuals in the field, procurement opportunities for private sector businesses, career information, press releases from 2001 to the present, and general descriptions of technology used by GCHQ in areas such as computer architecture and networking, software development, and telecommunication.

Security Service (MI-5)

The Security Service, commonly called MI-5, dates to the October 1909 establishment of a Secret Service Bureau as a means of protecting British naval ports against German espionage.[50] MI-5 responsibilities include protecting British national security against threats from espionage, terrorism, sabotage, and the efforts of foreign agents and powers to subvert parliamentary democracy by industrial, political, or violent means.[51] MI-5's statutory basis stems from the 1989 Security Service Act, which places it under the home secretary's authority; the 1994 Intelligence Services Act, which requires MI-5 to report to the Intelligence and Security Committee; and the 2000 Regulation of Investigatory Powers Act, which established officials to authorize communication intercepts and examine complaints filed against the service under the 1998 Human Rights Act.[52]

MI-5's website (www.mi5.gov.uk/) provides additional information about service activities including a statement of purpose and values, career opportunities, general description of its working activities, its accountability to other governmental authorities, historical information, myths about its operations, and details about information resources it has declassified.

Secret Intelligence Service (MI-6)

The Secret Intelligence Service, commonly called MI-6, answers to the foreign secretary. It began in 1909 with the Secret Service Bureau's establishment.[53] MI-6's responsibilities, according to the 1994 Intelligence Services Act, are to obtain and provide information about the actions or intentions of individuals and organizations outside the British isles that may threaten British national security.[54]

MI-6 does not have a publicly accessible website. However, information about some of its activities can be obtained from the Foreign and Commonwealth Office website (www.fco.gov.uk/), from the Cabinet Office's Intelligence and Security Committee, and through parliamentary debate transcripts.

National Archives—Public Records Office

The National Archives was created following the April 2003 merger of the Public Record Office and Historical Manuscripts Commission and serves as a focal point for researching British national history with particular emphasis on British government documents.[55]

The National Archives website (www.nationalarchives.gov.uk/) lists documents that have been publicly released including newly declassified documents, images from the 2003 exhibit "Secrets and Spies," information about accessible records and images from government agencies, and material on archival preservation of digital information.

National Audit Office

The National Audit Office (NAO) reports to Parliament on central government spending and conducts financial audits of governmental departments and agencies.[56] British governmental auditing is first mentioned in a 1314 reference to an auditor of the exchequer. The 1983 National Audit Act made NAO part of the House of Commons and gave the auditor general the power to report to Parliament on how economically and effectively government agencies used public funds.[57]

The website www.nao.gov.uk/ has an overview of NAO's work, press releases from November 1994 to the present, information on ongoing projects such as a report on battlefield helicopters, *Annual Reports* from 1999 to the present, and reports on individual government agency programs from the 1998–1999 parliamentary session to the present. Examples of NAO reports include *Ministry of Defence: Training New Pilots* (2000), *Ministry of Defence: Maximising the Benefits of Defence Equipment Cooperation* (2001), *Ministry of Defence: Helicopter Logistics* (2002), *Ministry of Defence: The Construction of Nuclear Submarine Facilities at Devonport* (2002), and *Ministry of Defence: Through-Life Management* (2003).

Parliament

Parliament is the United Kingdom's principal legislative body and a major source of British political, legal, and national security information. Parliamentary debates, particularly those that take place in the House of Commons, can contain useful information about British national security policy. During "Prime Minister's Questions," a weekly event, members of the House of Commons—the lower but most powerful house of Parliament—ask the prime minister questions about a public policy issues, including national security.[58] General access to Parliament's website is provided at www.parliament.uk/. Many parliamentary debates and committee hearings are webcast at www.parliamentlive.tv/.

House of Commons and House of Lords Debates

Parliament's website has the complete text of British parliamentary debates from *Hansard,* the printed publication containing House of Commons debates (November 1988–present) and House of Lords debates (November 1994–present). Participants in House of Commons debates include key British national security policy makers such as the prime minister, defence minister, and home secretary, who are all

House of Commons members. "Prime Minister's Questions," when the prime minister answers questions from members of Parliament, is also part of House of Commons debates.

Other useful general resources available on the parliamentary website are the full text of public laws from 1988 to the present, House of Lords judgments in legal cases from 1996 to the present, the text of bills being considered by Parliament and information on their status, biographical information on members of Parliament, and manuals on parliamentary procedure and the legislative process.

Parliamentary committees are also useful sources of national security–related information.

House of Commons Defence Committee

The House of Commons Defence Committee, consisting of eleven members, provides oversight of spending, administration, and policy conducted by the Ministry of Defence and related organizations.[59]

The Defence Committee's website (www.parliament.uk/parliamentary_committees/defence_committee.cfm) has a roster of current members, press releases, announcements of future meetings, the text of committee reports from 1997 to the present, and hearing transcripts from 1999 to the present. Examples of Defence Committee reports include *The Adaptation of the Treaty on Conventional Forces in Europe* (2000), *Draft Export Control and Nonproliferation Bill* (2001), *Threat from Terrorism* (2001), *The Future of NATO* (2002), *Arms Control and Disarmament (Inspections) Bill* (2003), and *Missile Defence: Government Response* (2003).

House of Commons Home Affairs Committee

The Home Affairs Committee is responsible for examining spending, policy, and administration of the Home Office and associated governmental organizations including the Crown Prosecution Service.[60]

The website (www.parliament.uk/parliamentary_committees/home_affairs_committee.cfm) includes a listing of the committee's eleven members, press releases and announcements of future meetings, hearing transcripts from 2001 to the present, and the text of committee reports from 1997 to the present. Examples of Home Affairs Committee reports on national security issues are *Accountability of the Secret Service* (1999), *Border Controls* (2001), *The Anti-Terrorism, Crime, and Security Bill* (2001), and *Extradition Bill* (2002).

House of Commons Library Research Reports

House of Commons Library research reports provide objective and factual information on a variety of public policy issues for British parliamentarians.[61] These reports are available from 1998 to the present and are accessible at www.parliament.uk/parliamentary_publications_and_archives/research_papers.cfm. Sample reports are *The Landmines Bill* (1998), *European Defence: From Portschach to Helsinki* (2000),

The Anti-Terrorism, Crime, and Security Bill Parts VI and VII: Pathogens, Toxins, and Weapons of Mass Destruction (2001), *The Anti-Terrorism, Crime, and Security Act 2001: Disclosure of Information* (2002), *Defence Statistics* (2002), *Ballistic Missile Defence* (2003), *The Conflict in Iraq* (2003), and *Iraq: Law of Occupation* (2003).

Other Foreign Governments

National security is a global concern with often diverse regional, cultural, and ethical aspects affecting each country uniquely.

India

India's importance in global national security developments is reflected by its 1998 nuclear tests, its ongoing security rivalry with neighboring Pakistan over the disputed region of Kashmir, its concern over and periodic intervention in Sri Lanka's civil war, and its contentious relationship with China.[62]

The Ministry of Defence website (http://mod.nic.in/) has information about India's military and national security policy. Accessible resources include descriptions of departmental organizational structure, recruitment and training information, coverage of defense research and development, and links to the Indian Armed Forces website (http://armedforces.nic.in/). Publications include the newsletter *Sainak Samachar* (2000–present), the ministry's *Annual Report* (1999/2000–present), *Reforming the National Security System: Recommendations of the Group of Ministers* (2001), and *National Security Environment: An Overview* (n.d.)

Israel

The national security information produced by the Israeli government reflects Israel's perspectives on the national security issues it confronts such as Palestinian hostility as manifested by suicide bombings, the ongoing security challenges it faces from its Arab neighbors, and the complexities of its relationship with the United States, which has its own security interests in the Middle East and a desire to achieve a lasting peace between Israel and its neighbors.[63]

The Israel Defense Force (IDF) website (www.idf.il/) provides historical information on IDF operations, news releases from 2000 to the present, the names of key IDF officials, a listing of chiefs of staff from 1948 to the present, information on IDF organizational components such as the Air Force and National Defense College, and a basic Israeli military doctrinal statement. Reports and statistics provided include *Civil Defense in a State of Emergency: Instruction for the Civilian Population* (n.d.), *Monthly Analysis of All Terrorist Incidents since September 2000* (2003), *In the Event of a Genuine Alert: Information on Civil Defense for the Family* (2003), and *The Battle in Jenin: The Israel Defence Force's Response to the Report by Amnesty International* (2003).

New Zealand

New Zealand is allied with the United States and Australia on most national security matters. Some concerns have been raised since the 1980s by New Zealand, however, about the maintenance of a U.S. nuclear weapons arsenal. The Ministry of Defence advises the government on defending New Zealand and its interests and is responsible for acquiring military equipment and for auditing and assessing New Zealand's military forces.[64]

The Ministry of Defence website (www.defence.govt.nz/) has materials explaining New Zealand's perspectives on national and international security issues including press releases, departmental organization information, and the status of military procurement activities. Accessible policy documents and reports include *Review of the Options for an Air Combat Capability* (2001), *Maritime Force Review* (2002), *Departmental Forecast Report of the New Zealand Defence Force for the Year Ending 30 June 2004* (2003), and *Defence Long-Term Development Plan* (2003).

Singapore

Singapore, an Asian island city-state, is an important center of international trade and serves geographically as a gateway to Southeast Asia, Indonesia and Oceania, and the South China Sea. Singapore was dramatically affected by World War II, as a result of its capture and occupation by Japan, and likely would be engaged in an international crisis or conflict involving Southeast Asian maritime areas.[65]

The Ministry of Defence website (www.mindef.gov.sg/) contains information on registering for national service, press releases, information about military training activities, links to Singaporean military branches, the text of relevant national statutes, a RealPlayer video entitled *The Singapore Armed Forces (SAF) Story* (2002), and publications including *Defending Singapore in the 21st Century* (2000) and the annual *Survival, Security, and Success* (2001–present).

South Africa

South Africa is sub-Saharan Africa's richest and most powerful nation. Located at the strategically important Cape of Good Hope, South Africa is a potentially important player in African and regional international security issues. It continues to make the transition from apartheid and must confront the impact of widespread HIV/AIDS (human immunodeficiency virus/acquired immune deficiency syndrome) infection.[66]

The Department of Defence website (www.mil.za/) has information on South Africa military policies, links to individual armed forces branch websites, the department's HIV/AIDS policy, and news releases from 2000 to the present. Access is also provided to reports including *Defence in a Democracy: South African White Paper on Defence* (1996), *Department of Defence Annual Report* (1997–present), *A Determination of South African Defence Requirements: A Vision for 2015 and Beyond* (2000), the monthly magazine *South African Soldier* (May 2001–present), and *Strategic Plan for Department of Defence 2002/2003* (2002).

International Government Organizations

International government organizations can be regional groupings of nations such as NATO with common international security objectives; entities such as the entire

UN, which seeks to have at least minimal influence on issues affecting localized or overall international security policy; and UN component organizations such as the International Atomic Energy Agency (IAEA), which seeks to prevent the spread of nuclear weapons.

European Parliament—Committee on Foreign Affairs, Human Rights, Common Security, and Defence Policy

The European Parliament since 1979 has been the legislative arm of the European Union (EU). Consisting of 626 members elected every five years, it passes laws affecting most Europeans in a variety of public policy areas from its main venue in Strasbourg, France.[67] The European Parliament's website (www.europarl.eu.int/) posts resources from its Committee on Foreign Affairs, Human Rights, Common Security, and Defence Policy.

The committee's oversight responsibilities encompass what it sees as the European Union common foreign and security policy including defense and disarmament policies, relations with non-EU countries and international government organizations concerning EU foreign and security policies, and other foreign and security policy matters.[68]

The website www.europarl.eu.int/committees/afet_home.htm has biographical information about the committee's 138 members and substitute members, a calendar of meetings and agendas, links to the text of EU security policy documents, hearing transcripts from 1995 to the present, and the text of committee reports from 1994 to the present. Examples of accessible committee reports are *Report on the Commission Recommendation for a Council Direction Authorising the Commission to Negotiate a Stabilisation and Association Agreement with the Former Yugoslav Republic of Macedonia* (2000), *Report on the Council's Fourth Annual Report According to Operative Provision 8 of the European Union Code of Conduct on Army Exports* (2003), and *Report on the New European Security and Defence Architecture: Priorities and Deficiencies* (2003).

European Union Common Foreign and Security Policy

The European Union Common Foreign and Security Policy seeks unified EU stances in the areas of foreign and security policy. The division among member nations such as the United Kingdom, France, and Germany over taking military action against Iraq in 2003 illustrates the difficulties of achieving such policy uniformity.[69]

The website www.europa.eu.int/institutions/cfsp/index_en.htm has links to the European Institute for Security Studies (ISS) and European Union Satellite Centre (EUSC), which began operations in 2002.[70]

Located in Paris, ISS responsibilities include researching and debating security and defense issues relevant to the EU, maintaining contacts with national security institutes within and external to the EU, providing analysis for EU officials, and developing transatlantic dialogue on security issues among the United States, Canada, and European countries.[71] The ISS website (www.iss-eu.org/) provides information on fellowship opportunities, institutional activities, and links to full-text research reports such as Chaillot Reports and Occasional Papers. Examples of these materials are *From Cooperation to Integration: Defence and Aerospace Industries in Europe* (2000), *The Southern Balkans: Perspectives from the Region* (2001), *Enlargement: A New NATO* (2001), *International Terrorism and Europe* (2002), *EU Cooperative Threat Reduction Activities in Russia* (2003), and *The European Union and the Crisis in the Middle East* (2003).

EUSC is located in Torrejon, Spain, near Madrid, and its institutional responsibilities involve analyzing and exploiting geospatial satellite imagery to support EU common foreign and security policy objectives.[72] EUSC's website (www.eusc.org/) contains information about the centre's mission, job openings, news releases, and information on courses it offers such as Interpreting Nuclear Installations Using Commercial Satellite Imagery. It does not offer any reports on its work, although one accessible document is *Staff Regulations of the European Union Satellite Centre* (2002) taken from the EU's *Official Journal*.

North Atlantic Treaty Organization

The North Atlantic Treaty Organization is located in Brussels, Belgium. It is a military alliance whose members include the United States, Canada, and a growing number of European countries dedicated to preserving their national security and commitments to democratic governance. NATO was established in 1949.[73]

Detailed information about NATO activities can be found at www.nato.int/, including historical information on the alliance's formation, information on ongoing NATO activities in Afghanistan, and Windows Media video clips. Accessible publications include the text of the original *North Atlantic Treaty* (1949) and the texts of accession of new NATO members such as *Protocol of the North Atlantic Treaty on the Accession of the Republic of Lithuania* (2003). Additional information resources and documents are the periodical *NATO Review* (1991–present), *NATO Handbook* (2001), *NATO-Ukraine Action Plan* (2002), *The Disposal of Albania's Anti-Personnel Mine Stockpiles* (2003), *The Prague Summit and NATO's Transformation* (2003), and the text of all NATO ministerial summits from 1949 to the present.

Organization for Security and Co-operation in Europe

The Organization for Security and Co-operation in Europe is headquartered in Vienna, Austria, and consists of fifty-five member nations from Central Asia, Europe, and North America. OSCE's purpose is serving as an early warning mechanism to prevent conflict between member countries through programs in arms control, preventive diplomacy, confidence- and security-building measures, human rights, election monitoring, and various other activities.[74]

The website www.osce.org/ provides information about OSCE and its work. Accessible resources include Quicktime and RealPlayer videos about OSCE activities, descriptions of ongoing projects, and publications such as *Annual Report on OSCE Activities* (1993–present) and *Handbook* (2002).

United Nations

The United Nations strives to play a significant role in international security development, deploying its peacekeeping forces to international crisis areas. Its subsidiary institutions such as the Security Council and International Atomic Energy Agency attempt to influence international security issues.[75]

The overall UN website (www.un.org/) provides links to United Nations component part websites; a news center featuring press releases, webcasts, and information on international crisis areas such as Iraq and Liberia; the text of briefings by the secretary general and other leading officials; documents from many UN agencies; and subject-specific resource links such as peace and security, human rights, and international law.

Paper copies of many UN documents can be found in UN depositories globally. The United Nations Dag Hammarskjold Library at www.un.org/Depts/dhl/deplib/countries/ has a list of these facilities. Access to UN information resources is also provided by commercial services such as Readex Corporation's *Access UN*.

Security Council

The UN Security Council is responsible for maintaining international peace and security according to UN principles; investigating disputes that might cause international friction; recommending solutions to such disputes; determining what actions, if any, are appropriate against international aggressors; and taking military actions against such aggressors. The controversy over the lead-up to the U.S. war against Iraq, which began in 2003, demonstrates the Security Council's weakness in promoting or enforcing its vision of international security.[76]

The Security Council's website (www.un.org/Docs/sc/) contains materials describing the council's mission and activities, such as the text of the UN's organic document, the *United Nations Charter;* current-year country reports to the Security Council describing security threats they face; information on the council's organizational structure; the council's *Annual Report 2001–2002* (2002); and selected Security Council meeting webcasts (2001–present). Additional materials include council meeting transcripts (1994–present), the text of all Security Council resolutions (1946–present), Security Council presidential press statements (2001–present), and council mission reports including *Report of the Security Council Mission to East Timor and Indonesia* (2000), *Report of the Security Council Mission to Kosovo and Belgrade, Federal Republic of Yugoslavia* (2002), and *Report of the Security Council Mission to West Africa* (2003).

Security Council Counterterrorism Committee

The Security Council's Counterterrorism Committee was established on September 28, 2001, by Security Council Resolution 1373, which condemned the September 11, 2001, terrorist attacks. The committee, consisting of representatives from the council's fifteen member states, monitors implementation of the resolution and seeks to increase the capabilities of nations to fight terrorism.[77]

The website www.un.org/Docs/sc/committees/1373/ contains information about the committee's establishment, information on how countries affected by terrorism can receive technical and other assistance, guidelines on working with experts and the Security Council to combat terrorism, and listings of existing international antiterrorism conventions. Reports from several nations describe their antiterrorism activities.

United Nations Monitoring, Inspection, and Verification Commission

The United Nations Monitoring, Inspection, and Verification Commission (UNMOVIC) was created from UN Security Council Resolution 1284 on December 17, 1999. Its purpose was continuing the work of the former United Nations Special Commission (UNSCOM) to disarm Iraq's weapons of mass destruction and ensure Iraqi adherence to its agreements with the UN to not produce such prohibited weapons.[78]

The website www.unmovic.org/ provides listings of UNMOVIC leaders and key personnel, the website of its predecessor organization (UNSCOM), and the text of press briefings made in Baghdad, Iraq, from November 2002 to March 2003. A number of UNMOVIC reports are provided including *First Quarterly Report of the Executive Chairman* (2000), *Organizational Plan for the United Nations Monitoring, Verification, and Inspection Commission* (2000), the text of UNMOVIC briefings to the UN Security Council during 2002–2003, *Twelfth Quarterly Report of the Executive Chairman* (2003), *Draft Work Programme* (2003), and *Unresolved Disarmament Issues: Iraq's Proscribed Weapons Programmes* (2003).

International Atomic Energy Agency

The International Atomic Energy Agency (IAEA) is headquartered in Vienna, Austria, and assists member UN nations in developing nuclear energy and technology for peaceful uses, developing nuclear safety standards, ensuring through its inspection system that member nations are complying with their obligations under the Nuclear Nonproliferation Treaty (NPT) and other nonproliferation agreements.[79]

IAEA's website (www.iaea.org/worldatom/) provides information resources such as press releases, employment opportunities, selected Quicktime and RealPlayer multimedia clips, information on IAEA inspection activities in Iraq and North Korea, and the text of international nuclear legal agreements such as the *Nonproliferation Treaty* (1970). Accessible full-text publications include *IAEA Safeguards Glossary* (2001), *Regulatory Inspection of Nuclear Facilities and Enforcement by the Regulatory Body: Safety Guidance* (2002), *Country Nuclear Power Profiles* (2002), and *Handbook on Nuclear Law* (2003).

Department for Disarmament Affairs

The UN's Department for Disarmament Affairs (DDA) seeks to promote international disarmament by assisting the UN secretary general, member states, and other groups in the elimination of weapons of mass destruction, illegal arms trafficking, and growing weapons stockpiles.[80]

The website http://disarmament.un.org/dda.htm contains information about DDA's organizational structure, links to pertinent UN General Assembly resolutions and decisions from 1997 to the present, and descriptions of organizational activities in areas such as weapons of mass destruction, conventional arms, terrorism, and regional disarmament in, for example, Africa, North and South America, and Asia. Accessible publications include excerpts from *UN Disarmament Yearbook* (1997–present) and the complete text of the quarterly *DDA Update* (October 1998–present) along with reports such as *Disarmament: A Basic Guide* (2001), *Symposium on Terrorism and Disarmament* (2001), the annual *United Nations Register of Conventional Arms* (2001–present) and *Objective Information on Military Matters, Including Transparency of Military Expenditures* (2001–present), and *A Disarmament Agenda for the 21st Century* (2002).

Organisation for the Prohibition of Chemical Weapons

The Organisation for Prohibition of Chemical Weapons (OPCW) is located in The Hague, Netherlands, and is responsible for implementing provisions of the 1992 Chemical Weapons Convention (CWC). The CWC seeks to eliminate chemical weapons from world military arsenals and produce international cooperation in chemistry for peaceful purposes to enhance international security, stability, and economic development.[81]

OPCW's website (www.opcw.org/) has historical information on chemical weapons development and international disarmament efforts, information on the CWC's projected international chemical weapons destruction timetable, a review of CWC's weapons inspection and verification process, speeches by the CWC director-general, and press release from 1997 to the present.

Available publications include the texts of the *Biological Weapons Convention* (1978) and CWC (1992) as well as other international disarmament agreements, legal documents such as *An Integrated Approach to National Implementing Legislation: Model Act Developed by the Organisation of Eastern Caribbean States* (2000), and information on the number of countries that have ratified the CWC.

United Nations Institute for Disarmament Research

The United Nations Institute Disarmament Research (UNIDIR) is located in Geneva, Switzerland. It serves as an intergovernmental entity within the UN conducting research on disarmament and security to assist the international community in its disarmament thoughts, decisions, and policy making.[82]

UNIDIR's website (www.unidir.org/) includes descriptions of research activity in areas such as land mines, missiles, peacekeeping, and small arms; organizational information; and databases such as the *UN Small Arms Conference* and a listing of international disarmament research institutes and their locations. Accessible full-text publications include older issues of the periodical *Disarmament Forum* (1999–present) and reports including *Missile Defence, Deterrence, and Arms Control: Contradictory Aims or Compatible Goals?* (2002) and *The Scope and Implications of a*

Tracing Mechanism for Small Arms and Light Weapons (2003). Excerpts are also provided from other publications including *Disarmament—Rethinking the Price Tag: A Methodological Inquiry into the Costs and Benefits of Arms Control* (2002) and *Internal Conflict and Regional Security in South Asia: Approaches, Perspectives, and Policies* (2003). A catalog listing of UNIDIR publications is also provided.

Notes

1. For an overview of parliamentary governmental structure, see Sydney Dawson Bailey, *British Parliamentary Democracy* (Boston: Houghton Mifflin, 1971).

2. Examples of works stressing comprehensive examinations of Australian national security history and policy include Carl Oatley, *Australia's National Security Framework: A Look to the Future* (Canberra, Australia: Australian Defence Studies Centre, 2000); Peter Dennis and others, *The Oxford Companion to Australian Military History* (Melbourne, Australia: Oxford University Press, 1995); David M. Horner and others, *The Australian Centenary History of Defence*, 7 vols. (Melbourne, Australia: Oxford University Press, 2001); and Xavier Pons, *A Sheltered Land* (St. Leonards, New South Wales: Allen and Unwin, 1994).

3. Australia, Department of Defence, "Homepage" (n.d.), 1 (www.defence.gov.au/), accessed October 30, 2003.

4. Royal Australian Air Force, "Genesis of the Air Force" (n.d.), 1 (www.defence.gov.au/raaf/history/air_force_fought/genesis.htm), accessed October 30, 2003. For additional background, see Alan Stephens, *Power Plus Attitude: Ideas, Strategy, and Doctrine in the Royal Australian Air Force* (Canberra, Australia: AGPS Press, 1992); and Alan Stephens, *The Australian Centenary History of Defence*, Vol. 2: *The Royal Australian Air Force* (South Melbourne, Australia: Oxford University Press, 2001).

5. Royal Australian Air Force, Aerospace Centre, "About the Aerospace Centre" (n.d.), 1 (www.defence.gov.au/RAAF/aerospace/about.htm), accessed October 30, 2003.

6. For historical and contemporary coverage of Australian Army developments, see Royal Australian Army, Army History Unit, "Australian Army-History" (n.d.), 1 (www.defence.gov.au/army/ahu/history/federation.htm), accessed October 30, 2003; Jeffrey Grey, *The Australian Centenary History of Defence*, Vol. 1: *The Australian Army* (Melbourne, Australia: Oxford University Press, 2001); David Horner, ed., *The Army and the Future: Land Forces in Australia and South-East Asia* (Canberra, Australia: Directorate of Departmental Publications, Defence Centre for Director of Army Activities and Public Affairs, 1993); John L. Mordike, *An Army for a Nation: A History of Australian Military Developments, 1880–1914* (North Sydney, Australia: Allen and Unwin, 1992); Michael Evans, *Forward from the Past: The Development of Australian Army Doctrine, 1972–Present* (Canberra, Australia: Land Warfare Studies Centre, 1999); Australia, Directorate of Army Public Affairs, *The Australian Army: A Brief History*, rev. ed. (Canberra, Australia: Defence Publishing Service, 2000); Albert Palazzo, *The Australian Army: A History of Its Organisation 1901–2001* (South Melbourne, Australia: Oxford University Press, 2001); and John G. Caligari, *The Army's Capacity to Defend Australia Offshore: The Need for a Joint Approach* (Canberra, Australia: Australian National University, Strategic and Defence Studies Centre, 2000).

7. Australian Army, Land Warfare Studies Centre, "Our Charter" (n.d.), 1 (www.defence.gov.au/army/LWSC/mainpages/about.htm), accessed October 30, 2003.

8. For additional historical background, see Royal Australian Navy, "Royal Australian Navy" (n.d.), 1 (www.navy.gov.au/), accessed October 30, 2003. See also David M. Stevens, *The Australian Centenary History of Defence*, Vol. 3: *The Royal Australian Navy* (Melbourne, Australia: Oxford University Press, 2001); David Stevens and John Reeve, eds., *Southern Trident:*

Strategy, History, and the Rise of Australian Naval Power (Crows Nest, New South Wales: Allen and Unwin, 2001); Navy Public Relations, *History of the Royal Australian Navy* (Sydney, Australia: Navy Public Relations, 1990); Thomas R. Frame, *Pacific Partners: A History of Australian-American Naval Relations* (Sydney, Australia: Hodder and Stoughton, 1992); and John Bach, *The Australia Station: A History of the Royal Navy in the South West Pacific, 1821–1913* (Kensington, New South Wales: New South Wales University Press, 1986).

9. Royal Australian Navy, Sea Power Centre, "Defence Instructions (Navy) ADMIN 3-103" (n.d.), 1–2 (www.navy.gov.au/spc/orgstrucmission.htm), accessed October 30, 2003.

10. Background on Australian intelligence can be found in Jeffrey Richelson and Desmond Ball, *The Ties That Bind: Intelligence Cooperation between the UKUSA Countries—The United Kingdom, the United States of America, Canada, Australia, and New Zealand* (Sydney, Australia: George Allen and Unwin, 1985); Anthony Bergin and Robert Hall, eds., *Intelligence and Australian National Security* (Canberra, Australia: Australian Defence Studies Centre, 1994); and Wayne Gobert, *The Origins of Australian Diplomatic Intelligence in Asia, 1933–1941* (Canberra, Australia: Australian National University, Strategic and Defence Studies Centre, 1992).

11. Australian Secret Intelligence Service, "About ASIS" (2003), 1–2 (www.asis.gov.au/aboutasis.html), accessed October 30, 2003.

12. Australian Secret Intelligence Service, "About ASIS," 2–3.

13. See Australian Security Intelligence Organisation, "About ASIO: Prime Minister's Memorandum to the Director-General of Security, Being a Directive for the Establishment and Maintenance of a Security Service" (2003). 1 (www.asio.gov.au/About/Timeline/Content/Directive.htm), accessed October 30, 2003; and Frank Cain, *The Australian Security Intelligence Organization: An Unofficial History* (Richmond, Victoria, Australia: Spectrum Publications, 1994).

14. Australian Security Intelligence Organisation, "What Is ASIO" (2003), 1 (www.asio.gov.au/About/Content/what.htm), accessed October 30, 2003.

15. Australia, Defence Intelligence Organisation, "DIO: About DIO" (n.d.), 1 (www.defence.gov.au/dio/maindx.htm), accessed October 30, 2003.

16. Australia, Defence Signals Directorate, "About DSD" (n.d.), 1 (www.dsd.gov.au/about_dsd/), accessed October 30, 2003.

17. Australia Inspector General of Intelligence and Security, "About IGIS" (n.d.), 1 (www.igis.gov.au/about.html), accessed October 30, 2003.

18. Australia, Office of National Assessments, "About ONA" (n.d.), 1 (www.ona.gov.au/), accessed October 30, 2003.

19. Australian National Audit Office, "About Us" (2000), 1 (www.anao.gov.au/WebSite.nsf/Lookup%20CorporateDocuments/About%20US!OpenDocument), accessed October 30, 2003. For an organizational history, see John Wanna, Christine Ryan, and Chew Ng, *From Accounting to Accountability: A Centenary History of the Australian National Audit Office* (St. Leonard's, New South Wales: Allen and Unwin, 2001).

20. For background, see Gordon Stanley Reid and Martyn Forrest, *Australia's Commonwealth Parliament 1901–1988: Ten Perspectives* (Melbourne, Australia: Melbourne University Press, 1988).

21. Australia, Parliament, Joint Standing Committee on Foreign Affairs, Defence, and Trade, "Committee Establishment, Role, and History" (2002), 1 (www.aph.gov.au/house/committee/jfadt/establ.htm), accessed October 30, 2003.

22. Australia, Parliament, Parliamentary Joint Committee on ASIO, ASIS, and DSD, "Committee Establishment, Role, and History" (2002), 1 (www.aph.gov.au/house/committee/pjcaad/role.htm), accessed October 30, 2003.

23. Examples of publications examining various aspects of Canadian national security policy include John Gellner, *The Defence of Canada: Requirements, Capabilities, and the National Will* (Toronto, Canada: Canadian International Institute of International Affairs, 1985); Nathaniel French Caldwell, *Arctic Leverage: Canadian Sovereignty and Security* (New York: Praeger, 1990); Ann Denholm Crosby, *Dilemmas in Defence Decision-Making: Constructing Canada's Role in NORAD, 1958–96* (New York: St. Martin's Press, 1997); John A. English, *Lament for an Army: The Decline of Canadian Military Professionalism* (Concord, Ontario, Canada: Irwin, 1998); Greg Donaghy, ed., *Canada and the Early Cold War, 1943–1957* (Ottawa, Canada: Department of Foreign Affairs and International Trade, 1998); David Rudd and Nicholas Furneaux, *Fortress North America? What Continental Security Means for Canada* (Toronto, Canada: Canadian Institute of Strategic Studies, 2002); Norman Hillmer and Maureen Appel Molot, eds., *A Fading Power: Canada among Nations 2002* (Don Mills, Ontario, Canada: Oxford University Press, 2002); Andrew Richter, *Avoiding Armageddon: Canadian Military Strategy and Nuclear Weapons, 1950–63* (Vancouver, Canada: University of British Columbia Press, 2002); and Canada, Department of National Defence, *Canadian Security and Military Preparedness: The Government's Response to the Report of the Standing Senate Committee on National Security and Defence* (Ottawa, Canada: Department of National Defence, 2002).

24. Canada, Department of National Defence, "About DND/CF: Main Roles" (2002), 1 (www.forces.gc.ca/site/about/roles_e.asp), accessed October 30, 2003.

25. Canada, Department of National Defense, Directorate of History and Heritage, "About Us" (2002), 1 (www.forces.gc.ca/hr/dhh/engraph/about_e.asp), accessed October 30, 2003.

26. Canadian Forces, "Air Force: Mission and Roles" (2002), 1 (www.airforce.dnd.ca/today1_e.htm), accessed October 30, 2003. For historical background, see William Alexander Binney, *The Creation of a National Air Force* (Toronto and Ottawa, Canada: University of Toronto Press and Department of National Defence, Canadian Government Publications Centre, Supply and Services Canada, 1986); and Brereton Greenhouse and Hugh A. Halliday, *Canada's Air Forces, 1914–1999* (Montreal, Canada: Art Global, 1999).

27. For current mission statement and historical background, see Canadian Forces, "Army Life: Mandate" (2003), 1 (www.army.forces.gc.ca/lf/English/1_1_1.asp), accessed October 30, 2003; Canada, Department of National Defense, *The Future Land Force: Canada's Army into the 21st Century* (Ottawa, Canada: Department of National Defense, 1994); and J. L. Granatstein, *Canada's Army: Waging War and Keeping the Peace* (Toronto, Canada: University of Toronto Press, 2002).

28. For further historical and policy background on Canada's Navy, see Marc Milner, *Canada's Navy: The First Century* (Toronto, Canada: University of Toronto Press, 1999); Michael L. Hadley and others, eds., *A Nation's Navy: In Quest of Canadian Naval Identity* (Montreal and Kingston, Canada: McGill-Queen's University Press, 1996); and Peter T. Haydon and Ann L. Griffiths, eds., *Canada's Pacific Naval Presence: Purposeful or Peripheral* (Halifax, Canada: Centre for Foreign Policy Studies, 1999).

29. Canadian Security Intelligence Service, "The CSIS Mandate" (2001), 4–5 (www.csis-scrs.gc.ca/eng/backgrnd/back1_e.html), accessed October 30, 2003. For additional historical background, see Richard Cleroux, *Official Secrets: The Story Behind: The Canadian Security Security Intelligence Service* (Montreal, Canada: McGraw-Hill Ryerson, 1990); and J. L. Granatstein and David Stafford, *Spy Wars: Espionage and Canada from Gouzenko to Glasnost* (Toronto, Canada: Key Porter Books, 1990).

30. Canada, Department of the Solicitor General, "Inspector General, Canadian Security Intelligence Service" (2002), 1 (www.sgc.gc.ca/igcsis/index_e.asp), accessed October 30, 2003.

31. For background on the Royal Canadian Mounted Police and one perspective on its historical intelligence activities, see Nora Kelly, *The Royal Canadian Mounted Police: A Century of*

History 1873–1973 (Edmonton, Canada: Hurtig, 1973); and Steve Hewitt, *Spying 101: The RCMP's Secret Activities at Canadian Universities, 1917–1977* (Toronto, Canada: University of Toronto Press, 2002).

32. Royal Canadian Mounted Police, Criminal Intelligence Program, "Using Intelligence to Prevent Crime" (2003), 1 (www.rcmp.ca/crimint/ci_aboutcid_e.htm), accessed October 30, 2003.

33. Canada, Security Intelligence Review Committee, "General Functions" (2001), 1 (www.sirc-csars.gc.ca/4000.html), accessed October 30, 2003.

34. Department of the Solicitor General of Canada, "Overview of the Organization" (2002), 1 (www.sgc.ca/about/overview_e.asp), accessed October 30, 2003.

35. For background and an overview, see Allan Kornberg and William Mishler, *Influence in Parliament, Canada* (Durham, N.C.: Duke University Press, 1976).

36. Canada, Parliamentary Library, "Virtual Library" (n.d.), 1 (www.parl.gc.ca/common/Library.asp?Language=E&Parl=37& Ses=2), accessed October 30, 2003.

37. Canada, Office of the Auditor General, "Vision" (2003), 1 (www.oag-bvg.gc.ca/domino/oag-bvg.nsf/html/menue.html), accessed October 30, 2003. For additional institutional background, see Sonja Sinclair, *Cordial but Not Cosy: A History of the Office of the Auditor General* (Toronto, Canada: McClelland and Stewart, 1979); Fergus M. Thompson, "Legislative Financial Audit in Canada: A Developmental History of the Auditor General's Office," M.A. thesis, Carleton University, 1981; and Canada, Office of the Auditor General, *Auditing for Parliament* (Ottawa, Canada: Office of the Auditor General, 1991).

38. Examples of works on British national security policy include Internal Centre for Security Analysis, *Coalitions and the Future of UK Security Policy: A Whitehall Paper* (London, England: Royal United Services Institute for Defense Studies, 2000); Andrew W. Cox and Stephen Kirby, *Congress, Parliament, and Defence: The Impact of Legislative Reform on Defence Accountability in Britain and America* (Basingstoke, United Kingdom: Macmillan, 1986); Stuart Croff and others, Britain and Defense, 1945–2000: A Policy Re-evaluation (Harlow, United Kingdom: Longman, 2001); Lawrence Freedman, *The Politics of British Defence, 1979–1998* (Basingstoke, United Kingdom, and New York: McMillian and St. Martin's Press, 1999); and Dan Keohane, *Security in British Politics, 1945–99* (Basingstoke, United Kingdom: Macmillan, 2000).

39. Analyses of British prime ministers and their exercise of power include James P. Barber, *The Prime Minister since 1945* (Oxford, England: Basil Blackwell, 1991); David Dilks, *The Office of Prime Minister in Twentieth-Century Britain* (Hull, England: University of Hull Press, 1993); Dennis Kavanagh and Anthony Seldon, *The Powers behind the Prime Minister: The Hidden Influence of Number Ten* (London, England: HarperCollins, 1999); and Patricia Lee Sykes, *Presidents and Prime Ministers: Conviction Politics in the Anglo-American Tradition* (Lawrence: University Press of Kansas, 2000).

40. United Kingdom, Cabinet Office, "An Introduction to the Cabinet Office" (2002), 1 (www.cabinet-office.gov.uk /min-org/organisation/), accessed October 30, 2003. For historical background and contemporary perspective, see Peter Hennessy, *The Blair Centre: A Question of Command and Control? A Political Commentary* (London, England: Public Management Foundation, 1999); Richard Kenneth Mosley, *The Story of the Cabinet Office* (London, England, and New York: Routledge and Kegan Paul and Humanities Press, 1969); and John F. Naylor, *A Man and an Institution: Sir Maurice Hankey, the Cabinet Secretariat, and the Custody of Cabinet Secrecy* (Cambridge, England: Cambridge University Press, 1984).

41. United Kingdom, Cabinet Office, Intelligence and Security Committee, "Intelligence and Security Committee" (2003), 1 (www.cabinet-office.gov.uk/intelligence), accessed October 30, 2003.

42. United Kingdom, Home Office, "Welcome to the Home Office" (2003), 1 (www.homeoffice.gov.uk/), accessed October 30, 2003. For institutional background, see Jill Pellew, *The Home Office, 1848–1914: From Clerks to Bureaucrats* (London, England: Heinemann Educational, 1982).

43. United Kingdom, Ministry of Defence, "Defence Mission" (2002), 1 (www.mod.uk/aboutusmission.htm), accessed October 30, 2003.

44. United Kingdom, Ministry of Defence, "History" (2002), 1 (www.mod.uk/aboutus/history.htm), accessed October 30, 2003. For additional Ministry of Defence background, see Paul Smith, ed., *Government and the Armed Forces in Britain, 1856–1990* (London, England: Hambledon, 1996); and Franklyn A. Johnson, *Defence Ministry: The British Ministry of Defence, 1944–1974* (London, England: Duckworth, 1980).

45. United Kingdom, Royal Air Force, "The Royal Air Force-History" (2003), 6 (www.raf.mod.uk/history/line1780.html), accessed October 30, 2003. For additional historical background, see also Chaz Bowyer, *History of the RAF* (Twickenham, United Kingdom: Hamlyn, 1985); Sir David Lee, *Flight from the Middle East: A History of the Royal Air Force in the Arabian Peninsula and Adjacent Territories, 1945–1972* (London, England: Her Majesty's Stationary Office, 1980); and Roy C. Nesbit, *An Illustrated History of the RAF* (London, England: Hutchinson, 1980).

46. For historical background, see Corelli Barnett, *Britain and Her Army, 1509–1970: A Military, Political, and Social Survey* (London, England: Allen Lane, 1970); Christopher Chant, *The Handbook of British Regiments* (London, England: Routledge and Kegan Paul, 1988); Eric Grove, *The Army and British Security after the Cold War: Defence Planning for a New Era* (Camberley, United Kingdom: Strategic and Combat Studies Institute, 1996); Ian V. Hogg, *The British Army in the 20th Century* (London, England: Ian Allan, 1985); and David Chandler, gen. ed., *The Oxford History of the British Army* (Oxford, England: Oxford University Press, 1996).

47. See United Kingdom, Royal Navy, "Today's Royal Navy" (2003), 1 (www.royal-navy.mod.uk/static/content/3788.html), accessed October 30, 2003; Paul M. Kennedy, *The Rise and Fall of British Naval Mastery*, 3d ed. (London, England: Fontana, 1991); Arthur J. Marder, *From the Dreadnought to Scapa Flow: The Royal Navy in the Fisher Era, 1904–1919*, 5 vols. (London, England: Oxford University Press, 1961–1970); J. R. Hill, ed., *The Oxford Illustrated History of the Royal Navy* (Oxford, England: Oxford University Press, 1995); and David A. Thomas, *A Companion to the Royal Navy* (London, England: Harrap, 1988).

48. Examples of histories on overall British intelligence operations or specific agencies include Richard J. Aldrich, *The Hidden Hand: Britain, America, and Cold War Secret Intelligence* (London, England: John Murray, 2001); Christopher Andrew, *Her Majesty's Secret Service: The Making of the British Intelligence Community* (New York: Viking, 1986); Stephen Dorril, *The Silent Conspiracy: Inside the Intelligence Services in the 1990s* (London, England: Heinemann, 1993); Richard J. Aldrich, ed., *Espionage, Security, and Intelligence in Britain, 1945–1970* (Manchester, England: Manchester University Press, 1998); Francis H. Hensley, *British Intelligence in the Second World War: Its Influence on Strategy and Operations*, 6 vols. (London: Her Majesty's Stationary Office, 1979–1990); and Nigel West, *The Friends: Britain's Post-War Secret Intelligence Operations* (Dunton Green, United Kingdom: Coronet, 1988).

49. See United Kingdom, Government Communications Headquarters, "About GCHQ: FAQ" (2002), 1 (www.gchq.gov.uk/about/), accessed October 30, 2003. For additional background on the Government Communications Headquarters and British intelligence cryptography, see Francis H. Hensley and Alan Stripp, eds., *Codebreakers: The Inside Story of Bletchley Park* (Oxford, England: Oxford University Press, 2001); Ted Enever, *Britain's Best Kept Secret: Ultra's Base at Bletchley Park* (Stroud, United Kingdom: Bramley, 1999); and Hugh Lanning and

Richard Norton-Taylor, *A Conflict of Loyalties: GCHQ 1984–1991* (Cheltenham, United Kingdom: New Clarion, 1991).

50. United Kingdom, Security Service, "A Brief History of the Service: Introduction" (n.d.), 1 (www.mi5.gov.uk/history/history_1.htm) accessed October 30, 2003.

51. United Kingdom, Security Service, "The Law—Security Service Act 1989, Chapter 5—The Security Service" (n.d.), 1 (www.mi5.gov.uk/law/law1_1.htm), accessed October 30, 2003.

52. United Kingdom, Security Service, "Accountability and Funding—Oversight in Law" (n.d.), 1 (www.mi5.gov.uk/accountability_funding/accountability_1.htm), accessed October 30, 2003.

53. For information on MI-6's historical origins, see Andrew, *Her Majesty's Secret Service*, 59–61; Oliver Hoare, ed., *British Intelligence in the Twentieth Century: A Missing Dimension?* (London, England: Frank Cass, 2003); and Alan Judd, *The Quest for C: Sir Mansfield Cumming and the Founding of the British Secret Service* (London, England: HarperCollins, 1999).

54. United Kingdom, Her Majesty's Stationary Office, "Intelligence Services Act 1994" (2000), 1 (www.legislation.hmso.gov.uk/acts/acts1994/Ukpga_19940013_en_2.html), accessed October 30, 2003.

55. See United Kingdom, National Archives, "About the National Archives" (2003), 1 (www.nationalarchives.gov.uk/about/default.htm), accessed October 30, 2003; United Kingdom, Public Records Office, *The Public Records Office: Souvenir Guide* (Kew, England: PRO Publications, 1998); and United Kingdom, Public Records Office, *SOE Operations in the Balkans: A Guide to the Records in the Public Record Office* (Kew, England: Public Record Office, 1998).

56. See United Kingdom, National Audit Office, "About Us: The Role of the National Audit Office" (n.d.), 1 (www.nao.gov.uk/about/role.htm), accessed October 30, 2003; and United Kingdom, National Audit Office, *Helping the Nation Spend Wisely* (London, England: National Audit Office, 2003).

57. United Kingdom, National Audit Office, "About Us: The History of the National Audit Office" (n.d.), 1–2 (www.nao.gov.uk/about/history.htm), accessed October 30, 2003.

58. For institutional historical overview of the British Parliament, see Jeffrey Goldsworthy, *The Sovereignty of Parliament: History and Philosophy* (Oxford, England: Clarendon Press, 1999); History of Parliament Trust, *The History of Parliament on CD-ROM* (Cambridge, England: Cambridge University Press with the History of Parliament Trust, 1998); and Peter Spufford, *Origins of the English Parliament* (London, England: Longmans, 1967).

59. United Kingdom, Parliament, House of Commons, Defence Committee, "Defence Committee" (2003), 1 (www.parliament.uk/parliamentary_committees/defence_committee.cfm/), accessed October 30, 2003.

60. United Kingdom, Parliament, House of Commons, Home Affairs Committee, "Home Affairs Committee" (2003), 1 (www.parliament.uk/parliamentary_committees/home_affairs_committee.cfm), accessed October 30, 2003.

61. United Kingdom, Parliament, House of Commons Library, "Library Research Papers" (2003), 1 (www.parliament.uk/parliamentary_publications_and_archives/research_papers.cfm), accessed October 30, 2003.

62. Significant works on Indian national security policy issues include Damon Bristow, *India's New Armament Strategy: A Return to Self-Sufficiency?* (London, England: Royal United Services Institute for Defence Studies, 1995); Devin T. Hagerty, *The Consequences of Nuclear Proliferation: Lessons from South Asia* (Cambridge, Mass.: MIT Press, 1998); Ross Babbage and Sandy Gordon, eds., *India's Strategic Future: Regional, State, or Global Power?* (New York: St. Martin's Press, 1992); George Perkovich, *India's Nuclear Bomb: The Impact on Global Proliferation* (Berkeley: University of California Press, 1999); Brahma Chellaney, ed., *Securing India's Future in the New Millenium* (New Delhi, India: Orient Longman, 1999); and Jasjit Singh, *India's Defence Spending: Assessing Future Needs* (New Delhi, India: Knowledge World in association

with Institute for Defence Studies and Analyses, 2000).

63. Sample works on Israeli national security include Eliot A. Cohen and others, *Knives, Tanks, and Missiles: Israel's Security Revolution* (Washington, D.C.: Washington Institute for Near East Policy, 1998); Uri Bar-Joseph, ed., *Israel's National Security towards the 21st Century* (London, England: Frank Cass, 2001); and Ariel Levite, *Offense and Defense in Israeli Military Doctrine* (Boulder, Colo.: Westview Press, 1990).

64. New Zealand, Ministry of Defence, "Homepage" (2003), 1 (www.defence.govt.nz/), accessed October 30, 2003. For additional background on New Zealand's national security situation, see George Bowen, *Defending New Zealand: New Zealand's Search for Security 1945–1985* (Auckland, New Zealand: Addison Wesley Longman, 1997); and New Zealand, Ministry of Defence, *The Shape of New Zealand's Defence: A White Paper* (Wellington, New Zealand: Ministry of Defence, 1997).

65. For perspectives on Singapore's security situation, see Choy Dawen and others, *Creating the Capacity to Change: Defence Entrepreneurship for the 21st Century* (Singapore: Pointer, Journal of the Singapore Armed Forces and Singapore Armed Forces Technology Institute Military History Institute, 2003); Tim Huxley, *Defending the Lion City: The Armed Forces of Singapore* (St. Leonards, New South Wales: Allen and Unwin, 2000); and Singapore, Ministry of Defence, *Defending Singapore in the 21st Century* (Singapore: Ministry of Defence, 2000).

66. Analyses of South Africa's security situation include Anton DuPlessia, *South Africa and the South Atlantic Ocean: A Maritime-Strategic Analysis* (Pretoria, South Africa: University of Pretoria Institute for Strategic Studies, 1987); and Peter Stiff, *Warfare by Other Means: South Africa in the 1980s and 1990s* (Alberton, South Africa: Galago Publications, 2001).

67. European Parliament, "Overview of the European Parliament" (2002), 1 (www.europarl.eu.int/presentation/default_en.html), accessed October 30, 2003. For additional background on this institution, see Richard S. Katz and Bernhard Wessels, eds., *The European Parliament, the National Parliaments, and European Integration* (Oxford, England, and New York: Oxford University Press, 1999); and Francis Jacobs and others, *The European Parliament* (New York: Stockton Press, 1995).

68. European Parliament, "Rules of Procedure of the European Parliament: Annex VI Powers and Responsibilities of Standing Committees, 15th ed." (2003), 1 (www2.europarl.eu.int/omk/sipade2?PROG=RULES-EP&L=EN&REF=RESP-AFET), accessed October 30, 2003.

69. For examples of varying assessments on the propriety and efficacy of a common European Union security policy, see Andrew M. Dorman, *European Adaptation to Expeditionary Warfare: Implications for the U.S. Army* (Carlisle Barracks, Pa.: U.S. Army War College Strategic Studies Institute, 2003); Trevor C. Salmon and Alistair J. K. Shepherd, *Toward a European Army: A Military Power in the Making?* (Boulder, Colo.: Lynne Rienner Publishers, 2003); and U.S. Congress, House Committee on International Relations, *European Common Foreign, Security, and Defense Policies: Implications for the United States and Atlantic Alliance*, 106th Cong., 2d sess., 2000.

70. European Union, "Decentralised Bodies of the European Union: Common Foreign and Security Policy" (n.d.), 1 (www.europa.eu.int/institutions/cfsp/index_en.htm), accessed October 30, 2003.

71. European Union, Institute for Security Studies, "An Institution at the Service of CFSP" (2002), 8 (www.iss-eu.org/about/brochure.pdf), accessed October 30, 2003.

72. European Union Satellite Centre, "The Centre" (n.d.), 1 (www.eusc.org/html/centre.html), accessed October 30, 2003.

73. See North Atlantic Treaty Organization, "What Does NATO Do?" (n.d.), 1 (www.nato.int/issues/faq/index.htm#A1), accessed October 30, 2003. For institutional historical background, see Don Cook, *Forging the Alliance: NATO, 1945–1950* (London, England: Secker

and Warburg, 1989); Peter Duignan, *NATO: Its Past, Present, and Future* (Stanford, Calif.: Hoover Institution Press, 2000); and Gustav Schmidt, ed., *A History of NATO: The First Fifty Years* (New York: Palgrave, 2001).

74. Organization for Security and Cooperation in Europe, "About the OSCE" (n.d.), 1 (www.osce.org/general/), accessed October 30, 2003. For additional background on the Organization for Security and Cooperation in Europe, see Stuart Croft and others, *The Enlargement of Europe* (Manchester, England, and New York: Manchester University Press and St. Martin's Press, 1999); P. Terrence Hopman, *Building Security in Post–Cold War Eurasia: The OSCE and U.S. Foreign Policy* (Washington, D.C.: U.S. Institute of Peace, 1999); and Janie Leatherman, *From Cold War to Democritic Peace: Third Parties, Peaceful Change, and the OSCE* (Syracuse, N.Y.: Syracuse University Press, 2003).

75. General histories of the United Nations and its attempts to influence international security policy making include Dimitris Bourantonis, *The United Nations and the Quest for Nuclear Disarmament* (Aldershot, United Kingdom, and Brookfield, Vt.: Dartmouth, 1993); Max Harrelson, *Fires All around the Horizon: The UN's Uphill Battle to Preserve the Peace* (New York: Praeger, 1989); Townsend Hoopes and Douglas Brinkley, *FDR and the Creation of the UN* (New Haven, Conn.: Yale University Press, 1997); and Evan Luard, *A History of the United Nations*, 2 vols. (New York: St. Martin's Press, 1982).

76. See United Nations Security Council, "UN Security Council: Functions and Powers" (n.d.), 1 (www.un.org/Docs/sc/unsc_functions.html), accessed October 30, 2003. For additional background on the Security Council, see Andrew Boyd, *Fifteen Men on a Powder Keg: A History of the U.N. Security Council* (New York: Stein and Day, 1971); Bruce Russet, ed., *The Once and Future Security Council* (New York: St. Martin's Press, 1997); Istvan S. Pogany, *The Security Council and the Arab-Israeli Conflict* (New York: St. Martin's Press, 1984); and Daneesh Sarooshi, *The United Nations and the Development of Collective Security: The Delegation by the UN Security Council of its Chapter VII Powers* (New York: Oxford University Press, 2000).

77. United Nations Security Council Counter-Terrorism Committee, "Mandate" (2003), 1 (www.un.org/Docs/sc/committees/1373/), accessed October 30, 2003.

78. United Nations Monitoring, Verification, and Inspection Commission, "UNMOVIC: Basic Facts" (2003), 1 (www.un.org/Depts/unmovic/new/pages/index.asp), accessed October 30, 2003.

79. International Atomic Energy Agency, "IAEA Mission Statement" (2003), 1 (www.iaea.org/worldatom/About/Profile/mission.html), accessed October 30, 2003. For a historical overview, see David Fischer, *History of the International Atomic Energy Agency: The First Forty Years* (Vienna, Austria: International Atomic Energy Agency, 1997).

80. United Nations, Department for Disarmament Affairs, "Vision Statement" (2003), 1 (http://disarmament2.un.org/dda-vision.htm), accessed October 30, 2003.

81. Organisation for the Prohibition of Chemical Weapons, "OPCW Mission Statement" (n.d.), 1 (www.opcw.org/html/intro/mission_statement.html), accessed October 30, 2003. For additional background, see Thomas Bernauer, *The Chemistry of Regime Formation: Explaining International Cooperation for a Comprehensive Ban on Chemical Weapons* (Geneva, Switzerland: United Nations Institute for Disarmament Research, 1993); and Lisa Woollomes Tabassi, comp. and ed., *OPCW: The Legal Texts* (The Hague and Cambridge, Mass.: T. M. C. Asser Press and Kluwer Law International, 1999).

82. United Nations Institute for Disarmament Research, "About UNIDIR" (2003), 1 (www.unidir.org/html/en/about.html), accessed October 30, 2003.

CHAPTER 13

Foreign Research Institutions

Interest in researching national security policy is not restricted to the United States. National security–oriented research institutions are found in countries around the world. These institutions can be government-funded, parts of academic institutions, or commercial organizations. They represent diverse national and ideological perspectives, which provide insight into how issues are viewed outside of the United States.

Australia

Australian research institutes dealing with national security policy are concerned, for example, with Australian military policy, issues affecting Australian security such as turmoil in Indonesia and other regional areas, and the implications of Australian military participation in Operation Iraqi Freedom.

Australian Defence Studies Centre

Located in Campbell, Australian Capital Territory, the Australian Defence Studies Centre (ADSC) is part of the University of New South Wales and the Australian Defence Force Academy. Established in 1987, ADSC promotes applied research on Australian defense. It seeks to focus attention on Australian defense and security issues including those affecting Asian and Pacific states near Australia.[1]

The website http://idun.its.adfa.edu.au/ADSC/ has announcements of upcoming events, biographies of resident scholars and visiting fellows, and descriptions of books written by ADSC personnel. Accessible reports include working papers such as "The Use of Military Force in Kosovo" (1999), "Australia's National Security Framework: A Look to the Future" (2000), "Security, People-Smuggling, and Australia's New Afghan Refugees" (2001), "Australia-India Security Relations: Common Interest or Common Disinterest?" (2001), and "Ministers, Media, and the Military: Reflections on Certain Maritime Incidents" (2002).

Australian Strategic Policy Institute

The Australian Strategic Policy Institute (ASPI) is located in Barton, Australian Capital Territory. As a government-funded but independent entity, ASPI is charged with educating Australians about the security challenges their country faces and helping the federal government make better informed policy decisions to enable its military forces to meet those challenges.[2]

Further information about ASPI activities can be found at www.aspi.org.au/. Available materials include information about ASPI organizational components including the Budget and Management Program, Operations and Capability Program, and Strategy and International Program; news releases (2001–present); media references to ASPI activities; and upcoming events and publications.

Accessible publications include *Beyond Bali: ASPI's Strategic Assessment* (2002), *Australia's Defence after September 11: A Quick Guide to the Issues* (2002), *Setting a Course for Australia's Naval Shipbuilding and Repair Industry* (2002), *Building the Peace: Australia and the Future of Iraq* (2003), *Danger and Opportunity: Australia and the North Korea Crisis* (2003), and *Sinews of War: The Defence Budget of 2003 and How We Got There* (2003). Website users can read and post e-mail comments about these works.

Strategic and Defence Studies Centre

Founded in 1966, the Strategic and Defence Studies Centre (SDSC) is located in Canberra, Australia, and is part of Australian National University's Research School of Pacific and Asian Studies. SDSC studies strategic issues concerning East Asia and the Pacific with particular emphasis on issues affecting Australian strategic interests in Southeast Asia and the Southwest Pacific.[3]

The website http://rspas.anu.edu.au/sdsc/ has information about SDSC graduate programs in strategy and defense, information about and the research interests of SDSC faculty, information on SDSC's Boeing Library, and listings and abstracts for selected working papers and related publications dating back to the 1980s. The full text of recent *Viewpoint* opinion pieces are provided, including "Pea Soup of Intelligence on Iraq" (2003) and "Intelligence on Iraq's WMD: The Case of the Missing Biological Weapons" (2003).

Bulgaria—Institute for Security and International Studies

The Institute for Security and International Studies (ISIS) is based in Sofia, Bulgaria, and is part of the International Relations Security Network hosted by the Partnership for Peace, which consists of North American and European nations. ISIS objectives include studying Bulgarian foreign and national security policy, European integration and Euroatlantic security institutions, Balkan and Black Sea regional security, and conducting quantitative analysis and computer simulation of security issues.[4]

The website www.isn.ethz.ch/isis/ provides information on ISIS activities and projects, staffing levels, and access to publications including the institute's *Annual*

Report (1995–present) and the periodicals *Balkan Regional Profile* (1999–present) and *Black Sea Basin Regional Profile* (1999–present). Numerous reports are also accessible including *Civil-Military Relations in South Eastern Europe: A Survey of the National Perspectives and of the Adaptation Process to the Partnership for Peace Standards* (n.d.), *Confidence and Security in the Balkans: The Role of Transparency in Defence Budgeting* (1996), *Security Risks and Instabilities in Southeastern Europe: Recommended Strategies to the EU in Process of Differentiated Integration of the Region by the Union* (2000), *The Balkans and the Caucasus: Conceptual Stepping-Stones towards the Formation of a New Single Geoeconomic, Geopolitical, and Geostrategic Region* (2002), and *Control, Cooperation, Expertise: Civilians and the Military in Bulgarian Defence Planning Experience* (2003).

Canada

Canadian national security research institutes examine issues such as nuclear proliferation and terrorism, and they analyze the role of Canadian military forces in international peacekeeping or other military operations. These organizations also produce information resources on the strengths and weaknesses of Canadian military forces and appropriate roles for these forces given existing governmental expenditures and force capabilities.

Canadian Institute of Strategic Studies

The Canadian Institute of Strategic Studies (CISS) is located in Toronto, Canada. Established in 1976, CISS serves as an independent information and research source on strategic and security issues affecting Canada. It provides outreach through seminars, publications, and educational activities for the Canadian public and government.[5]

The institute's website (www.ciss.ca/) provides announcements of upcoming events, research fellow listings, information on obtaining media commentary from CISS personnel, and membership information. Site contents also include abstracts of CISS *Strategic Outlook* series publications (1999–present) and descriptions of institute-produced books and the *McNaughton Papers* series. Full-text access is provided for the *Commentary* opinion series, which includes *Is the Cupboard Bare? The Canadian Forces and Iraq* (2002), *Kim, Saddam, and the Nuclear Danger* (2002), *The Enemy of My Enemy: The Odd Link between Ansar Al-Islam, Iraq, and Iran* (2003), and *Unjustified Optimism in Iraq?* (2003).

Centre for Security and Defence Studies—Carleton University

The Centre for Security and Defence Studies (CSDS) is part of Ottawa, Canada's Carleton University. CSDS members and faculty are drawn from interdisciplinary schools and departments at Carleton. The centre's mission includes enhancing graduate and undergraduate teaching in international conflict analysis and defense and security studies; supporting outreach activities within Canada's government, school boards, media, and nongovernmental entities; and promoting research and publication on security issues with particular emphasis on their relevance for Canada. CSDS work revolves around four interdisciplinary modules: Force and Statecraft; Partnering, Peacekeeping, and Peacebuilding; Military and Society; and Intelligence and Policy. They integrate centre research, teaching, and outreach activities.[6]

Further information about CSDS is accessible at www.carleton.ca/csds/. Online materials include event listings (2000–present), a link to a model NATO conference website, information on the interdisciplinary program modules, and faculty biographies. Accessible research papers from 1997 to the present include *Making the Impossible Possible: The PLA's Cross-Strait Operations in the 21st Century* (1999), *Canada's Communications Security Establishment from Cold War to Globalisation* (2000), *Intelligence and Information Superiority in the Future of Canadian Defence Policy* (2001), *Canadian Defence and the Canada-U.S. Strategic Partnership* (2002), and *Countering Complexity: An Analytical Framework to Guide Counter-Terrorism Policy-Making* (2003).

Conference of Defence Associations

The Conference of Defence Associations (CDA) is based in Ottawa, Canada. Established in 1932 and with a membership exceeding 600,000, CDA seeks to study defense and security problems and promote what it sees as the well-being and efficiency of Canada's military forces.[7]

CDA's website (www.cda-cdai.ca/) provides links to the websites of other Canadian associations concerned with national security issues and the text of public presentations and parliamentary committee testimony by CDA personnel. A number of reports and publications are accessible including *Stability and Prosperity: The Benefits of Investment in Defence* (2000), annual meeting *Proceedings* (2001–present), *Caught in the Middle: An Assessment of the Operational Readiness of the Canadian Forces* (2001), and *A Nation at Risk: The Decline of the Canadian Forces* (2002).

Council for Canadian Security in the 21st Century

The Council for Canadian Security in the 21st Century (CCS21), in Calgary, Canada, was organized in 2001 by individuals who wanted to get the Canadian government to undertake a defense and security policy review in the aftermath of the September 11, 2001, terrorist attacks in the United States.[8]

CCS21's website (www.ccs21.org/) lists individual organization members including former military personnel and academics, contact information, and further descriptions of organizational objectives. A number of research reports are also provided including *The Future of Canada's Security and Defence Policy: Critical Infrastructure Protection and DND Policy and Strategy* (n.d.), *Canadian Defence and Security in the 21st Century: To Secure a Nation* (2001), *Canada and Africa: Security Policy Paper* (n.d.), *Defence Export Regulations: Sustaining a Viable Canadian Defence Industry* (2001), and *The People's Defence Review* (2002).

Research Group in International Security

The Research Group in International Security (REGIS) was formed in 1996 as a cooperative venture of the University of Montreal and McGill University in Montreal, Canada, to integrate the activities of researchers, students, and others specializing in international security. Its mission is to offer comprehensive undergraduate and graduate curriculum, train graduate students with the skills required by governmental and nongovernmental security organizations, support promising academic researchers, expand scientific knowledge of international security, make this knowledge publicly available, increase interaction between English- and French-speaking international security researchers, and stimulate cooperation and maximize security studies resources at the University of Montreal and McGill University.[9]

The REGIS website (ww2.mcgill.ca/regis/) lists affiliated faculty, information on REGIS-sponsored events, descriptions of undergraduate and graduate courses, program information, and links to works written by affiliated scholars. Access is provided to working papers including "When (and How) Regions Become Peaceful: Explaining Transitions from War to Peace" (2001), "International and Transatlantic Images of Belonging: The United States and Europe in the 21st Century" (2001), "Does Offense-Defense Theory Have a Future?" (2001), and "Norm-Building in Security Spaces: The Emergence of the Light Weapons Problematic" (2001).

University of Calgary—Centre for Military and Strategic Studies

The University of Calgary's Centre for Military and Strategic Studies (CMSS) was established in 1981 and acquired its present name in 1999.[10] CMSS objectives include studying Canadian soldiers and Canadian military, security, and defense issues; examining international military, security, and defense issues; providing advanced educational programs for military personnel and civilians; and fostering informed public discussion and analysis.[11]

The CMSS website (www.stratnet.ucalgary.ca/) has biographies and research activities of centre fellows and information on the master of strategic studies program curriculum including descriptions of courses such as Canada in the Second World War and Applied Ethics and Military Force.

Numerous publications are provided including abstracts and selected articles from *Journal of Military and Strategic Studies* (2000–present), the newsletter *News and Views* (1999–present), *Annual Military and Strategic Studies Colloquium Proceedings* (1999 and 2000), and reports such as *Benchmark: Media Coverage of the Canadian Forces 1994–2000* (2001), *Public Participation in a Canadian Defence Policy Review* (2002), and *Professionalism in the Canadian Armed Forces: Bureaucracy, Inclusiveness, and Independence* (2003).

University of Manitoba—Centre for Defence and Security Studies

Located in Winnipeg, Canada, the Centre for Defence and Security Studies (CDSS) is part of the University of Manitoba's Political Studies Department. Founded in 1986,

CDSS gained its current name in 1993 and engages in research in all areas of national and international security on an interdisciplinary basis with other Canadian and international organizations.[12]

The CDSS website (www.umanitoba.ca/centres/defence/) lists center faculty and their areas of interest, which include European security architecture, North American security, and fissile material and nuclear technology proliferation. Also accessible is information on previous and upcoming CDSS events. The centre's website includes listings of its occasional papers published since 1988, such as *Canada's Defence Industries and Europe 1992: A Preliminary Investigation* (1990), *Canada and Ballistic Missile Defence* (1998), and *Canadian Security and Defence Policy: Continentalism and Internationalism* (2002).

York Centre for International and Security Studies

The York Centre for International and Security Studies (YCISS), located at York University in Toronto, Canada, is dedicated to studying international peace and security issues and supports collaborative interdisciplinary projects and academic programs in these areas.[13] The YCISS website (www.yorku.ca/yciss/) has listings of affiliated faculty and researchers, details of previous and upcoming events, student support programs, and methodological descriptions of centre research interests. Full-text access is provided to selected publications from the YCISS Occasional Paper (1990–present) and Working Paper (1991–present) series. Occasional Papers include *The Evolution of Strategic Thinking at the Canadian Department of National Defence, 1950–1960* (1996), *Blackened Faces and Ticker Tape Parades: Situating the Leviathan in Lakota and Euroamerican Conceptions of War* (1998), *Global Cultural Change and the Transnational Campaign to Ban Antipersonnel Landmines: A Research Agenda* (2000), and *Incorporating Peacebuilding into Mine Action Programmes* (2002). Accessible Working Papers include "Maritime Strategy and the New Law of the Sea: Losers and Gainers, With a Focus on Southeast Asia" (1996) and "Homeland Defence and the Re/Territorialization of the State" (2003).

Denmark—Danish Institute of International Affairs

The Danish Institute of International Affairs (DIIA) is located in Copenhagen, Denmark, and was established in 1995. Its mission is enhancing Danish research, analysis, and information activities in international affairs and foreign policy. Its organizational structure consists of a research and analysis department, which became known as the Institute of International Studies after December 31, 2002.[14]

The website www.dupi.dk/ contains information about past DIIA-sponsored events, descriptions of research projects such as Denmark's Security Policy Position during the Cold War, and a description of DIIA's library. Access is provided to a number of English language publications such as the institute's working paper series, which includes "Greenland's Geopolitical Reality and Its Political-Economic Consequences" (2001), "Danish Security Policy Over the Last 50 Years—Long-Term Essential Security Priorities" (2001), "Countering International Terrorism: The United Nations and Global Capacity Building" (2002), "A New Kind of War: Strategic Culture and the War on Terrorism" (2003), and "Pacifism or Activism: Towards a Common Strategic Culture within the European Security and Defence Policy?" (2003).

Finland—Finnish Institute of International Affairs

The Finnish Institute of International Affairs (FIIA) was founded in 1961 and is located in Helsinki, Finland. A private institution managed by the Foundation for Foreign Policy Research, FIIA aims to help Finns understand international affairs and to maintain close relationships with universities and governmental policymaking institutions. Key areas of FIIA research are Finnish foreign and security policy, Nordic-Baltic regional security, European Union (EU) foreign and security policy, and Russian-EU relations.[15]

Additional information on FIIA is accessible through its website (www.upi-fiia.fi/), which includes descriptions of institute research areas and contact personnel, a listing of Foundation for Foreign Policy Research directors, details of institute-hosted events (1999–present), and links to related research centers. Accessible security policy reports include *The Korean Peninsula: Is Kim Dae-Jung's Pursuit of a Korean Confederation Realistic?* (1999), *The Making of the European Union's Common Strategy on Russia* (2000), *The Northern EU: National Views on the Emerging Security Dimension* (2000), *The EU Common Strategy on Russia: Learning the Grammar of the CFSP* (2001), *Soft Security Problems in Northwest Russia and Their Implications for the Outside World* (2001), *Et Tu Brute! Finland's NATO Option and Russia* (2002), and *Maintaining a Balance of Power That Favors Human Freedom: The Finnish Strategic Experience* (2003).

Germany—German Institute for International Politics and Security

The German Institute for International Politics and Security (GIIPS) is an independent research center advising the German government on German foreign and security policy. Established in 1962 at Ebenhausen near Munich, Germany, GIIPS was relocated to Berlin in 2001, has nearly 150 staffers, and receives its funding from the German government.[16]

The GIIPS website (www.swp-berlin.org/) features German and English language content. English language material includes biographical information on institute researchers and their interests and descriptions of research units such as those covering EU enlargement, European and Atlantic security, and the Russian Federation and Newly Independent States. Examples of accessible research reports are *Combatting the Terrorist-Criminal Nexus* (2001), *Germany and the Middle East: Interests and Options* (2002), *Security Challenges in the Caucasus and Central Asia—A German and European Perspective* (2003), *After the Iraq War: Repercussion in the Levante* (2003), and *Iran and Its Neighbors: Diverging Views on a Strategic Region* (2003).

India

Indian national security research centers examine, for example, the nuclear arsenals of India and Pakistan, India's security relations with China, international terrorism, and the role of Kashmir in Indian national security policy decision making.

Institute for Defence Studies and Analysis

The Institute for Defence Studies and Analysis (IDSA) is located in New Delhi, India. Established in 1965, IDSA is an independent institution engaged in studying various aspects of national and international security and receives funding from India's defense and foreign ministries.[17] Further information about IDSA can be obtained at www.idsa-india.org/. Accessible resources include faculty and organizational department listings, position openings, and announcements of upcoming events. Available publications include articles from the journal *Strategic Analysis* (1997–present) and descriptions of recently published IDSA books such as *Jihadis in Jammu and Kashmir: A Portrait Gallery* (2002) and *Iraq War 2003: Rise of the "Unilateralism"* (2003).

Institute for Peace and Conflict Studies

The Institute for Peace and Conflict Studies (IPCS) is located in New Delhi, India, and was established in 1996. IPCS is an independent think tank that focuses on South Asian security issues. It brings together strategic thinkers, academics, and former members of India's armed and police forces to analyze national security issues such as arms control, disarmament, nonproliferation, Indo-Pakistan relations, and Chinese security polices.[18]

IPCS's website (www.ipcs.org/) features a "What's New" section, summaries of IPCS-sponsored seminars (1997–present), online debate forums on security topics such as Operation Iraqi Freedom, and descriptions of ongoing IPCS projects such as the possibility of nuclear war between India and Pakistan. Examples of accessible publications include the periodical *Peace and Conflict* (2002–present) and reports and commentaries such as *Kashmir: The Road Ahead* (2002), *India-U.S. Relations: Promoting Synergy* (2003), *Redefining the Non-Proliferation Norm* (2003), *Preemptive Strike: Will It Secure Indian Interests?* (2003), and *Madrassas in Pakistan* (2003).

Israel

Israeli national security research organizations examine an array of issues including the readiness of Israel's military forces, responding to terrorism, regional security issues such as oil and water, and descriptions and analysis of important historical and contemporary military operations.

Begin-Sadat Center for Strategic Studies

The Begin-Sadat Center for Strategic Studies (BSCSS) is located at Bar-Ilan University in Ramat-Gan, Israel. Founded in 1991 by Canadian Jewish community leader Thomas Hecht in honor of Israeli prime minister Menachem Begin (1977–1983) and Egyptian president Anwar Sadat (1970–1981), BSCSS seeks to provide policy-driven research on Middle East peace and security issues and sponsor conferences on these issues. Its research interests encompass Israeli strategic thinking, Israeli public opinion on national security, terrorism and low-intensity violence, Eastern

Mediterranean security, military industries, future Israeli defense forces, and other subjects.[19]

The website www.biu.ac.il/Besa/ provides further information about BSCSS organizational activities. Available resources include researcher biographies and listings of BSCSS-sponsored events from 1997 to the present. Full-text publications include the Bar-Ilan University *Bulletin* (1997–present), the journal *Middle East Review of International Affairs* (1997–present), and reports such as *Advanced Technology and Future Warfare* (1996), *Maps of Israeli Interests in Judea and Samaria* (1997), *The Vulture and the Snake Counter Guerilla Air Warfare: The War in Southern Lebanon* (1998), *Fatal Choices: Israel's Policy of Targeted Killing* (2002), and *Arms Control and Nonproliferation Developments in the Middle East: 2000–1* (2002).

Institute for Advanced Strategic and Political Studies

The Institute for Advanced Strategic and Political Studies (IASPS) is a Jerusalem, Israel-based research institution founded in 1984 that seeks to train Israel's top university graduates in economics and strategic studies from a conservative ideological perspective.[20]

The IASPS website (www.iasps.org.il/) provides fellowship program information, op-eds written by institute personnel, and information about organizational entities such as the Division for Economic Policy Research and Division for Research in Strategy. Examples of full-text research reports from the IASPS Research Papers in Strategy series are *Succession in Saudi Arabia: The Not So Silent Struggle* (1997), *The Afghan Vortex* (2000), *The Geopolitics of Water* (2000), *Turkey: The Key to Caspian Oil and Gas* (2001), and *Russia and the Mideast Vacuum* (2001).

Jaffee Center for Strategic Studies

The Jaffee Center for Strategic Studies (JCSS) is part of Tel Aviv University in Tel Aviv, Israel. Founded in 1977 as the Center for Strategic Studies, JCSS received its current name in honor of benefactors Mr. and Mrs. Mel Jaffee. Governed by an international and Israeli Board of Trustees, JCSS conducts interdisciplinary and nonpartisan research on international security issues with particular emphasis on Israeli national security.[21]

The JCSS website (www.tau.ac.il/jcss/) features a "What's New" page, descriptions of center-sponsored events (2000–present), biographies of affiliated scholars, transcripts of media appearances by JCSS personnel, and links to selected national security research institute websites. Available full-text publications include the newsletter *JCSS Bulletin* (1995–present), the periodical *Strategic Assessment* (1998–present), the op-ed anthology *Tel Aviv Notes* (2000–present), and the most recent edition of the annual *Middle East Strategic Balance*. Additional accessible reports include *Beyond the Veil: Israel-Pakistan Relations* (2000), *Egypt and Israel in Arms Control and Regional Security (ACRS): Concerns in a Regional Arms Control Process* (2001), *Israel Public Opinion on National Security 2002* (2002), and *The Battle of Jenin: A Case Study in Israel's Communication Strategy* (2003).

Japan—Institute for International Policy Studies

The Institute for International Politics Studies (IIPS), in Tokyo, Japan, was founded in 1988 by former Japanese prime minister Yasuhiro Nakasone. It conducts research on international security, economic, energy, and environmental issues affecting Japan and the global community.[22]

Additional information about IIPS can be acquired from its website (www.iips.org/). Accessible resources include institutional background information, descriptions of ongoing research projects, biographies of affiliated scholars, and information on IIPS-sponsored events. Examples of accessible publications include tables of contents and selected article abstracts from the journal *Asia-Pacific Review* (1994–present) and text from selected policy papers (1992–present) including *Corporate Risk and Information Security* (2001), *Energy Security: Strategic Viewpoints* (2002), and *The Post-9/11 Paradigm Shift and Its Effects on East Asia* (2003).

New Zealand—Centre for Strategic Studies

The Centre for Strategic Studies (CSS) is part of Victoria University in Wellington, New Zealand. CSS was founded in 1993, and its institutional mandate is promoting New Zealand's understanding about the external security environment within which the country exists in the twenty-first century and researching and commenting on these security issues.[23]

Further information about CSS activities and research can be found at www.vuw.ac.nz/css/. Resources provided include listings of center personnel, details on past CSS-sponsored seminars, and descriptions of books written by affiliated scholars. Free publications include the periodical *Strategic Briefing Papers* (1999–present) and reports such as *Revolution in Military Affairs: A New Zealand View, Part I* (1998), *Piracy: The Context for New Zealand and Its Defense Force* (1999), *Russia in Asia: Unwelcome Intruder or Accommodative Player?* (2000), and *The Context and Risk of Organised Illegal Immigration to New Zealand: An Exploration in Policy Relevant Research* (2000).

Pakistan—Institute of Strategic Studies—Islamabad

The Institute of Strategic Studies–Islamabad (ISSI) is a nonprofit research organization set up to promote expanded understanding and objective analysis of regional and global strategic issues with a particular emphasis on how such issues affect Pakistan.[24]

ISSI's website (www.issi.org.pk/) includes biographies and research interests of affiliated scholars, maps of the line of control between India and Pakistan in Kashmir, and links to relevant South Asian and international security websites. Accessible information resources include the journal *Strategic Studies* (2000–present); issue briefs on topics such as nuclear arms control, Afghanistan, and Central Asian countries (2001–present); and papers such as "Nuclear Safety and Terrorism: A Case Study of India" (2001), "The Bush Doctrine: Redefining Deterrence" (2002), and "Communal Violence in India: Hindu-Muslim Riots in Gujarat" (2002).

Singapore—Institute of Defense and Strategic Studies

The Institute of Defence and Strategic Studies (IDSS) was established in 1996 as an independent research entity at Singapore's Nanyang Technological University. The institute's mission is researching security, strategic, and international issues; providing general and graduate education in strategic studies, defense management, and defense technology; and promoting joint exchange programs and organizing seminars on relevant topics to other Asia-Pacific strategic and policy communities.[25]

The website www.idss.edu.sg/ includes news references to IDSS personnel and activities, listings of administrators and staff along with their research interests, and descriptions of courses offered under IDSS auspices such as Management of Defence Technology, Foreign Policy and Security Issues in Southeast Asia, and Selected Topics in Strategic Studies—Chinese Security and Military Policy.

Accessible IDSS working papers and related publications from 1998 to the present include "IDSS Panel Dialogue on the Future of Indonesia's Islam: The Quest for an Equilibrium" (n.d.), "Crisis and Transformation: ASEAN in the New Era" (2001), "Reconceptualizing the PLA Navy in Post-Mao China: Functions, Warfare, Arms, and Organization" (2002), "Seeking Security in the Dragons Shadow: China and Southeast Asia in the Emerging Asian Order" (2003), "The War on Terror and the Future of Indonesian Democracy" (2003), and "The Correlates of Nationalism in Beijing Public Opinion" (2003).

South Africa

South African research institutions covering national security policy address topics as varied as the role of diamonds in armed conflict, child soldiers, terrorism, and the security situation in countries such as Zimbabwe.

Centre for Conflict Resolution

The Centre for Conflict Resolution (CCR) is affiliated with the University of Cape Town in South Africa. CCR seeks to promote constructive and cooperative approaches to conflict resolution and violence reduction and conducts mediation, training, education, and research activities to facilitate these objectives.[26]

Further information about CCR and its activities can be obtained at http://ccrweb.ccr.uct.ac.za/. This website features information about CCR activities and publications such as recent issues of the journal *Track Two* and reports including *Crisis Resolution and Conflict Management in Africa* (1998), *Ethnic Conflict and Its Management* (1998), and *An Overview of Small Arms Production, Export, and Ownership in South Africa* (2000).

Institute for Security Studies

The Institute for Security Studies (ISS) is located in Pretoria, South Africa, and has a branch office in Capetown. Founded in 1991, ISS is a nonprofit research institute with fifty employees from six African countries. Its institutional mission is conducting applied research on regional and national security and disseminating research results to encourage other countries, particularly African countries, to promote political and security cooperation. ISS concentrates its research on arms management, African security analysis, peace missions, crime, and security sector transformation.[27]

The website www.iss.co.za/ has organizational information and descriptions of past ISS-sponsored events. Accessible full-text publications on African security issues include newsletters such as *Focus on Small Arms in Africa* (2002–present) and the scholarly journal *African Security Review* and its predecessors (1992–present).

The ISS Occasional Papers series is accessible from 1996 to the present and includes analyses such as *Early Warning and Conflict in Africa* (1996), *Renaissance Peacekeeping: A South African Solution to Conflict in the Democratic Republic of Congo (DRC)* (1999), *South African Police Service (SAPS) Border Control Units: An Evaluation of the New Detached Duties* (2001), *Diamonds and Other Precious Stones in Armed Conflicts and Law Enforcement Cooperation in Southern Africa* (2002), *AIDS, Security, and Governance in Southern Africa: Exploring the Impact* (2003), and *Offsetting the Costs of South Africa's (SA's) Strategic Defence Package* (2003).

The website also provides access to institute monographs produced from 1996 to the present. Representative examples include *Franco-South African Dialogue: Sustainable Security in Africa* (2000), *Fear in the City: Urban Terrorism in South Africa* (2001), *Africa and Terrorism: Joining the Global Campaign* (2002), *Policing the Ports: Illicit Trafficking in South Africa* (2003), *From Child Soldier to Ex-Fighter: Female Fighters, Demobilisation, and Reintegration in Ethiopia* (2003), and *Zimbabwe's Turmoil: Problems and Prospects* (2003).

Available online are descriptions of books that ISS has published and the text of selected books such as *Society under Siege*, Vol. III: *Managing Arms in South Africa* (2000) and *Angola's War Economy: The Role of Oil and Diamonds* (2000).

Sri Lanka—Regional Centre for Strategic Studies

The Regional Centre for Strategic Studies (RCSS) is located in Colombo, Sri Lanka, and is an independent nongovernmental collaborative institution focusing on South Asian international and strategic issues. Institutional objectives are to provide a facility for studying and researching South Asian strategic studies, sponsor and coordinate such research among scholars and professionals, and collaborate with other institutions on these issues.[28]

Additional details about RCSS activities are available at www.rcss.org/. Accessible resources include descriptions of books written by center-affiliated scholars, the RCSS *Newsletter* (1999–present), and reports from 1998 to the present such as *Coping with Disorder: Strategies to End Internal Wars in South Asia* (2000), *Defence Expenditures in South Asia: India and Pakistan* (2000), *Third-Generation Indian Perceptions of the Kashmir Issue* (2001), and *Government and Defence Spending: Views from South Asia* (2001).

Sweden—Stockholm International Peace Research Institute

The Stockholm International Peace Research Institute (SIPRI) was established as a legal foundation by the Swedish Parliament in 1966. Its mission is conducting research to promote international peace and the peaceful resolution of international conflicts as well as research on arms control and military armaments. It seeks to use what it sees as hard facts and data in its research to produce impartial information, although its general ideological position is similar to that held by European Social Democratic political parties.[29]

The SIPRI website (www.sipri.se/) has a "What's New" page; descriptions of SIPRI project areas including armed conflict and conflict management, arms transfers, European security and arms control, and Russia's security agenda; Quicktime video presentations by institute scholars; databases on military expenditures and national export control systems; information on SIPRI's library; and employment opportunities.

Publications produced by SIPRI include the annual *SIPRI Yearbook,* with chapter excerpts from 1993 to the present accessible online. The website has a catalog listing SIPRI publications (1969–present) and information on ordering these publications, many which are published by Oxford University Press. Examples of accessible full-text reports include *Preventing Violent Conflict: The Search for Political Will, Strategies, and Effective Tools* (2000), *The New Security Dimensions: Europe after NATO and the EU Enlargements* (2001), *Missile Defence and the ABM Treaty: A Status Report* (2001), *The Adapted CFE Treaty and the Admission of the Baltic States to NATO* (2002), *Armament and Disarmament in the Caucasus and Central Asia* (2003), and *The Future of the United Nations Register of Conventional Arms* (2003).

Switzerland

The presence of many United Nations institutions in Switzerland and that country's traditional policy of armed neutrality in national security issues help enhance the study of national security policy by institutions within Switzerland. Arms control, European security policy, and terrorism are some of the topics analyzed by Swiss national security research institutes.

Center for Security Studies

The Center for Security Studies (CSS) was founded in 1986 and maintains a staff of approximately seventy-five research and teaching personnel. CSS is part of the Swiss Federal Institute of Technology in Zurich, Switzerland, and specializes in national and international security studies. It carries out its activities through research, teaching, and networking with other academic research institutions and consulting with the Swiss government.[30]

The CSS website (www.fsk.ethz.ch/) features descriptions of ongoing center research projects such as Regionalization of Russian Foreign and Security Policy, Parallel History Project on NATO and the Warsaw Pact, Information Age Security, and Democratization of Armed Forces in Southeastern Europe; biographies and research interests of CSS personnel; and listings of previous CSS-sponsored events.

Numerous English language reports are also accessible including *Regionalization of Russian Foreign and Security Policy: The Case of Kursk Oblast* (2001), *The Internet and the Changing Face of International Relations and Security* (2001), *The International Critical Information Infrastructure Roundtable: An Inventory of Protection Practices in Eight Countries* (2002), *The Transformation of Terrorism: The "New Terrorism," Impact Scalability, and the Dynamic of Reciprocal Threat Perception* (2003), *Unraveling the European Security and Defence Policy Conundrum* (2003), and *Ready for Peace? The Implementation of the Good Friday Agreement in Northern Ireland 1998–2002* (2003).

Geneva Centre for Security Policy

The Geneva Centre for Security Policy (GCSP) is an international foundation based in Geneva and created as part of Switzerland's participation in the Partnership for Peace. GCSP's mandate includes providing expert international security policy training for diplomats and other foreign and defense ministry officials; defining, contributing, and advancing international security studies research and conference activities; and facilitating cooperative networking with countries, experts, and institutions specializing in this field.[31]

GCSP's website (www.gcsp.ch/) includes training course descriptions, descriptions of past conferences including papers presented, and alumni information. Full-text resources include selected conference proceedings such as *Turkey and the West* (2001) and assorted papers including *Arms Control in Reluctant Installments: Iraq and North Korea* (2000), *Implementation of Multilateral Arms Control Agreements: Question of Compliance, Nuclear Tests* (2000), *Terrorism: Threat and Responses* (2001), and *The Development of a Common European Security and Defence Policy by the European Union and Its Possible Consequences for Switzerland* (2001).

International Relations and Security Network

The International Relations and Security Network (IRSN) is part of the Center for Security Studies at the Swiss Federal Institute of Technology in Zurich, Switzerland. With thirty professional staff members and seventy partner organizations internationally, IRSN seeks to integrate information technology and the international security community by promoting knowledge and information exchange among individuals and organizations working in international security issues.[32]

IRSN's website (www.isn.ethz.ch/) has staff listings, Reuters news reports on international security issues, an events calendar of international security–related conferences, the Facts on International Relations and Security Trends (FIRST) database compiled from SIPRI and other sources, an international security acronyms glossary, and links to international security research organization websites. Publications provided include the bimonthly newsletter *Russian Regional Report*

(1996–present), the journal *Information and Security* (1998–present), and links to publications produced by other international security research organizations.

Taiwan—Taiwan Security Research

Taiwan Security Research (TSR) was founded in 1997 as part of the Political Science Department at National Taiwan University in Taipei, Taiwan. Its mission is providing objective and balanced information on security issues affecting Taiwan and the Asia-Pacific region.[33]

TSR's website (http://taiwansecurity.org/) features news and other information resources on topics such as U.S.-China engagement, the People's Liberation Army, missile buildup and defense, Taiwanese politics, Japan policy, and China's economic and social developments contributed by international media and scholarly sources. Papers from 1998 to the present are provided including "The Challenge to Political Negotiation across the Taiwan Strait" (1998), "The Taiwan Relations Act: Durable Agreement or Fraying Framework?" (1999), "Navigating the Taiwan Strait: Deterrence, Escalation Dominance, and U.S-China" (2002), "Taiwan Independence and the U.S. Response" (2002), and "Taiwan Strait II: The Risk of War" (2003).

United Arab Emirates—Emirates Center for Strategic Studies and Research

The Emirates Center for Strategic Studies and Research (ECSSR) is located in Abu Dhabi, United Arab Emirates. It conducts research on national security and economic health for the United Arab Emirates and the Persian Gulf region, facilitates the scholarly exchange of ideas and information, and assists and promotes the professional development of United Arab Emirates nationals through training programs.[34]

ECSSR's website (www.ecssr.ac.ae/) has information on the United Arab Emirates, descriptions of organizational entities such as the Department of Strategic Studies, and information and summaries of center-sponsored conferences and lectures. Additional content includes summaries of ECSSR books such as *Air/Missile Defense, Counter-Proliferation, and Security Policy Planning* (1999), *The Balance of Power in South Asia* (2000), and *The Gulf: Future Security and British Policy* (2000) along with summaries of research papers such as "Integrated Middle East Regional Approaches to Unconventional Arms Control and Disarmament" (1999), "Iran, Between the Gulf and the Caspian Basin: Strategic and Economic Implications" (2000), and "Turkish-Israeli Relations: From the Periphery to the Center" (2001).

United Kingdom

The United Kingdom has played a historically and contemporarily significant role in international security issues. British institutions conduct research on civil-military relations and disarmament, British military policy, and national security policy making in other countries.

Acronym Institute for Disarmament Diplomacy

Located in London, England, the Acronym Institute for Disarmament Diplomacy (AI) was established in 1995 as the Disarmament Intelligence Review and acquired its present name in 1997. AI's institutional mission is working with policymakers and nongovernmental organizations to promote nonproliferation and nuclear disarmament by publishing information and advocating available negotiating opportunities.[35]

AI's website (www.acronym.org.uk/) features a calendar of upcoming international disarmament conferences and news reports on disarmament-related subjects such as the Chemical Weapons Convention, Comprehensive Nuclear Test Ban Treaty, British disarmament policy, and South Asian nuclear developments. Available publications include the newsletter *Disarmament Review* (1996–present) and reports such as *A Comprehensive Test-Ban Treaty: Signed But Not Sealed* (1997) and *The Non-Proliferation Treaty: Challenging Times* (2000).

Civil-Military Relations in Central and Eastern Europe Internet Resource Center

Civil-Military Relations in Central and Eastern Europe Internet Resource Center (CMR) is part of the University of London's Kings College. CMR examines changes in civil-military relationships in Central and Eastern Europe following communism's demise. Research objectives include identifying development patterns in civil-military relationships in these regions, examining changes in these relationships and their relative importance, and assessing the impact of these changes and the outreach policies toward Central and Eastern Europe by organizations such as NATO, the European Union, and the Organization for Security and Cooperation in Europe.[36]

The website http://civil-military.dsd.kcl.ac.uk/ has listings of CMR-funding sources, CMR-sponsored event descriptions, contact information, and bibliographic citations to civilian-military relations resources. Examples of accessible papers include "Democratic Control of the Armed Forces in Central and Eastern Europe: A Framework for Understanding Civil-Military Relations" (1999), "Professionalization of Armed Forces in Central and Eastern Europe: A Background Paper" (2000), and "The Armed Forces and Society in Post-Communist Europe: Legitimacy and Change" (2002).

Conflict, Security, and Development Group

The Conflict, Security, and Development Group (CSDG) is located at the University of London's King College. CSDG was formed in 1999 at the request of the British Department for International Development to examine operational and policy challenges related to security sector reform. CSDG's primary focus is examining possible relationships among economic development, conflict, and national security. It publishes research on related topics such as light weapons proliferation, military demobilization, and police reform.[37]

CSDG's website (http://csdg.kcl.ac.uk/) features a map, listings and research interests of affiliated personnel, and institutional descriptive information. Accessible publications include *Bulletin* briefings (1999–present), select articles from the scholarly journal *Conflict, Security, and Development* (2001–present), and papers such as "Security Reform in Democratic Nigeria" (2000), "Reforming Southeast Asia's Security Sectors" (2001), "Off-Budget Military Expenditure and Revenue: Issues and Policy Perspectives for Donors" (2002), and "Security Sector Transformation in Post-Conflict Societies" (2002).

Conflict Studies Research Centre

The Conflict Studies Research Centre (CSRC), located in Camberley, Surrey, England, was founded in 1972 and serves as part of the British Army's Doctrine and Development Directorate. Its mission is analyzing long-term instability and military and security practices in Central and Eastern Europe and the former Soviet Union.[38]

CSRC's website (www.csrc.ac.uk/) features a "What's New" page, links to Russian and Eastern European security-oriented websites, and organization and contact information. Accessible full-text reports from 1999 to the present include the quarterly periodical *Russian Chronology* (1998–present) and monographs such as *Small Arms Transfers and Disarmament: A Security Leitmotif for Tajikistan in the Late 1990s?* (1999), *Chechnya: Dynamics of War Brutality and Stress* (2001), *The Recreation of Russia's Ground Forces High Command: Prepared for Future War?* (2002), *Manpower Problems of the Russian Armed Forces* (2002), *Vladimir Putin and Russia's Special Services* (2002), *New Documents on Ukraine's Security Policy: A Sound Basis for Action?* (2003), *Perspectives on Ethno-Nationalist/Separatist Terrorism* (2003), and *Uzbekistan and the Threat from Islamic Extremism* (2003).

International Institute for Strategic Studies

The International Institute for Strategic Studies (IISS) is based in London, England. Founded in 1958, it has a staff of fifty and approximately 2,140 members.[39] The institute's mission is providing objective information on international strategic issues for political, diplomatic, military, journalistic, academic, and general audiences.[40]

Detailed information about IISS programs and activities can be found at www.iiss.org/. Materials include press references to IISS experts or work, institutional experts' biographies and research interests, and information on IISS research program areas such as European security, Middle East, new terrorism, and Russia and Eurasia.

Full-text access is provided to the current IISS *Newsletter* and the journal *Russian Regional Perspectives*. Summaries are provided to articles from the journal *Survival* (2000–present), the current issue of the annual periodical *Military Balance*, and to the IISS monographic series Adelphi Papers (1996–present). The Adelphi Papers series is likely to be found in many university research libraries. Some titles are *Ballistic Missile Defence and Strategic Stability* (2000), *German Military Reform and*

European Security (2001), *Disintegrating Indonesia: Implications for Regional Security* (2002), *Iraq at the Crossroads: State and Society in the Shadow of Regime Change* (2003), and *Political Islam in Southeast Asia: Moderates, Radicals, and Terrorists* (2003).

Jane's Information Group

Jane's Information Group (JIG) is headquartered in Coulson, Surrey, England, and has offices in various international venues. Founded in 1898, JIG is a leading provider of intelligence and analysis on international security issues and has a reputation for accuracy, authoritativeness, and impartiality. Its products provide defense news and analysis, individual country security and threat appraisals, military systems and equipment information, orders of battle and military deployment information on the world's militaries, and international geopolitical intelligence and news analysis.[41]

The website www.janes.com/ contains information about JIG and its products and services, which are available in many academic and military libraries internationally. These publications include periodicals such as *Intelligence Review* and *International Defence Review* along with annual compilations such as *All the World's Aircraft*, *Jane's Fighting Ships*, *Jane's Land-Based Air Defence*, *Jane's Missiles and Rockets*, and *Jane's Naval Weapons Systems*. Online access to these publications is provided to subscribers receiving print versions of these resources.

Lancaster University—Centre for Defence and International Security Studies

The Centre for Defence and International Studies (CDISS) conducts interdisciplinary research on defense and security issues of concern to the United Kingdom and other countries and is based in Lancaster University's Department of Politics and International Relations, where it was established in 1990.[42]

The CDISS website (www.cdiss.org/) features descriptions of research programs covering aerospace power, civil-military relations, military technology, sea-lane security, and other subjects. Sample publications are *The Chinese Missile Threat: A Photo Essay* (1996), *Hypersonic Vehicles: Back to the Future* (1997), and *North Korea's Musudan-Ri Launch Vehicle* (1999). The website also lists anticipated future research topics dealing with ballistic missiles.

Royal United Services Institute

The Royal United Services Institute (RUSI), in London, England, was founded in 1831 by the Duke of Wellington. RUSI seeks to promote, debate, report on, and provide options on national defense and international security issues to government, military, political, diplomatic, academic, commercial, media, law enforcement, and other interested individuals and organizations.[43] The RUSI website (www.rusi.org/) provides the text of current press releases and information on receiving them by e-mail. It has links to RUSI study program websites: "Asia," "European Security," "Homeland Security and Resilience," "Middle East and North Africa," and "UK Armed Forces." The website has the current issue of the periodical *Chinese Military Guide*. Tables of contents are provided for a number of RUSI publications including *RUSI Journal* (February 2000–present) and the *Newsbrief* newsletter (January 2000–present). RUSI members receive full-text access to these and other publications.

The website also has listings for most volumes of the RUSI Whitehall Papers monographic series (1990–present). Titles include *The Transformation of the Polish Armed Forces—Preparing for NATO* (1999), *The Aegean Sea: Bridge or Barrier* (2001), *Hanging Together: Military Interoperability in an Age of Technical Innovation* (2003), and *Empires in Conflict: The Growing Rift between Europe and the United States* (2003).

Notes

1. Australian Defence Studies Centre, "Who We Are" (2003), 1 (http://idun.its.adfa.edu.au/ADSC/who.htm), accessed September 17, 2003.

2. Australian Strategic Policy Institute, "About Us" (n.d.), 1–2 (www.aspi.org.au/about.cfm), accessed September 17, 2003.

3. Strategic and Defence Studies Centre, "About the SDSC" (n.d.), 1 (http://rspas.anu.edu.au/sdsc/aboutus.html), accessed September 18, 2003.

4. Institute for International Security Studies, "Objectives" (n.d.), 1 (www.isn.ethz.ch/isis/alle/objectives.htm), accessed September 18, 2003.

5. Canadian Institute of Strategic Studies, "About Us" (n.d.), 1 (www.ciss.ca/aboutus.htm), accessed September 18, 2003.

6. Centre for Security and Defence Studies, "About the Centre" (n.d.), 1 (www.carleton.ca/csds/about_the_centre.html), accessed September 19, 2003.

7. Conference of Defence Associations, "About CDA" (2003), 1 (www.cda-cdai.ca/about.htm), accessed September 19, 2003.

8. Council for Canadian Security in the 21st Century, "Welcome to the Council for Canadian Security in the 21st Century WWW Site" (2003), 1 (www.ccs21.org/main.htm), accessed September 22, 2003.

9. Research Group in International Security, "Programme Information" (2000), 1–2 (ww2.mcgill.ca/regis/themes.htm), accessed August 19, 2003.

10. Centre for Military and Strategic Studies, "History" (n.d.), slide 2 (www.stratnet.ucalgary.ca/about/ report/2), accessed September 22, 2003.

11. Centre for Military and Strategic Studies, "About CMSS—Centre Objectives" (n.d.), 1 (www.stratnet.ucalgary.ca/about/object.html), accessed September 22, 2003.

12. Centre for Defence and Security Studies, "Information about CDSS" (n.d.), 1 (www.umanitoba.ca/centres/defence/), accessed September 23, 2003.

13. York Centre for International and Security Studies, "Welcome" (n.d.), 1 (www.yorku.ca/yciss/ welcome/welcome_main.htm), accessed September 24, 2003.

14. Danish Institute of International Affairs, "About DUPI" (n.d.), 1 (www.dupi.dk/www.dupi.dk/htdocs/re_en_omd/), accessed September 25, 2003.

15. Finnish Institute of International Affairs, "What Is the FIIA" (n.d.), 1 (www.upi-fiaa.fi/english/institute/institute_main.htm), accessed September 25, 2003.

16. German Institute for International Politics and Security, "Stiftung Wissenschaft und Politik (SWP)" (2003), 1 (www.swp-berlin.org/english/index_e.html), accessed September 26, 2003.

17. Institute for Defence Studies and Analysis, "Homepage" (n.d.), 1 (www.idsa-india.org/), accessed September 26, 2003.

18. Institute of Peace and Conflict Studies, "About Us" (2002), 1 (www.ipcs.org/ipcs/aboutUs.jsp?status=Objectives&mod=a), accessed September 26, 2003.

19. Begin-Sadat Center for Strategic Studies, "About Us" (n.d.), 1–2 (www.biu.ac.il/Besa/about.html), accessed September 29, 2003.

20. Institute for Advanced Strategic and Political Studies, "About Us" (n.d.), 1 (www.israeleconomy.org/about.htm), accessed September 29, 2003.

21. Jaffee Center for Strategic Studies, "About JCSS" (n.d.), 1–3 (www.tau.ac.il/jcss/about.html), accessed September 29, 2003.

22. Institute for International Policy Studies, "About IIPS" (n.d.), 1 (www.iips.org/page2.html), accessed October 1, 2003.

23. Centre for Strategic Studies, "Welcome to the CSS" (n.d.), 1 (www.vuw.ac.nz/css/), accessed October 1, 2003.

24. Institute of Strategic Studies Islamabad, "Homepage" (n.d.), 1 (www.issi.org.pk/), accessed October 1, 2003.

25. Institute of Defence and Strategic Studies, "About Us" (n.d.), 1 (www.idss.edu.sg/abuts_01.htm), accessed October 1, 2003.

26. Centre for Conflict Resolution, "About the Centre for Conflict Resolution" (n.d.), 1 (http://ccrweb.ccr.uct.ac.za/about.html), accessed October 2, 2003.

27. Institute for Strategic Studies, "Approach and Focus: History of the ISS" (n.d.), 1 (www.iss.co.za/about/app_focus.htm), accessed October 8, 2003.

28. Regional Center for Strategic Studies, "About RCSS" (n.d.), 1 (www.rcss.org/about.html), accessed October 3, 2003.

29. Stockholm International Peace Research Institute, "About SIPRI: A Brief History of SIPRI" (n.d.), 1 (http://about.sipri.se/history/), accessed October 3, 2003. For additional historical background, see Frank Blackaby, *How SIPRI Begun: SIPRI Continuity and Change 1966–1996* (Stockholm, Sweden: Stockholm International Peace Research Institute, 1996).

30. Center for Security Studies, "About Us" (n.d.), 1 (www.fsk.ethz.ch/about/about_us/about_us.htm), accessed October 4, 2003.

31. Geneva Centre for Security Policy, "About the GCSP" (2000), 1 (www.gcsp.ch/e/_navtop.htm), accessed October 4, 2003.

32. International Relations and Security Network, "Welcome" (2002), 1 (www.isn.ethz.ch/extended/index.cfm?service=about), accessed October 4, 2003.

33. Taiwan Security Research, "About TSR" (n.d.), 1 (http://taiwansecurity.org/TSR-About-TSR.htm), accessed October 4, 2003.

34. Emirates Center for Strategic Studies and Research, "ECSSR Mission" (n.d.), 1 (www.ecssr.ac.ae/03uae.intro3.html), accessed October 6, 2003.

35. Acronym Institute for Disarmament Diplomacy, "About the Acronym Institute" (2003), 1 (www.acronym.org.uk/acroinst.htm), accessed October 6, 2003.

36. Civil-Military Relations in Central and Eastern Europe, "Project Aims and Objectives" (2000), 1–2 (http://civil-military.dsd.kcl.ac.uk/project/aims_and_objectives.htm), accessed October 6, 2003.

37. Conflict, Security, and Development Group, "Profile" (n.d.), 1–2 (http://csdg.kcl.ac.uk/Profile/profile.html), accessed October 6, 2003.

38. Conflict Studies Research Centre, "About CSRC" (2001), 1 (www.csrc.ac.uk/pages/about_csrc.htm), accessed October 6, 2003.

39. "Associations Unlimited: International Institute for Strategic Studies" (n.d.), 1 (www.galenet.com/servlet/AU), accessed October 7, 2003.

40. International Institute for Strategic Studies, "About IISS" (n.d.), 1 (www.iiss.org/aboutiiss.php), accessed October 7, 2003.

41. Jane's Information Group, "About Jane's" (n.d.), 1 (www.janes.com/company/about/), accessed October 7, 2003. For a portrait of Jane's Information Group (JIG) founder Fred Jane and a historical overview of *Jane's Fighting Ships,* a key JIG publication, see Bert Chapman, "The Origins and Development of Jane's Fighting Ships," *Reference Services Review,* 21 (1) (1993): 71–78.

42. Centre for Defence and International Security Studies, "About CDISS" (1997), 1 (www.cdiss.org/descript.htm), accessed October 7, 2003.

43. Royal United Services Institute, "About the Institute" (2001), 1 (www.rusi.org/about.html), accessed October 8, 2003. For additional historical background on the Royal United Services Institute, see Michael D. Welch, *Science and the British Officer: The Early Days of the Royal United Services Institute for Defence Studies, 1829–1869* (London, England: Royal United Services Institute for Defence Studies, 1998).

CHAPTER 14

Selected Indexes, Journals, Series, and Scholars

Commercially produced periodicals indexes, major journals produced by academic publishers, monograph book series, and scholars enhance understanding of national security–related issues and theories.

Periodical Indexes

Periodical indexes are available that cover national security policy literature. Many U.S. and foreign academic research libraries have print or electronic versions of these indexes, or both, in their collections. Access to them depends on the agreements negotiated between subscribing libraries and the commercial publishers of the indexes. Electronic versions usually can be used only by students or faculty at academic institutions. In some cases, users need their university identification to register for access to online indexes. In other cases, users not affiliated with these institutions may not have to register and may access databases on a computer terminal in the university's library system or from a computer within the university's Internet protocol (IP) domain, which can include any computer on a given campus.

"Air University Library Index to Military Periodicals"

"Air University Library Index to Military Periodicals" (AULIMP) is produced by Air University Library at Maxwell Air Force Base, in Alabama. It indexes articles from military periodicals from 1989 to the present. It is freely accessible to the public at www.au.af.mil/au/aul/muir1/aulimp.htm. Users can check local libraries to see if they have paper or electronic copies of the articles.

America: History and Life

America: History and Life (AHL) is produced by ABC Clio publishers in Santa Barbara, California. It indexes articles, dissertations, book chapters, and books on American and Canadian history, covering 1450 to the present. AHL is primarily available in medium or large academic research libraries.

"Catalog of Government Publications"

The "Catalog of Government Publications" (CGP) is produced by the U.S. Government Printing Office (GPO). CGP is an online version of the *Monthly Catalog of U.S. Government Publications,* which lists publications U.S. federal depository libraries are eligible to receive. CGP is freely accessible to the public at www.gpoaccess.gov/cgp/, covers publications from January 1994 to the present, and provides links to online versions of many of these publications as well as detailed bibliographic information, which can be used to locate print versions at federal depository libraries. A related GPO product, "New Electronic Titles" (www.access.gpo.gov/su_docs/locators/net/), lists online links to newly available electronic U.S. government publications from 2000 to the present. The publications are listed by three to four date ranges per month.

Congressional Information Service Index

While not strictly a journal or periodical article index, the *Congressional Information Service Index* (CIS Index) is an essential resource for those studying governmental national security policy. Produced by LexisNexis subsidiary Congressional Information Service in Bethesda, Maryland, the CIS Index covers congressional committee hearings and publications from 1970 to the present. Print versions appear as a monthly index and as abstract volumes, which cumulate into annual index and abstract volumes and an annual legislative histories volume. The CIS Index has detailed bibliographic citations to congressional publications and the names of witnesses testifying before congressional committees. "Congressional Universe," a related Internet service from the Congressional Information Service, is also available.

"Ebsco Host's Military and Government Collection"

"Ebsco Host's Military and Government Collection" (EHMGC) offers access to more than three hundred military and government periodicals dating back to the middle 1980s. Access to some full-text articles is provided.

Historical Abstracts

Historical Abstracts (HA) is produced by ABC-Clio. It indexes articles, dissertations, book chapters, and books on national and international history outside North America, covering 1450 to the present.

> ## Superintendent of Documents Classification System
>
> The Superintendent of Documents (SuDoc) classification system is used to classify U.S. government publications distributed to federal depository libraries by the U.S. Government Printing Office (GPO). GPO is responsible for maintaining and updating the system, which is based on the federal agency producing the document. Each letter, number, and mark of punctuation within a SuDoc number are important because they tell something about an agency producing a document, the type of publication it is, and the publication year. For instance, a publication with the SuDoc number D 1.1:003 is the Department of Defense (DOD) annual report to Congress for federal fiscal year 2003. Publications with the SuDoc stem D 1.2 are general DOD publications, such as *On-Site Inspections under the CFE Treaty: A History of the On-Site Inspection Agency and CFE Treaty Implementation, 1990–1996* (D 1.2:C 76/12). Other general SuDoc number stems for DOD and military agencies are D 103 for the U.S. Army Corps of Engineers, D 114 for the U.S. Army Military History Center, D 205 for the Navy Judge Advocate General, D 221 for the Naval Historical Center, and D 301 for the Air Force Department. General information about the SuDoc classification system can be found on GPO's website at www.access.gpo.gov/su_docs/fdlp/pubs/explain.html.
>
> SuDoc numbers can change when a government agency producing those publications has its name changed or that agency's functions are transferred into a new agency. For instance, publications produced by the U.S. Customs Service were classified under the SuDoc stem T 17 when this agency was part of the Treasury Department. Following the 2003 creation of the Department of Homeland Security and the transfer of Customs Service functions to this new department, its publications were classified under the SuDoc stem HS 4.100. Such agency SuDoc number changes will be tracked by most federal depository library online catalog systems.

LexisNexis Government Periodicals Index

LexisNexis Government Periodicals Index (GPI) is published by LexisNexis Inc. subsidiary Congressional Information Service (CIS). It provides access to 170 U.S. government agency periodicals from 1988 to the present.

Public Affairs Information Service International

Public Affairs Information Service International (PAIS) is owned by the Online Computer Library Consortium (OCLC) in Dublin, Ohio. PAIS International offers access to scholarly public affairs literature from journal articles, books, book chapters, and selected U.S. government documents. Information on this service can be found at www.pais.org/, and many academic libraries subscribe to its print or online services.

"Staff College Automated Periodicals Index"

"Staff College Automated Periodicals Index" (SCAMPI) is a cooperative effort by the Joint Forces Staff College Library, National Defense University Library, and Defense Technical Information Center. It indexes popular and scholarly militarily oriented publications and selected General Accounting Office and RAND Corporation reports from 1997 to the present. SCAMPI also lists the journals it indexes and provides links to journal home pages, if available, through its website (www.dtic.mil/dtic/scampi/).

Worldwide Political Science Abstracts

Worldwide Political Science Abstracts (WPSA) is published by Cambridge Scientific Abstracts based in Bethesda, Maryland. WPSA indexes articles from political science journals from 1975 to the present and provides some retrospective coverage from 1960 to 1974.

Scholarly Journals

A large variety of scholarly journals covering national security policy are published in numerous countries. Among the topics they discuss are civil-military relations, defense economics, military sociology, nuclear strategy, and terrorism.[1] Scholarly journals also review books and other scholarly literature. These journals accept articles that have gone through the peer review process in which experts and scholars in a particular field who serve on a journal's editorial board review the content of submitted articles to determine their suitability for publication.

Many scholarly journals are available in print and electronic formats in U.S. and foreign academic libraries. However, many of these journals are published by commercial for-profit publishers. As a result, articles are highly unlikely to be freely available on the Internet. College and university libraries that have print copy subscriptions may have negotiated and paid for electronic access to these journals through contractual agreements with publishers. The agreements may restrict access to electronic journals to users who are part of a university community such as faculty and students with university identification numbers. The agreements also may stipulate that only computers in the university's IP range or in the university's library be used.

A useful directory to scholarly and popular periodicals is *Ulrich's International Periodicals Directory*. This annual multivolume set, published by R. R. Bowker, is a staple resource in many academic library reference collections for locating periodical information.

Two projects provide access to a large numbers of electronic journals on various subjects: JSTOR and TDNet. JSTOR provides access to recent and historical issues of scholarly journals in many social science disciplines and is available to members of participating academic institutions. Information about JSTOR is accessible at www.jstor.org/.[2] TDNet is an Israeli-based company providing access to electronic journal articles in multiple subjects by many academic libraries and research institutions.

Armed Forces and Society

Armed Forces and Society is produced by the InterUniversity Seminar on Armed Forces and Society (IUS) hosted at the University of Maryland. Published quarterly by Transaction Publishers, its International Standard Serial Number (ISSN) is 0095-327X, and general information about the journal and IUS can be accessed at www.bsos.umd.edu/ius/main/Journal.htm. Published since 1975, samples of recent *Armed Forces and Society* articles include "Toward Civilian Supremacy: Civil-Military Relations in Taiwan's Democratization" (fall 2002) and "The Reconstruction of Culture, Citizenship, and Military Service" (spring 2003).

Astropolitics: The International Journal of Space Power and Policy

Astropolitics: The International Journal of Space Power and Policy began production in 2003 and is published by the British-based Frank Cass publishers. Three issues are expected to be published per year. The journal's ISSN is 1477-7622, and its website is www.astropolitics.org/. Sample articles are "Totem and Taboo: Depolarizing the Space Weaponization Debate" (summer 2003) and "The Advent of Space Weapons" (summer 2003).

Civil Wars

Civil Wars is published quarterly by Frank Cass, its ISSN is 1369-8249, and general information can be obtained from the publisher's website (www.tandf.co.uk/journals/titles/13698249.asp). The journal has been published since 1998. Sample articles are "The Initiating and Magnifying Factors in Algeria's Civil Conflict" (spring 2001) and "Chechnya: The Causes of a Protracted Post-Soviet Conflict" (winter 2002).

Cold War History

Cold War History is produced by the Department of International History at the London School of Economics and Political Science and is published three times a year by Frank Cass. The ISSN is 1468-2745. The journal has been published since 2000, and general information about it can be found at www.tandf.co.uk/journals/titles/14682745.asp. Sample articles are "Driving the Soviets Up the Wall: A Super-Ally, a Superpower, and the Building of the Berlin Wall" (August 2000) and "Khruschev and the Berlin Crisis: Soviet Brinksmanship Seen from Inside" (January 2003).

Comparative Strategy

Comparative Strategy is cosponsored by the National Institute for Public Policy (near Washington, D.C.) and the Center for Strategic Studies at the University of Reading (in the United Kingdom) and is published by Taylor and Francis Group. Publication frequency is quarterly, the journal's ISSN is 0149-5933, and general information about it is accessible at www.tandf.co.uk/journals/titles/01495933.asp. It has been published since 1982. Recent sample articles are "Evolving Russian Perspectives on

Missile Defense: The Emerging Accommodation" (October-December 2002) and "Promoting Freedom and Democracy: Fighting the War of Ideas against Islamic Terrorism" (July–September 2003).

Contemporary Security Policy

Contemporary Security Policy is published three times a year by Frank Cass. Its ISSN is 1352-3260, and it has been published since 1980. General information on this journal is accessible at www.tandf.co.uk/journals/titles/13523260.asp. Recent articles include "Travels with Charlemagne: Metaphor, Myth, and the Future of Franco-German Security and Defence Cooperation" (April 2002) and "Risks of Nuclear Terror: Vulnerabilities to Theft and Sabotage at Nuclear Weapons Facilities" (December 2002).

CQ Weekly Report

CQ Weekly Report, called *Congressional Quarterly Weekly Report* until April 1998, is published by Congressional Quarterly Inc. in Washington, DC. It has been published since 1945, and its ISSN is 0010-5910. General information about this publication, which chronicles congressional legislative activity, can be found through the publisher's website (www.cq.com/). Examples of recent articles dealing with national security policy are "Homeland Security Bill's Momentum Unfazed by Cries of Underfunding" (July 12, 2003) and "Homeland Department Gets the Dollars, Along with a Number of Strings" (September 27, 2003).

Defence Studies

Defence Studies is published three times a year by Frank Cass. Its ISSN is 1470-2436, and it began publishing in 2001. General information about *Defence Studies* can be obtained through its website (www.tandf.co.uk/journals/titles/14702436.asp). Representative articles are "Is the West's Reliance on Technology the Panacea for Future Conflict or its Achilles' Heel?" (summer 2001), "The Continuing Relevance of Strategic Studies in the Post–Cold War Era" (summer 2001), and "Network Centric Warfare and the Death of Operational Art" (spring 2002).

European Security

European Security, published three times annually by Frank Cass, has been published since 1992. Its ISSN is 0966-2839. Information on its purpose and content are accessible at www.tandf.co.uk/journals/titles/09662839.asp. Examples of featured articles are "The European Security and Defence Policy: What Impact on the EU's Approach to Security Challenges?" (summer 2002) and "Spain's Pursuit of Security in the Western Mediterranean" (summer 2002).

Intelligence and National Security

Intelligence and National Security is published by Frank Cass. It appears quarterly, its ISSN is 0268-4527, and it has been published since 1986. General information on editorial content is provided at www.tandf.co.uk/journals/titles/02684527.asp. Sample articles include "The Problem with Glass Houses: The Soviet Recruitment and Deployment of SS Men as Spies and Saboteurs" (autumn 2000), "Enigmatic Variations: The Development of National Intelligence Assessment in Australia" (summer 2001), and "Towards Postmodern Intelligence" (autumn 2002).

International Journal of Intelligence and Counterintelligence

International Journal of Intelligence and Counterintelligence is published quarterly by Taylor and Francis. Its ISSN is 0885-0607, and it has been published since 1988. General information on this journal can be found at www.tandf.co.uk/journals/titles/08850607.asp. Representative articles are "GOP Oversight of Intelligence in the Clinton Era" (January 2002), "GAO versus the CIA: Uphill Battles against an Overpowering Force" (July 2002), "Partisanship and the Decline of Intelligence Oversight" (spring 2003), and "Pakistan's ISI: The Invisible Government" (fall 2003).

International Peacekeeping

International Peacekeeping is published quarterly by Frank Cass. Its ISSN is 1353-3312, it has been published since 1994, and information about its editorial focus can be found at www.tandf.co.uk/journals/titles/13533312.asp. Sample articles are "Improving the UN's Capacity for Conflict Prevention" (spring 2002), "The Global Impact of HIV/AIDS on Peace Support Operations" (autumn 2002), and "Conflict Prevention: Old Wine in New Bottles" (spring 2003).

International Security

International Security is produced at the Belfer Center for Science and International Affairs (BCSIA) at Harvard University's John F. Kennedy School of Government and published by Massachusetts Institute of Technology (MIT) Press. Produced quarterly, it has been published since 1976. Its ISSN is 0162-2889. General information on *International Security* can be found through the Belfer Center's website (http://bcsia.ksg.harvard.edu/) and the publisher's site (http://mitpress.mit.edu/). Examples of recent articles are "The United States and Terrorism in Southwest Asia: September 11 and Beyond" (winter 2001), "Navigating the Taiwan Strait: Deterrence, Escalation Dominance, and U.S.-China Relations" (fall 2002), "Nuclear Deterrence Theory, Nuclear Proliferation, and National Missile Defense" (spring 2003), and "Command of the Commons: The Military Foundations of U.S. Hegemony" (summer 2003).

Journal of Battlefield Technology

The *Journal of Battlefield Technology* is published three times a year by Argos Press in Red Hill, Australian Capital Territory, Australia. Its ISSN is 1440-5113, and it has been published since 1998. Information about the journal, the first page of articles and article abstracts from the current issue, and the table of contents from all issues are accessible at www.argospres.com/jbt/. Sample *Journal of Battlefield Technology* articles include "Technology Insertion to Develop Mortar Systems for the Modern Battlefield," (July 2002) and "A Method for Predicting Natural Fragmentation of Warheads" (July 2003).

Journal of Cold War Studies

Journal of Cold War Studies is produced quarterly by Harvard University's Project on Cold War Studies and published by MIT Press. Its ISSN is 1520-3972, and it has been available since 1999. General information about the journal can be found at www.fas.harvard.edu/~hpcws/journal.htm and through the MIT Press website at http://mitpress.mit.edu/. Sample articles include "Cold War under Ice: The Army's Bid for a Long-Range Nuclear Role, 1959–1963" (fall 2001), "The Carter Administration and Italy: Keeping the Communists Out of Power without Interfering" (summer 2002), and "The Prelude to Nationwide Surveillance in East Germany: Stasi Operations and Threat Perceptions, 1945–1953" (spring 2003).

Journal of Conflict and Security Law

Journal of Conflict and Security Law is published biannually by Oxford University Press. Its ISSN is 1467-7954, it has been published since 1996, and general information on it can be found at www3.oup.co.uk/jnls/list/jconsl/. Recent articles are "Starting from Scratch: The Military Discipline System of the East Timor Defence Force" (October 2002) and "The UN Security Council and New Threats to Peace: Back to the Future" (December 2003).

Journal of Contingencies and Crisis Management

Journal of Contingencies and Crisis Management is published quarterly by Blackwell Publishing. Its ISSN is 0966-0879, it has been published since 1993, and general information on it is accessible at www.blackwellpublishing.com/journal.asp?ref=0966-0879. Examples of recent articles are "Landmines and Local Community Adaptation" (June 2002) and "Surveillance and Security: A Dodgy Relationship" (March 2003).

Journal of Military Ethics: Normative Aspects of the Use of Military Force

Journal of Military Ethics: Normative Aspects of the Use of Military Force is published biannually by Taylor and Francis. Its ISSN is 1502-7570, it has been published since 2002, and general information about the journal is accessible at www.tandf.co.uk/journals/titles/15027570.asp. Recent articles are "The Moral Limits of Military Deception" (January 2002) and "The Role of the 'International Community' in Just War Tradition—Confronting the Challenges of Humanitarian Intervention" (July 2003).

Journal of Military History

Journal of Military History is published quarterly by the Society for Military History in Leavenworth, Kansas. Its ISSN is 0026-3931, and it has been published since 1937. Information about the journal and the tables of contents for issues from 1997 to the present are accessible at www.smh-hq.org/jmh/. Recent articles include "Southern by the Grace of God But Prussian by Common Sense: James Longstreet and the Exercise of Command in the U.S. Civil War" (October 2002), "An Inward Looking Time: The United States Army, 1973–1976" (April 2003), and "Jim Crow and Uncle Sam: The Tuskegee Flying Units and the U.S. Army Air Forces in Europe during World War II" (July 2003).

Journal of Slavic Military Studies

Journal of Slavic Military Studies is published quarterly by Frank Cass. Its ISSN is 1351-8046, it has been published since 1988, and general information on its contents is accessible at www.tandf.co.uk/journals/titles/13518046.asp. Recent articles include "Russian Chemical Weapons: Proliferation or Destruction?" (March 2002), "Russia and NATO toward the Twenty-first Century: Conflicts and Peacekeeping in Bosnia-Herzegovina and Kosovo" (June 2002), and "The Future of the Russian Sea-Based Deterrent" (March 2003).

Journal of Strategic Studies

Journal of Strategic Studies is published quarterly by Frank Cass. Its ISSN is 0140-2390, it has been published since 1978, and general information about its editorial focus is accessible at www.tandf.co.uk/journals/titles/01402390.asp. Recent articles featured in this journal include "NATO's New Strategic Concept: Coherent Blueprint or Conceptual Muddle?" (September 2000), "The Second Nuclear Age: Proliferation Pessimism versus Sober Optimism in South Asia and East Asia" (December 2001), and "Uncertain Courses: Theater Missile Defence and Cross-Strait Competition" (September 2002).

Low Intensity Conflict and Law Enforcement

Low Intensity Conflict and Law Enforcement is published three times a year by Frank Cass. Its ISSN is 0966-2847, it has been published since 1994, and general information about its contents can be found at www.tandf.co.uk/journals/titles/09662847.asp. Sample articles are "Waco: Failures in Crisis Management and the Misapplication of Coercive Diplomacy" (spring 2000), "An Alternative Strategy for Fighting Cocaine Trafficking in Bolivia" (autumn 2002), and "Transnational Threats: Falling Through the Cracks" (spring 2003).

National Interest

National Interest is published quarterly by National Affairs Inc. in New York City. Its ISSN is 0084-9382, it has been published since 1985, and general information on this journal is accessible at www.nationalinterest.org/. Recent articles include "The Law of War: How Osama Slipped Away" (winter 2001–2002), "Reforging the Atlantic Alliance" (fall 2002), "Migration and the Dynamics of Empire" (spring 2003), and "Leashing the Dogs of War" (fall 2003).

National Journal

National Journal is published weekly by the Washington, D.C.-based National Journal group and provides coverage of federal government policy and political developments. Its ISSN is 0027-9560, it has been published since 1969, and general information on its work is accessible at www.nationaljournal.com/. Recent articles include "Get Used to It: Europe Is Not a Status Quo Power" (December 21, 2002), "Iraq Is Not Vietnam" (April 12, 2003), and "Nuclear Scorpions in the Asian Bottle" (October 4, 2003).

Proceedings: U.S. Naval Institute

Proceedings: U.S. Naval Institute is published monthly by the U.S. Naval Institute, which is a member association and interest group of U.S. Navy, U.S. Marine Corps, and U.S. Coast Guard professionals based in Annapolis, Maryland. The publication's ISSN is 0041-798X, it has been published since 1874, and general information on the journal is accessible at www.usni.org/proceedings/proceedings.htm. Sample articles include "Gender and the Civil-Military Gap" (January 2000), "Are We Already Transformed?" (January 2002), "Sea Warrior: Maximizing Human Capital" (June 2003), and "Coast Guard Must Play in Overseas War Plans" (October 2003).

Security Studies

Security Studies is published quarterly by Frank Cass. Its ISSN is 0963-6412, it has been published since 1991, and general information on the journal's philosophy is accessible at www.tandf.co.uk/journals/titles/09636412.asp. Representative articles include "Mission Impossible? Preventing Deadly Conflict in the African Great Lakes Region" (autumn 2001), "Shaping Military Doctrine in France: Decisionmakers between International Power and Domestic Interests" (winter 2001–2002), "Between the Bear and the Phoenix: The United States and the European Defense Community, 1950–54" (summer 2002), and "The Operational Identity of Humanitarian Military Intervention" (autumn 2002).

Small Wars and Insurgencies

Small Wars and Insurgencies is published three times per year by Frank Cass. Its ISSN 0959-2318, it has been published since 1990, and general information about it is accessible at www.tandf.co.uk/journals/titles/09592318.asp. Sample articles include "Special Forces for Counter Revolutionary Warfare: The South African Case" (summer 2001), "FM 3-0 Operations: The Effect of Humanitarian Operations on U.S.

Army Doctrine" (spring 2002), and "A Clash of Wills: Hizballah's Psychological Campaign against Israel in South Lebanon" (fall 2002).

Studies in Conflict and Terrorism

Studies in Conflict and Terrorism is published six times a year by Taylor and Francis. Its ISSN is 1057-610X, it has been published since 1978, and general information on its mission is accessible at www.tandf.co.uk/journals/titles/1057610X.asp. Representative articles include "Cults, Violence, and Religious Terrorism: An International Perspective" (October 2001), "How Do We Know We're Winning the War against Terrorists? Issues in Measurement" (May 2002), "Die and Let Die: Exploring Links between Suicide Terrorism and Terrorist Use of Chemical, Biological, Radiological, and Nuclear Weapons" (January 2003), and "Saddam Hussein: Political Psychological Profiling Results Relevant to His Possession, Use, and Possible Transfer of Weapons of Mass Destruction (WMD) to Terrorist Groups" (September 2003).

Survival

Survival is published quarterly by Oxford University Press and produced by the International Institute for Strategic Studies. Its ISSN is 0039-6338, it has been published since 1959, and general information about its contents is accessible at http://survival.oupjournals.org/. Recent articles include "A Saudi Nuclear Option" (summer 2001), "South-West Asia after the Taliban" (spring 2002), "The Palestinian Strategic Impasse" (winter 2002–2003), and "China and America: Trouble Ahead?" (autumn 2003).

Terrorism and Political Violence

Terrorism and Political Violence is published quarterly by Frank Cass. Its ISSN is 0954-6553, it has been published since 1989, and general information about its coverage is available at www.tandf.co.uk/journals/titles/0956553.asp. Recent article samples include "Beating the Water: The Terrorist Search for Power, Control, and Authority" (summer 2000), "Covert Biological Weapons Attacks against Agricultural Targets: Assessing the Impact against U.S. Agriculture" (autumn 2001), and "Troops Defending the Homeland: The Posse Comitatus Act and the Legal Environment for a Military Role in Domestic Counter Terrorism" (autumn 2002).

Global Crime (formerly *Transnational Organized Crime*)

Global Crime is published quarterly by Frank Cass and examines cross-border criminal activities such as trafficking in drugs, people, and weapons and money laundering.[3] Its ISSN is 1357-7387, it has been published since 1999, and general information on it is accessible at www.tandf.co.uk/journals/titles/13577387.asp. Representative sample articles include "The Links between Transnational Organized Crime and Terrorism" (winter 2000) and "Transnational Chinese Organized Crime: Activities, Patterns, and Emerging Trends" (fall–winter 2002).

> ## Library of Congress Subject Headings
>
> Library of Congress Subject Headings (LCSH) are terms designated by the Library of Congress (LC) to enable users to search library online catalogs for books on a particular subject. Most library "Online Public Access Catalogs" (OPAC) allow users to search for books held in a collection using keywords. Although learning LCSH takes some time, it can prove a more precise method of searching a library's OPAC. For example, using the LCSH term "United States Armed Forces Appropriations and Expenditures" as a subject search on an OPAC will yield better results than using the more general "American and military and spending."
>
> Furthermore, search results for an individual book will highlight other LCSHs used by LC to classify that book. By clicking on those LCSHs, the library's OPAC will search for other books on that subject that were not retrieved in the initial search. Many academic libraries have the multivolume LCSH publications, which are produced and updated by LC.

■ Monographic Series

Monographic series are books on a particular subject or groups of subjects produced by publishers to further knowledge and understanding. Such works can be historical overviews and analyses, present groundbreaking theories, be interdisciplinary in their coverage, stimulate often-contentious scholarly debate, and even come to be recognized as classics in a particular discipline. Many academic libraries make a regular practice of purchasing and collecting all or some titles in monographic series produced by scholarly publishers on topics of interests to their respective clienteles.

Monographic series are searchable by title in the "Online Public Access Catalogs" of most public and academic libraries. As a result, the number of titles in a particular monographic series can easily be determined, and researchers thus can quickly determine how many titles their library owns. Many scholarly publishers produce monographic series on national security–oriented topics that can be ordered from online booksellers such as Amazon.com.

Annals of Communism—Yale University Press

Annals of Communism is published by Yale University Press. This series presents works on documents covering the history of the Soviet Union and international communism from Russian national and Communist Party archives that have not been accessible to Western or Russian scholars.[4] Fifteen titles have been produced in the series since 1995 according to the publisher's website (www.yale.edu/annals/). National security–oriented works include *The Secret World of American Communism* (1995) by Harvey Klehr and others, *The Soviet World of American Communism* by Harvey Klehr and others (1998), *The Road to Terror: Stalin and the Self-Destruction of the Bolsheviks, 1932–1939* by Arch Getty and Oleg Naumov (1999), and *Spain Betrayed: The Soviet Union in the Spanish Civil War* by Ronald Radosh and others (2001).

The website also contains information on forthcoming works from this series including *The Assassination of Sergei Kirov and the Great Terror,* the three-volume *The History of the Gulag, 1918–1989,* and *The Siege of Leningrad.*

BCSIA Studies in International Security—Massachusetts Institute of Technology Press

The Belfer Center for Science and International Affairs Studies in International Security series is published by MIT Press. BCSIA is affiliated with Harvard University's John F. Kennedy School of Government.

The series consisted of thirty-seven titles as of April 2004 according to the MIT Press website (http://mitpress.mit.edu/). These works cover 1994 to the present and include *America's Achilles' Heel: Nuclear, Biological, and Chemical Terrorism and Covert Attack* by Richard Falkenrath and others (1998), *Biological Weapons: Limiting the Threat* edited by Joshua Lederberg (1999), *Soldiers and Civilians: The Civil-Military Gap and American National Security* edited by Peter Feaver and Richard Kohn (2001), and *First to Arrive: State and Local Responses to Terrorism* edited by Juliette Kayyem and Robyn Pangi (2003).

Cambridge Studies in International Relations

Cambridge Studies in International Relations is produced by Cambridge University Press. The series consisted of one hundred eighteen titles in April 2004 according to the publisher's website (www.cup.org/). Works in this series, which date back to 1990, include *Arms and the State* by Keith Krause (1995), *The Dynamic of Secession* by Viva Ona Bartkus (1999), *Regions of War and Peace* by Douglas Lemke (2002), and *Deterrence Now* by Patrick M. Morgan (2003).

Contributions in Military Studies

Contributions in Military Studies is produced by Greenwood Press, which is a subsidiary of Praeger Press. This series, which covers 1972 to the present, consists of 226 titles according to an April 2004 search of Greenwood's website (www.greenwood.com/). Representative works include *Implosion: Downsizing the U.S. Military, 1987–2015* by Bart Brasher (2000), *Battling for Bombers: The U.S. Air Force Fights for Its Modern Strategic Aircraft Programs* by Frank Donnini (2000), *Defense Relations between Australia and Indonesia in the Post–Cold War Era* by Bilveer Singh (2002), and *The Cross and the Trenches: Religious Faith and Doubt among British and American Great War Soldiers* by Richard Schweitzer (2003).

Cornell Studies in Security Affairs

Cornell Studies in Security Affairs is produced by Cornell University Press. It had sixty-one titles as of April 2004 according to the publisher's website (www.cornellpress.cornell.edu/). Works in this series, which covers 1984 to the present,

> ## Dewey Decimal Classification System
>
> The Dewey Decimal classification system is used to catalog books by public libraries, smaller academic libraries, and, occasionally, by a few larger academic libraries. The system classifies books by a numbering system that groups areas of human knowledge into a decimalized numeric format ranging from 000 to 999. Within this broad format, the 300s cover the social sciences and the 900s cover history and geography. All numbers and letters in a book's Dewey call number provide bibliographic information about the subject, author, and publication year. For example, the book *Ground Warfare: An International Encyclopedia* was assigned the Dewey Decimal number 355.003 G918 2002; *From Theater Missile Defense to Antimissile Offensive Actions: A Near-Term Strategic Approach*, 358.17 K868f 1999; and *Nation against State: A New Approach to Ethnic Conflicts and the Decline of Sovereignty*, 940 G715N 1993. An introduction to the Dewey Decimal system is provided by the Online Computer Library Consortium at www.oclc.org/dewey/.

include *Military Organizations, Complex Machines: Modernization in the U.S. Armed Forces* by Chris Demchak (1991), *Causes of War: Power and the Roots of Conflict* by Stephen Van Evera (1999), *The Origins of Major War* by Dale Copeland (2000), *The Transformation of American Air Power* by Benjamin Lambeth (2000), and *Corporate Warriors: The Rise of the Privatized Military Industry* by P. W. Singer (2003).

Eastern European Studies—Texas A&M University Press

Eastern European Studies is published by Texas A&M University Press. The series, available since 1995, consisted of twenty-six titles in April 2004 according to the publisher's website (www.tamu.edu/upress/). Examples of works include *Genocide in Bosnia: The Policy of "Ethnic Cleansing"* by Norman Cigar (1995), *Serbia's Secret War: Propaganda and the Deceit of History* by Philip Cohen (1997), *War in Chechnya* by Stasys Knezys and Romanas Sedlickas (1999), *The Muslim-Croat Civil War in Central Bosnia: A Military History, 1992–1994* by Charles Shrader (2003), and *The First Domino: International Decision Making during the Hungarian Crisis of 1956* by Johanna Granville (2004).

Foreign Policy, Security, and Strategic Studies—McGill-Queen's University Press

Foreign Policy, Security, and Strategic Studies is produced by McGill-Queens University Press in Montreal, Quebec, and Kingston, Ontario, Canada. This series had seven titles as of April 2004 according to the publisher's website (www.mqup.mcgill.ca/). These works cover 1999–present and include *The Future of NATO: Enlargement, Russia, and European Security* by Charles-Philippe David and Jacques Levesque (1999),

Power versus Prudence: Why Nations Forgo Nuclear Weapons by T. V. Paul (2000), *From Peacekeeping to Peacemaking: Canada's Response to the Yugoslav Crisis* by Nicholas Gammer (2001), and *The Revolution in Military Affairs* by Elinor Sloan (2002).

Modern War Studies—University Press of Kansas

Modern War Studies is a monographic series produced by the University Press of Kansas. Consisting of 131 titles as of April 2004, a listing of titles in this series is accessible at the publisher's website (www.kansaspress.ku.edu/). The series covers 1986 to the present. Works include *Bernard Brodie and the Foundations of American Nuclear Strategy* by Barry Steiner (1991), *Warmaking and American Democracy: The Struggle Over Military Strategy, 1700 to the Present* by Michael Pearlman (1999), *America's Space Sentinels: DSP Satellites and National Security* by Jeffrey Richelson (1999), *Hammer and Rifle: The Militarization of the Soviet Union, 1926–1933* by David Stone (2000), *Military Justice in America: The U.S. Court of Appeals for the Armed Forces, 1775–1980* by Jonathan Lurie (2001), *Airpower in Small Wars: Fighting Insurgents and Terrorists* by James Corum and Wray Johnson (2003), and *Stalin's Secret War: Soviet Counterintelligence against the Nazis, 1941–1945* by Robert Stephan (2003).

The New Cold War History—University of North Carolina Press

The New Cold War History series is published by the University of North Carolina Press and seeks to provide new interpretations on this historical period in the wake of the opening of Soviet, East European, and Chinese archives to scholarly research.[5] According to the publisher's website (http://uncpress.unc.edu/), the series consisted of thirteen titles in April 2004. Available since 1998, works include *China and the Vietnam Wars, 1950–1975* by Qiang Zhai (2000), *Mao's China and the Cold War* by Chen Jian (2001), *Dealing with the Devil: East Germany, Détente, and Ostpolitik, 1969–1973* by M. E. Sarotte (2001), *A Bitter Peace: Washington, Hanoi, and the Making of the Paris Agreement* by Pierre Aselin (2002), and *Germany's Cold War: The Global Campaign to Isolate East Germany, 1949–1969* by William Glenn Gray (2003).

Nuclear Age Series—Stanford University Press

The Nuclear Age Series, published by the Stanford University Press, consists of sixteen titles covering national security aspects of the nuclear age. These titles cover works that have been published or republished from 1989 to the present according to the publisher's website (www.sup.org/). Examples of works from this series include *A Preponderance of Power: National Security, the Truman Administration, and the Cold War* by Melvyn Leffler (1992), *Cardinal Choices: Presidential Science Advising from the Atomic Bomb to SDI* by Gregg Herken (2000), *Toward Nuclear Abolition: A History of the World Nuclear Disarmament Movement, 1971–Present* by Lawrence Wittner (2003), and *Averting "Final Failure": John F. Kennedy and the Secret Cuban Missile Crisis Meetings* by Sheldon Stern (2003).

Princeton Studies in International History and Politics

Princeton Studies in International History and Politics is published by Princeton University Press. The series consisted of thirty-three titles in April 2004 according to the publisher's website (www.pup.princeton.edu/catalogs/series/psihp.html). Sample titles in this series, which covers 1993–present, are *Useful Adversaries: Grand Strategy, Domestic Mobilization, and Sino-American Conflict, 1947–1958* by Thomas Christensen (1996), *Does Conquest Pay? The Exploitation of Occupied Industrial Societies* by Peter Liberman (1998), *Stay the Hand of Vengeance: The Politics of War Crimes Tribunals* by Gary Jonathan Bass (2000), *In the Shadow of the Garrison State: America's Anti-Statism and Its Cold War Grand Strategy* by Aaron Friedberg (2000), and *Rhetoric and Reality in Air Warfare: The Evolution of British and American Ideas about Strategic Bombing, 1914–1945* Tami Davis Biddle (2002).

Smithsonian History of Aviation and Spaceflight Series

Published by the Smithsonian Institution Press, the Smithsonian History of Aviation and Spaceflight Series consists of works examining how aviation and spaceflight have transformed cultural, military, political, and social thought.[6] This series consisted of forty-one titles in April 2004 according to the Smithsonian Institution Libraries online catalog (www.siris.si.edu). Examples of titles in this series, which covers 1991–present, are *To Command the Sky: The Battle for Air Superiority Over Germany, 1942–1944* by Stephen McFarland and Wesley Phillips Newton (1991), *America's Pursuit of Precision Bombing, 1910–1945* by Stephen McFarland (1995), *Eye in the Sky: The Story of the Corona Spy Satellites* edited by Dwayne Day and others (1999), *The Forgotten Air Force: French Air Doctrine in the 1930s* by Anthony Christopher Cain (2002), *Cold War Laboratory: RAND, the Air Force, and the American State, 1945–1950* by Martin Collins (2002), and *The Kremlin's Nuclear Sword: The Rise and Fall of Russia's Strategic Nuclear Forces, 1945–2000* by Steven Zaloga (2002).

Studies in Canadian Military History—University of British Columbia Press and Canadian War Museum

Studies in Canadian Military History is a joint venture of the University of British Columbia Press and the Canadian War Museum. The series consists of works examining aspects of Canadian military history from a variety of intellectual and interdisciplinary approaches.[7] Four titles were in the series as of April 2004 according to the publisher's website (www.ubcpress.ca/books/series_military.html). Titles in this series, which covers 2002–present, include *The Halifax Explosion and the Royal Canadian Navy: Inquiry and Intrigue* by John Griffith Armstrong (2002), *Avoiding Armageddon: Canadian Thinking on Nuclear Weapons and Military Strategy, 1950–1963* by Andrew Richter (2002), *A War of Patrols: Canadian Army Operations in Korea* by William Johnston (2003), and *Frigates and Foremasts: The North American Squadron in Nova Scotian Waters, 1745–1815* by Julian Gwyn (2003).

> **Library of Congress Classification System**
>
> The Library of Congress Classification System (LC) is used by most medium and large academic libraries in the United States to catalog books and journals. Developed and maintained by the U.S. Library of Congress, the system breaks human knowledge into areas based on an alphanumeric classification system. Books are classified by letters and numbers reflecting information about the subject, author, and publication year. For example, books classified by the letters *E* and *F* are about American history; *J*, political science; *U*, military science; and *V*, naval science.
>
> Within political science's *J* classification, books on international relations are broadly classified between JZ 2 and JZ 6530, and books on international relations dealing with armed conflict, war, and order are classified between JZ 6378 and JZ 6405. For example, *Traditions of War: Occupation, Resistance, and the Law* is classified as JZ6387.N33 1999.
>
> Military science books are put into several disciplinary subclassifications such as UB for military administration and UB 250–UB 271 for military intelligence and UG for military engineering in the U.S. Air Force and UG 622–UG 1435 for air warfare and UG 730–UG 735 for air defenses. For example, *Go Spy the Land: Military Intelligence in History* is classified as UG250.G6 1992; *Air Power: A Centennial Appraisal*, UG625.M37 1994; and *The Emerging Shield: The Air Force and the Evolution of Continental Air Defense, 1945–1960*, UG733.S33 1990.
>
> Detailed information about LC classification can be found at http://lcweb.loc.gov/catdir/cpso/lcco/lcco.html, which is maintained by LC's Cataloging Policy and Support Office.

Studies in International Security and Arms Control—Stanford University Press

Studies in International Security and Arms Control is a Stanford University Press monographic series that produced five titles between 1976 and 1994. These titles are accessible through the publisher's website (www.sup.org/). Titles include *China Builds the Bomb* by John Lewis and Xue Litai (1988), *Uncertain Partners: China, Mao, and the Korean War* by Sergei Goncharov and others (1994), and *China's Strategic Seapower: The Politics of Force Modernization in the Nuclear Age* by John Lewis and Xue Litai (1994).

Studies in War, Society, and the Military—University of Nebraska Press

Studies in War, Society, and the Military is a University of Nebraska Press series. There were ten titles in this series as of April 2004 according to the publisher's website (www.nebraskapress.unl.edu/). The series, published from 1997 to the present, includes *The Rise of the National Guard: The Evolution of the American Militia,*

1865–1920 by Jerry Cooper (1997), *The Grand Illusion: The Prussianization of the Chilean Army* by William Sater and Holger Herwig (1999), *The Challenge of Change: Military Institutions and New Realities, 1918–1941* edited by Harold Winston and David Mets (2000), *Civilians in the Path of War* edited by Mark Grimsley and Clifford Rogers (2002), and *Arabs at War: Military Effectiveness, 1948–1991* by Kenneth Pollack (2002).

Texas A&M University Military History Series

Texas A&M University Press publishes the Texas A&M University Military History Series. The series, which covers 1987 to the present, had ninety-four titles as of April 2004 according to the publisher's website (www.tamu.edu/upress/). Sample titles are *War Machines: Transforming Technologies in the U.S. Military, 1920–1940* by Timothy May (2001), *Australia's Vietnam War* by Jeff Doyle and others (2002), *Striving for Air Superiority: The Tactical Air Command in Vietnam* by Craig Hannah (2002), *Victory on the Potomac: The Goldwater-Nichols Act Unifies the Pentagon* by James R. Locher III (2002), *Red Wings Over the Yalu: China, the Soviet Union, and the Air War in Korea* by Xiaoming Zhang (2002), and *Gentleman Soldier: John Clifford Brown and the Philippine-American War* edited by Joseph McCallus (2003).

Scholars

Scholars contribute to and influence the debate over national security policy regarding topics as diverse as asymmetric warfare, civil-military relations, homeland security, military procurement, nuclear strategic thought, and the revolution in military affairs. The number of U.S. and international scholars conducting national security policy research is at least several hundred and may be greater than one thousand. These individuals are primarily concentrated in academic institutions and think tanks around the world. They thus are given the opportunity and institutional support to disseminate their research through scholarly journal articles, books, government-contracted reports, press conferences, television and other media appearances, classroom instruction, and on the Internet. Many of these scholars have also served in government.[8]

The work of eight scholars—Eliot Cohen, Anthony Cordesman, James Corum, Colin Gray, John Mearsheimer, Michael O'Hanlon, Barry Posen, and Larry Wortzel—helped sculpt late twentieth and early twenty-first century scholarly debate on national security policy research. These individuals brought diverse ideological and methodological approaches to their research.

Eliot Cohen

Eliot Cohen serves as professor and director of the Strategic Studies Program at the Paul H. Nitze School of Advanced International Studies (SAIS) at Johns Hopkins University. He received academic degrees from Harvard University in 1977, 1979, and 1982, and he has professional memberships in the American Political Science Association, International Institute for Strategic Studies, and Inter-University

Seminar on Armed Forces and Society. He has also held academic appointments at Harvard University and the U.S. Navy War College.[9]

Cohen's research interests are the relationship between military institutions and political culture, the relationship between political objectives and military means, and the factors determining military success. Cohen considers his work as falling within the discipline of political science and as reflecting the Clausewitzian dictum that war is a continuation of politics by other means.[10]

Cohen's work includes *Commandos and Politicians: Elite Military Units in Modern Democracies* (Cambridge, Mass.: Harvard University Center for International Affairs, 1978); *Soldiers and Citizens: Dilemmas of Military Service* (Ithaca, N.Y.: Cornell University Press, 1985); *Gulf War Airpower Survey*, 5 vols. (Washington, D.C.: Department of the Air Force, 1993); and *Supreme Command: Soldiers, Statesmen, and Leaders in Wartime* (New York: Free Press, 2002). Cohen has also contributed articles to journals such as *Foreign Affairs* and *International Security*.[11]

Supreme Command presents case studies of how the active involvement and strategic insight of political leaders such as Abraham Lincoln, Winston Churchill, Georges Clemenceau, and David Ben-Gurion produced positive results from military campaigns that their nation participated in when they were in leadership positions. They continuously questioned and prodded military leaders to bring a fresh perspective to military campaigns. They also recognized the importance of political as well as military objectives.[12]

A biography of Cohen is accessible at the SAIS website at http://apps.sais-jhu.edu/faculty_bios/faculty_bio1php?ID=12.

Anthony Cordesman

Anthony Cordesman holds the Arleigh A. Burke Chair in Strategy at the Center for Strategic and International Studies (CSIS). His expertise encompasses Middle East and South Asian security issues, U.S. national security, defense intelligence, and the military balance. He appears regularly as a national security analyst for ABC News.

Cordesman has served in a variety of governmental positions including the Office of Secretary of Defense's intelligence assessment director, a national security assistant to Sen. John McCain (R-Ariz.), and other positions in the Departments of Defense, Energy, and State. During his tenure at CSIS, Cordesman has been involved in projects regarding the Persian Gulf and U.S. homeland security.[13]

Cordesman's articles have appeared in journals such as *Middle East Policy* and *Parameters*. He also has written, for example, *The Gulf and the West: Strategic Relations and Military Realities* (Boulder, Colo.: Westview Press, 1988); *Iran's Military Forces in Transition* (Westport, Conn.: Praeger, 1999); *Lessons of the Air and Missile Campaign in Kosovo* (Westport, Conn.: Praeger, 2001); *Strategic Threats and National Missile Defenses* (Westport, Conn.: Praeger, 2002); and *Terrorism, Asymmetric Warfare, and Threats* (Westport, Conn.: Praeger, 2002).

Further information about Cordesman is accessible on the CSIS website at http://csis.org/experts/4cordesm.htm. The website also has writings by Cordesman on contemporary national security issues.

James Corum

James Corum is professor of comparative military studies at Air University's School of Advanced Air and Space Studies. He received a B.A. from Gonzaga University in 1975, an M.A. in history from Brown University in 1976, a master of literature in history from Oxford University in 1984, and a Ph.D. in history from Queens University in 1990. Corum has served in the U.S. Army and as an instructor at Queens University. He has been at the School of Advanced Air and Space Studies since 1991.[14]

Corum's research interests focus on German military history and the role of airpower in military operations. His works include *The Roots of Blitzkrieg: Hans von Seeckt and German Military Reform* (Lawrence: University Press of Kansas, 1992), which examines the emergence of German military doctrine between World War I and World War II; *The Luftwaffe: Creating the Operational Air War, 1918–1940* (Lawrence: University Press of Kansas, 1997), which portrays the development and evolution of German military aviation doctrine and strategy during the interwar period; and *Airpower in Small Wars: Fighting Insurgents and Terrorists* (Lawrence: University Press of Kansas, 2003), which studies the role played by airpower in twentieth-century counterinsurgency and antiterrorist operations in conflicts such as the Greek Civil War, French colonial interventions in Vietnam and Algeria, and ongoing counterdrug operations in Latin America.

Corum is a member of the American Historical Association and the Society for Military History. His articles have appeared in journals such as *Aerospace Power Journal, Journal of Military History, Journal of Strategic Studies,* and *New Zealand Army Journal.*[15] Listings of Corum's writings and professional activities are available on the School of Advanced Air and Space Studies website (www.au.af.mil/au/sass/Corum%20vitae.htm).

Colin Gray

Colin Gray is a professor of international politics and strategic studies at the University of Reading, England. He received a B.A. from Manchester University and a Ph.D. from Oxford University. He has held academic positions at the University of Lancaster, University of British Columbia, Hull University, and York University. Gray has worked at the International Institute for Strategic Studies and the Hudson Institute, and he was a founder of the National Institute for Public Policy. He has advised the American and British governments on national security–related issues, and his research interests include modern strategic studies, U.S. foreign and defense policies, the intellectual history of strategic ideas, revolutions in military affairs, and weapons of mass destruction.[16] Gray's articles have been published in journals such as *Comparative Strategy, International Security, Joint Force Quarterly, Naval War College Review, Parameters,* and *Strategic Review.* His books include *House of Cards: Why Arms Control Must Fail* (Ithaca, N.Y.: Cornell University Press, 1992); *Weapons Don't Make War: Policy, Strategy, and Military Technology* (Lawrence: University Press of Kansas, 1993); *The Second Nuclear Age* (Boulder, Colo.: Lynne Rienner, 1999); *Strategy for Chaos: Revolutions in Military Affairs and the Evidence of History* (London,

England: Frank Cass, 2002); and *The Sheriff: America's Defense of the New World Order* (Lexington: University Press of Kentucky, 2004).[17]

General information about Gray and listings of his publications are accessible at www.rdg.ac.uk/AcaDepts/lp/PolIR/polsbiogs/CSG.html.

John Mearsheimer

John Mearsheimer is the R. Wendell Harrison Distinguished Professor of Political Science and codirector of the Program on International Security Policy at the University of Chicago, where he has taught since 1982. He received a B.S. from the U.S. Military Academy in 1970, an M.A. from the University of Southern California in 1974, and a Ph.D. from Cornell University in 1981. His professional career has included service in the U.S. Army and U.S. Air Force, an internship at the U.S. Arms Control and Disarmament Agency, and a Brookings Institution research fellowship. Mearsheimer is a member of the Inter-University Seminar on Armed Forces and Society and was elected to the American Academy of Arts and Sciences in 2003.[18]

Books authored by Mearsheimer include *Conventional Deterrence* (Ithaca, N.Y.: Cornell University Press, 1983); *Liddell Hart and the Weight of History* (Ithaca, N.Y.: Cornell University Press, 1988); and *The Tragedy of Great Power Politics* (New York: Norton, 2001). *Conventional Deterrence* examines how wars originate and the role played by conventional military forces in deterring war. Mearsheimer analyzes Allied forces unwillingness to attack Germany between March 1939 and May 1940, Germany's decision to initiate war during this same period, the role of conventional deterrence in the Arab-Israeli conflict, and prospects for conventional deterrence in Central Europe in the early 1980s given the existing NATO-Warsaw Pact conventional force structures and doctrine.

Liddell Hart and the Weight of History is a critical analysis of British military strategist Sir Basil Henry Liddell Hart (1895–1970). In this work, Mearsheimer seeks to describe and appraise the substance of Hart's military thought with particular emphasis on the "indirect approach" to military strategy that he advocated; examine the origins and evolution of Liddell Hart's thoughts on tactics, strategy, and grand strategy; determine whether Liddell Hart should be regarded as the ideological progenitor of Germany's blitzkrieg doctrine used at the start of World War II; evaluate Liddell Hart's interwar policy-making role; and analyze how Liddell Hart was able to restore his historical reputation from being associated with the British government's prewar appeasement policy toward Nazi Germany.[19]

In *The Tragedy of Great Power Politics,* Mearsheimer presents the concept of offensive realism as the reason that nations battle for international superiority to ensure their survival. He offers historical and contemporary examples of how such turmoil is an inherent part of international political, economic, and military life and urges the United States to remain true to the realist principles he believes have served it well throughout its history.[20]

Articles by Mearsheimer have appeared in journals and periodicals such as *Foreign Affairs, Foreign Policy, International Security,* and *The New Republic.* General information about him is available at http://political-science.uchicago.edu/faculty/mearsheimer.html.

Michael O'Hanlon

Michael O'Hanlon serves as senior fellow in defense strategy at the Brookings Institution and adjunct professor of international affairs at Columbia University and Georgetown University. He received a B.A. in 1982, M.S.E. in 1987, M.A. in 1988, and Ph.D. in 1991 from Princeton University. He has been a research assistant at the Institute for Defense Analyses and a defense and foreign policy budget analyst for the Congressional Budget Office.[21]

O'Hanlon's areas of expertise include arms treaties, Asian and European security issues, homeland security, Iraq policy, military technology, and U.S. national strategy and budget.[22] His articles have appeared in journals such as *Foreign Affairs, International Security, Orbis,* and *Survival.* He is a member of the Council on Foreign Relations and the International Institute for Strategic Studies.[23]

O'Hanlon has authored or coauthored numerous works including *Saving Lives with Force: Military Criteria for Humanitarian Intervention* (Washington, D.C.: Brookings Institution Press, 1997); *How to Be a Cheap Hawk: The 1999 and 2000 Defense Budgets* (Washington, D.C.: Brookings Institution Press, 1998); *Winning Ugly: NATO's War to Save Kosovo* (Washington, D.C.: Brookings Institution Press, 2000); *Defending America: The Case for Limited National Missile Defense* (Washington, D.C.: Brookings Institution Press, 2001); and *Crisis on the Korean Peninsula: How to Deal with a Nuclear North Korea* (New York: McGraw-Hill, 2003).

General information on O'Hanlon and his commentary on current security policy issues are accessible at www.brookings.edu/scholars/mohanlon.htm.

Barry Posen

Barry Posen is professor of political science at the Massachusetts Institute of Technology and is affiliated with that institution's Security Studies Program. He received a B.A. from Occidental College in 1974 and an M.A. and Ph.D. from the University of California–Berkeley in 1976 and 1981, respectively. He was assistant professor of political science at Princeton University from 1984 to 1987. He has been at MIT since 1987. Posen's professional memberships include the Council on Foreign Relations and the International Institute for Strategic Studies.[24]

Posen's books include *The Sources of Military Doctrine: France, Britain, and Germany between the World Wars* (Ithaca, N.Y.: Cornell University Press, 1984); and *Inadvertent Escalation: Conventional War and Nuclear Risks* (Ithaca, N.Y.: Cornell University Press, 1991). *The Sources of Military Doctrine* examines how interwar British, French, and German military doctrinal developments influenced their military operations at the outset of World War II and the possible relevance of those developments to the U.S.-Soviet strategic balance. *Inadvertent Escalation* seeks to demonstrate how the interface between conventional military operations and nuclear forces could increase conflict escalation pressures for nations with conventional and nuclear weapons.[25] Posen has contributed articles to journals such as *Foreign Policy, International Security, Security Studies,* and *World Politics.* Information about Posen's publications and recent course syllabi are accessible at http://web.mit.edu/polisci/faculty/B.Posen.html.

Larry Wortzel

Larry Wortzel is vice president and director of the Kathryn and Shelby Cullom Davis Institute for International Studies at the Heritage Foundation. He received a B.A. from Columbus College (Georgia) and an M.A. and Ph.D. from the University of Hawaii—Manoa. Wortzel has served as a military attaché at the U.S. Embassy in China and worked as the director of the U.S. Army War College's Strategic Studies Institute before joining the Heritage Foundation in 1999.[26]

Wortzel's areas of expertise are China, Asia, intelligence, national security, and military strategy. His articles have appeared in *Jane's Intelligence Review* and *Parameters.* Books he has written or edited include *China's Military Modernization* (Westport, Conn.: Greenwood Press, 1988); *Dictionary of Contemporary Chinese Military History* (Westport, Conn.: Greenwood Press, 1999); *The Chinese Armed Forces in the 21st Century* (Carlisle, Pa.: U.S. Army War College Strategic Studies Institute, 1999); *The Asia-Pacific in the U.S. National Security Calculus for a New Millennium* (Carlisle, Pa.: U.S. Army War College Strategic Studies Institute, 2000); and *The Lessons of History: The Chinese People's Liberation Army at 75* (Carlisle, Pa.: U.S. Army War College Strategic Studies Institute, 2003).

Further information on Wortzel, including the text of recent writings and media appearances, are accessible on the Heritage Foundation website at www.heritage.org/About/Staff/LarryWortzel.cfm.

Notes

1. For a useful, though somewhat dated, review of military periodicals, see Michael Unsworth, ed., *United States and Selected International Journals and Newspapers* (New York: Greenwood Press, 1990).

2. For a history of JSTOR, see Roger C. Schonfeld, *JSTOR: A History* (Princeton, N.J.: Princeton University Press, 2003).

3. Frank Cass Publishers, "Transnational Organized Crime" (2003), 1 (www.frankcass.com/jnls/toc.htm), accessed October 22, 2003.

4. Yale University Press, "Annals of Communism" (n.d.), 1 (www.yale.edu/annals/AOC_statement.html), accessed October 24, 2003.

5. University of North Carolina Press, "Series Descriptions," (n.d.), 4 (http://uncpress.unc.edu/bm-series.html), accessed October 23, 2003.

6. Smithsonian National Air and Space Museum, "NASM Publications: Smithsonian History of Aviation and Spaceflight Series" (2003), 1 (www.nasm.edu/nasm/pubs/avseries.html), accessed October 23, 2003.

7. University of British Columbia Press, "Studies in Canadian Military History Series" (n.d.), 1 (www.ubcpress.ca/books/series_military.html), accessed October 23, 2003.

8. One example is Condoleezza Rice, who served in the George W. Bush administration as national security adviser. See Biography Resource Center, "Condoleezza Rice" (2003), 1–5 (www.galenet.com/servlet/BioRC), accessed October 25, 2003.

9. Biography Resource Center, "Eliot Asher Cohen" (2003), 2 (www.galenet.com/servlet/BioRC), accessed October 25, 2003.

10. Biography Resource Center, "Eliot Asher Cohen."

11. Biography Resource Center, "Eliot Asher Cohen."

12. Biography Resource Center, "Eliot Asher Cohen," 1–2.

13. Center for Strategic and International Studies, "Anthony Cordesman" (2003), 1 (http://csis.org/html/4cordesm.htm), accessed October 27, 2003.

14. See Biography Resource Center, "James Sterling Corum" (2003), 2 (www.galenet.com/servlet/BioRC), accessed October 28, 2003; and Air University, School of Advanced Air and Space Studies, "Curriculum Vitae: James Sterling Corum" (n.d.), 1 (www.au.af.mil/sass/Corum%20vitae.htm), accessed October 28, 2003.

15. Biography Resource Center, "James Sterling Corum."

16. See Reading University Politics Department, "Professor Colin S. Gray" (n.d.), 1 (www.rdg.ac.uk/AcaDepts/lp/PolIR/polsbiogs/CSG.html), accessed October 28, 2003; and U.S. Army War College, *Maintaining Effective Deterrence: Biographical Sketch of the Author* (Carlisle Barracks, Pa.: U.S. Army War College, Strategic Studies Institute, 2003), iv (www.carlisle.army.mil/ssi/pubs/2003/maindetr/maindeter.pdf), accessed October 28, 2003.

17. U.S. Army War College, *Maintaining Effective Deterrence*.

18. See University of Chicago, Political Science Department, "John Mearsheimer" (2003), 1 (http://political-science.uchicago.edu/faculty/mearsh.htm), accessed October 28, 2003; and Biography Resource Center, "John Joseph Mearsheimer" (2002), 2 (www.galenet.com/servlet/BioRC), accessed October 28, 2003.

19. John J. Mearsheimer, *Liddell Hart and the Weight of History* (Ithaca, N.Y.: Cornell University Press, 1988), 5–9.

20. John J. Mearsheimer, *The Tragedy of Great Power Politics* (New York: W.W. Norton and Company, 2001), 402.

21. Biography Resource Center, "Michael Edward O'Hanlon" (2002), 3 (www.galenet.com/servlet/BioRC), accessed October 29, 2003.

22. Brookings Institution, "Scholars: Michael O'Hanlon" (n.d.), 1 (www.brookings.edu/scholars/mohanlon.htm), accessed October 29, 2003.

23. Brookings Institution, "Michael O'Hanlon," (2002), 1 (www.brookings.edu/rios/data/sources/onepagebio/e7dac134818bff3b4bd390a141465.pdf), accessed October 29, 2003.

24. Biography Resource Center, "Barry R. Posen" (2002), 1 (www.galenet.com/servlet/BioRC), accessed October 29, 2003.

25. Barry R. Posen, *Inadvertent Escalation: Conventional War and Nuclear Risks* (Ithaca, N.Y.: Cornell University Press, 1991), ix.

26. See U.S. Army War College Strategic Studies Institute, *The Asia-Pacific in the U.S. National Security Calculus for a New Millennium: Biographical Sketches of the Authors* (Carlisle Barracks, Pa.: U.S. Army War College Strategic Studies Institute, 2000), v (www.carlisle.army.mil/ssi/pubs/2000/calculus/calculus.pdf), accessed October 29, 2003; and Heritage Foundation, "About the Heritage Foundation—Our Staff: Larry M. Wortzel, Ph.D." (2003), 1–3 (www.heritage.org/About/Staff/LarryWortzel.cfm), accessed October 29, 2003.

Acronyms

ACA: Arms Control Association
ACC: Air Combat Command
ACS: Army Chemical School
ACSC: Air Command and Staff College
ACSS: Africa Center for Strategic Studies
ACUS: Atlantic Council of the United States
ACWA: Assembled Chemical Weapons Assessment
ADAMS: Agencywide Documents Access and Management System
ADF: Australian Defence Force
ADSC: Australian Defence Studies Centre
AEI: American Enterprise Institute for Public Policy Research
AFAA: Air Force Audit Agency
AFCA: Air Force Communications Agency
AFCA: Army Airways Communication System
AFC2ISRC: Air Force Command and Control and Intelligence, Surveillance, and Reconnaissance Center
AFDC: Air Force Doctrine Center
AFFTC: Air Force Flight Test Center
AFGC: Air Force General Counsel
AFHRA: Air Force Historical Research Agency
AFHSO: Air Force History Support Office
AFIS: American Forces Information Service
AFIT: Air Force Institute of Technology
AFIWC: Air Force Information Warfare Center
AFNA: Air Force News Agency
AFOSR: Air Force Office of Scientific Research
AFRL: Air Force Research Laboratory
AFSC: Air Force Safety Center
AFSC: Air Force Space Command
AGC: Army General Counsel
AHL: *America: History and Life*
AIA: Air Intelligence Agency
AIA: Army International Affairs
AMSP: Advanced Military Studies Program
AMWS: Army Mountain Warfare School
ANAO: Australian National Audit Office
ANG: Air National Guard
ANG: Army National Guard
ANL: Argonne National Laboratory
ANSER: Advancing National Strategies and Enabling Results Institute for Homeland Security
AOASF: Advanced Operational Arts Studies Fellowship
APCSS: Asia-Pacific Center for Security Studies
APG: Aberdeen Proving Ground
APHIS: Animal and Plant Health Inspection Service
ARC: Archival Research Catalog
ARI: Army Research Institute for the Behavioral and Social Sciences
ARL: Army Research Laboratory
ASB: Army Science Board
ASD-C3I: assistant secretary of defense for command, control, communications, and intelligence
ASIO: Australian Security Intelligence Organisation
ASIS: Australian Secret Intelligence Service
ASPI: Australian Strategic Policy Institute
ATSDIO: assistant to the secretary of defense for intelligence oversight
AU: Air University
AULIMP: "Air University Library Index to Military Periodicals"
AVIP: Anthrax Vaccination Immunization Program
AWC: Air War College
BAC: Bureau of Arms Control
BASIC: British-American Security Information Council

BCSIA: Belfer Center for Science and International Affairs
BDS: Bureau of Diplomatic Security
BI: Brookings Institution
BIS: Bureau of Industry and Security
BMDS: Ballistic Missile Defense System
BN: Bureau of Nonproliferation
BNL: Brookhaven National Laboratory
BPMA: Bureau of Political-Military Affairs
BSCSS: Begin-Sadat Center for Strategic Studies
BTSD: Border and Transportation Security Directorate
BUMED: Bureau of Medicine and Surgery
BVC: Bureau of Verification and Compliance
C4I: command, control, communications, computers, and intelligence
CADRE: College of Aerospace Doctrine, Research, and Education
CALL: Center for Army Lessons Learned
CARL: Combined Arms Research Library
CAS3: Combined Arms and Services Staff School
CBACI: Chemical and Biological Arms Control Institute
CBIRF: Chemical Biological Incident Response Force
CBO: Congressional Budget Office
CBP: U.S. Customs and Border Protection
CCBS: Center for Civilian Biodefense Strategies
CCC: Center for Contemporary Conflict
CCIPS: Computer Crime and Intellectual Property Section
CCMR: Center for Civil-Military Relations
CCR: Center for Counterproliferation Research
CCR: Centre for Conflict Resolution (South Africa)
CDA: Conference of Defence Associations (Canada)
CDC: Centers for Disease Control and Prevention
CDE: College of Distance Education
CDI: Center for Defense Information
CDISS: Centre for Defence and International Studies (United Kingdom)
CDSS: Centre for Defence and Security Studies (Canada)
CEIP: Carnegie Endowment for International Peace
CENTCOM: Central Command

CFE: Conventional Forces in Europe Treaty
CFR: *Code of Federal Regulations*
CGA: U.S. Coast Guard Academy
CGLP: Coast Guard Legal Program
CGP: "Catalog of Government Publications"
CGPACS: Center for Global Peace and Conflict Studies
CGSC: Command and General Staff College
CHAMPUS: Civilian Health and Medical Program of the Uniformed Services
CHDS: Center for Hemispheric Defense Studies
CI: Cato Institute
CIA: Central Intelligence Agency
CIAO: Columbia International Affairs Online
CIAO: Critical Infrastructure Assurance Office
CIDRAP: Center for Infectious Disease Research and Policy
CILHI: Central Identification Laboratory
CINFINIS: Cebrowski Institute for Information Innovation and Superiority
CISAC: Center for International Security and Cooperation
CIS Index: *Congressional Information Service Index*
CISS: Canadian Institute of Strategic Studies
CITR: Center for International Threat Reduction
CITS: Center for International Trade and Security
CJSEW: Center for Joint Services Electronic Warfare
CLAMO: Center for Law and Military Operations
CMC: Classification Management Committee
CMH: Center for Military History
CMR: Civil-Military Relations in Central and Eastern Europe Internet Resource Center
CMSS: Centre for Military and Strategic Studies (Canada)
CNO: chief of naval operations
CNS: Center for Nonproliferation Studies
CNCS: College of Naval Command and Staff
CNW: College of Naval Warfare
CNWS: Center for Naval Warfare Studies
CS: Counterespionage Section
CSBA: Center for Strategic and Budgetary Assessments
CSC: Command and Staff College

CSCE: Commission on Security and Cooperation in Europe
CSDG: Conflict, Security, and Development Group
CSDS: Centre for Security and Defence Studies (Canada)
CSI: Center for the Study of Intelligence
CSI: Combat Studies Institute
CSIS: Canadian Security Intelligence Service
CSIS: Center for Strategic and International Studies
CSL: Center for Strategic Leadership
CSLD: Center for Strategic Leadership Development
CSP: Center for Security Policy
C-SPAN: Cable Satellite Public Affairs Network
CSRC: Computer Security Resource Center
CSRC: Conflict Studies Research Centre
CSS: Center for Security Studies (Switzerland)
CSS: Centre for Strategic Studies (New Zealand)
CSSPAP: Computer System Security and Privacy Advisory Board
CTIW: Center on Terrorism and Irregular Warfare
CTNSP: Center for Technology and National Security Policy
CWC: 1992 Chemical Weapons Convention
DACOWITS: Defense Advisory Committee on Women in the Services
DARPA: Defense Advanced Research Projects Agency
DCA: Defense Commissary Agency
DCAA: Defense Contract Audit Agency
DCLM: Department of Command, Leadership, and Management
DCMA: Defense Contract Management Agency
DDA: Department for Disarmament Affairs
DDRS: Declassified Documents Reference System
DDTC: Directorate of Defense Trade Controls
DEA: Drug Enforcement Administration
DENIX: Defense Environmental Information Network and Information Exchange
DFAS: Defense Finance and Accounting Service
DHH: Directorate of History and Heritage (Canada)
DHS: Department of Homeland Security
DI: Directorate of Intelligence
DIA: Defense Intelligence Agency
DIIA: Danish Institute of International Affairs
DIILS: Defense Institute of International Legal Studies
DIO: Defence Intelligence Organisation (Australia)
DISA: Defense Information Systems Agency
DITT: Defense Information Technology Testbed
DLA: Defense Logistics Agency
DLSA: Defense Legal Services Agency
DMA: Defense Mapping Agency
DMSO: Defense Modeling and Simulation Office
DMSPO: Department of Military Strategy, Planning, and Operations
DNA: deoxyribonucleic acid
DND: Department of National Defence (Canada)
DNFSB: Defense Nuclear Facilities Safety Board
DNSS: Department of National Security and Strategy
DOD: Department of Defense
DODIG: Department of Defense Office of Inspector General
DOE: Department of Energy
DOT: Department of Transportation
DOT&E: director for operational test and evaluation
DPB: Defense Policy Board
DPMO: Defense Prisoner of War/Missing Personnel Office
DR&E: defense research and engineering
DSB: Defense Science Board
DSCA: Defense Security Cooperation Agency
DSD: Defence Signals Directorate (Australia)
DSS: Defense Security Service
DS&T: Directorate of Science and Technology
DTIC: Defense Technical Information Center
DTRA: Defense Threat Reduction Agency
ECSSR: Emirates Center for Strategic Studies and Research
EFOIA: Electronic Freedom of Information Act
EHMGC: "Ebsco Host's Military and Government Collection"
EIA: Energy Information Administration
EM: Office of Environmental Management
EOIR: Executive Office for Immigration Review
EPA: Environmental Protection Agency
EPME: Enlisted Professional Military Education

EPRD: Emergency Preparedness and Response Directorate
EU: European Union
EUSC: European Union Satellite Centre
EWC: East-West Center
EWS: Expeditionary Warfare School
FAA: Federal Aviation Administration
FAS: Federation of American Scientists
FATC: Field Artillery Training Command
FBI: Federal Bureau of Investigation
FBIS: Foreign Broadcast Information Center
FDA: Food and Drug Administration
FDLP: Federal Depository Library Program
FEMA: Federal Emergency Management Agency
FIIA: Finnish Institute of International Affairs
FISA: 1978 Foreign Intelligence Surveillance Act
FISC: Foreign Intelligence Surveillance Court
FISSEA: Federal Information Systems Security Educators Association
FLETC: Federal Law Enforcement Training Center
FM: field manual
FMC: Federal Maritime Commission
FOIA: Freedom of Information Act
FPRI: Foreign Policy Research Institute
FRUS: *Foreign Relations of the United States*
GAO: General Accounting Office
GCHQ: Government Communications Headquarters (United Kingdom)
GCSP: Geneva Centre for Security Policy
GIIPS: German Institute for International Politics and Security
GPI: *LexisNexis Government Periodicals Index*
GPO: U.S. Government Printing Office
GPS: global position satellite
GSA: General Services Administration
HA: *Historical Abstracts*
HF: Heritage Foundation
HHS: Department of Health and Human Services
HI: Hoover Institution on War, Revolution, and Peace
HIV/AIDS: human immunodeficiency virus/ acquired immune deficiency syndrome
HLSC: Henry L. Stimson Center
HLSPC: Homeland Security Planners Course
HMD: History and Museums Division

HO: Home Office
HSPD: Homeland Security Presidential Directives
HTML: hypertext markup language
IAEA: International Atomic Energy Agency
IAIPD: Information Analysis and Infrastructure Protection Directorate
IASPS: Institute for Advanced Strategic and Political Studies
IC: Intelligence Community
ICAF: Industrial College of the Armed Forces
IDA: Institute for Defense Analyses
IDF: Israel Defense Force
IDSA: Institute for Defence Studies and Analysis (India)
IDSS: Institute of Defence and Strategic Studies (Singapore)
IFPA: Institute for Foreign Policy Analysis
IGIS: Inspector General Canadian Security Intelligence Service
IGIS: Inspector General of Intelligence and Security (Australia)
IIPS: Institute for International Policy Studies (Japan)
IISS: International Institute for Strategic Studies
I&LD: Installations and Logistics Departments
INEEL: Idaho National Engineering and Environmental Laboratory
INF: Intermediate Nuclear Forces Treaty
INFOSEC: Center for Information Security Studies
INL: Bureau of International Narcotics and Law Enforcement Affairs
INRA: International Negotiations and Regional Affairs
INSCOM: Army Intelligence and Security Command
INSP: International Nuclear Safety Program
INSS: Institute for National Strategic Studies
IP: Internet protocol
IPCS: Institute for Peace and Conflict Studies
IPP: Initiatives for Proliferation Prevention
IPS: Institute for Policy Studies
IRMC: Information Resources Management College
IRSN: International Relations Security Network
IS: Infantry School
ISA: assistant secretary of defense for international security affairs

ISCAP: Interagency Security Classification Appeals Panel
ISIS: Institute for Security and International Studies (Bulgaria)
ISOO: Information Security Oversight Office
ISS: European Institute for Security Studies
ISS: Institute for Security Studies (South Africa)
ISSI: Institute of Strategic Studies–Islamabad
ITC: U.S. International Trade Commission
IUS: InterUniversity Seminar on Armed Forces and Society
JAG: Judge Advocate General
JATV: Joint Asset Total Visibility
JCIWS: Joint Command, Control, and Information Warfare School
JCS: Joint Chiefs of Staff
JCSS: Jaffee Center for Strategic Studies
JCWS: Joint and Combined Warfighting School
JEL: Joint Electronic Library
JFSC: Joint Forces Staff College
JIG: Jane's Information Group
JINSA: Jewish Institute for National Security Affairs
JPEC: Joint Planning and Execution Committee
JPOC: Joint Planning Orientation Course
JSTARS: Joint Surveillance Target Attack Radar System
KAPL: Knolls Atomic Power Laboratory
KCP: Kansas City Plant
LANL: Los Alamos National Laboratory
LBNL: Lawrence Berkeley National Laboratory
LC: Library of Congress
LCSH: Library of Congress Subject Headings
LLNL: Lawrence Livermore National Laboratory
LWSC: Land Warfare Studies Centre (Australia)
MAGTF: Marine Air Ground Task Force
MATCOM: Material Command
MCCDC: Marine Corps Combat Development Command
MCDP: Marine Corps Doctrinal Publications
MCI: Marine Corps Institute
MCRC: Marine Corps Research Center
MCSC: Marine Corps Systems Command
MCU: Marine Corps University
MCWAR: Marine Corps War College
MCWL: Marine Corps Warfighting Laboratory
MD: Management Directorate
MDA: Missile Defense Agency

MHI: Military History Institute
MI-5: Security Service (United Kingdom)
MI-6: Secret Intelligence Service (United Kingdom)
MIA: missing in action
MIT: Massachusetts Institute of Technology
MOD: Ministry of Defence (United Kingdom)
m&s: modeling and simulation activities
MSC: Military Sealift Command
NACIC: National Counterintelligence Council
NACOA: National Advisory Committee on Oceans and the Atmosphere
NAIL: National Archives Information Locator
NAMRL: Naval Aerospace Medical Research Laboratory
NAO: National Audit Office (United Kingdom)
NARA: National Archives and Records Administration
NAS: National Academy of Sciences
NATO: North Atlantic Treaty Organization
NAVAIR: Naval Air Systems Command
NAVFAC: Naval Facilities Engineering Command
NAVSEA: Naval Sea Systems Command
NBAR: National Bureau of Asian Research
NBC: nuclear, biological, and chemical threats
NBL: New Brunswick Laboratory
NCA: National Command Authorities
NCC: Naval Command College
NCCA: Naval Center for Cost Analysis
NCI: Nuclear Control Institute
NCIC: Network Centric Innovation Center
NCIS: Naval Criminal Investigative Service
NCIX: National Counterintelligence Executive
NDIC: National Drug Intelligence Center
NDMS: National Disaster Medical System
NDU: National Defense University
NEMRE: Nuclear Explosion Monitoring, Research, and Engineering Program
NESA-CSS: Near East South Asia Center for Strategic Studies
NEST: Nuclear Emergency Search Team
NGC: Navy General Counsel
NGIA: National Geospatial Intelligence Agency
NHC: Naval Historical Center
NI: Nautilus Institute
NIAID: National Institute of Allergy and Infectious Diseases
NIC: National Intelligence Council

NIEs: National Intelligence Estimates
NIH: National Institutes of Health
NIMA: National Imagery and Mapping Agency
NIPO: Navy International Programs Office
NIPP: National Institute for Public Policy
NIS: Newly Independent States
NISP: National Industrial Security Program
NISPPAC: National Industrial Security Program Policy Advisory Committee
NIST: National Institute of Standards and Technology
NJAG: Navy Judge Advocate General
NMIC: National Maritime Intelligence Center
NNSA: National Nuclear Security Administration
NORAD: North American Aerospace Defense Command
NORTHCOM: Northern Command
NPRST: Navy Personnel Research, Studies, and Technology
NPS: Naval Postgraduate School
NPT: Nuclear Nonproliferation Treaty
NRC: Nuclear Regulatory Commission
NRL: Naval Research Laboratory
NRO: National Reconnaissance Office
NSA: National Security Agency
NSA: National Security Archive
NSAM: National Security Action Memorandums
NSC: National Security Council
NSC: Naval Staff College
NSDD: National Security Decision Directives
NSDM: National Security Decision Memoranda
NSEP: National Security Education Program
NSGC: National Strategic Gaming Center
NSNFP: National Spent Nuclear Fuel Program
NSPD: National Security Presidential Directives
NSSM: National Security Study Memoranda
NSTC: National Science and Technology Council
NSWC: Naval Surface Warfare Center
NTIP: Naval Treaty Implementation Program
NTIS: National Technical Information Service
NTP: National Transportation Program
NTS: Nevada Test Site
NUWC: Naval Undersea Warfare Center
NVR: Naval Vessel Register
NWC: Naval War College
NWDC: Navy Warfare Development Command

NWTRB: Nuclear Waste Technical Review Board
OAG: Office of Auditor General (Canada)
OC: Ordnance Corps
OCRWM: Office of Civilian Radioactive Waste Management
ODP: Office for Domestic Preparedness
OE: Office of Enforcement
OEA: Office of Economic Adjustment
OFAC: Office of Foreign Assets Control
OGC: Office of the General Counsel
OIA: Office of International Affairs
OIG: Office of Inspector General
OIPR: Office of Intelligence Policy and Review
OIS: Office of Intelligence and Security
OMB: Office of Management and Budget
ONA: Office of National Assessments (Australia)
ONA: Office of Net Assessment
ONDCP: Office of National Drug Control Policy
ONI: Office of Naval Intelligence
ONR: Office of Naval Research
OPAC: "Online Public Access Catalogs"
OPCW: Organisation for Prohibition of Chemical Weapons (the Netherlands)
OPNAV: Office of the Chief of Naval Operations
ORNL: Oak Ridge National Laboratory
OSC: Office of Site Closure
OSCE: Organization for Security and Cooperation in Europe
OSD: Office of the Secretary of Defense
OSHA: Occupational Safety and Health Administration
OSTI: Office of Scientific and Technical Information
OSTP: Office of Science and Technology Policy
OTA: Office of Technology Assessment
OWCI: Office of War Crimes Issues
PACDIS: Program in Arms Control, Disarmament, and International Security
PACOM: Pacific Command
PA&E: Office of the Director, Program Analysis and Evaluation
PAIS: *Public Affairs Information Service International*
PCARSS: Plant Clearance Automated Reutilization Screening System

PCAST: President's Council of Advisors on Science and Technology
PCIPB: President's Critical Infrastructure Protection Board
PD: Presidential Directive
PDA: Project on Defense Alternatives
PDB: President's Daily Brief
PDD: Presidential Decision Directive
PDD 63: Presidential Decision Directive 63
PDF: portable document format
PERSCOM: Personnel Command
PISDES: Pacific Institute Studies in Development, Environment, and Security
PJCAAD: Parliamentary Joint Committee on ASIO, ASIS, and DSD
PKI: Public Key Infrastructure
PLA: People's Liberation Army (China)
PME: professional military education
PNL: Pacific Northwest Laboratory
POW: prisoner of war
PP: Pantex Plant
PP&O: Plans, Policies, and Operations Department
P&R: Programs and Resources Department
PSGS: Program on Science and Global Security
RA: Royal Army (United Kingdom)
RAA: Royal Australian Army
RAAF: Royal Australian Air Force
RAF: Royal Air Force (United Kingdom)
RAN: Royal Australian Navy
RANSAC: Russian American Nuclear Security Advisory Council
RCISS: Ridgway Center for International Security Studies
RCMP: Royal Canadian Mounted Police
RCSS: Regional Centre for Strategic Studies (Sri Lanka)
REDES: Research and Education in Defense and Security Studies Seminar
REGIS: Research Group in International Security
RMA: revolution in military affairs
RN: Royal Navy (United Kingdom)
RUSI: Royal United Services Institute
SAASS: School of Advanced Air and Space Studies
SAB: Scientific Advisory Board
SAIS: Johns Hopkins Center for Strategic and Advanced International Studies
SAIS: Paul H. Nitze School of Advanced International Studies
SAMS: School of Advanced Military Studies
SAW: School of Advanced Warfighting
SBCCOM: Soldier and Biological Chemical Command
SCAMPI: "Staff College Automated Periodicals Index"
SCP: School for Command Preparation
SD: Safety Division
SDSC: Strategic and Defence Studies Centre (Australia)
SEVIS: Student and Exchange Visitor Information System
SIAD: Statistical Information Analysis Division
SIGINT: signals intelligence
SIPRI: Stockholm International Peace Research Institute
SIRC: Security Intelligence Review Committee
SJA: Staff Judge Advocate
SMDC: Space and Missile Defense Command
SMSC: Space and Missile Systems Center
SNL: Sandia National Laboratories
SNSEE: School for National Security Executive Education
SOCOM: Special Operations Command
SOUTHCOM: Southern Command
SPAWAR: Space and Naval Warfare Systems Command
SPD: Space Policy Directorate
SPR: Strategic Petroleum Reserve
SRDC: Spacecraft Research and Design Center
SRS: Savannah River Site
SSI: Strategic Studies Institute
SSP: Security Studies Program
SSS: Selective Service System
START: Strategic Arms Reduction Talks Treaty
STD: Science and Technology Directorate
STI: scientific and technical information
STINET: Scientific and Technical Information Network
STRATCOM: Strategic Command
SuDoc: Superintendent of Documents classification system
SWD: Surface Warfare Directorate
TECOM: Training and Education Command
TISS: Triangle Institute for Security Studies
TRADOC: Training and Doctrine Command
TRANSCOM: Transportation Command

TRC: Terrorism Research Center
TSA: Transportation Security Administration
TSR: Taiwan Security Research
UCMJ: Uniform Code of Military Justice
UN: United Nations
UNIDIR: United Nations Institute Disarmament Research
UNMOVIC: United Nations Monitoring, Inspection, and Verification Commission
UNSCOM: United Nations Special Commission on Iraq
URLs: uniform resource locators
USACE: U.S. Army Corps of Engineers
USAF: U.S. Air Force
USAFA: U.S. Air Force Academy
USAFSS: U.S. Air Force Security Service
USAMRICD: U.S. Army Medical Research Institute of Chemical Disease
USAWC: U.S. Army War College
USCG: U.S. Coast Guard
USDA: U.S. Department of Agriculture
USEUCOM: European Command
USIP: U.S. Institute of Peace
USJFCOM: Joint Forces Command
USMA: U.S. Military Academy
USMC: U.S. Marine Corps
USML: United States Munition List
USN: U.S. Navy
USNA: U.S. Naval Academy
USNO: U.S. Naval Observatory
WHINSEC: Western Hemisphere Institute for Security Cooperation
WHMO: White House Medical Unit
WHMO: White House Military Office
WNC: World News Connection
WPNAC: Wisconsin Project on Nuclear Arms Control
WPSA: *Worldwide Political Science Abstracts*
WWICS: Woodrow Wilson International Center for Scholars
YMP: Yucca Mountain Project

Index

ABC Clio publishers, 381
Aberdeen Proving Ground, 28, 151, 159, 160
Abraham, Spencer, 126n35, 203
Abrams tank, 47, 92
Academic Engagement Program, 5
Academic institutions
    libraries, 380, 382, 383, 391
    See also specific institution names
Access UN, 348
Accounting and auditing
    Air Force, 145
    Australia, 332
    Canada, 337
    Defense Department, 34, 35
    federal government programs, 245–246
    United Kingdom, 342
    See also Office of Inspector General
Accounting Standards Advisory Board, 35
Acheson, Dean, 297
Acquisition and procurement
    advisory commission report, 255
    agency jurisdiction, 30, 34, 155–156, 173
    congressional oversight, 235, 236
    military education, 14
Acquisition Department, 14
Acronym Institute for Disarmament Diplomacy, 374
Actual Operations Branch, 156
Adams, John, 171
Addresses of military personnel, 27, 45
Adelphi Papers, 375
Administration and management, 27–28
Administrative Office of the U.S. Courts, 279
Administrative Procedure Act of 1946, 290
Advanced Gun System, 178
Advanced Law Enforcement Photography Training Program, 102
Advanced Military Studies Program, 7

Advanced Operational Arts Studies Fellowship, 7
Advanced Research Program, 9
Advanced Technology Office, 33
Advanced Tomahawk Weapons Control System, 178
Advancing National Strategies and Enabling Results (ANSER) Institute for Homeland Security, 297
Advisory Committee on Human Radiation Experiments, 260
Advisory Committee on Nuclear Waste, 202
Advisory Committee on Reactor Safeguards, 202
Advisory organizations and commissions, 253–276
Advisory Panel to Assess Domestic Response Capabilities for Terrorism Involving Weapons of Mass Destruction, 261
Aerospace and Materials Science, 148
Aerospace Centre (Australia), 328
Aerospace industry, 269–270
Aerospace intelligence, 214
Aerospace warfare, 4
Afghanistan, 269, 347, 368
    agency jurisdiction, 26, 45, 216
    foreign government actions, 328, 333, 334, 335, 338, 340
    unified combatant command, 137
AF News, 141
Africa
    agency jurisdiction, 31, 52, 199, 211
    congressional oversight, 241
    military education, 10
    research institute studies, 314, 315
    UN disarmament activities, 350
    unified combatant commands, 138, 139
Africa Center for Strategic Studies, 52
African Affairs Office, 31

Africa Policy Information Center, 315
Agencywide Documents Access and Management System, 202
Agriculture, 99
Agriculture Department, 97, 99, 103
Air and Space Power Journal, 4
Air Combat Command, 142
Air Command and Staff College, 3, 4, 142–143
Air Corps Tactical School, 142
Air Force (Canada), 334–335
Air Force Academy, 2, 144
Air Force and National Defense College, 344
Air Force Audit Agency, 145
Air Force Broadcasting Service, 141
Air Force Command and Control and Intelligence, Surveillance, and Reconnaissance Center, 145
Air Force Command and Control Battlelab, 63, 145
Air Force Communications Agency, 145–146
Air Force Cryptologic Support Center, Securities Directorate, 147
Air Force Department, 41, 136, 322
  agencies and operations, 141–150
  civilian law enforcement, 278
  educational institutions, 2, 3, 142–144, 148
  establishment and mission, 141
  intelligence agencies, 214–215
  senior leadership, 149
Air Force Doctrine Center, 146
Air Force Electronic Warfare Center, 147
Air Force Experimentation Office, 145
Air Force Flight Test Center, 146
Air Force General Counsel, 286–287
Air Force Historical Research Agency, 146–147
Air Force History Support Office, 147
Air Force Information and News Center, 141
Air Force Information Warfare Center, 147, 214
Air Force Institute of Technology, 148
Air Force Judge Advocate General's Department, 284
Air Force Link, 142
Air Force Material Command, 149
Air Force News Agency, 141
Air Force News Service, 141
Air Force Office of Scientific Research, 148
Air Force One, 124
Air Force Research Laboratory, 148–149
Air Force Safety and Inspection Center, 149
Air Force Safety Center, 149
Air Forces Command, 149
Air Force Security Service, 214
Air Force Space Command, 149–150
Air Force Test Pilot School, 146
Air Intelligence Agency, 147, 214–215, 265
Air Mobility Command, 140
Air National Guard, 143
Airport security. *See* Aviation security
Airpower, 399
Air Research and Development Command, 148
Air School of Application, 148
Air University, 3–4, 142, 143, 148, 282–283
"Air University Library Index to Military Periodicals," 380
Air University Press, 143–144
Air Vehicles, 148
Air War College, 3, 4, 16, 143, 282
Alaska, 241
Algeria, 60
America: History and Life, 381
American, British, Canadian, and Australian Armies Program, 151
American Continental Army, 150
American Embassy, 246
American Enterprise Institute for Public Policy Research, 296–297
American Forces Information Service, 27
Animal and Plant Health Inspection Service, 99
Animal health, 99, 103
Annals of Communism (monograph series), 391–392
Antarctica, 139
Anthrax, 74, 77, 97, 98, 107, 219, 312, 313
Anthrax Vaccination Immunization Program, 43–44
Antiballistic Missile Treaty of 1972, 110
Antiproliferation. *See* Proliferation, nonproliferation, and counterproliferation
Antiterrorism. *See* Terrorism and counterterrorism
Appellate courts, 279
Appointment power, 64*n*1
Appropriations. *See* Budgets and appropriations
Arab-Israeli conflict, 400
Archival Research Catalog, 193
Archives and records
  declassified government documents, 305, 315
  security classification, 193–194

United Kingdom, 341–342
See also National Archives and Records Administration
Arctic National Wildlife Refuge, 241
Arctic region, 139
Argonne National Laboratory, 76–77, 85
Argos Press, 386
Armed Forces and Society, 384
Armed services
   congressional oversight, 234–235, 239–240
   website, 25
   See also Military entries and specific service departments
Armed services academies, 2–3
Armor Center, 151
Armor School, 151
Arms control agreements, 401
   compliance verification, 40, 76, 87, 92, 110, 112–113, 174
Arms control and disarmament
   advisory commission report, 256
   agency jurisdiction, 31, 32, 40, 76, 82, 87, 110, 199
   international government organizations, 347
   military education, 10
   research institute studies, 297, 301, 307–308, 321, 371, 373, 374
   UN agencies, 349–351
Arms Control and Disarmament Program, 313
Arms Control Association, 297
Arms Export Control Act, 114
Army (Canada), 335
Army Air Force, 321
Army Airways Communication System, 145
Army and Air Force Hometown News Service, 141
Army Biomedical Laboratory, 159
Army Chemical School, 152
Army Corps of Engineers, 26, 92, 157, 234
Army Department, 41, 136, 322
   agencies and operations, 150–162
   civilian law enforcement, 278
   educational institutions, 2, 4–7, 154–155, 157, 159–160
   establishment and mission, 150
   intelligence agencies, 215–216
   newspapers, 153
   office of the secretary, 26
   senior leadership, 152

Army Europe, 26
Army General Counsel, 287
Army Industrial College, 13, 55
Army Intelligence and Security Branch, 215
Army Intelligence and Security Command, 215–216
Army Intelligence Master Plan, 216
Army Intelligence School, 215
Army International Affairs, 160
Army International Affairs Plan, 155, 160
Army Judge Advocate General's Corps, 284–285
Army Missile Defense Command, 162
Army Mountain Warfare School, 152
Army National Guard, 152–153
Army-Navy Staff College, 15, 60
Army Ordnance Department, 161
Army Rangers, 159
Army Research Institute for the Behavioral and Social Sciences, 153
Army Research Laboratory, 154
Army Science Board, 154, 155
Army Space Command, 162
Army War College, 4–5, 16, 154–155, 258, 278, 324
Arnold, Henry, 146
Arroyo Center, 322
Artillery training, 158
Art of War Department, 5
Asia, 319, 350, 401, 402. *See also* specific countries and geographic regions
Asian and Pacific Affairs Office, 31–32
Asia-Pacific Center for Security Studies, 44
Asia-Pacific region
   agency jurisdiction, 31–32, 44, 58
   congressional oversight, 241
   foreign government organizations, 331
   military education, 10
   research institute studies, 298, 315, 322, 360, 373
   unified combatant command, 139
Aspin, Les, 257
Assembled Chemical Weapons Assessment, 61
Assistant secretary for policy and international affairs, 90
Assistant secretary of defense for command, control, communications, and intelligence, 46, 62
Assistant secretary of defense for international security affairs, 31

Assistant secretary of defense for legislative affairs, 25, 26
Assistant secretary of defense for networks and information integration, 25, 26
Assistant secretary of defense for public affairs, 25, 27
Assistant secretary of defense for research and development, 37
Assistant secretary of defense for special operations and low-intensity conflict, 31, 139
Assistant secretary of the Army (acquisition, logistics, and technology), 155–156
Assistant to the president for national security affairs, 121
Assistant to the secretary of defense for intelligence oversight, 25, 27
Astrometry, 172
Astronomical and timing data, 172
Astropolitics: The International Journal of Space Power and Policy, 384
Asymmetric conflict, 10, 58
AT&T, 93
Atkinson, Richard C., 126*n*35
Atlantic Alliance, 297
Atlantic Command, 138
Atlantic Council of the United States, 297–298
Atlantic Fleet, 169
Atlantic Ocean, 139
Atlantic Undersea Test and Evaluation Center, 174
Atmospheric and oceanic policy, 255
Atmospheric and space sciences, 173
Atomic bomb, 196
Atomic Energy Commission, 76, 79, 81, 85, 90, 92, 93, 202
Auditing. *See* Accounting and auditing; Office of Inspector General
Australia, 151, 344
  government organizations, 327–333
  research institutions, 359–360
Australia Group, 314
Australian Defence Force, 328
Australian Defence Force Academy, 359
Australian Defence Studies Centre, 359
Australian National Audit Office, 332
Australian National University, 360
Australian Parliament, 332
Australian Parliamentary Library, 333
Australian Secret Intelligence Service, 330

Australian Security Intelligence Organisation, 330–331
Australian Strategic Policy Institute, 360
Austrian National Defence Academy, 315
Aviation Command and Control Branch, 165
Aviation Department, 165
Aviation history, 395
Aviation Logistics Support Branch, 165
Aviation medicine, 170
Aviation Safety Division, 149
Aviation security, 257
  advisory commission reports, 258, 269
  agency jurisdiction, 93, 104, 115–117
Aviation Security Act of 1990, 223
Aviation Weapons Branch, 165

B-52 Close Air Support Enhancement, 145
Balkan states, 260, 360
Ballistic Missile Defense Organization, 42, 239
Ballistic Missile Defense System, 42
Ballistic Missile Launch Notification Agreement of 1988, 110
Bancroft, George, 169
Bangladesh, 60
Banking and finance infrastructure, 223, 268
Bank Secrecy Act, 101
Bar-Ilan University, 366
Base Closure Account, 234
Bases, military. *See* Military installations
Basic Combat Training Brigade, 159
Battelle Corporation, 86, 92
Bay of Pigs, 210
Bechtel Corporation, 79
Begin, Menachem, 366
Begin-Sadat Center for Strategic Studies, 366–367
Behavioral science, 153
Belfer Center for Science and International Affairs, 311–312, 386
  Studies in International Security, 392
Bendix Corporation, 81
Ben-Gurion, David, 398
Berlin, 137
Berlin Airlift, 196
Bills and resolutions, 229–230
bin Laden, Osama, 45, 213, 260, 269
Biological weapons. *See* Chemical and biological weapons
Biotechnology, 54, 211, 301

Black Sea, 360
Blackwell Publishing, 387
Blair, Tony, 338
Bloomberg School of Public Health, 312
Board of Immigration Appeals, 106
Boeing Library, 360
Bolling Air Force Base, 147
Bolton, John, 113
Bomb Line Unit (BLU-118/B) Thermobaric Warhead, 40
Bomb squads, 93
Border and Transportation Security Directorate, 100
Border security, 101–102, 239
Bosnia, 260
Botulin toxin, 77, 96, 98, 312, 313
Bowtie investigation, 107
Bradley, Omar, 154
Bremer, L. Paul, 267
Bremer Commission, 267
Bright Star exercises, 137
Britain. *See* United Kingdom
British-American Security Information Council, 298
Brookhaven National Laboratory, 77
Brookhaven Science Associates, 77
Brookings Institution, 298
Brown, Harold, 37, 263
Browne, John C., 126*n*35
Budget and Management Program, 360
Budgets and appropriations
    congressional support agency, 244–245
    executive agency, 122–122
    House committees, 234, 235
    research institute studies, 300
    Senate committees, 239, 249
Buildings and facilities
    federal buildings management, 190
    See also Military installations
Bulgaria, 360–361
Bundy, McGeorge, 198
Bureau of Arms Control, 109, 110
Bureau of Citizenship and Immigration Services, 100–101
Bureau of Customs, 101
Bureau of Diplomatic Security, 109, 110
Bureau of Export Administration, 72
Bureau of Industry and Security, 72–73, 292, 314

Bureau of Intelligence and Research, 222–223
Bureau of International Narcotics and Law Enforcement Affairs, 109, 111
Bureau of Navigation, 217
Bureau of Nonproliferation, 109, 111–112
Bureau of Political-Military Affairs, 109, 112, 113
Bureau of the Census, 242
Bureau of Verification and Compliance, 110, 112–113
Burgess, Guy, 107
Bush, George H. W., 61, 208
    commissions and advisory organizations, 257–259
    presidential library, 201
Bush, George W., 119, 195
    commissions and advisory organizations, 269–271
    national security policy planning, 62, 120
    trade policy, 192
    war on terrorism, 213, 269, 288, 289
Business and industry protection, 220–221
BWXT Pantex, 92

C-5 Galaxy cargo plane, 141
Cabinet meeting minutes, 315
Cabinet Office, 338, 341
Cable News Network (CNN), 216
Cable Satellite Public Affairs Network (C-SPAN), 198, 231
California, 290
Cambridge Scientific Abstracts, 383
Cambridge Studies in International Relations (monograph series), 392
Cambridge University Press, 392
Camp David, 123, 124
Camp Pendleton, 163
Canada, 103, 151
    government organizations, 327, 333–337
    history studies, 381, 395
    research institutions, 361–364
    unified combatant command, 138
Canadian Broadcasting Corporation, 307
Canadian Forces, 334–335
Canadian Institute of Strategic Studies, 361
Canadian Parliament, 336–337
Canadian Parliamentary Library, 337
Canadian Security Intelligence Service, 335
Canadian War Museum, 395

Capability Assessment Branch, 165
Caribbean region, 139, 255
Carleton University, 361
Carnegie, Andrew, 299
Carnegie Endowment for International Peace, 299
Carnegie Foundation, 305
Carter, Hodding, III, 200
Carter, Jimmy, 200, 224
Casualty and Memorial Affairs Operations Center, 158–159
"Catalog of Government Publications," 381
Cato Institute, 299
Cebrowski Institute for Information Innovation and Superiority, 10
Census Bureau, 242
Center for Army Lessons Learned, 6, 156
Center for Asian Security Studies, 319
Center for Asia-Pacific Policy, 322
Center for Autonomous Underwater Vehicle Research, 172
Center for Central European and Eurasian Studies, 317
Center for Civilian Biodefense Strategies, 312
Center for Civil-Military Relations, 10, 172
Center for Contemporary Conflict, 10, 172
Center for Counterproliferation Research, 52, 53, 56
Center for Defense Information, 299–300
Center for East-West Policy, 313
Center for Emerging Threats and Capabilities, 167
Center for Global Peace and Conflict Studies, 312
Center for Global Security Research, 82
Center for Hemispheric Defense Studies, 53–54
Center for Infectious Disease Research and Policy, 313
Center for Information Security Studies, 10
Center for Information Systems Security Studies and Research, 10, 11, 172
Center for International Security and Cooperation, 313
Center for International Studies, 318
Center for International Threat Reduction, 87–88
Center for International Trade and Security, 313–314

Center for Joint Services Electronic Warfare, 10, 11
Center for Law and Military Operations, 285
Center for Medicare and Medicaid Services, 96
Center for Middle East Policy, 317
Center for Middle East Public Policy, 322
Center for Military History, 156
Center for Naval Warfare Studies, 9, 175
Center for Nonproliferation Studies, 314
Center for Northeast Asian Policy Studies, 298
Center for Russia and Eurasia, 322, 323
Center for Security Policy, 300
Center for Security Studies, 371, 372
Center for Strategic and Budgetary Assessments, 300
Center for Strategic and International Studies, 17, 300–301, 315
Center for Strategic Leadership, 4–5, 155
Center for Strategic Leadership Development, 14
Center for Strategic Studies (Israel), 367
Center for Strategic Studies (United Kingdom), 384
Center for Teaching and Learning, 169
Center for Technology and National Security Policy, 54
Center for the Study of Chinese Military Affairs, 54, 56
Center for the Study of Intelligence, 209–210
Center for the Study of Mobile Devices and Communications, 10
Center for the Study of Professional Military Ethics, 169
Center on Terrorism and Irregular Warfare, 10, 11, 172
Centers for Disease Control and Prevention, 44, 77, 96, 98, 99
Central America, 139, 253, 255
Central Asia, 80, 368
Central Command, 12, 136, 137
Central Documents Office, 39
Central Europe, 317, 374, 375, 400
Central Identification Laboratory, 157
Central Intelligence Agency, 213, 282
    advisory commission report, 265
    agencies and operations, 207–212
    agency jurisdiction, 109, 199
    congressional oversight, 234, 237, 239

declassified documents access, 291–292, 315
establishment and mission, 41, 99, 121
research institute studies, 302
Centre for Conflict Resolution (South Africa), 369
Centre for Defence and International Studies (United Kingdom), 376
Centre for Defence and Security Studies (Canada), 363–364
Centre for Military and Strategic Studies (Canada), 363
Centre for Security and Defence Studies (Canada), 361–362
Centre for Strategic Studies (New Zealand), 368
Chandler, William E., 218
Chelyabinsk launch site, 221
Chemical and Biological Arms Control Institute, 301
Chemical and Biological Defense Program, 77
Chemical and biological weapons
  arms control, disarmament, and threat reduction, 40, 77, 301, 350
  bioterrorism resources, 96–99, 313
  counterproliferation, 53
  decontamination formulations, 93
  defense, 33, 61, 76, 77, 152, 159, 161, 188, 223, 312
  incident response force, 163, 269
Chemical Biological Incident Response Force, 163
Chemical demilitarization, 61, 80, 161, 234
Chemical Incidents Reports Center, 188
Chemical Safety and Hazard Investigation Board, 188
Chemical Warfare Service, 161
Chemical Weapons Convention, 73, 110, 161, 297, 350, 374
Cheney, Dick, 17
Chernobyl nuclear plant, 80
Cheyenne Mountain Operations Center, 138
Chief of naval operations, 168–169
Child soldiers, 369
China, 118, 257, 344
  advisory commission, 270–271
  agency jurisdiction, 54, 56, 221
  research institute and scholarly studies, 314, 316, 318, 365, 366, 373, 402
  unified combatant command, 139

Chifley, Ben, 330
Churchill, Winston, 398
Circuit courts, 279
Citizenship, 100
Civil Engineer and Services School, 148
Civilian Health and Medical Program of the Uniformed Services, 63
Civil liberties, 107, 238, 261
Civil-military relations, 10, 13, 52, 172, 373
Civil-Military Relations in Central and Eastern Europe Internet Resource Center, 374
Civil service, 236, 242
Civil War, 156, 278
Civil Wars, 384
Classification Management Committee, 194
Classification system
  government documents, 382
  security classification procedures, 193–194, 262
Classified Information Procedures Act, 105
Clean Air Act Amendments of 1990, 188
Clemenceau, Georges, 398
Climate change, 319
Clinton, Bill, 33, 108, 221
  commissions and advisory organizations, 260–269
  national security policy planning, 42, 120, 121
Clinton Presidential Materials Project, 119, 201, 225
Coast Guard, 99, 100, 115
  education and training, 2, 9
  mission and operations, 101, 188, 290
Coast Guard Academy, 2
Coast Guard Hearings Office, 287
Coast Guard Intelligence Coordination Center, 218
Coast Guard Legal Program, 287
Code of Federal Regulations, 290, 291
Cohen, Eliot, 397–398
Cohen, William S., 33
Colby, William E., 198
Cold case squad, 218
Cold war
  agency jurisdiction, 32, 120, 196
  declassified documents access, 315
  research institute and scholarly studies, 364, 384, 387, 394
Cold War History, 384

College of Aerospace Doctrine, Research, and Education, 3, 4, 143
College of Distance Education, 8
College of International Security Studies, 50
College of Naval Command and Staff, 8, 9
College of Naval Warfare, 8, 9
College of Security Studies, 44
Colleges and universities
 libraries, 380, 382, 383, 391
 See also specific institution names
Columbia International Affairs Online, 314–315
Columbia University Press, 314
Combat Studies Institute, 6, 157
Combat Training Center Branch, 156
Combest, Larry, 262
Combined Arms and Services Staff School, 6
Combined Arms and Tactics Directorate, 159
Combined Arms Research Library, 6, 157
Command and control, 10, 80, 177
Command and Control Integration Division, 165
Command and Control Systems School, 167
Command and General Staff College, 3, 5–7, 157
Command and Staff College, 7
Command, control, communications (C3), 35
Command, control, communications, computers, and intelligence (C4I), 14–15
Commander in chief, 25, 119, 291
Commerce. *See* Trade issues
Commerce Department, 72–75, 264
Commissaries, 34
Commission on Higher Education of the Middle States Association, 13
Commission on Integrated Long-Term Strategy, 254
Commission on Merchant Marine and Defense, 254
Commission on Protecting and Reducing Government Secrecy, 262
Commission on Roles and Capabilities of the U.S. Intelligence Community, 262–263
Commission on Roles and Missions of the Armed Forces, 263
Commission on Security and Cooperation in Europe, 244
Commission on the Future of the U.S. Aerospace Industry, 269
Commissions and advisory organizations, 253–276
Commission to Assess the Organization of the Federal Government to Combat the Proliferation of Weapons of Mass Destruction, 263–264
Commission to Assess U.S. National Security Space Management and Organization, 264–265
Committee on Classification of Personnel in the Army, 153
Committee on Expenditures in Executive Departments, 242
Committee on Foreign Affairs, Human Rights, Common Security, and Defence Policy, 346
Committees, congressional. *See* House and Senate entries
Common Operating Environment, 36
Communications, 124, 145–146, 177, 340–341
Communications and Directives Directorate, 49
Communications and Information Systems Directorate, 141
Communism studies, 391–392
Comparative Strategy, 384–385
Comprehensive Nuclear Test Ban Treaty, 92, 297, 374
Comptroller (undersecretary of defense), 25, 29–30
Computational and Information Sciences Directorate, 154
Computer Crime and Intellectual Property Section, 104, 105
Computer Emergency Response Team, 44
Computer security. *See* Cybersecurity
Computer Security Resource Center, 74
Computer System Security and Privacy Advisory Board, 74
Concurrent resolutions, 229
Conference committees, 232
Conference Directorate, 56
Conference of Defence Associations, 362
Conflict resolution, 191, 312, 348, 369, 371
Conflict, Security, and Development Group, 374–375
Conflict Studies Research Centre, 375
Congress, 229–252
 bills and resolutions, 229–230
 committee activity reports, 233

committee hearings, 230–231
committee reports, 231–232
floor debate, 233
legislative calendars, 233
national security committees, 233–244
oversight of national security policy, 231
support agencies, 244–247
Congressional Budget and Impoundment Control Act of 1974, 235, 244
Congressional Budget Office, 231, 244–245
Congressional committees and subcommittees. *See* House and Senate entries
Congressional Information Service, 381, 382
Congressional Information Service Index, 381
Congressional Quarterly Inc., 277, 385
Congressional Quarterly Weekly Report, 385
Congressional Record, 233
Congressional Research Service, 229, 231, 238, 241, 246, 265
Congressional Universe, 233, 381
Conservative policy research, 296, 303
Constitutional powers and requirements, 25, 72, 119, 229, 231, 232, 279, 291
Constructive Directorate, 160
Contemporary Security Policy, 385
Continental Congress, 150, 162, 168, 237
Continental Navy of the American Revolution, 168
Contraband materials detection, 80, 101
Contract auditing, 34
Contract management, 34–35
Contributions in Military Studies (monograph series), 392
Controlled Substances Act, 106
Conventional Forces in Europe Treaty, 40, 110
Cooperative Threat Reduction Scorecard, 40
Cooper Library, 94
Coordinator for counterterrorism, 110, 113
Cordesman, Anthony, 398
Cornell Studies in Security Affairs (monograph series), 392–393
Cornell University Press, 392
Corona satellite program, 209, 221
Corum, James, 399
Cost Analysis Tools Division, 170
Cost control, 256
Cost Research and Operations Division, 170
Council for Canadian Security in the 21st Century, 362

Counterdrug programs. *See* Drug abuse and trafficking
Counterespionage Section, 105
Counterfeiting, 103, 117
Counterintelligence. *See* Intelligence entries
Counterintelligence, Foreign Disclosure, and Security Directorate, 216
Counterintelligence/Human Intelligence Plans and Policy Branch, 217
Counterproliferation. *See* Proliferation, nonproliferation, and counterproliferation
Counterterrorism. *See* Terrorism and counterterrorism
Counterterrorism Committee, 348–349
Court of Appeals for the Armed Forces, 283
Court of Military Appeals, 282
Courts-martial, 283, 289
Court system, 279–281
CQ Weekly Report, 385
Criminal Division, 105
Criminal Intelligence Program, 336
Criminal investigations, 105, 109, 218–219
Criminal organizations, 323, 390
Criminal tribunals, 115
Crisis Decision Exercise, 15
Critical Incident Response Training Program, 102
Critical Infrastructure Assurance Office, 72, 73
Critical Infrastructure Training Program, 102
Crown Prosecution Service, 343
Cryptological agencies, 219–220
C-SPAN, 198, 231
Cuba, 199
Cuban Missile Crisis, 197–198, 210, 220
Customs and Border Protection, 101–102
Customs Service, 99, 101
CyberCemetery, 268
Cybersecurity (computer security)
    agency jurisdiction, 105, 106, 109, 123, 192, 219, 223–224
    congressional oversight, 239

Danish Institute of International Affairs, 364–365
Deaf Smith nuclear site, 95
Decision-making training, 5, 33
Decision Strategies Department, 175
Declassified Documents Reference System, 315
Defence Academy (United Kingdom), 339

Defence Act, 329
Defence Committee (United Kingdom), 343
Defence Intelligence Organisation (Australia), 331
Defence Scientific Advisory Council (United Kingdom), 339
Defence Signals Directorate (Australia), 331
Defence Studies, 385
Defend America, 45
Defense Advanced Research Projects Agency, 33–34
Defense Advisory Committee on Women in the Services, 28, 43, 45
Defense Almanac, 25
Defense and Intelligence Acronyms, 210
Defense Base Closure and Realignment Commission, 265
Defense Commissary Agency, 34
Defense Communications Agency, 35
Defense Communications System, 35
Defense Contract Audit Agency, 34
Defense Contract Management Agency, 34–35
Defense Conversion Commission, 257
Defense Department, 109, 283, 311
    advisory commission reports, 254, 257, 263–265, 268, 270, 271
    affiliated institutions, 43–64
    agencies and responsibilities, 33–43
    congressional oversight, 234–235, 237, 239
    establishment and mission, 41, 99, 121
    Office of the Secretary, 25–33
    policy-making role, 25
    reorganization, 12
    website, 25
Defense Economic Adjustment Program, 61
Defense Environmental Information Network and Information Exchange, 45–46
Defense Finance and Accounting Service, 35
Defense Horizon reports series, 54
Defense Information System Network, 36
Defense Information Systems Agency, 35–36
Defense Information Technology Contracting Organization, 36
Defense Information Technology Testbed, 46
Defense Institute of International Legal Studies, 287–288
Defense Intelligence Agency, 26, 37, 208, 212–213, 237
Defense Legal Services Agency, 288
DefenseLink Freedom of Information Act, 46–47
Defense Logistics Agency, 36–37, 239
Defense Mapping Agency, 219
Defense Message System, 36
Defense Modeling and Simulation Office, 47
Defense Nuclear Facilities Safety Board, 78, 189, 234
Defense Office of Hearings and Appeals, 288
Defense Policy Board, 37
Defense Prisoner of War/Missing Personnel Office, 31, 32
Defense research and engineering, 28
Defense Science Board, 37–38
Defense Security Cooperation Agency, 26, 31, 32, 175, 287
Defense Security Service, 38–39
Defense Security Service Academy, 38
Defense Special Weapons Agency, 40
Defense Supply Agency, 36
Defense Supply Center, 36
Defense Task Force, 316
Defense Technical Information Center, 39, 57, 155, 383
Defense Threat Reduction Agency, 26, 40, 282
Defense Total Asset Visibility Implementation Plan, 51
Defense trade controls, 113–114
Defense trade shows, 33
Defense Virtual Library, 39
Demining, 112, 234
Denmark, 364–365
Department for Disarmament Affairs, 349–350
Department for International Development, 374
Department of Agriculture, 97, 99, 103
Department of Command, Leadership, and Management, 5
Department of Commerce, 72–75, 264
Department of Commerce and Labor, 72
Department of Defence (Australia), 328
Department of Defence (South Africa), 345
Department of Defense (U.S.). *See* Defense Department
Department of Defense Reorganization Act of 1986 (Goldwater-Nichols Act), 11–13, 16, 41–42, 58, 257
Department of Education, 13, 96
Department of Energy. *See* Energy Department

Department of Energy Organization Act of 1977, 76
Department of Foreign Affairs, 109
Department of Health and Human Services, 50, 72, 96–99, 260
Department of Health, Education, and Welfare, 96
Department of Homeland Security. *See* Homeland Security Department
Department of Justice. *See* Justice Department
Department of Labor, 72
Department of Military Strategy, Planning, and Operations, 5
Department of National Defence (Canada), 334–335
Department of National Security and Strategy, 5
Department of State. *See* State Department
Department of Strategic Studies, 373
Department of the Treasury. *See* Treasury Department
Department of Transportation. *See* Transportation Department
Department of Veterans Affairs, 50, 260, 268
Depleted Uranium Library, 47–48
Deployment Health Support Directorate, 47
Depot of Charts and Instruments, 172
Depth and Simultaneous Attack Battle Lab, 158
Deputy secretary of defense, 25, 27
Deputy undersecretary of defense for industrial affairs, 48
Deputy undersecretary of the Air Force— international affairs, 150
Deterrence, 10, 304, 400
Deutch, John, 263
Deutch-Specter Commission, 263–264
Dewey Decimal classification system, 393
Diamond trade, 369
Digital National Security Archive, 305
Dingell, John D., 236
Diplomatic security, 110–111
Directorate for Information Operations and Reports, 48–49
Directorate for Press Operations, 27
Directorate for Public Inquiry and Analysis, 27
Directorate of Defense Trade Controls, 110, 113–114
Directorate of History and Heritage, 334

Directorate of Intelligence, 208
Directorate of Science and Technology, 208–209
Director for operational test and evaluation, 25, 28
Director of administration and management, 25, 27–28
Director of defense research and engineering, 25, 28
Director of program analysis and evaluation, 25, 28–29
Disabled employees, 35
Disarmament. *See* Arms control and disarmament
Disarmament Intelligence Review, 374
Disaster management. *See* Emergency management
District courts, 279
District of Columbia, 236, 242
Division for Economic Policy Research, 367
Division for Research in Strategy, 367
Division of Military Information, 215
DNA analysis, 32, 107
Doctrine and Development Directorate, 375
Doctrine Department, 176
Domestic preparedness. *See* Emergency management
Domestic Surveillance Oversight Act of 2003 (proposed), 281
Douglas Aircraft Company, 321
Drug abuse and trafficking
  agency jurisdiction, 101, 105–106, 108, 109, 111, 117, 118, 122–123, 218
  congressional jurisdiction, 240, 243–244
  research institute and scholarly studies, 323, 390
Drug Enforcement Administration, 104, 105
Duke University, 324
"Duty, Honor, and Country" (motto), 3
Dwight D. Eisenhower Library and Museum, 196–197
Dynes, Robert, 126*n*35

East Asia, 211, 241, 360
East Asia Nonproliferation Program, 314
Eastern Europe, 80, 320, 374, 375
Eastern European Studies (monograph series), 393
East Timor, 335
East-West Center, 315

"Ebsco Host's Military and Government Collection," 381
E coli bacteria, 34
E-commerce, 36
Economic Adjustment Agency, 61
Economic and financial crimes, 106, 117–118, 218
Economic competitiveness, 74
Economic Espionage Act of 1996, 220
Economic sanctions, 117, 118
Economics Department, 14
Economic Studies Division, 170
Economist, 307
Edgewood Arsenal, 159
Education
 national security, 59, 61
 professional military. *See* Military education and training
Education Department, 13, 96
Edwards Air Force Base, 146
Egypt, 137
E. I. DuPont de Nemours and Company, 93
Eisenhower, Dwight D., 154, 198, 224
 presidential library, 196–197
Electronic Briefing Books, 305
Electronic Freedom of Information Act, 30, 73, 169, 210–211, 281–282
Electronic warfare, 11
11th Marine Expeditionary Unit, 163
El Salvador, 255
Embassies and consulates, 246
Emergency management
 advisory commission reports, 261, 268–269
 agency jurisdiction, 96, 97, 102, 152, 189–190, 223
 congressional oversight, 239
Emergency Preparedness and Response Directorate, 100
Emirates Center for Strategic Studies and Research, 373
Energy Department, 59, 72, 202, 282, 311
 advisory commission reports, 260, 264
 agencies and responsibilities, 76–96
 congressional oversight, 234, 236, 237, 239, 240
 defense nuclear facilities safety, 189
 directives, regulations, policies, and standards, 78
 intelligence agencies, 208, 221–222
 oversight and performance assurance, 89
 policy adviser, 907
Energy geopolitics, 211
Energy Information Administration, 79
Energy infrastructure, 223, 268
Energy Research and Development Administration, 76, 79, 201
England, 339. *See also* United Kingdom
Enhanced Performance Center, 160
Enlisted Professional Military Education, 7, 8
Environmental policy, 320
Environmental programs
 counterterrorism and emergency response, 96
 depleted uranium, 47–48
 military installations, 45–46
 nuclear energy and weapons production, 77, 79, 88
Environmental Protection Agency, 96, 188
Environment, Safety, and Health Researchers Workstation, 79
Ethnic conflict, 313, 316, 323
Ethnic Conflict Program, 316
Ethnic studies, 316
Eurasia, 211, 301, 317, 322, 323, 375
Eurasia Policy Studies, 319
Europe
 agency jurisdiction, 36, 49–50, 80, 211
 congressional oversight, 241
 international government organizations, 346–347
 military education, 10
 research institute and scholarly studies, 314, 317, 320, 374, 375, 393, 400, 401
 unified combatant commands, 136, 137
European Command, 136, 137
European Institute for Security Studies, 346–347
European Parliament—Committee on Foreign Affairs, Human Rights, Common Security, and Defence Policy, 346
European Security, 385
European Union, 346–347, 374
European Union Satellite Centre, 346, 347
Europe Field Command, 36
Executive branch agencies. *See* specific department names
Executive Office for Asset Forfeiture, 117
Executive Office for Immigration Review, 104, 106

Executive Office of the President, 72, 119–124
Executive Order 10656, 224
Executive Order 12333, 208, 213
Executive Order 12472, 35
Executive Order 12829, 193, 194
Executive Order 12958, 193, 194, 222
Executive Order 12961, 50
Executive Order 12968, 222
Executive Order 13122, 292
Executive Order 13224, 118
Executive Order 13231, 123
Executive Order 13233, 195
Executive Order 13284, 292
Executive Order 13301, 291
Executive orders, 119, 120, 291, 292
Executive power, 64n1
Expeditionary Warfare, Information Electronics, and Surveillance, 177
Expeditionary Warfare School, 7, 8, 167
Experiment Operations Division, 167
Experiment Plans Division, 167
Explosives, 80, 93, 192
Export controls, 72–73, 87, 101, 264, 314
Export License Division, 175

Federal Aviation Administration, 104, 115–116, 223, 258
Federal Aviation Agency, 115
Federal Bureau of Investigation, 104, 109, 282
    advisory commission reports, 258, 267, 271
    congressional oversight, 237
    declassified documents access, 315
    mission and operations, 106–108, 223
    research institute studies, 302, 307
Federal Communications Commission, 211
Federal Computer Incident Response Center, 190
Federal court system, 279–281
Federal depository libraries, 136, 230, 232, 233, 247, 253, 277, 279, 291, 292, 381, 382
Federal Emergency Management Agency, 45, 189–190, 268
Federal Information Systems Security Educators Association, 74
Federal Institute of Technology, 371, 372
Federal Law Enforcement Training Center, 102
Federal Maritime Commission, 190
Federal Property and Administrative Services Act of 1949, 190
Federal Protective Service, 190
Federal Register, 120, 281, 290–292
Federal Register Act of 1934, 290
Federal Reporter, 279
Federal Supplement, 279
Federated Assessment and Targeting Enhancements, 145
Federation of American Scientists, 120, 246, 260, 264, 267, 301–302, 321
Fermi, Enrico, 76
Field Artillery School, 158
Financial and economic crimes, 106, 117–118, 218
Financial Crimes Enforcement Network, 117–118
Financial management, 29–30, 34, 35
FindLaw, 280
Finnish Institute of International Affairs, 365
Fire Administration, 188, 190
Fire Dynamic Simulator, 74
First responders, 138, 162, 268
Fiscal Division (Marine Corps), 167
Fletcher School of Law and Diplomacy, 317
Flight tests, 146
Floor debate, 233
Foley, Thomas S., 37
Food and Drug Administration, 96, 97, 99
Food safety and security, 97, 99, 313
Foot-and-mouth disease, 34, 103
Ford, Gerald R., 199
Ford Foundation, 305, 321, 324
Foreign Affairs, Defense, and Trade Division, 246
Foreign Agents Registration Act, 105
Foreign and Commonwealth Office, 341
Foreign Area Officer Program, 50, 150
Foreign assets control, 118
Foreign assistance, 241
Foreign Broadcast Information Center, 211–212
Foreign Broadcast Information Service, 211
Foreign Broadcast Monitoring Service, 211
Foreign government organizations, 327–345
    Australia, 328–333
    Canada, 333–337
    India, 344
    Israel, 344
    New Zealand, 344–345
    Singapore, 345
    South Africa, 345
    United Kingdom, 338–344

Foreign intelligence. *See* Intelligence entries
Foreign Intelligence Surveillance Act of 1978, 108, 280
Foreign Intelligence Surveillance Court, 107, 109, 280–281
Foreign Liaison Directorate, 216
Foreign Military Financing Program, 234
Foreign military sales, 31, 32, 150, 175
Foreign Military Studies Office, 156
Foreign Policy Research Institute, 316
Foreign Policy, Security, and Strategic Studies (monograph series), 393–394
Foreign Press Center, 246
Foreign relations, congressional oversight, 237–238, 241–242
Foreign Relations of the United States, 114
Foreign research institutions, 359–379
Forensic science, 106, 219
Forms Program, 47
Forrestal, James, 303
Fort Belvoir, 215
Fort Benning, 64, 159
Fort Huachuca, 215, 284
Fort Knox, 151
Fort Leavenworth, 5, 156, 157, 160
Fort Leonard Wood, 152
Fort McNair, 13
Fort Meade, 214
Fort Monroe, 162
Fort Sill, 158
Fossil Energy Petroleum Reserves, 94
Foster Fellows Visiting Scholars Program, 113
Foundation for Foreign Policy Research, 365
Four Pillars Enterprise Company, 220
Fourth Amendment, 281
France, 346
Frank Cass (publisher), 384–386, 388–390
Franklin, Benjamin, 237
Franklin Delano Roosevelt Presidential Library and Museum, 195–196
Freedom of Information Act, 29, 30, 46–47, 85, 107, 145, 210, 281–282, 305
Future Warfighting Division, 165

General Accounting Office, 17, 231, 245–246, 383
General counsel offices, 286–288
General Counterdrug Intelligence Plan, 108
General Dennis J. Reimer Training and Doctrine Digital Library, 158, 159, 162

General Services Administration, 190–191
Geneva Centre for Security Policy, 372
Geneva Conventions, 285
Genocide, 115, 260
Geography issues, 223
Geological Survey, 221
George Bush Presidential Library and Museum, 201
George C. Marshall Center for European Security Studies, 49–50
Georgetown University, 300
George Washington University, 305
Georgia, Republic of, 304
Geospatial intelligence, 219, 347
Gerald R. Ford Library and Museum, 199
German Institute for International Politics and Security, 365
Germany, 196, 257, 346, 365, 399, 400
Gilmore, James, 261
Gilmore Commission, 261
Gingrich, Newt, 37
Global climate change, 319
Global Combat Support System, 36
Global Command and Control System, 36
Global Crime, 390
Global position satellites, 33
Global Security, 302
Goddard, George M., 215
Goldwater, Barry, 11, 12
Goldwater-Nichols Act of 1986, 11–13, 16, 41–42, 58, 257
Gore, Al, 267, 269
Gore Commission, 269
Government buildings
  management, 190
  See also Military installations
Government Communications Headquarters, 338, 340–341
Government documents
  archives and records administration, 192–193
  classification system, 382
  regulatory issues, 290–292
Government Printing Office, 243, 247, 381, 382
"GPO Access," 120, 229–233, 277–279, 291, 292
Grace, J. Peter, 256
Grace Commission, 256
Grant programs, 223
Grassley, Charles E., 281
Gray, Alfred, 166
Gray, Colin, 399–400

Great Britain. *See* United Kingdom
Greenwood Press, 392
Gregg-Graniteville Library, 94
Grenada, 11, 156
Ground Safety Division, 149
Guatemala, 210, 255
Gulflink, 50–51
Gulf of Mexico, 138, 139
Gulf War Medical Research Library, 50

Hague Convention, 285
Haiti, 260
Hanford nuclear site, 92, 95, 189
Hanssen, Robert, 302
Hart, Gary, 253, 261
Hart-Rudman Commission, 253, 261–262
Harvard University, 153, 311, 318, 386, 387, 392
Hazardous materials transport, 84
Health and Human Services Department, 50, 72, 96–99, 260
Health and safety, 301
   Air Force, 149
   aviation medicine, 170
   bioterrorism resources, 96–99
   depleted uranium, 47–48
   Gulf War illnesses, 50–51
   Marine Corps, 167–168
   military installations, 45–46
   nuclear facilities, 79
Health care, 63–64, 171
Hecht, Thomas, 366
Helms, Richard, 199
Helsinki Final Act, 244
Hemorrhagic fevers, 312
Henry VIII (king of England), 339
Henry Hofheimer lecture series, 58
Henry L. Stimson Center, 302–303
Heritage Foundation, 303
Herter, Christian, 297
Hickam Air Force Base, 157
Historian's Office, 110, 114
Historical Abstracts, 381
Historical Manuscripts Commission, 341
Historical Office, 27, 28
   State Department, 114
   See also Military history
History and Museums Division, 163–164
History Department, 160
HIV/AIDS, 345
HMS *Invincible*, 340

Holt, Rush, 252n74
Home Affairs Committee, 343
Homeland security, 291
   advisory commission report, 261–262
   agency jurisdiction, 54
   congressional oversight, 239
   research institute and scholarly studies, 297, 301, 401
Homeland Security Act of 2002, 41, 100, 239, 278
Homeland Security Department, 72, 74, 190, 287
   agencies and responsibilities, 99–104
   congressional oversight, 242
   establishment and mission, 99, 100
Homeland Security Information Center, 75
Homeland Security Planners Course, 14, 15
Homeland Security Presidential Directives, 120
Home Office, 339, 343
Homosexuals, 260
Honeywell Corporation, 81
Hoover, Herbert, 194, 316
Hoover Institution on War, Revolution, and Peace, 316
House Appropriations Committee, 231, 234, 239
House Armed Services Committee, 16, 230, 231, 234–235, 257
House Budget Committee, 222, 235–236
House Energy and Commerce Committee, 236
House Government Reform Committee, 231, 236–237
House International Relations Committee, 237–238, 241
House Judiciary Committee, 238–239
House Merchant Marine Panel, 235
House Morale, Welfare, and Recreation Panel, 235
House of Commons (Canada), 336
   Standing Committee on National Defence and Veterans Affairs, 337
House of Commons (United Kingdom), 327, 338, 342–344
House of Lords, 338, 342–343
House of Representatives (Australia), 332
House of Representatives (U.S.), 229, 278, 327
House Panel on Military Education, 16–18, 257–258
House Permanent Select Intelligence Committee, 237, 265

House Select Committee on Homeland Security, 239
House Special Oversight Panel on Department of Energy Reorganization, 239
House Special Oversight Panel on Terrorism, 235
House Subcommittee on Crime, Terrorism, and Homeland Security, 238
House Subcommittee on Cybersecurity, Science, and Research and Development, 239
House Subcommittee on Defense, 234
House Subcommittee on Emergency Preparedness and Response, 239
House Subcommittee on Energy and Power, 236
House Subcommittee on Energy and Water Development, 234
House Subcommittee on Foreign Operations, Export Financing, and Related Programs, 234
House Subcommittee on Human Intelligence, Analysis, and Counterintelligence, 237
House Subcommittee on Immigration and Claims, 238
House Subcommittee on Infrastructure and Border Security, 239
House Subcommittee on Intelligence and Counterterrorism, 239
House Subcommittee on Intelligence Policy and National Security, 237
House Subcommittee on Military Construction, 234
House Subcommittee on Military Installations and Facilities, 235
House Subcommittee on Military Personnel, 235
House Subcommittee on Military Procurement, 235
House Subcommittee on Military Readiness, 235
House Subcommittee on National Security, Veterans Affairs, and International Relations, 236
House Subcommittee on Oversight and Investigations, 236
House Subcommittee on Rules, 239
House Subcommittee on Technical and Tactical Intelligence, 237
House Subcommittee on Technology Procurement Policy, 236
House Subcommittee on Terrorism and Homeland Security, 237

Hudson Institute, 317
Humanitarian missions, 10
Human radiation experiment, 92, 260
Human Resources Command, 158–159
Human rights, 115, 210, 244, 320, 347, 348
Human Rights Act of 1998, 341
Hungary, 197
Hunt, William H., 217
Hussein, Saddam, 137, 269
Hyde, Henry, 64

IC21: The Intelligence Community in the 21st Century, 265
Idaho National Engineering and Environmental Laboratory, 79–80, 83
Imagery and Geospatial Plans and Policy Branch, 217
Imagery and mapping, 219, 302
Immigration, 100–101, 106, 201, 238, 243
Immigration and Naturalization Service, 99, 100, 104, 106
Impact Acceleration Injury Database, 170
India, 60, 139, 327, 344, 365–366, 368
Indonesia, 359
Industrial affairs, 48
Industrial College of the Armed Forces, 13–14, 55, 58
Industrial security, 38–39, 220–221
Infantry School, 159
Information Analysis and Infrastructure Protection Directorate, 74, 100, 223
Information Analysis Centers, 39
Information assurance, 11, 33, 36, 58, 340–341
Information classification procedures, 193–194, 262
Information Exploitation Office, 33
Information resources management, 13, 46, 55–56
Information Resources Management College, 13, 55–56
Information Security Oversight Office, 193–194
Information Security Resource Center, 92
Information Systems Division, 156
Information systems management, 35–36
Information technology, 10, 54, 211, 372
Information Technology and Operations Center, 160
Infrastructure protection
  advisory commission report, 268–269

agency jurisdiction, 73–74, 76, 93, 112, 123, 223–224
congressional oversight, 239
Initiatives for Proliferation Prevention, 80
Inspector General Act Amendments of 1988, 118
Inspector General Act of 1978, 75, 89
Inspector General Canadian Security Intelligence Service, 335
Inspector General of Intelligence and Security, 331
Inspectors general. *See* Office of Inspector General
Installations and Logistics Departments, 164
Institute for Advanced Strategic and Political Studies, 367
Institute for Defence Studies and Analysis (India), 366
Institute for Defense Analyses, 303–304
Institute for Disarmament Research, 350–351
Institute for Foreign Policy Analysis, 317
Institute for International Policy Studies, 368
Institute for National Security Studies, 144–145
Institute for National Strategic Studies, 52, 54, 56–57
Institute for Peace and Conflict Studies, 366
Institute for Policy Studies, 304
Institute for Security and International Studies (Bulgaria), 360–361
Institute for Security Studies, 369–370
Institute of Defence and Strategic Studies (Singapore), 369
Institute of International Studies (Denmark), 364
Institute of International Studies (Stanford University), 313
Institute of Medicine, 192
Institute of Strategic Studies–Islamabad, 368
Intellectual property protection, 105, 241, 289
Intelligence acronyms, 210
Intelligence activities
 advisory commission reports, 262, 264, 265, 268
 agencies and operations, 106, 108–109, 207–228
 Australia, 330–332
 Canada, 335–336
 congressional oversight, 234, 237, 239, 242–243
 Defense Department oversight, 27
 drug intelligence, 108
 judiciary role, 280–281
 military agencies, 214–219
 research institutions, 323–324
 scholarly journals, 385, 386
 United Kingdom, 340–341, 376
Intelligence and National Security, 385–386
Intelligence and Security Committee, 341
Intelligence Authorization Act of 1992, 208
Intelligence Authorization Act of 1995, 262
Intelligence Community, 208
Intelligence Estimates Branch, 217
Intelligence Operations and Personnel Resource Branch, 217
Intelligence Oversight Board, 224
Intelligence Plans and Policy/Tactical Exploitation of National Capabilities Program, 217
Intelligence Programs and Budget Branch, 217
Intelligence Security Committee, 338–339
Intelligence Services Act of 1994, 341
Intelligence Services Act of 2001, 330
Interagency Commission on Crime and Security in U.S. Seaports, 266
Interagency Security Classification Appeals Panel, 194
Interagency Working Group on Counterterrorism, 113
Intercontinental ballistic missiles, 256
Intermediate Nuclear Forces Treaty, 40
International Agreements Division, 175
International Atomic Energy Agency, 77, 86–87, 346, 348, 349
International Center for Terrorism Studies, 306
International Criminal Court, 33
International Criminal Court Treaty, 33
International government organizations, 345–351
International Institute for Strategic Studies, 375–376, 390
International Journal of Intelligence and Counterintelligence, 386
International law, 348
International Law Department, 9, 175
International Narcotics Control Effort program, 111
International Negotiations and Regional Affairs, 31, 33
International Nuclear Safety Program, 80
International Peacekeeping, 386

International Relations and Security Network, 360, 372–373
International Security, 311, 386
International Security and Defense Policy Center, 322
International security policy, 31
International Security Studies, 315
International Technology Programs Office, 28
International Traffic in Arms Regulations, 114
Internships, 36
InterUniversity Seminar on Armed Forces and Society, 384
Inventory of International Nonproliferation Organizations and Regimes, 314
Ira C. Eaker College for Professional Development, 3, 4, 282
Iran, 256–257, 267
Iran hostage crisis, 200
Iraq
 agency jurisdiction, 45
 foreign government actions, 329, 338, 340
 1991 war, 18, 257
 research institute and scholarly studies, 302, 308, 316, 401
 2003 war, 212, 269, 346
 UN agencies, 40, 348, 349
 unified combatant command, 137
Irregular warfare, 10, 11. *See also* Terrorism and counterterrorism
Israel, 60, 196, 304, 344, 366–367
Israel Defense Force, 344
Italy, 246, 318

Jaffee, Mel, 367
Jaffee Center for Strategic Studies, 367
Jane's Information Group, 376
Japan, 196, 368, 373
Jewish Institute for National Security Affairs, 304
Jimmy Carter Library and Museum, 200
Job announcements, 36
John D. and Catherine T. MacArthur Foundation, 305
John F. Kennedy Library and Museum, 197–198
John F. Kennedy School of Government, 311, 386, 392
John M. Olin Institute for Strategic Studies, 318
Johns Hopkins Center for Strategic and Advanced International Studies, 318
Johns Hopkins University, 312, 318
Johnson, Lyndon B., 120, 198
Joint Advisory Committee on Nuclear Weapons Surety, 28
Joint and Combined Staff Officer School, 58
Joint and Combined Warfighting School, 14, 58
Joint Center for Regulatory Studies, 296
Joint Chiefs of Staff, 12, 40–42, 121, 136, 168, 212, 213, 307
Joint Command, Control, and Information Warfare School, 14–15, 58
Joint Electronic Library, 43, 52, 57
Joint Expeditionary Force Experiment 2004, 145
Joint Forces Command, 136, 138
Joint Forces Quarterly, 1
Joint Forces Staff College, 13, 14, 16, 18, 58, 383
Joint Information Operations Center, 214
Joint Interoperability Test Command, 36
Joint Military Intelligence College, 210, 213
Joint National Integration Center, 43
Joint Non-Lethal Weapons Directorate, 163
Joint Planning and Execution Committee, 15
Joint Planning Orientation Course, 14, 15
Joint resolutions, 229
Joint Services Electronic Warfare Program, 11
Joint Standing Committee on Foreign Affairs, Defence, and Trade (Australia), 332
Joint Total Asset Visibility, 51
Joint Vision 2010, 51
Joint Vision 2020, 51–52
Joint warfare, 51–52
Jones, James L., 216
Journal of Battlefield Technology, 386–387
Journal of Cold War Studies, 387
Journal of Conflict and Security Law, 387
Journal of Contingencies and Crisis Management, 387
Journal of Military Ethics: Normative Aspects of the Use of Military Force, 387
Journal of Military History, 388
Journal of Slavic Military Studies, 388
Journal of Strategic Studies, 388
JSTOR, 383
Judge Advocates General, 283–286
Justice Department, 72, 99, 223, 260, 281
 agencies and responsibilities, 104–109
 information access site, 30, 104, 282

Kahn, Herman, 317
Kansas City Plant, 81
Kashmir, 344, 365, 368
Kathryn and Shelby Cullom Davis Center for International Studies, 303
Kazakhstan, 40, 314
Kelly Air Force Base, 141
Kennedy, John F., 120, 224
 presidential library, 197–198
Kennedy School of Government, 311, 386, 392
King's College, 374
Kirtland Air Force Base, 149
Kissinger, Henry, 199, 255
Kissinger Commission, 255
Knolls Atomic Power Laboratory, 81
Korea. *See* North Korea; South Korea
Korean Airlines Flight 007, 108
Korean War, 32, 196, 220
Kosovo, 335
Krushchev, Nikita, 198
Kuwait, 257
Kwajolein Atoll, 28

Laboratories
 national, 76–77, 79–83, 85, 86, 92, 93
 university, 99
Labor Department, 72
Lackland Air Force Base, 147, 214
Laird, Melvin, 62
Lancaster University, 376
Land Transportation Antiterrorism Training Program, 102
Land Warfare Studies Centre, 329
Langley Air Force Base, 142, 145
Lansing, Robert, 110
Latin America, 10, 210, 211, 255
Lattimore, Owen, 107
Law enforcement
 by armed forces, 278
 FBI duties and services, 106–108
 global cooperation, 109
 police reform, 374
 training resource, 102
Law of War, 285
Law of Warfare Program, 167
Lawrence Berkeley National Laboratory, 81–82
Lawrence Livermore National Laboratory, 82
Leadership Development Program, 6, 157
Leahy, Patrick J., 251*n*70, 281

Legal and regulatory resources, 277–295
 federal court system, 279–281
 Freedom of Information Act, 281–282
 military law, 283–290
 U.S. Code, 278–279
 U.S. government documents regulatory issues, 290–292
 U.S. laws, 277
 U.S. Statutes at Large, 278
Legislation on Foreign Relations, 238
Legislative affairs, 26–27
Legislative calendars, 233
Legislative Reference Service, 288
Legislative Reorganization Act of 1946, 239
Legislative Reorganization Act of 1970, 246
Legislative Research Service, 246
Lejeune, John, 164
Lemay, Curtis, 146
LexisNexis Government Periodicals Index, 382
LexisNexis Inc., 233, 277, 279, 280, 381, 382
Liberia, 302, 348
Libertarian policy research, 299
Libraries
 Army, 158
 classification systems, 393, 396
 college and university, 380, 382, 383, 391
 congressional, 230
 federal depository, 136, 230, 232, 233, 247, 253, 277, 279, 291, 292, 381, 382
 House of Commons, 343–344
 Joint Electronic, 57
 law school, 292
 National Defense University, 58, 383
 presidential, 120, 193, 194–201
Library of Congress, 229, 246
 Law Library, 230
Library of Congress Classification System, 396
Library of Congress Subject Headings, 391
Liddell Hart, Basil Henry, 400
Life Saving Service, 2
Lincoln, Abraham, 398
Lists of Sections Affected, 290, 292
Live fire programs, 28
Lockheed Martin Company, 81, 93
Logistics and mobilization, 58
Logistics Command, 164
Logistics Directorate, 160
Logistics support, 36, 155, 164

Logistics, Support Maintenance, and Modernization Division, 174
London School of Economics and Political Science, 384
Lop Nor test site, 221
Los Alamos National Laboratory, 80, 82–83
Los Angeles Air Force Base, 150
Low-intensity conflict, 139
Low Intensity Conflict and Law Enforcement, 388
Lyndon Baines Johnson Library and Museum, 198

MacArthur, Douglas, 196
MacArthur Foundation, 305
MacDill Air Force Base, 137
MacLean, Donald, 107
Mahaley, Joseph, 222
Management Directorate, 100
Management Headquarters, 27
Manhattan Engineering District, 82
Manhattan Project, 86
Manpower and Reserve Affairs Department, 164
Manual for Courts-Martial United States (2000), 283
Mapping and imagery, 219, 302
Marine Air Ground Task Force Staff and Training Program, 164–165
Marine and atmospheric science, 255
Marine Corps, 136, 139
    agencies and operations, 162–168
    congressional oversight, 240
    educational institutions, 7–8, 166–167
    establishment and mission, 162–163
    headquarters, 163
Marine Corps Combat Development Command, 8, 165
Marine Corps Combat Development Plan, 167
Marine Corps Commandant Staff Judge Advocate, 285–286
Marine Corps Doctrinal Publications, 166
Marine Corps Doctrine Division, 165–166
Marine Corps Institute, 166
Marine Corps Intelligence Department, 216–217
Marine Corps Mountain Warfare Training Center, 168
Marine Corps Research Center, 8
Marine Corps Systems Command, 166
Marine Corps University, 7–8, 166–167
Marine Corps War College, 7, 167
Marine Corps Warfighting Laboratory, 167
Marine One, 124
"Marines' Hymn," 164
Maritime Administration, 115, 116
Maritime Battle Center, 176
Maritime issues, 101, 190, 329–330
Marshall, George C., 196
Marshall Center, 49–50
Mason, Theodorus B. M., 218
Massachusetts Institute of Technology, 318
Massachusetts Institute of Technology Press, 311–312, 386, 387, 392
Material Command, 154
Materials Protection, Control, and Accounting Program, 77
Materials technology, 77, 173, 211
Mathematics and Space Sciences, 148
Maxwell Air Force Base, 3, 142, 143, 146, 284
McCain, John, 251n70
McGill-Queen's University Press, 393
McGill University, 363
McNair Papers, 56
McNamara, Robert S., 198, 212
Mearsheimer, John, 400
Mechanical Engineering Research Center, 160
Medical Research and Material Command, 159
Medical Research Division, 159
Medical Research Institute of Chemical Defense, 151, 159
Medline, 98
Medsearch, 50
Merchant marine, 116, 235, 254
Merchant Marine Academy, 235
Metro Boston Transit Authority, 307
Mexico, 103, 138
Microsystems Technology Office, 33
Middle East, 344
    agency jurisdiction, 32
    military education, 10
    research institute and scholarly studies, 298, 301, 304, 314, 316, 317, 322, 366–367, 375, 398, 400
Middle East Program, 316
Middle States Association of Colleges and Schools, 14
Milhollin, Gary, 307
Militarily Critical Technologies List, 39

Military Academy (West Point), 2–3, 157, 159–160
Military acronyms, 137, 162
Military agencies, 136–187
   Air Force, 141–150, 214–215
   Army, 150–162, 215–216
   Marine Corps, 162–168, 216–217
   Navy, 168–178, 217–219
   unified combatant commands, 136–141
Military assistance, 32
Military Assistance Program, 234
Military bases. *See* Military installations
Military chain of command, 42
Military commission trials, 288–289
Military demobilization, 374
Military departments. *See* specific service departments
Military draft, 203
Military education and training, 1–24
   armed services academies, 2–3, 144, 159–160, 169–170
   assessment and improvements, 16–18, 257–258
   congressional oversight, 234, 239
   graduate and postgraduate education, 3–11, 52–61, 142–144, 148, 154–155, 157, 166–167, 172–173, 175
   international programs, 32, 49–50
   joint education, 3, 11–16
Military engineers, 157
Military forces
   advisory commission report, 263
   women in service, 45, 257, 259
Military history, 320
   Air Force, 146–147
   Army, 5, 6, 156
   Canada, 334, 395
   Marine Corps, 163–164
   Navy, 171
   scholarly journals and series, 388, 397
Military History Institute, 4, 5, 155
Military History Instructional Support Team, 6
Military installations
   base closures, 265
   commissaries management, 34
   congressional oversight, 234, 235, 239
   economic adjustment, 61–62
   environmental, safety, and health programs, 45–46

   international force basing, 33
   shore facilities, 171
Military intelligence agencies, 208, 214–219
Military Intelligence Corps, 215
Military Intelligence Division, 211
Military law, 282–290
Military Manpower Task Force, 254–255
Military registration, 203
Military Reservations Division, 215
Military Sealift Command, 141, 169
Military Sea Transportation Service, 169
Military Staff Committee, 41
Military Traffic Management Command, 141
Military workforce statistics, 48–49
Mine Ban Treaty, 174
Ministry of Defence
   India, 344
   New Zealand, 345
   Singapore, 345
   United Kingdom, 307, 339
Missile defense, 10, 42–43, 110
Missile Defense Agency, 37, 42–43
Missile Defense Command, 162
Missile Technology Control Regime, 314
Missing in action, 32, 210
Mission Systems Division, 147
Modeling and simulation activities, 11, 47, 54, 59, 160
Modern War Studies (monograph series), 394
Money laundering, 102, 106, 109, 117, 390
Monographic series, 391–397
Monterey Institute of International Studies, 314
Monthly Catalog of U.S. Government Publications, 381
Morocco, 60
Moscow Treaty, 110
Mountain warfare, 152
Moynihan, Daniel Patrick, 262
Multizone Airflow and Contaminant Transport Analysis Software, 74
Murmansk Initiative, 77
MX missile, 256

Nakasone, Yasuhiro, 368
Nanotechnology, 211
Nanyang Technological University, 369
Narcotics trafficking. *See* Drug abuse and trafficking
National Academy of Engineering, 192

National Academy of Sciences, 192, 307
National Advisory Committee on Oceans and the Atmosphere, 255
National Aeronautics and Space Administration, 270
National Affairs Inc., 388
National Air Intelligence Center, 214
National Archives (United Kingdom), 341–342
National Archives and Records Administration, 120, 211, 219, 221
    congressional oversight, 242
    establishment and operations, 192–194
        federal laws and regulations repository, 277, 290
        presidential libraries management, 119, 194–201
National Archives Information Locator, 193
National Audit Act of 1983, 342
National Audit Office, 342
National Bipartisan Commission on Central America, 255
National Bureau of Asian Research, 319
National Bureau of Standards, 74
National Cargo Security Council, 223
National Center for Strategic Studies, 16
National Center for Unconventional Thought, 306
National City Marine Terminal, 290
National Command Authorities, 35
National Commission for the Review of the National Reconnaissance Office, 266–267
National Commission on Terrorism, 267
National Commission on Terrorist Attacks Upon the United States, 213, 270
National Communications System, 35
National Council for Science and the Environment, 246
National Counterintelligence Council, 220
National Counterintelligence Executive, 220–221
National Cyber Security Division, 223–224
National Defense Authorization Act of 1999, 261
National Defense Authorization Act of 2001, 64, 269, 270
National Defense Authorization Act of 2002, 264
National Defense Authorization Act of 2004, 219
National Defense University, 13–16, 18, 43, 52–61, 210, 258

National Defense University Library, 58, 383
National Defense University Press, 56
National Disaster Medical System, 96, 97
National Drug Intelligence Center, 104, 108
National Foreign Intelligence Program, 237
National Geospatial Intelligence Agency, 219
National Guard, 26, 47, 143, 152, 240, 278
National Homeland Security Agency, 262
National Imagery and Mapping Agency, 219, 237, 266
National Industrial Security Program, 38, 193, 194
    Policy Advisory Committee, 194
National Infrastructure Protection Center, 223
National Institute for Public Policy, 304–305, 384
National Institute of Allergy and Infectious Diseases, 96, 98
National Institute of Justice, 104
National Institute of Standards and Technology, 63, 72, 74–75
National Institutes of Health, 96, 98, 99
National Intelligence Council, 211, 212, 262
National Intelligence Estimates, 212, 302
National Interest, 388–389
National Journal, 389
National Journal Group, 389
National laboratories, 76–77, 79–83, 85, 86, 92, 93
National Library for the Environment, 246
National Library of Medicine Biodefense and Bioterrorism, 96, 98
National Maritime Intelligence Center, 218
National Military Establishment, 26
National Narcotics Leadership Act of 1988, 122
National Nuclear Security Administration, 80, 83
National Oceanic and Atmospheric Administration, 255
National Partnership for Reinventing Government, 267–268
National Performance Review, 267–268
National Reconnaissance Office, 221, 237, 266–267
National Research Council, 192
National Science and Technology Council, 123
National Science and Technology, Policy, Organization, and Priorities Act of 1976, 123
National Security Act Amendments of 1949, 168

National Security Action Memoranda, 120, 197
National Security Act of 1947, 26, 40, 41, 99, 121, 141, 150, 207
National security adviser, 121
National Security Agency, 26, 207, 208, 219–220, 237, 265
National Security Archive, 305
National Security Council, 119
    advisory commission reports, 256–257, 262, 264, 269
    declassified documents access, 315
    documents, 120, 199
    establishment and operations, 99, 121, 193, 254
    military and intelligence advice provided to, 12, 41, 209
National Security Decision Directives, 120, 121, 200
    Directive 47, 97
National Security Decision Memoranda, 199
National Security Directives, 201
National security education, 59, 61
National Security Education Act of 1991, 59
National Security Education Board, 59
National Security Education Fund, 59
National Security Education Program, 59
National Security Education Trust Fund, 59
National Security Health Policy Center, 306
National Security Presidential Directives, 120
National Security Research Division, 322
National Security Reviews, 201
National Security Studies program, 317
National Security Study Memoranda, 199
National Simulation Center, 160
National Spent Nuclear Fuel Program, 83–84
National Strategic Gaming Center, 56, 59
National Taiwan University, 373
National Technical Information Service, 72, 75, 211
National Technical Intelligence, 10
National Training Center, 156
National Transportation Program, 84
National War College, 13, 15–17, 58, 60, 258
Nautical Almanac Office, 172
Nautilus Institute, 319–320
Naval Academy (Annapolis), 3, 169–170
Naval Aerospace Medical Research Laboratory, 170

Naval Air Systems Command, 170
Naval Center for Space Science and Nanoscience Institute, 173
Naval Command College, 8, 9
Naval Cost Analysis Division, 170
Naval Criminal Investigative Service, 217, 218
Naval Facilities Engineering Command, 171
Naval Fires Control System, 178
Naval Historical Center, 168, 171
Naval Information Warfare Activity, 218
Naval Institute, 389
Naval Medical Command, 171
Naval Medicine Online, 171
Naval Nuclear Propulsion Program, 81
Naval Observatory, 172
Naval Postgraduate School, 10–11, 172–173
Naval Research Laboratory, 11, 173
Naval Sea Systems Command, 173
Naval Staff College, 8, 9
Naval Surface Warfare Center, 173–174
Naval Treaty Implementation Program, 174
Naval Undersea Warfare Center, 173, 174
Naval Vessel Register, 174–175
Naval War College, 8–9, 16, 17, 168, 175
Naval War College Press, 9, 175
Navy (Canada), 335
Navy Board, 339
Navy Department, 30, 101, 136, 162
    agencies and operations, 168–178
    congressional oversight, 240
    educational institutions, 3, 8–11, 169–170, 172–173, 175
    establishment and mission, 41, 168
    intelligence agencies, 217–219
Navy General Counsel, 289
Navy International Programs Office, 175–176
Navy Judge Advocate General, 283, 286
Navy Personnel Readiness and Community Support Department, 176
Navy Personnel Research, Studies, and Technology, 176
Navy Satellite Operations Center, 11
Navy Warfare Development Command, 176
Near East, 32, 211, 241. *See also* Middle East
Near East and South Asian Affairs Office, 32
Near East-South Asia Center for Strategic Studies, 60–61

Nellis Air Force Gunnery and Bombing Range, 84
Net assessments, 62
Net Evaluation Capabilities Subcommittee, 62
Network Centric Innovation Center, 176–177
Networks and information integration, 26
Nevada Operations Office, 84–85
Nevada Test Site, 84, 92
New Brunswick Laboratory, 85
The New Cold War History (monograph series), 394
"New Electronic Titles," 381
Newly Independent States Nonproliferation Program, 314
Newspapers and news agencies
  Air Force, 141
  Army, 153
  foreign broadcasts monitoring, 211–212
New York Times, 62, 307
New Zealand, 327, 344–345, 368
Nicaragua, 255, 257
Nichols, William F., 12
Night Vision Acuity Tester, 170
Nixon, Richard M., 195, 198
Nixon Presidential Materials Staff, 198
Nonproliferation. *See* Proliferation, nonproliferation, and counterproliferation
North America, 350
North American Aerospace Defense Command, 138, 333
North Atlantic Treaty Organization, 196, 327, 333, 338, 345
  agency jurisdiction, 28, 31, 47, 50
  congressional oversight, 234, 239
  members and operations, 347
  research institute studies, 304, 374
North Carolina State University, 324
Northeast Home Heating Oil Reserve, 95
Northern Command, 137, 138
North Korea, 92, 118, 139, 349
Northwest National Security Analysis Team, 92
Nuclear accidents, 258–259
Nuclear Age Series, 394
Nuclear Control Institute, 305–306
Nuclear Emergency Search Team, 83
Nuclear energy research and development, 77, 85, 86, 349
Nuclear Energy, Science, and Technology Office, 85–86

Nuclear Explosion Monitoring, Research, and Engineering Program, 86
Nuclear facilities
  licensing and inspection, 202
  safety, 78, 80, 189
  security, 83
  site closures, 91
Nuclear fuel disposal, 83–84, 92
Nuclear nonproliferation. *See* Proliferation, nonproliferation, and counterproliferation
Nuclear Nonproliferation Treaty, 40, 349
Nuclear propulsion technology, 81
Nuclear Regulatory Commission, 84, 88
  congressional oversight, 234, 239
  establishment and operations, 201–202
Nuclear Risk Reduction Centers Agreement of 1988, 110
Nuclear Safeguards and Nonproliferation Support Program, 85
Nuclear security, 77, 86–87, 111, 306–307
Nuclear waste, 77, 84, 88, 95, 202–203
Nuclear Waste Policy Act Amendments of 1987, 88, 95
Nuclear Waste Policy Act of 1982, 88, 95
Nuclear Waste Technical Review Board, 202–203, 234
Nuclear weapons
  assembly and disassembly plant, 92–93
  depleted uranium, 47–48
  design laboratory, 82
  environmental management, 77, 79, 88
  explosion monitoring, 86
  intelligence operations, 222
  Nevada test site, 84–85
  non-nuclear components production, 81
  release of declassified information, 91–92
  reliability assurance, 82–83, 85, 87, 93–94
  threat reduction, 40

Oakley, Robert, 200
Oak Ridge National Laboratory, 86–88
Occupational Safety and Health Administration, 188
Ocean, Atmosphere, and Space Department, 177
Oceanic and atmospheric policy, 255
Ocean transport, 169
Offensive realism, 400
Office for Domestic Preparedness, 102, 104

Office of Assistant Secretary for Aviation and International Affairs, 115, 116
Office of Auditor General (Canada), 337
Office of Audits, 114
Office of Chemical and Biological Weapons Conventions, 110
Office of Civilian Radioactive Waste Management, 88
Office of Classified and Controlled Information Review, 222
Office of Contingency Planning and Peacekeeping, 112
Office of Conventional Arms Control, 110
Office of Counterintelligence, 221, 222
Office of Counterproliferation and Biological Defense, 61
Office of Cyber Security and Special Reviews, 89
Office of Demand Reduction, 122
Office of Economic Adjustment, 61–62
Office of Electricity and Natural Gas Analysis, 90
Office of Emergency Management Oversight, 89
Office of Energy Emergencies, 90
Office of Enforcement, 117–118
Office of Environmental Management, 77–78, 88–89, 91
Office of Environment, Safety, and Health Evaluations, 89
Office of Foreign Assets Control, 117, 118, 314
Office of Foreign Visits, Assignments, and Travel, 222
Office of Headquarters Security Operations, 222
Office of Homeland Security, 99
Office of Independent Oversight and Performance Assurance, 89
Office of Information and Privacy, 30, 282
Office of Information and Regulatory Affairs, 122
Office of Inspections, 114
Office of Inspector General
    Air Force, 149
    Commerce Department, 72, 75
    Defense Department, 29
    Energy Department, 89–90
    Health and Human Services Department, 96, 98–99
    Justice Department, 104, 108
    State Department, 110, 114–115
    Transportation Department, 115, 117
    Treasury Department, 117, 118
See also Accounting and auditing
Office of Intelligence, 221, 222
Office of Intelligence and Security, 223
Office of Intelligence Policy and Review, 104, 108–109, 281
Office of International Affairs, 109
Office of International Materials Protections and Emergency Cooperation, 77
Office of International Negotiations and Regional Affairs, 31, 33
Office of International Programs, 202
Office of International Security Negotiations, 110
Office of International Security Operations, 112
Office of Investigations
    Nuclear Regulatory Commission, 202
    State Department, 114
Office of Isotopes for Medicine and Science, 85
Office of Justice Programs, 102
Office of Law Revision Counsel, 278, 279
Office of Management and Budget, 119, 121–122, 264
Office of Management and Information Resources, 89
Office of Mine Action Initiatives and Partnerships, 112
Office of National Assessments, 331–332
Office of National Drug Control Policy, 119, 122–123
Office of Naval Intelligence, 217–218, 265
Office of Naval Intelligence Detachment, 9
Office of Naval Research, 168, 173, 177
Office of Net Assessment, 62
Office of Newly Independent States, Russian, and Middle Eastern Affairs, 90
Office of Nuclear Material Safety and Safeguards, 202
Office of Nuclear Materials Management Policy, 90
Office of Nuclear Reactor Regulation, 202
Office of Nuclear Security and Incident Response, 202
Office of Plutonium and Special Materials Inventory, 222
Office of Policy and International Affairs, 90
Office of Public Affairs and Public Diplomacy, 110
Office of Safeguards and Security Evaluations, 89

Office of Science and Technology Integration, 167
Office of Science and Technology Policy, 119, 123, 259
Office of Scientific and Technical Information, 90–91
Office of Security, 221, 222
Office of Security and Intelligence Oversight, 114
Office of Site Closure, 91
Office of Space Reconnaissance, 266
Office of State and Local Affairs, 122
Office of Strategic and Theater Defenses, 110
Office of Strategic Negotiations and Implementation, 110
Office of Strategic Services, 41
Office of Strategic Transition, 110
Office of Technology Assessment, 247
Office of the Assistant Secretary of Defense for Special Operations and Low-Intensity Conflict, 139
Office of the Chief Administrative Hearing Officer, 106
Office of the Chief Immigration Judge, 106
Office of the Chief of Naval Operations, 168
Office of the Deputy Chief of Staff of the Secretary of the Army for Intelligence, 216
Office of the Deputy Under Secretary of Defense for Installations and Environment, 45
Office of the Director, Program Analysis and Evaluation, 28–29
Office of the Executive Secretary, 29
Office of the Federal Register, 277, 290
Office of the General Counsel, 169, 288, 289
Office of the Secretary of Defense, 25–33
Office of the Secretary of the Navy, 286
Office of War Crimes Issues, 110, 115
Official Secrets Act, 327
Offutt Air Force Base, 140
O'Hanlon, Michael, 401
Oil (petroleum) supply, 94–95, 234, 241
O'Leary, Hazel 91
Online Computer Library Consortium, 382
"Online Public Access Catalogs," 391
OpenNet, 91–92
Open skies agreements, 116–117
Operational test and evaluation, 28, 173–174
Operation Anaconda, 137, 216

Operation Desert Storm, 12, 18, 50, 147, 257, 268
Operation Enduring Freedom, 12, 26, 137, 328, 333, 338
Operation Falconer, 329
Operation Iraqi Freedom, 12, 137, 328, 333, 338, 359, 366
Operation Just Cause, 201
Operation Overlord, 334
Operations Capability Program, 360
Operations Department, 176
Operations Directorate, 160
Operations Division, 163
Operations Support Division, 147
Operation Telic, 340
Operation Urgent Fury, 11, 156
Operation Veritas, 340
Ordnance Center, 151
Ordnance Corps, 160–161
Ordnance Museum, 161
Organisation for Prohibition of Chemical Weapons (the Netherlands), 350
Organization for Security and Co-operation in Europe, 244, 327, 347, 374
Organized crime, 106, 109
Orlando, Ernest, 81
OTA Legacy, 247
Outreach programs, 14, 54, 56, 59, 302, 324, 361, 374
Overseas Security Advisory Council, 110
Oxford University Press, 387, 390

Pacific Command, 44, 137, 139
Pacific Institute Studies in Development, Environment, and Security, 320
Pacific Northwest Center for Global Security, 92
Pacific Northwest Laboratory, 77, 80, 92
Packard, David, 255
Packard Commission, 58, 255–256
Pakistan, 344, 365, 366, 368
Palestine, 344
Panama, 139, 201, 257
Panama Canal Treaty, 200
Pantex Army Ordnance Plant, 92
Pantex Plant, 92–93, 189
Parliament
    Australia, 332–333
    Canada, 336–337
    United Kingdom, 342–344

Parliamentary Joint Committee on ASIO, ASIS, and DSD, 333
Partnership for Peace Consortium, 50, 360, 372
Passport fraud, 110
Pastor, Robert A., 200
Patriot Advanced Capability-3 system, 42
Peacekeeping Institute, 155
Peacekeeping operations, 10, 260, 302, 335, 348, 386
Penkowsky, Oleg, 210
Pennyhill Press, 246
Pentagon, 45, 269
People's Liberation Army (China), 54, 373
Periodical indexes, 380–383
Perry, William J., 53
Pershing, John J., 154
Persian Gulf region, 302, 373
Persian Gulf War, 18, 50–51, 201, 268
Personnel Command, 158
Personnel identification, 157
Personnel policy, 30–31, 235, 240
Personnel Progression, Performance, and Security Department, 176
Personnel research, 176
Personnel security, 38–39, 110–111
Personnel Security Investigations Program, 38
Peterson Air Force Base, 138, 149
Petroleum supplies, 94–95, 234, 241
Philby, Kim, 107
Philippines, 139, 196
Physics and Electronics, 148
Physics research, 77, 81
Pius XII (pope), 196
Plague, 98, 312
Plans, Policies, and Operations Department, 163
Plans, Requirements, and Resource Division, 147
Plant Clearance Automated Reutilization Screening System, 34–35
Platform Program Support Division, 170
Plum Island Animal Disease Center, 103
Poindexter, John, 200
Political-military affairs, 112, 160, 398
Pollack, Kenneth, 316
Polygraph examinations, 219
Polygraph Institute, 38
Port security, 101, 266
Posen, Barry, 401–402

Posse Comitatus Act, 278
Postal Service, 242
Potomac Institute for Policy Studies, 306
Powell, Colin, 200
Powell, Jody, 200
Powers, Gary, 210
Praeger Press, 392
Presidential Commission on the Assignment of Women in the Armed Forces, 259
Presidential Decision Directives, 120
    Directive 61, 222
    Directive 62, 223
    Directive 63, 73, 223
    Directive 75, 220
    NSC-24, 220
Presidential Directives, 200
Presidential libraries, 120, 193, 194–201
Presidential Libraries Act of 1955, 194
Presidential Libraries Act of 1986, 195
Presidential Records Act of 1978, 195
Presidential speeches and proclamations, 119–120, 291
President's Advisory Committee on Gulf War Veterans Illnesses, 50, 268
President's Blue Ribbon Commission on Defense Management, 58, 255–256
President's Board of Consultants on Foreign Intelligence Activities, 224
President's Commission on Aviation Security and Terrorism, 258
President's Commission on Catastrophic Nuclear Accidents, 258–259
President's Commission on Critical Infrastructure Protection, 223, 268–269
President's Commission on Strategic Forces, 256
President's Council of Advisors on Science and Technology, 123, 259
President's Critical Infrastructure Protection Board, 119, 123
President's Daily Brief, 213
President's Foreign Intelligence Advisory Board, 223–224
President's Private Sector Survey on Cost Control in the Federal Government, 256
President's Special Review Board, 256
Price-Anderson Amendments Act of 1988, 258
Primary Source Media, 315
Prime minister, 338, 342, 343

Princeton Studies in International History and Politics, 395
Princeton University, 247, 320
Princeton University Press, 395
Prisoners of war, 32, 210, 291
Privacy Act of 1974, 222
Proceedings: U.S. Naval Institute, 389
Procurement. *See* Acquisition and procurement
Professional military education. *See* Military education and training
Professional Military Education: An Asset for Peace and Progress, 17
Profumo, John, 107
Program analysis and evaluation, 28–29
Program in Arms Control, Disarmament, and International Security, 320
Program on Science and Global Security, 320–321
Programs and Resources Department, 167
Programs Division, 167
Project Air Force, 322, 323
Project Management Office, 94
Project Matrix, 74
Project on Cold War Studies, 387
Project on Defense Alternatives, 321
Project RAND, 321
Proliferation, nonproliferation, and counterproliferation
   advisory commission report, 263–264
   agency jurisdiction, 32, 40, 53, 61, 76, 77, 80, 82, 86–87, 92, 111–112, 192
   congressional jurisdiction, 234, 240
   military education, 10
   research institute studies, 301, 304–307, 314, 316, 321, 374
   UN agency, 349
   unified combatant command, 139
Proliferation Research and Assessment Program, 314
Public affairs, 27
Public Affairs Information Service International, 382
Publications Board, 75
Publications Directorate, 56
Public Health Security and Bioterrorism Preparedness and Response Act of 2002, 97
Public Health Service, 96
Public Key Infrastructure Program Management Office, 62–63
Public Papers of the President, 198, 200, 201

Public Records Office, 341
Puerto Rico, 38, 138

al Qaeda, 45, 216, 238, 260, 269, 289
Quadrennial Defense Review, 262
Quayle, Dan, 37
Quirin, Ex parte (1942), 289

Radiation experiments, 92, 260
Radiation Exposure Compensation Act of 1990, 260
Radioactive wastes, 84, 88
RAND Corporation, 37, 261, 321–323, 383
Readex Corporation, 348
Reagan, Ronald, 95, 120, 208, 213
   commissions and advisory organizations, 253–257
   presidential library, 200
Realism, 400
Red Cross, 45
Rehnquist, Janet, 99
Reimer Digital Library, 158, 159, 162
Regional Centre for Strategic Studies (Sri Lanka), 370
Regional security, 10, 31
Regional Strategy and Planning Department, 5
Regulation of Investigatory Powers Act of 2000, 341
Regulatory resources. *See* Legal and regulatory resources
Religion studies, 316
Reorganization Plan No. 7 of 1961, 190
Requirements and Solutions Analysis Branch, 147
Research and development
   armed service departments, 148–149, 153–154, 173, 177
   congressional oversight, 235, 247
   Defense Department, 28, 33–34, 37–38
   national laboratories, 76, 77, 79, 81, 82
Research and Development Network, 39
Research and Education in Defense and Security Studies Seminar, 53
Research Directorate, 56
Research Division, 156
Research Group in International Security, 363
Research institutions, 296, 311, 359, 397. *See also* specific institution names
Research School of Pacific and Asian Studies, 360

Reserve Intelligence Detachment, 217
Reserve Officers Training Corps, 17
Resolutions and bills, 229–230
Revenue Cutter Service, 2
Revenue Marine, 101
Rewards for Justice program, 113
Rhode Island, 174
Rice, Condoleeza, 403n8
Richard M. Scaife Initiative on the End of Communism, 316
Richard Nixon Library, 198
Ridgway, Matthew, 323
Ridgway Center for International Security Studies, 323
Rivlin, Alice, 244
Rocky Flats Depot, 189
Rogers, William J., 200
Rome, U.S. embassy in, 246
Ronald Reagan Ballistic Missile Test Site, 28
Ronald W. Reagan Presidential Library and Museum, 200
Roosevelt, Franklin D., 194, 195
Rosenberg, Julius and Ethel, 210
Rostow, Walt, 198
Royal Air Force, 339–340
Royal Army, 340, 375
Royal Australian Air Force, 328
Royal Australian Army, 329
Royal Australian Navy, 329
Royal Canadian Mounted Police, 335, 336
Royal Navy, 340
Royal United Services Institute, 376–377
R. R. Bowker (publisher), 383
Rudman, Warren B., 225, 253, 261, 263
Rudman Report, 225
Rumsfeld, Donald H., 42, 59, 199
Rusk, Dean, 198
Russell, Richard B., 198
Russia
  agency jurisdiction, 40, 77, 86, 211
  research institute studies, 301, 306–307, 314, 316, 320, 322, 323, 371, 375
  unified combatant command, 139
Russian American Nuclear Security Advisory Council, 306–307
Rwanda, 115, 260

Saban Center for Middle East Policy, 298
Sadat, Anwar, 366
Safeguards and Arms Control Division, 77

Safety. *See* Health and safety
Safety Division, 167–168
Safety Issues Directorate, 149
Salmonella, 77
Salvation Army, 45
Sandia National Laboratories, 92, 93
Satellite surveillance, 209, 219, 221, 266–267, 347
Satellites, 33, 322
Saudi Arabia, 37
Savannah River Site, 93–94, 189
Schlesinger, James R., 37
Scholarly journals, 383–390
Scholars, 397–402
School for Command Preparation, 6, 157
School for National Security Executive Education, 61
School of Advanced Air and Space Studies, 3, 4, 143
School of Advanced Military Studies, 6, 7, 157
School of Advanced Warfighting, 7, 8
School of Application, 7, 166
School of Application for Cavalry and Infantry, 5, 157
School of Instruction for the Revenue Marine, 2
School of Marine Air Ground Task Force Logistics, 7, 8
School of Public and International Affairs, 323
School of Systems and Logistics, 148
Schools of Combined Arms and Staff Services, 157
Science and technology
  advisory commission report, 259
  agency jurisdiction, 123, 192
  congressional oversight, 241, 247
  research institute studies, 301–302, 306
  See also Research and development
Science and Technology Directorate, 100
Scientific Advisory Board, 148
Scientific and technical information, 39, 75, 90–91
Scientific and Technical Information Network, 39, 155
Scott Air Force Base, 140, 145
Scowcroft, Brent, 199, 256
Scowcroft Commission, 256
Sea Bed Arms Control Treaty, 174
Seaport security, 101, 266
Seaport Security Antiterrorism Training Program, 102

Sea Power Centre (Australia), 329–330
Search warrants, 281
Sea transport, 169
Secret Intelligence Service (MI-6), 338, 341
Secret Service, 100, 103–104
Secret Service Bureau, 341
Secure Socket Layering, 136
Security assistance, 32–33, 112, 175, 234, 241
Security Assistance Directorate, 175
Security classification procedures, 193–194, 262
Security Clearance Review Program, 288
Security clearance system, 27, 38–39, 193–194, 219, 262, 288
Security Division, 163
Security education, 38, 59, 61
Security, Education, Training, and Awareness Program, 38
Security Intelligence Review Committee, 336
Security Investment Program, 234
Security Management Online, 266
Security Policy Staff, 222
Security sector reform, 374
Security Service (MI-5), 338, 341
Security Service Act of 1989, 341
Security Studies, 389
Security Studies Program, 318–319
Selective Service System, 203, 235, 240
Senate (Australia), 332
Senate (Canada), 336
Senate (U.S.), 229, 232, 327
Senate Appropriations Committee, 231, 239
Senate Armed Services Committee, 230, 231, 234, 238–240
Senate Budget Committee, 240
Senate Caucus on International Narcotics Control, 243–244
Senate Energy and Natural Resources Committee, 240–241
Senate Foreign Relations Committee, 238, 241–242
Senate Governmental Affairs Committee, 242
Senate Judiciary Committee, 243
Senate Permanent Subcommittee on Investigations, 242
Senate Select Committee on Intelligence, 242–243
Senate Subcommittee on Administrative Oversight and the Courts, 243
Senate Subcommittee on African Affairs, 241
Senate Subcommittee on Airland Forces, 240
Senate Subcommittee on Antitrust, Competition, Business, and Consumer Rights, 243
Senate Subcommittee on Crime and Drugs, 243
Senate Subcommittee on Defense, 239
Senate Subcommittee on East Asian and Pacific Affairs, 241
Senate Subcommittee on Emerging Threats and Capabilities, 240
Senate Subcommittee on Energy and Water Development, 239
Senate Subcommittee on Energy Research, Development, Production and Regulation, 241
Senate Subcommittee on European Affairs, 241
Senate Subcommittee on Foreign Operations, Export Financing, and Related Programs, 239
Senate Subcommittee on Forests and Public Land Management, 241
Senate Subcommittee on Immigration, 243
Senate Subcommittee on International Economic Policy, Export, and Trade Promotion, 241
Senate Subcommittee on International Operations, 241
Senate Subcommittee on International Security, Proliferation, and Federal Services, 242
Senate Subcommittee on Military Construction, 239
Senate Subcommittee on National Parks, Historic Preservation, and Recreation, 241
Senate Subcommittee on Near Eastern and South Asian Affairs, 241
Senate Subcommittee on Oversight of Government Management, Restructuring, and the District of Columbia, 242
Senate Subcommittee on Personnel, 240
Senate Subcommittee on Readiness and Management Support, 240
Senate Subcommittee on Seapower, 240
Senate Subcommittee on Strategic Forces, 240
Senate Subcommittee on Technology, Terrorism, and Government Information, 243
Senate Subcommittee on the Constitution, 243
Senate Subcommittee on Water and Power, 241
Senate Subcommittee on Western Hemisphere, Peace Corps, Narcotics, and Terrorism, 241

Sensors and Electron Devices Directorate, 154
Separation of powers, 327
7th Army, 26
70th Intelligence Wing, 214
Sherman, William Tecumseh, 1
Shipbuilding Support Office, 174
Shipp, Billy, 80
Shipping Act of 1948, 190
Shipping regulation, 190
Ship registry, 174–175
Signals intelligence, 340–341
Signals Intelligence and Science Commands Plans and Policy Branch, 217
Simulation and modeling activities, 11, 47, 54, 59, 160
Singapore, 327, 345, 369
67th Information Operations Wing, 214
6901st Special Communications Center, 147
Skelton, Ike, 16, 17, 58, 257
Skelton Panel, 16–18, 257–258
Slip laws, 277–278
Slip opinions, 280
Small Craft Enforcement Training Program, 102
Smallpox, 98, 312
Small wars, 58
Small Wars and Insurgencies, 389–390
Smithsonian History of Aviation and Spaceflight Series, 395
Smithsonian Institution Press, 395
Smuggling, 101, 323
Social sciences, 153
Society for Military History, 388
Software engineering, 80
Soldier and Biological Chemical Command, 151, 161
Solicitor General (Canada), 336
Somalia, 260
South Africa, 327, 345, 369–370
South America, 139, 350
South Asia
  agency jurisdiction, 32, 60, 211
  congressional oversight, 241
  research institute and scholarly studies, 301, 314, 316, 320, 366, 368, 370, 374, 398
Southeast Asia, 360
Southeast Asian Studies, 319
Southern Command, 137, 139
South Korea, 139
South Vietnam, 199
Southwest Border Initiative program, 106
Soviet-Eastern Europe Research and Training Act, 223
Soviet Union (former), 257
  advisory commission report, 254
  agency jurisdiction, 40, 80, 86, 111, 120, 197
  intelligence coverage, 210, 220, 221
  research institute studies, 313, 375
  unified combatant command, 140
  See also Russia
Space and Missile Defense Command, 162
Space and Missile Systems Center, 150
Space and Naval Warfare Systems Command, 177
Space-borne assets, 264–265
Space Command (Air Force), 149–150
Space Command (Army), 162
Spacecraft Research and Design Center, 10, 11
Spaceflight history, 395
Space Policy Directorate, 43, 63
Space science, 173
Spanish-American War, 2
Special Defense Acquisition Fund, 234
Special Operations Command, 137, 139–140
Special Operations Division, 167
Special Security Office/Special Intelligence Communications Branch, 217
Specter, Arlan, 263, 281
Sputnik, 197
Sri Lanka, 344, 370
"Staff College Automated Periodicals Index," 383
Standards of Conduct Office, 288
Stanford University, 313, 316
Stanford University Press, 394, 396
State Department, 60, 72, 246
  advisory commission report, 264
  congressional oversight, 234, 237, 239, 241
  declassified documents access, 315
  intelligence activities, 208, 222–223
  mission and operations, 109–115, 258
  security assistance programs, 33
Statistical information
  Defense Department military and civilian workforce, 48–49
  energy information, 79
Statistical Information Analysis Division, 48–49
Steel trade, 191–192
Stimson, Harry, 196, 302

Stockdale, James, 169
Stockholm International Peace Research Institute, 371
Stockpile Stewardship Program, 82, 87
Strategic Air Command, 140
Strategic and Defence Studies Centre (Australia), 360
Strategic Arms Reduction Talks Treaty, 40, 174
Strategic Command, 137, 140, 162
Strategic Command Field Office, 36
Strategic Defense Initiative Organization, 42
Strategic Forum series, 56
Strategic Initiatives Group, 163
Strategic National Stockpile Program, 98
Strategic Petroleum Reserve, 94–95, 201
Strategic Research Department, 9, 175
Strategic Studies Group, 9, 175
Strategic Studies Institute, 4, 5, 155
Strategy and International Program, 360
Strategy and Plans Division, 163
Stratfor, 323–324
Student and Exchange Visitor Information System, 101
Student worker programs, 36
Studies and Analysis Division, 165
Studies in Canadian Military History (monograph series), 395
Studies in Conflict and Terrorism, 390
Studies in International Security and Arms Control (monograph series), 396
Studies in War, Society, and the Military (monograph series), 396–397
Subcommittees, congressional. *See* House and Senate entries
Substance Abuse and Mental Health Services Administration, 96
Substate groups, 11
Suez Canal, 197
Suharto, Mohamed, 199
Superintendent of Documents classification system, 382
Support Equipment Aircraft Launch and Recovery Equipment, 170
Supreme Court, 279–280, 283
Supreme Court Reporter, 280
Surface Warfare Directorate, 177–178
Survivability and Lethality Directorate, 154
Survival, 390
Sustainable development, 320

Sweden, 371
Switzerland, 371–373
Syria, 267
Systems and Engineering Department, 43

Tactical Exploitation of National Capabilities Program, 217
Tactile Situation Awareness System, 170
Taiwan, 271, 373
Taiwan Security Research, 373
Tariff Act of 1930, 191
Tariff Commission, 191
Taylor, Charles, 302
Taylor, Maxwell, 198
Taylor, Myron, 196
Taylor and Francis Group, 384, 386, 387, 390
TDNet, 383
Technical Applications Center, 86
Technical information, 39, 75, 90–91
Technical Information Program, 90
Technology transfer, 241
Tel Aviv University, 367
Telecommunications, 223, 268
Terrorism and counterterrorism
　advisory commission, 267
　agency jurisdiction, 45, 76, 77, 82, 93, 96, 102, 106, 109, 113, 117–118, 139, 172
　congressional jurisdiction, 234, 236, 240
　investigation of Sept. 11, 2001, attack, 270
　military education, 10, 11
　research institute and scholarly studies, 301, 307, 316, 390
　UN committee, 348–349
Terrorism and Political Violence, 390
Terrorism Research Center, 307
Terrorist Financing Rewards Program, 118
Test and Evaluation Department, 43
Texas A&M University, 201
　Military History Series, 397
Texas A&M University Press, 393, 397
Think tanks, 296, 311, 359, 397. *See also* specific research institutions
"Thomas" (Library of Congress), 229, 230, 232, 233
Thomson and Gale Company, 315
Threat reduction, 40
Tiananmen Square massacre, 257
Total Force, 52
Tower, John, 256

Tower Commission, 256
Trade Act of 1974, 191
Trade issues
    advisory commission report, 270–271
    agency jurisdiction, 72–75, 99, 101, 113–114, 117, 118, 190, 191
    congressional oversight, 241
    research institute studies, 313–314
Trade secret protection, 220–221
Trading with the Enemy Act, 118
Training and Doctrine Command, 6, 162
Training and Education Command, 168
Training Systems Instructional Systems, 170
Transaction Publishers, 384
Transnational Organized Crime. See *Global Crime*
Transparency in Armaments Agreement, 174
Transportation
    hazardous materials, 84
    waterborne commerce, 190
    White House, 124
Transportation Command, 137, 140–141, 169
Transportation Department, 72, 84, 99, 101, 104, 188
    intelligence activities, 223
    mission and operations, 115–117
Transportation security, 223. *See also* Aviation security
Transportation Security Administration, 99, 104
Treasury Department, 72, 99, 101–103
    congressional oversight, 237
    mission and operations, 107, 117–119
Treasury Secretary, 262
Treaties. *See* Arms control agreements
Treaty ratification requirement, 232, 241
Triangle Institute for Security Studies, 324
TriCare, 63–64
Truman, Harry S., 84, 118, 196
Truman Presidential Museum and Library, 196
Tufts University, 317
Tularemia, 98, 312

U-2 spy plane incident, 197, 210
Ukraine, 40, 314
Ulrich's International Periodicals Directory, 383
Undersea Vehicles Group, 174
Undersecretary of defense (comptroller), 25, 29–30

Undersecretary of defense for acquisition, technology, and logistics, 25, 26, 30, 33, 48, 51
Undersecretary of defense for personnel and readiness, 25, 26, 30–31
Undersecretary of defense for policy, 26, 31
Underwater Sound Reference Division, 174
Unified Agenda, 291
Unified combatant commands, 136–141
Unified Command Plan, 137, 141
Uniform Code of Military Justice, 282–283
United and Strengthening America by Providing Appropriate Tools Required to Intercept and Obstruct Terrorism (USA PATRIOT) Act, 107, 281
United Arab Emirates, 373
United Kingdom, 107, 151, 172, 307, 346
    government organizations, 327, 338–344
    research institutions, 373–377
United Nations, 109, 327, 346, 348–351, 371
United Nations Dag Hammarskjold Library, 348
United Nations Department for Disarmament Affairs, 349–350
United Nations Institute for Disarmament Research, 350–351
United Nations Military Staff Committee, 41
United Nations Monitoring, Inspection, and Verification Commission, 349
United Nations Security Council, 348
    Counterterrorism Committee, 348–349
United Nations Special Commission on Iraq, 40, 349
United States Commission on International Narcotics Control, 243
United States Military Personnel Center, 158
United States Munition List, 113
United States Reports, 280
United States Space Command, 63
United States Supreme Court Reports Lawyers Edition, 280
Universities and colleges. *See* specific institution names
University laboratories, 99
University libraries, 380, 382, 383, 391
University of British Columbia Press, 395
University of Calgary, 363
University of California, 82
University of California–Berkeley, 81
University of California–Irvine, 312

University of Cape Town, 369
University of Chicago, 76
University of Georgia, 313, 314
University of Illinois, 320
University of London, 374
University of Manitoba, 363
University of Maryland, 384
University of Michigan, 199
University of Minnesota–Minneapolis, 313
University of Montreal, 363
University of Mounted Warfare, 151–152
University of Nebraska Press, 396
University of New Mexico, 93
University of New South Wales, 359
University of North Carolina–Chapel Hill, 324
University of North Carolina Press, 394
University of North Texas, 260, 268
University of Pittsburgh, 323
University of Reading, 384
University of South Carolina, 94
University of Tennessee, 86
University of Texas, 198
University of Wisconsin–Madison, 307
University Press of Kansas, 394
University Publications of America, 246
Upton, Emory, 1
Uranium, 47–48
U.S. Air Force. *See* Air Force Department
USA PATRIOT Act, 107, 281
U.S. Army. *See* Army Department
U.S. Attorneys, 105
U.S.-China Economic and Security Review Commission, 270–271
U.S. Coast Guard. *See* Coast Guard
U.S. Code, 278–279
U.S. Commission on National Security/21st Century, 253, 261–262
U.S. Institute of Peace, 191
U.S. International Trade Commission, 191–192
U.S. laws, 277
U.S. Marine Corps. *See* Marine Corps
U.S. Navy. *See* Navy Department
U.S.-Russia Strategic Offensive Reductions Treaty (Moscow Treaty), 110
U.S.-Russian Security Programs Division, 77
USS *Dallas,* 175
USS *Iowa,* 175
USS *John Stennis,* 175

U.S. Statutes at Large, 278
U.S. Treasury, 89
Uzbekistan, 83

Vance, Cyrus, 200
Vandenberg Air Force Base, 221
Vehicle Ambush Countermeasures Training Program, 102
Vehicle Technology Directorate, 154
Veneman, Ann M., 59
Vernon County (ship), 175
Vessel register, 174–175
Veterans Affairs Department, 50, 260, 268
Veterans Health Administration, 97
Victoria University, 368
Video Imaging Capacity Enhancement, 145
Vietnam, 199
Vietnam War, 32, 198, 210, 315
Viral hemorrhagic fevers, 312
Virgin Islands, U.S., 138
Virtual Directorate, 160
Visa fraud, 110

Wagner, Arthur L., 215
Wales, 339
Walker, Robert S., 269
War, Law of, 285
War crimes, 115, 302
War Department, 41, 150, 156, 161, 211
Warfare Analysis and Research Department, 9
War Gaming Department, 9, 175
War-gaming exercises, 56, 59, 155
War Office, 339
War on terrorism, 269. *See also* Terrorism and counterterrorism
Washington, George, 154
Washington Post, 62
Water systems, 223, 268
Weapons and Materials Research Directorate, 154
Weapons and Systems Development Energetics Test Ranges, 170
Weapons of mass destruction
  military education, 10
  threat reduction, 40
  See also Chemical and biological weapons; Nuclear weapons
Weapons of Mass Destruction Training Program, 102

Weapons, Space, and Nuclear Safety Division, 149
Weapons System Evaluation Group, 303
Weatherhead Center for International Affairs, 318
Weinberger, Caspar W., 254
Wellington (duke), 376
West, Brian, 224
Western cultural identity, 316
Western Hemisphere Affairs Office, 32
Western hemisphere defense studies, 53–54
Western Hemisphere Institute for Security Cooperation, 64
Westinghouse Savannah River Company, 93
Westlaw, 279, 280
West Point, 2, 159
West Publishing, 277
White House, 45, 315
White House Commission on Aviation Safety and Security (Gore Commission), 104, 269
White House Communications Agency, 36, 124
White House Medical Unit, 124
White House Military Office, 119, 123–124
White House Transportation Agency, 124
White Sands Missile Range, 154
William Clinton Presidential Materials Project, 119, 201, 225
Wilson, Woodrow, 308
Wisconsin Project on Nuclear Arms Control, 307–308
Women, 45, 257, 259
Woodrow Wilson International Center for Scholars, 308
Woodrow Wilson School of Advanced International Affairs, 247
Woodrow Wilson School of Public and International Affairs, 320
World Bank, 241
World News Connection, 211–212
World Trade Center, 74, 269
World Trade Organization, 241
World War I, 316
World War II, 195–196, 400, 401
Worldwide Military Command and Control System, 35
Worldwide Political Science Abstracts, 383
Wortzel, Larry, 402
Wright-Patterson Air Force Base, 148, 214

Y-12 National Security Complex, 87
Yale University, 315
Yale University Press, 391
Yeager, Chuck, 146
York Centre for International and Security Studies, 364
York University, 364
Yucca Mountain Project, 88, 95, 202, 203
Yugoslavia, 115

Zimbabwe, 369
Zimmerman Library Government Information Department, 93
Zinni, Anthony, 58

Citations of Authors

Abelson, Donald E., 308n1
Aldrich, Richard J., 355n48
Aldridge, James F., 180n39
Allen, James S., 66n33
Amato, Ivan, 186n116
Anderson, Oscar Edward, 130n83
Andrew, Christopher, 225n4, 355n48, 356n53
Arnold, Peri, 133n145

Babbage, Ross, 356n62
Bach, John, 351n8
Bailey, Sydney Dawson, 351n1
Ball, Desmond, 352n10
Ball, Harry P., 20n19, 182n59
Ball, Howard, 295n33
Bamford, James, 227n40
Barber, James P., 354n39
Bar-Joseph, Uri, 357n63
Barnett, Corelli, 355n46
Barry, John, 71n103
Bass, Gary Jonathan, 295n33
Batten, Donna, 227n37
Bebbington, William P., 129n72
Bergin, Anthony, 352n10
Berman, Larry, 134n149
Bernauer, Thomas, 358n81
Bernier, Bernard A., Jr., 271n2
Binney, William Alexander, 353n26
Blackaby, Frank, 378n29
Bland, Larry I., 69n64
Boies, John L., 324n1
Boll, Michael M., 272n3
Borch, Frederic L., 294n23
Borowski, Harry R., 179n17
Bourantonis, Dimitris, 358n75
Bowen, George, 357n64
Bowman, William, 272n6

Bowyer, Chaz, 355n45
Boyd, Andrew, 358n76
Brinkley, Douglas, 358n75
Bristow, Damon, 356n62
Brown, James, 272n3
Burns, William F., 24n86
Bush, George H. W., 273n14

Cain, Frank, 352n13
Caldwell, Dan, 186n120
Caldwell, Nathaniel French, 353n23
Caligari, John G., 351n6
Canedy, Susan, 183n82
Carnes, Mark C., 126n32
Carroll, James D., 251n68
Carroll, Thomas Patrick, 225n4
Carsey, Thomas M., 248n11
Casey, Dennis F., 226n15
Challaney, Brahma, 356n62
Chandler, David, 355n46
Chant, Christopher, 355n46
Chapman, Anne W., 183n82
Chapman, Bert, 125n24, 203n4, 379n41
Chubin, Daryl E., 134n152
Clarke, Richard A., 276n60
Cleroux, Richard, 353n29
Clifford, Kenneth J., 184n83
Cohen, Elliot A., 357n63
Cole, Alice C., 65n2
Collins, Martin J., 326n26
Condit, Doris M., 65n3
Condit, Kenneth W., 67n46
Cook, Don, 357n73
Cope, John A., 18n1
Cox, Andrew W., 354n38
Cox, Richard J., 205n32, n37
Crackel, Theodore J., 19n8, 183n73

448

Critchlow, Donald T., 309*n*7
Croft, Stuart, 358*n*74
Crosby, Ann Denholm, 353*n*23

Darling, Arthur B., 225*n*3
Dastrup, Boyd L., 20*n*26, 182*n*65, *n*69
Davidson, Eugene, 295*n*33
Davidson, Michael J., 294*n*19
Davies, Kirk L., 294*n*19
Davis, Richard L., 19*n*12
Dawen, Choy, 357*n*65
Day, Dwayne A., 180*n*40, 227*n*44
Dennis, Peter, 351*n*2
Dertouzos, James N., 324*n*1
Diamond, Nancy, 134*n*152
Dick, Steven J., 185*n*113
Dilkes, David, 354*n*39
Donaghy, Greg, 353*n*23
Donnini, Frank P., 19*n*12
Donovan, Arthur, 272*n*5
Dorman, Andrew M., 357*n*69
Dorril, Stephen, 355*n*48
Doubler, Michael D., 181*n*54
Drucker, Arthur J., 181*n*55
Duignan, Peter, 357*n*73
DuPlessia, Anton, 357*n*66
Dupuy, William E., 183*n*82

Edwards, Lee, 309*n*19
Efflandt, Scott, 18*n*2
Enever, Ted, 355*n*49
English, John A., 353*n*23
Ennels, Jerome A., 19*n*12
Etheridge, Elizabeth W., 130*n*82
Evans, Michael, 351*n*6

Fabian, Larry L., 309*n*8
Fairchild, Byron R., 67*n*46
Fehner, Terrence R., 125*n*15
Filtner, David, 271*n*1
Finlayson, Kenneth, 182*n*71
Finnegan, John Patrick, 226*n*21, *n*22, *n*23
Fiore, James J., 128*n*63
Fischer, David, 358*n*79
Fitzgerald, Randall, 272*n*12
Fleitz, Frederick H., 273*n*25
Forrest, Martyn, 352*n*20
Frame, Thomas R., 351*n*8

Freedman, Lawrence, 354*n*38
Furneaux, Nicholas, 353*n*23
Futrell, Robert Frank, 179*n*19

Garraty, John A., 126*n*32
Gellner, John, 353*n*23
Generous, William T., Jr., 294*n*21
Genovese, Michael A., 133*n*145
Gertz, Bill, 273*n*25
Ghamari-Tabrizi, Sharon, 325*n*14
Gibson, Andrew, 272*n*5
Gittins, Richard A., 294*n*19
Gobert, Wayne, 352*n*10
Goin, Peter, 127*n*43
Goldberg, Alfred, 65*n*2, *n*3, 70*n*102
Goldberg, Sheldon A., 179*n*17
Goldman, Emily O., 186*n*120
Goldsworthy, Jeffrey, 356*n*58
Gordon, Sandy, 356*n*62
Gough, Terrence J., 182*n*63
Graham, Hugh Davis, 134*n*152
Granatstein, J. L., 353*n*27, *n*29
Grandstaff, Mark R., 19*n*12
Greenhouse, Brereton, 353*n*26
Grey, Jeffrey, 351*n*6
Griffith, Robert K., 272*n*6
Griffiths, Ann L., 353*n*28
Grove, Eric, 355*n*46
Gurney, Gene and Clare, 133*n*139
Gusterson, Hugh, 126*n*34

Hadley, Michael L., 353*n*28
Hagerty, Devin T., 356*n*62
Hall, Robert, 352*n*10
Halliday, Hugh A., 353*n*26
Hanson, Victor Davis, 276*n*60
Harden, Victoria Angela, 130*n*87
Harrelson, Max, 358*n*75
Harrison, Cynthia, 293*n*4, *n*5
Hattendorf, John B., 21*n*44, 186*n*123
Haydon, Peter T., 353*n*28
Haynes, John Earl, 227*n*41
Heilbron, J. L., 126*n*32
Hendrickson, Ryan C., 273*n*25
Hennessy, Peter, 354*n*40
Hensley, Francis H., 355*n*48, *n*49
Herken, Gregg, 134*n*152
Hewitt, Steve, 353*n*31

Hilgartner, Stephen, 204n20
Hill, J. R., 355n47
Hillmer, Norman, 353n23
Hoare, Oliver, 356n53
Hogan, David W., Jr., 181n47
Hogg, Ian V., 355n46
Holder, Leonard, Jr., 18n2, 24n86
Holt, Cora J., 179n18
Hone, Thomas, 185n103
Hooks, Gregory M., 324n1
Hoopes, Townsend, 358n75
Hopkins, J. C., 179n17
Hopman, P. Terrence, 358n74
Horner, David M., 351n2, n6
Houghton, Amo, 251n73
Howarth, Stephen, 185n102
Huxley, Tim, 357n65

Jacobs, Francis, 357n67
Jenkins, Brian Michael, 276n60
Johnson, Franklyn A., 355n44
Johnson, Leland, 127n47, 129n70
Johnson, Loch, 225n3
Judd, Alan, 356n53

Katz, Richard S., 357n67
Kauchak, Marty, 71n103
Kauffman, George B., 126n32
Kavanagh, Dennis, 354n39
Keaney, Thomas A., 19n10, 22n60
Keller, Bill, 71n103
Keller, Mollie, 131n102
Kelly, Nora, 353n31
Kennedy, George C., 19n10, 22n60
Kennedy, Paul M., 355n47
Kenney, Steven H., 24n86
Keohane, Dan, 354n38
Kirby, Stephen, 354n38
Kitsos, Thomas, 272n7
Klehr, Harvey, 227n41
Koh, Harold Hongju, 273n13
Kohn, Richard H., 294n19
Korb, Lawrence J., 67n46
Kornberg, Allan, 354n35
Krepon, Michael, 186n120

LaFantasie, Glenn W., 225n2
Langley, Harold D., 185n112
Lanham, Charles T., 182n71

Lanning, Hugh, 355n49
Larsgaard, Mary Lynette, 227n37
Latell, Brian, 227n44
Leatherman, Janie, 358n74
Lee, David, 355n45
Leighton, Richard M., 65n3, 70n101
Lemann, Nicholas, 71n103
Levine, Charles H., 272n12
Levite, Ariel, 357n63
Lewis, Leslie, 183n80
Linowes, David F., 271n1
Lipson, Gerald, 272n12
Locher, James R., III, 22n59, n60
Loeb, Paul Rogat, 128n66
Loeber, Charles R., 125n15
Logsdon, John M., 227n44
Lovell, John P., 19n3, n6, n8, 179n26
Lowenthal, Mark M., 134n147
Luard, Evan, 358n75
Lurie, Jonathan, 294n21

Maltzman, Forrest, 293n7
Mann, Alfred K., 134n152
Marder, Arthur J., 355n47
Markusen, Ann, 324n1
Marshall, Gabriel G., 226n15
Matchette, Robert B., 204n24, n25, 225n11
Matheny, Albert R., 295n36
Matthews, James K., 179n18, 185n104
Mazuzan, George T., 206n44
McDonald, Forrest, 133n145
McFarland, Stephen L., 179n19
McMichael, Scott R., 182n71
Melanson, Philip H., 131n108
Mellor, Tony, 65n14, n15, n16, n17, n18, 66n21, n23, n27, n29, n30, n37, 71n103, 130n80
Merrill, John, 186n121
Milkis, Sidney M., 133n145
Millet, Allen R., 184n83
Milner, Marc, 353n28
Mishler, William, 354n35
Mojtabai, A. G., 129n68
Molot, Maureen Appel, 353n23
Mordike, John L., 351n6
Morehead, Joe, 124n12, 227n37, 247n4, 248n5, 292n1, n2, n3, n7, 295n37, n38, n39
Morrison, Larry R., 180n31
Mosher, Frederick C., 134n149
Mosley, Richard Kenneth, 354n40

Moynihan, Daniel Patrick, 274n33
Murray, Williamson, 18n2, 23n77, 24n86

Naylor, John F., 354n40
Neilson, Keith, 19n10, 22n60
Nenninger, Timothy K., 20n26
Nesbit, Roy C., 355n45
Newton, Wesley Phillips, 19n12
Ng, Chew, 352n19
Norton-Taylor, Richard, 355n49

Oatley, Carl, 351n2

Pace, Steve, 180n33
Packard, Wyman H., 226n31, n32
Palazzo, Albert, 351n6
Patterson, David S., 225n2
Pellew, Jill, 355n42
Perkovich, George, 356n62
Peters, W. R., 129n69
Plischke, Elmer, 132n102
Pogany, Istvan S., 358n76
Pogue, Forrest C., 69n64
Pons, Xavier, 351n2
Poole, Walter S., 67n46
Posner, Richard A., 293n4
Powell, S. Steven, 309n21
Powers, Paul A., 131n99
Prados, John, 134n147
Prince, Carl E., 131n102

Ragsdale, Lyn, 133n145
Ranelagh, John, 225n3
Reams, Bernard D., 248n5
Reardon, Steven L., 65n3
Reed, Brian, 18n2
Reeve, John, 351n8
Reid, Gordon Stanley, 352n20
Reigel, Stanley A., 295n36
Relyea, Harold C., 204n28
Rettig, Richard A., 183n72
Ricci, David M., 308n1
Rice, Condoleeza, 273n14
Richelson, Jeffrey T., 225n8, 227n44, 352n10
Richter, Andrew, 353n23
Ricks, Thomas R., 66n35
Rives, Jack L., 294n19
Roberts, Marcia, 131n108
Robin, Ron Theodore, 308n1

Rose, Richard, 134n149
Rudd, David, 353n23
Rudgers, David F., 225n3
Ruffner, Kevin C., 227n48
Rundquist, Barry S., 248n11
Ruppenthal, Roland G., 66n33
Russet, Bruce, 358n76
Rutenberg, David C., 66n33
Ryan, Christine, 352n19

Salmon, Trevor C., 357n69
Sapolsky, Harvey M., 186n128
Sarooshi, Daneesh, 358n76
Schaffer, Daniel, 127n47
Schmidt, Gustav, 357n73
Schnabel, James F., 67n46
Schoenbrod, David, 295n36
Schonfeld, Roger C., 402n2
Schwartz, Bernard, 293n7
Scowcroft, Brent, 273n14
Seidel, Robert W., 126n32
Seldon, Anthony, 354n39
Shallat, Todd A., 182n67
Shepherd, Alistair J. K., 357n69
Shrader, Charles R., 66n33
Shroyer, Jo Ann, 126n35
Siegel, Jay M., 294n27
Sinclair, Sonja, 354n37
Singh, Jasit, 356n62
Skelton, Ike, 24n84
Smart, Jeffrey K., 183n79
Smith, Bromley K., 134n147
Smith, James Allen, 308n1, 309n7, n14
Smith, Paul, 355n44
Snyder, William P., 272n3
Spector, Ronald H., 21n44, 186n123
Spufford, Peter, 356n58
Stafford, David, 353n29
Stephens, Alan, 351n4
Sterling, Keir B., 183n76
Stevens, David M, 351n8
Stiehm, Judith Hicks, 20n19, 182n59
Stiff, Peter, 357n66
Strickland, Donald A., 309n16
Strickland, Lee, 293n9, n10
Stripp, Alan, 355n49
Stubbs, Walter, 248n7
Sweetman, Jack, 19n9
Sykes, Patricia Lee, 354n39

Tabassi, Lisa Woollomes, 358n81
Theis, John J., III, 133n145
Thelan, David P., 273n13
Thomas, David A., 355n47
Thomas, Evan, 71n103
Thompson, Fergus M., 354n37
Thorne, C. Thomas, Jr., 225n2
Titus, A. Costandina, 127n43
Trask, David F., 132n122
Trask, Roger R., 65n2, 70n102, 251n64
Treese, Joel D., 248n17
Trest, Warren A., 179n19
Tutchings, Terrence R., 271n1

Ulmer, S. Sidney, 294n21
Unsworth, Michael, 402n1

Van Creveld, Martin, 66n33
Vitas, Robert A., 24n86
Walch, Timothy, 204n21
Walker, J. Samuel, 206n44
Wallace, Lane E., 66n40, 67n41
Walsh, Edward, 126n35
Walsh, Lawrence E., 273n13

Wanna, John, 352n19
Watson, Robert J., 65n3, 67n46
Weigley, Russell F., 18n2, 181n47
Welch, Michael D., 379n43
Wessels, Bernhard, 357n67
West, Nigel, 355n48
Wheeler, Russell R., 293n4, n5
Whitnah, Donald Robert, 133n134
Williams, Bruce Alan, 295n36
Wilnik, Jay, 272n3
Wilson, Don W., 205n36
Wolanin, Thomas R., 271n1
Wood, Karen A., 271n2
Woodward, Bob, 276n60
Wyld, Lionel D., 186n121

York, Byron, 275n52

Zegart, Amy B., 67n46
Zeidner, Joseph, 181n55
Zelikow, Philip, 273n14
Zink, Steven D., 271n2, 272n10, n12
Zwirn, Jerrold, 247n2